Modern
REAL ESTATE
Practice in Illinois

SEVENTH EDITION REVISED

Filmore W. Galaty,
Wellington J. Allaway,
Robert C. Kyle,
Laurie S. MacDougal,
Consulting Editor

Dearborn™
Real Estate Education

This publication is designed to provide accurate and authoritative information in regard to the subject matter covered. It is sold with the understanding that the publisher is not engaged in rendering legal, accounting, or other professional advice. If legal advice or other expert assistance is required, the services of a competent professional should be sought.

President: Dr. Andrew Temte
Chief Learning Officer: Dr. Tim Smaby
Vice President, Real Estate Education: Asha Alsobrooks
Development Editor: Trude Irons

MODERN REAL ESTATE PRACTICE IN ILLINOIS SEVENTH EDITION REVISED
©2012 Kaplan, Inc.
Published by DF Institute, Inc., d/b/a Dearborn Real Estate Education
332 Front St. S., Suite 501
La Crosse, WI 54601
www.dearborn.com

Printed in the United States of America
12   13   14   10   9   8   7   6   5   4   3   2   1
ISBN: 978-1-4277-3930-8 / 1-4277-3930-7
PPN: 1510-707A

Contents

Preface

Whether you are preparing for the Illinois real estate licensing examination, fulfilling a college or university requirement, looking for specific guidance about buying a home or investment property, or simply expanding your understanding of this fascinating field, you can rely on *Modern Real Estate Practice in Illinois Seventh Edition Revised* for accurate and comprehensive information in a format that is easy to use.

■ TEXT FEATURES

- *Key Terms,* at the beginning of each chapter, point out important vocabulary words and are helpful for study and review.
- *Illinois-specific laws and practice issues* are clearly highlighted for easy study and classroom emphasis.
- The *For Example* feature adds real-life examples and case studies to illustrate key concepts.
- *In Practice* sections reinforce course material by showing how the concepts are likely to be played out in actual practice.
- *Math Concepts,* marked with an icon, help students learn basic real estate math skills and their applications.
- *Margin Boxes* direct readers' attention to important concepts and contain tips for more effective studying.
- Inclusive *Chapter Summaries* help students easily refer to and retain key information from the chapter.
- *Chapter review questions and practice exams*, containing national and Illinois-specific questions, provide a good sampling of the types of questions on the real estate licensing examination.
- The *Math FAQs* section contains more than 30 pages covering real estate problems involving fractions, decimals, and measurements. Twenty-five sample questions and an answer key with solutions are included.
- The latest *AMP Outline* for the national broker's exam is included, along with chapter references for each topic.

■ NEW TO THE SEVENTH EDITION REVISED

- New content topics have been added, such as:
  — Managing Broker Responsibilities
  — Business Planning
  — IRS Tax Considerations
  — Safety Concerns
  — Errors and Omissions Insurance
  — Short Sales
  — Securing Management Business

— New Opportunities
— Community Association Management

■ All forms are updated to include the latest versions:
— New Settlement Statement (HUD-1)
— Good Faith Estimate (GFE)
— Buyer Agency Checklist
— Seller Agency Checklist
— Seller Disclosure
— Exclusive Buyer Representation/Exclusive Right to Purchase Contract
— Confirmation of Consent to Dual Agency
— Sponsoring Broker-Salesperson Contract
— Listing Agreement
— Disclosure of Contemporaneous Offers
— Property Disclosure Report
— Additional Designated Agent
— Notice of No Agency Relationship
— Buyer Information Checklist

Questions and answers are updated to reflect the current business climate.

Web links are located in Appendix A, in chapter-by-chapter order.

One thing, however, has stayed the same. The two fundamental goals of *Modern Real Estate Practice in Illinois* are to help students understand the dynamics of the real estate industry in Illinois and pass their state licensing exam. In this edition, we've met that challenge, providing the critical information students need to pass the real estate examination, buy or sell property, or establish a real estate career.

■ A FINAL NOTE

We like to hear from our readers. Like the many instructors who have helped us develop each edition and the real estate professionals who have been willing to share their expertise, you are a partner in the *Modern Real Estate Practice* book series. The only way we can be sure we've succeeded—and know what we need to improve—is if you tell us.

Your comments help us evaluate the current edition and continue to improve future editions. Please take a few moments to let us know what you thought of this edition of *Modern Real Estate Practice in Illinois*. Did it help you? Has your understanding of the real estate industry increased? How did you do in your real estate course or on your license exam? What additional or different information would improve the book? Please let us know what you thought of this edition at *contentinquiries@dearborn.com*.

Thank you for your help and for joining the ranks of successful users of *Modern Real Estate Practice in Illinois*.

Acknowledgments

The publishers convey gratitude and appreciation to the instructors and other real estate professionals whose invaluable suggestions and advice help *Modern Real Estate Practice in Illinois* remain the state's leading real estate principles text.

■ CONSULTING EDITOR

Laurie MacDougal has worked in the real estate industry since 1975. She is a real estate educator with the Chicago Association of REALTORS® and its affiliates. Laurie has taught all levels of real estate licensing courses, and is best known for her ongoing involvement with real estate broker prelicensing, continuing education, and sales training courses. In addition, she founded and operates Laurmac Learning Center, which provides customized training for the real estate and mortgage brokerage industries.

Laurie served as consulting editor on *Modern Real Estate Practice in Illinois*, Fifth Edition, Fifth Edition Update, Sixth Edition, and Seventh Edition. Her other products include *Illinois Broker Management*, *Illinois Real Estate Broker Post-Licensing*, and *Illinois Real Estate Managing Broker Prelicensing*.

Beyond the classroom, Laurie's real estate experience of three-plus decades includes industrial and commercial development, property management, economic development, and residential real estate sales. Currently, she provides consulting services to numerous real estate–related organizations regarding license law and compliance issues.

Laurie has appeared as an industry expert on NBC *Nightly News* and CLTV segments, discussing real estate–related news.

■ REVIEWERS

This edition of *Modern Real Estate Practice in Illinois* would not have been possible without the input of real estate instructors and the feedback of real estate professionals. For their comments, suggestions, and contributions, the publishers wish to especially thank Michael Fair, Director, Illinois Academy of Real Estate; Francis Patrick Murphy, JD, Chicago Association of REALTORS®, Carol Carlson-Nofsinger, J.D., instructor at the College of DuPage. A special word of thanks to Gerald R. Cortesi, instructor at Harper College and Oakton College.

Each new edition of *Modern Real Estate Practice in Illinois* builds on earlier editions. The authors would like to thank the following individuals for their assistance with prior editions of this book:

Jean Bartholomew

Elyse Berns

Maureen Cain

Patrick Cal

William Carmody

Sandra CeCe

Michael Fair

Kerry Kidwell

Maureen LeVanti

Deborah Lopes

Vincent Lopez

Rose McDonald

Laurie MacDougal

Clarke Marquis

Sam Martin

Lynda McKay

Susan Miranda

Robert Mocella

Francis Patrick Murphy

Wayne Paprocki

Joyce Bea Sterling

Dawn Svenningsen

Alan Toban

Casey Voris

Barry Ward

Terry W. Watson

Mary Wezeman

Martha Williams

CHAPTER 1

Introduction to the Real Estate Business

■ **LEARNING OBJECTIVES** *When you've finished reading this chapter, you should be able to*

■ **identify** the various careers available in real estate and the professional organizations that support them;

■ **describe** the five categories of real property;

■ **explain** the operation of supply and demand in the real estate market;

■ **distinguish** the economic, political, and social factors that influence supply and demand; and

■ **define** the following *key terms*

brokerage	market	sponsoring broker
Federal Reserve Board	real estate licensee	supply and demand

■ A VERY BIG BUSINESS

Real estate transactions are taking place all around us, all the time. When a commercial leasing company rents space in a shopping center or the owner of a building rents an apartment , it's a real estate transaction. If an appraiser gives an expert opinion of the value of farmland or a bank lends money to purchase an office building, it's a real estate transaction. Most common of all, when a family sells its old home to buy a new one or steps into the housing market for the first time, it's a real estate transaction. Consumers of real estate services include home buyers and sellers, tenants and landlords, investors, and developers. Nearly everyone at some time is an active participant in the real estate industry.

All this adds up to big business—complex transactions that involve billions of dollars every year.

The services of highly trained individuals are required: attorneys, bankers, appraisers, abstract and title insurance agents, architects, surveyors, accountants, tax experts, home inspectors, and many others, in addition to buyers and sellers. All these people depend on the skills, knowledge, and integrity of licensed real estate professionals.

■ REAL ESTATE: A BUSINESS OF MANY SPECIALIZATIONS

Despite the size and complexity of the real estate business, many people think of it as being made up of only brokerage. Actually, the real estate industry is much broader than that. Appraisal, property management, financing, subdivision and development, home inspection, counseling, education, and auctioning are all separate businesses within the real estate field. To succeed in this complex industry, every real estate professional must have a basic knowledge of these specialties.

Brokerage   *Brokerage* is the business of bringing people together in a real estate transaction. A **real estate licensee** acts as a point of contact between two or more people in negotiating the sale, purchase, or rental of property. A real estate licensee may be the agent for the buyer, for the seller, or for both. The property may be residential, commercial, or industrial. Illinois license categories include broker, managing broker, and leasing agent. A managing broker may be designated to supervise other licensees and run an office. All licensees are employed by their sponsoring broker, who must hold a managing broker license, and they conduct brokerage activities on behalf of the sponsoring broker. *Leasing agents* bring together tenants and prospective rental properties. The **sponsoring broker** is ultimately responsible for the actions of all licensees working under the umbrella of that particular firm. Please note the salesperson license category is being phased out and all existing salesperson licenses will terminate on May 1, 2012. Effective May 1, 2011, two main categories of licensure will exist: managing broker and broker. There will be no changes to the leasing agent requirements.

Appraisal   *Appraisal* is the process of estimating a property's market value based on established methods and the appraiser's professional judgment. Although real estate training will give brokers and managing brokers some understanding of the valuation process, most lenders require that a professional appraisal by a licensed appraiser accompany a loan package. The appraisal substantiates the sales price of the home and assists the lender in determining maximum loan amount. Appraisals are also used for refinancing and insurance purposes. Detailed expertise in all the methods of valuation is required. Appraisers must be licensed or certified for any federally related loan transaction.

Property management   A *property manager* is a person or company hired to maintain and manage property on behalf of its owner. By hiring a property manager, the owner is relieved of many day-to-day management tasks, such as finding new tenants, collecting rents, altering or constructing new space for tenants, ordering repairs, and generally maintaining the property. The scope of the manager's work depends on the terms of the individual employment contract, known as a *property management agreement*. Whatever tasks are specified, the property manager must protect the owner's investment and maximize the owner's return on his investment.

Financing *Financing* is the business of providing the funds that make real estate transactions possible. Most transactions are financed by means of mortgage loans or trust deed loans secured by the property. Individuals involved in financing real estate may work in commercial banks, mortgage banking, or mortgage brokerage companies. A growing number of real estate brokerage firms affiliate with mortgage brokers to provide consumers with one-stop-shopping real estate services. Mortgage brokers and the loan officers working for them must be licensed and registered in Illinois.

Subdivision and development *Subdivision* is the splitting of a single property into smaller parcels. *Development* involves the construction of improvements on the land. These improvements may be either on-site or off-site. Off-site improvements such as water lines and storm sewers are made on public lands to serve the new development. On-site improvements are additions or enhancements within the buildings or lots being sold that increase the value of the properties within the development. On-site improvements include roads and infrastructure, new buildings, or private wells made on individual parcels. While subdivision and development normally are related, they are independent processes that can occur separately.

Home inspection *Home inspection* is a profession that allows practitioners to combine their interest in real estate with their professional skills and training in the construction trades or in engineering. Professional home inspectors conduct a thorough visual survey of a property's structure, systems, and site conditions and prepare an analytical report that is valuable to both purchasers and homeowners. In Illinois, home inspectors must be licensed.

Professional inspections occur on other types of property as well. Commercial properties may undergo an environmental assessment to determine the probability of hazardous substances being present on the property.

Counseling *Counseling* involves providing clients with competent independent advice based on sound professional judgment. A real estate counselor helps clients choose among the various alternatives involved in purchasing, using, or investing in property. A counselor's role is to furnish clients with the information needed to make informed decisions. Professional real estate counselors must have a high degree of industry expertise.

Education *Real estate education* is available to both practitioners and consumers. Colleges and universities, private schools, and trade organizations all conduct real estate courses and seminars, from the principles of a prelicensing program to the technical aspects of tax and exchange law. State licensing laws establish the minimum educational requirements for obtaining—and keeping—a real estate license. Continuing education (CE) helps ensure that licensees keep their skills and knowledge current.

Auctioning   Buying or selling real estate at auction uses an open and competitive bidding process to transfer property. In Illinois, as in many states, auctioneers have licensing requirements.

Other areas   Many other real estate career options are available. Practitioners will find that real estate specialists are needed in a variety of business settings. *Lawyers* who specialize in real estate are always in demand. Large *corporations* with extensive land holdings often have their own *real estate* and *property tax departments*. Local governments must staff both *zoning boards* and *assessment offices*.

■ PROFESSIONAL ORGANIZATIONS

Many trade organizations serve the real estate business. The largest is the National Association of REALTORS® (NAR), whose Web site is *www.realtor.org*. The NAR sponsors various affiliated organizations that offer professional designations to brokers, managing brokers, and other professionals who complete required courses in areas of special interest. Members subscribe to a Code of Ethics and are entitled to be known as REALTORS® or REALTOR-ASSOCIATES®. You must be a member of NAR to use the term REALTOR®.

The NAR has the following affiliated institutes, societies, and councils:

- Counselors of Real Estate (CRE)
- Commercial Investment Real Estate Institute (CIREI)
- Institute of Real Estate Management (IREM)
- REALTORS® Land Institute (RLI)
- REALTORS® National Marketing Institute (RNMI)
- Certified Real Estate Brokerage Manager (CRB)
- Certified Residential Specialist (CRS)
- Graduate, Real Estate Institute (GRI)
- Council of Residential Specialists (CRS)
- Society of Industrial and Office REALTORS® (SIOR)
- Women's Council of REALTORS® (WCR)

The National Association of Real Estate Brokers (NAREB), whose members are known as *Realtists*, also adheres to a code of ethics. The NAREB arose out of the early days of the civil rights movement as an association of racial minority real estate brokers in response to the conditions and abuses that eventually gave rise to fair housing laws. Today, the NAREB remains dedicated to equal housing opportunity.

The National Association of Hispanic Real Estate Professionals (NAHREP) is the largest minority trade group in the real estate industry. Its mission is to increase the rate of sustainable Hispanic home ownership by empowering real estate professionals that serve the Hispanic community.

The Asian Real Estate Association of America (AREAA) is a non-profit professional trade organization dedicated to promoting sustainable homeownership opportunities in Asian American communities.

Other professional associations include the following:

- American Society of Appraisers (ASA)
- National Association of Independent Fee Appraisers (NAIFA)
- Real Estate Educators Association (REEA)
- Real Estate Buyer's Agent Council (REBAC)
- National Association of Exclusive Buyer's Agents (NAEBA)
- Building Owners and Managers Association (BOMA)
- Certified Commercial Investment Managers (CCIM)
- American Society of Home Inspectors® (ASHI)

Members are expected to comply with the Standards of Practice and Code of Conduct as set forth by each organization.

Types of Real Property

Just as there are areas of specialization within the real estate industry, there are different types of property in which to specialize. Real estate can be classified as

Five Categories of Real Property

1. Residential
2. Commercial
3. Industrial
4. Agricultural
5. Special Purpose

- *residential*—all property used for single-family or multifamily housing, whether in urban, suburban, or rural areas;
- *commercial*—business property, including office space, shopping centers, stores, theaters, hotels, and parking facilities;
- *industrial*—warehouses, factories, land in industrial districts, and power plants;
- *agricultural*—farms, timberland, ranches, and orchards; or
- *special purpose*—churches, schools, cemeteries, and government-held lands.

The market for each of these types of property can be subdivided into the *sales market*, which involves the transfer of title and ownership rights, and the *rental market*, in which space is used temporarily by lease.

IN PRACTICE Although it is possible for a single real estate firm or an individual real estate licensee to perform all the services and handle all the classes of property discussed in this chapter, this rarely is done. While a broad range of services may be available, most firms and professionals specialize to some degree. Some licensees perform only one service for one type of property or client, such as residential sales or commercial leasing. Under one brokerage firm's roof, however, there may be many specializations.

"One-stop shopping" (collecting many specialties under one roof) has become a major umbrella for today's specialization trend, allowing those specialized parts to form a cohesive whole. Having one firm offer brokerage, appraisal, financing, and title insurance services provides added value, convenience, and possible cost savings to the consumer while adding increased profitability to brokerage companies. On the other hand, there is the potential for a conflict of interest. Consult an attorney to ensure proper procedures are followed.

■ THE REAL ESTATE MARKET

A **market** is a place where goods can be bought and sold. A market may be a specific place, such as the village square, or it may be a vast, complex, worldwide economic system for moving goods and services. In either case, the function of a market is to provide a setting in which supply and demand can establish market value, making it advantageous for buyers and sellers to trade.

Supply and Demand

The forces of **supply and demand** in the market determine how prices for goods and services are set. Essentially, when supply increases and demand remains stable, prices go down; when demand increases and supply remains stable, prices go up. Greater supply means producers need to attract more buyers, so they lower prices. Greater demand means producers can raise their prices because buyers compete for the product.

> When supply increases and demand remains stable, prices go down. When demand increases and supply remains stable, prices go up.

Supply and demand in the real estate market   Two characteristics of real estate govern the way the market reacts to the pressures of supply and demand: uniqueness and immobility. *Uniqueness* means that no matter how similar two parcels of real estate may appear, they are never *exactly* alike. Each occupies its own unique geographic location, and two properties are never exactly the same inside. *Immobility* refers to the fact that property cannot be relocated to satisfy demand where supply is low. Nor do buyers necessarily make relocation decisions based on greater housing supply in a certain locale. For these reasons, real estate markets are *local markets*. Each geographic area has different types of real estate and different conditions that drive prices. In these defined hubs of activity, real estate offices can keep track of types of property in demand and specific parcels available.

IN PRACTICE   Technological advances and market changes have widened the real estate professional's local market. No longer limited to a single small area, licensees must track trends and conditions in a variety of different and sometimes distant local markets. Technological devices—computers, the Internet, cell phones, e-fax, global positioning systems, and an ever-expanding gallery of other tools—help real estate practitioners stay on top of their wide-ranging markets.

> *Uniqueness* and *immobility* are the two characteristics of land that have the most impact on market value.

Because of real estate's uniqueness and immobility, the market generally adjusts slowly to the forces of supply and demand. Although a home offered for sale can be withdrawn in response to low demand and high supply, it is much more likely that oversupply will result in a lower price. When *supply* is low, on the other hand, a high demand may not be met because development and construction are lengthy processes. As a result, development tends to occur in uneven spurts of activity.

Even when supply and demand can be forecast with some accuracy, natural disasters can disrupt market trends. Similarly, sudden changes in financial markets, unemployment, and foreclosures can dramatically disrupt a seemingly stable market.

> **Demand and Price**
> Price follows demand: High demand, high prices; low demand, low prices.

Because some forces in these cycles are unpredictable, the best approach is to assume that "good markets don't always last." Skilled real estate licensees are aware of and recognize predictable indicators of the cycles so they can better assist clients in making intelligent sales and purchase decisions.

Factors that tend to affect the *supply side* of the real estate market's supply and demand balance include the labor force, construction and material costs, government controls, and financial policies.

Factors Affecting Supply

Labor force and construction costs   A shortage of skilled labor or building materials or an increase in the cost of materials can decrease the amount of new construction. Construction permit fees and high property transfer costs can also discourage development. An attempt may be made to pass increased construction costs along to buyers and tenants in the form of higher prices and increased rents, which can further slow the market.

Factors that affect the supply of real estate are
- labor force,
- construction costs,
- government controls, and
- government financial policies.

Government controls and financial policies   The government's monetary policy can have a substantial impact on the real estate market. The **Federal Reserve Board** establishes a discount rate of interest for the money it lends to its member banks. That rate has a direct impact on the interest rates that banks charge to borrowers. These interest rates play a significant part in people's ability to buy homes. The Federal Reserve Board attempts to keep the rates at a level that will keep the market moving without leading to inflation.

Governmental agencies, such as the Federal Housing Administration (FHA) and the Department of Veterans Affairs (VA), also have impact by insuring or guaranteeing loans. They are intended to benefit the economy, the consumer, and housing purchases.

Virtually any government action has some effect on the real estate market. Even eminent domain used to "take" land for a highway project may shift the supply or value of land in a local market.

Policies on the taxation of real estate can have both significant and complex effects on the real estate market. Real estate taxation is a necessary source of revenue for local governments. High taxes may deter investors but may be necessary to maintain continued economic growth within the community. Tax incentives can attract new business and industries. With these enterprises come increased employment and expanded residential real estate markets.

Local governments also can influence supply. Land-use controls, building codes, and zoning ordinances help shape the character of a community and control the use of land.

Factors Affecting Demand

Factors that tend to affect the *demand side* of the real estate market include population, demographics, and employment and wage levels.

Factors that affect the demand for real estate are

■ population,
■ demographics, and
■ employment and wage levels.

Population   Shelter is a basic human need, so the demand for housing grows with the population. Although the total population of the country continues to rise, the demand for real estate increases at a faster rate in some areas than in others. In some locations, growth has ceased altogether as the population has declined. This may be due to economic changes (e.g., high unemployment), social concerns (e.g., going green), or population changes (e.g., shifts from colder to warmer climates). The result can be a drop in demand for real estate in one area matched by an increased demand elsewhere.

Demographics   *Demographics* is the study and description of population. The population of a community is a major factor in determining the quantity and type of housing in that community. Family size, the ratio of adults to children, the ages of children, the number of retirees, family income, lifestyle, and the growing number of single-parent and empty-nester households are all demographic factors that contribute to the amount and type of housing needed.

IN PRACTICE   Niche marketing refers to a subset of the market, both in the products and the people who will buy the product. The phrase may reference a specific group in a specific geographical area or property category. It can also refer to the demographics that it is intended to impact. For example, target marketing to specific demographic populations such as the baby boomers (born between 1946–1964), Generation X (born between 1965–1976), and Millennials (born between 1977–1998) or bilingual agents fluent in Spanish and English marketing to Hispanic consumers. By understanding the various niches, real estate licensees are better able to service buyers and sellers on their purchase and sale decisions.

Employment and wage levels   Decisions about whether to buy or rent and how much to spend on housing are closely related to income. When job opportunities are scarce or wage levels low, demand for real estate usually drops.

■ SUMMARY

As we've seen, the real estate market depends on a variety of economic forces, such as interest rates and employment levels. To be successful, licensees must follow economic trends and anticipate where they will lead. How people use their income depends on consumer confidence. Consumer confidence is based not only on perceived job security but also on the availability of credit, the impact of inflation, and actions of the Federal Reserve Board. General trends in the economy, such as the availability of mortgage money and the interest rate that must be paid to have it, will strongly influence an individual's decision to invest in real estate.

Although brokerage is the most widely recognized real estate activity, the industry provides many other services. These include appraisal, property management, property development, counseling, property financing, and education. Most real estate firms specialize in only one or two of these areas; however, the highly complex and competitive nature of our society requires that a real estate licensee be knowledgeable in a number of fields.

Real property can be classified by its general use as residential, commercial, industrial, agricultural, or special purpose. Although many real estate licensees deal with more than one type of real property, they usually specialize to some degree. The trend toward one-stop shopping has added value to the consumers while increasing profitability for brokerage companies.

A market is a place where goods and services can be bought and sold and where price levels can be established based on supply and demand. Because of its unique characteristics, real estate is usually relatively slow to adjust to the forces of supply and demand.

Real estate supply and demand is affected by many factors, including changes in population and demographics, wage and employment levels, construction costs, availability of labor, and governmental monetary policy and controls. Demand influences supply. High demand, high prices; low demand, low prices.

Governmental agencies influence the market by insuring or guaranteeing loans.

CHAPTER 1 QUIZ

1. A professional estimate of a property's market value, based on established methods and using trained, professional judgment, is performed by a
   a. real estate broker.
   b. real estate appraiser.
   c. real estate counselor.
   d. home inspector.

2. In general, when the supply of a certain commodity increases
   a. prices tend to rise.
   b. prices tend to drop.
   c. demand tends to rise.
   d. demand is unchanged.

3. Which factor tends to affect supply in the real estate market?
   a. Population
   b. Demographics
   c. Government controls
   d. Employment

4. Which factor MOST likely influences the demand for real estate?
   a. Labor force
   b. Construction costs
   c. Wage levels and employment opportunities
   d. Government financial policies

5. Property management, leasing, appraisal, financing, and development are all examples of
   a. factors affecting demand.
   b. specializations within the real estate industry.
   c. non-real estate professions.
   d. government regulation of the real estate industry.

6. A REALTOR® is
   a. a specially licensed real estate broker.
   b. any real estate broker who assists buyers, sellers, landlords, or tenants in any real estate transaction.
   c. a member of the National Association of Real Estate Brokers who specializes in residential properties.
   d. a real estate licensee who is a member of the National Association of REALTORS®.

7. A major manufacturer of automobiles announces that it will relocate one of its factories, along with 2,000 employees, to a small town. What effect will this announcement MOST likely have on the small town's housing market?
   a. Houses likely will become less expensive as a result of the announcement.
   b. Houses likely will become more expensive as a result of the announcement.
   c. The announcement involves an issue of demographics, not a supply and demand issue; housing prices will stay about the same.
   d. The announcement involves an industrial property; residential housing will not be affected.

8. A licensee who has several years of experience in the industry decided to retire from actively marketing properties. Now this licensee helps clients choose among the various alternatives involved in purchasing, using, or investing in property. What is the licensee's profession?
   a. Real estate counselor
   b. Real estate appraiser
   c. Real estate educator
   d. REALTOR®

9. The words *broker* and REALTOR® are
   a. interchangeable.
   b. different categories of membership in the National Association of REALTORS®.
   c. different titles offered by separate professional organizations.
   d. unrelated; a broker is a real estate licensee, and a REALTOR® is a member of the National Association of REALTORS®.

10. Schools would be considered part of which real estate classification?
    a. Special-purpose
    b. Industrial
    c. Commercial
    d. Government-held

11. When demand for a commodity decreases and supply remains the same
    a. price tends to rise.
    b. price tends to fall.
    c. price is not affected.
    d. the market becomes stagnant.

12. A licensed real estate professional acting as a point of contact between two or more people in negotiating the purchase of a property is known as a(n)
    a. leasing agent.
    b. sponsoring broker.
    c. property manager.
    d. appraiser.

13. All of the following would affect supply EXCEPT
    a. population.
    b. construction costs.
    c. governmental controls.
    d. the labor force.

14. All of the following are categories of the uses of real property EXCEPT
    a. residential.
    b. developmental.
    c. agricultural.
    d. industrial.

15. All of the following would affect demand EXCEPT
    a. population.
    b. demographics
    c. wage levels.
    d. fiscal policy.

16. All of the following affect how quickly the forces of supply and demand work EXCEPT
    a. degree of standardization of the product.
    b. mobility of the product.
    c. degree of standardization of the product's price.
    d. mobility of the parties to the transaction.

17. A real estate professional who performs a visual survey of a property's structure and systems and prepares an analytical report for a purchaser or an owner is acting as a(n)
    a. educator.
    b. appraiser.
    c. property manager.
    d. home inspector.

18. When the supply of a commodity decreases while demand remains the same
    a. price tends to rise.
    b. price tends to drop.
    c. price tends to not be affected.
    d. price tends to go in the direction of supply.

19. When responsible for maintaining a client's property and maximizing the return on the client's investment, a real estate licensee is serving as a(n)
    a. rental agent.
    b. building maintenance specialists.
    c. property manager.
    d. investment counselor.

20. Detailed information about the age, education, behavior, and other characteristics of members of a population group is called
    a. population analysis.
    b. demographics.
    c. family lifestyles
    d. household data.

CHAPTER 2

Real Property and the Law

■ **LEARNING OBJECTIVES**   *When you've finished reading this chapter, you should be able to*

- ■ **identify** the rights that convey with ownership of real property and the characteristics of real estate;

- ■ **describe** the difference between real and personal property, and the various types of personalty;

- ■ **explain** the types of laws that affect real estate;

- ■ **distinguish** among the concepts of land, real estate, and real property; and

- ■ **define** the following *key terms*

accession	fixture	Real Estate License Act of 2000 (the Act)
air rights	improvement	
appurtenance	land	real property
attachment	location	severance
bill of sale	manufactured housing	situs
bundle of legal rights	personal property	subsurface rights
chattels	personalty	surface rights
deed	real estate	trade fixture
emblements		

■ LAND, REAL ESTATE, AND REAL PROPERTY

The words *land*, *real estate*, and *real property* often are used interchangeably. To most people, they mean the same thing. Strictly speaking, however, these terms refer to different aspects of the same idea. To fully understand the nature of real estate and the laws that affect it, licensees must be aware of these subtle yet important differences.

Land

Land is defined as *the earth's surface extending downward to the center of the earth and upward to infinity*. The term includes permanent natural objects such as trees and water. (See Figure 2.1.)

Land includes not only the surface of the earth but also the underlying soil. Land also refers to objects that are naturally attached to the earth's surface, such as boulders and plants. Land includes the minerals and substances that lie far below the earth's surface (*subsurface*). It even includes the air above the earth, all the way up into space (*airspace*).

Real Estate

Real estate is defined as *land at, above, and below the earth's surface, plus all things permanently attached to it*. These attachments may be natural or artificial, such as buildings. (See Figure 2.1.)

F I G U R E   2.1

Land, Real Estate, and Real Property

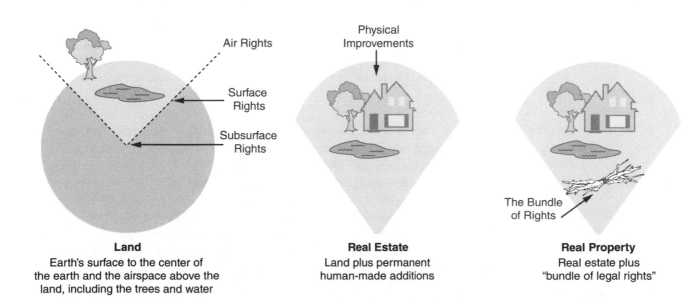

Land
Earth's surface to the center of the earth and the airspace above the land, including the trees and water

Real Estate
Land plus permanent human-made additions

Real Property
Real estate plus "bundle of legal rights"

The term *real estate* is similar to the term *land,* but it means much more. *Real estate* includes the natural land along with all human-made improvements. An **improvement** is any artificial addition to land, such as a building or a fence.

The term *improvement,* as used in the real estate industry, refers to any addition to the land. The word is neutral. It doesn't matter whether the artificial attachment makes the property better-looking or more useful, more or less valuable, the land still is said to be *improved.* Land also may be improved by streets, utilities, sewers, and other additions that make it suitable for building.

Real Property

The term *real property* is the broadest of all. It includes both land and real estate. **Real property** is defined as *the interests, benefits, and rights that are automatically included in the ownership of land and real estate.* (See Figure 2.1.)

Real property includes the surface, subsurface, airspace, any improvements, and the *bundle of legal rights*—the legal rights of ownership that attach to ownership of a parcel of real estate (discussed later in this chapter).

Real property often is coupled with the word **appurtenance.** An appurtenance is anything associated with the property, although not necessarily a direct part of it. Typical appurtenances include parking spaces in multiunit buildings, easements, water rights, and other improvements. An appurtenance is connected to the property, and ownership of the appurtenance normally transfers to the new owner when the property is sold.

IN PRACTICE When consumers talk about buying or selling homes, office buildings, and land, they often will call all these properties *real estate.* For practical purposes, the term is synonymous with *real property* as defined here. In everyday usage, then, remember that *real estate* has come to include the legal rights of ownership specified in the formal definition of *real property.* Sometimes people also use the term *realty* instead.

Surface, subsurface, and air rights The right to use the surface of the earth is referred to as a **surface right.** However, real property ownership also can include **subsurface rights,** which are the rights to the natural resources lying below the earth's surface. Although it may be difficult to imagine, the two rights are distinct. An owner may transfer her surface rights without transferring the subsurface rights.

■ **FOR EXAMPLE** A landowner sells the rights to any oil and gas found beneath her farm to an oil company. Later, the same landowner sells the remaining interests (the surface, air, and limited subsurface rights) to a buyer, reserving the rights to any coal that may be found in the land. This buyer sells the remaining land to yet another buyer but retains the farmhouse, stable, and pasture. After these sales, four parties now have ownership interests in the same real estate: (1) the original landowner owns all the coal; (2) the oil company owns all the oil and gas; (3) the first buyer owns the farmhouse, stable, and pasture; and (4) the second buyer owns the rights to the remaining real estate. (See Figure 2.2.)

F I G U R E   2.2

Surface and Subsurface Rights

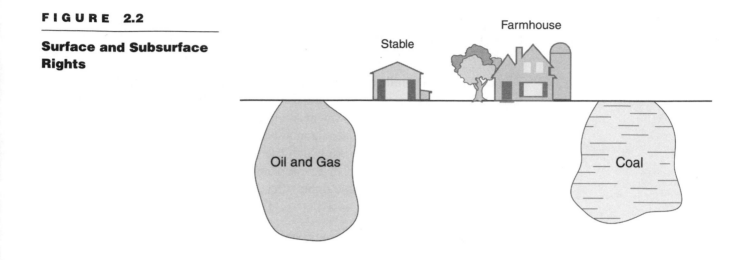

Air rights   The rights to use the space above the earth may be sold or leased independently, provided the rights have not been preempted by law. **Air rights** can be an important part of real estate, particularly in large cities where air rights over railroads must be purchased to construct office buildings. Examples of construction based on air rights include the MetLife Building in New York City and the Prudential Building in Chicago. To construct such a building, the developer must purchase not only the air rights but also numerous small portions of the land's surface for the building's foundation supports.

Before air travel was common, a property's air rights were considered to be unlimited, extending upward into the farthest reaches of outer space. However, now that air travel is common, the courts and the U.S. Congress have put limits on air rights. Today, the courts permit reasonable interference with air rights, such as that necessary for aircraft (and presumably spacecraft), so long as the owner's right to use and occupy the land is not unduly lessened. Governments and airport authorities often purchase adjacent air rights to provide approach patterns for air traffic.

With the continuing development of solar power, air rights, solar rights, and even "view" rights are being closely examined by the courts. A proposed tall building that blocks sunlight from a smaller, existing building may be held to be interfering with the smaller building's right to sunlight, especially if the smaller building is solar-powered. Air and solar rights are established by laws and ordinances that very widely from state to state.

■ OWNERSHIP OF REAL PROPERTY

Traditionally, ownership of real property is described as a **bundle of legal rights**. In other words, a purchaser of real estate actually buys the rights of ownership held by the seller. These rights include the

■ right of possession;
■ right to control the property within the framework of the law;
■ right of enjoyment (that is, to use the property in any legal manner);

■ right of exclusion (to keep others from entering or using the property); and

■ right of disposition (to sell, will, transfer, or otherwise dispose of or encumber the property).

The concept of a bundle of rights comes from old English law. In the Middle Ages, a seller transferred property by giving the purchaser a handful of earth or a bundle of bound sticks from a tree on the property, symbolizing the whole property. The purchaser, who accepted the bundle in a ceremony, became owner of the tree producing the sticks *and* the land to which the tree was attached. Because the rights of ownership (like the sticks) can be separated and individually transferred, the sticks became symbolic of those rights. (See Figure 2.3.)

■ REAL PROPERTY AND PERSONAL PROPERTY

Property may be classified as either real or personal. **Personal property**, sometimes called **personalty**, is *all property that can be owned and that does not fit the definition of real property.*

An important distinction between the two is that personal property is movable. Items of personal property, also referred to as **chattels**, include such tangibles as chairs, tables, clothing, money, bonds, and bank accounts. Trade fixtures are included in this category. They, too, are frequently referred to as *chattels.*

Manufactured Housing

Manufactured housing is defined as *dwellings that are not constructed at the site but are built off-site and trucked to a building lot where they are installed or assembled.* Manufactured housing includes modular, panelized, precut, and mobile homes. Generally, however, the term *mobile home* is used to refer to factory-built housing constructed before 1976. Use of the term *mobile home* was phased out with the passage of the National Manufactured Housing Construction and Safety Standards Act of 1976

F I G U R E   2.3

The Bundle of Legal Rights

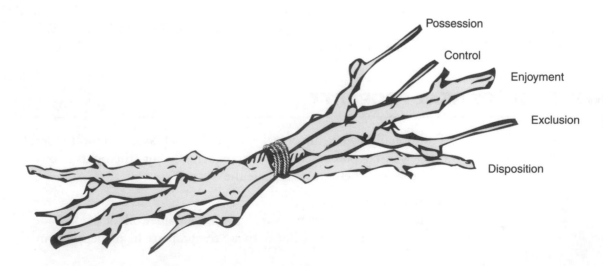

Possession

Control

Enjoyment

Exclusion

Disposition

when manufactured homes became federally regulated. Nevertheless, the term *mobile home* is still commonly used among licensees. Most states have agencies that administer and enforce the federal regulations for manufactured housing.

The distinction between real and personal property is not always obvious. Manufactured housing, for example, is generally considered personal property even though its mobility may be limited to a single trip to a park or development to be hooked up to utilities. Manufactured housing may, however, be considered real property if it becomes permanently affixed to the land. The distinction is generally one of state law. Whether manufactured housing is characterized as real or personal property may have an effect on how it is taxed. Real estate licensees should be familiar with local laws before attempting to sell manufactured housing. Some states permit only specially licensed dealers to sell such housing; other states require no special licensing.

Plants

Trees and crops generally fall into one of two classes. (1) Trees, perennial shrubbery, and grasses that do not require annual cultivation are considered real estate. They attach to the land. (2) Annually cultivated crops such as wheat, corn, vegetables, and fruit, known as **emblements**, are generally considered personal property. As long as an annual crop is growing, it will stay with the real property unless other provisions are made in the sales contract.

In Illinois

When Illinois farmland is sold, it is customary for possession to be transferred to the buyer on March 1. March 1 is chosen because it falls after the last year's crops have been harvested and before the new crops are planted. Because of this "standard" date, no special provisions are required regarding the annual crops. However, when possession is transferred to the buyer on March 1, it also is customary for the buyer to assume full payment of the current year's tax bill *without proration*. This is because she will receive the full benefit of the new crop for that tax year.

The legal term for plants that do not require annual cultivation (such as trees and shrubbery) is *fructus naturales* (fruits of nature); emblements are known in the law as *fructus industriales* (fruits of industry).

If the sale is closed at another time during the year and before the crops are harvested, the sales contract should indicate whether the growing crops are included in the sales price. Sometimes, when the crop is included in the sale, the buyer reimburses the seller for crop-related costs already incurred, such as seed, planting, fertilizing, and spraying. As for farm leases, if an owner wishes to break a lease with a tenant, notification must be given by November 1. This produces the least interference with the cycle of spring planting and fall harvesting. ■

An item of real property can become personal property by **severance**. For example, a growing tree is *real estate* until the owner cuts it down, *severing* it from the property. Similarly, an apple becomes personal property once it is picked from a tree, and a wheat crop becomes personal property once harvested.

It also is possible to change personal property into real property through a process known as annexation. For example, a landowner buys cement, stones, and sand, mixes them into concrete, and constructs a sidewalk across her land. This landowner has effectively converted personal property (cement, stones, and sand) into real property (a sidewalk).

Licensees need to know whether property is real or personal for many reasons. An important distinction arises, for instance, when the property is transferred from one owner to another. *Real property* is conveyed by **deed**, while *personal property* is conveyed by a **bill of sale**.

Classifications of Fixtures

In considering the differences between real and personal property, it is necessary to distinguish between a *fixture* and *personal property*.

Legal Tests of a Fixture

1. Method of attachment
2. Adaptation to real estate
3. Agreement

Fixtures A **fixture** is *personal property that has been so affixed to land or a building that, by law, it becomes part of the real property*. Examples of fixtures are heating systems, elevator equipment in high-rise buildings, radiators, kitchen cabinets, attached bookcases, light fixtures, and plumbing fixtures. Almost any item that has been added as a permanent part of a building is considered a fixture. During the course of time, the same materials may be both real and personal property, depending on their use and location.

Legal tests of a fixture The overall test that is used in determining whether an item is a fixture or personal property is a question of intent. (See Figure 2.4.)

Did the person who installed the item intend for it to remain permanently on the property or for it to be removable in the future? In determining intent, courts use three basic tests:

1. *Method of attachment*—How permanent is the method of attachment? Can the item be removed without causing damage to the surrounding property?
2. *Adaptation to real estate*—Is the item being used as real property or personal property?
3. *Agreement*—Have the parties agreed in writing on whether the item is real or personal property? What does the contract say?

Although these tests may seem simple, court decisions have occasionally been inconsistent. Property that appears to be permanently affixed sometimes has been ruled to be personal property, while property that seems removable has been ruled a fixture. It is important that an owner clarify what is to be sold with the real estate at the very beginning of the sales process.

At the time a property is listed, the seller and real estate agent should discuss which items will be included in the sale. Any item that the seller does not want included in the sale should be replaced prior to public viewing. The written sales contract between the buyer and the seller should *list articles included in the sale if any doubt exists as to whether they are personal property or fixtures*.

FIGURE 2.4

Legal Tests of a Fixture

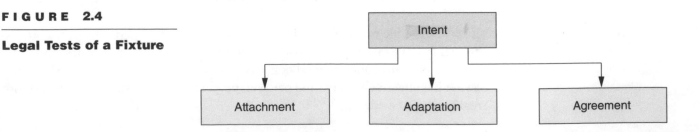

Trade fixtures   A special category of fixture includes property used in the course of business. An article owned by a tenant and attached to a rented space or building or used in conducting a business is a trade fixture, also called a *chattel fixture*. Some examples of trade fixtures are bowling alleys, store shelves, bars, and restaurant equipment. Agricultural fixtures, such as chicken coops and tool sheds, also are included in this category. Trade fixtures must be removed on or before the last day the property is rented. The tenant is responsible for any damage caused by the removal of a trade fixture. Trade fixtures that are not removed become the real property of the landlord. Acquiring the property in this way is known as accession.

Personal property that "turns into" real property does so by **attachment**. However, in commercial real estate, if trade fixtures (personal property) are not removed, they become real property of the landlord. Acquiring property in this way is known as **accession**.

■ **FOR EXAMPLE**   A pizza parlor leases space in a small shopping center. The restaurateur bolted a large iron oven to the floor of the unit. When the pizza parlor goes out of business or relocates, the restaurateur will be able to remove the pizza oven if the bolt holes in the floor can be repaired. The oven is a trade fixture. On the other hand, if the pizza oven was brought into the restaurant in pieces, welded together, and set in concrete, the restaurateur might not be able to remove it without causing structural damage. In that case, the oven might become a fixture.

Trade fixtures differ from other fixtures in these ways:

- Fixtures belong to the owner of the real estate, but trade fixtures are usually owned and installed by a tenant for the tenant's use.
- Fixtures are considered a permanent part of a building, but trade fixtures are removable. Trade fixtures may be attached to a building so they appear to be fixtures, but can be carefully removed.

Legally, fixtures are real property, so they are included in any sale or mortgage. Trade fixtures, however, are considered personal property and are not included in the sale or mortgage of real estate, except by written agreement.

■ CHARACTERISTICS OF REAL ESTATE

Real estate possesses seven basic characteristics that define its nature and affect its use. These characteristics fall into two broad categories—*economic* characteristics and *physical* characteristics.

Economic Characteristics

The economic characteristics of land affect its investment value. These four characteristics are *scarcity*, *improvements*, *permanence of investment*, and *location (situs)*.

Scarcity   We usually do not consider land a rare commodity, but only a quarter of the earth's surface is dry land; the rest is water. The total available supply of land is not limitless. While a considerable amount of land remains unused or uninhabited, the supply in a given location or of a particular quality is generally considered to be limited.

Improvements   Building an improvement on one parcel of land can affect the land's value and use as well as that of neighboring tracts and whole communities. For example, constructing a new shopping center or selecting a nuclear power site or toxic waste dump can dramatically shift land values in a large area.

Permanence of investment   The capital and labor used to build an improvement represent a large fixed investment. Although even a well-built structure can be razed to make way for a newer building, improvements such as drainage, electricity, water, and sewage systems often remain. The return on such investments tends to be long term and relatively stable.

Location   This economic characteristic, sometimes called area preference or **situs**, does not directly refer to a geographic location but rather to people's preferences for given areas. It is the unique quality of these preferences that results in different values for similar units. *Location is the most important economic characteristic of land.*

■ **FOR EXAMPLE**   A river runs through a town, dividing the town more or less in half. Houses on the north side of the river sell for an average of $170,000. On the south side of the river, identical houses sell for more than $200,000. The only difference is that homebuyers think that the south area is a better neighborhood, even though no obvious difference exists between the two equally pleasant sides of town.

Physical Characteristics

Land has three main physical characteristics: *immobility*, *indestructibility*, and *uniqueness*.

Immobility   It is true that some of the substances of land are removable and that topography may shift. Nevertheless, *the geographic location of any given parcel of land can never be changed*. It is fixed or *immobile*.

Indestructibility   Land also is *indestructible*. This permanence of land, coupled with the long-term nature of most improvements, tends to stabilize investments in real estate.

The fact that land is indestructible does not change the fact that man-made *improvements* on land depreciate and can become obsolete, which *may* dramatically reduce the land's value. This gradual depreciation should not be confused with the knowledge that the economic desirability of a given location can change.

Uniqueness   No two parcels of land are ever exactly the same. Although they may be very similar, all parcels differ geographically because each parcel has its own location. The characteristics of each property, no matter how small, differ from those of every other. An individual parcel has no substitute because each is unique. The uniqueness of land also is referred to as *nonhomogeneity*.

Heterogeneity

Four Economic Characteristics of Real Estate

1. Scarcity
2. Improvements
3. Permanence of investment
4. Location *or*

Area of Preference

SIPA

Physical Characteristics of Real Estate

1. Immobility
2. Indestructibility
3. Uniqueness

■ **FOR EXAMPLE**   Because of the uniqueness of property, a person who contracts to buy a new condominium apartment, say, Unit 305, cannot have Unit 307 substituted at the closing, even though the two units appear to be identical. The buyer could sue for *specific performance* (asking the seller to "perform" on the promise of Unit 305) based on the *uniqueness* of real estate.

■ LAWS AFFECTING REAL ESTATE

The unique nature of real estate has given rise to an equally unique set of laws and rights. Even the simplest real estate transaction involves a body of complex laws. Licensees must have a clear and accurate understanding of the laws that affect real estate.

Seven Sources of Law

1. United States Constitution
2. Laws passed by Congress
3. Rules of the regulatory agencies
4. State constitutions
5. State statutes
6. Local ordinances
7. Common law

The specific areas important to the real estate practitioner include law of contracts, general property law, law of agency, and the state's real estate license law. All of these will be discussed at length later in this book. Federal regulations (such as environmental laws) as well as federal, state, and local tax laws also play an important role in real estate transactions. Finally, state and local land-use and zoning laws, as well as environmental regulations, have a significant impact on the practice of real estate, too.

Laws come from seven different sources. They are the *United States Constitution, laws passed by Congress, rules of the regulatory agencies, state constitutions, state statutes, local ordinances,* and *common law* (common usage and court decisions).

A real estate practitioner can't be an expert in all areas of real estate law. However, licensees should know and understand some basic principles. Perhaps most important is the ability to recognize which problems should be referred to a real estate attorney. Only attorneys are trained and licensed to prepare documents defining or transferring rights in property and to give advice on matters of law. *Under no circumstances may a real estate licensee act as an attorney unless she is also a licensed attorney representing a client in only that capacity.*

In Illinois

Key Law for Illinois

The Illinois Real Estate License Act of 2000
■ Click on *www.ilga.gov*
■ Click on *Illinois Compiled Statutes*
■ Click on *Chapter 225 Professions and Occupations*
■ Scroll to *225 ILCS 454*

The practice of real estate in Illinois is governed by the **Real Estate License Act of 2000 (the Act)**, as amended in 2010, and rules established by the Illinois Department of Financial and Professional Regulation. This license law is *Public Act 96-856, Chapter 225 of the Illinois Compiled Statutes, Act 454.* Other laws affecting real estate in Illinois may be found throughout the Illinois compiled statutes, but many of those addressing real property are in *Chapter 765, ILCS.* ■

Because real estate practitioners are involved with other people's real estate and money, the need for regulation of their activities has long been recognized. The purpose of real estate license law is to protect the public from fraud, dishonesty, and incompetence in real estate transactions. All 50 states, the District of Columbia, and all Canadian provinces have passed laws that require real estate practitioners to be licensed. Although state license laws are similar in many broad respects, they may differ on key points, from the amount of education required for a license to appropriate approaches for handling agency relationships. In practice, those differences sometimes are quite significant.

Note: The Real Estate License Act of 2000 is discussed in Chapter 14.

■ SUMMARY

Although most people think of land as the surface of the earth, land actually includes the earth's surface, the mineral deposits under the earth, and the air above the earth. The term *real estate* further expands this definition to include all natural and man-made improvements attached to the land. The term *real property* describes real estate plus the bundle of legal rights associated with its ownership. A buyer of real estate purchases from the seller the legal rights to use the land in certain ways, going back to the old English transfer of bundle rights—the symbolic few branches from a tree. The various rights to the same parcel of real estate may be owned and controlled by different parties. For instance, one person may own the surface rights, one the air rights, and one the subsurface rights.

All property that does not fit the definition of real estate is classified as personal property (or chattels). When articles of personal property are attached to real estate, they may become fixtures and as such are considered part of the real estate. However, personal property attached to real property by a tenant for business purposes is called a trade fixture, and it remains personal property, transportable by the tenant at the end of the lease. The special nature of land as an investment is apparent in both its economic and physical characteristics. The economic characteristics are scarcity, improvements, permanence of investment, and location (situs). The physical characteristics of land are that it is immobile, indestructible, and unique.

Even the simplest real estate transaction reflects a complex body of laws. They are the United States Constitution, laws passed by Congress, rules of the regulatory agencies, state constitutions, state statutes, local ordinances, and common law (shaped by common usage and court decisions).

All 50 states, the District of Columbia, and Canadian provinces have some type of licensing requirement for real estate practitioners. Real estate licensees have an obligation to be familiar with the real estate laws and licensing requirements not only for their own states but for any areas into which their practice may extend.

CHAPTER 2 QUIZ

1. One defining difference between real estate (real property) and personal property is
   - a. real estate includes land and all things permanently attached, while personal property includes property that is movable.
   - b. real estate includes land and the rights and interests inherent in the ownership of land, while personal property includes only air and mineral rights.
   - c. real estate includes the trees and air rights, while personal property includes the house and its contents.
   - d. real estate includes annual crops, while personal property includes mineral rights.

2. A bookstore owner rents space in a commercial building. The bookstore has large tables fastened to the walls where customers are encouraged to sit and read. Shelves create aisles from the front of the store to the back. The shelves are bolted to both the ceiling and the floor. Which of the following best characterizes the contents of the bookstore?
   - a. The shelves and tables are trade fixtures and will be sold when the owner sells the building.
   - b. The shelves and tables are trade fixtures and must be removed before the bookstore's lease expires.
   - c. Because the bookstore is a tenant, the shelves and tables are fixtures and may not be removed except with the owner's permission.
   - d. Because the shelves and tables are attached to the building, they are treated the same way as other fixtures.

3. The term *nonhomogeneity* refers to
   - a. scarcity.
   - b. immobility.
   - c. uniqueness.
   - d. indestructibility.

4. Another term for personal property is
   - a. realty.
   - b. fixtures.
   - c. chattels.
   - d. fructus naturales.

5. When an owner of real estate sells the property to someone else, which of the "sticks" in the bundle of legal rights is she using?
   - a. Exclusion
   - b. Legal enjoyment
   - c. Control
   - d. Disposition

6. A man inherited a farm from his uncle. As a new owner, the first thing he did with the vacant property was to remove all the topsoil, which he sold to a landscaping company. He then removed a thick layer of limestone and sold it to a construction company. Finally, he dug 40 feet into the bedrock and sold it for gravel. When the farm owner died, he left the farm to his daughter. Which of the following statements is *TRUE*?
   - a. The daughter inherits nothing because the farm no longer exists.
   - b. The daughter inherits a large hole in the ground, but it is still a farm, down to the center of the earth.
   - c. The daughter owns the gravel, limestone, and topsoil, no matter where it is.
   - d. The man's estate must restore to its original condition.

7. The buyer and the seller of a home are debating whether a certain item is real or personal property. The buyer says it is real property and should convey with the house; the seller says it is personal property and would not convey without a separate bill of sale. In determining whether an item is real or personal property, a court would NOT consider which of the following?

   a. The cost of the item when it was purchased
   b. Whether its removal would cause severe damage to the real estate
   c. Whether the item is clearly adapted to the real estate
   d. Any relevant agreement of the parties in their contract of sale

8. Which of the following would BEST describe the economic characteristics of real estate?

   a. Location, uniqueness, and indestructibility
   b. Scarcity, immobility, and improvements
   c. Heterogeneity, location, and improvements
   d. Scarcity, improvements, and area preference

9. An owner decides to sell her house and takes the antique front door with her when she moves. In the absence of any provision in the contract, is the owner allowed to remove the door?

   a. Yes, the owner can remove the door, and the act would be known as *accession*.
   b. No, this act of *severance* is not allowed at time of selling because the door is a fixture.
   c. No, this would be *conversion*.
   d. Yes, the owner can remove the door, and the act would be known as *separation*.

10. When the buyer moved into a newly purchased home, the buyer discovered that the seller had taken the electric lighting units that were installed over the vanity in the bathroom. The seller had not indicated that these would be removed. Which of the following is TRUE?

    a. Installed lighting units normally are considered to be real estate fixtures.
    b. The lighting fixtures belong to the seller because he installed them as personal property.
    c. These lighting fixtures are considered trade fixtures, and could be removed.
    d. Original lighting fixtures are real property, but replacement lighting would be personal property and can be taken by the seller.

11. A homeowner is building a new enclosed front porch on his home. A truckload of lumber has been left in his driveway for use in building the porch. At this point, the lumber is considered what kind of property?

    a. A fixture, because it will be permanently affixed to existing real property
    b. Personal property
    c. A chattel that is real property
    d. A trade fixture or chattel fixture

12. Intent of the parties, method of attachment, adaptation to real estate, and agreement between the parties are the legal tests for determining whether an item is

    a. a trade fixture or personal property.
    b. real property or real estate.
    c. a fixture or personal property.
    d. an improvement.

13. Parking spaces in multiunit buildings, water rights, and other improvements are classified as

    a. trade fixtures.
    b. emblements.
    c. subsurface rights.
    d. appurtenances.

14. A person buys a parcel of natural forest. The person then immediately cuts down all the trees and constructs a large shed out of old sheets of rusted tin for storing turpentine, varnish, and industrial waste products. Which of the following statements is *TRUE* about this rusty shed?

    a. The owner's action constitutes improvement of the property.
    b. The shed is personal property.
    c. If the owner is in the business of storing toxic substances, the shed is a trade fixture.
    d. Altering the property in order to construct a shed is not included in the bundle of rights.

15. The phrase *bundle of legal rights* is properly included in

    a. the definition of real property.
    b. a legal description.
    c. real estate transactions.
    d. leases for less than one year.

16. Which of the following is an example of an appurtenance?

    a. Personal property
    b. Water rights
    c. A fixture
    d. A trade fixture

17. All of the following are included in the right to control one's property *EXCEPT*

    a. the right to sell the property to a neighbor.
    b. the right to exclude utility meter readers.
    c. the right to erect "No Trespassing" signs.
    d. the right to enjoy profits from its ownership.

18. According to law, a trade fixture is usually treated as

    a. a fixture.
    b. an easement.
    c. personalty.
    d. a license.

19. A buyer is interested in a house that fits most of her needs, but it is located in a busy area where she is not sure she wants to live. Her concern about the property's location is called

    a. physical deterioration.
    b. area preference.
    c. permanence of investment.
    d. immobility.

20. Which of the following is considered personal property?

    a. Wood-burning fireplace
    b. Awnings
    c. Bathtubs
    d. Patio furniture

3

Concepts of Home Ownership

■ **LEARNING OBJECTIVES** *When you've finished reading this chapter, you should be able to*

- ■ **identify** the various types of housing choices available to homebuyers;
- ■ **describe** the issues involved in making a home ownership decision;
- ■ **explain** the tax benefits of home ownership and the provisions of changes to the tax code;
- ■ **distinguish** the various types of homeowners' insurance policy coverage; and
- ■ **define** the following *key terms*

boot	equity	PITI (principal, interest,
coinsurance clause	homeowners' insurance	taxes, and insurance)
Comprehensive Loss	policy	replacement cost
Underwriting Exchange	liability coverage	replacement cost policies
(CLUE)		

■ HOME OWNERSHIP

People buy homes for both psychological and financial reasons. To many, home ownership is a sign of financial stability. It is an investment that can appreciate in value and provide federal income tax deductions. Home ownership also imparts benefits that are less tangible but no less valuable: pride, security, and a sense of belonging to the community.

Types of Housing

As our society evolves, the needs of its homebuyers become more specialized. Some housing types are not only innovative uses of real estate, but they also incorporate a variety of ownership concepts. These different forms of housing respond to the demands of a diverse marketplace.

Apartment complexes are groups of apartment buildings with any number of units in each building. The buildings may be lowrise or highrise, and the amenities may include parking, security, clubhouses, swimming pools, tennis courts, and even golf courses.

The *condominium* is a popular form of residential ownership, particularly for people who want the security of owning property without the care and maintenance a house demands. Condominium owners share ownership of common facilities such as halls, elevators, swimming pools, clubhouses, tennis courts, and surrounding grounds. Management and maintenance of building exteriors and common facilities are provided by the governing association or by outside contractors, with expenses paid out of monthly assessments charged to owners.

A *cooperative* is similar to a condominium in that it also may offer units with shared common facilities. The owners, however, do not actually own the units. Instead, they buy *shares of stock* in the corporation that holds title to the building. Owners receive proprietary leases that entitle them to occupy particular units. Like condominium unit owners, cooperative unit owners pay their share of the building's expenses.

Planned unit developments (PUDs), sometimes called *master-planned communities*, merge such diverse land uses as housing, recreation facilities, and commercial concerns in one self-contained development. PUDs are planned under special zoning ordinances. These ordinances permit maximum use of open space by reducing lot sizes and street areas. Owners do not have direct ownership in the common areas. A community association is formed to maintain these areas with fees collected from the owners. A PUD may be a small development of just a few homes or an entire planned city.

Retirement communities, or *active adult communities*, many of them in temperate climates, often are structured as PUDs. They may provide shopping, recreational opportunities, and healthcare facilities in addition to residential units.

Highrise developments, sometimes called *mixed-use developments* (MUDs), combine such elements as office space, stores, theaters, and apartment units into a single vertical community. MUDs are usually self-contained, offering convenient options (such as a spa or exercise facility) to those living there.

Converted-use properties are factories, warehouses, office buildings, hotels, schools, churches, and other structures that have been converted to residential use. Developers often find renovation of such properties more aesthetically and economically appealing than demolishing a perfectly sound structure to build something new. An abandoned warehouse may be transformed into luxury loft condominium units, a closed hotel may reopen as an apartment building, or an old factory may be recycled into a profitable shopping mall.

Manufactured housing, including mobile homes, was once considered useful only as temporary residences. Now, however, such homes are more often permanent principal residences or stationary vacation homes. Increased living space now available in the newer models combined with low cost has made such homes an attractive option for many. Housing parks make residential environments possible with community facilities; semi-permanent home foundations; and hookups for gas, water, and electricity.

Modular homes, also referred to as *prefabricated homes*, are also gaining in popularity as the price rises for newly constructed homes (i.e., homes built on a construction site). Each room in a modular home is pre-assembled at a factory, driven to the building site on a truck, and then lowered onto its foundation by a crane. Later, workers finish the structure and connect plumbing and wiring. Entire developments can be built at a fraction of the time and cost of conventional construction.

Time-shares allow multiple purchasers to share ownership of a single property, usually a vacation home. Each owner is entitled to use the property for a certain period of time each year, usually a specific week. In addition to the purchase price, each owner pays an annual maintenance fee.

■ HOUSING AFFORDABILITY

Congress, state legislatures, and local governments work diligently to increase the affordability of housing. Because more homeowners mean more business opportunities, real estate and related industry groups have a vital interest in ensuring affordable housing for all segments of the population.

In recent years, creative financing, low-interest loans, and interest-only loans helped make housing costs more manageable. As a result, 67.5 percent of households were homeowners by the end of 2008, according to the U.S. Bureau of the Census. By 2010, however, easy money for home loans was all but over, and unemployment had risen, making it more difficult for buyers to save the down payment and closing costs needed to secure a mortgage loan.

Certainly, not everyone wants to or should own a home. Home ownership involves substantial commitment and responsibility. People whose work requires frequent moves or whose financial position is uncertain particularly benefit from renting. Renting also provides more leisure time by freeing tenants from management and maintenance.

Those who choose home ownership must evaluate many factors before they decide to purchase property. The purchasing decision must be weighed carefully in light of each individual's financial circumstances. Renters can probably make a higher mortgage payment than their current rent payment, without requiring a pay increase, because of the tax savings realized by home ownership.

The decision of buying or renting property involves considering

■ how long a person wants to live in a particular area,
■ a person's financial situation,

- housing affordability,
- current mortgage interest rates,
- tax consequences of owning versus renting property, and
- what may happen to home prices and tax laws in the future.

Mortgage terms and payment plans are two of the biggest factors when deciding whether to own or rent a home. Although many loan programs of the past are either not offered or offered only to highly cautioned borrowers, liberalized mortgages are still available to those who qualify. For example, the Federal Housing Administration (FHA) and the Department of Veterans Affairs (VA) have programs with low down payments and lower credit score requirements.

Ownership Expenses and Ability to Pay

Home ownership involves many expenses, including utilities (such as electricity, natural gas, and water), trash removal, sewer charges, and maintenance and repairs. Owners also must pay real estate taxes and buy property insurance, and they must repay the mortgage loan with interest. This is what lenders refer to as PITI (principle, interest, taxes, and insurance); those expenses that comprise a monthly payment.

Mortgage Terms

To determine whether a prospective buyer can afford a certain purchase, most lenders use automated underwriting and credit scoring. In the past, the formula for homebuyers who were able to provide at least 10 percent of the purchase price as a down payment was that the monthly cost of buying and maintaining a home—mortgage payments, both principal and interest, plus taxes and insurance impounds—could not exceed 28 percent of gross (i.e., pretax monthly income). The payments on all debts—normally including long-term debt such as car payments, student loans, or other mortgages—could not exceed 36 percent of monthly income. Expenses such as insurance premiums, utilities, and routine medical care were not included in the 36-percent figure but were considered to be covered by the remaining 64 percent of the buyer's monthly income. These formulas may vary, however, depending on the type of loan program and the borrower's earnings, credit history, number of dependents, and other factors. But today, credit scores play a key role when lending institutions decide whether to lend money. (Note that these financial qualification ratios are true for most Fannie Mae and Freddie Mac conforming mortgages, but loans with more liberal ratios are available.)

■ **FOR EXAMPLE** Prospective homebuyers want to know how much house they can afford to buy. The buyers have a gross monthly income of $5,000. The buyers' allowable housing expense, using the 28 percent and 36 percent ratios, may be calculated as follows:

Ratio 1:
$5,000 gross monthly income × 28% = $1,400 total housing expense allowed.

Ratio 2:
$5,000 gross monthly income × 36% = $1,800 total housing expense and other long-term debt allowed.

Memory Tip

The basic costs of owning a home—mortgage *Principal, Interest, Taxes,* and *Insurance*—can be remembered by the acronym **PITI.**

A home purchased at a price of $350,000 ($70,000 down) on a 30-year loan, six percent interest, will ultimately cost the consumer more than $590,000.

Both ratios need to be met independently in most loan scenarios.

In this case, $1,400 (Ratio 1) plus existent debt ($800 indicated) = $2,200. $2,200 exceeds the dollar amount for Ratio 2 (a maximum of $1,800), so Ratio 2 is not met.

If actual debts exceed the amount allowed and the borrower is unable to reduce them, the monthly payment would have to be lowered proportionately using some other loan package or by purchasing a less expensive property. *Debts and housing payment combined cannot exceed 36 percent of gross monthly income.*

Investment Considerations

Current market value –
Property debt = Equity

Purchasing a home offers several financial advantages to a buyer. First, if the property's value increases, a sale could bring in more money than the owner paid, creating a long-term gain. Second, as the total mortgage debt is reduced through monthly payments, the owner's actual ownership interest in the property increases. This increasing ownership interest is called **equity** and represents the paid-off share of the property held free of any mortgage. A tenant accumulates a good credit rating by paying the rent on time, but a homeowner's *mortgage payments build equity and, thus, increase net worth.* Equity also builds when the property's value rises through area appreciation. The third financial advantage of home ownership is in tax deductions available to homeowners but not to renters.

Tax Benefits

To encourage home ownership, the federal government allows homeowners certain income tax advantages. Homeowners may deduct from their income some or all of the mortgage interest paid as well as real estate taxes and certain other expenses identified on page 31. Tax considerations may be an important part of any decision to purchase a home.

In the late 1990s, the federal government enacted several federal tax reforms that significantly changed the importance of tax considerations for most homesellers. For instance, $500,000 is now excluded from capital gains tax for profits on the sale of a principal residence by married taxpayers who file jointly. Taxpayers who file singly are entitled to a $250,000 exclusion. The exemption may be used repeatedly, as long as the homeowners have both owned and occupied the property as their residence for at least two of the past five years.

First-time homebuyers may make penalty-free withdrawals from their tax-deferred individual retirement funds (IRAs) for down payments on their homes. However, these withdrawals are still subject to income tax. The limit on such withdrawals is $10,000 and must be spent entirely within 120 days on a down payment to avoid any penalty.

In short, the changes in tax laws have generally benefited home ownership, which is good news for homeowners and real estate licensees.

The *Tax Reconciliation Act of 2006* provides capital gains tax breaks. As it relates to homeownership, the tax rate for long-term capital gains was reduced. The maximum tax rate on an individual's long-term capital gains was reduced to 15 percent in 2003 through 2008. For taxpayers in the 10–15 percent ordinary income tax rate brackets, the rate on long-term capital gains was reduced to 5 percent in 2003 through 2007, and to 0 percent for 2008 through 2010. After 2010, the long-term capital gains tax rate will be 20 percent (10 percent for taxpayers in the 15 percent tax bracket) if the original rates are not extended before that time.

Exchanges

Real estate investors can defer taxation of capital gains by making property exchanges. Even property that has appreciated greatly since its initial purchase may be exchanged for other property. A property owner will incur tax liability on a sale only if additional capital or property is also received; the tax is *deferred*, not *eliminated*. Whenever the investor sells the property, the capital gain will be taxed. In many states, state income taxes can also be deferred by using the exchange form of property transfer.

To qualify as a tax-deferred exchange, the properties involved must be of *like kind* as defined under Section 1031 of the Internal Revenue Code. The exchanged property must be real estate of equal value and same use. Any additional capital or personal property included in the transaction to even out the value of the exchange is called **boot.** The IRS requires tax on the boot to be paid at the time of the exchange by the party who receives it. The value of the boot is added to the basis of the property for which it is given. Tax-deferred exchanges are governed by strict federal requirements, and competent guidance from a tax professional is essential.

Tax deductions   Homeowners may deduct from their gross income any of the following:

- Real estate taxes (but *not* interest paid on overdue taxes)
- Mortgage interest payments on most first and second homes (the combined amount of acquisition indebtedness cannot exceed $1,000,000, and the combined amount of home equity indebtedness cannot exceed $100,000)
- Certain loan origination fees in the year of purchase (rules differ for refinance and equity loans)
- Loan discount points in the year of purchase (whether paid by the buyer or the seller)
- Loan prepayment penalties

IN PRACTICE   Note that appraisal fees, notary fees, preparation costs, mortgage insurance premiums, and VA funding fees are not interest but are part of the cost of acquiring a home. When it is sold at a later date, these charges can be figured into the cost *basis*. Points are deductible in the year of a house purchase if certain criteria are met. Points are deducted over the life of the loan for a refinance. Note that real estate licensees should not provide tax advice, and homeowners should consult with accountants or attorneys about home ownership or investment tax deductions. The rules are complicated and constantly changing.

■ HOMEOWNERS' INSURANCE

A home is often the largest investment people will ever make. Most homeowners see the importance of protecting their investment by insuring it. Lenders usually require that a homeowner obtain insurance when a debt is secured by the property. While owners can purchase individual policies that insure against destruction of property by fire or windstorm, injury to others, and theft of personal property, most buy a combined **homeowners' insurance policy** to cover all these risks.

Coverage and Claims

The most common homeowners' policy is called a *basic form*. It provides property coverage against

- fire and lightning,
- glass breakage,
- windstorm and hail,
- explosion,
- riot and civil commotion,
- damage by aircraft,
- damage from vehicles,
- damage from smoke,
- vandalism and malicious mischief,
- theft, and
- loss of property removed from the premises when it is endangered by fire or other perils.

A broad-form policy also is available. It covers
- falling objects;
- damage due to the weight of ice, snow, or sleet;
- collapse of all or part of the building;
- bursting, cracking, burning, or bulging of a steam or hot water heating system or of appliances used to heat water;
- accidental discharge, leakage, or overflow of water or steam from within a plumbing, heating, or air-conditioning system;
- freezing of plumbing, heating, and air-conditioning systems and domestic appliances; and
- injury to electrical appliances, devices, fixtures, and wiring from short circuits or other accidentally generated currents.

Further insurance is available from policies that cover almost all possible perils. Special apartment and condominium policies generally provide fire and windstorm, theft, and public **liability coverage** for injuries or losses sustained within the unit. However, they do not usually cover losses or damages to the structure. The basic structure, in such cases, is insured by either the landlord or the condominium owner's association.

A third party, such as an insurance company, often settles any covered insurance claim. When this happens, the third party generally acquires the right to any legal damages available to the insured. This right is called *subrogation*. (In other words, if a house burns down due to a utility company's negligence, and the insured accepts compensation from the insurance company, then the insurance company gains the rights related to possible further payment for damages from the utility company.) Most homeowners' insurance policies contain a **coinsurance clause**. This provision usually requires that the owner maintain insurance equal to a specified percentage (usually 80 percent) of the **replacement cost** of the dwelling (not including the price of the land). An owner who has this type of policy may make a claim for the full cost of the repair or replacement of the damaged property without deduction for depreciation or annual wear and tear.

■ **FOR EXAMPLE**   A homeowners' insurance policy is for 80 percent of the replacement cost of the home, or $80,000. The home is valued at $100,000, and the land is valued at $40,000. The homeowner sustains $30,000 in fire damage to the house. The homeowner can make a claim for the full cost of the repair or replacement of the damaged property without a deduction for depreciation. However, if the owner has insurance of only $70,000, the claim will be handled in one of two ways. The owner will receive either actual cash value (replacement cost of $30,000 less depreciation cost of say $3,000, or $27,000), or the claim will be prorated by dividing the percentage of replacement cost actually covered (0.70) by the policy minimum coverage requirement (0.80). So, 0.70 divided by 0.80 equals 0.875, and $30,000 multiplied by 0.875 equals $26,250.

Comprehensive Loss Underwriting Exchange

Comprehensive Loss Underwriting Exchange (CLUE) is a database of consumer claim history that enables insurance companies to access prior claim information in the underwriting and rating process. The database contains up to five years of personal property claim history. The reports include policy information such as name, date of birth, policy number, and claim information date (date and type of loss, amounts paid, and description of property covered).

IN PRACTICE   Water-related problems have emerged in some properties over time. In particular, significant problems can occur with synthetic stucco exterior finishes and mold. The *exterior insulating finishing system* (EIFS) is a highly effective moisture barrier that also tends to *seal in* moisture—trapping water in the home's walls and resulting in massive wood rot. Frequently, the effects of the rotting cannot be seen until the damage is extensive and sometimes irreparable. If a homeowner suspects that EIFS was used on their home and is causing damage, the homeowner should have the property inspected. Some insurance companies refuse to cover homes with EIFS exteriors, and class action lawsuits have been brought against builders by distressed homeowners.

■ FEDERAL FLOOD INSURANCE PROGRAM

The National Flood Insurance Act of 1968 was enacted by Congress to help owners of property in flood-prone areas by subsidizing flood insurance and by taking land-use and land-control measures to improve future management for floodplain areas. The Federal Emergency Management Agency (FEMA) administers the flood insurance program. The Army Corps of Engineers has prepared detailed maps that identify specific flood-prone areas throughout the country. To finance property with federal or federal-related mortgage loans, owners in flood-prone areas known as special flood hazard areas (SFHAs) are required to obtain flood insurance. The insurance agent must receive a copy of an elevation certificate, a form supplied by a licensed surveyor before determining the appropriate insurance rate. Homeowners' insurance policies always exclude floods, so flood coverage must always be purchased as a totally separate policy.

In designated areas, flood insurance is required on all types of buildings—residential, commercial, industrial, and agricultural—for either the value of the property or the amount of the mortgage loan, subject to the maximum limits available. Policies are written annually and can be purchased from any licensed property insurance broker, the National Flood Insurance Program (NFIP), or the designated servicing companies in each state.

Flood Insurance: What's Covered and What's Not

FEMA defines a flood as "a general and temporary condition of partial or complete inundation of two or more acres of normally dry land or two or more properties from

- an overflow of inland or tidal waves;
- an unusual and rapid accumulation or runoff of surface waters;
- mudflows or mudslides on the surface of normally dry land; or
- the collapse of land along the shore of a body of water (under certain conditions)."

The physical damage to a building or personal property directly caused by a flood is covered by flood insurance policies. For example, damage from sewer backups is covered if it results directly from flooding. Flood policies exclude coverage for losses such as swimming pools, cars, money, animals, groundcover, or underground systems.

Policies are of two types: replacement cost value (RCV) or actual cost value (ACV). Deductibles and premiums vary accordingly.

IN PRACTICE Massive losses in the NFIP due to the Mississippi floods in 1993 caused Congress to pass laws that greatly increase the number of properties that are required to be covered by the NFIP. This requirement results not only in higher expenses for the buyer but also negatively affects property values. Agents should pay attention to what property is in a flood zone and communicate that to potential buyers.

■ SUMMARY

Current trends in home ownership include cooperatives, apartment complexes, condominiums, planned unit developments (PUDs), retirement communities, highrise developments, converted-use properties, modular homes, mobile homes, time-shares/time-uses, and of course, residential housing. Prospective buyers should be aware of the many advantages and disadvantages in home ownership. While a homeowner gains financial security and pride of ownership, both the initial price and the continuing expenses must be considered.

One of the many income tax benefits available to homeowners is the ability to deduct mortgage interest payments (with certain limitations) and property taxes from federal income taxes. Up to $250,000 (filing singly) or $500,000 (married, filing jointly) in house sale profits can now be excluded from capital gains tax. The exemption may be used repeatedly, but the homeowners must have occupied the property for at least two years out of the last five.

To protect their investment in real estate, most homeowners purchase insurance. A basic form homeowners' insurance policy covers fire, theft, and liability, and it can be extended to cover other risks. Many homeowners' policies contain a coinsurance clause that stipulates that the policyholder must maintain insurance in an amount equal to 80 percent of the replacement cost of the home. If this percentage is not met, the policyholder receives only partial compensation for repair costs if a loss occurs. Guaranteed replacement cost policies, with coinsurance met, offer the most security by providing full replacement coverage. Actual cash value policies usually subtract depreciation before determining compensation and result in lower compensation.

The Comprehensive Loss Underwriting Exchange (CLUE) is a database of consumer claim history that enables insurance companies to access prior claim information in the underwriting and rating process.

The federal government requires flood insurance for federally regulated or federally insured mortgage loans for properties located in special flood hazard areas (SFHAs). Lenders may notify buyers of the need for flood insurance during the loan acquisition process, but many buyers will want to know prior to purchase. Sellers who know of a floodplain on their property must disclose it. Floodplain maps, which change from time to time, may be acquired through local government offices or insurance companies.

CHAPTER 3 QUIZ

1. Which of the following is *NOT* a cost or expense of owning a home?
   a. Interest paid on borrowed capital
   b. Homeowners' insurance
   c. Maintenance and repairs
   d. Taxes on personal property

2. Homeowners may deduct all of the following expenses when preparing their income tax return EXCEPT
   a. real estate taxes.
   b. mortgage interest on a first home.
   c. mortgage interest on a second home.
   d. mortgage interest on a third home.

3. A couple paid $56,000 for their property 20 years ago. Today, the market value is $119,000, and they owe $5,000 on their mortgage. With regard to this situation, which of the following is *TRUE?*
   a. The $63,000 difference between the original investment and the market value is their tax basis.
   b. The $114,000 difference between the market value and the mortgage is their equity.
   c. The $63,000 difference between the original investment and the market value will be used to compute the capital gains.
   d. The $114,000 difference between the market value and the mortgage is their replacement cost.

4. A building that is remodeled into residential units and is no longer used for the purpose for which it was originally built is an example of
   a. a converted-use property.
   b. urban homesteading.
   c. planned unit development.
   d. a modular home.

5. A highrise development that includes office space, stores, theaters, and apartment units is an example of which of the following?
   a. Planned unit development (PUD)
   b. Mixed-use development (MUD)
   c. Converted-use property
   d. Special cluster zoning

6. Each room of a house was preassembled at a factory, driven to the building site on a truck, and then lowered onto its foundation by a crane. Later, workers finished the structure and connected plumbing and wiring before the owners moved in. Which term *BEST* describes this type of home?
   a. Mobile
   b. Modular
   c. Manufactured
   d. Converted

7. A single woman bought a home 18 months ago and is now selling because she found a new job in another city. A married couple, (who file joint taxes), have owned their nine-bedroom home for three years. Now, the couple wants to move to a small condominium unit. A single man who owned his home for 17 years, sold it, and will use the proceeds from the sale to purchase a larger house. Based on these facts, which of these people is entitled to the $500,000 exclusion?
   a. The single woman
   b. The married couple
   c. The married couple and the single man
   d. The single woman and the single man

8. When married homeowners (who file jointly) realize a profit from the sale of their home that exceeds $500,000, which of the following is *TRUE?*
   a. The homeowners will not pay capital gains tax if they are over 55.
   b. Up to $125,000 of the excess profit will be taxed as a capital gain.
   c. The excess gain will be taxed at the homeowners' income tax rate.
   d. The excess gain will be taxed at the current applicable capital gains rate.

9. Theft, smoke damage, and damage from fire are covered under which type of homeowners' insurance policy?

a. Basic form
b. Broad form
c. Coinsurance
d. National Flood Insurance Program policies

10. One result of the capital gains tax law is that most homeowners

a. will pay capital gains tax at an 8 percent lower rate on their home sales.
b. may use the one-time $500,000 exclusion if they file their taxes jointly.
c. may use the $250,000 exclusion if they lived in the property for two out of the last five years.
d. will be permitted to use the $125,000 over-55 exclusion more than once.

11. In 2011, a buyer paid two discount points at the closing. Which of the following is NOT deductible from his gross income?

a. Mortgage interest payments on a principal residence
b. Real estate taxes (except for interest on overdue taxes)
c. The gain realized from the sale or exchange of a principal residence
d. Loan discount points

12. A lot is valued at $25,000, and the house is valued at $75,000. If the house is totally destroyed by fire, under a guaranteed replacement cost policy with a coinsurance clause, which of the following would MOST likely occur?

a. The insurance company would pay $100,000 to the owner.
b. The insurance company would pay $75,000 to the owner.
c. The insurance company would pay $60,000 to the owner.
d. The insurance company would pay $80,000 to the owner.

13. A homeowner has $80,000 in equity in his primary residence of three years. The owner sells the residence for $135,000. The broker's commission was 5.5 percent, and other selling expenses amounted to $1,200. What is the owner's taxable gain on this transaction?

a. $61,425
b. $47,575
c. $0
d. $46,375

14. A man incurs the following expenses: (1) $9,500 in interest on a mortgage loan on his residence; (2) $800 in real estate taxes plus a $450 late payment penalty; and (3) a $1,000 loan origination fee paid in the course of purchasing his home. How much may be deducted from his gross income?

a. $9,800
b. $10,500
c. $11,300
d. $11,750

15. A community that merges housing, recreation, and commercial units into one self-contained development is called

a. MUD.
b. PUD.
c. cooperative.
d. condominium.

16. Efforts to increase home ownership include

a. requiring higher down payments.
b. requiring higher credit scores.
c. penalizing first-time homebuyers for using funds from IRAs.
d. lower closing costs for first-time homebuyers.

17. The real cost of owning a home includes certain costs/expenses that many people overlook. Which of the following is NOT such a cost/expense of home ownership?

a. Income lost on cash invested in the home
b. Interest paid on borrowed capital
c. Maintenance and repair expenses
d. Personal property taxes

18. Which of the following is never covered in any homeowners' insurance policy?
    a. Fire and lightening
    b. Explosion
    c. Windstorm and hail
    d. Flood

19. Which clause is found in most homeowners' insurance policies?
    a. Property improvement clause
    b. Coinsurance clause
    c. Co-ownership clause
    d. Property devaluation clause

20. That portion of the value of an owners' property value that exceeds the amount of their mortgage debt is called
    a. equality.
    b. escrow.
    c. surplus.
    d. equity.

CHAPTER

4

Real Estate Agency

When you've finished reading this chapter, you should be able to

- ■ **identify** the various types of agency relationships common in the real estate profession and the characteristics of each;

- ■ **describe** the fiduciary duties involved in an agency relationship;

- ■ **explain** the process by which agency is created and terminated and the role of disclosure in agency relationships;

- ■ **distinguish** the duties owed by an agent to her client from those owed to customers; and

- ■ **define** the following *key terms*

agency	cooperative commission	listing agreement
agency coupled with an interest	customer	material fact
	designated agent	Megan's Law
agent	dual agency	ministerial acts
Article 15 of the Real Estate License Act of 2000	express agency	negligent misrepresentation
	express agreement	
	fiduciary relationship	principal
brokerage agreement	fraud	puffing
buyer agency	general agency	ready, willing, and able buyer
buyer agency agreement	general agent	
client	gratuitous agency	seller disclosure form
commingling	implied agency	single agency
compensation	implied agreement	special agent
confidentiality	latent defect	subagent
consumer	law of agency	universal agent

39

■ INTRODUCTION TO REAL ESTATE AGENCY

The relationship between a real estate licensee and the parties involved in a real estate transaction is not a simple one. In addition to the parties' assumptions and expectations, the licensee is subject to a wide range of legal and ethical requirements designed to protect the seller, the buyer, and the transaction itself. **Agency** is the word used to describe that special relationship. Agency is governed by two kinds of law: *common law*, the rules of a society established by tradition and court decisions, and *statutory law*, the laws, rules, and regulations enacted by legislatures and other governing bodies.

> In Illinois

Agency relationships in Illinois are governed under statutory law. The body of law on which Illinois agency is based is Article 15 of the Real Estate License Act of 2000. ■

The History of Agency

The fundamentals of agency law have remained largely unchanged for hundreds of years. However, the application of the law has changed dramatically, especially in recent years, particularly in residential transactions. As states enact legislation that defines and governs the real estate licensee-client relationship, licensees are re-evaluating their services. They must determine whether they will represent the seller, the buyer, (or the landlord or tenant) or both in a transaction. They also must decide how they will cooperate with other licensees depending on which party the licensee represents.

Even as the laws change, the underlying assumptions that govern the agency relationship remain intact. The principal-agent relationship evolved from the master-servant relationship in English common law. The loyalty replaced the servant's personal interests as well as any loyalty the servant might owe others.

> "Do my actions and words represent my client's best interests?" The answer should always be "Yes."

In today's agency relationship, the agent owes the principal similar loyalty—above any personal interests of the agent. The real estate licensee is regarded as an expert on whom the principal can rely for specialized professional advice.

■ LAW OF AGENCY

> In Illinois

The **law of agency** defines the rights and duties of the principal and the agent. It applies to a variety of business transactions. Both contract law and real estate licensing laws—in addition to the law of agency—interpret the relationship between real estate licensees and their clients. The law of agency is a common-law concept. In Illinois, the *Real Estate License Act of 2000* is given precedence in defining legal real estate agency concepts. Insofar as real estate is considered, Illinois is a statutory agency state that has replaced common-law duties with statutory duties. ■

Definitions

Legally, *agency* refers to a strict, defined legal relationship. In the case of real estate, agency is a relationship that a broker, managing broker, or leasing agent (representing the sponsoring broker) may have with buyers, sellers, landlords, or tenants. Those who hire are *clients*, and those who are hired are agents. A real estate licensee becomes an agent, through a contractual agreement, whether expressed or implied. At this point, the real estate licensee actually becomes a legal, loyal agent obligated to work for the client's best interests at all times, so long as those interests are within the law.

The Term *Agency*

In a broader sense than the agent-client relationship, the relationship of the broker, managing broker, or leasing agent with the sponsoring broker is also called a **general agency** because they represent the sponsoring broker in all daily actions. Contracts most effectively establish the agent-client relationship.

Definitions—Statutory (Real Estate License Act of 2000)

Key terms of the law of agency under Article 15 of the Real Estate License Act of 2000 are defined as follows:

In Illinois

- **Agent**—The individual who is authorized and consents to represent the interests of another person. In the real estate business, a firm's sponsoring broker is the agent and shares this responsibility with the licensees who work for them.
- **Agency**—A relationship in which a consumer has given consent (express or implied) to a real estate licensee to represent the consumer in a real property transaction. Consent may be given to a licensee directly or through an affiliated licensee.
- **Brokerage agreement**—An agreement, made verbally or set out in writing, for an agent or firm to provide brokerage services to a consumer and to receive compensation for providing those services.
- **Client**—The person or entity that a licensee represents in a real property transaction.
- **Compensation**—Payment (monetary or otherwise) made to a person or entity for executing services for a client or customer.
- **Consumer**—A person or entity for whom an agent provides services, which are only to be provided by a licensee, or a person or entity who seeks such services from a licensee.
- **Confidential information**—Information given by a client to a licensee during the term of a brokerage agreement that (1) the client requests (in writing or verbally) the licensee keep in confidence; (2) relates to the client's negotiating position; or (3) could do damage to the client's negotiating position if disclosed. This information must not be shared *unless* the client gives authorization for the licensee to share the information, the information must be shared by law, or the information is revealed by some person or entity other than the licensee.

- ■ **Customer**—A person or entity for whom a licensee is providing services (excluding ministerial acts) but who is not *represented* by the licensee in an agency relationship.
- ■ **Ministerial acts**—Informative or clerical service provided by a licensee to a consumer; providing ministerial acts is not equivalent to active representation. ■

> An agent works *for* the client and *with* the *customer*.

There is a distinction between the level of services a licensee (as agent) provides to a **client** and the level of services a licensee may provide to a **customer**. The client is the **principal** to whom her agent gives advice and counsel. The agent is entrusted with certain confidential information and has fiduciary responsibilities (sometimes called *statutory responsibilities*) to the principal.

In contrast, the customer is entitled to factual information and honest dealings as a consumer but never receives advice and counsel or confidential information about the principal. The real estate licensee may provide ministerial acts to the customer but, as an agent, *works for* the client.

The relationship between the principal and agent must be consensual; that is, the principal delegates authority and the agent consents to act. The parties must agree to form the relationship.

Just as the agent owes certain duties to the principal, the principal has responsibilities toward the agent. The principal's primary duties are to comply with the brokerage agreement and cooperate with the agent. The principal must not hinder the agent and must deal with the agent in good faith. The principal also must compensate the agent according to the terms of the brokerage agreement.

Fiduciary/Statutory Responsibilities

> **Memory Tip**
>
> **Remember COLD AC**
>
> The six common-law fiduciary duties may be remembered by the acronym **COLD AC**: Care, Obedience, Loyalty, Disclosure, Accounting, and Confidentiality.

The agency agreement usually authorizes the real estate licensee to act for the principal. The agent's **fiduciary relationship** of trust and confidence means that the real estate licensee owes the principal certain duties. These duties were not simply moral or ethical; they formed the common law of agency and now are the basis for statutory laws governing real estate transactions. *Under the common law of agency, an agent owes the principal the duties of care, obedience, loyalty, disclosure, accounting, and confidentiality.* Table 4.1 illustrates the agent's obligations to the buyer.

Care   Agents must exercise a reasonable degree of care while transacting the business entrusted to them by the principal. Principals expect the agent's skill and expertise in real estate matters to be superior to that of the average person. The agent should know all facts pertinent to the principal's affairs, such as the physical characteristics of the property being transferred and the type of financing being used.

If the agent represents the seller, care and skill include helping the seller arrive at an appropriate listing price, discovering and disclosing facts that affect the seller, and properly presenting the contracts that the seller signs. It also means properly marketing the property and helping the seller evaluate the terms and conditions of offers to purchase.

TABLE 4.1

Obligations to Buyer

Seller's Broker	Buyer's Broker
Responsibilities	
Be honest with buyer but responsible to seller, including duty of skill and care to promote and safeguard seller's best interests	Be fair with seller but responsible to buyer, including duty of skill and care to promote and safeguard buyer's best interests
Earnest Money Deposit	
Collect amount sufficient to protect seller	Suggest substantial deposit indicating sincerity in offer; put money in interest-bearing account if required by state law; suggest that forfeiture of earnest money be sole remedy if buyer defaults
Seller Financing	
Can discuss but should not encourage financing terms and contract provisions unfavorable to seller, such as (1) no due-on-sale clause, (2) no deficiency judgment (nonrecourse), (3) unsecured note. If a corporate buyer, suggest seller require personal guaranty	Suggest terms in best interests of buyer, such as low down payment, deferred interest, long maturity dates, no due-on-sale clause, long grace period, nonrecourse
Property Condition	
Require seller to fill out all disclosure forms	Require that seller sign property condition statement and confirm representations of condition; require soil and termite inspections, if appropriate; look for negative features and use them to negotiate better price and terms
Documents	
Give buyer a copy of important documents, such as mortgage to be assumed, declaration of restrictions, title report, condominium bylaws, house rules	Research and explain significant portions of important documents affecting transaction, such as prepayment penalties, subordination, right of first refusal; refer buyer to expert advisers when appropriate
Negotiation	
Use negotiating strategy and bargaining talents in seller's best interests	Use negotiating strategy and bargaining talents in buyer's best interests
Showing	
Show buyer properties in which broker's commission is protected, such as in-house or MLS-listed properties. Pick best times to show properties. Emphasize attributes and amenities	Search for best properties for buyer to inspect, widening marketplace to for-sale-by-owner properties, lender-owned (REO) properties, probate sales, unlisted properties. View properties at different times to find negative features, such as evening noise, afternoon sun, traffic congestion
Property Goals	
Be more concerned with sale of seller's property that fits buyer's stated objectives	Counsel buyer as to developing accurate objectives; may find that buyer who wants apartment building might be better off with duplex at half the price or that buyer looking for vacant lot would benefit more from investment in improved property
Offers	
Transmit all offers to seller. Consult with seller about possible action steps (e.g., accept offer, counteroffer, reject offer)	Help buyer prepare strongest offer
Possession Dates	
Consider best date for seller in terms of moving out, notice to existing tenants, impact on insurance, risk of loss provision	Consider best date for buyer in terms of moving in, storage, favorable risk of loss provision if fire destroys property before closing

TABLE 4.1

Obligations to Buyer (Continued)

Seller's Broker	Buyer's Broker
Default	
Discuss remedies upon default by either party. Point out to seller any attempt by buyer to limit liability (nonrecourse, deposit money is sole liquidated damages)	Suggest seller's remedy be limited to retention of deposit money; consider having seller pay buyer's expenses and cancellation charges if seller defaults
Efficiency	
As listing broker, expend much time and effort in helping seller sell property	Broker's role is to assist buyer in locating and acquiring best property, not to sell buyer a particular property
Negotiation	
Use negotiating strategy and bargaining talents in seller's best interests	Use negotiating strategy and bargaining talents in buyer's best interests
Appraisal	
Unless asked, no duty to disclose low appraisal or fact broker sold similar unit yesterday for $10,000 less	Suggest independent appraisal be used to negotiate lower price offer; review seller's comparables from buyer's perspective

An agent who represents the buyer is expected to help the buyer locate suitable property and evaluate property values, neighborhoods and property conditions, financing alternatives, and offers and counteroffers with the buyer's interest in mind.

An agent who does not make a reasonable effort to properly represent the interests of the principal could be found by a court to have been negligent. The agent is liable to the principal for any loss resulting from the agent's negligence or carelessness. The standard of care will vary from market to market and depends on the expected behavior for a particular type of transaction in a particular area.

IN PRACTICE Because real estate licensees have, under the law, enormous exposure to liability, nearly all sponsoring brokers purchase errors and omissions (E&O) insurance policies for their firms. Similar to malpractice insurance in the medical and legal fields, E&O policies cover liability for errors and negligence in the usual listing and selling activities of a real estate office. Errors and omissions insurance is required by virtually all sponsoring brokers in Illinois. However, *no insurance policy will protect a licensee from litigation arising from criminal acts*. Insurance companies normally exclude coverage for violations of fair housing laws and antitrust laws as well.

Obedience The fiduciary relationship obligates the agent to act in good faith at all times, obeying the principal's instructions in accordance with the contract. However, that obedience is not absolute. The agent may not obey instructions that are unlawful or unethical. On the other hand, an agent who exceeds the authority assigned in the contact will be liable for any losses that the principal suffers as a result.

■ **FOR EXAMPLE** A seller tells the listing agent, "I don't want you to show this house to any minorities." Because refusing to show a property to someone on the basis of race is illegal, the agent must not follow the seller's instructions and should withdraw from the agency. Violating fair housing laws is illegal, and the duty of obedience never extends to illegal actions.

Loyalty   The principal's interests come first, even above the self-interest of the agent. Agents must not consider how the result of negotiations will serve their own interests (for instance, by providing them with commission); each agent must perform all services with the goal of promoting the principal's interests. By law, in all fifty states, agents are not permitted to buy property listed with them for their accounts—or buy or sell property in which they have personal interest—unless they have made that interest known to the principal or purchaser and received that party's consent.

In Illinois   Illinois license law prohibits an agent from acting as a dual agent in any transaction to which the agent is a party. The agent must be particularly sensitive to any possible conflicts of interest. ■

Disclosure   It is the agent's duty to keep the principal informed of all facts or information that could affect a transaction. Duty of disclosure includes disclosure of relevant information or material facts that the agent knows or should have known.

The agent is obligated to discover facts that a reasonable person would feel are important in choosing a course of action, regardless of whether those facts are favorable or unfavorable to the principal's position. The agent may be held liable later for a mistake on these issues.

In Illinois   The Illinois Residential Real Property Disclosure form shifts the responsibility for full disclosure from the real estate agent to the seller. It requires that sellers of one- to four-unit residential properties fill out property disclosure forms revealing any material defects they are aware of in the real estate for sale. The completed forms shall be given to buyers before an offer is made. If the disclosure form is delivered after the offer has been accepted and if it has any negative disclosures, the buyer has three days to cancel the contract. Furthermore, *if the seller learns of a new problem after a contract is signed and up until closing, disclosure must be made in writing to the buyer.* In the latter case, the buyer does *not* have the power to simply cancel the contract. Compensation may be negotiated or the problem remedied by the seller. ■

Disclosure forms are usually completed by the seller before he signs the listing agreement or at the time of signing. Regardless of the seller's completion of the disclosure form, the seller's agent is required to disclose all material defects known to her, including in cases where the agent knows that the seller has misrepresented the extent or existence of property defects or has not fully disclosed them. *An agent for a buyer must disclose deficiencies of a property as well.* (See Figure 4.1.)

Accounting   Most states' license laws require that agents periodically report the status of all funds or property received from or on behalf of the principal. Similarly, most state license laws require that licensees give accurate copies of all documents to all affected parties and keep copies on file for a period of time.

FIGURE 4.1

Residential Real Property Disclosure Report

Illinois Association of REALTORS®
RESIDENTIAL REAL PROPERTY DISCLOSURE REPORT

NOTICE: THE PURPOSE OF THIS REPORT IS TO PROVIDE PROSPECTIVE BUYERS WITH INFORMATION ABOUT MATERIAL DEFECTS IN THE RESIDENTIAL REAL PROPERTY. THIS REPORT DOES NOT LIMIT THE PARTIES RIGHT TO CONTRACT FOR THE SALE OF RESIDENTIAL REAL PROPERTY IN "AS IS" CONDITION. UNDER COMMON LAW SELLERS WHO DISCLOSE MATERIAL DEFECTS MAY BE UNDER A CONTINUING OBLIGATION TO ADVISE THE PROSPECTIVE BUYERS ABOUT THE CONDITION OF THE RESIDENTIAL REAL PROPERTY EVEN AFTER THE REPORT IS DELIVERED TO THE PROSPECTIVE BUYER. COMPLETION OF THIS REPORT BY SELLER CREATES LEGAL OBLIGATIONS ON SELLER THEREFORE SELLER MAY WISH TO CONSULT AN ATTORNEY PRIOR TO COMPLETION OF THIS REPORT.

Property Address: _____

City, State & Zip Code: _____

Seller's Name: _____

This report is a disclosure of certain conditions of the residential real property listed above in compliance with the Residential Real Property Disclosure Act. This information is provided as of _____, 20____, and does not reflect any changes made or occurring after that date or information that becomes known to the seller after that date. The disclosures herein shall not be deemed warranties of any kind by the seller or any person representing any party in this transaction.

In this form, "am aware" means to have actual notice or actual knowledge without any specific investigation or inquiry. In this form a "material defect" means a condition that would have a substantial adverse effect on the value of the residential real property or that would significantly impair the health or safety of future occupants of the residential real property unless the seller reasonably believes that the condition has been corrected.

The seller discloses the following information with the knowledge that even though the statements herein are not deemed to be warranties, prospective buyers may choose to rely on this information in deciding whether or not and on what terms to purchase the residential real property.

The seller represents that to the best of his or her actual knowledge, the following statements have been accurately noted as "yes" (correct), "no" (incorrect) or "not applicable" to the property being sold. If the seller indicates that the response to any statement, except number 1, is yes or not applicable, the seller shall provide an explanation, in the additional information area of this form.

YES   NO   N/A
1. ____ ____ ____ Seller has occupied the property within the last 12 months. (No explanation is needed.)
2. ____ ____ ____ I am aware of flooding or recurring leakage problems in the crawlspace or basement.
3. ____ ____ ____ I am aware that the property is located in a flood plain or that I currently have flood hazard insurance on the property.
4. ____ ____ ____ I am aware of material defects in the basement or foundation (including cracks and bulges).
5. ____ ____ ____ I am aware of leaks or material defects in the roof, ceilings or chimney.
6. ____ ____ ____ I am aware of material defects in the walls or floors.
7. ____ ____ ____ I am aware of material defects in the electrical system.
8. ____ ____ ____ I am aware of material defects in the plumbing system (includes such things as water heater, sump pump, water treatment system, sprinkler system, and swimming pool).
9. ____ ____ ____ I am aware of material defects in the well or well equipment.
10. ____ ____ ____ I am aware of unsafe conditions in the drinking water.
11. ____ ____ ____ I am aware of material defects in the heating, air conditioning, or ventilating systems.
12. ____ ____ ____ I am aware of material defects in the fireplace or woodburning stove.
13. ____ ____ ____ I am aware of material defects in the septic, sanitary sewer, or other disposal system.
14. ____ ____ ____ I am aware of unsafe concentrations of radon on the premises.
15. ____ ____ ____ I am aware of unsafe concentrations of or unsafe conditions relating to asbestos on the premises.
16. ____ ____ ____ I am aware of unsafe concentrations of or unsafe conditions relating to lead paint, lead water pipes, lead plumbing pipes or lead in the soil on the premises.
17. ____ ____ ____ I am aware of mine subsidence, underground pits, settlement, sliding, upheaval, or other earth stability defects on the premises.
18. ____ ____ ____ I am aware of current infestations of termites or other wood boring insects.
19. ____ ____ ____ I am aware of a structural defect caused by previous infestations of termites or other wood boring insects.
20. ____ ____ ____ I am aware of underground fuel storage tanks on the property.
21. ____ ____ ____ I am aware of boundary or lot line disputes.
22. ____ ____ ____ I have received notice of violation of local, state or federal laws or regulations relating to this property, which violation has not been corrected.
23. ____ ____ ____ I am aware that this property has been used for the manufacture of methamphetamine as defined in Section 10 of the Methamphetamine Control and Community Protection Act.

Note: These disclosures are not intended to cover the common elements of a condominium, but only the actual residential real property including limited common elements allocated to the exclusive use thereof that form an integral part of the condominium unit.
Note: These disclosures are intended to reflect the current condition of the premises and do not include previous problems, if any, that the seller reasonably believes have been corrected.

If any of the above are marked "not applicable" or "yes", please explain here or use additional pages, if necessary:

_____

_____

_____

Check here if additional pages used: ____

Seller certifies that seller has prepared this statement and certifies that the information provided is based on the actual notice or actual knowledge of the seller without any specific investigation or inquiry on the part of the seller. The seller hereby authorizes any person representing any principal in this transaction to provide a copy of this report, and to disclose any information in the report, to any person in connection with any actual or anticipated sale of the property.

Seller: _____ Date: _____

Seller: _____ Date: _____

PROSPECTIVE BUYER IS AWARE THAT THE PARTIES MAY CHOOSE TO NEGOTIATE AN AGREEMENT FOR THE SALE OF THE PROPERTY SUBJECT TO ANY OR ALL MATERIAL DEFECTS DISCLOSED IN THIS REPORT ("AS IS"). THIS DISCLOSURE IS NOT A SUBSTITUTE FOR ANY INSPECTIONS OR WARRANTIES THAT THE PROSPECTIVE BUYER OR SELLER MAY WISH TO OBTAIN OR NEGOTIATE. THE FACT THAT THE SELLER IS NOT AWARE OF A PARTICULAR CONDITION OR PROBLEM IS NO GUARANTEE THAT IT DOES NOT EXIST. PROSPECTIVE BUYER IS AWARE THAT HE MAY REQUEST AN INSPECTION OF THE PREMISES PERFORMED BY A QUALIFIED PROFESSIONAL.

Prospective Buyer: _____ Date: _____ Time: _____

Prospective Buyer: _____ Date: _____ Time: _____

108 Revised 08/09   COPYRIGHT © BY ILLINOIS ASSOCIATION OF REALTORS®

Source: Published with Permission, Illinois Association of REALTORS®.

FIGURE 4.1

Residential Real Property Disclosure Report (continued)

RESIDENTIAL REAL PROPERTY DISCLOSURE ACT
ARTICLE 2: DISCLOSURES
765 ILCS 77/5 et seq.

Section 5: As used in this Act, unless the context otherwise requires the following terms have the meaning given in this section:

"Residential real property" means real property improved with not less than one nor more than four residential dwelling units; units in residential cooperatives; or, condominium units including the limited common elements allocated to the exclusive use thereof that form an integral part of the condominium unit.

"Seller" means every person or entity who is an owner, beneficiary of a trust, contract purchaser or lessee of a ground lease, who has an interest (legal or equitable) in residential real property. However, "seller" shall not include any person who has both (i) never occupied the residential real property and (ii) never had the management responsibility for the residential real property nor delegated such responsibility for the residential real property to another person or entity.

"Prospective buyer" means any person or entity negotiating or offering to become an owner or lessee of residential real property by means of a transfer for value to which this Act applies.

Section 10. Except as provided in Section 15, this Act applies to any transfer by sale, exchange, installment land sale-contract, assignment of beneficial interest, lease with an option to purchase, ground lease or assignment of ground lease of residential real property.

Section 15. The provisions of the Act do not apply to the following:

(1) Transfers pursuant to court order, including, but not limited to, transfers ordered by a probate court in administration of an estate, transfers between spouses resulting from a judgment of dissolution of marriage or legal separation, transfers pursuant to an order of possession, transfers by a trustee in bankruptcy, transfers by eminent domain and transfers resulting from a decree for specific performance.

(2) Transfers from a mortgagor to a mortgagee by deed in lieu of foreclosure or consent judgement, transfer by judicial deed issued pursuant to a foreclosure sale to the successful bidder or the assignee of a certificate of sale, transfer by a collateral assignment of a beneficial interest of a land trust, or a transfer by a mortgagee or a successor in interest to the mortgagee's secured position or a beneficiary under a deed in trust who has acquired the real property by deed in lieu of foreclosure, consent judgement or judicial deed issued pursuant to a foreclosure sale.

(3) Transfers by a fiduciary in the course of the administration of a decedent's estate, guardianship, conservatorship, or trust.

(4) Transfers from one co-owner to one or more other co-owners.

(5) Transfers pursuant to testate or intestate succession.

(6) Transfers made to a spouse, or to a person or persons in the lineal line of consanguinity of one or more of the sellers.

(7) Transfers from an entity that has taken title to residential real property from a seller for the purpose of assisting in the relocation of the seller, so long as the entity makes available to all prospective buyers a copy of the disclosure form furnished to the entity by the seller.

(8) Transfers to or from any governmental entity.

(9) Transfers of newly constructed residential real property that has not been occupied.

Section 20. A seller of residential real property shall complete all applicable items in the disclosure document described in Section 35 of this Act. The seller shall deliver to the prospective buyer the written disclosure statement required by this Act before the signing of a written agreement by the seller and prospective buyer that would, subject to the satisfaction of any negotiated contingencies, require the prospective buyer to accept a transfer of the residential real property.

Section 25. Liability of seller. (a) The seller is not liable for any error, inaccuracy, or omission of any information delivered pursuant to the Act if (i) the seller had no knowledge of the error, inaccuracy, or omission, (ii) the error, inaccuracy, or omission was based on a reasonable belief that a material defect or other matter not disclosed had been corrected, or (iii) the error, inaccuracy, or omission was based on information provided by a public agency or by a licensed engineer, land surveyor, structural pest control operator, or by a contractor about matters within the scope of the contractor's occupation and the seller had no knowledge of the error, inaccuracy or omission.

(b) The seller shall disclose material defects of which the seller has actual knowledge.

(c) The seller is not obligated by this Act to make any specific investigation or inquiry in an effort to complete the disclosure statement.

Section 30. Disclosure supplement. If prior to closing, any seller has actual knowledge of an error, inaccuracy, or omission in any prior disclosure document after delivery of that disclosure document to a prospective buyer, that seller shall supplement the prior disclosure document with a written supplemental disclosure.

Section 35. Disclosure report form. The disclosures required of a seller by this Act, shall be made in the following form: [form on reverse side]

Section 40. Material defect. If a material defect is disclosed in the Residential Real Property Disclosure Report, after acceptance by the prospective buyer of an offer or counter-offer made by a seller or after the execution of an offer made by a prospective buyer that is accepted by the seller for the conveyance of the residential real property, then the Prospective Buyer may, within three business days after receipt of that Report by the prospective buyer, terminate the contract or other agreement without any liability or recourse except for the return to prospective buyer of all earnest money deposits or down payments paid by prospective buyer in the transaction. If a material defect is disclosed in a supplement to this disclosure document, the prospective buyer shall not have a right to terminate unless the material defect results from an error, inaccuracy, or omission of which the seller had actual knowledge at the time the prior disclosure document was completed and signed by the seller. The right to terminate the contract, however, shall no longer exist after the conveyance of the residential real property. For purposes of the Act the termination shall be deemed to be made when written notice of termination is personally delivered to at least one of the sellers identified in the contract or other agreement or when deposited, certified or registered mail, with the United States Postal Service, addressed to one of the sellers at the address indicated in the contract or agreement, or, if there is not an address contained therein, then at the address indicated for the residential real property on the Report.

Section 45. This Act is not intended to limit or modify any obligation to disclose created by any other statute or that may exist in common law in order to avoid fraud, misrepresentation, or deceit in the transaction.

Section 50. Delivery of the Residential Real Property Disclosure Report provided by this Act shall be by:

1) personal or facsimile delivery to the prospective buyer;

2) depositing the report with the United States Postal Service, postage prepaid, first class mail, addressed to the prospective buyer at the address provided by the prospective buyer or indicated on the contract or other agreement, or

3) depositing the report with an alternative delivery service such as Federal Express, UPS, or Airborne, delivery charges prepaid, addressed to the prospective buyer at the address provided by the prospective buyer or indicated on the contract or other agreement.

For purposes of the Act, delivery to one prospective buyer is deemed delivery to all prospective buyers. Delivery to authorized individual acting on behalf of a prospective buyer constitutes delivery to all prospective buyers. Delivery of the Report is effective upon receipt by the prospective buyer. Receipt may be acknowledged on the Report, in an agreement for the conveyance of the residential real property, or shown in any other verifiable manner.

Section 55. Violations and damages. If the seller fails or refuses to provide the disclosure document prior to the conveyance of the residential real property, the buyer shall have the right to terminate the contract. A person who knowingly violates or fails to perform any duty prescribed by any provision of the Act or who discloses any information on the Residential Real Property Disclosure Report that he knows to be false shall be liable in the amount of actual damages and court costs, and the court may award reasonable attorney fees incurred by the prevailing party.

Section 60. No action for violation of the Act may be commenced later than one year from the earlier of the date of possession, date of occupancy or date of recording of an instrument of conveyance of the residential real property.

In Illinois

Illinois licensees are required to deliver true copies of all executed sales contracts to the people who signed them within 24 hours. In Illinois, all funds entrusted to a licensee must be deposited in a special escrow account by the next business day following the signing of a sales contract or lease. **Commingling** such monies with the licensee's personal or general business funds is illegal. **Conversion**, the practice of using those escrow funds as the licensee's own money, is illegal as well. Licensees should be aware that records of escrow account transactions and reconciliations must be kept on file for at least *five years.* ∎

Confidentiality **Confidentiality** is a key element of fiduciary duties. Client information obtained during the term of the brokerage agreement must be kept confidential. For example, when the principal is the seller, the agent may not reveal such things as the principal's willingness to accept less than the listing price or urgency to sell, *unless* the principal has authorized the disclosure. If the principal is the buyer, the agent may not disclose that the buyer will pay a higher price, is under a tight moving schedule, or other facts that might harm the principal's bargaining position.

These statutory duties, based on (but replacing) common-law duties, are set forth in Article 15 of the Real Estate License Act of 2000. According to this statute, the agent must

- perform the terms of the brokerage agreement between a sponsoring broker and the client;
- promote the best interests of the client by
    - seeking a transaction at the price and terms stated in the brokerage agreement or at a price and terms otherwise acceptable to the client,
    - timely presenting all offers to and from the client, unless the client has waived this duty,
    - disclosing to the client material facts concerning the transaction of which the licensee has actual knowledge, unless that information is confidential information,
    - timely accounting for all money and property received in which the client has, may have, or should have had an interest,
    - obeying specific directions of the client that are not otherwise contrary to applicable statutes, ordinances, or rules, and
    - acting in a manner consistent with promoting the client's best interests as opposed to a licensee's or any other person's self-interest;
- exercise reasonable skill and care in the performance of brokerage services;
- keep confidential all confidential information received from the client; and
- comply with all the requirements of the Act and all applicable statutes and regulations, including fair housing and civil rights.

An agent may not disclose personal, confidential information about her principal. However, known material facts about the property's physical condition or its environs must always be disclosed. A **material fact** is any fact that, if known, might reasonably be expected to affect the course of events.

| In Illinois | Under Section 15-15 (2) (C) of the Act, material facts do not include the following when located on or related to real estate that is not the subject of the transaction: |

- Physical conditions that do not have a substantial adverse effect on the value of the real estate
- Fact situations
- Occurrences ■

Opinion versus Fact

Real estate licensees and other staff members must always be careful about the statements they make. They must be sure that the customer understands whether the statement is an opinion or a fact. Statements of *opinion* are permissible only as long as they are offered as opinions and without any intention to deceive.

Statements of *fact* must be accurate. Exaggeration of a property's benefits is called **puffing**. While puffing is legal, licensees must ensure that none of their statements can be interpreted as fraudulent. **Fraud** is the intentional misrepresentation of a material fact in such a way as to harm or take advantage of another person. That includes not only making false statements about a property but also intentionally concealing or failing to disclose important facts.

The misrepresentation or omission does not have to be intentional to result in licensee liability. *A negligent misrepresentation occurs when the licensee should have known that a statement about a material fact was false.* If the buyer relies on the licensee's statement, the licensee is liable for any damages that result. Similarly, a licensee who accidentally fails to perform some act—for instance, forgetting to deliver a counteroffer—may be liable for damages that result from such a negligent omission.

■ **FOR EXAMPLE** While showing a potential buyer an average-looking house, the broker described even its plainest features as "charming" and "beautiful." Because the statements were obviously the broker's personal opinions designed to encourage a positive feeling about the property (or puff it up), the truth or falsity of the statements is not an issue. A broker was asked by a potential buyer if a particular neighborhood was safe. The broker knew that the area was experiencing a skyrocketing rate of violent crime but assured the buyer that no problem existed. The broker also neglected to inform the buyer that the lot next to the house the buyer was considering had been sold to a waste disposal company for use as a toxic dump. Both might be examples of fraudulent misrepresentation.

If a contract to purchase real estate is obtained as a result of fraudulent misstatements, the contract may be disaffirmed or renounced by the purchaser. In such a case, the licensee not only loses a commission but can be liable for damages if either party suffers loss because of the misrepresentation. If the licensee's misstatements were based on the owner's own inaccurate statements and the licensee had no independent duty to investigate their accuracy, the licensee may be entitled to a commission, even if the buyer rescinds the sales contract.

In Illinois

An Illinois licensee may be held liable to the buyer under the *Illinois Consumer Fraud and Deceptive Practices Act*. Licensees found in violation of this act may be required to pay the plaintiffs' attorneys' fees and court costs in addition to damages. The act prohibits the use, within a trade or profession, of any deception, fraud, false promise, misrepresentation or concealment, suppression, or omission of any material fact with the intent that others rely on it. A real estate brokerage business clearly fits within the meaning of the act, and the courts of Illinois have ruled accordingly. ■

Latent Defects

The seller has a duty to disclose any known latent defects that threaten structural soundness or personal safety. A structural defect that would not normally be uncovered over the course of an ordinary inspection (due to the placement or type of defect, for instance) is referred to as a **latent defect**. Buyers have been able to either rescind the sales contract or receive damages when a seller fails to reveal known latent defects. The courts also have decided in favor of the buyer when the seller neglected to reveal violations of zoning or building codes.

In addition to the seller's duty to disclose latent defects, the seller's licensed real estate agent has an independent duty to conduct a reasonably competent and diligent inspection of the property. It is the licensee's duty to discover any material facts that may affect the property's value or desirability, whether or not they are known to or disclosed by the seller. Any such material facts discovered by the licensee must be disclosed to prospective buyers. If the licensee should have known about a substantial defect that is detected later by the buyer, the licensee may be liable to the buyer for any damages resulting from that defect. The statute of limitations is one year for buyer action.

■ **FOR EXAMPLE** The listing broker knew that a house had been built on a landfill. A few days after the house was listed, another broker in the same real estate office noticed that the living room floor was uneven and sagging in places. In some states, both brokers have a duty to conduct further investigations into the structural soundness of the property. In other states, no such duty exists, but the listing broker would have the duty of discussing the issue with the seller and advising the buyer to have an inspection performed. They cannot simply ignore the problem or place throw rugs over particularly bad spots and hope buyers won't look underneath. If the seller refuses to disclose the problem, then the broker should refuse the listing.

In Illinois

The Illinois Appellate Court, in *Harkala v. Wildwood*, 1st Dist. (1990), held there was no breach of duty to a party in a real estate transaction "unless the realtor could have discovered the falsity of the representation by exercise of ordinary care" and cited *Munjal v. Baird & Warner, Inc., et al.*, 2nd Dist. (1985), which held that a broker or salesperson has no duty to discover "latent material defects" in a property if a seller has not disclosed these defects to her prior to sale. The Harkala decision further held that using the phrase "good buy" was not a violation of the Consumer Fraud Act absent knowledge of latent defects. This decision underscored the need to find ways by which a licensee could obtain relevant information about a listed property from the seller to avoid future litigation from unhappy buyers. Although sellers do have a duty to disclose those issues of which they are aware, buyers are increasingly being held responsible for discovering issues of which they are concerned. ◼

IN PRACTICE   Even the most conscientious licensees can commit errors or inadvertently omit required steps during a real estate transaction; in some cases these mistakes can have negative financial repercussions for one or more of the parties involved. When a lawsuit arises as a result of errors or omissions, licensees can rely on a type of business liability insurance called errors and omissions insurance to help cover the cost of defending the suit.

Stigmatized Properties

Stigmatized properties are those properties that society has branded undesirable because of events that occurred there. *Stigma* is the continuing negative association with or feeling about the property. Typically, the stigma is a criminal event such as homicide, gang-related activity, or a tragedy such as suicide. Properties have even been stigmatized by rumors that they are haunted. Because of the potential liability to a licensee for inadequately researching and disclosing material facts concerning a property's condition, licensees should seek legal counsel when dealing with a stigmatized property.

In Illinois	*Article 15 of the Real Estate License Act of 2000* states that in dealing with specific situations related to disclosure, *"no cause of action shall arise against a licensee for the failure to disclose that an occupant of that property was afflicted with HIV or any other medical condition or that the property was the site of an act or occurrence which had no effect on the physical condition of the property or its environment or the structures located thereon."*

Article 15, Section 15–20, continues:

- ◼ "... no cause of action shall arise against a licensee for the failure to disclose a fact situation on property that is not the subject of the transaction."
- ◼ "... no cause of action shall arise against a licensee for the failure to disclose physical conditions, located on property that is not the subject of the transaction, that do not have a substantial adverse effect on the value of the real estate that is the subject of the transaction."

For any action brought under Article 15, "the court may in its discretion, award only actual damages and court costs or grant injunctive relief, when appropriate."

Any action brought under Article 15 must commence within two years after the person bringing the action knew or should have known of such act or omission. In no event can the action be brought more than five years after the date on which the act or omission occurred. If the person entitled to bring the action is under the age of 18 or under legal disability, the period of limitation shall not begin to run until the disability is removed. ◼

The *buyer's agent* is the one to suggest the *highest range of prices* the buyer should consider, based on comparable values and current market. The agent's aim is to help the buyer get the *lowest price possible, given all other buyer concerns and needs.* The buyer's agent discloses information about how long a property has been listed or why the owner is selling, if known. Of course, a *seller's* agent who discloses such information violates the agent's fiduciary/statutory duties of loyalty to the seller.

The seller's disclosure form is a good guide to follow for what *must* be disclosed to all parties by the listing side of a transaction. In all other respects, unless it is illegal or a material fact about the property itself, the seller's agent should follow the seller's lawful instructions. A buyer's agent should be on watch and do what research is possible. When in doubt, consult the sponsoring broker.

Megan's Law

At the state level, Megan's Law is a general name for laws requiring law enforcement authorities to make information available to the public regarding registered sex offenders. Individual states decide what information will be made available and how it is to be disseminated. Commonly included information includes the offender's name, picture, address, incarceration date, and nature of crime. The information is often displayed on public sites but can also be published in newspapers and pamphlets or disseminated through various other means.

At the federal level, Megan's Law is known as the Sexual Offender Act of 1994 and requires persons convicted of sex crimes against children to notify local law enforcement of any change of address or employment after release from custody (such as prison or a psychiatric facility). The notification requirement may be imposed for a fixed period of time—usually at least ten years—or permanently.

Some states may legislate registration for all sex crimes, even if no minors were involved. It is a felony in most jurisdictions to fail to register or fail to update information.

| In Illinois | As noted, Article 15, Section 15–20, of the Act states, "No cause of action shall arise against a licensee for the failure to disclose . . . fact situations on property that is not the subject of the transaction . . ."

Listing agents have no legal duty to disclose that a known sex offender resides in a property near a listed home, but skilled buyer's agents should be watchful for any signals of hard-to-identify issues. Sex offender location lists are public information, and a buyer's agent should refer a buyer client to such lists if asked. When in doubt, consult an attorney. ■

Creation of Agency

An agency relationship may be based on a formal agreement between the parties, an **express agency,** or it may result from the parties' behavior, an **implied agency**.

Express agency The principal and agent may enter into a contract, or an **express agreement**, in which the parties formally express their intention to establish an agency and state its terms and conditions. The agreement may be either oral or written. An agency relationship between a seller and a sponsoring broker generally is created by a written employment contract, commonly referred to as a **listing agreement**, that authorizes the sponsoring broker (or their designated licensees) to find a buyer or tenant for the owner's property. An express agency relationship between a buyer and a sponsoring broker is created by a **buyer agency agreement**. Similar to a listing agreement, it stipulates the activities and responsibilities the buyer expects from the sponsoring broker (or their designated licensees) in finding the appropriate property for purchase or rent.

In Illinois	The Real Estate License Act of 2000 requires that all exclusive brokerage agreements must be in writing. ∎

Implied agency An agency also may be created by **implied agreement**. This occurs when the actions of the parties indicate that they have mutually consented to an agency. A licensee acts on behalf of another as agent. Even though the licensee may not have consciously planned to create an agency relationship, the parties can create one *unintentionally*, *inadvertently*, or *accidentally* by their actions.

∎ **FOR EXAMPLE** Prospective buyers enter a real estate office asking to see a property listed with another brokerage. A real estate licensee immediately calls the sellers' agent and makes an appointment to show the property. Without discussing the available agency options or having the customers sign a written agency agreement, the licensee drives them to the house. Through the actions of the licensee, the customers think they are being represented.

Compensation *The source of compensation does not determine agency.* A real estate agent does not necessarily represent the person who pays her commission. In fact, agency can exist even if no fee is involved; it is called a **gratuitous agency**. The written brokerage agreement should state how the agent is being compensated and explain all the alternatives available.

In Illinois	In Illinois, compensation does not determine the agency relationship. Both buyer's and seller's real estate agents are often paid by the seller in a **cooperative commission** arrangement. The seller first pays the listing sponsoring broker, and the listing sponsoring broker cuts a check to the cooperating sponsoring broker. Sometimes the seller pays only the listing sponsoring broker and the buyer pays the buyer's sponsoring broker. Regardless of the particular arrangement, the licensee is required to inform clients in each transaction of how the sponsoring broker will be compensated and how the commission will be split with sponsoring brokers representing other parties. ∎

Termination of Agency

An agency may be terminated for any of the following reasons:

- Death or *incapacity* of either party
- Destruction or condemnation of the property
- Expiration of the terms of the agency
- Mutual agreement by all parties to the contract
- Breach by one of the parties, in which case the breaching party might be liable for damages

- By operation of law, as in bankruptcy of the principal (bankruptcy terminates the agency contract, and title to the property transfers to a court-appointed receiver)
- Completion, performance, or fulfillment of the purpose for which the agency was created

| In Illinois |

A definite termination date must be included in a brokerage agreement. Automatic extension clauses are illegal under Illinois law. ■

An **agency coupled with an interest** is an agency relationship in which the agent has an interest in the subject of the agency, such as the property being sold. An agency coupled with an interest cannot be revoked by the principal or be terminated on the principal's death.

■ **FOR EXAMPLE**   A broker agrees to provide the financing for a condominium building being constructed by a developer in exchange for the exclusive right to sell the units once the building is completed. The developer may not revoke the listing agreement once the broker has provided the financing because this is an agency coupled with an interest.

■ TYPES OF AGENCY RELATIONSHIPS

What an agent may do as the principal's representative depends solely on what the principal authorizes the agent to do.

Limitations on an Agent's Authority

A **universal agent** is a person empowered to do anything the principal could do personally. The universal agent's authority to act on behalf of the principal is *virtually unlimited*.

| In Illinois |

In Illinois, a written power of attorney is required to create a universal agency. ■

> A **general agent** represents the principal *generally*; a **special agent** represents the principal only for a *specific act*, such as the sale of a house.

A **general agent** may represent the principal in a broad range of matters related to a particular business or activity. The general agent may, for example, bind the principal to any contract within the scope of the agent's authority. A property manager is typically considered a general agent to the property owner. Brokers and managing brokers are *general agents to their sponsoring broker*.

A **special agent** is authorized to represent the principal in one specific act or business transaction only, under detailed instructions. *A real estate licensee usually is a "special" agent to a client.* If hired by a seller, the licensee is limited to finding a ready, willing, and able buyer for the property. A special agent for a buyer (buyer's agent) has the limited responsibility of finding a property that fits the buyer's criteria.

As a special agent, the licensee may not bind the principal to a contract. The principal makes all contractually related decisions and will sign on her own. A *special power of attorney* is another legal means of authorizing an agent to carry out only a specified act or acts.

Finally, a **designated agent** is a person authorized by the sponsoring broker to act as the agent of a specific principal. A designated agent is the *only* licensee in the company who has a fiduciary responsibility toward that principal. When one licensee in the company is a designated agent, the others are free to act as agents for the other party in a transaction. In this way, two licensees from the same real estate company may represent opposite sides in a property sale without entering dual agency.

| In Illinois | Designated agency is recognized in Illinois. A sponsoring broker entering into a brokerage agreement may specifically designate those licensees employed by or affiliated with the sponsoring broker to act as legal agents of that client to the exclusion of all other licensees employed by or affiliated with the sponsoring broker. The sponsoring broker will not be considered to be acting for more than one party in a transaction if the licensees specifically designated as legal agents of a person are not representing more than one party in a transaction. (See Figures 4.2 and 4.3.)

The sponsoring broker must take care to protect confidential information disclosed by a client to her designated agent. A designated agent may disclose to her sponsoring broker or persons specified by the sponsoring broker confidential information of a client for the purpose of seeking advice or assistance for the benefit of the client in regard to a possible transaction. The sponsoring broker cannot disclose confidential information unless otherwise required by this act or requested or permitted by the client who originally disclosed the confidential information. ■

Single Agency

When an agent or firm represents *only one* party (buyer, seller, landlord, or tenant) exclusively in a real estate transaction, this relationship is referred to as **single agency**. The agent and firm's fiduciary and statutory duties are provided only to that one party (the principal); the other party in the transaction is referred to as the customer.

While a single agency licensee may represent both sellers and buyers, that licensee cannot represent both *in the same transaction*. This avoids conflict and results in client-based service and loyalty to *only* one client. On the other hand, it traditionally rules out the sale of in-house listings to represented buyers.

Buyer Agency

Many licensees involved with residential property are discovering opportunities for buyer representation. Some licensees have become specialists in the emerging field of **buyer agency,** even representing buyers exclusively.

A *buyer agency* relationship is established in the same way as any other agency relationship: by contract, agreement, or implication. The buyer's agent may receive a fee from the buyer or share in the seller-paid commission to the listing sponsoring broker or both, depending on the terms of the agency agreement.

| In Illinois | In Illinois, it is common for the listing sponsoring broker to split the listing commission with the buyer's sponsoring broker. ■

F I G U R E   4.2

Disclosure of Buyer's Designated Agent

ILLINOIS ASSOCIATION OF REALTORS®
DISCLOSURE OF BUYER'S DESIGNATED AGENT

_____ (Brokerage company hereinafter referred to
as "Broker") designates _____ ("Designated Agent") as the legal
agent(s) of _____ (hereinafter referred to as "Buyer") for the purpose of
representing Buyer in the acquisition of real estate by Buyer. Buyer understands and agrees that neither
Broker nor any other sales associates affiliated with Broker (except as provided for herein) will be acting
as legal agent of the Buyer. Broker shall have the discretion to appoint a substitute or additional
designated agent for Buyer as Broker determines necessary. Buyer shall be advised within a reasonable
time of any such substitution or addition.

Broker acknowledges and agrees that Buyer has no current exclusive Buyer representation agreement
with any other real estate agent or firm. Buyer represents that if Buyer previously entered into an
exclusive Buyer representation agreement(s) that they have expired and/or have been terminated.
Further, Buyer agrees to immediately inform Designated Agent if Designated Agent is showing to Buyer a
property previously shown to Buyer.

Buyer, by continuing to work with Buyer's Designated Agent, acknowledges that the representations and
agreements made above are true and correct.

BUYER REPRESENTATION OPTIONS

Check the box that applies

☐ Use **IAR Terms of Non-Exclusive Buyer Representation,** if Buyer does not choose to enter a buyer
brokerage representation agreement.

  ▪ Use form number 341.

NOTE: If Buyer consents to Dual Agency, use form number 335, Disclosure and Consent to Dual Agency,
together with form number 341.

☐ Use **IAR Non–Exclusive Buyer Representation Contract**, if Buyer does not want an exclusive
agency relationship with Broker, but will sign a non-exclusive agreement.

  ▪ Use form number 339 with Disclosure and Consent to Dual Agency
  ▪ Use form number 339a if Broker's office policy does not allow disclosed dual agency or if Buyer
does not consent to dual agency.

☐ Use **IAR Exclusive Buyer Representation/Exclusive Right to Purchase Contract**, if Buyer will
enter exclusive agency relationship with Broker.

  ▪ Use form number 338 with Disclosure and Consent to Dual Agency
  ▪ Use form number 338a if Broker's office policy does not allow disclosed dual agency or if Buyer
does not consent to dual agency.

Date copy furnished to Buyer: _____ By: _____

_____   _____
Buyer's Signature **(OPTIONAL)**   Buyer's Signature **(OPTIONAL)**

(NOTE: Give copy to Buyer and retain copy for Brokerage company file.)

Form 349 2/17/10   Copyright by Illinois Association of REALTORS®

F I G U R E   4.3

Additional Designated Agent

ILLINOIS ASSOCIATION OF REALTORS®
ADDITIONAL AGENT DESIGNATION

(Use this form when naming an additional designated legal agent
to represent a seller-client, buyer-client or tenant/lessee client)

_____ ("Broker") is designating the licensee named below
as an additional designated agent for the client named below.

Additional Designated Agent: _____
                                                     (print or type name)

Additional Designated Agent Signature: _____

Additional Designated Agent shall serve you as one of your agents until such time as
(check all that apply)

☐   terminated by the client or Broker

☐   for the time period beginning _____, 2_____ until _____, 2_____.

Broker: _____
                                              (signature)

Client Name: _____
                                    (print or type)

Property Address (if listing): _____

Form 340 12/9/09   Copyright by Illinois Association of REALTORS®

Property Management Agency

An owner may employ a sponsoring broker to market, lease, maintain, or manage the owner's property. Such an arrangement is known as *property management*. The sponsoring broker is made the agent of the property owner through a property management agreement. As in any other agency relationship, the sponsoring broker has a fiduciary responsibility to the client-owner.

Dual Agency

In **dual agency**, the agent represents two principals in the same transaction. Dual agency requires equal loyalty to two separate principals at the same time. The challenge is to fulfill the fiduciary obligations to one principal without compromising the interests of the other, especially when the parties' interests may not only be separate but even opposite. While practical methods of ensuring fairness and equal representation exist, it should be noted that a dual agent can never fully represent either party's interests. (See Figure 4.4.)

Disclosed dual agency Real estate licensing laws permit dual agency only if the buyer and seller are informed and consent to the licensee's representation of both in the same transaction. Although the possibility of conflict of interest still exists, disclosure is intended to minimize the risk for the licensee by ensuring that both principals are aware of the effect of dual agency on their respective interests. The disclosure alerts the principals that they may have to assume greater responsibility for protecting their interests than they would if each had independent representation. Because the duties of disclosure and confidentiality are limited by mutual agreement, they must be carefully explained to the parties in order to establish informed consent. (See Figure 4.5 for the required dual agency disclosure language and see Figure 4.6 for the confirmation of consent to dual agency language.)

Considerable debate focuses on whether licensees can properly represent both the buyer and seller in the same transaction, even though the dual agency is disclosed.

Confirmation of Consent to Dual Agency

Because of the obvious risks inherent in dual agency—ranging from conflicts of interest to outright abuse of trust—the practice is illegal in some states. In states where dual agency is permitted (i.e., Illinois), all parties must consent to the arrangement, preferably in writing.

FIGURE 4.4

Dual Agency

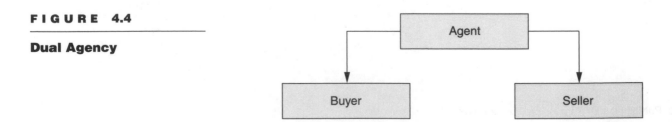

FIGURE 4.5

Disclosure and Consent to Dual Agency

ILLINOIS ASSOCIATION OF REALTORS®
DISCLOSURE AND CONSENT TO DUAL AGENCY
(DESIGNATED AGENCY)

NOTE TO CONSUMER: THIS DOCUMENT SERVES THREE PURPOSES. FIRST, IT DISCLOSES THAT A REAL ESTATE LICENSEE MAY POTENTIALLY ACT AS A DUAL AGENT, THAT IS, REPRESENT MORE THAN ONE PARTY TO THE TRANSACTION. SECOND, THIS DOCUMENT EXPLAINS THE CONCEPT OF DUAL AGENCY. THIRD, THIS DOCUMENT SEEKS YOUR CONSENT TO ALLOW THE REAL ESTATE LICENSEE TO ACT AS A DUAL AGENT. A LICENSEE MAY LEGALLY ACT AS A DUAL AGENT ONLY WITH YOUR CONSENT. BY CHOOSING TO SIGN THIS DOCUMENT, YOUR CONSENT TO DUAL AGENCY REPRESENTATION IS PRESUMED.

The undersigned _____, ("Licensee"),
(insert name(s) of Licensee undertaking dual representation)

may undertake a dual representation (represent both the seller or landlord and the buyer or tenant) for the sale or lease of property. The undersigned acknowledge they were informed of the possibility of this type of representation. Before signing this document please read the following:

Representing more than one party to a transaction presents a conflict of interest since both clients may rely upon Licensee's advice and the client's respective interests may be adverse to each other. Licensee will undertake this representation only with the written consent of ALL clients in the transaction.

Any agreement between the clients as to a final contract price and other terms is a result of negotiations between the clients acting in their own best interests and on their own behalf. You acknowledge that Licensee has explained the implications of dual representation, including the risks involved, and understand that you have been advised to seek independent advice from your advisors or attorneys before signing any documents in this transaction.

WHAT A LICENSEE CAN DO FOR CLIENTS WHEN ACTING AS A DUAL AGENT

1. Treat all clients honestly.
2. Provide information about the property to the buyer or tenant.
3. Disclose all latent material defects in the property that are known to the Licensee.
4. Disclose financial qualification of the buyer or tenant to the seller or landlord.
5. Explain real estate terms.
6. Help the buyer or tenant to arrange for property inspections.
7. Explain closing costs and procedures.
8. Help the buyer compare financing alternatives.
9. Provide information about comparable properties that have sold so both clients may make educated decisions on what price to accept or offer.

WHAT LICENSEE CANNOT DISCLOSE TO CLIENTS WHEN ACTING AS A DUAL AGENT

1. Confidential information that Licensee may know about a client, without that client's permission.
2. The price or terms the seller or landlord will take other than the listing price without permission of the seller or landlord.
3. The price or terms the buyer or tenant is willing to pay without permission of the buyer or tenant.
4. A recommended or suggested price or terms the buyer or tenant should offer.
5. A recommended or suggested price or terms the seller or landlord should counter with or accept.

If either client is uncomfortable with this disclosure and dual representation, please let Licensee know. You are not required to sign this document unless you want to allow the Licensee to proceed as a Dual Agent in this transaction.

By signing below, you acknowledge that you have read and understand this form and voluntarily consent to the Licensee acting as a Dual Agent (that is, to represent BOTH the seller or landlord and the buyer or tenant) should that become necessary.

CLIENT:_____   **CLIENT:**_____

Date:_____   Date:_____

| Document presented on _____, 20____ By: _____ (Broker/Licensee Initials) |

LICENSEE:_____

Date:_____

Form 335 3/9/10   Copyright by Illinois Association of REALTORS®

F I G U R E 4.6

Confirmation of Consent to Dual Agency

ILLINOIS ASSOCIATION OF REALTORS®
CONFIRMATION OF CONSENT TO DUAL AGENCY

The undersigned confirm that they have previously consented to_____

_____, ("Licensee"), acting as a Dual Agent

(insert Licensee's name(s))

in providing brokerage services on their behalf and specifically consent to Licensee acting as a Dual
Agent in regard to the transaction for the property located at.

_____.

(insert address)

Signature of client(s):   _____   Date:_____

_____   Date:_____

_____   Date:_____

_____   Date:_____

Form 336 2/2000   Copyright© by Illinois Association of REALTORS®

In the Illinois Appellate Court case of *W. E. Erickson v. Chicago Title Insurance Company*, 1st Dist. (1994) concurred with the ruling in *Zimmerman v. Northfield Real Estate, Inc.*, 1st Dist. (1986), that licensees who attempt to avoid liability to buyers through the use of a waiver or an exculpatory clause in the sales contract will probably be unsuccessful where a positive duty has been imposed by law. In *Zimmerman*, the licensee "broker" included the following in the sales contract:

> *Purchaser acknowledges that neither the seller, broker, or any of their agents have made any representations with respect to any material fact relating to the real estate unless such representations are in writing and further that the purchaser has made such investigations as purchaser deems necessary or appropriate to satisfy that there has been no deception, fraud, false pretenses, misrepresentations, concealments, suppressions, or omission of any material fact by the seller, the broker, or any of their agents relating to the real estate, its improvements, and included personal property.*

The court refused to enforce the clause because it clearly violated public policy, particularly that which is expressed within the Illinois Real Estate License Act and the rules. ■

■ **FOR EXAMPLE**   A real estate licensee is the agent for the owner of a large mansion. A prospective buyer comes into the licensee's office and asks her to represent him in a search for a modest home. After several weeks of activity, including low offers unsuccessfully negotiated by the licensee, the prospective buyer spots the "For Sale" sign in front of the mansion. He tells the licensee that he wants to make an offer and asks for the licensee's advice on a likely price range. The licensee is now in the difficult position of being a dual agent. She represents the seller, who naturally is interested in receiving the highest possible price, and the buyer, who is interested in making a successful low offer.

Designated agency is a process that avoids dual agency that may occur during an *in-house* sale in which two different agents are involved. Under designated agency, the sponsoring broker designates one agent to represent the seller and one agent to represent the buyer. Designated agency is legal in Illinois. However, designated agency does not apply to a single agent who represents both parties at the same time in the same transaction.

Undisclosed dual agency   A licensee may not intend to create a dual agency. It may occur unintentionally or inadvertently. Sometimes the cause is carelessness. Other times the licensee does not fully understand her fiduciary responsibilities. Some licensees lose sight of legal obligations when they focus intensely on bringing buyers and sellers together. For example, a licensee representing the seller might tell a buyer that the seller will accept less than the listing price to entice the buyer into making an offer. Or the listing licensee might try to persuade the seller to accept an offer that is really in the buyer's interest. Giving a buyer any specific advice on how much to offer can lead the buyer to believe that the licensee represents the buyer's interests and is acting as the buyer's advocate.

Any of these actions create an *implied* agency with the buyer and violate the duties of loyalty and confidentiality to the principal-seller. Because neither party has been informed of that situation and been given the opportunity to seek separate representation, the interests of both are jeopardized. This undisclosed dual agency is a violation of licensing laws. It can result in rescission of the sales contract, forfeiture of commission, or filing of a suit for damages.

Disclosure of Agency

Real estate licensees are required to disclose the parties they represent. Understanding the scope of the service a party can expect from the agent allows consumers to make an informed decision about whether to seek their own representation.

In Illinois | *Licensees are considered to be representing the consumer they are working with as the consumer's designated agent, unless there is a written agreement between them specifying a different relationship or if the licensee is performing only ministerial acts on the consumer's behalf. (See Figure 4.7.)*

Ministerial acts are defined as acts performed for a consumer that are informative or clerical in nature and do not rise to the level of active representation on behalf of a consumer. Examples of ministerial acts include

- responding to phone inquiries by consumers as to the availability and pricing of brokerage services;
- responding to phone inquiries from a consumer concerning the price or location of property;
- attending an open house and responding to questions about the property from a consumer;
- setting an appointment to view property;
- responding to questions of consumers walking into a licensee's office concerning brokerage services offered or particular properties;
- accompanying an appraiser, inspector, contractor, or similar third party on a visit to a property;
- describing a property or the property's condition in response to a consumer inquiry;
- completing business or factual information for a consumer on an offer or contract to purchase on behalf of a client;
- showing a client through a property being sold by an owner on her own behalf; or
- referring to another broker or service provider. ■

In Illinois | Article 15, Section 15-35, discusses agency relationship disclosure. It requires that a consumer be advised in writing that a designated agency relationship exists, unless there is a written agreement between the sponsoring broker and the consumer providing for a different brokerage relationship. This must occur no later than beginning to work as a designated agent on behalf of the consumer. The name or names of her designated agent or agents must be in writing, and the sponsoring broker's compensation and policy with regard to cooperating with sponsoring brokers who represent other parties in a transaction must be disclosed.

A licensee must also disclose in writing to a customer that the licensee is not acting as the agent of the customer at a time intended to prevent disclosure of confidential information from a customer to a licensee, but in no event later than the preparation of an offer to purchase or lease real property. (See Figures 4.8 and 4.9.) ■

F I G U R E   4.7

Notice of No Agency Relationship

ILLINOIS ASSOCIATION OF REALTORS

NOTICE OF NO AGENCY RELATIONSHIP

Name of "Sales Associate"_____

Name of Brokerage Company_____

Property Address_____

☐ **NOTICE OF NO AGENCY RELATIONSHIP**
(Check here if you represent either seller or buyer)

Thank you for giving Sales Associate the opportunity to_____

_____
(Insert description of work, i.e. showing property of a FSBO)
in regard to the above mentioned property.

Sales Associate's broker has previously entered into an agreement with a client to provide certain real estate brokerage services through a Sales Associate who acts as that client's designated agent. As a result, Sales Associate will not be acting as your agent but as the agent of the _____(insert buyer or seller).

☐ **NOTICE OF MINISTERIAL ACTS**
(Check here if you do not represent either buyer or seller at this time)

Thank you for giving Sales Associate the opportunity to _____

_____
(Insert description of work, i.e. listing presentation)
in regard to the above mentioned property.

Under State law this activity does not result in the Sales Associate acting as your agent. Should you decide to enter into a real estate brokerage services agreement with Sales Associate's broker, then Sales Associate can be designated as your agent.

THIS NOTICE OF NO AGENCY IS BEING PROVIDED AS REQUIRED BY STATE LAW.

_____   Date_____
Sales Associate Signature

_____   _____
Customer Signature   Customer Signature

_____   _____
Print Customer's Name   Print Customer's Name

Date_____   Date_____

FORM 350   10/27/03   Copyright by Illinois Association of REALTORS

Source: Published with Permission, Illinois Association of REALTORS®.

Buyer Agency Checklist

     ILLINOIS ASSOCIATION OF REALTORS
BUYER AGENCY CHECKLIST

INITIAL CONTACT WITH CONSUMER

[ ]   Inquire into whether consumer is being represented by another licensee. If so, find out whether it is exclusive or non-exclusive.

[ ]   Advise consumer (prospective buyer-client) of the designated agency relationship that will exist unless there is written agreement providing for a different relationship.

[ ]   Advise consumer about how compensation to buyer agent works.

[ ]   Complete and have buyer sign the appropriate Buyer Representation Contract.

[ ]   Advise consumer regarding the potential for dual agency and provide Disclosure and Consent to Dual Agency form. Must get buyer's signature on form before entering into dual agency situation.

[ ]   Advise buyer of name and designated agent(s) in writing.

AFTER RECEIVING SIGNED BUYER REPRESENTATION CONTRACT

[ ]   If additional designated agent(s) are named after initial disclosure, give notice using Additional Agent Designation form.

[ ]   Advise buyer that only the designated agents are his/her legal agents and that other agents of the same company do not represent buyer.

[ ]   Caution buyer not to discuss confidential information with any agent other than the designated agent(s).

WHEN SHOWING PROPERTY

[ ]   Check the MLS or with the seller (if not represented) or seller's agent regarding cooperating compensation.

[ ]   If you are showing your own listing, make sure both seller and buyer have signed the Disclosure and Consent to Dual Agency form and inform both parties that you are acting as a dual agent.

WHEN PRESENTING CONTRACTS

[ ]   If in a dual agency situation, advise the parties of their right to seek independent advice from an advisor or attorney before signing any documents such as a contract to purchase.

[ ]   When possible, before buyer makes an offer, obtain seller's Residential Real Property Disclosure form from seller and give to buyer for his/her review.

[ ]   If acting as dual agent, ensure that Confirmation of Consent to Dual Agency language appears in the contract, in a rider, or is provided in a separate form.

EXECUTION OF CONTRACT

[ ]   If acting as dual agent, see that Confirmation of Consent to Dual Agency language is initialed by the parties, or if provided in its own separate from, see that the parties sign it.

[ ]   If one party no longer consents to dual agency, immediately refer the party to a new agent. You may not receive a referral fee unless disclosure is made to both buyer and seller.

[ ]   If seller has not previously provided the Residential Real Property Disclosure Report, request that seller do so at this time. Retain a copy for our files.

Form 343 2/2000   Copyright by Illinois Association of REALTORS

FIGURE 4.9

Seller Agency Checklist

  ILLINOIS ASSOCIATION OF REALTORS
SELLER AGENCY CHECKLIST

NOTE: No subagency is allowed; therefore, you are seller's agent only when taking a listing.

INITIAL CONTACT WITH CONSUMER

[ ]   Upon initial contact, if the consumer is shopping for an agent you may want to disclose to the consumer in writing that unless the consumer chooses to work with you that you will not be considered as the consumer's agent.

[ ]   Inquire into whether consumer has any agency relationship with another licensee. If so, find out when that relationship terminates.

[ ]   Advise the consumer (prospective seller-client) of the designated agency relationship that will exist unless there is written agreement providing for a different relationship.

[ ]   Advise consumer about compensation and whether broker will share compensation with other brokers representing buyers in a transaction.

[ ]   Complete and have seller sign Exclusive Right to Sell Contract.

[ ]   Advise consumer regarding dual agency and provide Disclosure and Consent to Dual Agency form. Must get seller's signature on form before entering into dual agency situation.

[ ]   Advise seller of name of designated agent(s) in writing.

AFTER RECEIVING SIGNED SELLER REPRESENTATION CONTRACT

[ ]   Discuss how appointments will be made.

[ ]   Discuss with seller how other agents working with prospective buyers, even agents of this company, are agents for the buyer, and seller should use caution not to disclose confidential information.

[ ]   Caution seller not to disclose confidential information to anyone other than the designated agent(s).

[ ]   Explain open house procedures to sellers. Include explanation as to whether someone other than the designated agent may be sitting the open house.

[ ]   If additional designed agent(s) are named after initial disclosure, give notice to seller using Additional Agent Designation forms.

WHEN MAKING APPOINTMENTS FOR THE SELLER

NOTE: License Law considers licensee working with buyer to be buyer's agent, confirm this.

[ ]   If contacted by buyer directly, ask if buyer is working with another agent.

Form 345 2/2000   Copyright by Illinois Association of REALTORS

F I G U R E   4.9

Seller Agency Checklist (continued)

[ ]   If buyer is not working with another agent, advise buyer of the designated agency or dual agency relationship that will exist if buyer works with you.

    [ ]   If buyer desires representation, seek a buyer representation contract. (See Buyer Agency Checklist).

    [ ]   If buyer wants representation but not dual agency then seek a buyer representation contract unless you already represent the seller of the property the buyer is interested in, in which case you should then refer the buyer to another sales associate in the office.

    [ ]   If buyer is interested in seeing only one particular listing and does not want to be represented, evaluate whether you are performing "Ministerial Acts". If so, provide agency disclosure (use Notice of No Agency Relationship form).

[ ]   If you are not seller's designated agent, notify seller's designated agent of appointment and whether buyer is represented by an agent.

[ ]   Record proper information on appointment sheet.

[ ]   Scheduler should inform seller of appointment and confirm with seller that buyer is not represented or is represented by a buyer's agent.

WHEN ACCEPTING A CONTRACT TO PURCHASE FROM BUYER OR BUYER'S AGENT

[ ]   Make sure that seller(s) has (have) filled out and signed the Residential Real Property Disclosure Report. Provide it to buyer and get signature before contract is accepted. Keep a copy for our files.

[ ]   If acting as a disclosed dual agent, make sure buyer(s) and seller(s) are provided with the Confirmation of Dual Agency form and that they sign or initial it before or at time contract is executed.

    [ ]   If one party no longer consents to dual agency, immediately refer the party to a new sales associate. You may not receive a referral fee unless disclosure is made to both seller and buyer.

[ ]   Present contract to seller.

[ ]   If contract is accepted, deposit any earnest moneys received into broker's special account.

Form 345 2/2000   Copyright by Illinois Association of REALTORS

■ CUSTOMER-LEVEL SERVICES

Even though an agent's primary responsibility is to the principal, the agent also has duties to third parties. Any time a licensee works with a third party or a customer, the licensee is responsible for adhering to state and federal consumer protection laws as well as to the ethical requirements imposed by professional associations and state regulators.

In Illinois

An agent's primary responsibility is to the principal, and Illinois courts have long held that the contractual principal-agent relationship as defined in a listing agreement or buyer agency agreement gives the seller or buyer a cause of action against the licensee who breaches her fiduciary duties to the client. The courts have not demanded fiduciary duty to third parties. However, Illinois license law does set forth the duties that licensees owe to third-party customers (buyers or sellers). Licensees are to treat all customers honestly. They cannot negligently or knowingly give customers false information.

An agent owes a customer the duties of reasonable care and skill, honest and fair dealing, and disclosure of known facts.

Finally, licensees must disclose all material adverse facts about the physical condition of the property to the customer that are actually known by the licensee and that could not be discovered by a reasonably diligent inspection of the property by the customer.

In Illinois, *a licensee may be held liable to a seller or buyer if the licensee misrepresents material facts about a property and if the seller or buyer suffers monetary loss through reliance on these statements.* The licensee's loyalty to the principal is no defense even though the principal may have ordered the agent to misrepresent. *Licensees have a duty to prospective sellers and buyers to disclose all material information within their knowledge.* If the licensee knowingly makes untrue statements, Illinois courts will have no difficulty in finding the licensee liable to the appropriate party.

Furthermore, liability may be imposed when the licensee is aware of facts that tend to indicate she is making a false statement. For instance, if the seller tells his agent/licensee that "the roof was replaced last year," and the agent has good reason to believe that statement is untrue, the licensee should attempt to ascertain the truth and pass the correct information on to the buyer. However, if the client provided the false information and the licensee did not have knowledge that the information was false, the licensee will not be held liable to the customer.

Licensees who attempt to avoid liability to buyers through the use of a waiver or an exculpatory clause in the sales contract will probably be unsuccessful. ■

■ SUMMARY

The common law of agency has historically governed the principal-agent relationship. Agency relationships may be expressed either by the words of the parties or by written agreement, or they may be implied by the parties' actions. In single agency relationships, the licensee or agent represents one party, either the buyer or the seller, in the transaction. In some states, if the agent elicits the assistance of other licensees who cooperate in the transaction, the other licensees may become subagents of the principal. Any blanket offering of subagency by a multiple listing service (MLS) in Illinois is illegal.

Many states, including Illinois, are dominated by non-single agency firms. These firms work with both buyers and sellers, including buyers and sellers in the same transaction. They will consider dual agency in the event it develops or will assign designated agents to each of the two parties (usually a seller and a buyer) should a conflict develop. Many states, including Illinois, have adopted statutes that replace the common law of agency and amplify it.

Representing two opposing parties in the same transaction constitutes dual agency. Licensees must be careful not to create dual agency when none was intended. This unintentional or inadvertent dual agency can result in the sales contract being rescinded and the commission being forfeited or in a lawsuit. Disclosed dual agency requires that both principals be informed of and consent to the licensee's multiple representation. In any case, the prospective parties in any transaction should be informed about agency alternatives and the ways in which client-level versus customer-level services differ. Many states, including Illinois, have mandatory agency disclosure laws. The source of compensation for the client services does not determine which party is represented.

Licensees have certain duties and obligations to their customers as well. Consumers are entitled to fair and honest dealings and to the information necessary for them to make informed decisions. This includes accurate information about the property. Some states, including Illinois, have mandatory property disclosure laws.

Real estate license laws and regulations govern the professional conduct of brokers, managing brokers, and leasing agents. The license laws are enacted to protect the public by ensuring a standard of competence and professionalism in the real estate industry.

Stigmatized housing remains a controversial issue in many states. In many states, buyers' agents bear more burden for disclosure of known stigmas than do sellers' (listing) agents.

Stigmas to a property are disclosed only when they constitute a material fact and affect the physical condition of the property. Normally, ghosts or past crimes on a property would not be disclosed. Federal law prohibits disclosure of HIV or other medically related conditions except by permission or direction of the seller/owner.

In Illinois   Article 15 of the Real Estate License Act of 2000, as amended in 2010, has fully superseded any previous agency law. Illinois agency law currently presumes that a broker or managing broker who is working with a seller represents the seller (client relationship). A licensee working with a buyer is presumed to represent the buyer. Written disclosure is required for any other arrangement.

The Illinois Real Estate License Act of 2000, along with the rules governing permitted dual agency, always must be disclosed in writing, to be legal. Merely designating one licensee to represent sellers and another to represent buyers does not by itself constitute dual agency. Licensees operate as designated agents most of the time. Agency relationship disclosures require written notice to the consumer of the name or names of the designated agent; that a designated agency relationship exists, unless there is a written agreement providing otherwise; and the sponsoring broker's compensation and policy with regard to compensation cooperation with other sponsoring brokers. Dual agency, however, occurs if the same agent represents both parties in a transaction. Then additional designated agents sometimes need to be made so that two licensees are involved (each representing only one party) unless a disclosed dual agency is agreed to in writing. Even disclosed dual agency is frowned upon by many and is likely to continue to be controversial. ■

CHAPTER 4 QUIZ

1. Which of the following *BEST* describes an agent?
   a. A person who gives someone else the legal power to act on her behalf
   b. A person who is in a customer-agent relationship
   c. A person who is placed in a position of trust and confidence
   d. Two agents who work for the same brokerage firm

2. A seller listed his property with SXS Realty. The agency relationship between the seller and the sponsoring broker would be what type of agency?
   a. Special
   b. General
   c. Implied
   d. Universal

3. Which of the following statements is *TRUE* of a real estate broker acting as the agent of the seller?
   a. The broker is obligated to render faithful service to the seller.
   b. The broker can disclose personal information to a buyer if it increases the likelihood of a sale.
   c. The broker can agree to a change in price without the seller's approval.
   d. The broker can accept a commission from the buyer without the seller's approval.

4. A seller lists his home with a real estate broker for $289,500. Later the same day, a potential buyer comes into the broker's office and asks for general information about homes for sale in the $250,000–$300,000 price range. Based on these facts, which of the following statements is *TRUE*?
   a. The seller and potential buyer are both the broker's customers.
   b. The seller is the broker's client; the potential buyer is a customer.
   c. The broker owes fiduciary duties to both the seller and the potential buyer.
   d. If the potential buyer asks the broker to be his buyer representative, the broker must decline because of the pre-existing agreement with the seller.

5. A licensee who has contracted with a condominium owner to manage a highrise apartment is probably a
   a. transactional broker.
   b. buyer's agent.
   c. general agent.
   d. special agent.

6. Which of the following events will terminate an agency in a broker-seller relationship?
   a. The broker discovers that the market value of the property is such that she will not make an adequate commission.
   b. The owner declares personal bankruptcy.
   c. The owner abandons the property.
   d. The broker appoints other brokers to help sell the property.

7. In Illinois, a real estate broker hired by an owner to sell a parcel of real estate must comply with
   a. the federal common law of agency, although a state agency statute may exist that abrogates common law.
   b. undisclosed dual agency requirements.
   c. the concept of caveat emptor as codified in Illinois law.
   d. the Illinois statute governing agency relationships.

8. A broker is hired by a first-time buyer to help the buyer purchase a home. The buyer confides to the broker that being approved for a mortgage loan may be complicated by the fact that the buyer filed for bankruptcy two years ago. When the buyer offers to buy a home, what is the broker's responsibility?
   a. The broker should let the buyer know a broker has a responsibility to disclose the buyer's financial situation to the local multiple listing service.
   b. The broker has a duty to be honest to the sellers. The broker should not lie about the buyer's financial circumstances but may present them in the best possible terms.
   c. The broker should have the buyer qualified by a lender and then politely refuse to answer any questions that would violate the duty of confidentiality.
   d. The broker has no responsibility whatsoever toward the sellers because the broker is the buyer's agent.

9. A broker lists a residence. For various reasons, the owner of the residence must sell the house quickly. To expedite the sale, the broker tells a prospective purchaser that the seller will accept at least $5,000 less than the asking price for the property. Based on these facts, which of the following statements is TRUE?
   a. The broker has not violated his agency responsibilities to the seller.
   b. The broker should have disclosed this information, regardless of its accuracy.
   c. The disclosure was improper, regardless of the broker's motive.
   d. The relationship between the broker and the seller is referred to as a general agency relationship.

10. A buyer who is a client of the broker wants to purchase a house that the broker has listed for sale. Which of the following statements is TRUE?
    a. Illinois law no longer regulates this situation.
    b. The broker should refer the buyer to another broker to negotiate the sale.
    c. The seller and buyer must be informed of the situation and agree to the broker's representation of both of them.
    d. The buyer should not have been shown a house listed by the broker.

11. A buyer comes into a real estate broker's office and asks the broker to represent her while searching for a home in the $190,000–$200,000 price range. The broker recalls a house for sale by owner listed at $198,000. The broker calls the owner of the house, asking for permission for his client to see the house. Based on these facts, which of the following statements is TRUE?
    a. Both the buyer and for-sale-by-owner seller are customers of the broker.
    b. The for-sale-by-owner seller is the broker's customer; the buyer is a client.
    c. The buyer is the broker's customer; the for-sale-by-owner seller is the broker's client.
    d. The broker is now a dual agent.

12. A real estate licensee was representing a buyer. At their first meeting, the buyer explained that he planned to operate a dog grooming business out of any house he bought. The licensee did not check the local zoning ordinances to determine in which parts of town such a business could be conducted. Which agency duty did the licensee violate?

    a. Care
    b. Obedience
    c. Loyalty
    d. Accountability

13. Broker A tells a prospective buyer, "This property has the most beautiful view." In fact, the view includes the back of a shopping center. In a separate transaction, Broker B fails to mention to some enthusiastic potential buyers that a six-lane highway is planned for construction within ten feet of a house the buyers think is perfect. Based on these facts, which of the following statements is *TRUE*?

    a. Broker A has committed fraud.
    b. Broker B has committed puffing.
    c. Both brokers are guilty of intentional misrepresentation.
    d. Broker A is merely puffing; Broker B has misrepresented the property.

14. Under Illinois agency law, which of the following is *TRUE*?

    a. The law codifies the common-law concept of caveat emptor by eliminating any assumption of a buyer's right to representation or disclosure.
    b. Sponsoring brokers may designate which agent represents which party.
    c. Sellers are not legally obligated to make any disclosures regarding the known physical condition of the property.
    d. Dual agency is outlawed.

15. A sponsoring broker listed and sold a home. The seller had told the sponsoring broker that the home was structurally sound. This information was passed on to a prospective buyer by one of the licensee's sponsored by the broker. If the sponsoring broker has no way of knowing that this information is false, who will likely be held liable if a latent defect is later discovered?

    a. The sponsored licensee
    b. The seller
    c. The seller and the sponsored licensee
    d. The buyer will lose because a buyer must carefully inspect or bear the loss

16. In real estate transactions, the term *fiduciary* typically refers to the

    a. sale of real property.
    b. person who gives someone else the legal power to act on her behalf.
    c. person who has legal power to act on behalf of another.
    d. agent's relationship to the principal.

17. A real estate licensee's responsibility to keep the principal informed of all the facts that could affect a transaction is the duty of

    a. care.
    b. disclosure.
    c. obedience.
    d. accounting.

18. Which of the following would be considered dual agency?

    a. A licensee acting for both the buyer and the seller in the same transaction
    b. Two brokerage companies cooperating with each other
    c. A licensee representing two or more sellers at the same time
    d. A licensee listing and then selling the same property

19. In a dual agency situation, a licensee may represent both the seller and the buyer if
    a. the licensee informs either the buyer or the seller of this fact.
    b. the buyer and the seller are related by blood or marriage.
    c. both parties give their informed consent, in writing, to the dual agency.
    d. both parties are represented by attorneys.

20. Designated agency is MOST likely to occur when
    a. there is a client-buyer and a customer-seller.
    b. the seller and the buyer are represented by different companies.
    c. both the buyer and the seller are customers.
    d. the buyer and the seller are represented by the same company.

CHAPTER 5

Real Estate Brokerage

■ **LEARNING OBJECTIVES** *When you've finished reading this chapter, you should be able to*

■ **identify** the role of technologies, personnel, and license laws in the operation of a real estate business;

■ **describe** the various types of antitrust violations common in the real estate industry and the penalties involved with each;

■ **explain** how a licensee's compensation is usually determined;

■ **distinguish** employees from independent contractors and explain why the distinction is important; and

■ **define** the following *key terms*

allocation of customers or markets	fiduciary standard	price-fixing
antitrust laws	group boycotting	procuring cause
CAN-SPAM Act of 2003	independent contractor	professional real estate services
commission	Junk Fax Prevention Act of 2005	ready, willing, and able buyer
cooperative commission	managing broker	sponsoring broker
employee	National Do Not Call Registry	tie-in agreement
errors and omissions insurance	personal assistant	

■ REAL ESTATE BROKERAGE

Brokerage is simply the business of bringing parties together. A real estate license is required to exchange, purchase, or lease real property for others and to charge a fee for these services. The broker means an individual, partnership, limited liability company, corporation, or registered limited liability company. Until April 30, 2012, broker does not mean a real estate salesperson or leasing agent. After that date, however, brokerage services will be between a sponsoring (or managing) broker and the consumer: buyers, sellers, landlords, and/or tenants as the salesperson's license is being phased out.

A **brokerage** business may take many forms. It may be a sole proprietorship (a single-owner company), a corporation, or a partnership. The office may be independent or part of a regional or national franchise. The business may consist of a single office or multiple branches. The brokerage office may be located in a downtown highrise, a suburban shopping center, or the sponsoring broker's home. A typical real estate brokerage may specialize in one kind of transaction or service, or it may offer a variety of services.

No matter what form it takes, a real estate brokerage has the same demands, expenses, and rewards as any other small business. The real estate industry, after all, is made up of thousands of individual businesses operating in defined local markets. A real estate broker faces many of the same challenges as an entrepreneur in any other industry. In addition to mastering the complexities of real estate transactions, the real estate broker must be able to handle the day-to-day details of running a business and to set effective policies for every aspect of the brokerage operation. This includes maintaining space and equipment, hiring employees and real estate licensees, determining compensation, directing staff and sales activities, and implementing procedures to follow in carrying out agency duties. Each state's real estate license laws and regulations establish the business activities and methods of doing business that are permitted.

Although brokerage firms vary widely in size and style, few brokerage firms today perform their duties without the assistance of real estate licensees associated with the firm. Much of the business's success hinges on the relationship between sponsoring brokers and their sponsored licensees. Illinois has defined the roles and responsibilities in 1450 Real Estate License Act of 2000.

In Illinois

Every real estate office must have a sponsoring or managing broker of record, neither of which is required to be the owner of the business. After April 30, 2012, all licensees acting as a managing broker or self-sponsored broker must have a managing broker's license or acquire one within 90 days after being named managing broker. ■

Sponsoring brokers   By Section 1450.100 definition, the sponsoring broker is the entity holding the company real estate license, whether the entity is an individual who operates as a sole proprietorship, partnership, limited liability company, corporation or registered limited liability partnership. A sponsoring broker may be self-sponsored. There may be only one sponsoring broker for any one real estate company. A sponsoring broker may authorize a managing broker to issue sponsor cards in the name of the sponsoring broker.

Likewise, the sponsoring broker may assign escrow account bookkeeping duties to a qualified company employee or independent contractor and may delegate authorized individuals to sign on behalf of the sponsoring broker. The sponsoring broker may authorize company personnel to sign contracts entered into by the sponsoring broker according to the sponsoring broker's company policy. Even though the sponsoring broker may delegate authority, ultimately, the sponsoring broker is responsible for all activities.

Managing brokers A managing broker has taken additional courses and received a managing broker license. A sponsoring broker may also be the managing broker of an office or may appoint a managing broker to serve as the managing broker of several branch offices, or different managing brokers may be responsible for individual branch offices. In any event, the managing broker is responsible for the supervision of all real estate activities performed by affiliated licensees.

Additionally, each managing broker is responsible for record keeping as mandated by Rule 1450.180, maintenance of the employment agreements entered into with each sponsored licensee (Rule 1450.160), and if escrow monies are maintained, the managing broker must comply with each part of Rule 1450.155.

Sponsored licensees Until April 30, 2012, sponsored licensees may include those holding a salesperson's license or a broker's license. Article 5, Section 5-26 of the Real Estate License Act of 2000 states that "no new salesperson licenses shall be issued after April 30, 2011, and all existing salesperson licenses shall terminate on May 1, 2012." After April 30, 2012, only two types of licenses will be issued: broker and managing broker. Both brokers and managing brokers can work under the supervision of a sponsoring broker. A sponsoring broker may assign supervisory responsibilities to an affiliated managing broker.

Independent Contractors:

- Do not work employer-determined hours
- Do not receive scheduled salaries
- Must be self-starters
- Decide when and how to do their work
- Are paid irregularly based on project completion (e.g., a completed sale)

Independent contractor versus employee Every sponsoring broker who hires licensees or has an independent contractor relationship with a licensee must have a *written employment agreement* with each licensee. The agreement defines the employment or independent contractor relationship, including supervision, duties, compensation, and termination. The employment agreement must be dated and signed by both parties. Termination is not intended to indicate that a specific termination date is required but rather allows for negotiation as to the term of the employment agreement. An executed copy of the employment agreement must be provided to the sponsored licensees.

A sponsoring broker is required by the federal government to withhold Social Security tax and income tax from wages paid to employees. The sponsoring broker is also required to pay unemployment compensation tax on wages paid to one or more employees as defined by state and federal laws. In addition, employees might receive benefits such as health insurance, profit-sharing plans, or workers' compensation.

FIGURE 5.1

Sample Employment Agreement

ILLINOIS ASSOCIATION OF REALTORS®
SPONSORING BROKER-SALESPERSON CONTRACT

THIS AGREEMENT made and entered into this _____ day of _____, 2___, by and between _____
hereinafter referred to as "Sponsoring Broker", and _____, hereinafter referred to as "Salesperson".

WITNESSETH:

WHEREAS, Sponsoring Broker is duly licensed and does engage in business as a real estate broker in the City of _____
State of Illinois;

WHEREAS, Salesperson is now duly licensed and does engage in business as a real estate salesperson, and whereas, it is deemed to be to the mutual advantage of Sponsoring Broker and Salesperson to enter into this contract upon the terms and conditions hereinafter set forth.

NOW, THEREFORE, for and in consideration of the mutual covenants and promises herein contained and each act done pursuant hereto the undersigned hereby enter into the following agreement:

1. Facilities and Sales Effort.

   A. Salesperson agrees to proceed diligently, faithfully, loyally, legally and within his/her best efforts to sell, trade, lease or rent any and all real estate listed with Sponsoring Broker (except for any special listings which are exclusively placed by Sponsoring Broker with another salesperson), to solicit additional listings and customers for Sponsoring Broker, and otherwise to promote the business of serving the public in real estate transactions to the end that each of the parties hereto may derive the greatest profit possible.

   B. Sponsoring Broker agrees for the convenience of Salesperson to provide desk space, clerical service and office facilities at the office of Sponsoring Broker presently maintained at _____, _____,
   Illinois, and/or at such other places as Sponsoring Broker may from time to time utilize.

   C. Sponsoring Broker agrees to make available to the Salesperson all current listings of the office, except such as the Sponsoring Broker, for valid and usual business reasons, may place exclusively in the temporary possession of some other salesperson, and agrees, upon request, to provide assistance and full cooperation to the salesperson.

2. Termination.

   A. This agreement, and the relationship created hereby, may be terminated by either party hereto, with or without cause, at any time upon _____ (_____) days written notice given to the other; but the rights of the parties to any commissions which accrued prior to said notice shall not be divested by the termination of this agreement except as stipulated herein.

   B. Upon termination of this agreement, all negotiations commenced by Salesperson during the term of this agreement shall continue to be handled through Sponsoring Broker and with such assistance by Salesperson as is reasonable under all the circumstances. Salesperson shall be compensated according to the Commission Schedule referred to in paragraph 5, after deduction of all appropriate expenses.

   C. Salesperson, upon such termination, shall furnish Sponsoring Broker with a bona fide list of all prospects, leads and probable transactions developed by Salesperson, or upon which Salesperson shall have been engaged with respect to any transaction completed subsequent to termination of this agreement in which Salesperson has rendered assistance in accordance with this paragraph. Except as provided in subparagraph B above, Salesperson shall not be compensated in respect to any transaction completed subsequent to termination of this agreement unless agreed to in writing by Sponsoring Broker.

   D. Upon termination of this agreement, Salesperson further agrees not to furnish to any person, firm, company or corporation engaged in the real estate business any information as to Sponsoring Broker's clients, customers, properties, prices, terms of negotiations nor Sponsoring Broker's policies or relationships with clients and customers nor any other information concerning Sponsoring Broker and/or his/her business. Salesperson shall not, after termination of this agreement, remove from the files or from the office of the Sponsoring Broker any maps, books and publications, card records, investor or prospect lists, or any other material, files or data, and it is expressly agreed that the aforementioned records and information are the property of Sponsoring Broker. Salesperson shall be entitled to photostats of certain instruments pertaining to transactions in which Salesperson has a bona fide interest, and Sponsoring Broker shall not unreasonably withhold the same from Salesperson.

3. Automobile. It is agreed that Salesperson shall furnish his/her own automobile and pay all expenses thereof and that Sponsoring Broker shall have no responsibility therefore. Salesperson agrees to carry public liability insurance upon that automobile with minimum limits of $ _____ for each person and $ _____ for each accident and with property damage limit of $ _____.

4. Real Estate Licenses, Insurance and Dues. Salesperson shall pay all of the cost of his/her own real estate license and his/her dues for membership in the National Association of REALTORS®, Illinois Association of REALTORS® and the _____
Board/Association of REALTORS® and any associations, membership organizations or trade associations to which Salesperson wishes to belong. Salesperson shall obtain and pay for errors and omissions insurance with a company and in an amount acceptable to Sponsoring Broker.

5. Commissions.

   A. The commissions and fees for services rendered in the sale, rental, trade or leasing of real estate shall be those stated in the Sponsoring Broker's policy manual or other similar written document and shall be payable to the Sponsoring Broker. In no event shall Salesperson charge less than the commission or fee established by the Sponsoring Broker without the prior consent of the Sponsoring Broker. If Sponsoring Broker shall have entered into a special contract or agreement pertaining to any particular transaction the Sponsoring Broker shall advise Salesperson of such special arrangement. Commissions, when earned and paid pursuant to this agreement, shall be divided between Sponsoring Broker and Salesperson, after deduction of all expenses, according to the Salesperson's commission schedule as adopted by Sponsoring Broker from time to time. Sponsoring Broker shall notify Salesperson of any change in said commission schedule.

   B. In the event that two (2) or more salespeople under contract with Sponsoring Broker participate in a transaction and claim a commission thereon, then and in that event the amount of the commissions allocable to each salesperson shall be divided equally among the salespeople or otherwise according to a written agreement among said salespeople.

   C. In no case shall Sponsoring Broker be personally liable to Salesperson for any commission not collected, nor shall Salesperson be personally liable to Sponsoring Broker for any commission not collected. If commissions have been or are to be collected from the party or parties for whom the service was performed, it is agreed that such sums shall be deposited with the Sponsoring Broker and subsequently divided according to the terms of this agreement.

   D. The division and distribution of the earned commissions as provided herein, which may be paid to or collected by Sponsoring Broker, but from which Salesperson is due certain commissions, shall take place as soon as practicable after collection and receipt of such commissions. However, Sponsoring Broker is first entitled to reimbursement for any expenses incurred such as attorney's fees, revenue stamps, abstract costs or expenses incurred in the collection of the commission with respect to any transaction.

*WITNESS the signature of the parties hereto on the day and year first above written in duplicate.

SPONSORING BROKER   SALESPERSON

_____

By: _____   _____

Capacity _____

*Original signature required on each copy

Form 201
9/2002 Copyright© Illinois Association of REALTORS®   Page 1 of 2

FIGURE 5.1

Sample Employment Agreement (continued)

6. Supervision.

   A. Salesperson agrees to abide by the requirements and standards of Sponsoring Broker as set forth in Sponsoring Broker's Office Policy Manual.

   B. If Salesperson needs consultation in a transaction or situation, Salesperson agrees to seek the counsel of Sponsoring Broker or his/her designee.

7. Listings, Correspondence, Records and Forms.

   A. Salesperson agrees that any and all listings of property, and all actions taken in connection with the real estate business, shall be taken by Salesperson in the name of Sponsoring Broker. Such listings shall be filed with Sponsoring Broker within twenty-four (24) hours after receipt of same by Salesperson. All listings shall be and remain the separate and exclusive property of Sponsoring Broker unless otherwise agreed by the parties hereto.

   B. It is agreed by the parties hereto that all correspondence received, copies of all correspondence written, plats, listing information, memoranda, files, photographs, reports, legal opinions, accounting information, and any and all other instruments, documents or information of any nature whatsoever concerning transactions handled by Sponsoring Broker or by Salesperson, or jointly, are and shall remain the property of Sponsoring Broker, provided, however, that Salesperson is entitled to a copy of each upon reasonable request.

   C. The parties hereto shall mutually approve and agree upon all correspondence from the office of Sponsoring Broker pertaining to transactions being handled, in whole or in part, by Salesperson.

   D. The parties hereto agree that forms to be used by the Salesperson will be those provided or otherwise approved by the Sponsoring Broker.

   E. Sponsoring Broker shall have the right to review and approve all completed contracts and completed forms before they are presented to clients for signature.

8. Independent Contractor.

   A. This agreement does not constitute a hiring by either party. The parties hereto are and shall remain independent contractors bound by the provisions hereof. This agreement shall not be construed as a partnership, and neither party hereto shall be liable for any obligation incurred by the other except as provided elsewhere herein. Sponsoring Broker shall not withhold from Salesperson's commission any amounts for withholding or employment taxes or any other items. Salesperson will not be treated as an employee for federal and state tax purposes and will be responsible for the payment of any and all federal or state taxes based upon commissions earned and received. Sponsoring Broker will not make any premium payments or contributions for any workmen's compensation or unemployment compensation for Salesperson.

   B. Sponsoring Broker agrees to serve as Salesperson's sponsor as required by the Illinois Real Estate License Act of 2000, as amended, 225 ILCS 454/10-20 (a).

9. Default and Hold Harmless. The parties hereto mutually agree that if either party shall be in default of or breach any of the terms and conditions of this Contract and such default or breach shall result in any loss or damage to the other party, then and in that event, the defaulting party hereby agrees to pay to the other party any such loss or damage and further agrees to hold the other party harmless from any claim, demand, cause of action, or lawsuit which may result from or be caused by such breach of this Contract.

10. Ethics, Laws, and Trade Organizations.

    A. Salesperson and Sponsoring Broker each agree to conduct his/her business and regulate his/her habits and working hours so as to maintain and to increase the good will, business, profits and reputation of Sponsoring Broker and Salesperson, and the parties agree to conform to and abide by all laws, rules and regulations applicable to real estate brokers and real estate salespeople. Specifically, Salesperson and Sponsoring Broker shall be governed by the Code of Ethics of the National Association of REALTORS®, the Real Estate License Act of the State of Illinois, the constitution and bylaws of the local real estate board, the rules and regulations of any multiple listing service with which Sponsoring Broker now and in the future may be affiliated, and any further modifications or additions to the foregoing.

    B. Salesperson acknowledges Sponsoring Broker's commitment and support for all state, federal fair housing and antitrust laws and further understands the Sponsoring Broker expects Salesperson to be knowledgeable concerning these laws and to conduct his/her business practices accordingly.

11. Litigation and Controversies.

    A. In the event that Salesperson does not wish to enter into the following actions jointly with Sponsoring Broker, the Salesperson hereby grants to Sponsoring Broker the power of attorney in his/her name, place and stead to institute an action in a court of competent jurisdiction concerning commissions or other matters related to the conduct of such real estate business of Sponsoring Broker and Salesperson as have been pursued by the parties under this Agreement; to conduct the same to a final decision; to negotiate settlements; to defend actions, suits or proceedings pertaining to said real estate business; to employ counsel and to settle or pursue matters to a final conclusion in such manner and upon such terms as to Sponsoring Broker may seem expedient or desirable.

    B. In the event any transaction in which Salesperson is involved results in a dispute, litigation or legal expense, Salesperson shall cooperate fully with Sponsoring Broker. It is the policy to avoid litigation whenever possible, and Sponsoring Broker, within his/her discretion may determine whether or not any litigation or dispute shall be prosecuted, defended, compromised or settled, and the terms and conditions of any compromise or settlement, or whether or not legal expense shall be incurred; provided, however, that no compromise or settlement involving the payment of money or anything of value by Salesperson, or the foregoing of any commission not challenged or subject to dispute or portion thereof due Salesperson, shall be accepted by Sponsoring Broker without the written consent of Salesperson.

    C. Salesperson shall notify Sponsoring Broker of any transaction in which Salesperson is involved which Salesperson has reason to believe may result in litigation or arbitration involving the Sponsoring Broker.

12. Expenses. Sponsoring Broker shall not be liable to Salesperson for any expenses incurred by Salesperson or for any of his/her acts, nor shall Salesperson be liable to Sponsoring Broker for Sponsoring Broker's office help or expenses or any of Sponsoring Broker's acts, other than as specifically provided for herein.

13. Miscellaneous.

    A. Heirs, Successors and Assigns. This agreement shall be binding upon and the benefits shall inure to the heirs, successors and assigns of the parties hereto.

    B. Notices. All notices provided for under this agreement shall be in writing and shall be sufficient if sent by certified mail to the last known address of the party.

    C. Governing Law. This agreement shall be governed by the laws of the State of Illinois.

    D. Assignment. This assignment is personal to the parties hereto and may not be assigned, sold or otherwise conveyed by either of them.

    E. Waiver. The failure of any party hereto to enforce at any time any of the provisions or terms of this agreement shall not be construed to be a waiver of such provision or term, nor the right of any party thereafter to enforce such term or provision.

    F. Entire Agreement. This agreement constitutes the entire agreement between the Sponsoring Broker and Salesperson and there are no agreements or understandings concerning such agreement which are not fully set forth herein.

    G. Severability. If any provision of this agreement is invalid or unenforceable in any jurisdiction, the other provisions herein shall remain in full force and effect in such jurisdiction and shall be liberally construed in order to effectuate the purpose and intent of this agreement, and the invalidity or unenforceability of any provision of this agreement in any jurisdiction shall not affect the durability or enforceability of such provision in any other jurisdiction.

A sponsoring broker's relationship with a sponsored licensee who is an **independent contractor** is very different.

A licensee must meet three specific criteria set out by the IRS in the Internal Revenue Code to be treated as an independent contractor for federal tax purposes, the following criteria must be met:

■ Individual must hold an active real estate license
■ Individual must agree in writing not to be treated as an employee for federal tax purposes; and
■ At least 90 percent of the individual's income must be derived from sales rather than hours worked.

An employment agreement between the sponsoring broker and managing broker is also required even if the managing broker is the sole owner in the sponsoring brokerage (regardless of the business type: LLC, LLP, and so on).

IN PRACTICE   The sponsoring broker must have a written employment agreement for all sponsored licensees both for independent contractors and for employees including licensed personal assistants. Specific legal and tax questions regarding independent contractors should be referred to a competent attorney or an accountant.

IRS Tax Considerations: Independent Contractor/Regular Employee

One of the most important decisions a sponsoring broker needs to make is how to classify workers for tax purposes. Determining employee classification should always be discussed with a tax professional. This section is not intended to provided tax advice; it is only to provide information to help a business owner better utilize a tax professional. The relationship between the sponsoring broker and the person who performs services for that broker is viewed by the IRS in its Publication 15-A (2010), *Employer's Supplemental Tax Guide*, as a statutory nonemployee.

The IRS has three categories of statutory nonemployees: direct sellers, licensed real estate agents, and certain companion sitters. The IRS has two requirements for the statutory nonemployee:

■ Payment or compensation for the service must be directly related to sales or other work output and not on the number of hours worked.
■ The workers have contracts specifying that they will not be treated as regular employees for tax purposes.

Workers who meet these two requirements will be treated as self-employed or independent contractors.

A sponsoring broker's relationship with a licensee who is an independent contractor can be very different from the relationship with an employee. As the name implies, independent contractors usually have a more flexible work schedule than that of employees. A broker may determine what the independent contractors do (especially because the contractors represent the broker as the broker's agents) but cannot dictate how they do it. As such, a company can expect independent contractors to comply with its policies and procedures. An independent contractor's income is typically commission-based. Independent contractors are responsible for paying their own income taxes and Social Security taxes.

It is not unusual for the IRS to investigate independent contractor and regular employee statuses in real estate offices. Under the qualified real estate category in the Internal Revenue Code, three requirements must be met in order to apply independent contractor status to an individual:

- The individual must have a current real estate license.
- The individual must have a written contract with the sponsoring broker specifying that the licensee will not be treated as a regular employee for federal tax purposes and that the taxes will be paid by the licensee.
- At least 90 percent of an individual's income as a licensee must be based on sales production and not on the number of hours worked.

In Illinois

Illinois real estate laws do not currently define the concept of a team, although the laws that define activities that require a real estate license in Illinois apply to them.

The sponsoring broker must consider whether licensed real estate team members should be treated as independent contractors or employees under the Internal Revenue Code and the Fair Labor Standards Act, to name a couple of applicable statutes.

If a licensed team member is a statutory independent contractor, this might be true for tax purposes only. For other purposes, the licensee might be a common law employee; in that case, Illinois workers' compensation laws might apply.

A licensed team member must have a written employment contract/independent contractor agreement with the sponsoring broker.

Unlicensed team members are regular employees. Either the sponsoring broker or a licensed team member might compensate them. The sponsoring broker will want to ensure that proper withholding requirements are met if a team member is compensating the regular employee. It is vital to consult an attorney and a competent tax advisor on these issues.

Similarly, the use of an unlicensed personal assistant, whether or not a member of a team, must comply with the laws that determine who is an independent contractor. By definition, the unlicensed personal assistant does not meet the safe harbor provisions of an independent contractor and would likely need to be paid as a regular employee. If the safe harbor provisions do not apply, then the employer should review the IRS test, with the advice of a tax professional, to determine if the worker meets the criteria.

The managing broker must remember that determining whether a worker is or is not an independent contractor is primarily done for tax purposes and has no impact on activities that require an Illinois real estate license. ■

Managing Broker Responsibilities

The **managing broker** has supervisory responsibilities for all licensees in one or, in the case of a multioffice company, more than one office appointed by the sponsoring broker. Sometimes, in the case of a sole proprietorship, the managing broker and the sponsoring broker are one and the same. If they are not the same, the sponsoring broker can delegate the issuance of sponsor cards to the managing broker.

Maintenance of licenses   Sponsoring brokers are required to notify IDFPR in writing of the names and license numbers of all managing brokers employed by the sponsoring broker and the office or branch offices for which each managing broker is responsible. The managing broker must have a current active managing broker's license.

Unexpected loss of managing broker   If a sponsoring and/or managing broker dies or a managing broker leaves a branch office unexpectedly, a request may be made to IDFPR within 15 days of this development to grant an extension for continued office operations. The extension may be granted for up to 60 days. In the case of an owner's death, a representative of the estate could operate the office for up to 60 days. In most cases of loss of a sponsoring or managing broker, a licensed managing broker assumes the management of the office. The appointed licensee must sign a written promise to personally supervise the office operations and accept responsibility for the office until a permanent replacement is located.

Death of self-sponsored broker   IDFPR will honor the order of a court of competent jurisdiction appointing a legal representative for the sole purpose of closing out the affairs of a deceased or disabled broker who was a sole proprietor. The court order is honored until the real estate brokerage operation is closed but does not allow the brokerage to actively engage in the brokerage business.

Renewals   When a managing broker receives renewal application form from IDFPR, the managing/sponsoring broker must notify the licensee of the receipt in person within seven days or by registered or certified mail or some other form of signature delivery within ten days. The notice will inform the licensee that any undeliverable renewal form will be returned to IDFPR. When a managing broker receives a renewal application form from IDFPR for a licensee not supervised or sponsored by the managing or sponsoring broker, the renewal form must be returned immediately to IDFPR.

Change of business address   All managing brokers must notify IDFPR on business letterhead of any change of business address for any of the offices they manage within 24 hours of any change. Change of address filing is required for all offices and branch offices.

Advertising   Effective May 1, 2012, all managing broker licensees who are named as managing brokers with the Division must indicate this status on all advertising that includes their name. Those who hold the managing broker license, but are not named as managing broker with the Division, are not required to include their names. They may not represent or indicate that they are managing brokers, only brokers affiliated with the sponsoring broker.

Supervision A managing broker must exercise reasonable supervision over the activities of licensees and unlicensed personal assistants working in those offices managed by the managing broker. These supervisory duties include the following:

- Implementation of office policies and procedures established by the sponsoring broker
- Training of licensees or unlicensed assistants
- Assisting licensees as necessary in real estate transactions
- Supervising escrow accounts over which the sponsoring broker has delegated responsibility to the managing broker in order to ensure compliance with the escrow account provisions of the Act
- Supervising all advertising of any service for which a license is required
- Familiarizing sponsored licensees with the requirements of federal and state laws relating to the practice of real estate
- Compliance with the rules for licensees and offices under his supervision

The sponsoring broker is ultimately responsible for the actions of all sponsored licensees including those of managing brokers as well as proper maintenance of escrow funds.

Termination of Sponsorship

If a salesperson, broker, leasing agent, or licensed personal assistant terminates employment with the sponsoring broker for any reason, the licensee must obtain his license from the sponsoring broker, or managing broker, if so designated by the sponsoring broker. The sponsoring broker signs and dates the license, which indicates that the relationship has been terminated. The sponsoring broker must send the Illinois Department of Financial and Professional Regulation (IDFPR) a copy of the terminated license within two days of the termination or be subject to discipline for failure to do so. The signed license automatically becomes inoperative, as does the licensee's ability to practice real estate, until a new sponsorship is designated.

If the licensee is simply changing brokers, the new sponsoring broker must immediately complete a sponsor card (45-day permit) for the licensee to carry until a new license and pocket card (with the new firm's name indicated as sponsor) arrives. The sponsoring broker prepares and sends a duplicate sponsor card to IDFPR for this transition period, along with the original endorsed license from the previous sponsoring broker within 24 hours of sponsorship along with the required fee.

Planning

Planning is the most fundamental management activity. Almost every business decision is guided by a **business plan**. Planning takes time and money; however, the resources devoted to planning are relatively small in comparison to the benefits of a sound plan that is followed and reviewed often. It is useful for building credibility with others outside your company. For the plan to be effective, it must be flexible and measurable, but, most important, it must be achievable.

The development of the business plan begins with creating a mission statement. This statement identifies the company's purpose for being in business and sets the course, purpose, and tone of the organization. The mission statement provides the focus for the company. Everything else in the business plan supports the mission statement.

The mission statement identifies specific objectives or goals for accomplishing the mission. These are the end results to be achieved. Goals must be translated into specific words that tell exactly how to focus the company's resources. Goals have several characteristics. They must

- be specific or identifiable;
- be measurable;
- be attainable; and
- have beginning and ending dates.

Each of the goals is supported by strategies that prescribe the methodology used in accomplishing that specific goal. Strategies include things needing to be done to overcome any obstacles or enhancement of resources. They also help to eliminate nonproductive activities. Lastly, activities or tasks must be designed to carry out the strategies to accomplish the goal. To summarize, the mission statement provides an overall view of where the company is going. The objectives or goals spell out specifically what the company wants to achieve. The strategies are the broad courses of action thought to accomplish the goal. Finally, the tasks are the specific day-to-day activities that will make the strategies a reality.

Preparing a Policy and Procedures Manual

A **policy and procedures manual** should be written and should serve as a risk management tool for the company. In preparing the manual, the writer should be positive. For example, one should use the "it's okay to" approach rather than "don't do this" approach. The Illinois Association of REALTORS® (IAR) has a *Sample Office Policy Manual* that can serve as a general guideline in developing your policy manual. The table of contents from this manual, shown in Figure 5.2, serves as a guideline for topics to include in a policy and procedures manual.

Policies and procedures are extremely beneficial for the following reasons:

- Establishing a clear understanding of the relationship between broker and sponsored licensees as well as administrative functions versus staff functions
- Working to resolve conflicts before they come up
- Building confidence that everyone knows what the rules are and how the company is supposed to operate
- Giving guidance for many of the situations licensees face on a day-to-day basis

Keep in mind that the policy and procedures manual is not a sales training manual. Obviously, the policy manual cannot become the complete solution to every policy issue. When a decision cannot be made easily about a specific problem, the manual should state how it is to be interpreted and who will do the interpretation.

FIGURE 5.2

Sample Policy and Procedures Manual

Table of Contents
Company Mission Statement
Statement of Business Principles
Equal Employment Opportunity Policy
Policy Against Sexual Harassment
Independent Contractor/Employment Agreement
Use of Personal Assistants
Office Hours
Holidays and Holiday Hours
Office Opening and Closing Procedures
Smoking Policy
Training Program and Schedule
Sales Meetings/Property Inspections
Inquiries/Visits by Government Officials
Subpoenas and Summonses
Agent Safety
Functions of Unlicensed Office Personnel
Payments to Unlicensed Persons
Sample Brokerage Relationship Policies
Cooperation and Compensation Policy
Agency Disclosure Policy
Mandatory Buyer-Agency Events
Strongly Recommended Buyer-Agency Events
Agency and Confidentiality
Fair Housing Policy
Antitrust Policy
Listing Procedures
Buyer Qualification Policy
Sales Contract Policy
Advertising Policy
Risk Reduction Policy
Business Items List
E-mail and Internet Policy
Acknowledgment and Agreement
Agency "Dos and Don'ts"

Source: *Sample Office Policy Manual*, © 2000 Illinois Association of REALTORS®, with permission of Bruce Aydt and the Missouri Association of REALTORS®.

Safety Concerns: Appointments and Showings

Real estate agents enjoy working with the public and have historically felt safe while performing their jobs, but the trend has shifted in recent years, with a number of agents robbed, raped, and murdered while showing homes and other properties.

Many real estate firms have responded to the violence by incorporating safety procedures into their procedure manual as a way to help keep their agents safe. Licensees can help minimize risks by implementing the following suggestions.

■ Ask the customer for work, home, and cell phone numbers and a physical address. Verify the information by calling the customer at one or more of the numbers.
■ Give someone in your office an itinerary of properties you plan to show and then check back in often by cell phone.

- Do not meet unknown customers at a property. Require that they meet you at your office. Make sure someone writes down their license plate number and the type of car they are driving.
- Never get into a car with someone you don't know. Use your vehicle for showings or ask your customer to follow you in another car.
- Program your cell phone to dial 911 at the touch of a button.
- Never work at a public open house by yourself.
- Do not show vacant properties by yourself unless you know your customers, and never show properties after dark.
- Keep pepper spray or Mace® handy.
- Always follow the customers into the property and let them enter while you stay by the door.
- Pay attention to exits.
- Ask someone else to accompany you to show or list property if you feel uncomfortable about the people with whom you are working. Don't assume that women are safer customers than men. Women are as just as capable of armed robbery and sometimes work with a partner who waits at the house for the two of you to arrive.

For offices that don't have office safety procedures, the National Association of REALTORS® and other state and local associations have developed safety guidelines that will aid licensees when showing or listing properties and holding open houses.

Business Planning

To stay on top of changes in the real estate industry and practice, as well as keeping up with emerging technologies, brokers should review and update policy manuals regularly.

In Illinois   The Real Estate License Act of 2000 Section 10-40 requires that "every brokerage company or entity, other than a sole proprietorship with no other sponsored licensees, shall adopt a company or office policy dealing with topics" such as

- the agency policy of the entity;
- fair housing, nondiscrimination, and harassment;
- confidentiality of client information; and
- advertising. ■

Errors and Omissions Insurance

Sponsoring or managing brokers have an array of issues and options to consider when deciding to obtain an **errors and omissions insurance** (E&O) policy. In general, they need to determine what level of protection to seek in the policy and how to tailor the coverage to their sponsoring/managing practice. Because insurance policies and practices vary from company to company, the sponsoring or managing broker must be careful to review any specific policy intended for the office and should discuss coverage with more than one insurance provider before obtaining coverage.

Brokers are licensed professionals who are held to fiduciary standards. A **fiduciary standard** is a legal standard that holds a licensee to the highest ethical standards that the law provides. Licensees have the duties of advice and counsel to the represented client and must be fair, honest, and accurate in dealing with consumers and customers whom they do not represent. In this regard, the broker is treated no differently than a doctor, lawyer, or other licensed professional acting in a confidential environment. However, unlike a doctor or a lawyer, the broker is expected to engage in sales activities that can conflict with the duties owed by a fiduciary. This conflict can create significant professional liability exposure for the real estate licensee.

The classes of services performed by licensees shape the types of liability claims most often filed against real estate licensees. Real estate licensees may represent buyers, sellers, lessors, and lessees. They coordinate a variety of services, such as insurance, title, loan origination, home inspection, and legal. In addition, they often function as independent professionals managing their own offices, advertising campaigns, and other related business functions. In providing these services, licensees become vulnerable to potential liabilities.

Licensees earn a specified commission or negotiated fee (typically based on some percentage of the final sale price or annual rental cost) as they help secure buyers or tenants for various kinds of real property usually owned by third parties. Because earnings are a function of commission for each transaction, increasing the number of transactions increases the annual earnings. Dual agency also increases the total compensation through representation of both parties in the transaction but can also increase the possibility of conflicts of interest. In order to prevent a breach of fiduciary duty, licensees must know how to balance a client's specific requirements with the duties owned to third parties.

Liability claims can also arise from a number of related services provided occasionally for a separate fee basis or are incidental to the transaction. These include property appraisal, property management, auctioneering, consulting, and handling earnest monies or security deposits. The real estate licensee needs to be aware that not all these activities are covered by standard real estate broker's liability coverage forms. Some real estate licensee services require a special endorsement to the insurance policy for an additional premium; other services require the purchase of a separate insurance policy.

The most common errors and omissions claims against real estate licensees include the following:

- Mishandling monies (earnest money or security deposits) during transactions
- Making misstatements about material facts regarding the property, such as the presence of lead-based paint, asbestos, or radon
- Misrepresenting the property dimensions or failure to measure property dimensions accurately
- Disclosure of confidential information without authorization from the client
- Undisclosed dual agency
- Failure to identify the real or personal property correctly in the contract
- Mistakes regarding the property tax identification number (PIN) for the subject property or failure to provide an adequate legal description of the property
- Misrepresentations about financing arrangements

- Failure to disclose a financial interest in the customer who is negotiating with the client
- Failure to disclose financial relationships compensating the licensee in the transaction
- Violations of the federal Fair Housing Act and the Illinois Human Rights Act
- Breaching the terms of the listing or buyer agreement or the property management agreement

Policy Protection and Covered Services

A real estate licensee needs insurance protection from claims made by clients, customers, and consumers related to the provision of real estate activities, referred to as professional services by the insurance industry. The sponsoring/managing broker must determine whether the errors and omissions policy adequately addresses what

- services are covered,
- person(s) is(are) covered,
- damages are covered,
- defenses are covered, and
- territory is covered.

Real estate licensees should know whether the services they provide constitute professional services and are, thus, insurable under the policy. They should also be aware that professional services are defined differently in each insurer's policy.

Professional real estate services typically refer to services that require a person to have an Illinois real estate license in order to perform those services on behalf of clients, customers, and consumers. As a prerequisite for coverage, the licensee must possess all valid necessary licenses or certifications at the time of the act or omission giving rise to the claim and must be acting within the scope of the employment agreement, either written or oral. Sometimes insurance companies will include coverage for ancillary professional real estate services rendered by the insured for others, such as a notary public's duties.

Covered Defense Costs

Errors and omission policies may sometimes pay the costs involved in investigating, defending, and settling claims. These costs primarily involve attorney's fees but also include related expenses required by the claim settlement process. The sponsoring broker should determine whether defense costs are covered by the policy or in addition to the policy limits. If defense costs are covered within the policy limits, then as the legal fees increase, the limits of the coverage of the policy are proportionately reduced.

Excluded Coverage

Most E&O policies exclude certain ancillary real estate–related activities. These exclusions include a licensee's involvement in areas that do not require an Illinois real estate license, such as property development and insurance agency operations.

Depending on the insurer, coverage for such services may be bought back for an additional premium, if an insured's operations require such coverage. A real estate licensee who wants coverage for such services may obtain it by paying an additional premium or, depending on the limitations of the policy, by obtaining a separate policy. The sponsoring or managing broker should also be aware that violations of fair housing laws, some civil sanctions, and criminal act are not covered by E&O policies. Some policies will cover the legal defense for certain issues, such as discrimination, but not the damages awarded.

Other possible exclusions from coverage under E&O policies include the following:

- Bankruptcy of the insured
- Violation of securities law
- Wrongful termination
- Employee Retirement Income Security Act (ERISA) violations
- Claims by or against related entities
- Workers' compensation claims
- Personal injury claims
- Claims arising from usage of vehicles, aircraft, and watercraft
- Environmental issues, such as mold and asbestos
- Real estate owned by the insured
- Commission disputes

Because there can be coverage gaps between E&O policies and commercial general liability (CGL) policies, the sponsoring/managing broker should ensure that excluded coverage for bodily injury, property damage, and personal injury are covered by CGL policies or by special endorsement. Potential gap coverage between E&O policies and CGL policies should be discussed by the sponsoring broker with the insurer to best customize the coverage to the brokerage firm.

Covered Persons

E&O policies are intended to cover those licensees whose licenses are held by the sponsoring broker, as well as office staff and unlicensed assistants in an insured real estate broker's office who may be involved in a transaction—even if their function does not involve professional activities. Where the sponsoring broker is a business entity, such as a partnership, corporation, or limited liability company (LLC), these policies can include coverage for past and present partners, officers, directors, and regular employees. Because the nature of the claims against the policies can survive the death or incapacity of the insured, coverage should be structured to include the heirs, executors, administrators, and trustees in bankruptcy of the insured.

Independent Contractors

Most real estate offices that sell residential real estate will sponsor licensees who are treated as independent contractors. Therefore, it is important that the E&O

policies cover those independent contractors. The sponsoring/managing broker must keep in mind that unlicensed assistants cannot be treated as independent contractors because it is a violation of federal tax law. Therefore, the sponsoring/managing broker must be certain that the E&O policy is written to cover unlicensed assistants. A sponsoring broker must also address liability arising from predecessor firm issues. For example, brokerage firm A acquires brokerage firm B with at least 50 percent of brokerage firm B's licensees joining brokerage firm A or where brokerage firm A assumes at least 50 percent of brokerage firm B's assets and/or liabilities. Under these circumstances, a claim against a brokerage firm B licensee (for an incident prior to the acquisition) who currently works with brokerage firm A could become the obligation of brokerage firm A.

Covered Territory

Most E&O policies cover claims resulting from anywhere in the world, provided the claim and concomitant litigation is brought in the United States, its territories or possessions, or Canada. Actions conducted outside the United States will likely require additional coverage or a separate policy. The licensee should be aware that use of Web sites with their worldwide exposure might lead to claims and litigation outside the United States; a licensee would need a policy with unrestricted territorial coverage to address this issue.

Other Policy Issues

The sponsoring or managing broker should be aware of additional issues that might affect E&O coverage. The insurance claims process varies from insurer to insurer. Therefore, licensees need to understand the procedures of their provider. Some policy issues to be aware of include the following:

- Most E&O policies have liability caps that set a payment limit per claim and an aggregate payment limit; the licensee should obtain coverage that matches the licensee's liability exposure.
- There are two basic types of deductible provisions. One type of deductible applies to each error committed, and the other type applies to each claim filed. Limits per error are found in a nonaccumulation clause. For example, if a licensee represents a condo developer whose units have a series of claims filed for multiple coverage periods, the policy will restrict coverage to the monetary limit of the first coverage period. Also, most policies permit the insurer to assess the deductible even if the claim does not lead to a liability against the licensee if the insurer pays for the successful legal defense.
- Most E&O policies have provisions that limit payment to the amount offered in a settlement offer. If the licensee refuses the settlement and the subsequent trial judgment is higher than the settlement offer, then the licensee will be liable for the payment amount in excess of the settlement offer, as well as the defenses costs of the trial.
- All E&O policies have some additional conditions that are essential elements of the policy's coverage. All policies have subrogation provisions that allow the insurer the right to initial litigation where the insurer has paid on claims against the policy. Insurers require the insured to cooperate with the claims process and subsequent litigation and prohibit the insured from making voluntary settlements.

■ Problems may arise when one insured sues another insured. This can occur when one licensee sues another licensee in the sponsoring broker's office resulting from a claim arising from professional services provided (e.g., one agent selling another agent's property) in that office. The policy should include a special clause that ensures coverage for that type of claim.

■ Although most insurers limit coverage to the inception date of the policy, some insurers will consider providing first-time insurance buyers coverage for prior acts (for an additional premium). Generally, prior acts coverage is limited to retroactive claims for no more than five years. If the policy expires or is cancelled and is not replaced with a new policy with prior acts coverage, then the licensee must have an extended-reporting-period clause that allows a claim that occurred during the coverage period to be processed against the expired policy. This type of coverage is usually limited to no more than one to three years after expiration of the policy.

It is the duty of the sponsoring broker to determine what level of E&O insurance is necessary to meet the needs of the brokerage office.

Personal Assistants

A **personal assistant**, also known as a *real estate assistant* or *professional assistant*, is often a combination office manager, marketer, organizer, and facilitator with a fundamental understanding of the real estate industry. While an assistant does not need to have a real estate license, she is allowed to perform many more duties if holding a real estate license. (*In Illinois, there is no specific assistant's license.*)

The extent to which the assistant can help licensees with transactions is usually determined by state license laws. An unlicensed assistant may perform duties ranging from clerical and secretarial functions to answering phones. A licensed assistant can set up and host open houses, deal more extensively with clients, actively show houses, and assist in all aspects of a real estate transaction. In other words, a licensed assistant can perform any activity that any licensee is permitted to perform.

| In Illinois |

Section 1450.165 of the administrative rules specifies the permitted activities in which an unlicensed real estate assistant may engage. (See Figure 5.3.)

The Real Estate License Act of 2000 requires that *licensed personal assistants must have an employment agreement with the sponsoring broker* of the firm in which they are working, even though they are, in practice, working for an affiliate licensee. The sponsoring broker must pay licensed personal assistants. ■

Broker Compensation

The sponsoring broker's compensation is specified in the contract with the client.

Real estate license laws may stipulate that a *written agreement must establish compensation to be paid.* Compensation can be in the form of a commission (computed as a percentage of the total sales price), a flat fee, or an hourly rate. The amount of a broker's commission is negotiable in every case. Even subtle attempts to impose

F I G U R E   5.3

Licensed and Unlicensed Real Estate Assistants

An Unlicensed Real Estate Assistant May . . .

- answer the telephone, take messages, and forward calls to a licensee
- submit listings and changes to an MLS
- follow up on a transaction after a contract has been signed
- assemble documents for a closing
- secure public information documents from a courthouse, sewer district, water district, or other repository of public information
- have keys made for a company listing
- draft advertising and promotional materials for approval by a licensee
- place advertising in media
- record and deposit earnest money, security deposits, and rents
- complete contract forms with business and factual information at the direction of and with approval by a licensee
- monitor licenses and personnel files
- compute commission checks and perform bookkeeping activities
- place signs on property
- order items of routine repair as directed by a licensee
- prepare and distribute flyers and promotional information under the direction of and with approval by a licensee
- act as a courier to deliver documents, pick up keys, etc.
- place routine telephone calls on late rent payments
- schedule appointments for the licensee (does not include making phone calls, telemarketing, or performing other activities to solicit business on behalf of the licensee)
- respond to questions by quoting from published information
- sit at a property for a broker tour that is not open to the public
- gather feedback on showings
- perform maintenance, engineering, operations, or other building trades work and answer questions about such work
- provide security
- provide concierge services and other similar amenities to existing tenants
- manage or supervise maintenance, engineering, operations, building trades, and security
- perform other administrative, clerical, and personal activities for which a license under the Act is not required

An Unlicensed Real Estate Assistant May NOT. . .

- host open houses, kiosks, home show booths, or fairs
- show property
- interpret information on listings, titles, financing, contracts, closings, or other information related to a real estate transaction
- explain or interpret a contract, listing, lease agreement, or other real estate document with anyone outside the employing licensee's firm
- negotiate or agree to any commission, commission split, management fee, or referral fee on behalf of a licensee
- perform any other activity for which a real estate license under the Act is required

SOURCE: Sec. 1450.165, Rules for the Administration of the Real Estate License Act of 2000.

uniform commission rates are clearly a violation of antitrust laws. A sponsoring broker, however, may set the minimum commission rate acceptable for his own company.

The important point is that the broker and the client agree on a rate before the agency relationship is established.

In Illinois Only a licensed managing or sponsoring broker may collect a commission in Illinois; the managing or sponsoring broker then may share it with any licensees who are directly involved in or responsible for a given transaction. To collect a commission on a real estate transaction, the agent must have been "hired" by way of an agreement in which the principal (seller or buyer) agreed to pay a specified commission for services. The percentage of sales price or dollar amount of commission must have been expressed clearly in the agreement. If another real estate office "brought in" the buyer, the concept of **cooperative commission** allows the *listing broker* to pay the *selling broker* the amount of *cooperative commission* advertised in advance on the multiple listing service (MLS) listing. This check is issued by the listing broker's office to the selling broker's office, and checks then are cut by each of these sponsoring brokers to any respective salespersons (or other brokers working within the firm) who were directly involved in the transaction. ■

Cooperative Commission

Commission paid by the listing broker to the "cooperating broker" who has the buyer.

A commission is usually considered earned when the work for which the real estate broker was hired has been accomplished. Most sales commissions are payable when the sale is consummated by *delivery of the seller's deed*. This provision is generally included in the listing agreement. When the sales or listing agreement specifies no time for the payment of the broker's commission, the commission is usually earned when

- a completed sales contract has been executed by a ready, willing, and able buyer;
- the contract has been accepted and executed by the seller; and
- copies of the contract are in possession by all parties.

To be entitled to a sales commission, an individual must be

- a licensed real estate broker,
- the procuring cause of the sale, and
- employed by the buyer or the seller under a valid contract.

To be a *procuring cause*, the broker must have started a chain of events that resulted in a sale.

To be considered the **procuring cause** of a sale, the broker must have started or caused a chain of events that resulted in the sale. For example, activities such as conducting open houses, placing advertisements in the newspaper, and showing the house to the buyer are considered procuring cause. A broker who causes or completes such an action without a contract or without having been promised payment is a *volunteer* and may not legally claim compensation.

IN PRACTICE   Procuring cause disputes between brokers are usually settled through an arbitration hearing conducted by the local board or association. Disputes between a broker and a client may go to court. They may not be taken to the Division.

A *ready, willing, and able buyer* is one prepared to buy on the seller's terms and ready to complete the transactions.

A **ready, willing, and able buyer** is one who is *prepared to buy on the seller's terms and ready to take positive steps toward consummation of the transaction.* Once a seller accepts an offer from a ready, willing, and able buyer, the real estate broker is entitled to a commission. Courts may prevent the real estate broker from receiving a commission if the real estate broker knew the buyer was unable to perform. If the transaction is not consummated, the real estate broker may still be entitled to a commission if the seller

- had a change of mind and refused to sell,

- has a spouse who refused to sign the deed,
- had a title with uncorrected defects,
- committed fraud with respect to the transaction,
- was unable to deliver possession within a reasonable time,
- insisted on terms not in the listing (e.g., the right to restrict the use of the property), or
- had a mutual agreement with the buyer to cancel the transaction.

In Illinois

In Illinois, the closing of the sale is the usual proof in a court of law that the broker has produced a buyer and earned a commission. ■

Sales Force Compensation

The amount of compensation a licensee receives from a sale is set by mutual agreement between the affiliated licensees and their sponsoring brokers. This compensation agreement is included in the employment agreement. A sponsoring broker may agree to pay a fixed salary or a predetermined percentage based on transactions originated by a specific licensee. Some sponsoring brokers require that sales staff pay all or part of the expenses of advertising listed properties; this may be subtracted from commissions by agreement or be billed separately to the licensee.

In Illinois

In many states, including Illinois, it is illegal for a sponsoring broker to pay a commission to anyone *other than*

- a licensees under that same sponsoring broker; or
- another firm's sponsoring broker (cooperative commission) who then pays his own sponsored licensees involved.

Fees, commissions, or other compensation *cannot* be paid to unlicensed persons for services that legally require a real estate license. "Other compensation" includes certain items of personal property, such as a new television, or other premiums, such as vacations, given to nonlicensed persons to perhaps acquire names of "leads." This is not to be confused with referral fees paid between managing or sponsoring brokers for "leads," which are legal as long as the individuals are licensed.

Sponsoring brokers may pay their sponsored licensees their commissions directly or, under the Act, a licensee may form a *solely owned corporation* for the purpose of receiving compensation. That one-shareholder corporation cannot be licensed by the IDFPR. However, the licensee must file a copy of the certificate of incorporation issued by the Secretary of State with IDFPR. The corporation can receive compensation earned by that licensee only, both from real estate and non-real-estate-related activities. The corporation cannot be licensed and cannot be used by the licensee to perform real estate activities, sponsor or employ other licensees, or advertise itself to the public in the corporation's name. ■

IN PRACTICE All monies going in and out of real estate offices are handled by the sponsoring broker. This includes, but is not limited to, incentive prizes for selling agents, earnest money deposits, escrows, commissions, referral fees, licensed personal assistant wages, bonuses, thank-you surprises from buyers or sellers, and other monies or awards.

In Illinois   **Commissions and disclosures** The sponsoring broker's compensation and policy with cooperating brokers who represent other parties in a transaction must always be disclosed. If there is compensation from two parties to a transaction—from both the buyer and the seller—that needs to be disclosed in writing as well. If a licensee refers the client to another source for services related to the transaction and the licensee has an interest greater than 1 percent in that source, it must be disclosed. In addition, a licensee must disclose to a client all sources of compensation related to the transaction received by the licensee from a third party. ■

Commission Structures

Commission "splits" earned by sponsored licensees vary. Some firms have adopted a 100 percent commission plan. Sponsored licensees in these offices pay a monthly service charge or desk fee to their sponsoring brokers to cover the costs of office space, telephones, and supervision in return for keeping 100 percent of the commissions from the sales they negotiate. The 100 percent commission sponsored licensee pays all of his own expenses.

Other companies offer graduated commission splits based on a sponsored licensee's achieving specified production goals. For instance, a sponsoring broker might agree to split commissions 50/50 with a certain sponsored licensee until the sponsoring broker has earnings of $25,000 for the year from that sponsored licensees or 60/40 until the sponsoring broker's tally reaches $50,000. Past that point, the sponsored licensees portion of the split might go to 70 percent, 80 percent, or even 100 percent. Commission splits 80/20 or 90/10 are not unheard of for high producers. No matter how the licensee's compensation package is structured, *only the sponsoring broker can pay it.*

In cooperating transactions (usually stated as "co-op: X%" on the MLS sheet), the commission is paid by the sponsoring broker of the "list side" to the sponsoring broker of the "sell side," and then paid to the sponsored licensee who worked for or with the buyer. The listing sponsored licensee is similarly paid by the listing sponsoring broker.

In Illinois   If the commission is from a listing that has sold, the sponsoring broker of the listing firm is first paid by the seller. Then the sponsoring broker pays the sponsored licensee involved at the listing office and also pays the cooperating sponsoring broker at any other firm involved in the transaction. The cooperating sponsoring broker in turn issues the appropriate amount to the sponsored licensee involved at his office, based on their agreed-upon split. Sometimes a commission or fee does not involve a seller. It might come from a buyer who has agreed to a buyer agent fee. The same procedure applies: incoming funds always go to the sponsoring broker first; from there they are dispersed to others involved.

If a sponsored licensee had earned a commission but his employment had been terminated prior to the payment of the commission, the former sponsoring broker may pay the commission directly to the former associate, even if that former associate has a new sponsoring broker. ∎

MATH CONCEPTS

SHARING COMMISSIONS

A commission might be shared by many people: The listing managing broker, the listing broker, the selling managing broker, and the selling broker. Drawing a diagram can help you determine which person is entitled to receive what amount of the total commission.

For example, broker Ed, while working for managing broker Harry, took a listing on a $73,000 house at a 6 percent commission rate. Broker Tom, while working for managing broker Matt, found the buyer for the property. If the property sold for the listed price, the listing managing broker and the selling managing broker shared the commission equally and the selling managing broker kept 45 percent of what he received, how much did broker Tom receive? (If the managing broker retained 45 percent of the total commission he received, his broker would receive the balance: 100% − 45% = 55%.)

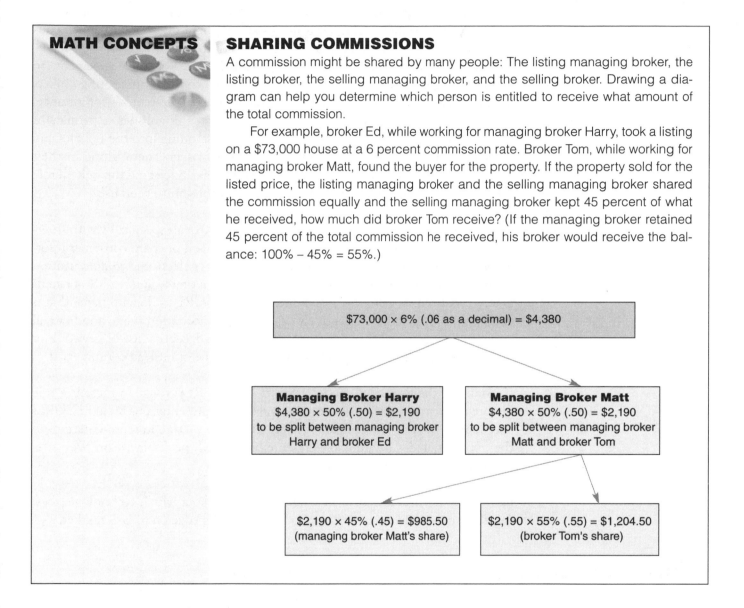

Legal Rights and Obligations

As each contract is prepared for signature during a real estate transaction, the **licensee** should advise the parties of the desirability of securing legal counsel to protect their interests. *Only a lawyer can offer legal advice.* Licensees are prohibited from practicing law.

Technology and Brokerage of the Future

The Internet has brought tremendous change to the real estate industry. Real estate practitioners and consumers rely heavily on the Internet for a variety of services. Practitioners use blogs to exchange information and vlogs to target out-of-area consumers looking for properties. Visitors to vlogs download videos and can see virtual tours of properties. Virtual staging is also used by practitioners to give consumers an idea of what a vacant property can look like to make it more appealing to sell.

Social networking sites such as Facebook, LinkedIn, YouTube, and Twitter are becoming increasingly useful in business—and the real estate industry is no different. Recognizing the value and pervasiveness of these sites, sponsoring brokers should set out clear guidelines in policy manuals and brokerage agreements to permit and guide the use of these technologies by licensees. Sponsoring brokers must also learn about the potential risks and liabilities of these sites—for instance, recognizing that communication through these sites establishes a permanent record of sorts—and should incorporate this understanding into the policies and guidelines they establish for licensees on the use of social networking in their businesses. They must also work to ensure that clients understand the helpful role these sites can play in real estate transactions and consent to their use.

In Illinois Section 10-35 of the Real Estate License Act of 2000 deals specifically with Internet and related advertising. Licensees intending to sell or share consumer information gathered from or through the Internet or other electronic communication media must disclose that intention to consumers in a timely and readily apparent manner. A licensee using the Internet cannot use a URL or domain name that is deceptive or misleading; deceptively or without authorization frame another real estate brokerage or MLS Web site; or engage in the deceptive use of keywords or other devices to direct, drive, or divert Internet traffic or mislead consumers. ■

In addition, the REALTOR® Code of Ethics requires REALTORS® to present a true picture in their advertising, marketing, and other representations including URLs and domain names. The obligation to present a true picture in representations to the public includes information presented, provided, or displayed on Web sites and that the information be current.

Real estate **licensees** must make careful decisions about which technologies best suit their needs and invest in them to have a cutting edge on today's market.

■ ANTITRUST LAWS

The real estate industry is subject to federal and state **antitrust laws.** These laws prohibit monopolies and any contracts, combinations, and conspiracies that unreasonably restrain trade—that is, acts that interfere with the free flow of goods and services in a competitive marketplace. The most common antitrust violations are price-fixing, group boycotting, allocation of customers or markets, and tie-in agreements.

Price-Fixing

Price-fixing is the practice of setting prices for products or services rather than letting competition in the open market establish those prices. In real estate, price-fixing occurs when competing real estate companies agree to set standard sales commissions, fees, or management rates or if they attempt illegal tying arrangements. *Price-fixing is illegal.* Real estate companies must independently determine any minimum commission rates or minimum fees. These decisions must be based on a company's business judgment and revenue requirements without input from other real estate companies.

MLSs, Boards of REALTORS®, and other professional organizations may not set fees or commission splits. They cannot deny membership to licensees based on the fees the licensees charge. Either practice could lead the public to believe that the industry not only sanctions the unethical practice of withholding cooperation from certain licensees but also encourages the illegal practice of restricting open-market competition.

The challenge for real estate licensees is to avoid even the impression of price-fixing. Hinting to prospective clients that there is a "going rate" of commission or a "normal" fee also implies that rates are, in fact, standardized, which must be avoided. The licensee must make it clear to clients that any stated minimum is only the firm's minimum. The specific commission is negotiable in a fair market.

> **Antitrust violations include**
>
> - price-fixing,
> - group boycotting,
> - allocation of customers,
> - allocation of markets, and
> - tie-in agreements.

Group Boycotting

Group boycotting occurs when two or more businesses conspire against another business or agree to withhold their patronage to reduce competition. Group boycotting is illegal under the antitrust laws.

■ **FOR EXAMPLE**   There are only two real estate companies in a small town. They agree that there are too many apartment finder services in town. They decide to refer all prospective tenants to the service operated by the niece of one of the sponsoring broker rather than handing out a list of all providers as they have done in the past. As a result, the sponsoring broker's niece runs the only apartment finder service in the town by the end of the year.

Allocation of Customers or Markets

Allocation of customers or markets involves an agreement among **real estate companies** to divide their markets and refrain from competing for each other's business. Allocations may be made on a geographic basis, with **real estate companies** agreeing to specific territories within which they will operate exclusively. The division also may occur by markets, such as by price range or category of housing. These agreements result in reduced competition.

Tie-in Agreements

Tie-in agreements, also known as *tying agreements*, are agreements to sell one product only if the buyer purchases another product as well. The sale of the first (desired) product is "tied" to the purchase of a second, less desirable, product.

■ **FOR EXAMPLE**   A sponsoring broker owns a vacant lot in a popular area of town. A builder wants to buy the lot and build three new homes on it. The sponsoring broker refuses to sell the lot to the builder unless the builder also agrees to purchase three other less desirable lots further east. This sort of tie-in arrangement violates antitrust laws.

Penalties

The penalties for violating antitrust laws are severe. For instance, under the *Sherman Antitrust Act*, people who fix prices or allocate markets may be subject to a maximum $1 million fine and up to ten years in prison. For corporations, the penalty may be as high as $100 million.

■ OTHER CONSUMER PROTECTION MEASURES

National Do Not Call Registry

In 2003, the Federal Communications Commission (FCC) established the **National Do Not Call Registry**. The registry is a list of phone numbers of consumers who do not want to be contacted by commercial telemarketers. It is managed by the FTC and is enforced by the FTC, the FCC, and state officials. The registry applies to any plan, program, or campaign to sell goods or services through interstate phone calls. The registry does not limit calls by political organizations, charities, collection agencies, or telephone surveyors.

Fortunately, the law establishes specific guidelines for when licensees may contact consumers, even when they are listed in the National Do Not Call Registry. Licensees are permitted to call consumers with whom they have an established business relationship up to 18 months following the consumer's last payment, purchase, or delivery. With consumers on the registry who have submitted applications or made inquiries, licensees are allowed additional contact for up to three months after the fact.

For example, it is permissible for a real estate licensee to call expired listings for the purpose of listing the property because the established business relationship exception permits the listing **licensee and the listing real estate company** to contact the seller for up to 18 months after the listing expiration date. Keep in mind that companies must also maintain a company-specific do-not-call list that applies as well.

Accessing the National Do Not Call Registry

Sellers, telemarketers, and other service providers must register to access the registry. The do-not-call registry may not be used for any purpose other than preventing telemarketing calls to the telephone numbers on the registry.

Regulators say that brokerage companies must have a do-not-call policy even if they do not engage in cold calling. A company that is a seller or telemarketer could be in violation of the law for placing any telemarketing calls (even to numbers *not* on the do-not-call registry) if the company does not have a policy for access to the registry. Violators may be subject to fines for each call placed.

To successfully avoid penalties ("safe harbor"), the seller or telemarketer must demonstrate the following:

- It has written procedures to comply with the do-not-call requirements.
- It trains its personnel in those procedures.
- It monitors and enforces compliance with these procedures.
- It maintains a company-specific list of telephone numbers it may not call.
- It accesses the national registry every 31 days before calling any consumer and maintains records documenting this process.
- It must show that any call made in violation of the do-not-call rules was the result of an error.

The best source of information about complying with the do-not-call rules is the FTC's Web sites: *www.donotcall.gov* and *www.ftc.gov*. They include business information about the registry.

The CAN-SPAM Act

The **CAN-SPAM Act of 2003** (Controlling the Assault of Non-Solicited Pornography and Marketing Act) establishes requirements for sending commercial e-mail; spells out penalties for those that don't comply, not just "spammers"; and gives consumers the right to have e-mailers stop e-mailing them.

The CAN-SPAM Act targets e-mail used to promote or advertise products and services (including online products and services) offered for commercial purposes. The act does not apply to "transactional or relationship content," that is, those messages meant to facilitate or alter existing customer agreements (for instance, by giving a customer additional information about an existing agreement or conducting business as part of an existing agreement); however, these e-mails must not explicitly or implicitly operate for the purposes of advertising or promotion, as this would be in violation of the law.

The CAN-SPAM Act is enforced by the FTC as well as by federal and state agencies, which have jurisdiction over the company or companies in question. In addition, companies that violate the CAN-SPAM Act can be sued by Internet service providers. Criminal sanctions can be brought against violators by the Department of Justice.

Briefly, the CAN-SPAM Act requires the following:

- *False or misleading header information is banned.* An e-mail's "From," "To," and routing information—including the original domain name and e-mail address—must be accurate and identify the person who initiated the e-mail.
- *Deceptive subject lines are prohibited.* The subject line cannot mislead the recipient about the contents or subject matter of the message.
- *E-mail recipients must have an opt-out method.* You must provide a return e-mail address or another Internet-based response mechanism that allows a recipient to ask you not to send future e-mail messages to that e-mail address and requests must be honored.

■ *Commercial e-mail must be identified as an advertisement and include the sender's valid physical postal address.*

Each violation is subject to fines. Deceptive commercial e-mails are also subject to laws banning false or misleading advertising. Additional fines are provided for commercial e-mailers who violate the rules and do any of the following:

■ "Harvest" e-mail addresses from Web sites or Web services that have published a notice prohibiting the transfer of e-mail addresses for the purpose of sending e-mail

■ Generate e-mail addresses using a "dictionary attack"—combining names, letters, or numbers into multiple permutations

■ Use scripts or other automated ways to register for multiple e-mail or user accounts to send commercial e-mail

■ Relay e-mails through a computer or network without permission—for example, taking advantage of open relays or open proxies without notification.

In Illinois   Licensees in Illinois should be aware that they are subject to additional regulation in their use of commercial e-mail, per the Illinois Electronic Mail Act. The use of e-mail communication and Web advertising is also restricted as laid out in "Rules" Section 1450.145. ■

The Junk Fax Prevention Act

The **Junk Fax Prevention Act of 2005** does not legalize unsolicited fax advertisements or solicitations but does allow for an established business relationship exception. As a general rule, a real estate licensee could not legally send an unsolicited commercial fax message without express written consent or without an established business relationship with the recipient.

Following are the provisions of the fax law:

■ Sets out guidelines for what constitutes an established business relationship (EBR) and reaffirms that EBR when customers pose exceptions to the ban on unsolicited commercial faxes

■ Does not place time limitations on EBRs

■ Requires companies to offer a free method by which fax recipients may opt out of receiving future fax communications. The opt-out method must be available at any time of day, every day; and the opt-out information must be made available on the first page of the fax.

■ Requires businesses to receive customer's written or oral consent to send fax advertising, or in the case of new business relationships, to send only to those customers who have provided their fax numbers willingly to some other source with permission for such use by other parties (including the sender)

■ Permits businesses to send faxes to numbers that they had access to via an EBR prior to July 9, 2005, when the act became law.

■ Requires businesses to receive direct consent from EBR customers for whom they did not already have fax numbers prior to the effective date of the legislation, or to obtain these numbers via some other source to which the EBR customer willingly provided them with permission for such use by other parties (including the sender)

In 2008 the FCC added the following clarifications to the law:

1. Senders have met the consent requirement if they buy the fax number(s) from companies who have obtained the information from published sources; however, if there are errors in the list, the sender could be held liable.
2. Senders must make a reasonable effort to ascertain whether recipients have given consent.
3. Senders are permitted to provide a Web site, which must be easily accessible and usable, through which recipients may opt out of receiving fax communications.

In Illinois State laws regarding unsolicited fax advertising have not been replaced or preempted by the federal law. Under Illinois law, for instance, sending unsolicited fundraising and advertising e-mails without the recipients' permission may be punishable by a $500 fine. ∎

■ STATE LICENSE LAWS

All 50 states, the District of Columbia, and all Canadian provinces license and regulate the activities of real estate professionals. While the laws share a common purpose, the details vary from state to state. Uniform policies and standards for administering and enforcing state license laws are promoted by an organization of state license law officials known as ARELLO—the Association of Real Estate License Law Officials.

Real estate license laws have been enacted to *protect the public* by ensuring a standard of competence and professionalism in the real estate industry. The laws achieve this goal by

■ establishing basic requirements for obtaining a real estate license and, in many cases, requiring continuing education to keep a license;
■ defining which activities require licensing;
■ describing the acceptable standards of conduct and practice for licensees; and
■ enforcing those standards through a disciplinary system.

The purpose of these laws is not merely to regulate the real estate industry. Their main objective is to make sure that the rights of purchasers, sellers, tenants, and owners are protected from unscrupulous or sloppy practices.

The laws are not intended to prevent licensees from conducting their businesses successfully nor are they meant to interfere in legitimate transactions. Laws cannot create an ethical or a moral marketplace. However, by establishing minimum levels of competency and limits of permitted behavior, laws can make the marketplace safer and more honest.

Each state has a licensing authority—a commission, a department, a division, a board, or an agency—that serves the needs of real estate licensees while protecting the public. This authority has the power to issue licenses, to make real estate information available to licensees and the public, and to enforce the statutory real estate law.

In Illinois	The Real Estate License Act of 2000 governs the licensing and activities of Illinois real estate licensees. The Act's intent is to evaluate the competency of persons engaged in the real estate business and to regulate this business for the protection of the public. Illinois license law consists of the "act" itself as well as the "rules," which interpret and implement it. ∎

■ SUMMARY

Real estate brokerage is the act of bringing people together, for a fee or commission, for the purpose of buying, selling, exchanging, or leasing real estate. New technologies are changing the way that brokerage offices are managed and operated. Social networking including blogs, vlogs, Facebook, You Tube, and Twitter is changing the way properties are marketed. To avoid liability and as a means of risk management, office policy manuals should contain language under which sponsored licensees may employ these methods in their real estate practices.

The use of licensed assistants is another way a real estate licensee may advance in a busy, demanding business. Licensed assistants must have an agreement with the sponsoring broker and must be paid by him. An unlicensed assistant may only engage in administrative or clerical functions on behalf of the licensee who hired the assistant.

The licensee's compensation in a real estate sale may take the form of a percentage commission, a flat fee, or an hourly rate. The licensee is considered to have earned a commission when he procures a ready, willing, and able buyer for a seller. Sponsored licensees who work under a sponsoring broker do so either as an employee or as an independent contractor. Either way, there must be a written employment agreement signed by both parties.

Federal and state antitrust laws prohibit licensees from conspiring to fix prices, engage in boycotts, allocate customers or markets, or establish tie-in agreements.

The National Do Not Call Registry is a list of consumer telephone numbers that do not want to be contacted by businesses who sell goods or services. Violators are subject to fines for each illegal call placed.

The CAN-SPAM Act establishes requirements for commercial e-mail, spells out penalties for e-mail senders, and gives consumers the right to have e-mailers stop sending e-mails to them. It is enforced by the FTC and the Department of Justice with fines levied per transgression.

The Junk Fax Prevention Act prohibits faxing unsolicited fax advertisements or solicitations but does allow for an established business relationship exception.

Real estate license laws and regulations govern the professional conduct of licensees. The license laws are enacted to protect the public by ensuring a standard of competence and professionalism in the real estate industry.

In Illinois

In Illinois, the Real Estate License Act of 2000, as amended in 2010, provides the guidelines for compliance in handling real estate activities.

The Electronic Mail Act imposes additional requirements upon senders of commercial e-mail messages over and above federal CAN-SPAM rules. ∎

CHAPTER 5 QUIZ

1. "To recover a commission for brokerage services, a sponsoring broker must be employed as the agent of the seller." Which of the following statements best explains the meaning of this sentence?

   a. The sponsoring broker must work in a real estate office.

   b. The seller must have made an express or implied agreement to pay a commission to the sponsoring broker for selling the property.

   c. The sponsoring broker must have asked the seller the price of the property and then found a ready, willing, and able buyer.

   d. The sponsoring broker must have one or more sponsored licensees employed in the office.

2. An Illinois real estate licensee who is engaged as an independent contractor

   a. is considered an employee by the IRS for tax purposes.

   b. must have a written contract with the sponsoring broker.

   c. must be covered by workers' compensation.

   d. may work as an independent contractor for two or more sponsoring brokers.

3. In Illinois, the usual "proof" that the listing broker has earned his commission is the

   a. submission to the seller of a signed offer from a ready, willing, and able buyer.

   b. closing of the sale.

   c. signing of an exclusive listing contract.

   d. deposit of the buyer's earnest money into escrow.

4. A broker listed the seller's home for $300,000. Before the listing contract expired, the broker brought the seller a full-price offer on the seller's terms, containing no contingencies. The seller then decided not to sell. Which of the following statements is *TRUE*?

   a. The broker has no reason to collect a commission in this case.

   b. The seller probably is liable for the commission.

   c. The broker must immediately file suit against the seller.

   d. The seller's only liability is to the buyer.

5. Under Illinois law, which of the following may an unlicensed assistant do?

   a. Negotiate compensation

   b. Engage in prospecting

   c. Sit at a property that is not open to the public

   d. Host a broker open house

6. According to the Illinois license law, a sponsored real estate licensee may not

   a. represent both buyer and seller.

   b. buy or sell real estate for himself.

   c. accept a commission from another broker unless previously earned.

   d. engage in dual agency.

7. A sponsoring broker must have a written employment agreement with which of these individuals?

   a. Independent contractors

   b. Licensed personal assistants

   c. Sponsored brokers

   d. All of the above

8. Two real estate companies agreed to boycott the services of the MNM Title Company so that the new TSK Title Company can take over MNM's market share. What is the act that the two real estate companies are violating?

   a. Antiboycotting Act
   b. Illinois Lincoln Antitrust Act
   c. Sherman Antitrust Act
   d. Land of Lincoln Fair Trade Act

9. The broker's commission was $8,200. If the commission rate was 6 percent, what was the selling price of the property?

   a. $136,666.67
   b. $154,232.50
   c. $132,666.67
   d. $175,452.48

10. A broker received $2,520 as the firm's 50 percent share of a commission. If the property sold for $72,000, what was the commission rate?

   a. 7 percent
   b. .07 percent
   c. 8 percent
   d. 6.5 percent

11. One general rule of the National Do Not Call Registry is

   a. states must maintain separate do-not-call lists.
   b. the national registry must be updated once a year.
   c. it is illegal to make an unsolicited phone call to a number listed on the national registry.
   d. real estate offices are exempt from the laws because they are not considered telemarketers.

12. Federal regulations on unsolicited e-mail

   a. require prior permission of recipients in order to send e-mail to them.
   b. require that e-mail lists be scrubbed every 31 days.
   c. exempt phone calls to individuals with whom the real estate office has a prior business relationship.
   d. require commercial e-mails to include a physical address, among other things, for the sender.

13. Which statement is TRUE regarding the Junk Fax Prevention Act of 2005?

   a. Real estate licensees are not required to search the national registry before making telemarketing calls to solicit listings or to solicit potential buyers.
   b. Real estate licensees are exempt from telemarketing laws.
   c. Real estate licensees may phone or fax any visitors to an open house who provide their phone numbers on a sign-in sheet, but only where the visitor is given either an option to opt out or notice that they will be called.
   d. Real estate licensees may not advertise their listings by faxing promotional flyers to a list of potential homebuyers with whom they do not have an existing business relationship.

14. Real estate licensees who are paid in a lump sum and who are personally responsible for paying their own taxes are probably

   a. nonexempt.
   b. buyer's broker.
   c. independent contractors.
   d. employees.

15. A licensee entered into a contract with her sponsoring broker, specifying that she is not an employee. In the past year, just less than half of the licensee's income from real estate activities came from sales commissions. The remainder was based on an hourly wage paid by the sponsoring broker for office administrative duties. Using these facts, it is MOST likely that the IRS would classify the licensee as

   a. self-employed.
   b. an employee.
   c. an independent contractor.
   d. a part-time real estate licensee.

16. Which of the following may a sponsoring broker dictate to an independent contractor?

   a. Number of hours the person would have to work
   b. Work schedule that the person would need to follow
   c. Sales meetings the person would need to attend
   d. Compensation the person would receive

17. After a particularly challenging transaction finally closes, the client gives the sponsored broker representing the client a check for $500 "for all your extra work." Which statement is *TRUE*?

    a. While such compensation is irregular, it is appropriate for the sponsored broker to accept the check.

    b. The sponsored broker may receive compensation only from the sponsoring broker.

    c. The sponsored broker should accept the check and deposit it immediately in a special escrow account.

    d. The sponsoring broker is entitled to 80 percent of the check.

18. The amount of commission paid to a sponsored licensee is determined by

    a. Illinois law.

    b. the local real estate board.

    c. mutual agreement with the sponsoring broker.

    d. mutual agreement with the client.

19. A sponsored licensee wants to receive a lump-sum payment at the end of each transaction. The sponsored licensee must meet all of the following requirements *EXCEPT*

    a. receive all income from the brokerage based on production, not time worked.

    b. be free from supervision by the sponsoring broker and/or office manager.

    c. hold a current real estate license.

    d. have a written agreement with the sponsoring broker stating that the sponsored licensee will not be treated as an employee for federal tax purposes.

20. A new sponsored real estate licensee wants to find new business among the firm's expired listings. Under the National Do Not Call Registry, for how long after the listing has expired may the licensee solicit business from the firm's previous listings?

    a. The licensee may not contact this individual if the individual is on the National Do Not Call Registry.

    b. Up to 30 days after the listing expired

    c. Up to 90 days after the listing expired

    d. Up to 18 months after the listing expired

CHAPTER 6

Brokerage Agreements

■ **LEARNING OBJECTIVES** *When you've finished reading this chapter, you should be able to*

■ **identify** the different types of listing and buyer representation agreements and their terms;

■ **describe** the ways in which a listing may be terminated;

■ **explain** the listing process and the parts of the listing agreement;

■ **distinguish** among the characteristics of the various types of listing and buyer representation agreements;

■ **define** the following *key terms*

buyer agency agreement	exclusive-right-to-sell listing	net listing
comparative market analysis (CMA)	market value	open listing
contemporaneous offers	minimum services	option listing
exclusive-agency listing	multiple listing service (MLS)	statute of frauds

■ BROKERAGE AGREEMENTS

Brokerage agreements are *employment contracts* for the personal professional services of the sponsoring broker, not for the transfer of real estate. The various types of brokerage agreements establish the basic relationship between the parties and provide different levels of rights and responsibilities for the sponsoring broker. Perhaps most important, brokerage agreements address the essential questions of exclusivity and compensation.

A listing agreement is an employment contract between a sponsoring broker and a seller; a buyer representation agreement is an employment contract as well because it establishes the rights and responsibilities of the sponsoring broker as agent for the buyer. A management contract sets up the relationship between the sponsoring broker and the owner of a rental property; it is discussed in detail in Chapter 17.

For the majority of real estate licensees, listing and buyer representation agreements are the fundamental, bedrock documents of the real estate profession.

In most states, either by **statutes of frauds** or by specific rules from real estate licensing authorities, exclusive brokerage agreements are required to be in writing to be enforceable in court. Oral agreements are not illegal but are not recommended because they cannot be enforced in court.

| In Illinois | In Illinois, per Section 1450.195, a brokerage agreement is either a written or oral agreement between a sponsoring broker and a consumer for licensed [real estate] activities to be provided to a consumer in return for compensation or the right to receive compensation from another. Brokerage agreements may constitute either a bilateral or a unilateral agreement between the sponsoring broker and the sponsoring broker's client depending upon the content of the brokerage agreement. All exclusive brokerage agreements must be in writing.

Also in Illinois, each broker agreement must clearly state that it is illegal for either the owner or the sponsoring broker to refuse to display or sell to any person because of one's membership in a protected class (e.g., race, color, religion, national origin, sex, ancestry, age, marital status, physical or mental handicap, familial status, or any other class protected by Article 3 of the Illinois Human Rights Act). ∎

Employment contracts with buyers and sellers create special agency relationships between the principal (the person who is being represented by the sponsoring broker) and the sponsoring broker (the agent). As agent, the sponsoring broker is authorized to represent the principal to third parties.

Under both the law of agency and most state license laws, only a sponsoring broker can act as the legal agent to list, sell, rent, or purchase another person's real estate and provide other services to a principal. All sponsored licensees of a sponsoring broker may perform these acts in the name of and under the supervision of the sponsoring broker only. Note that throughout this chapter, unless otherwise stated, the terms *broker*, *agent*, and *firm* are intended to include both a sponsoring broker and her sponsored licensees. In other words, a broker employment contract is ultimately between the principal (buyer or seller) and the sponsoring broker of the firm.

■ TYPES OF LISTING AGREEMENTS

Types of Listing Agreements

Several types of listing agreements exist. The type of contract determines the specific rights and obligations of the parties.

Exclusive-right-to-sell listing

One authorized broker receives a commission regardless of who sells the property.

Exclusive-right-to-sell listing agreements   In an **exclusive-right-to-sell listing**, one broker is appointed as the seller's sole agent. The listing broker is given the exclusive right, or *authorization*, to market the seller's property. If the property is sold while the listing is in effect, the seller must pay the broker a commission *regardless of who sells the property*: the listing broker, another broker, or even if the seller finds a buyer without the broker's assistance. Sellers benefit from this form of agreement because the broker feels freer to spend time and money actively marketing the property, making a timely and profitable sale more likely. From the broker's perspective, an exclusive-right-to-sell listing offers the greatest opportunity to receive a commission. The majority of residential listing agreements in Illinois are exclusive-right-to-sell listing agreements.

Exclusive-agency listing

■ There is one authorized broker.
■ Broker receives a commission only if she is the procuring cause.
■ Seller retains the right to sell without obligation.

Exclusive-agency listing agreement   In an **exclusive-agency listing**, one broker is authorized to act as the exclusive agent of the seller-principal. However, the seller retains the right to sell the property without obligation to the broker. The seller is obligated to pay a commission to the broker only if the listing broker or a cooperating broker has been the procuring cause of a sale. The seller retains the right to sell the property without financial obligation to the listing broker.

Open listing agreement   In an **open listing** (known in some areas as a *nonexclusive listing*), the seller retains the right to employ any number of brokers as agents. The brokers can act simultaneously, and the seller is financially obligated only to that broker who successfully produces a ready, willing, and able buyer. If the seller personally sells the property without the aid of any of the brokers, the seller is not obligated to pay a commission.

Open listing

■ There are multiple brokers.
■ Only the selling broker is entitled to a commission.
■ Seller retains the right to sell independently without obligation.

Negotiated terms of an open listing agreement should be in writing to protect the broker's ability to collect an agreed-on fee from the seller. Written terms may be in the form of a listing agreement (if the broker represents the seller) or a fee agreement (if the broker represents the buyer or the seller does not wish to be represented).

Net listing   A **net listing** provision specifies that the seller will receive a net amount of money from any sale, with the excess going to the listing broker as commission. The broker is free to offer the property at any price greater than the net amount the seller wants; the difference is the broker's fee. Because a net listing can create a clear conflict of interest between the broker's fiduciary responsibility to the seller and the broker's profit motive, net listings are illegal in many states and are discouraged in others.

In Illinois

In Illinois, net listings are legal but not recommended due to the potential for fraud. ■

In a net listing: Actual sale price − Seller-required sale price = Broker profit.

> **Net Listing**
>
> The broker is entitled to any amount exceeding the seller's stated net.

■ **FOR EXAMPLE** A broker lists a property. The agreement states that the minimum amount acceptable to the seller is $190,000. The list price is set much higher, but the only profit the broker will gain is the amount the property sells for over the $190,000 amount.

A number of situations could occur that make net listings ill-advised on the above property. For instance:

1. The broker advertises the property for $250,000. Given the above agreement, the broker pockets $40,000 when an offer and sale for $230,000 is made. *(Actual sale price [$230,000] minus seller-required sale price [$190,000] equals broker profit [$40,000])*. This is likely to provoke charges that the broker deliberately estimated fair market value on the low side so as to reap larger rewards. The seller loses money, and the broker may have her integrity questioned.

2. The property is marketed at $200,000. It sells for $190,000, with the seller accepting. The broker earns nothing, given the stated agreement, and must pay for her advertising campaign. If such a possibility is foreseen by a broker, owing to the very small gap between seller's desired list price and seller's required price, the agent may not feel motivated to spend money advertising or promoting the listing because it is anticipated that little or no commission may result. Both seller and broker may lose.

> **Option Listing**
>
> The broker has the right to purchase the property.

Option listing An **option listing** provision gives the broker the right to purchase the listed property at some point in the future. The specific length of the time period is by agreement and usually matches the length of the listing. Use of an option listing may open the broker to charges of fraud unless the broker is scrupulous in fulfilling all obligations to the property owner. In some states, a broker who chooses to exercise such an option must first inform the property owner of the broker's profit in the transaction and secure in writing the owner's agreement to it.

Note: An *option listing* differs from an *option contract*, the latter involving a consumer's option to purchase a given property.

Sometimes, brokers and sellers enter into *guaranteed sale agreements*, in which the broker agrees to buy the listed property if it fails to sell before the end of the listing period. Typically, these guarantees are made to the seller as an inducement to list the property with the broker.

> **In Illinois**

In Illinois, any exclusive listing agreement must be in writing and is subject to other legal requirements, noted in detail in the Illinois Real Estate License Act of 2000. ■

Special Listing Provisions

Multiple listing A *multiple listing* clause may be included in an exclusive listing. It is used by licensees who are members of a **multiple listing service (MLS)**. An

MLS is a marketing organization whose members make their listings available for showing and sale through all the other member licensees.

An MLS offers advantages to licensees, sellers, and buyers. Licensees develop a sizable inventory of properties to be sold and are assured a portion of the commission if they list property or participate in the sale of another licensee's listing. Sellers gain because the property is exposed to a much larger market. Buyers gain because of the variety of properties on the market.

The contractual obligations among the member licensees of an MLS vary widely. Most MLSs require that a licensees, turn over new listings to the service within a specific, fairly short period of time after the licensee obtains the listing. The length of time during which the listing licensee can offer a property to the public on her own without involving the MLS varies. Of course, sellers must be informed and give their written consent for any delay in notifying the MLS. This gives the listing company a strong chance to sell its own listing.

Under the provisions of most MLSs, a participating licensee makes a unilateral offer of cooperation and compensation to other member licensees, when the listing enters the MLS. The licensee must have the written consent of the seller to include the property in an MLS.

In Illinois

Under Illinois law, a licensee working with a buyer is not considered to be a subagent of the seller. *No offer of subagency can be made through an MLS in Illinois today.* Illinois law states that a buyer is represented as a client by the licensee with whom she is working unless that consumer *chooses* not to be. This approach makes it clear to all parties who is represented by whom.

Today it is illegal to offer subagency through an MLS in Illinois.

While a few buyers choose to remain as customers without representation, even that lack of agency is now subject to disclosure. Generally, a notice of no agency would be provided. *If nothing is said about agency, licensees are considered to be representing the consumer with whom they are working, either as a designated agent for the consumer (unless there is a written agreement to the contrary) or as a licensee if performing only ministerial acts.*

In spite of these relatively clear lines with regard to whose agent is whose, sellers often still pay the fees for both agents in a transaction. These fees are called *cooperative commissions.* In an Illinois MLS listing data sheet, this is typically stated as "co-op: X% or as a flat fee." *Paying someone a commission does not create agency in Illinois.* ■

IN PRACTICE   Technology has enhanced the benefits of MLS membership. In addition to providing instant access to information about the status of listed properties, MLSs often offer a broad range of other useful information about mortgage loans, real estate taxes and assessments, municipalities, and school districts. They are equally helpful to licensees who need to make a comparative market analysis (CMA) to determine the value of a particular property before suggesting an appropriate range of prices. Computer-assisted searches also help buyers select properties that best meet their needs.

■ TERMINATION OF LISTING AGREEMENTS

As previously stated, all Illinois exclusive brokerage agreements must be in writing. Because the licensee's services are unique, a brokerage agreement cannot be assigned to another licensee without the principal's written consent. The property owner cannot force the licensee to perform, but the licensee's failure to work diligently toward fulfilling the contract's terms constitutes a breach of the listing agreement. If the licensee cancels the listing, the seller may be entitled to sue the licensee for damages.

On the other hand, a property owner could be liable for damages to the licensee by refusing to cooperate with the licensee's reasonable requests, such as allowing the licensee to show the property to prospective buyers or refusing to proceed with a complete sales contract.

Listing agreements may be terminated for the following reasons:

- When the agreement's purpose is fulfilled, such as when a ready, willing, and able buyer has been found
- When the agreement's term expires
- If the property is destroyed or its use is changed by some force outside the owner's control, such as a zoning change or condemnation by eminent domain (See Chapter 7.)
- If title to the property is transferred by operation of law, as in the case of the owner's bankruptcy or foreclosure
- If the broker and the seller mutually agree to cancel the brokerage agreement
- If either the broker or seller dies or becomes incapacitated. If the sponsored licensee dies or becomes incapacitated, the brokerage agreement is still valid.

Expiration of Brokerage Agreement

In Illinois

All exclusive brokerage agreements should specify a definite period during which the broker is to be employed. In Illinois, as in most states, failing to specify a definite termination date in a listing is grounds for the suspension or revocation of a real estate license. ■

Automatic Extension

Courts in most states have discouraged the use of automatic extension clauses in exclusive listings. Automatic extension clauses are illegal in some states, and many listing contract forms specifically provide that there can be no automatic extensions of the agreement.

Pursuant to Section 10-25 of the Illinois Real Estate License Act of 2000, no licensee shall obtain any written brokerage agreement containing a clause automatically extending the period of the contract.

Broker Protection

In Illinois

Some listing contracts in Illinois and elsewhere contain a *broker protection clause*, also called a *safety* clause. This clause provides that the property owner will pay the listing broker a commission if, within a specified time period after the listing agreement expires, the owner transfers property title to someone who saw the property while it was listed with the broker. The protection clause protects brokers from losing a commission on a sale involving buyers who saw the property while it was listed and to discourage others from trying to reach private arrangements with sellers. ■

The length of time for a protection clause is set by agreement. Any new buyers the seller might procure on her own after expiration of the listing are not affected. To protect the owner and prevent liability of the owner for two separate commissions, this clause cannot be enforced if the property is relisted under a new contract with another brokerage firm.

| In Illinois | Each brokerage agreement for a residential property of four units or less that provides for a protection period subsequent to its termination date shall also provide that no commission or fee will be due and owing pursuant to the terms of the brokerage agreement if, during the protection period, a valid, written brokerage agreement is entered into with another licensed real estate broker. ■

■ THE LISTING PROCESS

Before signing a contract, the broker and seller must discuss a variety of issues. The seller's most critical concerns typically are the selling price of the property and the net amount she can expect to receive from the sale. The broker has several professional tools available to provide information about a property's value and to calculate the proceeds from a sale.

Pricing the Property

While it is the responsibility of the broker to advise and assist, it is the seller who must determine the listing price for the property. Because the average seller does not have the skills needed to determine a market-based listing price, brokers must be prepared to offer their knowledge and expertise.

The CMA

A *comparative market analysis*, or **CMA**, is an analysis of market activity among comparable properties. It is not the same as a formal appraisal.

Brokers can help sellers determine a listing price for the property by using a **comparative market analysis (CMA)**. A CMA analyzes properties similar to the subject property in size, location, and amenities. It is distinctly different from an appraisal report offered by a licensed appraiser that is based only on an analysis of properties that have actually sold.

The CMA is based on

- recently closed properties (solds),
- properties currently on the market (competition for the subject property), and
- properties that did not sell (expired listings in the area).

Sold prices represent what buyers have been willing to pay for similar properties in the neighborhood. Very often, the expired listing prices are those prices that buyers have not been willing to pay for a property similar to the subject property.

Current asking prices of current, similar properties on the market indicate the trend: asking prices lower than the "solds" indicate a slow or declining market. An optimistic market is indicated when the asking prices are higher than the "solds."

Although a CMA is not viewed as a formal appraisal, the broker uses many of the appraiser's methods and techniques in arriving at a reasonable value range. If no adequate comparisons can be made, or if the property is unique in some way, the broker may suggest that the seller have a professional appraiser conduct a detailed, formal estimate of the property's value. In most situations, the broker's sense of the local market and detailed knowledge of properties in a neighborhood contribute to a quality CMA.

Market Value

Market value is the most probable price a property would bring in an arm's-length transaction under normal conditions on the open market.

The figure sought in both CMAs and appraisals is the property's market value. **Market value** is *the most probable price a property would bring in an arm's-length transaction under normal conditions on the open market*. A CMA estimates market value as likely to fall within a range of values (e.g., $335,000 to $340,000). A formal appraisal indicates a specific value rather than a range. In both cases, the seller/principal must make the final decision on his asking price.

While it is the property owner's privilege to set whatever listing price he chooses, a broker should consider rejecting any listing in which the price is substantially exaggerated or severely out of line with the indications of the CMA or appraisal. These tools provide the best indications of what a buyer will likely pay for the property. An unrealistic listing price will make it difficult for the broker to properly market the seller's property within the agreed upon listing period. Furthermore, a buyer may have difficulty obtaining financing because the property did not appraise for the sale price.

IN PRACTICE   When helping a seller determine an appropriate listing price, the broker must give an estimate of value that is reasonable and as accurate as possible. Overpriced listings cost the broker time and money in wasted marketing and advertising and give sellers false hopes of riches to come. Additionally, some research suggests that listings priced too high in the beginning sell for less in the end than if they had been more moderately priced at the outset.

Seller's Return

The broker easily can calculate roughly how much the seller will net from a given sales price or what sales price will produce a desired net amount. (The Math Concepts accompanying this section illustrates how the various formulas are applied.)

Information Needed for Listing Agreements

Once the broker and the owner agree on a listing price, the broker must obtain specific, detailed information about the property. Obtaining as many facts as possible ensures that most contingencies can be anticipated. This is particularly important when the listing will be shared with other licensees through an MLS, and the other licensees must rely on the information taken by the listing broker.

MATH CONCEPTS

CALCULATING SALES PRICES, COMMISSIONS, AND NETS TO SELLER

When a property sells, the sales price equals 100 percent of the money being transferred. Therefore, if a broker is to receive a 6 percent commission, 94 per-cent will remain for the seller's other expenses and equity. To calculate a commission using a sales price of $225,000 and a commission rate of 6 percent, multiply the sales price by the commission rate:

$$\$225,000 \times 6\% = \$225,000 \times 0.06 = \$13,500 \text{ commission}$$

To calculate a sales price using a commission of $13,500 and a commission rate of 7 percent, divide the commission by the commission rate:

$$\$13,500 \div 7\% = \$13,500 \div 0.07 = \$192,857 \text{ sales price}$$

To calculate a commission rate using a commission of $8,200 and a sales price of $164,000, divide the commission by the sales price:

$$\$8,200 \div \$164,000 = 0.05, \text{ or } 5\% \text{ commission rate}$$

To calculate the net to the seller using a sales price of $125,000 and a commission rate of 8 percent, multiply the sales price by 100 percent minus the commission rate:

$$\$125,000 \times (100\% - 8\%) = \$125,000 \times (92\%) = \$125,000 \times 0.92 = \$115,000$$

The same result can be achieved by calculating the commission ($125,000 × 0.08 = $10,000) and deducting it from the sales price ($125,000 − $10,000 = $115,000); however, this involves unnecessary extra calculations.

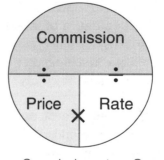

In summary: Sales price × Commission rate = Commission
Commission ÷ Commission rate = Sales price
Commission ÷ Sales price = Commission rate
Sales price × (100% − Commission rate) = Net to seller

Disclosures

Disclosure of agency relationships and property conditions has become the focus of consumer safeguards in recent years. Property condition disclosures normally cover a wide range of structural, mechanical, and other conditions that a prospective purchaser should know about to make an informed decision. Brokers should caution sellers to make truthful, careful disclosures to avoid litigation arising from fraudulent or careless misrepresentations. It is the broker's responsibility to see that the seller is aware of these mandatory disclosures.

In Illinois

Illinois requires that agents disclose whose interests they legally represent if the other party has no agent. It is important that the seller be informed of the brokerage company's policies about cooperating with other brokers. Seller disclosure of property conditions is also required by Illinois law. ■

■ THE LISTING AGREEMENT

A wide variety of listing agreement forms are available. Some brokers have attorneys draft contracts, some use forms prepared by their local REALTOR® association, and some use forms produced by state real estate licensing authorities. Some brokers use a separate information sheet (also known as a *profile* or *data sheet*) for recording property features. That sheet is wed to a second form containing the contractual obligations between the seller and the broker: listing price, duration of the agreement, signatures of the parties, and so forth. Other brokers use a single form. A sample listing agreement appears in Figure 6.1.

In Illinois

The listing contracts most commonly in use are prepared by local REALTOR® associations and their attorneys. These forms may vary slightly from area to area. ■

In Illinois

Illinois law requires that the following disclosures be included with listing contracts. ■

Disclosure of material facts A broker must not withhold material facts concerning a property of which she has knowledge from any purchaser, prospective purchaser, seller, lessee, lessor, or other party to the transaction. *Material facts* are any facts on which a reasonable person would base a contractual decision.

Disclosure of interest A broker must disclose in writing to the parties to the transaction her status as a broker and any direct or indirect interest she has or may have in the subject property. For example, if the buyer or seller is a licensed broker, this must be clearly stated in the contract.

Disclosure of special compensation A broker is prohibited from accepting "any finder fees, commissions, discounts, kickbacks, or other compensation from any financial institution, title insurance company, or any other person other than another licensee, without full disclosure in writing of such receipt to all parties to the transaction." Sponsored licensees receive any such compensation only through their respective sponsoring brokers.

Earnest money and purchaser default When any written listing includes a provision that the seller will not receive the earnest money deposit if the purchaser defaults, this fact must appear emphasized in letters larger than those otherwise used in the listing agreement.

Disclosure of property condition Seller disclosure of property conditions is required by law in Illinois. These disclosures normally cover a wide range of structural, mechanical, and other conditions that a prospective purchaser should know about to make an informed decision. Brokers should caution sellers to make truthful disclosures to avoid litigation arising from fraudulent or careless misrepresentations. A Property Disclosure Report must be given to the buyer before an offer is made and accepted or the buyer will have three days in which to rescind the contract, based on any negative disclosures. In Illinois, many listing brokers choose to leave the disclosure statement on display with their sellers and available in the home itself for all showings. In addition, a lead paint disclosure is required on any property built before 1978, and a radon disclosure is required of the seller.

FIGURE 6.1

Sample Listing Agreement

ILLINOIS ASSOCIATION OF REALTORS®
EXCLUSIVE SELLER REPRESENTATION CONTRACT
(DUAL AGENCY DISCLOSURE AND CONSENT INCLUDED)

1. In consideration of the services to be performed by_____, (Brokerage Company, hereinafter referred to as "Broker") and the commissions to be paid by _____, ("Seller"), the parties agree that Broker shall have the exclusive right to act as Seller's agent for the marketing and sale of Seller's property upon the following terms and conditions:

    Property Address:_____

    City: _____, Illinois Zip: _____

    Marketing Price: $_____

    Marketing Period: From _____ 2_____ through 11:59 p.m. on _____, 2_____.

    Seller understands that this exclusive right to represent Seller (Exclusive Representation) means that if the Seller sells the property identified above through the efforts of Broker and his agents or through another real estate office or agent, Seller will be obligated to compensate Broker pursuant to paragraph 3 of this Contract.

2. Broker agrees to provide those brokerage services set forth in Section 15-75 of the Illinois Real Estate License Act of 2000.

3. If during the term of this Contract Broker obtains an offer to purchase the property from a ready, willing, and able buyer at the marketing price, or if Seller enters into a contract or receives an offer from anyone to whom the property was presented during the term of this Contract, that results in a contract for the sale or exchange of the property at any price and upon any terms to which Seller consents, Seller shall be obligated to pay Broker a commission of _____ percent (___%) of the total purchase price of the sale or exchange. The full commission is to be paid at closing, which in the case of a sale on contract for deed shall be at the time buyer and Seller execute the initial contract or agreement for deed.

4. Seller agrees that such a commission shall be paid if the property is sold or exchanged by Seller within a protection period of _____ (___) days following the term of this Contract or any extensions thereof to anyone to whom the property was presented during the term of this Contract. However, this provision shall not apply if Seller has entered into a valid, written listing agreement with another licensed real estate broker during the protection period.

5. In the event a purchase contact is entered into and buyer defaults without fault on the Seller's part, Broker will waive the commission, and this agreement shall be continued from the date of default through the date provided in paragraph 1. Should Seller default on any contract for the purchase or exchange of the property, any commission owed under this agreement shall become payable immediately.

    [5. ALTERNATE TO BE SUBSTITUTED IN LIEU OF THE ABOVE ¶5.] In the event a purchase contract is entered into and buyer defaults with or without fault on the Seller's part, any commission owed under this contract shall become payable immediately. Should Seller default on any contract for the purchase or exchange of the property, any commission owed under this agreement shall become payable immediately.

6. When a contract to purchase is entered into for the purchase of Seller's property, the buyer may deposit earnest money with Broker. Broker will hold any such earnest money in a special, non-interest bearing escrow account on behalf of the buyer and Seller. At closing, the earnest money will be disbursed according to the terms of the contract to purchase. If the transaction fails to close:

    (a) due to fault of the Seller, the earnest money shall be returned to the buyer.

    [AS TO ¶S (b) THROUGH (d) BELOW, THE PARTIES SHOULD CHECK THE ONE PARAGRAPH WHICH APPLIES].

    ☐ (b) DUE TO FAULT OF THE BUYER, THE EARNEST MONEY SHALL FIRST GO TOWARD PAYING THE COMMISSION BROKER WOULD HAVE EARNED IN THE SALE, AND THE BALANCE, IF ANY, SHALL GO TO SELLER.

    ☐ (c) DUE TO FAULT OF THE BUYER, THE EARNEST MONEY SHALL BE DISTRIBUTED TO THE SELLER, LESS ANY COSTS OF ADVERTISING OR REASONABLE EXPENSES INCURRED BY BROKER.

    ☐ (d) due to fault of the buyer, the earnest money shall be distributed to the Seller.

7. Seller agrees that for the purpose of marketing Seller's property, Broker shall place Seller's property in the Multiple Listing Service(s) in which Broker is a member.

8. Seller makes the following elections with regard to having Sellers's property displayed on any Internet site:
    (circle YES or NO to all that apply)
    - Display listing on any Internet site: YES   NO
    - Display Seller's property address on Internet: YES   NO

    > **Seller understands and acknowledges that if seller circles "NO" for the above two options, consumers who conduct searches for listings on the Internet will not see the corresponding information about Sellers' property in response to their searches.**
    >
    > _____   _____   _____
    > **Seller's Initials**   **Seller's Initials**   **Date**

    - Allow for automatic valuation tools to be used for Seller's listing: YES   NO
    - Allow for blogging or comments to be used or made regarding Seller's listing: YES   NO

9. Seller(s) acknowledge(s) that they have been informed of the responsibilities imposed upon sellers under the Residential Real Property Disclosure Act. Seller agrees to comply with the requirements of this Act to the best of Seller's ability and to not knowingly give any false or inaccurate information regarding the disclosures required by that Act.

FIGURE 6.1

Sample Listing Agreement (continued)

10. Broker designates _____, ("Seller's Designated Agent"), a sales associate(s) affiliated with Broker as the only legal agent(s) of the Seller. Broker reserves the right to name additional designated agents when in Broker's discretion it is necessary. If additional designated agents are named, Seller shall be informed in writing within a reasonable time. (ADD IF DESIRED: Seller acknowledges that Seller's Designated Agent may from time to time have another sales associate, who is not an agent of Seller, sit an open house of Seller's property or provide similar support in the marketing of Seller's property.) Seller understands and agrees that this agreement is a contract for Broker to market Seller's property and that Seller's Designated Agent(s) is (are) the only legal agent(s) of Seller. Seller's Designated Agent will be primarily responsible for the direct marketing and sale of Seller's property.

11. Seller has been informed that potential buyers may elect to employ the services of a licensed real estate broker or sales associate as their own agent (buyer's agent).

12. **DISCLOSURE AND CONSENT TO DUAL AGENCY**

    NOTE TO CONSUMER: THIS SECTION SERVES THREE PURPOSES. FIRST, IT DISCLOSES THAT A REAL ESTATE LICENSEE MAY POTENTIALLY ACT AS A DUAL AGENT, THAT IS, REPRESENT MORE THAN ONE PARTY TO THE TRANSACTION. SECOND, THIS SECTION EXPLAINS THE CONCEPT OF DUAL AGENCY. THIRD, THIS SECTION SEEKS YOUR CONSENT TO ALLOW THE REAL ESTATE LICENSEE TO ACT AS A DUAL AGENT. A LICENSEE MAY LEGALLY ACT AS A DUAL AGENT ONLY WITH YOUR CONSENT. BY CHOOSING TO SIGN THIS SECTION, YOUR CONSENT TO DUAL AGENCY REPRESENTATION IS PRESUMED.

    The undersigned _____, ("Licensee"/"Seller's Designated Agent"), may
    (insert name(s) of Licensee undertaking dual representation)

    undertake a dual representation (represent both the seller or landlord and the buyer or tenant) for the sale or lease of property. The undersigned acknowledge they were informed of the possibility of this type of representation. Before signing this document please read the following:

    Representing more than one party to a transaction presents a conflict of interest since both clients may rely upon Licensee's advice and the client's respective interests maybe adverse to each other. Licensee will undertake this representation only with the written consent of ALL clients in the transaction.

    Any agreement between the clients as to a final contract price and other terms is a result of negotiations between the clients acting in their own best interests and on their own behalf. You acknowledge that Licensee has explained the implications of dual representation, including the risks involved, and understand that you have been advised to seek independent advice from your advisors or attorneys before signing any documents in this transaction.

    ### WHAT A LICENSEE CAN DO FOR CLIENTS WHEN ACTING AS A DUAL AGENT

    1. Treat all clients honestly.
    2. Provide information about the property to the buyer or tenant.
    3. Disclose all latent material defects in the property that are known to the Licensee.
    4. Disclose financial qualification of the buyer or tenant to the seller or landlord.
    5. Explain real estate terms.
    6. Help the buyer or tenant to arrange for property inspections.
    7. Explain closing costs and procedures.
    8. Help the buyer compare financing alternatives.
    9. Provide information about comparable properties that have sold so both clients may make educated decisions on what price to accept or offer.

    ### WHAT LICENSEE CANNOT DISCLOSE TO CLIENTS WHEN ACTING AS A DUAL AGENT

    1. Confidential information that Licensee may know about a client, without that client's permission.
    2. The price or terms the seller or landlord will take other than the listing price without permission of the seller or landlord.
    3. The price or terms the buyer or tenant is willing to pay without permission of the buyer or tenant.
    4. A recommended or suggested price or terms the buyer or tenant should offer.
    5. A recommended or suggested price or terms the seller or landlord should counter with or accept.

    If either client is uncomfortable with this disclosure and dual representation, please let Licensee know. You are not required to sign this section unless you want to allow the Licensee to proceed as a Dual Agent in this transaction.

    By initialing here and signing below, you acknowledge that you have read and understand this form and voluntarily consent to the Licensee acting as a Dual Agent (that is, to represent BOTH the seller or landlord and the buyer or tenant) should that become necessary.

    _____   _____   _____
    Seller's initials   Seller's initials   Date

13. Broker is authorized to show the property to prospective buyers represented by buyer's agents, and Broker, in its sole discretion, may pay a part of the above commission to buyer's agent or other cooperating agents. Broker is authorized in its sole discretion to determine with which brokers it will cooperate, and the amount of compensation that it will offer cooperating brokers in the sale of Seller's property. Seller acknowledges that the compensation offered to such cooperating brokers may vary from broker to broker.

14. Seller understands that Broker and/or Designated Agent may have previously represented a buyer who is interested in your property. During that representation, Broker and/or Designated Agent may have learned material information about the buyer that is considered confidential. Under the law, neither Broker nor Designated Agent may disclose any such confidential information to you.

FIGURE 6.1

Sample Listing Agreement (continued)

15. Seller understands and agrees that other sales associates affiliated w ith Broker, other than Seller' s Designated Agent(s), may represent the actual or prospective buy er of Seller's property. F urther, Seller understands and agrees that if the property is sold through the efforts of a sales associate affiliated with Broker who represents the buyer, the other sales associate affiliated with Broker will be acting as a buyer's designated agent.

16. Seller agrees to immediately refer to Seller's Designated Agent all prospective brokers or agents for buyers who contact Seller for any reason and to provide Seller's Designated Agent with their names and contact information.

17. Broker and Seller's Designated Agent are authorized in their sole discretion, to place a for sale sign on the property if permitted by law, to remove all other brokerage signs, to place a lockbox on the property, to have access to the property at all reasonable times for the purpose of showing it to prospective buyers, to cooperate with other brokers and to use pictures of the property and to expose property information and/or images to the Internet for marketing purposes.

18. Seller agrees to provide a limited home warranty program from _____ at a charge of $_____ plus options, if any. Seller acknowledges that the home warranty program is a limited warranty with a deductible. Seller acknowledges receipt of the application for such home warranty program. [STRIKE THROUGH IF NOT OFFERED].

19. Items such as wall-to-wall carpeting, garage door openers, smoke detectors, built-in appliances, light fixtures, landscaping and many indoor and outdoor decorative items may legally be "fixtures" and if so they must remain with the house unless specifically excluded in the Purchase Agreement. (Discuss this matter with Seller's Designated Agent to avoid uncertainty for all parties regarding what you may take and what should remain with the house, and make specific provisions for these items in the Purchase Agreement.)

20. Seller understands that the information w hich Seller provides to Seller' s Designated Agent as listing information will be used to advertise Seller's property to the public, and it is essential that this information be accurate. SELLER HAS EITHER REVIEWED THE MLS LISTING INPUT SHEET AND REPRESENTS THAT THE INFORMATION CONTAINED IN IT IS TRUE AND ACCURATE TO THE BEST OF SELLER'S KNOWLEDGE, OR SELLER UNDERST ANDS THAT THEY HAVE AN OBLIGATION TO PROVIDE ACCURATE, TRUTHFUL INFORMATION TO BE PUT IN THE MLS INPUT SHEET AND HEREBY PROMISES TO FULFILL THIS OBLIGATION. Although Seller is listing Seller's property in its present physical condition ("as is" condition), Seller understands that Seller may be held responsible by a buyer for any latent or hidden, undisclosed defects or concealed defects in the property which are known to Seller but which are not disclosed to the buyer.

21. Seller agrees to save and hold Broker harmless from any clai ms, disputes, litigation, judgm ents, and costs (including reaso nable attorney's fees) arising from Seller's breach of this agreement, from any incorrect information or misrepresentation supplied by Seller or from any material facts, including latent defects, that are known to Seller that Seller fails to disclose.

22. This contract shall be binding upon and inure to the benefit of the heirs, administrators, successors, and assigns of the parties hereto. This contract can only be amended by a writing signed by the parties.

THE PARTIES UNDERSTAND AND AGREE THAT IT IS ILLEGAL FOR EITHER OF THE PARTIES TO REFUSE TO DISPLAY OR SELL SELLER'S PROPERT Y T O ANY PERSON ON T HE BASIS OF RACE, COLOR, RELIGION, SEX , NAT IONAL ORIGIN, ANCESTRY, AGE, ORDER OF PROT ECTION STATUS, MARITAL STATUS, PHYSICAL OR MENT AL HANDICAP, MILIT ARY STATUS, SEXUAL ORIENTATION, UNFAVORABLE DISCHARGE FROM MILITARY SERVICE, FAMILIAL STATUS OR ANY OTHER CLASS PROTECTED BY ARTICLE 3 OF THE ILLINOIS HUMAN RIGHTS ACT. THE PARTIES AGREE TO COMPLY WITH ALL APPLICABLE FEDERAL, STATE AND LOCAL FAIR HOUSING LAWS.

Seller hereby acknowledges receipt of a signed copy of this agreement and all attachments. The attachments include the following: [HERE LIST ALL ATTACHMENTS]._____

_____.

(If seller is married both signatures are required)

SELLER:_____   _____, Broker

SELLER:_____   BY: _____   DATE: _____

ADDRESS:_____   _____   DATE: _____
_____   Seller's   Designated Agent

DATE:_____   PHONE:_____   OFFICE:_____

Once a long-lasting agreement has been finalized and signed by the broker and seller, Illinois law prohibits the broker from making any addition to, deletion from, or alteration of the written listing without the written consent of the principal. The broker must return a true copy of the listing agreement, signed by the seller and by the broker, to the principal within 24 hours of execution. ■

Listing Agreement Issues

Regardless of which form of listing agreement is used, the same considerations arise in most real estate transactions. This means that all listing contracts tend to require similar information. Nonetheless, brokers should review the specific forms used in their areas and refer to their state's laws for any specific requirements. Some of the considerations covered in a typical contract are discussed in the following paragraphs.

In Illinois

There is no required state form for any real estate contract in Illinois. However, all written exclusive listing agreements must include

- the list price of the property,
- the agreed-upon amount of commission and the time of payment,
- the duration of the agreement, with a definite termination date clearly set forth,
- the names of the broker and seller,
- signatures of both broker and seller,
- the identification of the property involved (address or legal description),
- the duties of the listing broker,
- a statement of nondiscrimination, and
- a statement regarding antitrust.

Licensees may not obtain written listings that contain blank spaces to be filled in later. ■

Type of listing agreement   The contract may be an exclusive-right-to-sell listing (the most common type), an exclusive-agency listing, an open listing, or a net listing (the last not recommended). The type of listing agreement determines the extent of a broker's authority to act on the principal's behalf. Most MLSs do not permit open listings to be posted in their systems.

Broker's authority and responsibilities   The contract should specify whether the broker may place a sign on the property and advertise and market the property or utilize social networking through Facebook or other similar sites. Another major consideration is whether the broker is permitted to authorize buyers' brokers through an MLS and the Internet. It should also address whether or not the broker may accept earnest money on behalf of the seller and the responsibilities for holding the funds. The broker does not have the authority to sign any legal documents or contracts without first obtaining a power of attorney from the seller or the seller's representative.

Names of all parties to the contract   Anyone who has an ownership interest in the property must be identified and must sign the listing to validate it. If the property is owned under some form of co-ownership, that fact should be clearly established. (See Chapter 8.)

In Illinois If a married couple is living in the listed property, both spouses must sign the listing, even if only one owns the property, in order to release homestead rights. If the property is in the possession of a tenant, that should be disclosed and instructions given on how the property is to be shown to a prospective buyer. ∎

Brokerage firm   The brokerage company name, the sponsoring broker, and the *designated agent* of the sponsoring broker must all be identified.

Listing price   This is the proposed gross sales price. The seller's proceeds will be reduced by unpaid real estate taxes, special assessments, mortgage or trust deed debts, and any other outstanding obligations.

Real property and personal property   Any real property to be removed from the premises by the seller and any personal property to be included in the sale for the buyer should be noted and be explicitly identified in the subsequent purchase contract. Some items that may later become points of negotiation might include major appliances, swimming pool and spa equipment, fireplace accessories, storage sheds, window treatments, stacked firewood, and stored heating oil.

Leased equipment   It must be determined if leased equipment—security systems, cable television boxes, water softeners, special antennas—will be left with the property. If so, the seller is responsible for notifying the equipment's lessor of the change of property ownership.

Description of the premises   In addition to the street address, the legal description, lot size, and tax parcel number (property index number or PIN) may be required for future insertion into a purchase offer.

In Illinois   The street address of the property is sufficient for listing agreements to be valid and enforceable under Illinois law. However, it is advisable to include the parcel number (or property index number, or PIN), and most listing agreements include a blank for it. This number can be acquired from the tax database. ∎

Proposed dates for the closing and the buyer's possession   These dates should be based on an anticipated closing date. The listing agreement should allow adequate time for the paperwork involved (including the buyer's qualification for any financing) and the physical moves to be arranged by the seller and the buyer.

The closing   An attorney, title company, or escrow company should be considered and retained as soon as possible. A designated party will be needed to complete the settlement statements, disburse the funds, and file the proper forms, such as documents to be recorded and documents to be sent to the IRS.

In some states brokers are more actively involved in this area. In Illinois, the attorney, title company, and lender dominate closing issues.

Evidence of ownership   A warranty deed, title insurance policy, or abstract of title with an attorney's opinion can be used for proof of title.

Encumbrances   All liens must be paid by the seller or be assumed by the buyer at the closing. Identify as much information as possible about existing loans, such as the name and address of each lender, the type of loan, the loan number, the loan balance, the interest rate, the monthly payment, and if the loan can be prepaid without penalty. Determine if the buyer can assume the present loan, and if so, under what circumstances and if there is any possibility of seller financing.

Physical encroachments on the property (such as a fence) and their legal implications are questions best referred to an attorney, even if they were noted in the listing file.

Zoning   Identify current zoning for the property.

Property taxes   Ask about current (or most recent year's) property taxes and determine the amount of any outstanding special assessments and whether they will be paid by the seller or assumed by the buyer.

Home warranty program   In some situations, it may be advisable to offer a "home warranty" with the property. Skillful brokers are able to explain these warranties that often benefit both the seller and the buyer. Most real estate offices have information about the different home warranty programs available to homeowners for use in brokers' presentations. (*Brokers must disclose in writing any monies sent to them by a home warranty company.*)

Commission   The circumstances under which a commission will be paid must be specifically stated in the contract. The fee can be either a percentage or a flat rate and is usually paid at closing directly by the seller or the party handling the closing. Negotiation of commission is a key discussion point in creating a listing contract. The commission amount is fully negotiable between parties.

| In Illinois | By law, written listing agreements in Illinois must state that no change in the amount of the commission or time of payment will be valid or binding unless the change is made in writing and signed by all parties. ■

Antitrust wording   Any assertion that a "set" or "standard" commission exists violates antitrust laws. Any sponsoring broker is free to set a *minimum* commission that will be accepted within a given office, but there is *no such thing as a standard commission*. The contract should indicate that all commissions have been negotiated between the seller and the broker. It is illegal for commissions to be set by any regulatory agency, trade association, or other industry organization.

Termination of the contract   A contract should provide some way for the parties to end it. Under what circumstances will the contract terminate? Can the seller arbitrarily refuse to sell or cooperate with the listing broker?

| In Illinois | If a listing agreement provides that, in the event of a default by a buyer, the broker's full commission or fees will be paid out of an earnest money deposit, with the remainder of the earnest money to be paid to the seller, the provision shall appear in the listing agreement in letters larger than those generally used in the listing agreement. ■

Broker protection ("carryover") clause   Brokers are well advised to protect their interests against possible fraud or a reluctant buyer's change of heart. There are various circumstances under which a broker is entitled to a commission, for a specified amount of time, after an agreement terminated.

Warranties by the owner   The owner is responsible for certain assurances and disclosures that are vital to the agent's ability to market the property successfully. Is the property suitable for its intended purpose? Does it comply with the appropriate zoning and building codes? Will it be transferred to the buyer in essentially the same condition as it was originally presented, considering repairs or alterations to be made as provided for in a purchase contract? Are there any known defects?

Indemnification ("hold harmless") wording   The seller and the broker may agree to hold each other harmless (i.e., not to sue one another) for any incorrect information supplied by one to the other. Indemnification may be offered regardless of whether the inaccuracies are intentional or unintentional.

In Illinois   A client shall not be vicariously liable for the acts or omissions of a licensee in providing brokerage services for or on behalf of the client. ∎

Nondiscrimination (equal opportunity) wording   The seller must understand that the property will be shown and offered without regard to the race, color, creed, or religious preference, national origin, family status, sex, age, or disability of the prospective buyer. Federal, state, and local fair housing laws protect a variety of different groups and individuals. For instance, on the state and local level, sexual orientation and source of finances are also often protected.

In Illinois   All Illinois written listing agreements must clearly state that it is illegal for either the owner or the broker to refuse to sell or show property to any person because of race, color, religion, national origin, sex, familial status, ancestry, citizenship status, age 40 and over, marital status, physical or mental disability, military service, unfavorable military discharge, sexual orientation, and order of protected status.

The Illinois Human Rights Act and information pertaining to it are available on the Internet. ∎

Minimum Services

All exclusive brokerage agreements must specify that the sponsoring broker, through its sponsored licensees, must provide the following required **minimum services:**

In Illinois

1. Accept delivery of and present to the client all offers and counteroffers to buy, sell, or lease the client's property or the property the client seeks to purchase or lease
2. Assist the client in developing, communicating, negotiating, and presenting offers, counteroffers, and notices that relate to the offers and counteroffers until a lease or purchase agreement is signed and all contingencies are satisfied or waived
3. Answer the client's questions relating to the offers, counteroffers, notices, and contingencies ∎

This applies to listing agreements as well as buyer agency agreements.

The signatures of the parties   All parties identified in the listing contract must sign the contract, including all individuals who have a legal interest in the property.

The date the contract is signed   This date may differ from the date the contract actually becomes effective (e.g., if a sponsored licensee takes the listing and then must have the sponsoring broker sign the contract to accept employment under its terms).

Additional information   Although not required on the listing agreement, the listing broker should also obtain any additional information that would make the property more appealing and marketable, such as neighborhood amenities. Such amenities might include information about schools, parks and recreational areas, places of worship, and public transportation.

IN PRACTICE   Anyone who takes a listing should use only the appropriate documents provided by the broker. Most brokers are conscientious and only use documents that have been carefully drafted or reviewed by an attorney for construction and legal language that complies with the appropriate federal, state, and local laws. Contracts should also give consideration to local customs, such as closing dates and the proration of income and expenses.

■ BUYER AGENCY AGREEMENTS

Like a listing agreement, a **buyer agency agreement** is an employment contract. In this case, the broker is employed as the buyer's agent. The buyer, rather than the seller, is the principal. The purpose of the agreement is to find a suitable property. A buyer agency agreement gives the buyer a degree of representation possible only in a fiduciary relationship. A buyer's broker must protect the buyer's interests at all points in the transaction.

Types of Buyer Agency Agreements

Three basic types of buyer agency agreements exist:

1. **Exclusive buyer agency agreement**—Also known as an *exclusive right to represent*, this is a true exclusive agency agreement. The buyer is legally bound to compensate the broker whenever the buyer purchases a property of the type described in the contract. The broker is entitled to payment regardless of whether she locates the property. Even if the buyer finds the property independently, the broker is entitled to payment. A sample exclusive buyer agency contract appears in Figure 6.2.
2. **Exclusive-agency buyer agency agreement**—Like an exclusive buyer agency agreement, this is an exclusive contract between the buyer and the broker. However, this agreement limits the broker's right to payment. Brokers are only entitled to payment if they locate the property the buyer ultimately purchases. The buyer retains the right to locate and buy property without financial obligation to the broker. Buyer brokers end up "educating" buyers

FIGURE 6.2

Exclusive Buyer Representation\Exclusive Right to Purchase Contract

ILLINOIS ASSOCIATION OF REALTORS®
EXCLUSIVE BUYER REPRESENTATION/EXCLUSIVE RIGHT TO PURCHASE CONTRACT
(DUAL AGENCY DISCLOSURE AND CONSENT INCLUDED)

In consideration of _____'s (Brokerage Company hereinafter referred to as "Broker") agreement to designate a sales associate affiliated with Broker to act as an agent of the Buyer for the purpose of identifying and negotiating to acquire real estate for _____ ("Buyer"), the Buyer hereby grants to Broker the relationship as marked in Section 1 of the Contract.

SECTION 1: TYPE OF REPRESENTATION
(Instruction: check the box next to desired choice):

☐ **Exclusive Representation.** Buyer understands that this exclusive right to represent Buyer (Exclusive Representation) means that if the Buyer makes an acquisition of property, whether through the efforts of Broker and his agents or through the efforts of another real estate office or agent, Buyer will be obligated to compensate Broker pursuant to Section 8 of this Contract. This Exclusive Agency shall be effective for the following area: _____.
The term "acquisition" shall include the purchase, lease, exchange or option of real estate.

☐ **Exclusive Right to Acquire.** Buyer understands that this "exclusive right to purchase" means that if Buyer acquires any property, whether through the efforts of the Buyer, Broker and his agents, another real estate agency besides Broker's, or other third party, Buyer will be obligated to compensate Broker pursuant to Section 8 of this Contract. This exclusive right to acquire shall be effective for the following area:_____"Acquisition" shall include the purchase, lease, exchange or option of real estate.

Broker designates and Buyer accepts_____ ("Buyer's Designated Agent") as the legal agent(s) of Buyer for the purpose of representing Buyer in the acquisition of real estate by Buyer. Buyer understands and agrees that neither Broker nor any other sales associates affiliated with Broker (except as provided for herein) will be acting as legal agent of the Buyer. Broker shall have the discretion to appoint a substitute designated agent for Buyer as Broker determines necessary. Buyer shall be advised within a reasonable time of any such substitution.

SECTION 2: TERM
This Contract shall be effective until 11:59 p.m. on _____, 2____, when it shall then terminate. This Contract is irrevocable and can be terminated prior to the termination date only by written agreement of the parties. If within ____ days after the termination of this Contract (i.e. the protection period), Buyer purchases any property to which Buyer was introduced by Buyer's Designated Agent, then Buyer agrees to pay Broker the compensation provided for in Section 8. However, no compensation will be due to Broker if, during this protection period, Buyer enters into a separate buyer representation agreement with another broker.

SECTION 3: BUYER'S DESIGNATED AGENT'S DUTIES
(a)   To use Buyer's Designated Agent's best efforts to identify properties listed in the multiple listing service that meet the Buyer's specifications relating to location, price, features and amenities, as identified on the attached Buyer's Information Checklist.
(b)   To arrange for inspections of properties identified by the Buyer as potentially appropriate for acquisition.
(c)   To advise Buyer as to the pricing of comparable properties.
(d)   To assist Buyer in the negotiation of a contract acceptable to the Buyer for the acquisition of property.
(e)   To provide reasonable safeguards for confidential information that the Buyer discloses to Buyer's Designated Agent.
(f)   Other services: _____.

SECTION 4: BROKER'S DUTIES
(a)   To provide through Buyer's Designated Agent, those brokerage services set forth in Section 15-75 of the Illinois Real Estate License Act of 2000.
(b)   To provide Buyer's Designated Agent with assistance and advice as necessary in Buyer's Designated Agent's work on Buyer's behalf.
(c)   To make the managing Broker, or his /her designated representative, available to consult with Buyer's Designated Agent as to Buyer's negotiations for the acquisition of real estate, who will maintain the confidence of Buyer's confidential information.
(d)   To make other sales associates affiliated with Broker aware of Buyer's general specifications for real property.
(e)   As needed, to designate one or more sales associates as Designated Agents of Buyer.

SECTION 5: BUYER'S DUTIES
(a)   To complete the Buyer's checklist which will provide Buyer's specifications for the real estate Buyer is seeking.
(b)   To work exclusively with Buyer's Designated Agent to identify and acquire real estate during the time that this Contract is in force.
(c)   To supply relevant financial information that may be necessary to permit Buyer's Designated Agent to fulfill Agent's obligations under this Contract.
(d)   To be available upon reasonable notice and at reasonable hours to inspect properties that seem to meet Buyer's specifications.
(e)   To pay Broker according to the terms specified in Section 8 of this Contract.

SECTION 6: REPRESENTING OTHER BUYER
Buyer understands that Buyer's Designated Agent has no duty to represent only Buyer, and that Buyer's Designated Agent may represent other prospective buyers who may be interested in acquiring the same property or properties that Buyer is interested in acquiring.

Form 338 REVISED 12/29/09   1/3   Copyright© by Illinois Association of REALTORS®

Source: Published with Permission, Illinois Association of REALTORS®.

F I G U R E   6.2

Exclusive Buyer Representation\Exclusive Right to Purchase Contract (continued)

SECTION 7: DISCLOSURE AND CONSENT TO DUAL AGENCY

NOTE TO CONSUMER: THIS SECTION SERVES THREE PURPOSES. FIRST, IT DISCLOSES THAT A REAL ESTATE LICENSEE MAY POTENTIALLY ACT AS A DUAL AGENT, THAT IS, REPRESENT MORE THAN ONE PARTY TO THE TRANSACTION. SECOND, THIS SECTION EXPLAINS THE CONCEPT OF DUAL AGENCY. THIRD, THIS SECTION SEEKS YOUR CONSENT TO ALLOW THE REAL ESTATE LICENSEE TO ACT AS A DUAL AGENT. A LICENSEE MAY LEGALLY ACT AS A DUAL AGENT ONLY WITH YOUR CONSENT. BY CHOOSING TO SIGN THIS SECTION, YOUR CONSENT TO DUAL AGENCY REPRESENTATION IS PRESUMED.

The undersigned _____,("Licensee"/"Buyer's
(insert name(s) of licensee

Designated Agent") may undertake a dual representation (represent both the seller or landlord and the buyer or tenant) for the sale or lease of property. The undersigned acknowledge they were informed of the possibility of this type of representation. Before signing this document please read the following:

Representing more than one party to a transaction presents a conflict of interest since both clients may rely upon Licensee's advice and the client's respective interests may be adverse to each other. Licensee will undertake this representation only with the written consent of ALL clients in the transaction.

Any agreement between the clients as to a final contract price and other terms is a result of negotiations between the clients acting in their own best interests and on their own behalf. You acknowledge that Licensee has explained the implications of dual representation, including the risks involved, and understand that you have been advised to seek independent advice from your advisors or attorneys before signing any documents in this transaction.

WHAT A LICENSEE CAN DO FOR CLIENTS WHEN ACTING AS A DUAL AGENT

1. Treat all clients honestly.
2. Provide information about the property to the buyer or tenant.
3. Disclose all latent material defects in the property that are known to the Licensee.
4. Disclose financial qualification of the buyer or tenant to the seller or landlord.
5. Explain real estate terms.
6. Help the buyer or tenant to arrange for property inspections.
7. Explain closing costs and procedures.
8. Help the buyer compare financing alternatives.
9. Provide information about comparable properties that have sold so both clients may make educated decisions on what price to accept or offer.

WHAT LICENSEE CANNOT DISCLOSE TO CLIENTS WHEN ACTING AS A DUAL AGENT

1. Confidential information that Licensee may know about a client, without that client's permission.
2. The price or terms the seller or landlord will take other than the listing price without permission of the seller or landlord.
3. The price or terms the buyer or tenant is willing to pay without permission of the buyer or tenant.
4. A recommended or suggested price or terms the buyer or tenant should offer.
5. A recommended or suggested price or terms the seller or landlord should counter with or accept.

If either client is uncomfortable with this disclosure and dual representation, please let Licensee know. You are not required to sign this section unless you want to allow the Licensee to proceed as a Dual Agent in this transaction.

By initialing here and signing below, you acknowledge that you have read and understand this form and voluntarily consent to the Licensee acting as a Dual Agent (that is, to represent BOTH the seller or landlord and the buyer or tenant) should that become necessary.

_____   _____   _____
Buyer's initials   Buyer's initials   Date

SECTION 8: COMPENSATION

Broker and Buyer expect that Broker's commission will be paid by the seller or seller's broker for Broker's acting as a cooperating agent. However, if Broker is not compensated by seller or seller's broker, or if the amount of compensation paid by seller or seller's broker is not at least _____% of the purchase price, then Buyer agrees to pay Broker the difference between_____% of the purchase price and what seller or seller's broker actually paid. This Section applies if the Buyer enters into a contract to acquire real estate during the term of this Contract or the protection period, and such contract results in a closed transaction. Any modification to this Section, including the commission to be paid to Broker, shall be by a separate written agreement to this Contract.

SECTION 9: PREVIOUS REPRESENTATION

Buyer understands that Broker and/or Designated Agent may have previously represented the seller from whom you wish to purchase property. During that representation, Broker and/or Designated Agent may have learned material information about the seller that is considered confidential. Under the law, neither Broker nor Designated Agent may disclose any such confidential information to you.

SECTION 10: FAILURE TO CLOSE

If a seller or lessor in an agreement made on behalf of Buyer fails to close such agreement, with no fault on the part of Buyer, the Buyer shall have no obligation to pay the commission provided for in Section 8. If such transaction fails to close because of any fault on the part of Buyer, such commission will not be waived, but will be due and payable immediately. In no case shall Broker or Buyer's Designated Agent be obligated to advance funds for the benefit of Buyer in order to complete a closing.

F I G U R E   6.2

Exclusive Buyer Representation\Exclusive Right to Purchase Contract (continued)

SECTION 11: DISCLAIMER
The Buyer acknowledges that Broker and Buyer's Designated Agent are being retained solely as real estate professionals, and not as attorneys, tax advisors, surveyors, structural engineers, home inspectors, environmental consultants, architects, contractors, or other professional service providers. The Buyer understands that such other professional service providers are available to render advice or services to the Buyer, if desired, at Buyer's expense.

SECTION 12: COSTS OF THIRD PARTY SERVICES OR PRODUCTS
Buyer agrees to reimburse Broker the cost of any products or services such as surveys, soil tests, title reports and engineering studies, furnished by outside sources immediately when payment is due.

SECTION 13: INDEMNIFICATION OF BROKER
Buyer agrees to indemnify Broker and Buyer's Designated Agent and to hold Broker and Buyer's Designated Agent harmless on account of any and all loss, damage, cost or expense, including attorneys' fees incurred by Broker or Buyer's Designated Agent, arising out of this Contract, or the collection of fees or commission due Broker pursuant to the terms and conditions of this Contract, provided the loss damage, cost, expense or attorneys' fees do not result because of Broker's or Buyer's Designated Agent's own negligence or willful and wanton misconduct.

SECTION 14: ASSIGNMENT BY BUYERS
No assignment of Buyer's interest under this Contract and no assignment of rights in real property obtained for Buyer pursuant to this Contract shall operate to defeat any of Broker's rights under this exclusive representation contract.

SECTION 15: NONDISCRIMINATION
THE PARTIES UNDERSTAND AND AGREE THAT IT IS ILLEGAL FOR EITHER OF THE PARTIES TO REFUSE TO DISPLAY OR SELL SELLER'S PROPERTY TO ANY PERSON ON THE BASIS OF RACE, COLOR, RELIGION, SEX, NATIONAL ORIGIN, ANCESTRY, AGE, ORDER OF PROTECTION STATUS, MARITAL STATUS, PHYSICAL OR MENTAL HANDICAP, MILITARY STATUS, SEXUAL ORIENTATION, UNFAVORABLE DISCHARGE FROM MILITARY SERVICE, FAMILIAL STATUS OR ANY OTHER CLASS PROTECTED BY ARTICLE 3 OF THE ILLINOIS HUMAN RIGHTS ACT. THE PARTIES AGREE TO COMPLY WITH ALL APPLICABLE FEDERAL, STATE AND LOCAL FAIR HOUSING LAWS.

SECTION 16: MODIFICATION OF THIS CONTRACT
No modification of any of the terms of this Contract shall be valid and binding upon the parties or entitled to enforcement unless such modification has first been reduced to writing and signed by the parties.

SECTION 17: ENTIRE AGREEMENT
This Contract constitutes the entire agreement between the parties relating to the subject thereof, and any prior agreements pertaining hereto, whether oral or written have been merged and integrated into this Contract.

This Contract may be executed in multiple copies and my signature as Buyer hereon acknowledges that I have received a signed copy.

_____   Accepted by:
Buyer

_____   _____, Broker
Buyer

Buyer's Address: BY:_____ DATE:_____

_____   _____ DATE:_____
                                                 Buyer's Designated Agent
_____

Date:_____   PHONE:_____OFFICE:_____

about the process and show many homes only to find that the buyers avoid compensation by working directly with an unlisted property owner, FSBO.

3. **Open buyer agency agreement**—This agreement is a nonexclusive buyer representation agreement between a broker and a buyer. It permits the buyer to enter into similar agreements with an unlimited number of brokers. The buyer is obligated to compensate only the broker who locates the property the buyer ultimately purchases.

Buyer Representation Issues

A broker and a buyer must discuss a number of issues before entering into a written buyer agency agreement. The broker should conduct a counseling session with the buyer to determine the buyer's needs and goals, financial capabilities, and motivation. This session gives the broker the ability to educate the buyer on the buying process and market conditions and to formulate a strategy for finding the right property. In addition, compensation needs to be addressed and negotiated in the event there is no offer of cooperative compensation from the listing broker to the buyer's broker.

The information learned about the buyer in the initial counseling session will be invaluable in the negotiation phase of the transaction.

The broker should make the same disclosures to the buyer that the broker would make in a listing agreement. The broker should explain the forms of agency available and the parties' rights and responsibilities under each type of agreement. The specific services provided to a buyer-client need to be clearly explained.

In Illinois   The source of compensation is not the factor that determines the relationship. A buyer's broker may be compensated by either the buyer or the seller. Compensation is always negotiable. ■

IN PRACTICE   In Illinois, it is common for the listing broker to split the listing fee with the buyer's broker. Note that this is a clear case where commission does not equate to agency or representation. Discussions regarding a commission or fee provided by the buyer may still take place. A broker is free to negotiate for compensation from any buyer for whom service was provided in an agency capacity. However, if the broker receives compensation from more than one source in a transaction, it always needs to be disclosed in writing to the involved parties. (See Figure 6.3.)

A buyer agent's duties include using the broker's best efforts to identify properties listed in the MLS that meet buyer's criteria, arrange for property inspections identified by buyer as potentially appropriate for purchase, advise buyer as to the pricing of comparable properties, assist buyer in the negotiation of a sales contract acceptable to buyer, and to provide confidentiality on any information that buyer discloses to the broker.

FIGURE 6.3

Buyer Information Checklist

ILLINOIS ASSOCIATION OF REALTORS
BUYERS INFORMATION CHECKLIST

1.   Name: _____

2.   Address: _____

3.   Telephone No.: _____ Fax No.: _____

4.   Area(s) requested: _____

5.   Approximate possession date: _____

6.   Specifications:

   a.   Bedrooms _____
   b.   Baths _____
   c.   Garage _____
   d.   Basement _____
   e.   Style _____
   f.   Lot Size _____
   g.   Features: _____
   h.   Remarks: _____

7.   Price range: _____
      How was this determined:

      ☐ Broker Pre-qualification
      ☐ Lender
      ☐ Other

8.   What do you consider a comfortable monthly mortgage payment?
      $_____

9.   How much do you plan to invest in the down payment?
      $_____ Source: _____

10.   Do you have a preference for any particular lender or mortgage broker?
      _____

11.   Other than the maximum price which you might be willing to pay for the property, is there any other information which you deem confidential and would not want disclosed?

                    ☐ Yes   ☐ No

      If yes, please state:_____

12.   In order to assist us in monitoring our commitment to Fair Housing, we request the following information. Your providing this information is completely voluntary and will not be made known to any sellers.

      Race: ☐ Black   ☐ White   ☐ Other
      ☐ Disabled
      ☐ Family with children
      ☐ Married

Form 344 2/2000   Copyright by Illinois Association of REALTORS

Source: Published with Permission, Illinois Association of REALTORS®.

FIGURE 6.3

Buyer Information Checklist (continued)

Signatures:

_____   _____
Agent   Buyer

_____   _____
Date   Date

                                                          _____
                                                          Buyer

                                                          _____
                                                          Date

13.   Source of Buyer:

☐ Personal referral   ☐ Ad call
☐ Floor call/walk in   ☐ Company referral
☐ Sign call   ☐ Met at open house

14.   How was property presented to Buyer?

☐ Buyer requested to see one specific home.
☐ Computer generated based on area stated by Buyer.
    (If so, attach computer search)

Properties and/or Areas Shown	Price	Date	Buyers Comments	Printed Listing Given
_____	_____	_____	_____	☐
_____	_____	_____	_____	☐
_____	_____	_____	_____	☐
_____	_____	_____	_____	☐
_____	_____	_____	_____	☐
_____	_____	_____	_____	☐
_____	_____	_____	_____	☐
_____	_____	_____	_____	☐
_____	_____	_____	_____	☐
_____	_____	_____	_____	☐
_____	_____	_____	_____	☐

Form 344 2/2000   Copyright by Illinois Association of REALTORS

■ QUALIFYING BUYER SERVICES

Qualifying Buyer Services

The buyer's broker provides the following services throughout the real estate transaction:

■ Needs assessment—Determine and evaluate the needs and wants of the buyer.

■ Property selection—Locate the best property for the buyer by notifying buyers of new listings and for-sale-by-owner properties. Remember, property selection need not be limited by price. In today's market, list prices can often be negotiated down.

■ Viewing properties—Provide an objective evaluation of the property and show buyers how to compare properties. Disclose material facts that are pertinent to the property.

■ Negotiate—Strategize with the buyer, suggesting techniques that strengthen the buyer's position. Then, implement those strategies on the buyer's behalf. Disclose any prior unsuccessful negotiations. Provide price counseling and prepare a comparative market analysis (CMA) on the property the buyer is considering.

■ Follow-up—Resolve any issues that could prevent a closing from occurring. Provide ongoing communications with the client, preferably by e-mail for maintaining records.

■ THE BUYING PROCESS

When the buyers have found the right property, the next step is to prepare and negotiate an offer that will lead to a signed sales contract between the seller and the buyer. The buyer's broker must prepare a CMA to establish a price for the buyer to offer. Factors to take into consideration include:

■ Property condition— Does the property need a lot of repairs?

■ Length of time on the market— This indicates the selling pace of the market, the level of inventory, or a potential problem with the property.

■ Supply and demand—Essentially, when supply increases and demand remains stable, prices go down; when demand increases and supply remains stable, prices go up. Greater supply means producers need to attract more buyers, so they lower prices. Greater demand means producers can raise their prices because buyers compete for the product.

■ Seller's motivation—Is the property in distress, pre-foreclosure, or requiring a short sale?

■ Terms and contingencies—The fewer the contingencies, the stronger the offer, making it more attractive to the seller or bank (if property is bank owned or requires bank approval for a short sale).

| In Illinois | The buyer's broker is obligated to keep confidential all confidential information received from the client. ■ |

When buyer brokers are working with two or more clients who are seeking similar properties in the same price range, the buyer's broker is permitted to show alternative properties to prospective buyers or tenants. Specifically, the buyer's broker does not breach a duty or obligation to the client by showing alternative properties to prospective buyers or tenants, by showing properties in which the client is interested to other prospective buyers or tenants, or by making or preparing **contemporaneous offers** or contracts to purchase or lease the same property.

However, brokers must provide written disclosure to all clients for whom the licensee is preparing or making contemporaneous offers or contracts to purchase or lease the same property and shall refer to another designated agent any client that requests such referral. (See Figure 6.4.)

■ TERMINATION OF BROKER EMPLOYMENT AGREEMENTS

A broker employment agreement is a contract between a broker and a seller or buyer. Its success depends on the broker's personal and professional efforts. Because broker services are unique, a broker cannot turn over the contract to another broker without the principal's written consent. The client cannot force the broker to perform, but the broker's failure to work diligently toward fulfilling the contract's terms constitutes abandonment of the contract. In the event the contract is abandoned or revoked by the broker, the principal is entitled to sue the broker for damages.

On the other hand, the principal might fail to fulfill the terms of the agreement. For instance, a property owner who refuses to cooperate with the broker's reasonable requests, such as allowing the broker to show the property to prospective buyers or refusing to proceed with a completed sales contract, could be liable for damages to the broker. If either party cancels the contract, one party may be liable for damages to the other.

An employment agreement may be canceled for the following reasons:

- When the agreement's purpose is fulfilled
- When the agreement's term expires without a successful transfer
- If the property is destroyed or its use is changed by some force outside the client's control, such as a zoning change or condemnation by eminent domain
- If title to the property is transferred by operation of law, as in the case of the client's bankruptcy or foreclosure
- If the broker and client mutually agree to end the agreement
- If either the broker or the client dies or becomes incapacitated
- If either the broker or client breaches the contract, the agreement is terminated and the breaching or canceling party may be liable to the other for damages.

FIGURE 6.4

Disclosure of Contemporaneous Offers

ILLINOIS ASSOCIATION OF REALTORS®
DISCLOSURE OF CONTEMPORANEOUS OFFERS

_____, an agent (hereinafter referred to as Designated Agent) with _____ (Brokerage company hereinafter referred to as Broker), is acting as Designated Agent for more than one prospective buyer or tenant who the Designated Agent has reason to believe are making or preparing to make contemporaneous offers to purchase or lease the property located at _____.

(street address or description of property).

At this time, buyers/tenants have the option of being referred to another designated agent who will serve as the agent for buyer/tenant.

Buyer elects: (choose one of the following)

☐　to remain with Designated Agent identified above notwithstanding that another client of Designated Agent may be making a contemporaneous offer to purchase or lease the real property identified above.

☐　to be referred to another designated agent who will act as agent for buyer/tenant in the making of an offer to purchase or lease the real property identified above.

Signed by: _____　dated _____
(Designated Agent)

Signed by: _____　dated _____
(Buyer or Tenant)

Signed by: _____　dated _____
(Buyer or Tenant)

Form 427 12/18/09　　　　　　　　　　　Copyright by Illinois Association of REALTORS®

| In Illinois | Except as may be provided in a written agreement between the broker and the client, neither a sponsoring broker nor any licensee affiliated with the sponsoring broker owes any further duties to the client after termination, expiration, or completion of performance of the brokerage agreement except: |

- to account for all monies and property relating to the transaction; and
- to keep confidential all confidential information received during the course of the brokerage agreement. ■

■ SUMMARY

To acquire an inventory of property to sell, brokers must obtain listings. Types of listings include exclusive-right-to-sell, exclusive-agency, and open listings. With an exclusive-right-to-sell listing, the seller employs only one broker and must pay that broker a commission regardless of whether it is the broker or the seller who finds a buyer, provided the buyer is found within the listing period.

Under exclusive agency, the broker is given the exclusive right to represent the seller, but the seller can avoid paying the broker a commission by selling the property to someone not procured by the broker.

With an open listing, to obtain a commission, the broker must find a ready, willing, and able buyer on the seller's terms before the property is sold by the seller or by another broker.

A multiple listing service (MLS) provision may appear in an exclusive-right-to-sell or an exclusive-agency listing. It gives the broker the additional authority and obligation to distribute the listing to other members of the broker's multiple listing organization, which enhances the odds of the property selling.

A net listing, which is illegal in some states and considered somewhat unethical in most areas, is based on the net price the seller will receive if the property is sold. The broker is free to offer the property for sale at the highest available price and will receive as commission any amount exceeding the seller's stipulated net. Net listings are legal in Illinois but not recommended.

An option listing, which also must be handled with caution, gives the broker the option to purchase the listed property if it does not sell in a specified amount of time.

When listing a property for sale, the seller is concerned about the selling price and the net amount due from the sale. A comparative market analysis (CMA) compares the prices of recently sold properties that are similar to the seller's property. The CMA or a formal appraisal report can be used to help the seller determine a reasonable listing price. The approximate amount the seller will net from the sale is calculated by subtracting the broker's commission, any other seller expenses (attorney, title search), and any existing liens (such as the mortgage) from the approximate sales price.

Listing contract forms typically are preprinted forms that include such information as the type of listing agreement, the broker's authority and responsibility under the listing, the listing price, the duration of the listing, information about the property, terms for the payment of commission, details regarding the buyer's possession, and nondiscrimination and antitrust laws. Detailed information about the property may be included in the listing contract or on a separate property data sheet.

Disclosure of the broker's agency relationships and agency policies are required. The seller will be expected to comply honestly with legally required disclosures of property conditions.

A buyer agency agreement ensures that a buyer's interest will be represented. Different forms of buyer agency agreements exist—an exclusive buyer agency, an exclusive-agency buyer agency, and open buyer agency. In an exclusive buyer agency, the broker is compensated regardless of whether the broker locates the property. In an exclusive-agency buyer agency, the broker is compensated only if the broker locates the property the buyer purchases. In open buyer agency, the buyer is obligated to compensate only the broker who locates the property the buyer purchases.

A buyer's broker is obligated to find a suitable property for the client, who is owed fiduciary or statutory duties of agency. Buyer agency is regulated by Illinois agency laws.

A buyer agent's duties include providing best efforts to identify properties listed in the MLS that meet buyer's criteria, arranging for property inspections identified by the buyer as potentially appropriate for purchase, advising the buyer about the pricing of comparable properties, assisting the buyer in the negotiation of a sales contract that is acceptable to the buyer, and providing confidentiality on all information that buyer discloses to agent.

A best practice is for the broker to conduct a counseling session with the buyer to determine the buyer's needs and goals, financial capabilities, and motivation. This gives the broker the ability to educate the buyer on the buying process and market conditions and to formulate a strategy for finding the right property.

Qualifying buyer services include needs assessment, property selection, viewing properties, negotiating, and follow-up.

The buying process includes the agent preparing a CMA for the buyer on the property selected then preparing and negotiating the offer that ultimately leads to a contract between the buyer and seller.

Listings and buyer agency agreements may be terminated for the same reasons as any other agency relationship.

In Illinois

In Illinois, a written exclusive or exclusive-right-to-sell listing agreement must include the list price, the basis for and time of payment of the commission, the term of the listing, the names and signatures of the listing broker and seller, and the address or legal description of the property.

All exclusive brokerage agreements must be in writing according to the Real Estate License Act of 2000. In addition, under the Act, all exclusive brokerage agreements must provide for minimum services.

Detailed information about a property should be included for the record in the listing contract or on a separate property data sheet. Full disclosure of the broker's agency relationship, any interest the broker has in the subject property, material facts pertaining to the property, any guaranteed sales agreement, or any special bonus or fee provided to an agent is required by Illinois law.

A broker who represents a seller may show alternative properties to prospective buyers or tenants. Likewise, a buyer's broker may show the same property to other buyers. However, when the broker is making or preparing offers on the same property, known as contemporaneous offers, the broker must provide written disclosure to the other clients, and if requested, must refer a buyer to another designated agent. ■

CHAPTER 6 QUIZ

1. A listing taken by a real estate licensee is an agreement between the seller and the
   a. sponsoring broker.
   b. local multiple listing service.
   c. sponsored licensee associated with the firm.
   d. local REALTOR® association.

2. Which of the following is a similarity between an exclusive-agency listing and an exclusive-right-to-sell listing?
   a. Under both, the seller retains the right to sell the real estate without the broker's help and without paying the broker a commission.
   b. Under both, the seller authorizes only one particular broker to show the property.
   c. Both types of listings give the responsibility of representing the seller to one broker only.
   d. Both types of listings are open listings.

3. The listing agreement expires on May 2. Which event would *NOT* terminate the listing?
   a. The agreement is not renewed after May 2.
   b. The broker dies on April 29.
   c. On April 15, the seller tells the broker that he is dissatisfied with the broker's marketing efforts.
   d. The seller's house is destroyed by fire on April 25.

4. The seller has listed his property under an exclusive-agency listing with the broker. If the seller sells the property himself during the term of the listing to someone introduced to the property by the seller, he will owe the broker
   a. no commission.
   b. the full commission.
   c. a partial commission.
   d. only reimbursement for the broker's costs.

5. A broker sold a residence for $235,000 and received $12,925 as her commission in accordance with the terms of the listing. What was the broker's commission rate?
   a. 5.5 percent
   b. 5.7 percent
   c. 6.25 percent
   d. 6.5 percent

6. Under a listing agreement, the broker is entitled to sell the property for any price, as long as the seller receives $185,000. The broker may keep any amount over $185,000 as a commission. This type of listing is called a(n)
   a. exclusive-right-to-sell listing.
   b. exclusive-agency listing.
   c. open listing.
   d. net listing.

7. Which of the following is a similarity between an open listing and an exclusive-agency listing?
   a. Under both, the seller avoids paying the broker a commission if the seller sells the property to someone the broker did not procure.
   b. Both grant a commission to any broker who procures a buyer for the seller's property.
   c. Under both, the broker earns a commission regardless of who sells the property as long as it is sold within the listing period.
   d. Both grant an exclusive right to sell to whatever broker procures a buyer for the seller's property.

8. The final decision on a property's listed price should be determined by the
   a. broker based on information from the local MLS.
   b. broker and the appraiser.
   c. broker and seller equally.
   d. seller based on the broker's CMAs.

9. Which of the following statements is *TRUE* of a listing contract?

    a. It is an employment contract for the personal and professional services of the broker.

    b. It obligates the seller to convey the property if the broker procures a ready, willing, and able buyer.

    c. It obligates the broker to work diligently for both the seller and the buyer.

    d. It automatically binds the owner, broker, and MLS to the agreed provisions.

10. A real estate company received a 6.5 percent commission on the sale of a property. The listing broker in the company received 40 percent of the commission, or $9,750. What was the selling price of the property?

    a. $55,000 $9750 \div 40\% = 24,375$

    b. $150,000 $24375 \ast 60\% = 14,625$

    c. $250,000

    (d.) $375,000 $24,375 \div 6.5\% = 375,000$

11. A seller listed her residence with a broker. The broker brought an offer at full price and terms of the listing from buyers who were ready, willing, and able to pay cash for the property. However, the seller changed her mind and rejected the buyers' offer. In this situation, the seller

    a. must sell her property.

    b. owes a commission to the broker.

    c. is liable to the buyers for specific performance.

    d. is liable to the buyers for compensatory damages.

12. A comparative market analysis

    a. is the same as an appraisal.

    b. can help the seller price the property.

    c. by law must be completed for each listing taken.

    d. should not be retained in the property's listing file.

13. A property was listed with a broker who belonged to a multiple listing service and was sold by another member broker for $153,500. The total commission was 6 percent of the sales price. The selling broker received 60 percent of the commission, and the listing broker kept the balance. What was the listing broker's commission?

    a. $3,684

    b. $4,464

    c. $5,526

    d. $36,840

14. A seller signs a listing agreement with a broker to sell his home. The agreement states that the broker will receive a 5.5 percent commission. The home sells for $387,000. What is the net amount that the seller will receive from the sale?

    a. $4,785

    b. $21,285

    c. $365,715

    d. $369,585

15. A real estate broker and a seller enter into a listing agreement that contains the following language: "Seller will receive $100,000 from the sale of the subject property. Any amount greater than $100,000 will constitute Broker's sole and complete compensation." Which of the following statements is *TRUE* regarding this agreement?

    a. This agreement is an example of an option listing.

    b. If the seller's home sells for exactly $100,000, the broker still will be entitled to receive the standard commission in the area.

    c. The broker may offer the property for any price over $100,000, but the agreement may be unethical.

    d. This type of listing is known as an open listing because the selling price is left open.

16. A broker enters into an agreement with a client. The agreement states, "In return for the compensation agreed upon, Broker will assist Client in locating and purchasing a suitable property. Broker will receive the agreed compensation regardless of whether Broker, Client, or some other party locates the property ultimately purchased by Client." What kind of agreement is this?

    a. Exclusive-agency listing
    b. Exclusive-agency buyer agency agreement
    c. Exclusive buyer agency agreement
    d. Open buyer agency agreement

In Illinois

17. Illinois licensees may

    a. submit a listing to the local MLS.
    b. refuse to show a property to racial minorities if their sellers so instruct them.
    c. advertise in their own name as long as they hold independent contractor status.
    d. never take open listings.

18. Under what conditions is a disclosure of contemporaneous offers required?

    a. When a buyer's agent is acting as designated agent for more than one buyer interested in buying the same property
    b. When a seller's agent is also representing the buyer on the same transaction
    c. When a buyer's agent does not want to engage in dual agency
    d. When a buyer wants the agent to also represent the seller on the sale of her property

19. Illinois requires that listing agreements contain a

    a. multiple listing service (MLS) clause.
    b. definite contract termination date.
    c. automatic extension clause.
    d. broker protection clause.

20. In Illinois, what brokerage agreements must be in writing?

    a. Any brokerage agreement
    b. Only listing agreements
    c. Exclusive brokerage agreements
    d. Those listed with a REALTOR®

Interests in Real Estate

■ **LEARNING OBJECTIVES**   *When you've finished reading this chapter, you should be able to*

■ **identify** the kinds of limitations on ownership rights that are imposed by government action and the form of conveyance of property;

■ **describe** the various estates in land and the rights and limitations they convey;

■ **explain** concepts related to encumbrances and water rights;

■ **distinguish** the various types of police powers and how they are exercised; and

■ **define** the following *key terms*

accretion	encroachment	license
appurtenant easement	encumbrance	lien
avulsion	Equity in Eminent Domain Act	life estate
condemnation	erosion	life tenant
deed restrictions	escheat	littoral rights
doctrine of prior appropriation	estates in land	party wall
dominant tenement	fee simple absolute	police power
easement	fee simple defeasible	quick-take
easement by condemnation	fee simple determinable	remainder interest
easement by necessity	fee simple estates	reversionary interest
easement by prescription	freehold estate	riparian rights
easement in gross	future interest	servient tenement
eminent domain	homestead	taxation
	leasehold estates	Uniform Probate Code
		unsecured debt

■ LIMITATIONS ON THE RIGHTS OF OWNERSHIP

Ownership of a parcel of real estate is not absolute, that is, it is dependent on the type of interest a person holds in the property. Keep in mind that a landowner's power to control her property relates to the landowner having title of the property and the bundle of legal rights that accompanies the title. Even the most complete ownership the law allows is limited by public and private restrictions. These restrictions are intended to ensure that one owner's use or enjoyment of her property does not interfere with others' use or enjoyment of their property or with the welfare of the general public. Real estate licensees should have a working knowledge of the restrictions that might limit current or future owners. For example, a zoning ordinance that will not allow a doctor's office to coexist with a residence, a condo association bylaw prohibiting resale without board approval, or an easement allowing the neighbors to use the private beach may not only burden today's purchaser but also deter a future buyer.

■ GOVERNMENTAL POWERS

Individual ownership rights are subject to certain powers, or rights, held by federal, state, and local governments. These limitations on the ownership of real estate are imposed for the general welfare of the community and, therefore, supersede the rights or interests of the individual. Government powers include police power, eminent domain, taxation, and escheat.

> **In Illinois**   The state and local government powers discussed in this section are all held by the state of Illinois and various county and municipal governing bodies. ■

Police Power

Every state has the power to enact legislation to preserve order, protect the public health and safety, and promote the general welfare of its citizens. That authority is known as a state's **police power**. The state's authority is passed on to municipalities and counties through legislation called *enabling acts*. What is identified as being in the public interest can vary considerably from state to state and region to region. For example, a police power is used to enact environmental protection laws, zoning ordinances, and building codes. Regulations that govern the use, occupancy, size, location, and construction of real estate also fall within the police powers.

Like the rights of ownership, the state's power to regulate land use is not absolute. The laws must be uniform and nondiscriminatory; that is, they may not operate to the advantage or disadvantage of any one particular owner or owners. (See Chapter 19.)

> **Memory Tip**
>
> Remember the four government powers as **PETE**:
> Police power
> Eminent domain
> Taxation
> Escheat

Eminent Domain

Eminent domain is the right of the government to acquire privately owned real estate for public use. **Condemnation** is the process by which the government exercises this right, by either judicial or administrative proceedings. In the taking of property, just compensation must be paid to the owner, and the rights of the property owner must be protected by due process of law.

Eminent domain is the government's right to acquire property for public use. *Condemnation* is the actual process of taking property.

Ideally, the public agency and the owner of the property in question agree on compensation through direct negotiation, and the government purchases the property for a price considered fair by the owner. In some cases, the owner may simply dedicate the property to the government as a site for a school, park, or another beneficial use. Sometimes, however, in cases where the owner's consent cannot be obtained, the government agency can initiate condemnation proceedings to acquire the property.

In Illinois

Local units of government and quasi-governmental bodies are given the power of eminent domain by the Illinois Constitution and by the Illinois Code of Civil Procedure. In certain situations, Illinois law permits a summary proceeding in which a plaintiff/condemnor may obtain immediate fee simple title to real property, including the rights of possession and use. Such a proceeding in Illinois is termed a **quick-take**.

In quick-take, the plaintiff must deposit a sum with the county treasurer that is preliminarily considered by the court to be *just compensation*; this can be litigated later. A quick-take might be appropriate, for instance, in the following circumstances:

- The state of Illinois or the Illinois Toll Highway Authority takes property to construct, maintain, and operate highways.
- A sanitary district takes property to remove obstructions in a river, such as the Des Plaines River or Illinois River.
- An airport authority takes property to provide additional land for airport purposes. ■

Generally, states delegate their power of eminent domain to quasi-public bodies and publicly held companies responsible for various facets of public service. For instance, a public housing authority might take privately owned land to build low-income housing, or the state's land-clearance commission or redevelopment authority could use the power of eminent domain to make way for urban renewal. If there were no other feasible way to accomplish its aims, a railway, utility company, or highway department might acquire farmland or residential properties to extend railroad tracks, bring electricity to a remote new development, or build a new highway.

In the past, the proposed use for taking property was to be for the public good. However, in June 2005, the U.S. Supreme Court in *Kelo v. City of New London*, significantly changed the definition of public use. The court held that local governments can condemn homes and businesses for private or economic development purposes.

In *Kelo v. City of New London*, a development agent, on behalf of the city, initiated condemnation proceedings on land owned by nine property owners who refused to have their property taken. The development plan involved land for commercial, residential, and recreational purposes. The court noted that the development plan was not going to benefit a particular class of identifiable individuals. Further, although the owners' properties were not blighted, the city determined that a program of economic rejuvenation was justified and entitled to deference. *Economic development* fit within the broad definition of *public purpose*. The court found that the city's proposed disposition of petitioners' properties qualified as a *public use* within the meaning of the Takings Clause of the Fifth Amendment of the U.S. Constitution.

In this case, the city had invoked a state statute that authorized the use of eminent domain to promote economic development. The court decision leaves it to the states to establish rules that cities must follow when exercising eminent domain powers. In response to this court decision, many state legislators are drafting legislation to impose a narrow definition of *public use* in eminent domain proceedings to stop condemnations justified on purely economic grounds.

| In Illinois | The **Equity in Eminent Domain Act** became effective in Illinois on January 1, 2007, following the *Kelo v. New London* Supreme Court case. The law places the obligation on government to prove that an area is blighted before forcing property owners to sell their property for private development projects. In addition, the act helps property owners receive fair market value for their property, requires relocation costs for displaced residents and businesses, and pays attorneys' fees when property owners successfully sue to keep their property. ∎ |

Taxation

Taxation is a charge on real estate to raise funds to meet the public needs of a government. Taxes on real estate include annual real estate taxes assessed by local and area governmental entities, including school districts; taxes on income realized by individuals and corporations on the sale of property; and special fees that may be levied for special projects. Nonpayment of taxes may give government the power to claim an interest in the property. (See Chapter 10.)

Escheat

Escheat (revert) is a process by which the state may acquire privately owned real or personal property. State laws provide for ownership to transfer, or **escheat**, to the state when an owner dies and leaves no heirs (as defined by the law) and there is no will or living trust instrument that directs how the real estate is to be distributed. In some states, real property escheats to the county where the land is located; in other states, it becomes the property of the state. Escheat is intended to prevent property from being ownerless or abandoned.

| In Illinois | In Illinois, real property will escheat to the *county* in which it is located rather than to the state. ∎ |

■ ESTATES IN LAND

An **estate in land** defines the degree, quantity, nature, and extent of an owner's interest in real property. Many types of estates exist, but not all interests in real estate are estates. To be an estate in land, an interest must allow possession, meaning the holding and enjoyment of the property either now or in the future, and must be measured according to time. Historically, estates in land have been classified primarily by their length of time of possession (i.e., as freehold estates and leasehold estates).

Freehold estates last for an indeterminable length of time, such as for a lifetime or forever. They include *fee simple* (also sometimes called an *indefeasible fee*), *defeasible fee*, and *life estates*. The first two of these estates continue for an indefinite period and may be passed along to the owner's heirs. A life estate is based on the lifetime of a person and ends when that individual dies. Freehold estates are illustrated in Figure 7.1.

Leasehold estates last for a fixed period of time. They include estates for years and estates from period to period. Estates at will and estates at sufferance also are leaseholds, though by their operation, they are not generally viewed as being for fixed terms.

In Illinois

The traditional freehold and leasehold estates found in most states are also recognized under Illinois law. ■

Fee Simple Estate

Because **fee simple estates** are of unlimited duration, they are said to run "forever." Upon the death of the owner, a fee simple passes to the owner's heirs or as provided by will. A fee simple estate is also referred to as an *estate of inheritance* (because that is how it passes unless the owner chooses to sell the property) or simply as *fee ownership*. There are two major divisions of fee ownership: fee simple absolute and fee simple defeasible.

FIGURE 7.1

Freehold Estates

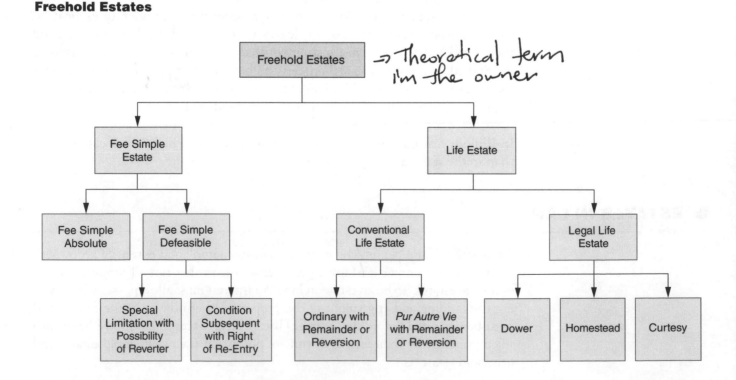

Fee simple absolute   A **fee simple absolute** estate is the highest interest in real estate recognized by law. Fee simple ownership is absolute ownership; the holder is entitled to all rights to the property. It is limited only by certain public and private restrictions, such as zoning laws and restrictive covenants.

Fee simple defeasible   A **fee simple defeasible** (or *defeasible fee*) estate is a qualified estate—that is, it is subject to the occurrence or nonoccurrence of some specified event. Two categories of defeasible estates exist: those *subject to a condition subsequent* or *by a fee simple determinable* (qualified by a special limitation).

A fee simple estate may be qualified by a *condition subsequent*. This means that the new owner must not perform some action or activity. The former owner retains a *right of re-entry* so that *if the condition is broken, the former owner can retake possession of the property through legal action.* Conditions in a deed under "condition subsequent" are different from restrictions or covenants because of the grantor's right to reclaim ownership. Possible reclamation of ownership does not exist under private restrictions made by builders or homeowner associations.

■ **FOR EXAMPLE**   An owner grants some land to her church "on the condition that there be no consumption of alcohol on the premises." This is a *fee simple subject to a condition subsequent.* If alcohol is consumed on the property, the former owner has the right to reacquire full ownership. It will be necessary for the grantor (or the grantor's heirs or successors) to go to court to assert that right.

A fee simple determinable is a fee simple defeasible estate that may be inherited. This estate is qualified by a special limitation (which is an occurrence or event). The language used to distinguish a special limitation—words such as *so long as* or *while* or *during*—is the key to creating this special limitation. The former owner retains a *possibility of reverter*. If the limitation is violated, the former owner (or heirs or successors) can reacquire full ownership with no need go the court. The deed is automatically returned to the former owner.

The right of reentry and possibility of reverter may never take effect. If they do, it will be only at some time in the future. Therefore, each of these rights is considered a **future interest.**

■ **FOR EXAMPLE**   When an owner gives land to a church, "so long as the land is used for only religious purposes," it is known as a *fee simple determinable.* The church had the full bundle of rights possessed by a property owner, but one of the "sticks" in the bundle is a control "stick," in this case. If the church ever decides to use the land for a nonreligious purpose, the original owner has the right to reacquire the land without going to court.

In Illinois

Because the right of re-entry and possibility of reverter can happen only in the future, they are considered future interests. While the condition passes from owner to owner forever, Illinois allows the original grantor's right of reverter to continue for only 40 years. After that time, the condition still may be enforced but no longer by the threat of losing the property. ■

Fee simple *determinable*:
"So long as"
"While"
"During"

Fee simple subject to a condition subsequent: "on condition that"

Memory Tip
■ *Determinable fee = Pre-determined events (re-version)*
■ *Special limitation = Specifically limited in advance*
■ *Defeasible with condition subsequent = Court subsequently must sanction re-entry*

Life Estate

A **life estate** is a freehold estate limited in duration to the life of the owner or the life of some other designated person or persons. Unlike other freehold estates, a life estate is not inheritable. It passes to future owners according to the prearranged provisions of the life estate.

A life tenant is not a renter like a tenant associated with a lease. A **life tenant** is entitled to the rights of ownership and can benefit from both possession and ordinary use and profits arising from ownership, just as if the individual were a fee simple. The life tenant's ownership may be sold, mortgaged, or leased, but it is always subject to the limitation of the life estate.

A life tenant's ownership rights are not absolute. The life tenant may not injure the property, such as by destroying a building or allowing it to deteriorate. In legal terms, such injury is known as *waste*. Those who eventually will own the property could seek an injunction against the life tenant or sue for damages if waste occurs.

Because the ownership will terminate on the death of the person against whose life the estate is measured, a purchaser, lessee, or lender can be affected if the life tenant has sold his rights. Because the interest is less desirable than a fee simple estate, the life tenant's limited rights must be disclosed if the property is sold. The new purchaser will lose the property at whatever point in time the original life tenant would have lost it.

Conventional life estate A *conventional life estate* is created intentionally by the owner. It may be established either by deed at the time the ownership is transferred during the owner's life or by a provision of the owner's will after the owner's death. The estate is conveyed to an individual who is called the life tenant. The life tenant has full enjoyment of the ownership for the duration of his life. When the life tenant dies, the estate ends and its ownership passes, often as a fee simple to another designated individual, or returns to the previous owner.

■ **FOR EXAMPLE** Anna, who has a fee simple estate in a property, conveys a life estate to Phil for Phil's lifetime. Phil is the life tenant. On Phil's death, the life estate terminates, and Anna once again owns the property. If Phil's life estate had been created by Anna's will, however, subsequent ownership of the property would be determined by the provisions of the will.

Pur autre vie A life estate also may be based on the lifetime of a person other than the life tenant. This is known as a life estate *pur autre vie* ("for the life of another"). Although a life estate is not considered an estate of inheritance, a life estate pur autre vie provides for the life tenant's "ownership" only until the death of the person against whose life the estate is measured.

■ **FOR EXAMPLE** Rita's good friend, Harry, struggles with finances, often not paying his apartment rent. Harry is set to inherit his family home after his father dies. In the meantime, Rita sets up a life estate pur autre vie giving Harry the rights of a life tenant to a cottage she owns. Harry's life tenancy terminates at the moment of his father's death, at which time ownership of the cottage will revert to Rita, Rita's heirs, or pass to a designated remainderman.

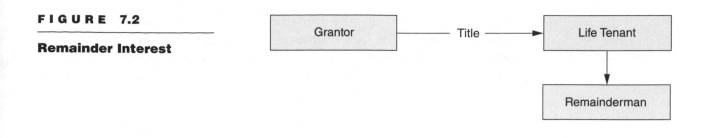

FIGURE 7.2

Remainder Interest

Remainder and reversion   The fee simple owner who creates a conventional life estate must plan for future ownership. When the life estate ends, it is replaced by a fee simple estate. The future owner of the fee simple estate may be designated in one of two ways:

1. **Remainder interest:** The creator of the life estate may name a *remainderman* as the person to whom the property will pass when the life estate ends. ("Remainderman" is the legal term; neither the term *remainderperson* nor the term *remainderwoman* is used legally.) (See Figure 7.2.)
2. **Reversionary interest:** The creator of the life estate may choose *not* to name a remainderman. In that case, the creator will recapture ownership when the life estate ends. The ownership is said to "revert to the original owner." (See Figure 7.3.)

■ **FOR EXAMPLE**   Craig conveys a ranch to Jean for Jean's lifetime and designates James to be the remainderman. While Jean is still alive, James owns a remainder interest, which is a nonpossessory estate; that is, James does not possess the property, but has an interest in it nonetheless. This is a future interest in the fee simple estate. If Jean should die, James automatically becomes the fee simple owner. On the other hand, Craig may convey a life estate in the ranch to Jean during and based on Jean's life. On Jean's death, ownership of the ranch reverts to Craig. Craig has retained a reversionary interest (also called a nonpossessory estate). Craig has a future interest in the ownership and may reclaim the fee simple estate when Jean dies. If Craig dies before Jean, Craig's heirs (or other individuals specified in Craig's will) will assume ownership of the ranch whenever Jean dies.

■ **IN PRACTICE**   Assisting a client with life estates, determinable fees, or fees with conditions subsequent should be the job of a skilled real estate attorney. Noting such situations in a sales transaction is, however, a responsibility of careful listing agents. In day-to-day practice, however, basic fee simple absolute—the simplest to understand form of ownership—will dominate.

Legal life estate   A *legal life estate* is not created voluntarily by an owner. Rather, it is a form of life estate established by state law. It becomes effective automatically when certain events occur. Dower, curtesy, and homestead are the legal life estates currently used in many states.

Legal Life Estate
■ Dower
■ Curtesy
■ Homestead

FIGURE 7.3

Reversionary Interest

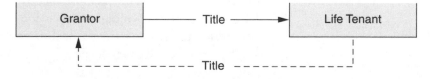

Dower and curtesy provide the nonowning spouse with a means of support after the death of the owning spouse. *Dower* is the life estate that a wife has in the real estate of her deceased husband. *Curtesy* is an identical interest that a husband has in the real estate of his deceased wife. In some states, dower and curtesy are referred to collectively as either dower or curtesy.

Dower and curtesy provide that the nonowning spouse has a right to a *one-half* or *one-third interest* in the real estate for the rest of the spouse's life, even if the owning spouse wills the estate to others. Because a nonowning spouse might claim an interest in the future, both spouses may have to sign the proper documents when real estate is conveyed. The signature of the nonowning spouse would be needed to release any potential common-law interests in the property being transferred.

In Illinois

Most separate or *marital property* states, including Illinois, have abolished the common-law concepts of dower and curtesy in favor of the **Uniform Probate Code**. This gives the surviving spouse the right to take what is called an *elective share* on the death of the other spouse. ■

A **homestead** is a legal life estate in real estate occupied as the family home. In effect, the home is protected from unsecured creditors during the occupant's lifetime. In states that have homestead exemption laws, a portion of the area or value of the property occupied as the family home is exempt from certain judgments for debts such as charge accounts and personal loans. The homestead is not protected from real estate taxes levied against the property or from a mortgage for the purchase or cost of improvements. In other words, if the debt is secured by the property, the property cannot be exempt from a judgment on that debt.

How does the homestead exemption actually work? The homestead merely reserves a certain amount of money for the family in the event of a court sale. On such a sale, any debts secured by the home, such as a mortgage, unpaid taxes, or mechanics' liens are paid from the proceeds first. The family then receives the amount reserved by the homestead exemption. Finally, whatever amount remains from the sale proceeds is applied to the family's unsecured debts, such as credit card debts.

In Illinois

Every homeowner in Illinois is entitled to a homestead estate up to a value of $15,000 for a single person and $30,000 for a married couple. The estate extends to all types of residential property including condominiums and cooperatives. Single persons, as well as householders with spouses and families, qualify.

No notice has to be recorded or filed to establish a homestead in Illinois. Therefore, prospective purchasers, lienholders, and other concerned parties are charged with inspecting a property to see if it serves as the residence of the potential debtor and if homestead estate rights can be claimed. ■

A family can have only one homestead at any one time. The Illinois homestead exemption is not applicable between co-owners but is applicable to any co-tenant's unsecured creditors. The exemption continues after the death of an individual for the benefit of the surviving spouse as long as she continues to occupy the homestead residence. It also extends for the benefit of all children living there until the youngest reaches 18 years of age.

A release, waiver, or conveyance of homestead is not valid unless it is expressed in writing and signed by the individual and his spouse, if applicable. The signatures of both spouses are always required on residential sales contracts, listing agreements, notes, mortgages, deeds, and other conveyances to release possible homestead rights, even if the property in question is owned solely by either the husband or the wife.

■ **FOR EXAMPLE**   Greenacre is Tony's Illinois homestead. In Illinois, the homestead exemption is $15,000. At a court-ordered sale, the property is purchased for $60,000. First, Tony's remaining $15,000 mortgage balance is paid, and then Tony receives $15,000. The remaining $30,000 is applied to Tony's unsecured debts. Of course, no sale would be ordered if the court could determine that nothing would remain from the proceeds for the unsecured creditors.

■ ENCUMBRANCES

Physical Encumbrances
- Restrictions
- Easements
- Licenses
- Encroachments

An **encumbrance** is a claim, charge, or liability that attaches to real estate. An encumbrance does not have a possessory interest in real property; it is not an estate. An encumbrance may decrease the value or obstruct the use of the property. In essence, an encumbrance is a right or an interest held by someone other than the property owner that affects title to the real estate but does not necessarily prevent a transfer of title.

Encumbrances may be divided into two classifications:

- *Liens*—(usually monetary charges)
- *Encumbrance*—restrictions, easements, licenses, and encroachments

Liens

A **lien** is a charge against property that provides security for a debt or an obligation of the property owner. If the obligation is not repaid, the lienholder is entitled to have the debt satisfied from the proceeds of a court-ordered or forced sale of the debtor's property. Real estate taxes, mortgages and trust deeds, judgments, and mechanics' liens all represent possible liens against an owner's real estate.

Deed Restrictions

Deed restrictions are private agreements that affect land use. Once placed in the deed by a previous owner, they "run with the land," limiting the use of the property and binding to all grantees. Deed restrictions are enforced by an owner of real estate and are included in the seller's deed to the buyer.

Covenants, conditions, and restrictions (CC&Rs) are private agreements that affect land use typically imposed by a developer or subdivider to maintain specific standards in a subdivision. CC&Rs are listed in the original development plans for the subdivision filed in the public record. They may be enforced by the original owner, developer, or by a homeowners' association.

Easements

An **easement** is the right to use the land of another for a particular purpose. It may exist in any portion of the real estate, including the airspace above or a right-of-way across the land. Easements are by agreement at any time or created by a seller when a property is conveyed.

An **appurtenant easement** is attached to the ownership of one parcel and allows the owner the use of a neighbor's land. For an appurtenant easement to exist, *two adjacent parcels of land must be owned by two different parties*. The parcel over which the easement runs is known as the **servient tenement;** the neighboring parcel that benefits is known as the **dominant tenement.** (See Figures 7.4 and 7.5.)

An appurtenant easement is part of the dominant tenement. If the dominant tenement is conveyed to another party, the beneficial easement transfers with the title, or "runs with the land." It will transfer with the deed of the dominant tenement forever unless the holder of the dominant tenement releases that right. Easements are considered encumbrances for disclosure, especially so for the servient tenement whose land is being used. While the easement must also be mentioned for a dominant tenement, the fact that it exists is often a marketing plus (such as an easement accessing a beach).

A **party wall** can be an exterior wall of a building that straddles the boundary line between two lots, or it can be a commonly shared partition wall between two connected properties. Each lot owner owns the half of the wall on his lot, and each lot owner has an appurtenant easement in the other half of the wall. A written party wall agreement must be used to create the easement rights. Expenses to build and maintain the wall are usually shared. A fence built on the lot line is treated

FIGURE 7.4

Easement Appurtenant

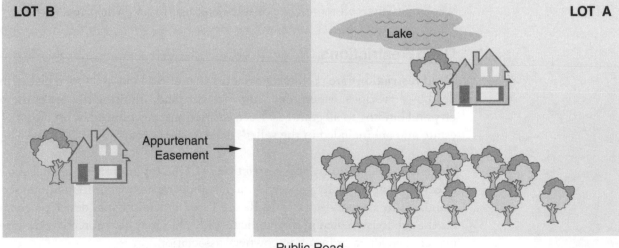

Public Road

The owner of Lot A has an appurtenant easement across Lot B to gain access to his property from the paved road. Lot A is dominant, and Lot B is servient.

FIGURE 7.5

Easement Appurtenant and Easement in Gross

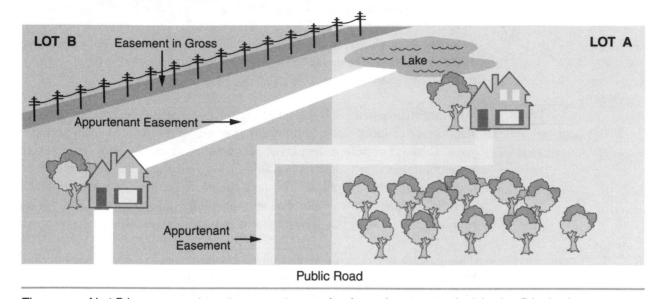

The owner of Lot B has an appurtenant easement across Lot A to gain access to the lake. Lot B is dominant and Lot A is servient. The utility company has an easement in gross across both parcels of land for its power lines. Note that Lot A also has an appurtenant easement across Lot B for its driveway. Lot A is dominant and Lot B is servient.

the same as a wall. A party driveway shared by and partly on the land of adjoining owners must also be created by written agreement, specifying responsibility for expenses. An **easement in gross** is an individual or company interest in or right to use someone else's land. (See Figure 7.5.) A railroad's right-of-way is an easement in gross, as are the rights-of-way of utility easements (such as for a pipeline or high-tension power line). Commercial easements in gross may be assigned, conveyed, and inherited. Personal easements in gross are usually not assignable. Generally, a personal easement in gross terminates on the death of the easement owner. An easement in gross is often confused with the similar but less formal *personal right of license*, discussed later in this chapter.

Creating an easement   An easement is commonly created by a written agreement between parties that establishes the easement right. It may be created by the grantor in a deed of conveyance, in which the grantor either reserves an easement over the sold land or grants the new owner an easement over the grantor's remaining land. Two other ways for an easement to be created are *easement by necessity* and *easement by prescription*.

Easement by necessity   An easement that is created when an owner sells a parcel of land that has no access to a street or public way except over the seller's remaining land is an **easement by necessity**. An easement by necessity is created by court order based on the principle that owners must have the right to enter and exit their land—the right of *ingress* (*enter*) and *egress* (*exit*); they cannot be landlocked.

Easement by prescription   If the claimant has made use of another's land for a certain period of time as defined by state law, an **easement by prescription**, or a *prescriptive easement*, may be acquired. The prescriptive period may vary from 10 years to 21 years in states. The claimant's use must have been continuous, exclusive, and without the owner's approval ("adverse"). The use must be visible, open, and notorious; that is, the owner must have been able to learn of it. A visible fence, continuous gardening on the back lot, or driving over property so often that ruts are visible are all examples.

In Illinois

To establish an easement by prescription in Illinois, the use must be adverse, exclusive, under claim of right, and continuous and uninterrupted for a period of *20 years*. Illinois law permits owners of pedestrian walkways in shopping centers and large commercial or industrial buildings to prevent the establishment of prescriptive easements by the public. To block the establishment of a prescriptive easement, the owner of any property must display signs or send a certified letter stating that access to or use of the property is by permission (and thus not adverse).

The concept of *tacking* provides that successive periods of continuous occupation by different parties may be combined (tacked) to reach the required total number of years necessary to establish a claim for a prescriptive easement. To tack on one person's possession to that of another, the parties must have been "successors in interest," such as an ancestor and his heir, a landlord and tenant, or a seller and buyer. ■

■ **FOR EXAMPLE**   Jana's property is located in a state with a prescriptive period of 20 years. For the past 22 years, Frank has driven his car across Jana's front yard every day to reach his garage with ease. Frank has an easement by prescription.

For 25 years, Linda has driven across Jana's front yard two or three times a year to reach her property when she's in a hurry. She does *not* have an easement by prescription because her use has not been continuous.

For 15 years, Elliot parked his car on Jana's property, next to Jana's garage. Six years ago, Elliot sold his house to Ned, who continued to park his car next to Jana's garage. Last year, Ned acquired an easement by prescription through *tacking*.

Easement by condemnation   An **easement by condemnation** is acquired for a public purpose, through the right of *eminent domain*. The owner of the servient tenement must be compensated for any loss in property value.

Terminating an easement   An easement terminates

- when the need no longer exists;
- when the owner of either the dominant or the servient tenement becomes the owner of both properties (also known as *termination by merger*);
- by release of the right of easement to the owner of the servient tenement;
- by abandonment of the easement (the intention of the parties is the determining factor);
- by non-use of a prescriptive easement;
- by adverse possession by the owner of the servient tenement;

- by destruction of the servient tenement (e.g., the demolition of a party wall);
- by lawsuit ("action to quiet title") against someone claiming an easement; or
- by property conversion (e.g., a residential use is converted to a commercial purpose).

Note: an easement may *not* automatically terminate for those reasons. Certain legal steps may be required.

License

A **license** is a personal *privilege* (not a right) to enter the land of another for a specific purpose. A license differs from an easement in that it can be terminated or canceled by the *licensor* (the person who granted the license) at any time. If the use of another's property is given orally or informally, it generally is considered to be a license rather than a personal easement in gross. A license ends on the death of either party or the sale of the land by the licensor.

■ **FOR EXAMPLE** One neighbor is asked by another for permission to park a boat in their driveway. The neighbor says, "Sure, go ahead!" The neighbor now has a license to park in the driveway, but the driveway owner may tell the neighbor to move the boat at any time. Similarly, a ticket to a theater or sporting event is a license: the holder is permitted to enter the facility and is entitled to a seat. However, if the ticketholder becomes rowdy or abusive, he may be asked to leave.

Encroachments

Survey sketch—Sketches only lot
Spot survey—Sketches lot *and* buildings

An **encroachment** occurs when all or part of a structure (such as a building, fence, or driveway) illegally extends beyond the land of its owner or beyond the legal building lines. An encroachment usually is disclosed by either a physical inspection of the property or a spot survey. A *spot survey* shows the location of all improvements located on a property and whether they extend over the lot or building lines. A spot survey is more informational and useful than a simple *survey sketch* with only the lot dimensions. If a spot survey and physical inspection show that a building encroaches on adjoining land, the neighbor may be able to either recover damages or secure removal of the portion of the building that encroaches. Unchallenged encroachments that last beyond a state's prescriptive period, however, may give rise to easements by prescription.

IN PRACTICE Because an undisclosed encroachment could create a serious situation if discovered late in a transaction, any known encroachments should be noted in a listing agreement and in the sales contract. Spot surveys provide evidence of encroachments. However, the new survey may only become available fairly late in the transaction process. For this reason, listing agents often encourage sellers to attach an existent survey to listing materials if one is available.

■ NATURE AND WATER: RIGHTS AND RESTRICTIONS

Whether for agricultural, recreational, or other purposes, waterfront real estate has always been desirable. Each state has strict laws that govern the ownership and use of water as well as the adjacent land. The laws vary among the states, but all are closely linked to climatic and topographic conditions. Where water is plentiful, for instance, many states rely on the simple parameters set by the common-law doctrines of riparian and littoral rights. Where water is scarce, a state may control all but limited domestic use of water according to the doctrine of prior appropriation.

Riparian Rights

Memory Tip

Riparian refers to rivers, streams, and similar waterways; *Littoral* refers to lakes, oceans, and similar bodies of water.

Riparian rights are common-law rights granted to owners of land along the course of a river, stream, or similar body of flowing water. Although riparian rights are governed by laws that vary from state to state, they generally include the unrestricted right to use the water. As a rule, the only limitation on the owner's use is that it cannot interrupt or alter the flow of the water or contaminate it in any way. In addition, an owner of land that borders a non-navigable waterway (that is, a body of water unsuitable for commercial boat traffic) owns the land under the water to the exact center of the waterway.

Land adjoining commercially navigable rivers, on the other hand, is usually owned to the water's edge, with the state holding title to the submerged land. (See Figure 7.6.) Navigable waters are considered public waterways on which the public has an easement or right to travel.

Littoral Rights

Closely related to riparian rights are the **littoral rights** of owners whose land borders commercially navigable lakes, seas, and oceans. Owners with littoral rights enjoy unrestricted use of available waters but own the land adjacent to the water only up to the mean high-water mark. (See Figure 7.7.) All land below this point is owned by the public.

Riparian and littoral rights are appurtenant (attached) to the land. The right to use the water belongs to whoever owns the bordering land and cannot be retained by a former owner after the land is sold.

FIGURE 7.6

Riparian Rights

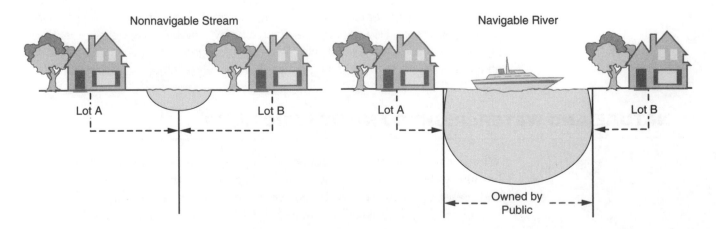

FIGURE   7.7

Littoral Rights

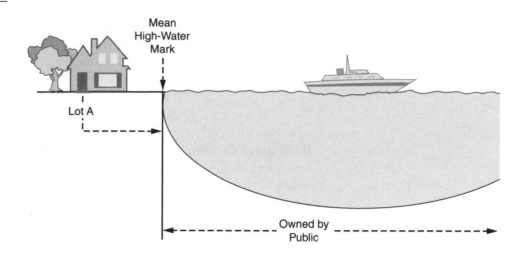

Accretion, Erosion, and Avulsion

The amount of land an individual owns may be affected by the natural action of water. An owner is entitled to all land created through **accretion**—increases in the land resulting from the deposit of soil by the water's action. (Such deposits are called *alluvion* or *alluvium*.) If water recedes, new land is acquired by *reliction*.

■   **FOR   EXAMPLE**   One famous example of soil deposits is visible in Galena, Illinois. The river running through town was large enough 150 years ago to help Galena become a major river port—the "largest in the West." Today, high and dry banks and old silt deposits can be seen that mark only faint memories of flowing water. In this case, accretion had a negative result. Because of silt deposits, the river became impassable by large ships within a few decades, changing the town's direction forever. Today, Galena is no longer a large trade port, but it has become a popular tourist destination with a rich history. It is also a prime example of major land, economic, and real estate development changes imposed by nature.

On the other hand, an owner may *lose land* through **erosion**. Erosion is the gradual and imperceptible wearing away of the land by natural forces such as wind, rain, and flowing water. Fortunately, erosion usually takes hundreds of years to have any noticeable effect on a person's property. Flash floods or heavy winds can increase the speed of erosion.

Avulsion is the sudden removal of soil by an act of nature. It is an event that causes the loss of land much less subtly than erosion. A major earthquake or a mudslide, for instance, can cause an individual's land holdings to become much smaller very quickly.

In Illinois

Those who sell Illinois real estate should be aware of the New Madrid fault, located mainly in Missouri but with potential impact on southern Illinois. Many geologists predict a serious New Madrid quake could occur at any time. ■

Doctrine of Prior Appropriation

In states where water is scarce, ownership and use of water are often determined by the **doctrine of prior appropriation**. Under this doctrine, the right to use any water, with the exception of limited domestic use, is *controlled by the state* rather than by the landowner adjacent to the water.

To secure water rights in prior appropriation states, a landowner must demonstrate to a state agency that he plans a *beneficial use* for the water, such as crop irrigation. If the state's requirements are met, the landowner receives a permit to use a specified amount of water for the limited purpose of the beneficial use. Although statutes governing prior appropriation vary from state to state, the priority of water rights is usually determined by the oldest recorded permit date.

Once granted, water rights attach to the land of the permit holder. The permit holder may sell a water right to another party. Issuance of a water permit does not automatically grant access to the water source. All rights of access over the land of another (easements) must be obtained by agreement from the property owner.

■ SUMMARY

Ownership of real estate is not absolute since a landowner's power to control that property is subject to public controls and private restrictions. Individual ownership rights are subject to certain powers held by federal, state, and local governments. Government powers include police power, eminent domain, taxation, and escheat.

An estate is the degree, quantity, nature, and extent of interest a person holds in land. Freehold estates are estates of indeterminate length and last until they are sold or the owner dies, and then they pass freely by will to stated parties. Less-than-freehold estates are called *leasehold estates*, and they involve landlords and rent rather than sales contracts and owners.

A freehold estate may be a fee simple estate or a life estate. A fee simple estate can be absolute (sometimes just called a *fee*) or defeasible (rights affected by the happening of some event). A fee simple absolute is the highest form of real estate ownership and comes with the most rights attached.

One type of defeasible fee, the fee simple determinable, is especially restrictive: The property automatically reverts to the original owner if a given promise or restriction is broken. Defeasible fees with condition subsequent must go to court for the original owner to gain right of re-entry over similar issues. Illinois limits right of reverter or re-entry by the original owner to a maximum length of 40 years. After that, the restrictions may still be enforced, but the original owner may not take back the property.

A conventional life estate is created by the owner of a fee estate and involves measuring limited ownership rights by the life of the owner, the life tenant, or a third party. On the death of this individual, ownership shifts based on the original owner's instructions in the life estate.

Legal life estates are created by law and are quite different from other life estates: these life estates involve long-lived (for the life of the property) monetary rights granted to homeowners and spouses of homeowners. Common legal life estates in the United States include dower and curtesy and homestead rights.

In Illinois

In Illinois, dower and curtesy has been replaced by spousal "elective shares," based on the Uniform Probate Code. Illinois offers homestead rights of $15,000 per individual ($30,000 for a married couple). This amount is protected from unsecured creditors. ■

Encumbrances against real estate can be legal or physical: liens, deed restrictions, easements such as driveways, licenses to use a property for a stated purpose, and physical encroachments such as fences or sheds built over a property line are all examples.

An easement is a right to use another's real estate. Easements are classified as interests in real estate but are not large enough in concept to be estates in land. There are two types of easements. Appurtenant easements involve two separately owned tracts. The tract benefited is known as the dominant tenement; the tract over which the easement is found is called the servient tenement. An easement in gross is a personal right, such as that granted to utility companies to maintain poles, wires, and pipelines. Personal easements in gross are possible and resemble a formalized license.

Easements may be created by agreement, express grant or reservation in a deed, by necessity, by prescription, or by condemnation. An easement can be terminated when the purpose of the easement no longer exists, by merger of both interests, or by release or abandonment of the easement.

A license is permission to enter another's property for a specific purpose. A license usually is created orally and is temporary; it can easily be ended by the property owner. A personal easement in gross is more formal than a license, in writing, and cannot be terminated without cause.

Ownership of land encompasses not only the land itself but also the right to use the water on or adjacent to it. Many states subscribe to the common-law doctrine of riparian rights, which allows ownership of non-navigable streams to their midpoint. Littoral rights are held by owners of land next to lakes and oceans; land rights here go to the mean high-water mark. In states where water is scarce, water use from natural flowing water is by doctrine of prior appropriation, and permits for water use are required, such as for watering crops.

In Illinois

Local units of government and quasi-governmental bodies are granted the power of *eminent domain* by the Illinois Constitution. A *quick-take* in Illinois is a fast proceeding to obtain title, such as for highway construction.

The Equity in Eminent Domain Act places the obligation on government to prove that an area is blighted before forcing property owners to sell their property for private development projects.

Real property escheats to the county in which it is located if no will was left and no heirs are found.

The period for an easement by prescription in Illinois is 20 years. ■

CHAPTER 7 QUIZ

1. A city decides to build a new library. Which of the following terms would *BEST* describe the action taken by the city to acquire the land for the new library?
   a. Zoning would allow the city to take the land by granting a variance for the library.
   b. County laws permit the city to take the land by escheat so long as the property owners are paid just compensation.
   c. The city has the right to take the land by eminent domain as long as just compensation is paid the property owners.
   d. The sheriff would sell the property at a public sale and pay the owners just compensation, and then the city could build the library.

2. A purchaser of real estate learned that his ownership rights could continue forever and that no other person could claim to be the owner or exert any ownership control over the property. This person owns a
   a. fee simple absolute interest.
   b. life estate.
   c. determinable fee estate.
   d. fee simple on condition.

3. A person owned the fee simple title to a vacant lot adjacent to a hospital and was persuaded to make a gift of the lot. She wanted to have some control over its use, so her attorney prepared her deed to convey ownership of the lot to the hospital "so long as it is used for hospital purposes." After completion of the gift, the hospital will own a
   a. fee simple absolute estate.
   b. license.
   c. fee simple determinable.
   d. leasehold estate.

4. Your neighbors regularly use your driveway to reach their garage, which is on their property. Your attorney explains that ownership of the neighbor's real estate includes an easement appurtenant giving them the right to do this. Your property is the
   a. dominant tenement.
   b. license property.
   c. a leasehold interest.
   d. servient tenement.

5. A tenant who rents an apartment from the owner of the property holds a(n)
   a. easement.
   b. license.
   c. freehold interest.
   d. leasehold interest.

6. If the owner of real estate does not take action against a persistent trespasser before the statutory period has passed, the trespasser may acquire
   a. an easement by necessity.
   b. a license.
   c. title by eminent domain.
   d. an easement by prescription.

7. A property owner wants to use water from a river that runs through his property to irrigate a potato field. To do so, the owner is required by his state's law to submit an application to the Department of Water Resources describing in detail the beneficial use he plans for the water. If the department approves the property owner's application, it will issue a permit allowing a limited amount of river water to be diverted onto the property. Based on these facts, it can be assumed that this property owner's state relies on which rule of law?
   a. Common-law riparian rights
   b. Common-law littoral rights
   c. Doctrine of prior appropriation
   d. Doctrine of highest and best use

8. Which is *NOT* a governmental power?

   a. Easement in gross
   b. Police power
   c. Eminent domain
   d. Taxation

9. Property deeded to a town "so long as" it is used "for recreational purposes" conveys a

   a. fee simple absolute.
   b. fee simple on condition precedent.
   c. leasehold interest.
   d. fee simple determinable.

10. A property owner has the legal right to pass over the land owned by her neighbor. This is a(n)

    a. estate in land.
    b. easement.
    c. police power.
    d. encroachment.

11. Which of the following is a legal life estate?

    a. Leasehold
    b. Fee simple absolute
    c. Homestead
    d. Determinable fee

12. A father conveys ownership of his residence to his daughter but reserves for himself a life estate in the residence. The interest the daughter owns during her father's lifetime is

    a. pur autre vie.
    b. a remainder.
    c. a reversion.
    d. a leasehold.

13. An owner has a fence on her property. By mistake, the fence extends one foot onto the property of a neighbor. The fence is an example of a(n)

    a. license.
    b. encroachment.
    c. easement by necessity.
    d. easement by prescription.

14. Encumbrances on real estate

    a. include easements and encroachments.
    b. make it impossible to sell the encumbered property.
    c. must all be removed before the title can be transferred.
    d. established by condition subsequent.

15. A person has permission from a property owner to hike on the owner's property during the autumn months. The hiker has a(n)

    a. easement by necessity.
    b. easement by prescription.
    c. determinable freehold interest.
    d. license.

16. In Illinois, the homestead exemption

    a. must be recorded with the county recorder to be in effect.
    b. is limited to $15,000 for single persons.
    c. can never be released.
    d. is limited to $15,000 per residence.

17. What can terminate an easement?

    a. Owner of either property becomes sole owner of both
    b. Continued use of the easement
    c. Release of the easement by the servient tenement
    d. Maintenance of the easement

18. In Illinois, a prescriptive easement may be

    a. established by 15 years of continuous, uninterrupted use without the owner's approval or permission.
    b. prevented by posting a "No Trespassing" sign in a prominent place on or near the boundary of the property.
    c. established by 20 years of continuous, uninterrupted, exclusive use under claim of right and without the owner's permission.
    d. defeated by showing that the adverse possession was not exercised by a single individual for the requisite period, but by successive parties in interest.

19. In Illinois, which of the following is *TRUE* when there is escheat of a decedent's real property?

a. The decedent's heirs must receive just compensation for the property's fair market value, measured at the time of the decedent's death.

b. The state laws of eminent domain apply.

c. Ownership of the property goes to the county in which it is located.

d. Ownership of the property goes to the state.

20. The type of easement that is a right-of-way for a utility company's power lines is a(n)

a. easement in gross.

b. easement by necessity.

c. easement by prescription.

d. nonassignable easement.

8

Forms of Real Estate Ownership

When you've finished reading this chapter, you should be able to

- ■ **identify** the four basic forms of co-ownership;

- ■ **describe** the ways in which various business organizations may own property;

- ■ **explain** how a tenancy in common, joint tenancy, and tenancy by the entirety are created and how they may be terminated;

- ■ **distinguish** cooperative ownership from condominium ownership; and

- ■ **define** the following *key terms*

common elements	limited liability company	severalty
community property	limited partnership	syndicate
condominium	marital property	tenancy by the entirety
cooperative	partition	tenancy in common
co-ownership	partnership	time-share estate
corporation	proprietary lease	time-share ownership
general partnership	right of survivorship	time-share use
joint tenancy	separate property	trust
joint venture		

■ FORMS OF REAL ESTATE OWNERSHIP

Real estate licensees provide buyers the information necessary for them to determine the type of ownership that best fit their needs. The choice of ownership will affect the ability to transfer the real estate, has tax implications, and decides rights to future claims.

Although the forms of ownership available are controlled by state laws, a fee simple estate may be held in three basic ways:

- ■ In *severalty*, where title is held by one individual
- ■ In *co-ownership*, where title is held by two or more individuals
- ■ In *trust*, where a third individual holds title for the benefit of another

■ OWNERSHIP IN SEVERALTY

Ownership in **severalty** occurs when property is owned by one individual or corporation. The term comes from the fact that this sole owner is "severed" or "cut off" from other owners. The severalty owner has sole rights to the ownership and sole discretion to sell, will, lease, or otherwise transfer part or all of the ownerships rights to another person. When a husband or wife owns property in severalty, state law may affect how ownership is held.

| In Illinois |

Sole ownership of property is quite common in Illinois, and title held in severalty presents no unique legal problems. However, when either a husband or wife owns property in severalty, lenders, grantees, and title insurers in Illinois usually require that the spouse sign in order to release any potential homestead rights. This is true for both listing and sales contracts. *A nonowning spouse who is a minor will also have to sign.* ■

■ CO-OWNERSHIP

When title to one parcel of real estate is held by two or more individuals, those parties are called *co-owners* or *concurrent owners*. Most states commonly recognize various forms of **co-ownership**. Individuals may co-own property as tenants in common, joint tenants, or tenants by the entirety, or they may co-own *community property* in states recognizing community property.

| In Illinois |

Illinois recognizes co-ownership and most traditional forms of co-ownership as discussed in this chapter *except* for community property (Illinois is a *marital property* state). Illinois also recognizes ownership in trust, in partnership, and by commercial entities such as corporations and limited liability companies. ■

Tenancy in Common

A parcel of real estate may be owned by two or more people as tenants in common. In a **tenancy in common,** each tenant holds an *undivided fractional interest* in the property. A tenant in common may hold, for example, a one-half or one-third interest in a property. *The physical property, however, is not divided into a specific half* *or third.* Hence, it is called an undivided fractional interest. The co-owners have *unity of possession*, meaning they are entitled to *possession* of the whole property. It is the ownership interest, not the property, that is divided.

The deed creating a tenancy in common may or may not state the fractional interest held by each co-owner. If no fractions are stated, the tenants are presumed to hold equal shares. For example, if five people hold title, each would own an undivided one-fifth interest.

Because the co-owners own separate interests, they can sell, convey, mortgage, or transfer their individual interests without the consent of the other co-owners. However, no individual tenant may transfer the ownership of the entire property. When one co-owner dies, the tenant's undivided interest passes according to the co-owner's will, heirs, or living trust.

In Illinois, a single deed may show the proportional interests of each tenant in common, *or* a separate deed issued to each tenant may show her individual proportional interest. When a single deed is used, lack of a description of each tenant's share means all tenants hold equal, undivided shares.

Tenants in common also hold their ownership interests in severalty. In other words, because the co-owners own separate interests, each can sell, convey, mortgage, or transfer their interest. The consent of the other co-owners is *not* needed. When one co-owner dies, the tenant's undivided interest passes according to the person's will. (See Figure 8.1.)

In Illinois, the law presumes that two or more owners hold title as tenants in common if the deed does not state specifically how title is to be held. ■

Joint Tenancy

Four Forms of Co-Ownership

1. Tenancy in common
2. Joint tenancy
3. Tenancy by the entirety
4. Community property

Most states recognize some form of **joint tenancy** in property owned by two or more people. The feature that distinguishes a joint tenancy from a tenancy in common is *unity of ownership*. Title is held as though all the owners, collectively, constitute one unit. Joint tenancy includes the **right of survivorship**. Upon the death of a joint tenant, the deceased's interest transfers directly to the surviving joint tenant(s). Essentially, there is one less owner. The joint tenancy continues until only one owner remains. This owner then holds title in severalty. The right

F I G U R E   8.1

Tenancy in Common

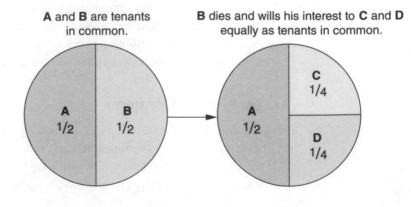

of survivorship applies only to the co-owners of the joint tenancy; it cannot pass to their heirs.

With each successive joint tenant death, the surviving joint tenants keep acquiring the deceased tenant's interest. The last survivor takes title in severalty and has all the rights of sole ownership, including the right to pass the property to any heirs. A will has no effect on a deceased joint tenant's property. (See Figure 8.2.)

Creating joint tenancies   A joint tenancy can be created only by the intentional act of conveying a deed or giving the property by will. It cannot be implied or created by operation of law. The deed must specifically state the parties' intention to create a joint tenancy, and the parties must be explicitly identified as joint tenants.

Four "unities" are required to create a joint tenancy:

1. Unity of *possession*—all joint tenants holding an undivided right to possession
2. Unity of *interest*—all joint tenants holding equal ownership interests
3. Unity of *time*—all joint tenants acquiring their interests at the same time
4. Unity of *title*—all joint tenants acquiring their interests by the same document

The four requirements for unities include the following:

- Title is acquired by one deed.
- The deed is executed and delivered at one time.
- The deed conveys equal interests to all of the parties.
- The parties hold undivided possession of the property as joint tenants.

> Typical wording in a deed creating a joint tenancy would be: *"To A and B as joint tenants and not as tenants in common."*

> **Memory Tip**
>
> The four unities necessary to create a joint tenancy may be remembered by the acronym **PITT**:
> Possession
> Interest
> Time
> Title

FIGURE 8.2

Joint Tenancy With Right of Survivorship

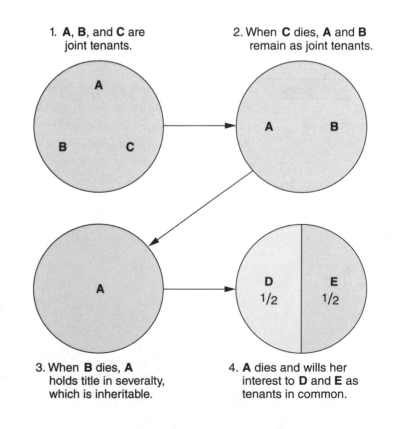

1. **A, B,** and **C** are joint tenants.

2. When **C** dies, **A** and **B** remain as joint tenants.

3. When **B** dies, **A** holds title in severalty, which is inheritable.

4. **A** dies and wills her interest to **D** and **E** as tenants in common.

In Illinois

Illinois allows a sole owner to execute a deed to herself and others "as joint tenants and not as tenants in common" in order to create a valid joint tenancy. ■

Terminating joint tenancies A joint tenancy is destroyed when any one of the four unities of joint tenancy is terminated. A joint tenant is free to convey interest in the jointly held property but doing so destroys the unities of time and title. The new owner cannot become a joint tenant and will hold interest as a tenant in common. Rights of other joint tenants, however, are unaffected.

■ **FOR EXAMPLE** A, B, and C hold title to a ranch as joint tenants. A conveys her interest to D. D now owns a fractional interest in the ranch as a tenant in common with B and C, who continue to own their undivided interest as joint tenants. (See Figure 8.3.) D is presumed to have a one-third interest, which may be reconveyed or left to D's heirs.

In Illinois

In the 1983 Illinois Supreme Court case *Minonk State Bank v. Gassman*, the court held that a joint tenant may unilaterally sever the tenancy by *conveying to* herself as a tenant in common even without the consent of co-owners. As a result, any owner holding property in a joint tenancy may elect, at any time, to become a tenant in common. At such time, that particular owner may will her interest to heirs or sell it. Any joint tenancy may be severed by mutual agreement of all cotenants, by conveying to third parties, or through a partition suit in the courts. ■

Termination of Co-Ownership by Partition Suit

Cotenants who wish to terminate their co-ownership may file an action in court to partition the property. **Partition** is a legal way to dissolve the relationship when the parties do not voluntarily agree to its termination. (A partition suit is also sometimes referred to as a *suit to partition*.) If the court determines that the land cannot be divided physically into separate parcels without destroying its value, the court will order the real estate sold. The proceeds of the sale will then be divided among the co-owners according to their fractional interests.

In Illinois

An Illinois partition suit may be filed by one or more of the owners in the circuit court of the county in which the subject parcel is located. The court appoints one or three commissioners who must, if possible, divide the property by legal description among the owners in title. If such division cannot be made without

FIGURE 8.3

Combination of Tenancies

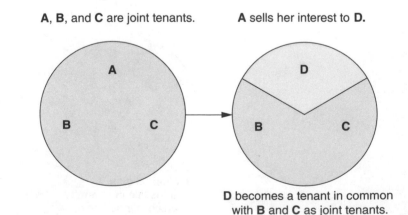

A, B, and C are joint tenants.

A sells her interest to D.

D becomes a tenant in common with B and C as joint tenants.

harming the rights of the co-owners, the commissioners must report a valuation of the property. The property is then offered for public sale at a price not less than two-thirds of the value as set by the commissioners.

All defendants to the suit (the co-owners who object to the partition) are required to pay their proportionate share of court costs and the lawyer fees of the plaintiff (the co-owner who is seeking partition). However, this requirement may be waived if the defendants have a sound and substantial defense. Upon completion of the sale, confirmation of the sale by the court, and delivery of a proper conveyance to the purchaser at the sale, the proceeds of the sale are delivered to the former cotenants according to the court order. Generally, the proceeds of the sale are divided among the former owners according to their fractional interests. ■

Tenancy by the Entirety

Tenancy by the entirety for married couples (a special joint tenancy):
- Right of survivorship
- No probate delays
- If lawsuits against spouse—no liens
- No half-interests
- To convey, *both* must sign
- Only for personal residence, homestead

Some states, including Illinois, allow husbands and wives to use a special form of co-ownership called **tenancy by the entirety** for their personal residence. In this form of ownership, each spouse has an equal, undivided interest in the property. (The term *entirety* refers to the fact that the owners are considered one indivisible unit: Under early common law, a married couple was viewed as one "legal person.") A husband and wife who are tenants by the entirety have rights of survivorship. During their lives, they can convey title only by a deed signed by both parties. One party cannot convey a one-half interest, and generally they have no right to partition or divide.

The main reason married couples own property by the entirety is that a lawsuit against one of the spouses will not put a lien on the house. A married couple owning property by the entirety would be eligible for homestead protection in the event of a judgment against either the husband or the wife. In addition, on the death of one spouse, the survivor automatically becomes the sole owner. Married couples often take title to property as tenants by the entirety so the surviving spouse can enjoy the benefits of ownership without the delay of probate proceedings.

In Illinois

Tenancy by the entirety is recognized in Illinois. To create a tenancy by the entirety, the deed must indicate that the property is to be owned "not as joint tenants or tenants in common, but as tenants by the entirety."

The Illinois Religious Freedom Protection and Civil Union Act was signed into law on January 31, 2011. The act's purpose is to provide persons entering into a civil union with the "obligations, responsibilities, protections, and benefits as are afforded or recognized by the law of Illinois to spouses." (750 ILCS 75/20) Civil union partners will be able to hold title to real property as tenants by the entirety after the act's effective date of June 1, 2011.

Memory Tip

The methods of terminating a tenancy by the entirety may be remembered by the acronym **JSDAD**: *Judgment Sale, Death, Agreement,* or *Divorce*

A tenancy by the entirety may be terminated in several ways:

- By a court-ordered sale of the property to satisfy a judgment against the husband and wife as joint debtors (the tenancy is dissolved so that the property can be sold to pay the judgment)

- By the death of either spouse (the surviving spouse becomes sole owner in severalty)

■ By agreement between both parties (through the execution of a new deed)

■ By divorce (which leaves the parties as tenants in common) ■

Community Property

Community property laws are based on the idea that a husband and wife, rather than merging into one entity, are equal partners in the marriage. Under community property laws, any property acquired during a marriage is considered to be obtained by mutual effort. As of 2010, nine states have adopted this concept; however, community property laws vary widely among the states. Essentially, all community property states recognize two kinds of property: separate property and community property.

Separate property is real or personal property that was owned solely by either spouse before the marriage. It also includes property acquired by gift or inheritance during the marriage, as well as any property purchased with separate funds during the marriage. Any income earned from a person's separate property belongs to that individual. Separate property can be mortgaged or conveyed by the owning spouse without the signature of the nonowning spouse.

Community property consists of all other property, both real and personal, acquired by either spouse during the marriage. Any conveyance or encumbrance of community property requires the signatures of both spouses. When one spouse dies, the survivor automatically owns one-half of the community property. The other half is distributed according to the deceased spouse's will.

If a community property spouse dies without a will, the other half is inherited by the surviving spouse or by the decedent's other heirs, depending on state law. *Community property does not provide an automatic right of survivorship as do joint tenancy and tenancy by the entirety.*

In Illinois

Illinois is *not* a community property state. However, as a **marital property** state, Illinois has certain similarities to community property states but with important differences. Illinois, too, breaks property down into two major categories based on marital status: marital property and nonmarital property. Illinois law recognizes that a husband and wife acquire joint rights in all property acquired after the date of marriage for the duration of the marriage. Illinois labels such property *marital property*, all of which will be divided between the two parties in the event of a divorce.

Nonmarital property is property that was acquired prior to the marriage or by gift or inheritance at any time, even during the marriage. If nonmarital property is exchanged for other property, if it increases in value, or if it returns income, the exchange, increase, or income also would be considered nonmarital property (property belonging to the individual). If nonmarital property is commingled with marital property, however, a presumption of *transmutation* is created: the resulting "mixed" property is presumed to be marital property. The spouses may execute an express contract agreeing to exclude certain property from being classified as marital property.

The *Illinois Marriage and Dissolution of Marriage Act* gives the courts flexibility in determining the precise division of marital property. This is a difference from community property states, which often impose a strict 50-50 division unless a prenuptial agreement is in place. ■

See Table 8.1 for a brief description of the forms of co-ownership.

■ TRUSTS

A **trust** is a device by which one person transfers ownership of property to someone else to hold or manage for the benefit of a third party. Perhaps a grandfather who wishes to ensure the college education of his granddaughter transfers his oil field to the grandchild's mother. He instructs the mother to use income from the trust to pay for the grandchild's college tuition. In this case, the grandfather is the *trustor*—the person who creates the trust. The granddaughter is the *beneficiary*—the person who benefits from the trust. The mother is the *trustee*—the party who holds legal title to the property and is entrusted with carrying out the trustor's instructions regarding the purpose of the trust. The trustee is a *fiduciary*, who acts in confidence or trust and has a special legal relationship with the beneficiary. The trustee's power and authority are limited by the terms of the trust agreement, will, or deed in trust.

IN PRACTICE   The legal and tax implications of setting up a trust are complex and vary widely from state to state. Attorneys and tax experts should always be consulted on the subject of trusts.

TABLE 8.1

Forms of Co-Ownership

	Property Held	Property Conveyed
Tenancy in Common	Each tenant holds a fractional undivided interest.	Each tenant can convey or devise his or her interest, but not entire interest.
Joint Tenancy	Unity of ownership. Created by intentional act; unities of possession, interest, time, title.	Right of survivorship; cannot be conveyed to heirs.
Tenancy by the Entirety	Husband and wife have equal undivided interest in their personal residence.	Right of survivorship; convey by deed signed by both parties. One party can't convey one-half interest.
Community Property	Husband and wife are equal partners in marriage. Real or personal property acquired during marriage is community property.	Conveyance requires signature of both spouses. No right of survivorship; when spouse dies, survivor owns one-half of community property. Other one-half is distributed according to will or, if no will, according to state law.

Most states allow real estate to be held in trust. Depending on the type of trust and its purpose, the trustor, trustee, and beneficiary can all be either people or legal entities, such as corporations. Trust companies are corporations set up for this specific purpose.

In Illinois Illinois permits real estate to be held in trust as part of a living or testamentary trust or as the sole asset in a land trust. ■

Real estate can be owned under living or testamentary trusts and land trusts. It also can be held by a group of investors in a real estate investment trust (REIT).

Living and Testamentary Trusts

A property owner may provide for her own financial care or for that of the owner's family by establishing a trust. This trust may be created by agreement during the property owner's lifetime (*living trust*, also called *inter vivos trust*) or established by will after the owner's death (*testamentary trust*). (Note that neither of these is related to the so-called living will, which deals with the right to refuse medical treatment.)

The person who creates the trust conveys real or personal property to a trustee (usually a corporate trustee), with the understanding that the trustee will assume certain duties. These duties may include the care and investment of the trust assets to produce an income. After paying the trust's operating expenses and trustee's fees, the income is paid to or used for the benefit of the beneficiary. The trust may continue for the beneficiary's lifetime, or the assets may be distributed when the beneficiary reaches a certain age or when other conditions are met.

Land Trusts

A few states, including Illinois, permit the creation of *land trusts*, in which real estate is the only asset. As in all trusts, the title to the property is conveyed to a trustee, and the beneficial interest belongs to the beneficiary. In the case of land trusts, however, the beneficiary usually is also the trustor. While the beneficial interest is personal property, the beneficiary retains management and control of the real property and has the right of possession and the right to any income or proceeds from its sale. Land trusts are frequently created for the conservation of farmland, forests, coastal land, and scenic vistas.

One of the distinguishing characteristics of a land trust is that the public records usually do not name the beneficiary. A land trust may be used for secrecy when assembling separate parcels. There are other benefits as well. A beneficial interest in a land trust is personal property and can be transferred by assignment, making the formalities of a deed unnecessary. The beneficial interest in property can be pledged as security for a loan without having a mortgage recorded. Because the beneficiary's interest is personal, it passes at the beneficiary's death under the laws of the state in which the beneficiary lived. If the deceased owned property in several states, additional probate costs and inheritance taxes can be avoided.

Have a trust for kids to avoid lawyers

Land Trusts
- Trustor often is beneficiary
- Trustee often is bank
- Beneficial interest is personal property
- Fully private ownership
- Useful in probate proceedings

A land trust ordinarily continues for a definite term, such as 20 years. If the beneficiary does not extend the trust term when it expires, the trustee is usually obligated to sell the real estate and return the net proceeds to the beneficiary.

In Illinois   Land trusts are used in Illinois. However, Illinois law requires that the trustee disclose the beneficiary's name to certain parties under specific circumstances.

The beneficiary's name must be revealed

- to the concerned housing authority within ten days after receiving a complaint of a violation of a building ordinance or law;
- when applying to any state of Illinois agency for a license or permit affecting the entrusted real estate;
- if selling the entrusted property by land contract (seller financing);
- if the trustee is named as a defendant in a private lawsuit or criminal complaint regarding the subject real estate (the beneficiary's identity can then be "discovered" by the plaintiff); or
- if a fire inspector or another officer is investigating arson. ■

A land trust ordinarily continues for a definite term, such as 20 years. If the beneficiary (who may also be the trustor or original owner) does not extend the trust term when it expires, the trustee usually is obligated to sell the real estate and return the net proceeds to the beneficiary.

IN PRACTICE   Licensees should be cautious in using the term *trust deed*. It can mean both a *deed in trust* (which relates to the creation of a living, testamentary, or land trust) and a *deed of trust* (a financing document similar to a mortgage). These documents are not interchangeable. Using an inaccurate term can cause serious misunderstandings.

Real Estate Investment Trust

By directing their funds into a real estate investment trust (REIT), real estate investors take advantage of the same tax benefits as do mutual fund investors. A real estate investment trust does not have to pay corporate income tax as long as 95 percent of its income is distributed to its shareholders. Certain other conditions also must be met. To qualify as a REIT, at least 75 percent of the trust's income must come from real estate. Investors purchase certificates in the trust, which in turn invests in real estate or mortgages (or both). Profits are distributed to investors.

Some advantages of the REIT are avoidance of corporate tax, centralized management, continuity of operation, transferability of interests, diversification of investment and the benefit of skilled real estate advice. Some of the disadvantages are that investments are passive in nature and usually restricted to very large real estate transactions. Losses cannot be passed through to the investor to offset her income and usually the trust must be registered with the Securities and Exchange Commission.

Other rules have been eased for when a sale constitutes a prohibited transaction, the amount of capital gain dividends a REIT may pay, penalties on distributions of deficiency dividends, definitions of rents and interest, treatment of shared appreciation mortgage income, and distribution requirements relating to income not accompanied by the receipt of cash.

■ OWNERSHIP OF REAL ESTATE BY BUSINESS ORGANIZATIONS

A business organization is a legal entity that exists independently of its members. Ownership by a business organization makes it possible for many people to hold an interest in the same parcel of real estate. Investors may be organized to finance a real estate project in various ways. Some provide for the real estate to be owned by the entity; others provide for direct ownership by the investors.

Partnerships

A **partnership** is an association of two or more persons who carry on a business for profit as co-owners. In a **general partnership,** all the partners participate in the operation and management of the business and share full liability for business losses and obligations. A **limited partnership,** on the other hand, consists of one or more general partners as well as limited partners. The business is run by the general partner or partners. The limited partners are not legally permitted to participate, and each can be held liable for business losses only to the extent of her investment. The limited partnership is a popular method of organizing investors because it permits investors with small amounts of capital to participate in large real estate projects with a minimum of personal risk.

General partnerships are dissolved and must be reorganized if one partner dies, withdraws, or goes bankrupt. In a limited partnership, however, the partnership agreement may provide for the continuation of the organization following the death or withdrawal of one of the partners.

In Illinois

Illinois has adopted the federal Uniform Partnership Act (UPA), which permits real estate to be held in the partnership name. The Uniform Limited Partnership Act (ULPA) also has been widely adopted. It establishes the legality of the limited partnership entity and provides that realty may be held in the limited partnership's name. Profits and losses are passed through the partnership to each partner, whose individual tax situation determines the tax consequences. ■

Corporations

A **corporation** is a legal entity (an artificial person) created under the authority of the laws of the state from which it receives its charter. A corporation is managed and operated by its *board of directors*. The *charter* sets forth the powers of the corporation, including its right to buy and sell real estate (based on a resolution by the board of directors). Because the corporation is a legal entity, it can own real estate in severalty or as a tenant in common. Some corporations are permitted by their charters to purchase real estate for any purpose; others are limited to purchasing only the land necessary to fulfill the entities' corporate purposes.

In Illinois

The creation and regulation of corporations in Illinois are governed by the Illinois Business Corporation Act. The federal Uniform Partnership Act also applies. ■

As a legal entity, a corporation continues to exist until it is formally dissolved. The death of one of the officers or directors does not affect title to property owned by the corporation.

Individuals participate, or invest, in a corporation by purchasing stock. Because stock is personal property, shareholders do not have direct ownership interest in real estate owned by a corporation. Each shareholder's liability for the corporation's losses is usually limited to the amount of her investment.

One of the main disadvantages of corporate ownership of income property is that the profits are subject to double taxation. As a legal entity, a corporation must file an income tax return and pay tax on its profits. The portion of the remaining profits distributed to shareholders as dividends is taxed again as part of the shareholders' individual incomes.

An alternative form of business ownership that provides the benefit of a corporation as a legal entity but avoids double taxation is known as an *S corporation*. Only the shares of the profits that are passed to the shareholders are taxed. The profits of the S corporation are not taxed. Though there is no limitation on the amount of corporate income for an S corporation, the shareholders are limited to 100.

S corporations are subject to strict requirements regulating their structure, membership, and operation. If the IRS determines that an S corporation has failed to comply with these detailed rules, the entity will be redefined as some other form of business organization, and its favorable tax treatment will be lost.

Syndicates and Joint Ventures

Generally speaking, a **syndicate** is two or more people or firms joined together to make and operate a real estate investment. A syndicate is not in itself a legal entity; however, it may be organized into a number of ownership forms, including co-ownership (tenancy in common, joint tenancy), partnership, trust, or corporation. A **joint venture** is a form of partnership in which two or more people or firms carry out a single business project. The joint venture is characterized by a time limitation resulting from the fact that the joint venturers do not intend to establish a permanent relationship.

Limited Liability Companies

The **limited liability company** (LLC) combines the most attractive features of limited partnerships and corporations. The members of an LLC enjoy the limited liability offered by a corporate form of ownership and the tax advantages of a partnership. In addition, the LLC offers flexible management structures without the complicated requirements of S corporations or the restrictions of limited partnerships. The structure and methods of establishing a new LLC or of converting an existing entity to the LLC form vary from state to state.

| In Illinois |

With passage of the Illinois Limited Liability Company Act in 1994, Illinois joined the majority of states that recognize limited liability companies as legitimate business organizations. ■

■ CONDOMINIUMS, COOPERATIVES, TOWN HOUSES, AND TIME-SHARES

A growing urban population, diverse lifestyles, changing family structures, and heightened mobility have created a demand for new forms of ownership. Condominiums, cooperatives, town houses, and time-share arrangements are four types of property ownership that have arisen in residential, commercial, and industrial markets to address our society's changing real estate needs.

Condominium Ownership

Condominium form of ownership has become increasingly popular throughout the United States. Condominium laws, often called *horizontal property acts*, have been enacted in every state. Under these laws, the owner of each unit holds a fee simple title to the unit. The individual unit owners also own a specified share of the undivided interest in the remainder of the building and land, known as the **common elements.** Common elements typically include such items as land, courtyards, lobbies, the exterior structure, hallways, elevators, stairways, and the roof, as well as recreational facilities such as swimming pools, tennis courts, and golf courses. (See Figure 8.4.) The individual unit owners own these common elements as *tenants in common*. As such, each has a fractional, undividable interest in the common locations, meaning the interest can be sold (along with the condo) but not any actual part of the common elements. State law usually provides, however, that unit owners do not have the same right to partition that other tenants in common have.

Condominium ownership is not restricted to highrise buildings. Lowrises, town houses, and detached structures can all be owned using the condominium type of ownership.

Creation of a condominium   Many states have adopted the Uniform Condominium Act (UCA). Under its provisions, a condominium is created and established when the owner of an existing building (or the developer of unimproved property) executes and records a detailed report and description of the property called a *declaration of condominium*.

FIGURE 8.4

Condominium Ownership

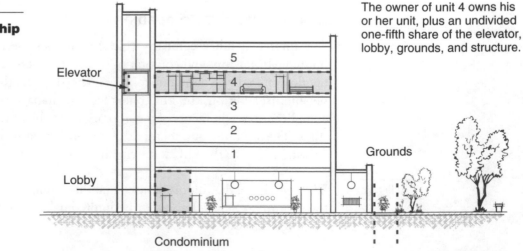

The owner of unit 4 owns his or her unit, plus an undivided one-fifth share of the elevator, lobby, grounds, and structure.

In Illinois

Illinois has *not* adopted the Uniform Condominium Act. In Illinois, creation of condominiums is governed by the Illinois Condominium Property Act (765 ILCS 605/). Under this law, an owner/developer may elect to submit a parcel of real estate as a condominium situation by recording a declaration to which is attached a three-dimensional plat of survey of the parcel showing the location and size of all units in the building. (*A building built on leased land may not be submitted for condominium designation in Illinois.*) Every unit purchaser acquires the fee simple title to the unit purchased, together with the percentage of ownership of the common elements that is set forth in the declaration and that belongs to that unit. This percentage is computed on the basis of the initial list prices of each unit.

Illinois Condominium Property Act

www.ilga.gov/
- Click on Illinois Compiled Statutes
- Click on Chapter 765
- Click on 765 ILCS 605/

The survey required with each declaration of condominium ownership must indicate the dimensions of each unit. This survey will show the outlines of the lot, the size and shape of each unit, and the elevation or height above base datum for the upper surface of the floor level and the lower surface of the ceiling level. The difference between these two levels represents the airspace owned in fee simple by the unit owner.

Many Illinois municipalities have adopted *conversion ordinances* to protect tenants in rental buildings whose owners wish to convert to condominiums. The ordinances also protect prospective purchasers. These laws typically allow tenants an opportunity to extend their leases and often guarantee first purchase rights. Additional protections often include disclosure of all material information, structural soundness of the building, adequacy of parking, and a variety of other concerns. These ordinances generally have been upheld by the courts as a valid exercise of police power. ∎

Ownership   Once the property is established as a condominium, each unit becomes a separate parcel of real estate that is owned in fee simple and may be held by one or more persons in any type of ownership or tenancy recognized by state law. A condominium unit may be mortgaged like any other parcel of real estate. The unit can usually be sold or transferred to whomever the owner chooses unless the condominium association provides for a right of first refusal. In such a case, the owner is required to offer the unit at the same price to the other owners in the condominium or the association before accepting an outside purchase offer.

Real estate taxes are assessed and collected on each unit as an individual property. Default in the payment of taxes or a mortgage loan by one unit owner may result in a foreclosure sale of that owner's unit. One owner's default, however, does not affect the other unit owners.

Operation and administration   The condominium property is administered by an association of unit owners, often called a *homeowners' association (HOA)*. The association may be governed by a board of directors or another official entity, and it may manage the property on its own or hire a property manager.

The association must enforce any rules it adopts regarding the operation and use of the property. The association is responsible for the maintenance, repair, cleaning, and sanitation of the common elements and structural portions of the property. It also must maintain fire, extended-coverage, and liability insurance.

The expenses of maintaining and operating the building are paid by the unit owners in the form of fees and assessments. Both fees and assessments are imposed and collected by the owners' association (see discussion of a PUD in Chapter 3). Recurring fees (referred to as *assessments* or *condo fees*) are paid by each unit owner. The fees often are due monthly, but the schedule may be quarterly, semiannually, or annually, depending on the provisions of the bylaws. The size of an individual owner's fee is generally determined by the size of the owner's unit. For instance, the owner of a three-bedroom unit pays a larger share of the total expense than the owner of a one-bedroom unit. If the fees are not paid, the association may seek a court-ordered judgment to have the delinquent owner's unit sold to cover the outstanding amount.

Special assessments are special payments required of unit owners to address some specific expense, such as a new roof. Assessments are structured in the same way as condo fees: owners of larger units pay proportionately higher assessments.

| In Illinois |

These general condominium guidelines apply under the Condominium Property Act in Illinois. However, the property may be removed from condominium status at any time by the unanimous consent of all owners and all lienholders, as evidenced by a recorded written instrument. All owners would then be tenants in common. ■

Cooperative Ownership

In a **cooperative**, a corporation holds title to the land and building. The corporation offers shares of stock to prospective tenants.

The price the corporation sets for each apartment becomes the price of the stock. The purchaser becomes a shareholder in the corporation by virtue of this stock ownership and receives a **proprietary lease** to the apartment for the life of the corporation. Because stock is personal property, the cooperative tenant-owners do not own real estate. Instead, they own an interest in a corporation that has only one asset: the building.

Operation and management The operation and management of a cooperative are determined by the corporation's bylaws. Through their control of the corporation, the shareholders of a cooperative control the property and its operation. They elect officers and directors who are responsible for operating the corporation and its real estate assets. Individual shareholders are obligated to abide by the corporation's bylaws.

An important issue in most cooperatives is the method by which shares in the corporation may be transferred to new owners. The bylaws may require that the board of directors approve any prospective shareholders. In some cooperatives, a tenant-owner must sell the stock back to the corporation at the original purchase price so that the corporation realizes any profits when the shares are resold. In others, if the stock is sold for the latest "going price" on the unit, stock profits may go to the departing tenant or at least be shared.

■ **FOR EXAMPLE** A controversial celebrity may attempt to move into a highly exclusive cooperative apartment building but be blocked by the cooperative's board. In refusing to allow a controversial personality to purchase shares, the board can cite the unwanted publicity and media attention other celebrity tenants might suffer.

The corporation incurs costs in the operation and maintenance of the entire parcel, including both the common property and the individual apartments. These costs include real estate taxes and any mortgage payments the corporation may have. The corporation also budgets funds for such expenses as insurance, utilities, repairs and maintenance, janitorial and other services, replacement of equipment, and reserves for capital expenditures. Funds for the budget are assessed to individual shareholders, generally in the form of monthly fees similar to those charged by a homeowners' association in a condominium.

Unlike in a condominium association, which has the authority to impose a lien on the title held by a unit owner who defaults on maintenance payments, the burden of any defaulted payment in a cooperative falls on the remaining shareholders. Each shareholder is affected by the financial ability of the others. For this reason, approval of prospective tenants by the board of directors frequently involves financial evaluation. If the corporation is unable to make mortgage and tax payments because of shareholder defaults, the property might be sold by court order in a foreclosure suit. This could destroy the interests of all shareholders, including those who have paid their assessments.

Advantages Cooperative ownership, despite its risks, has become desirable in recent years for several reasons. Lending institutions view the shares of stock as acceptable collateral for financing. The availability of financing extends the possible transfer of shares to modest purchasers in many co-ops. As a tenant-owner, rather than a tenant who pays rent to a landlord, the shareholder has some control over the property. Tenants in cooperatives also enjoy certain income tax advantages. The IRS treats cooperatives as it does fee simple interest in single homes or condominiums in regard to deductibility of loan interest, property taxes, and homesellers' tax exclusions. Finally, owners enjoy freedom from maintenance.

| In Illinois |

Illinois real estate licensees are permitted to list and sell cooperative units and interests without obtaining a securities license. ■

Town House Ownership

A **town house** is a popular form of housing in urban areas. The term *town house* is often used to describe any type of housing connected by common walls. In fact, the town-house concept is a cross between single-family houses and apartments. Normally, each town house has two floors and is located on a small lot.

Most town house developments are more similar to a PUD. Title to each unit and lot is vested in the individual owner. Each owner also has a fractional interest in the common areas and is proportionately financially responsible. Common areas may include open spaces, recreational facilities, driveways, and sidewalks. The owner may sell, lease, will, or otherwise transfer the dwelling unit. The rights to the use of the common areas pass with title.

Time-Share Ownership

Time-share ownership permits multiple purchasers to buy interests in real estate, usually a resort property. Each purchaser receives the right to use the facilities for a certain period of time. A *time-share estate* includes a real property interest in condominium ownership; a *time-share use* is a contract right in which a third party retains ownership of the real estate.

In Illinois

The promotion or sale of all time-share units is strictly regulated by the Illinois Real Estate Time-Share Act of 1999 (765 ILCS 101). The Time-Share Act now provides for minimum requirements of a time-share listing agreement. It provides for disclosures, in addition to those already required, to a prospective purchaser of a time-share that includes the status of assessments and real estate or personal property taxes. It also provides that a time-share resale agent have a real estate license unless the licensee sells less than eight time-shares per year. The Illinois Real Estate Time-Share Act of 1999 applies to both in-state and out-of-state time-share sales.

In addition, pursuant to the Real Estate License Act of 2000, a person who engages in the sale of time-shares must have a real estate license. Certain exemptions to the real estate licensing requirement apply:

- An exchange company registered under the Real Estate Time-Share Act of 1999 and their regular employees
- An existing time-share owner who, for compensation, refers prospective purchasers, but only if the existing time-share owner
  - refers no more than 20 prospective purchasers in any calendar year,
  - receives no more than $1,000, or its equivalent, for referrals in any calendar year; and
  - limits her activities to referring prospective purchasers of time-share interests to the developer or the developer's employees or agents and does not show, discuss terms or conditions of purchase, or otherwise participate in negotiations with regard to time-share interests. ■

A **time-share estate** is a fee simple interest. The owner's occupancy and use of the property are limited to the contractual period purchased. The owner is assessed for maintenance and common area expenses based on the ratio of the ownership period to the total number of ownership periods in the property. Time-share estates theoretically never end because they are real property interests. However, the physical life of the improvements is limited and must be looked at carefully when considering such a purchase.

The main difference between a time-share estate and a time-share use lies in the interest transferred to an owner by the developer of the project. A **time-share use** consists of the right to occupy and use the facilities for a certain number of years. At the end of that time, the owner's rights in the property terminate. In effect, the developer has sold only a right of occupancy and use to the owner, not a fee simple interest.

In Illinois

The Illinois Real Estate Time-Share Act of 1999 requires that all developers and their agents must register with the IDFPR and hold a real estate license unless the licensee sells less than eight time-shares per year. A time-share listing agreement must provide for minimum requirements. Each purchaser must be given a detailed *public offering statement* before signing the contract. The statement discloses extensive information about the property such as time periods, percentage of common expenses for each unit, use and occupancy restrictions, and total number of units. In addition, disclosures to purchasers must include the status of assessments and real estate or personal property taxes. The statement also must include information about the developer and property management.

Any purchase contract entered into by a purchaser of a time-share interest shall be voidable by the purchaser, without penalty, within five calendar days after the receipt of the public offering statement or the execution of the purchase contract, whichever is later. The purchase contract shall provide notice of the five-day cancellation period as well as the name and mailing address to which any notice of cancellation shall be delivered.

Upon such cancellation, the developer or resale agent shall refund to the purchaser all payments made by the purchaser, less the amount of any benefits actually received pursuant to the purchase contract. The refund shall be made within 20 calendar days after the receipt of the notice of cancellation, or receipt of funds from the purchaser's cleared check, whichever occurs later.

The Real Estate Time-Share Act of 1999 places developers and their agents under strict requirements regarding potential misrepresentation, such as predicting specific or immediate market value increases or disclosure of details of any prizes offered. Violations can result in the suspension or revocation of a certificate or permit issued under the act. ■

Membership camping is similar to time-share use. The owner purchases the right to use the developer's facilities, which usually consist of an open area with minimal improvements (such as camper and trailer hookups and restrooms). Normally, the owner is not limited to a specific time for using the property; use is limited only by weather and access.

IN PRACTICE   The laws governing the development and sale of time-share units are complex. In addition, the sale of time-share properties may be subject to federal securities laws. In many states, time-share properties are now subject to subdivision requirements. Real estate licensees providing assistance on time-shares need to be well-versed in the laws, benefits, and risks of such ownership and should counsel their clients to seek legal advice before purchasing.

■ SUMMARY

Sole ownership, or ownership in severalty, means that title is held by one natural person or legal entity. Under co-ownership, title can be held concurrently by more than one person or legal entity in several ways.

Tenancy in common provides that each party holds separate title but shares possession of the whole property with the other owners, each of which has separate interests. Upon the death of a tenant in common, her interest passes to any legal heirs. When two or more parties hold title to real estate in Illinois, they do so as tenants in common by default unless they express another intention.

Joint tenancy indicates two or more owners with the right of survivorship. The intention of the parties to establish a joint tenancy must be stated clearly. The four unities of possession, interest, time, and title (PITT) must be present.

Tenancy by the entirety, in those states where it is recognized (including Illinois), is a type of joint tenancy between husband and wife. It gives the couple the right of survivorship in all lands they acquired during marriage. During their lives, both must sign the deed for any title to pass to a purchaser. Liens may not be placed on a property held in this way if such liens are the result of one spouse's legal problems. Community property exists only in certain states, such as California. Usually, the property acquired by combined efforts during the marriage is community property, and each spouse owns one-half but with no right of survivorship. (Properties acquired by a spouse before the marriage and through inheritance or gifts during the marriage are considered separate property.)

Real estate ownership may be held in trust. All trusts involve three conceptual parts: trustor, trustee, and beneficiary. In a land trust (common in Illinois), the trustor and the beneficiary are typically the same party. To create any trust, the trustor conveys title and visible control to a third-party trustee, for the benefit of the beneficiary. Names of the owners of a land trust are not usually available except in court suits or building violations involving the subject property, arson investigations, or other legally noted exceptions.

Various types of business organizations may own real estate. A corporation is a legal entity and can hold title to real estate in severalty. While a partnership is technically not a legal entity, the Uniform Partnership Act and the Uniform Limited Partnership Act, adopted by most states, recognize a partnership as an entity that can own property in the partnership's name. A limited liability company (LLC) combines the limited liability offered by a corporate form with the tax advantages of a partnership without the complicated requirements of S corporations or the restrictions of limited partnerships. A syndicate is simply an association of two or more people or firms that invest in real estate. Many syndicates are joint ventures assembled for only a single project.

Cooperatives are a form of ownership in which actual title is held by one entity (a corporation or trust) that pays taxes, mortgage interest, and principal, as well as all operating expenses. Shareholders occupy the units, buy initial stock, and/or also pay monthly assessments in order to do so. They sometimes share in stock profits when they depart the building and their "shares" are sold.

In a condominium setting, each owner-occupant holds fee simple title to a unit plus a share of the common elements. Each unit owner receives an individual tax bill and may mortgage the unit. Her bankruptcy or default does not affect other building occupants. Expenses for operating the building are collected by an owners' association through monthly assessments.

A town house is a popular form of housing in urban areas. Normally, each town house has two floors and is located on a small lot.

Time-sharing enables multiple purchasers to own estates or "use interests" in real estate, with the right to use the property for a part of each year.

In Illinois

Illinois is a marital property state. Any property acquired during the marriage is likely to be viewed as marital, shared property unless it is by gift or inheritance to only one spouse. This is true even for real estate set up as ownership in severalty during the marriage. If nonmarital inherited property or gift monies are commingled, transmutation can legally transform them into marital property. Divorce laws in Illinois give courts flexibility in distributing marital property. ■

CHAPTER 8 QUIZ

1. The four unities of possession, interest, time, and title are associated with which of the following?
   a. Community property
   b. Severalty ownership
   c. Tenants in common
   d. Joint tenancy

2. What is the difference between tenancy in common and joint tenancy?
   a. Tenancy in common is characterized by right of survivorship; joint tenancy is characterized by unity of possession.
   b. Tenancy in common ownership must contain specific wording; joint tenancy is presumed by the law when two or more people own property unless the deed states otherwise.
   c. Under tenancy in common ownership, each owner has the right to sell, mortgage, or lease her interest without the consent of the other owners; this is not true in joint tenancy.
   d. Tenancy in common is an inheritable estate; joint tenancy is characterized by the right of survivorship.

3. Three women were concurrent owners of a parcel of real estate. When one woman died, her interest, according to her will, became part of her estate. The deceased was a
   a. joint tenant.
   b. tenant in common.
   c. tenant by the entirety.
   d. severalty owner.

4. A legal arrangement under which the title to real property is held to protect the interests of a beneficiary is a
   a. trust.
   b. corporation.
   c. limited partnership.
   d. general partnership.

5. Which statement is *TRUE* regarding a cooperative?
   a. Title to the land and building are held by different owners.
   b. Unit owners hold real property interests.
   c. Maintaining and operating a cooperative is paid for by the corporation from charges assessed to unit owners, generally in the form of monthly fees.
   d. Because their proprietary leases are real property, unit owners are exempt from the fees or assessments condominium owners are often required to pay for building maintenance and operation.

6. A man purchases an interest in a house. He is entitled to the right of possession only between July 10 and August 4 of each year. Which of the following is MOST likely the type of ownership the man purchased?
   a. Cooperative
   b. Condominium
   c. Time-share estate
   d. Life estate

7. Because a corporation is a legal entity (an artificial person), real estate owned by it is owned in
   a. trust.
   b. partnership.
   c. severalty.
   d. survivorship tenancy.

8. Which is a form of co-ownership?
   a. Severalty
   b. Sole owner
   c. Tenancy at will
   d. Joint tenancy

9. A married couple owns a mansion with a right of survivorship. Theirs is most likely
   a. severalty ownership.
   b. community property.
   c. a tenancy in common.
   d. an estate by the entirety.

10. Two people are co-owners of a small office building with the right of survivorship. One of the co-owners dies intestate and leaves nothing to be distributed to his heirs. Which of the following would explain why the second co-owner acquired the deceased's interest?
    a. Adverse possession
    b. Joint tenancy ✓
    c. Law of escheat
    d. Reversionary interest

11. Which of the following BEST proves one's right to live in a cooperative?
    a. Tax bill for the individual unit
    b. Existence of a reverter clause
    c. Shareholder's stock certificate ✓
    d. Right of first refusal

12. Which of the following statements applies to both joint tenancy and tenancy by the entirety?
    a. There is no right to file a partition suit.
    b. The survivor becomes a severalty owner. ✓
    c. A deed signed by one owner will convey a fractional interest.
    d. A deed will not convey any interest unless signed by both spouses.

13. If property is held by two or more owners as tenants with survivorship rights, the interest of a deceased cotenant will be passed to the
    a. surviving owner(s). ✓
    b. heirs of the deceased.
    c. state under the law of escheat.
    d. trust under which the property was owned.

14. Which of the following statements is TRUE according to the Illinois Real Estate Time-Share Act?
    a. Developers, but not their agents, are required to register with the IDFPR.
    b. Purchasers must be given a disclosure statement about the property immediately after signing the purchase contract.
    c. Purchasers have 24 hours in which to request a disclosure statement from a developer.
    d. The statute guarantees purchasers a five-day right to rescind a time-share purchase contract. ✓

15. The names of the beneficiaries of a land trust must be revealed by the trustee to
    a. any member of the public who is interested in the beneficiary's identity.
    b. any Illinois agency when applying for a license or permit affecting the entrusted real estate. ✓
    c. any unsecured creditor of the beneficiary.
    d. a licensed real estate broker if the broker is assisting in the sale or rental of the entrusted property.

16. Every co-owner of real estate in Illinois has the right to file a suit for partition when the property is held in which of the following ways?
    a. Joint tenancy or tenancy in common ✓
    b. Land trust
    c. Condominium or cooperative
    d. Time-share use or estate

17. Title to land in Illinois may be held and conveyed in which of the following ways?
    a. In the name of a partnership ✓
    b. As joint tenants only if the property is owned by a husband and wife as their principal residence
    c. As tenants in common with rights of survivorship
    d. All of the above

18. If the deed of conveyance to Illinois land transfers title to two or more co-owners without defining the character of the co-ownership, which of the following statements is *TRUE*?

a. The property is construed as being held in joint tenancy.

b. The co-owners are tenants in common.

c. While proper in some states, such a deed would be an invalid conveyance under Illinois law.

d. By statute, such co-owners would have the right of survivorship.

19. A and B held title to an apartment building as joint tenants with rights of survivorship. A and B had an argument, and A didn't like the possibility that B would acquire total ownership of the building if A died. Therefore, A executed a deed to himself as a tenant in common and later willed his interest to C. If these facts occurred in Illinois, which of the following statements accurately describes A's action?

a. A's action is illegal under Illinois law.

b. While not necessarily illegal, A's action has no effect on the joint tenancy.

c. A's goal of severing the joint tenancy can be accomplished only by a partition suit.

d. A's action legally severs the joint tenancy.

20. Which of the following is necessary to convert an apartment building to condominium ownership in Illinois?

a. The owner records a condominium declaration with a three-dimensional plat.

b. The owner must record a certificate stating that the current tenants have been duly surveyed and that a majority of all tenants are in favor of the conversion.

c. The existing tenants elect a board of directors having the power to act as legal administrator for the property, and the board petitions the state under the Condominium Property Act for certification as a condominium.

d. The owner must execute and record a declaration of condominium under the Uniform Condominium Act as adopted in Illinois.

CHAPTER 9

Legal Descriptions

■ **LEARNING OBJECTIVES**   *When you've finished reading this chapter, you should be able to*

■ **identify** the three methods used to describe real estate;

■ **describe** how a survey is prepared;

■ **explain** how to read a rectangular survey description;

■ **distinguish** the various units of land measurement; and

■ **define** the following *key terms*

air lots	legal description	ranges
base lines	lot-and-block (or recorded plat) system	rectangular (government) survey system
benchmarks	metes-and-bounds method	sections
correction line	monuments	survey
datum	plat map	townships
fractional sections	point of beginning (POB)	township lines
government check	principal meridians	township tiers
government lots		
government survey system		

■ DESCRIBING LAND

Consumers expect to become owners of every bit of land to which they are entitled. Ownership of land purchased must be precisely described in the legal documents. Though lawyers review the legal descriptions for accuracy, the real estate licensee needs to understand how the land is described and the reasoning behind that description.

A street address, while usually enough to find the location of a particular building, is not precise enough to describe legal ownership. Addresses change as streets are renamed, or rural roads might become public streets and growing communities. Sales contracts, deeds, and mortgages require a more specific (or *legally sufficient*) description of property to be binding.

A **legal description** is a detailed way of describing a parcel of land for documents such as deeds and mortgages that will be accepted in a court of law. The description is based on information collected through a **survey**—the process by which boundaries are measured by calculating the dimensions and area to determine the exact location of a piece of land. Courts have stated that a description is legally sufficient if it allows a surveyor to locate the parcel. In this context, *locate* means that the surveyor must be able to define the exact boundaries of the property. A street address will not tell a surveyor how large the property is or where it begins and ends. Several alternative systems of identification have been developed to express a legal description of real estate.

■ METHODS OF DESCRIBING REAL ESTATE

Three basic methods can be used to describe real estate:

1. Metes and bounds
2. Rectangular (or government) survey
3. Lot and block (recorded plat)

Although each method can be used independently, the methods may be combined in some situations. Some states use only one method; others use all three.

Metes-and-bounds descriptions were used in the original thirteen colonies and in those states that were being settled while the rectangular survey system was being developed. Today, as technology allows for greater precision and expanded record keeping, there is greater integration of land description information. Currently, the Federal Bureau of Land Management and the USDA Forest Service are developing the National Integrated Land System (NILS) in cooperation with states, counties, and private industry. This new system of land description is designed to be compatible with both the metes-and-bounds description and the rectangular survey system. The NILS has unified the worlds of surveying into the Graphic Information System (GIS) for the management of *cadastral* (public survey records) and land parcel information.

Metes-and-Bounds Method

The **metes-and-bounds method** is the oldest type of legal description. *Metes* means distance, and *bounds* means compass directions or angles. The method relies on a property's physical features to determine the boundaries and measurements of the parcel. A metes-and-bounds description always starts at a designated place on the parcel, called the **point of beginning (POB)**. From there, the surveyor proceeds around the property's boundaries. The boundaries are recorded by referring to linear measurements, natural and artificial landmarks (called *monuments*), and directions. A metes-and-bounds description always ends back at the POB so that the tract being described is completely enclosed.

Monuments are fixed objects used to identify the POB, the ends of boundary segments, or the location of intersecting boundaries. A monument may be a natural object, such as a stone, large tree, lake, or stream. It may also be a man-made object, such as a street, highway, fence, canal, or markers (iron pins or concrete posts) placed by surveyors. Measurements often include the words "more or less" because the location of the monuments is more important than the distances given in the wording. In other words, the actual distance between monuments takes precedence over any linear measurements in the description.

An example of a metes-and-bounds description of a parcel of land (pictured in Figure 9.1) follows:

> *A tract of land located in Old Town, Liberty County, Virginia, is described as follows: Beginning at the intersection of the east line of Jones Road and the south line of Old Road; then east along the south line of Old Road 200 feet; then south 15° east 216.5 feet, more or less, to the center thread of Town Creek; then northwesterly along the center line of said creek to its intersection with the east line of Jones Road; then north 105 feet, more or less, along the east line of Jones Road to the point of beginning.*

When used to describe property within a town or city, a metes-and-bounds description may begin as follows:

> *Beginning at a point on the southerly side of Kent Street, 100 feet easterly from the corner formed by the intersection of the southerly side of Kent Street and the easterly side of Broadway; then. . . .*

In this description, the POB is given by reference to the corner intersection. Again, the description must eventually close by returning to the POB.

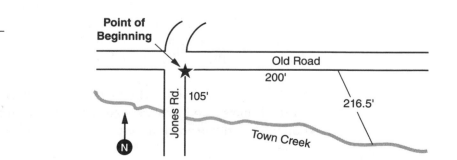

IN PRACTICE   Metes-and-bounds descriptions can be complex and should be handled with extreme care. When they include detailed compass directions or concave and convex lines, these descriptions can be hard to understand. Natural deterioration or destruction of the monuments in a description can make boundaries difficult to identify. For instance, "Raney's Oak" may have died long ago, and "Hunter's Rock" may no longer exist. Computer programs are available that convert the data of the compass directions and dimensions to a drawing that verifies that the description represents a closed figure. Professional surveyors should be consulted for definitive interpretations of any legal description.

| In Illinois |

Metes-and-bounds descriptions are used in Illinois when describing irregular tracts, portions of a recorded lot, or fractions of a section. Such descriptions always incorporate the rectangular survey method and refer to the section, township, range, and principal meridian of the land. These elements are described in the following section. ■

Rectangular (Government) Survey System

The **rectangular survey system**, sometimes called the **government survey system**, was established by Congress in 1785 to standardize the description of land acquired by the newly formed federal government. This system is based on two sets of intersecting lines: principal meridians and base lines. The **principal meridians** run north and south, and the **base lines** run east and west. Both are located by reference to degrees of longitude and latitude. Each principal meridian has a name or number and is crossed by a base line. Each principal meridian and its corresponding base line are used to survey a definite area of land, indicated on the map by boundary lines. There are 37 principal meridians in the United States.

Each principal meridian describes only specific areas of land by boundaries. No parcel of land is described by reference to more than one principal meridian. The meridian used is not necessarily the nearest one.

| In Illinois |

Locations in Illinois are described by their relation to one of the three meridians shown on the map in Figure 9.2. Note that only two of these three meridians actually run through Illinois, but nevertheless all are sometimes referenced in legal descriptions for Illinois properties.

The *Second Principal Meridian* is located in Indiana and controls that portion of Illinois lying south and east of Kankakee. The *Third Principal Meridian* begins at Cairo, at the junction of the Ohio and Mississippi rivers, and extends northward toward Wisconsin and near Rockford to the Illinois-Wisconsin border. The *Fourth Principal Meridian* begins near Beardstown and extends northward to the Canadian border. Surveys of land located in the western portion of Illinois use a base line for the Fourth Principal Meridian at Beardstown. Surveys of land in Wisconsin and eastern Minnesota are made from the Fourth Principal Meridian using a base line that is on the Illinois-Wisconsin border.

Not all property is described by reference to the nearest principal meridian. Notice on the Illinois map in Figure 9.2, a property on the western border of the Third Principal Meridian and just west of Rockford will be described by reference to the

FIGURE   9.2

**Rectangular Survey
System Map**

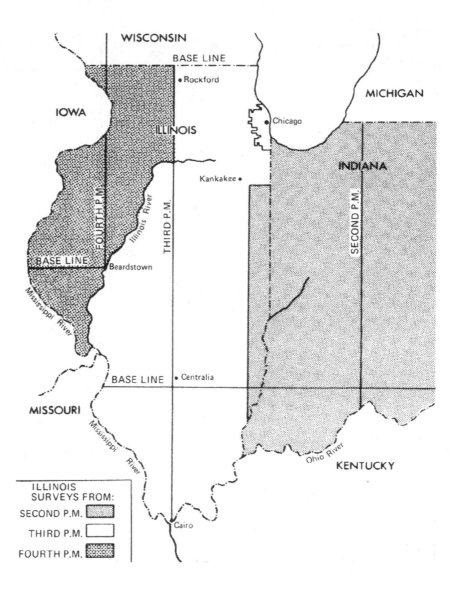

Fourth Principal Meridian. There are no options with regard to the meridians and base lines used to describe a particular property; once made, a legal description is not changed. ■

Further divisions are used in the same way as monuments in the metes-and-bounds method. They are

- townships,
- ranges,
- sections, and
- quarter-section lines.

Township tiers   Lines running east and west, parallel to the base line and six miles apart, are referred to as **township lines**. (See Figure 9.3.) They form strips of land called **township tiers**. These township tiers are designated by consecutive numbers north or south of the base line. For instance, the strip of land between 6 and 12 miles north of a base line is Township 2 North.

FIGURE   9.3

Township Lines

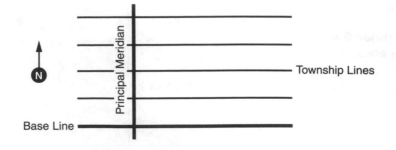

Ranges The land on either side of a principal meridian is divided into six-mile-wide strips by lines running north and south, parallel to the meridian. These north-south strips of land are called **ranges**. (See Figure 9.4.) They are designated by consecutive numbers east or west of the principal meridian. For example, Range 3 East would be a strip of land between 12 and 18 miles east of its principal meridian.

Township squares When the horizontal township lines and the vertical range lines intersect, they form squares. These township squares are the basic units of the rectangular survey system. (See Figure 9.5.) **Townships** are six miles square and contain 36 square miles (23,040 acres).

Note that although a township *square* is part of a township *tier*, the two terms do not refer to the same thing. Township tiers are the very long strips of six-mile-wide land running east and west. For this discussion, the word *township* used by itself refers only to the township *squares* formed by the vertical range lines intersecting the tiers.

Each township is given a legal description. The township's description includes the following:

- Designation of the township tier in which the township is located
- Designation of the range strip
- Name or number of the principal meridian for that area

■ **FOR EXAMPLE** In Figure 9.5, the gray shaded township is described as Township 3 North, Range 4 East of the Principal Meridian (an Illinois legal description would name the 2nd, 3rd, or 4th principal meridian, naming the meridian specifically). This township is the third strip, or tier, north of the base line, and it designates the township number and direction. The township is also located in the fourth range strip (those running north and south) east of the principal meridian. Finally, reference

Memory Tip

The directions of township lines and range lines may be easily remembered by thinking of the words this way:

FIGURE   9.4

Range Lines

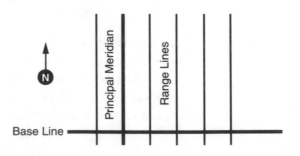

FIGURE 9.5

Townships in the Rectangular Survey System

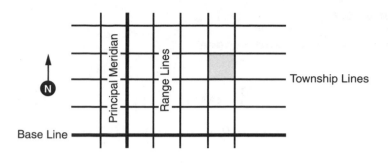

is made to the principal meridian because the land being described is within the boundary of land surveyed from that meridian. An actual description, then, might be abbreviated as T3N, R4E 4th Principal Meridian.

Sections   Each township contains 36 sections. Each section is one square mile, or 640 acres. Sections are numbered 1 through 36, as shown in Figure 9.6. Section 1 is always in the northeast, or upper right-hand, corner. The numbering proceeds right to left (backward), beginning in the upper right-hand corner. From there, the numbers drop down to the next tier and continue from left to right, then back from right again to left. By law, each section number 16 is set aside for school purposes. The sale or rental proceeds from section 16 were originally available for township school use. The schoolhouse was often located in this section so it would be centrally located for all of the students in the township. As a result, Section 16 is always referred to as the school section.

Sections (see Figure 9.6) are divided into halves (320 acres) and quarters (160 acres). In turn, each of those parts may be further divided into halves and quarters. The southeast quarter of a section, which is a 160-acre tract, is abbreviated SE¼. The SE¼ of the SE¼ of the SE¼ of Section 1 would be a ten-acre square in the lower right-hand corner of Section 1.

The rectangular survey system sometimes uses a shorthand method in its descriptions. For instance, a comma may be used in place of the word *of*: SE¼, SE¼, SE¼, Section 1. It is possible to combine portions of a section, such as NE¼ of SW¼ and N½ of NW¼ of SE¼ of Section 1, which could also be written NE¼, SW¼; N½, NW¼, SE¼ of Section 1. A semicolon means "and." Because of the word *and* in this description, tallying first the total amount of land on each side of "and" (or the semicolon), then adding those two numbers together for area, gives 60 acres.

Memory Tip

Townships are numbered in a backward **S-curve**, beginning at the upper right; right to left, then curving left to right, then right to left.

FIGURE 9.6

Sections in a Township

N

6	5	4	3	2	1
7	8	9	10	11	12
18	17	16	15	14	13
19	20	21	22	23	24
30	29	28	27	26	25
31	32	33	34	35	36

W   E

S

FIGURE 9.7

Counties, Townships, and Ranges

Counties, Townships and Ranges in Illinois
Showing Principal Meridians and Base Lines

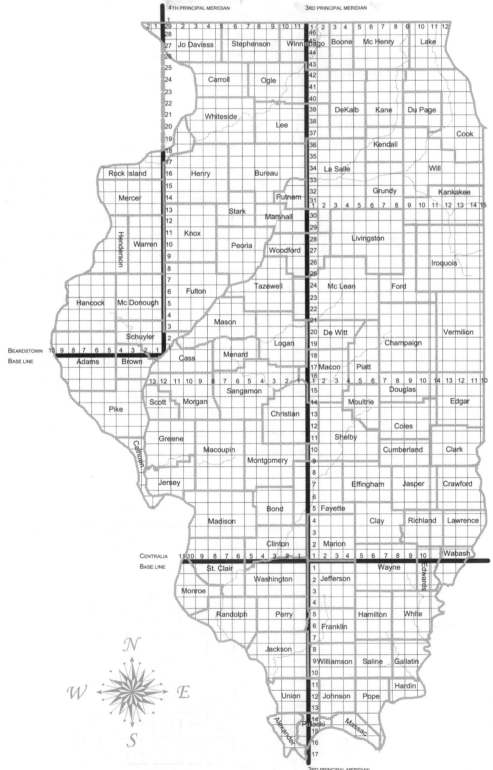

Correction lines Range lines are parallel only in theory. Due to the curvature of the earth, *range lines gradually approach each other.* If they are extended northward, they eventually meet at the North Pole. The fact that the earth is not flat, combined with the crude instruments used in early days, means that few townships are exactly six-mile squares or contain exactly 36 square miles. The system compensates for this "round earth problem" with correction lines. (See Figure 9.8.) Every fourth township line, both north and south of the base line, is designated a **correction line**. On each correction line, the range lines are measured to the full distance of six miles apart. Guide meridians run north and south at 24-mile intervals from the principal meridian. A **government check** is the irregular area created by these corrections; such an area is about 24 miles square.

Because most townships do not contain exactly 36 square miles, surveyors follow well-established rules of adjustment. These rules provide that any irregularity in a township must be adjusted in those sections adjacent to its north and west boundaries (Sections 1, 2, 3, 4, 5, 6, 7, 18, 19, 30, and 31). These are called *fractional sections.* All other sections are exactly one square mile and are known as *standard sections.* These provisions for making corrections explain some of the variations in township and section acreage under the rectangular survey system of legal description.

Fractional sections and government lots Undersized or oversized sections are classified as **fractional sections**. Fractional sections may occur for a number of reasons. In some areas, for instance, the rectangular survey may have been made by separate crews, and gaps less than a section wide remained when the surveys met. Other errors may have resulted from the physical difficulties encountered in the actual survey. For example, part of a section may be submerged in water.

FIGURE 9.8

A Section

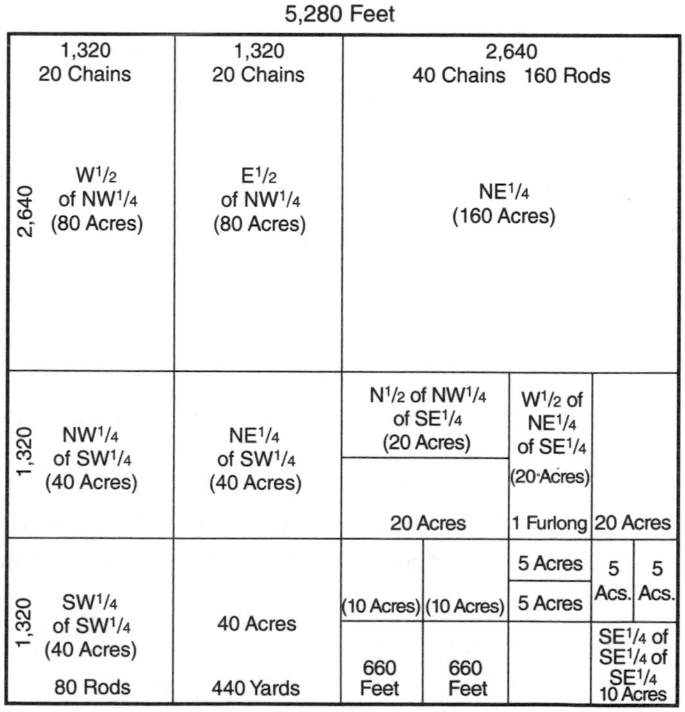

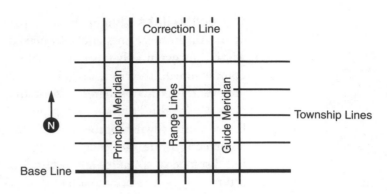

Areas smaller than full quarter-sections were numbered and designated as **government lots** by surveyors. These lots can be created by the curvature of the earth, by land bordering or surrounding large bodies of water, or by artificial state borders. An *overage* or a *shortage* was corrected whenever possible by placing the government lots in the north or west portions of the fractional sections. For example, a government lot might be described as *Government Lot 2 in the northwest quarter of fractional Section 18, Township 2 North, Range 4 East of the Salt Lake Meridian*.

Reading a rectangular survey description   To determine the location and size of a property described in the rectangular (or government) survey style, start at the end and work backward to the beginning. In other words, *analyze the legal description right to left*. For example, consider the following description:

> *The S½ of the NW¼ of the SE¼ of Section 11, Township 8 North, Range 6 West of the Fourth Principal Meridian.*

To locate this tract of land from the citation alone, first search for the Fourth Principal Meridian on a map of the United States. Then, on a regional map, find the township in which the property is located by counting six range strips west of the Fourth Principal Meridian and eight townships north of its corresponding base line. After locating Section 11, divide the section into quarters. Then divide the SE¼ into quarters, and then the NW¼ of that into halves. The S½ of that NW¼ contains the property in question.

In computing the size of this tract of land, first determine that the SE¼ of the section contains 160 acres (640 acres divided by 4). The NW¼ of that quarter-section contains 40 acres (160 acres divided by 4), and the S½ of that quarter-section—the property in question—contains 20 acres (40 acres divided by 2).

In general, if a rectangular survey description does not use the conjunction *and* or a semicolon (indicating two or more parcels are combined), the *longer* the description, the *smaller* the tract of land it describes.

Legal descriptions should always include the name of the county and state in which the land is located because meridians often relate to more than one state and occasionally relate to two base lines.

Must-Know Measurements

Sections are smaller than townships.
Township = 6 miles × 6 miles = 36 sections per township.
Section = 1 mile × 1 mile = 1 square mile
43,560 = square feet per acre
5,280 feet in a mile (one side of a section)

For example, the description "the southwest quarter of Section 10, Township 4 North, Range 1 West of the Fourth Principal Meridian" could refer to land in either Illinois or Wisconsin.

Metes-and-bounds descriptions within the rectangular survey system   Land in states that use the rectangular survey system also may require a metes-and-bounds description. This usually occurs in one of three situations: when describing an irregular tract; when a tract is too small to be described by quarter-sections; or when a tract does not follow the lot or block lines of a recorded sub-division or section, quarter-section lines, or other fractional section lines. The following is an example of a combined metes-and-bounds and rectangular survey system description (See Figure 9.10):

> *That part of the northwest quarter of Section 12, Township 10 North, Range 7 West of the Third Principal Meridian, bounded by a line described as follows: Commencing at the southeast corner of the northwest quarter of said Section 12 then north 500 feet; then west parallel with the south line of said section 1,000 feet; then south parallel with the east line of said section 500 feet to the south line of said northwest quarter; then east along said south line to the point of beginning.*

In Illinois   Metes-and-bounds descriptions may be included in the rectangular survey system used in Illinois when describing irregular or small tracts. ■

Lot-and-Block System

The third method of legal description is the **lot-and-block (recorded plat) system**. This system uses lot-and-block numbers referred to in a plat map filed in the public records of the county where the land is located. The lot-and-block system is often used to describe property in subdivisions and urban areas.

A lot-and-block survey is performed in two steps. First, a large parcel of land is described either by metes and bounds or by rectangular survey. Once this large parcel is surveyed, it is broken into smaller parcels. As a result, a lot-and-block legal description is always a smaller part of a metes-and-bounds or rectangular survey description. For each parcel described under the lot-and-block system, the lot refers to the numerical designation of any particular parcel. The block refers to the name of the subdivision under which the map is recorded. The block reference is drawn from the early 1900s, when a city block was the most common type of subdivided property.

FIGURE   9.10

Metes and Bounds with Rectangular Survey

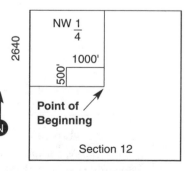

"Section 12, T10N, R7W,
Third Principal Meridian"

FIGURE 9.11

Subdivision Plat Map

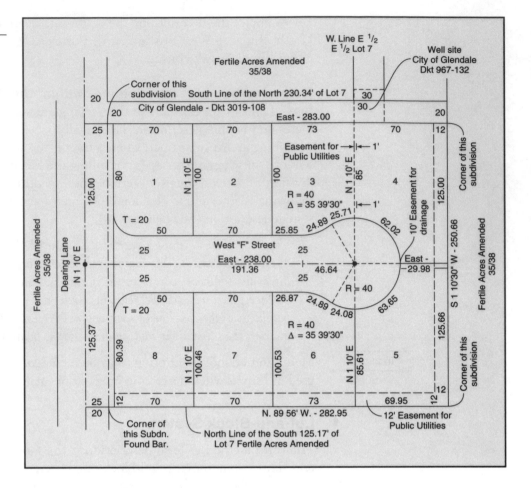

The lot-and-block system starts with the preparation of a *subdivision plat* by a licensed surveyor or an engineer. (See Figure 9.11.) On this plat, the land is divided into numbered or lettered lots and blocks, and streets or access roads for public use are indicated. Lot sizes and street details must be described completely and must comply with all local ordinances and requirements. When properly signed and approved, the subdivision plat is recorded in the county in which the land is located.

The plat becomes part of the legal description. In describing a lot from a recorded subdivision plat, three identifiers are used:

1. Lot-and-block number
2. Name or number of the subdivision plat
3. Name of the county and state

The following is an example of a lot-and-block description:

> *Lot 71, Happy Valley Estates 2, located in a portion of the southeast quarter of Section 23, Township 7 North, Range 4 East of the Seward Principal Meridian in _____ County, State of _____.*

Anyone who wants to locate this parcel would start with the map of the Seward Principal Meridian to identify the township and range reference. Then he would consult the township map of Township 7 North, Range 4 East, and the section map of Section 23. From there, he would look at the quarter-section map of the southeast quarter. The quarter-section map would refer to the plat map for the subdivision known as the second unit (second parcel subdivided) under the name of Happy Valley Estates.

Some subdivided lands are further divided by a later resubdivision. In the following example, one developer (Western View) purchased a large parcel from a second developer (Homewood). Western View then resubdivided the property into different-sized parcels:

> *Lot 4, Western View Resubdivision of the Homewood Subdivision, located in a portion of the west half of Section 19, Township 10 North, Range 13 East of the Black Hills Principal Meridian, _____ County, State of _____.*

In Illinois   The lot-and-block system is used in Illinois. Subdivision descriptions are the predominant method of describing developed land in this state. The plat of Prairie Acres Estates that appears in Figure 9.12 illustrates a subdivision map.

Under the Illinois Plat Act, when an owner divides a parcel of land into two or more parts, any of which is less than five acres, the parts must be surveyed and a plat of subdivision recorded. An exception to this would be the division of lots or

F I G U R E   9.12

Plat Map of Prairie Acres Estates

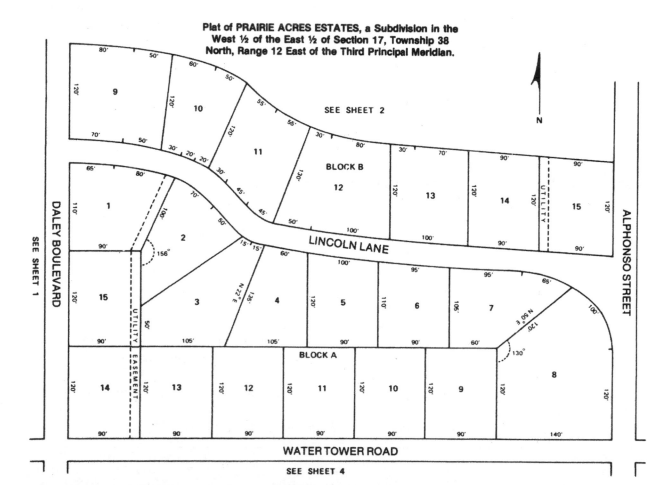

Recorded January 14, 1969, in Book 275, Page 1346, in Prairie County, Illinois.

blocks of less than one acre in any recorded subdivision that does not involve the creation of any new streets or easements of access. When a conveyance is made, the county recorder may require an affidavit that an exception exists.

The provisions of the Illinois Plat Act are complicated and subject to interpretation by each county recorder. Anyone attempting to record a document conveying land should consult a lawyer and the county recorder about the requirements involved. ■

IN PRACTICE   Real estate offices routinely have plat books available. These books have all the lots drawn and numbered for a given township area. If you have the legal description or the *property index number* (PIN) for a property, you can locate its basic dimensions and location using these books. The legal description and the PIN are the two non-street address forms of property identification commonly used. PINs are basically a condensed version of a legal description; they can be found for a given property by examining a survey, checking the tax database, or by calling the county.

■ PREPARING A SURVEY

Legal descriptions should not be altered or combined without adequate information from a surveyor or title attorney. A licensed surveyor is trained and authorized to locate and determine the legal description of any parcel of land. The surveyor does this by preparing two documents: a survey and a survey sketch. The *survey* states the property's legal description. The *survey sketch* shows the location and dimensions of the parcel. When a survey also shows the location, size, and shape of buildings on the lot, it is referred to as a *spot survey*.

IN PRACTICE   Because legal descriptions, once recorded, affect title to real estate, they should be prepared only by a professional surveyor.

MATH CONCEPTS

LAND ACQUISITION COSTS

To calculate the cost of purchasing land, use the same unit in which the cost is given. Costs quoted per square foot must be multiplied by the proper number of square feet; costs quoted per acre must be multiplied by the proper number of acres; and so on.

To calculate the cost of a parcel of land of three acres at $1.10 per square foot, convert the acreage to square feet before multiplying:

43,560 square feet per acre × 3 acres = 130,680 square feet

130,680 square feet × $1.10 per square foot = $143,748

To calculate the cost of a parcel of land of 17,500 square feet at $60,000 per acre, convert the cost per acre into the cost per square foot before multiplying by the number of square feet in the parcel:

$60,000 per acre ÷ 43,560 square feet per acre = $1.38 (rounded) per square foot

17,500 square feet × $1.38 per square foot = $24,150

Legal descriptions should be copied with extreme care. An incorrectly worded legal description in a sales contract may result in a conveyance of more or less land than the parties intended. For example, damages suffered from an incorrect description could be extensive if buildings and improvements need to be moved because the land upon which the improvements were made is not owned. Often, even punctuation is extremely critical.

Title problems can arise for the buyer who seeks to convey the property at a future date. Even if the contract can be corrected before the sale is closed, a real estate licensee risks losing a commission and may be held liable for damages suffered by an injured party because of an improperly worded legal description.

It is very important for real estate licensees to be aware of various surveys and their uses. Not all surveys include surveyor liability and warranties of accuracy. Some surveys, such as an Improvement Location Certificate (ILC), are not full surveys. ILCs are prepared in a shorter time frame and at less cost, providing only the location of the structures and improvements as related to property boundaries.

■ MEASURING ELEVATIONS

Just as surface rights must be identified, surveyed, and described, so must rights to the property above the earth's surface. Elevations are measured to determine the legal descriptions of air rights and condominium apartments. As discussed earlier, land includes the space above the ground. In the same way land may be measured and divided into parcels, the air itself may be divided. An owner may subdivide the air above his land into air lots. **Air lots** are composed of the airspace within specific boundaries located over a parcel of land.

The condominium laws passed in all states require that a registered land surveyor prepare a plat map that shows the elevations of floor and ceiling surfaces and the vertical boundaries of each unit with reference to an official datum (discussed later). A unit's floor, for instance, might be 60 feet above the datum, and its ceiling, 69 feet. Typically, a separate plat is prepared for each floor in the condominium building.

Subsurface rights can be legally described in the same manner as air rights. They are measured *below* the datum rather than above it. Subsurface rights are used not only for coal mining, petroleum drilling, and utility line location but also for multistory condominiums—both residential and commercial—that have several floors below ground level.

Datum

A **datum** is a point, line, or surface from which elevations are measured or indicated. For the purpose of the U.S. Geological Survey (USGS), *datum* is defined as the mean sea level at New York Harbor. However, virtually all large cities have local official datum that is used instead of the USGS datum. A surveyor would use a datum in determining the height of a structure or establishing the grade of a street.

In Illinois

The general datum plane used by Illinois surveyors is the USGS datum. ∎

Benchmarks As discussed earlier in this chapter, monuments traditionally are used to mark surface measurements between points. A monument could be a marker set in concrete, a piece of steel-reinforcing bar (rebar), a metal pipe driven into the soil, or simply a wooden stake stuck in the dirt. Because such items are subject to the whims of nature and vandals, their accuracy is sometimes suspect. As a result, surveyors instead rely heavily on benchmarks to mark their work accurately and permanently.

Benchmarks are permanent reference points that have been established throughout the United States. They are usually embossed brass markers set into solid concrete or asphalt bases. While used to some degree for surface measurements, their principal reference use is for marking datums.

IN PRACTICE All large cities have established a local official datum used in place of the USGS datum. For instance, the official datum for Chicago is known as the *Chicago City Datum*. It is a horizontal plane that corresponded to the low water level of Lake Michigan in 1847 (the year in which the datum was established) and is considered to be at zero elevation. Although a surveyor's measurement of elevation based on the USGS datum will differ from one computed according to a local datum, it can be translated to an elevation based on the USGS.

Location:
22 West 300 Birchwood
Drive, Glen Ellyn, IL
Benchmark:
22 miles west of Chicago's
State Street Benchmark

Cities with local datums also have designated official local benchmarks, which are assigned permanent identifying numbers. Local benchmarks simplify surveyors' work because the basic benchmarks may be miles away. A major one in Chicago is located at State and Madison Streets. It references non-city addresses extending far west of Cook County. County addresses beginning with 33 West or 25 West refer to number of miles west of State Street (*as the crow flies!*). Numbers 1 North or 4 South refer to miles north or south of Madison Street.

∎ LAND UNITS AND MEASUREMENTS

It is important to understand land units and measurements because they are integral parts of legal descriptions. Some commonly used measurements are listed in Table 9.1. Today, the terms *rods*, *cubic yards*, and *chains* are not often used.

TABLE 9.1

Units of Land Measurement

	Measurement
mile	5,280 feet; 1,760 yards; 320 rods
rod	16.5 feet; 5.50 yards
square mile	640 acres (5,280 × 5,280 = 27,878,400 ÷ 43,560)
acre	43,560 square feet; 160 sq. rods
cubic yard	27 cubic feet
square yard	9 square feet
square foot	144 square inches
chain	66 feet; 4 rods; 100 links
township	36 square miles; 6 miles × 6 miles
section	1 square mile; 640 acres; 1 mile × 1 mile

■ SUMMARY

A legal description is a precise method of identifying a parcel of land. Three methods of legal description can be used: metes-and-bounds method, rectangular (or government) survey system, and lot-and-block (plat map) system. A property's description should always be noted by the same method as the one used in previous documents.

The metes-and-bounds method uses direction and distance measurement to establish precise boundaries for a parcel. Monuments are fixed objects that establish these boundaries. Their physical location takes precedence over the written linear measurement in a document. When property is described by metes and bounds, the description begins and ends at the point of beginning (POB).

The rectangular (or government) survey system is used in most states. Illinois legal descriptions refer to three principal meridians, one of which is in Indiana (the second). Meridians in and near Illinois number from left to right on the map. A given property is not necessarily referenced by the closest meridian. Once a legal description has been made, it is permanent. With rectangular survey, each principal meridian and its corresponding base line are the primary reference points. Any parcel of land is surveyed from only one principal meridian and one base line.

East and west lines parallel with the base line form six-mile-wide strips called township tiers. North and south lines parallel with the principal meridian form six-mile-wide range strips. The resulting squares are 36 square miles in area and are called townships.

A sample legal description might partially read: Township 3 North, Range 4 East of the 2nd Principal Meridian. Legal descriptions are read left to right but are best analyzed right to left. Townships are divided into 36 sections, one square mile each. Each section has 640 acres, and each acre has 43,560 square feet. Section 16 is traditionally the school section; all other sections are numbered off in the township backwards in S-curves, starting with Section 1 in the upper right-hand corner.

Irregularities in using a square system to match a round planet are adjusted in the rectangular system by correction lines, which in turn form pockets of land called government checks.

When a tract of land is irregular, a surveyor can prepare a combination of methods: for instance, rectangular survey and metes-and-bounds description. Lot-and-block combined with rectangular survey is even more frequently utilized in describing suburban America.

Land in every state can be subdivided into lots and blocks by means of a plat map. An approved plat of survey is filed for record in the recorder's office of the county in which the land is located. A plat of subdivision gives the legal description of a building site in a town or city by lot, block, and subdivision in a section, township, and range of a principal meridian in a county and state. Lot and block, section, and township also comprise the essentials given in a property identification number (PIN), which also appears on tax information, surveys, and contracts.

Air lots, condominium descriptions, and other measurements of vertical elevations may be computed from the U.S. Geological Survey datum, which is the mean sea level in New York Harbor. Most large cities have established local survey datums for surveying within the areas—the Chicago City Datum is based on the low-level water mark of Lake Michigan in 1847. The elevations from these datums are further supplemented by reference points, called benchmarks, placed at fixed intervals from the datums. Benchmarks are used for vertical reference points but often supplement surface measurements.

CHAPTER 9 QUIZ

1. What is the proper description of this shaded area of a section?

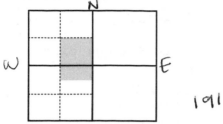

191

a. SW¼ of the NE¼ and the N½ of the SE¼ of the SW¼

b. N½ of the NE¼ of the SW¼ and the SE¼ of the NW¼

c. SW¼ of the SE¼ of the NW¼ and the N½ of the NE¼ of the SW¼

d. S½ of the SW¼ of the NE¼ and the NE¼ of the NW¼ of the SE¼

2. When surveying land, a surveyor refers to the principal meridian that is

188

a. nearest the land being surveyed.

b. in the same state as the land being surveyed.

c. not more than 40 townships or 15 ranges distant from the land being surveyed.

d. within the rectangular survey system area in which the land being surveyed is located.

3. In describing real estate, the system that uses feet, degrees, and natural and artificial markers as monuments is

a. rectangular survey.

b. metes and bounds.

c. government survey.

d. lot and block.

Questions 4 through 7 refer to the following illustration of a whole township and parts of the adjacent townships.

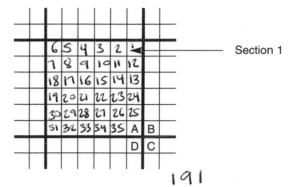

Section 1

191

4. The section marked A is which of the following?

a. School section

b. Section 31

c. Section 36

d. Government lot

5. Which of the following is Section 6?

191

a. A

b. B

c. C

d. D

6. The section directly below C is

a. Section 7.

b. Section 12.

c. Section 25.

d. Section 30.

7. Which of the following is Section D?

a. Section 1

b. Section 6

c. Section 31

d. Section 36

8. A buyer purchased a one-acre parcel for $2.15 per square foot. What is the selling price of the parcel?

$2.15 × 43,560

a. $344

b. $46,827

c. $1,376

d. $93,654

9. The legal description "the northwest ¼ of the southwest ¼ of Section 6, Township 4 North, Range 7 West" is defective because there is no reference to
   a. lot numbers.
   b. boundary lines.
   c. a principal meridian.
   d. a record of survey.

10. To keep the principal meridian and range lines as near to six miles apart as possible, a correction known as a *government check* is made. How large is a government check?
    a. 1 square mile
    b. 20 square miles
    c. 6 miles square
    d. 24 miles square

11. Fractional sections in the rectangular survey system along the northern or western borders of a check that are less than a quarter-section in area are known as
    a. fractional parcels.
    b. government lots.
    c. portional sections.
    d. fractional townships.

12. Buyer A purchased 4.5 acres of land for $78,400. An adjoining owner wants to purchase a strip of A's land measuring 150 feet by 100 feet. What should this strip cost the adjoining owner if A sells it for the same price per square foot originally paid for the property?
    a. $3,000
    b. $6,000
    c. $7,800
    d. $9,400

13. A property contained ten acres. How many lots of not less than 50 feet by 100 feet can be subdivided from the property if 26,000 square feet were dedicated for roads?
    a. 80
    b. 81
    c. 82
    d. 83

14. A parcel of land is 400 feet by 640 feet. The parcel is cut in half diagonally by a stream. How many acres are there in each half of the parcel?
    a. 2.75
    b. 2.94
    c. 5.51
    d. 5.88

15. The section due west of Section 18, Township 5 North, Range 8 West, is
    a. Section 19, T5N, R8W.
    b. Section 17, T5N, R8W.
    c. Section 13, T5N, R9W.
    d. Section 12, T5N, R7W.

In Illinois

16. Legal descriptions of land in Illinois usually are based on the
    a. rectangular survey system.
    b. Third, Fourth, and Fifth Principal Meridians.
    c. three base lines running through the central part of the state.
    d. nearest principal meridian.

17. Land in the northwest corner of Illinois is described with reference to which principal meridian?
    a. Second
    b. Third
    c. Fourth
    d. Fifth

Answer questions 18 through 20 using the information given on the plat of Prairie Acres Estates in Figure 9.12.

18. How many lots have easements?
    a. 3
    b. 4
    c. 6
    d. 7

19. Which of the following lots has the most frontage on Lincoln Lane?
    a. Lot 10, block B
    b. Lot 11, block B
    c. Lot 7, block A
    d. Lot 8, block A

20. "Beginning at the intersection of the east line of Daley Boulevard and the south line of Lincoln Lane and running south along the east line of Daley Boulevard a distance of 230 feet; then easterly parallel to the north line of Water Tower Road a distance of 195 feet; then north-easterly on a course of N22°E a distance of 135 feet; and then northwesterly along the south line of Lincoln Lane to the point of beginning." Which lots are described here?

a. Lots 13, 14, and 15, block A
b. Lots 9, 10, and 11, block B
c. Lots 1, 2, 3, and 15, block A
d. Lots 7, 8, and 9, block A

P. 197.

12) 78,400 / 196,020 sq ft = 0.4
15,000 sq ft × 0.4 = 6000.

Real Estate Taxes and Other Liens

■ **LEARNING OBJECTIVES** *When you've finished reading this chapter, you should be able to*

■ **identify** the various classifications of liens;

■ **describe** how real estate taxes are applied through assessments, tax liens, and the use of equalization ratios;

■ **explain** how nontax liens, such as mechanics' liens, mortgage liens, and judgment liens, are applied and enforced;

■ **distinguish** the characteristics of voluntary, involuntary, statutory, and equitable liens; and

■ **define** the following *key terms*

ad valorem tax	inheritance taxes	Special Service Areas
appropriation	involuntary lien	(SSAs)
attachment	judgment	redemption
encumbrance	lien	specific lien
equalization factor	lien waivers	statutory lien
equitable lien	lis pendens	subordination agreement
estate taxes	mechanic's lien	tax deed
general lien	mortgage lien	tax liens
general real estate tax	special assessment	tax sale

■ LIENS

The ownership of real estate is subject to certain obligations imposed by governmental powers, usually in the form of taxes. Creditors and courts can also make claims against property to secure payment for debts, by way of a *lien*.

A **lien** is a charge or claim against property that is made to enforce the payment of money. Whenever someone borrows money, the lender generally requires some form of security. *Security* (also referred to as *collateral*) is something of value that the borrower promises to give the lender if the borrower fails to repay the debt. When the lender's security is in the form of real estate, the security is called a lien.

> All liens are encumbrances, but not all encumbrances are liens.

Liens are not limited to security for borrowed money (such as *mortgage liens*). Liens can be enforced against property by a government agency to recover taxes owed by the owner (*tax liens*). A lien can be used to compel the payment of an assessment or other special charge as well. A *mechanic's lien* represents an effort to recover payment for work performed.

A lien represents only an interest in property; it does not constitute actual ownership of the property. It is an *encumbrance* on the owner's title. An **encumbrance** is any charge or claim that attaches to real property and lessens its value or impairs its use. An encumbrance does not necessarily prevent the transfer or conveyance of the property, but because it is "attached" to the property, it transfers along with it. Liens differ from other encumbrances, however, because they are financial or monetary in nature and attach to the property because of a debt.

Types of Liens

There are many different types of liens. One way liens are classified is by how they are created. A **voluntary lien** is created intentionally by the property owner's action, such as when someone takes out a mortgage loan. An **involuntary lien**, on the other hand, is not a matter of choice; it is created by law. It may be either statutory or equitable. A **statutory lien** is created by statute. A real estate tax lien, then, is an involuntary, statutory lien. It is created by statute without the property owner taking it on voluntarily. An **equitable lien** is created by a court to ensure the payment of a judgment as well as by agreement.

> **Memory Tip**
> Four ways to create a lien (VISE):
> Voluntary
> Involuntary
> Statutory
> Equitable

Liens also may be classified according to the type of property involved. **General liens** affect all the property, both real and personal, of a debtor. This includes judgments, estate and inheritance taxes, decedent's debts, corporate franchise taxes, and Internal Revenue Service taxes. A lien on real estate differs from a lien on personal property. A lien attaches to *real property* at the moment it is filed. In contrast, a lien does not attach to *personal property* until the personal property actually is levied on or seized by the sheriff.

Specific liens are secured by specific property and affect only that particular property. Specific liens on real estate include mechanics' liens, mortgage liens, real estate tax liens, and liens for special assessments and utilities. Specific liens can also secure personal property, as when a lien is placed on a car to secure payment of a car loan.

Effects of Liens on Title

The existence of a lien does not necessarily prevent a property owner from conveying title to someone else. The lien might reduce the value of the real estate, however, because few buyers will take on the risk of a property that has a lien on it.

Because the lien attaches to the property, not the property owner, a new owner could lose the property if the creditors take court action to enforce payment. Once properly established, a lien runs with the land and will bind all successive owners until the lien is paid in full.

IN PRACTICE   A buyer should insist on a title search before closing a real estate transaction so that any recorded liens are revealed. If liens are present, the buyer may decide to purchase at a lower price or at better terms, require the liens be paid, or refuse to purchase.

Priority of liens   Priority of liens refers to the order in which claims against the property will be satisfied. In general, the rule for priority of liens is "first to record, first in right." Liens take priority from the date they are recorded in the public records of the county in which the property is located.

There are some notable exceptions to this rule. For instance, real estate taxes and special assessments generally take priority over all other liens, regardless of the order in which the liens are recorded. This means that outstanding real estate taxes and special assessments are paid from the proceeds of a court-ordered sale first. The remainder of the proceeds is used to pay other outstanding liens in the order of their priority. Mechanics' liens take priority as provided by state law but never over tax and special assessment liens.

■ **FOR EXAMPLE**   A mansion is ordered sold by the court to satisfy the owner's debts. The property is subject to a $50,000 judgment lien, incurred as a result of a mechanic's lien suit. $295,000 in interest and principal remains to be paid on the mansion's mortgage. This year's unpaid real estate taxes amount to $5,000. The judgment lien was entered in the public record on February 7, 2011, and the mortgage lien was recorded January 22, 2009. If the mansion is sold at the tax sale for $375,000, the proceeds of the sale will be distributed in the following order:

1. $5,000 to the taxing bodies for this year's real estate taxes
2. $295,000 to the mortgage lender (the entire amount of the mortgage loan outstanding as of the date of sale)
3. $50,000 to the creditor named in the judgment lien
4. $25,000 to the owner (the proceeds remaining after paying the first three items)

However, if the mansion sold for $325,000, the proceeds would be distributed as follows:

1. $5,000 to the taxing bodies for this year's real estate taxes
2. $295,000 to the mortgage lender (the entire amount of the mortgage loan outstanding as of the date of sale)
3. $25,000 to the creditor named in the judgment lien
4. $0 to the owner

Although the creditor is not repaid in full, this outcome is considered fair for two reasons:

■   The creditor's interest arose later than the others, so the other interests took priority.

■   The creditor knew (or should have known) about priority creditors when credit was extended to the mansion owner, so the risk involved was clear (or should have been clear).

Subordination agreements are written agreements between lienholders to change the priority of mortgage, judgment, and other liens. Under a subordination agreement, the holder of a superior or prior lien agrees to permit a junior lienholder's interest to move ahead of her lien.

■ REAL ESTATE TAX LIENS

The ownership of real estate is always subject to certain government powers. One of these is the right of state and local governments to impose (levy) taxes to pay for their functions. Because the location of real estate is permanently fixed, the government can levy taxes with a high degree of certainty that the taxes will be collected. The annual taxes levied on real estate usually have priority over previously recorded liens, so they may be enforced by a court-ordered sale.

There are two types of real estate taxes: *general real estate taxes* (also called *ad valorem taxes*) and *special assessments* (or *improvement taxes*). Both are levied against specific parcels of property and automatically become **tax liens** on those properties.

General Tax (Ad Valorem Tax)

The general real estate tax, or ad valorem tax   *Ad valorem* is Latin for "according to value." Ad valorem taxes are based on the value of the property being taxed. They are specific, involuntary, statutory liens. They are charged by various government agencies and municipalities, including

■   states;
■   counties;
■   cities, towns, and villages;
■   school districts (local elementary and high schools, publicly funded junior colleges and community colleges);

- drainage districts;
- water districts;
- sanitary districts; and
- parks, forest preserves, recreation, and other public-use districts.

Real estate property taxes are a favored source of revenue for local governments because real estate cannot be hidden and is relatively easy to value. Property taxes pay for a wide range of government services and programs.

Exemptions from general taxes Most state laws exempt certain real estate from taxation. Such property must be used for tax-exempt purposes, as defined in the statutes. The most common exempt properties are owned by

- various municipal organizations (such as schools, parks, and playgrounds),
- cities and counties,
- state and federal governments,
- religious and charitable organizations,
- hospitals, and
- educational institutions.

Many state laws also allow special exemptions to reduce real estate tax bills for certain property owners or land uses. For instance, senior citizens frequently are granted reductions in the assessed values of their homes. Some state and local governments offer real estate tax reductions to attract industries and sports franchises. Many states also offer tax reductions for agricultural land.

In Illinois

Properties in Illinois that are totally exempt from paying general real estate taxes include schools, religious institutions, cemeteries, and charitable institutions, as well as those owned by federal, state, county, and local governments. Taxing districts may elect to exempt certain other properties (within limits), such as commercial and industrial properties.

Illinois property taxes are adjusted to reflect certain concessions given on owner-occupied residences. These properties are designated as *homesteads*. The *homestead exemption* (not to be confused with the *homestead estate*) reduces the assessed value of a property subject to taxes. Here are the basic exemptions:

1. The Homeowners' Exemption applies to owners of single-family homes, condominiums, cooperatives, and one- to six-unit apartment buildings. In some counties, owners must apply to the assessor for the exemption each year; in others, the exemption is automatically applied. The amount of exemption is currently $6,000.
2. The Senior Citizen's Homestead Exemption is available to homeowners over the age of 65. Seniors must prove age and ownership to the County Assessor by December 31 of the assessment year for which the application is made. These exemption amounts are subtracted from the property's equalized assessed value before the tax rate is applied. This exemption reduces the equalized assessed value of a senior's home by $4,000.
3. The Senior Citizen's Assessment Freeze Homestead Exemption program allows Illinois seniors to freeze their assessed valuation for the remainder of their lifetime once they have turned 65 if household income does not exceed $55,000. Annual application and proof of income must be filed with the county assessor.

4. The Homestead Improvement Exemption allows any Illinois homeowner who has recently improved her home (by adding a new family room, for instance) to forestall an increase in the home's overall assessed value for up to four years. This exemption is available up to an improvement value of $75,000.

Property owners may qualify for other tax concessions based on their status as disabled veterans or by virtue of improvements to the property, certain maintenance and repair expenses, solar heating, airport land, farmland, rehabilitation of historic buildings, and location within enterprise zones or tax concession districts. ■

IN PRACTICE   If there is a new addition or remodeling, the buyers' real estate agent should be aware of

- mechanics' liens, and
- four-year homestead improvement exemptions.

Assessment   Real estate is valued for tax purposes by county or township assessors or appraisers. This official valuation process is called *assessment*. A property's *assessed value* generally is based on the sales prices of comparable properties, although practices may vary. Land values may be assessed separately from buildings or other improvements, and different valuation methods may be used for different types of property. State laws may provide for property to be periodically reassessed.

In Illinois

In all counties except Cook, real property is assessed at 33⅓ percent of fair market value. (Depending on how the property is classified, real property in Cook County is assessed based on a sliding scale of percentages of fair market value, from 10 to 25 percent.) Real property is defined by the Illinois Revenue Act as including land, buildings, structures, improvements, and any other permanent fixtures attached to land.

To Determine Taxes
- Locate assessed value (usually ⅓ market value)
- Always "equalize" assessed value *first*
- Subtract any exemptions
- Multiply adjusted assessed value by tax rate = real estate taxes

Taxpayers who believe that errors were made in their property's assessment may file a complaint directly with the county assessor. If the taxpayer's complaint is denied, the decision may be appealed to an administrative board of review (in Cook County, the Board of Appeals). Alternatively, the taxpayer can bypass the county official and go directly to the board of review. If the taxpayer is dissatisfied with the board's decision, she may appeal to the Illinois Property Tax Appeal Board or to the circuit court of the county in which the property is located. ■

Equalization.   In some jurisdictions, when it is necessary to correct inequalities in statewide tax assessments, an **equalization factor** is used to achieve uniformity. An equalization factor may be applied to raise or lower assessments in a particular district or county. The basic assessed value of each property in the area is multiplied by the equalization factor to acquire an "equalized assessment," then any exemptions are subtracted, and last, the tax rate is applied.

MATH CONCEPTS

CALCULATING REAL ESTATE TAXES

Assessed value × Equalization factor – Exemptions × Tax rate = Annual tax

The assessments in one county are 20 percent lower than the average assessments throughout the rest of the state. This underassessment can be corrected by requiring the application of an equalization factor of 125 percent (1.25) to each assessment in that county. Therefore, a parcel of land assessed for tax purposes at $98,000 would be taxed on an equalized value of $122,500 ($98,000 × 1.25 = $122,500). At this point, the $5,500 homestead exemption would be subtracted. Then, if there were a $4,000 senior exemption, it would be subtracted next ($122,500 – $5,500 – $4,000 = $113,000 adjusted assessed value). Using this final equalized, adjusted assessed value, taxes would then be computed by multiplying by the proper tax rate.

In Illinois

The assessed valuation of real estate is adjusted yearly in each county by applying an equalization factor determined by the Property Tax Administration Bureau of the Department of Revenue. Assessed values are compared with selling prices to arrive at the equalization factor, and each county is assigned a multiplier to be used for equalization purposes. The equalizer is always applied first (equalizer times the basic value) before applicable homeowners' exemptions (if any) are subtracted from value. From the final equalized, adjusted assessed value, taxes are computed. *Any given parcel receives a full reassessment on a quadrennial (four-year) basis*, as mandated by the state. ■

Budgets and tax rates   The process of arriving at a real estate tax rate begins with the adoption of a *budget* by each taxing district. Each budget covers the financial requirements of the taxing body for the coming fiscal year. The fiscal year may be the January through December calendar year or some other 12-month period designated by statute. The budget must include an estimate of all expenditures needed for the year. In addition, the budget must indicate the amount of income expected from all fees, revenue sharing, and other sources. The net amount remaining to be raised from real estate taxes is then determined by the difference between these figures.

The next step is to spread out the needed monies among all the homeowners proportionately (based on values). The total monies needed for the coming fiscal year are divided by the total valuations of all real estate located within the taxing body's jurisdiction.

Proposed expense ÷ Total assessed property values = Tax rate

■ **FOR EXAMPLE**   A taxing district's budget indicates that $800,000 must be acquired from real estate taxes to pay for needed expenditures. The assessment roll (assessor's record) of all taxable real estate within the district equals $10 million. The tax rate is computed as follows:

$800,000 ÷ $10,000,000 = .080 or 8%

Appropriation   Formal **appropriation** is the way a taxing body actually authorizes the expenditure of funds and provides for the sources of the funding. Appropriation generally involves the adoption of an ordinance or the passage of a law that states the specific terms of the proposed taxation. The amount to be raised from the general real estate tax is then imposed on property owners through a tax levy. A *tax levy* is the formal action taken to impose the tax, usually by way of a vote of the taxing district's governing body.

Creating the tax bills   After appropriation, a property owner's tax bill is computed by applying the tax rate to the assessed valuation of the property.

Generally, one tax bill that incorporates all real estate taxes levied by the various taxing districts is prepared for each property. Some tax purposes or tax targets (like the park district) are split out and easily identifiable on most bills. In some areas, however, separate bills are prepared by each taxing body.

In Illinois   The county collector prepares and issues only one combined tax bill to each parcel of property. ■

■ **FOR EXAMPLE**   If a property is assessed for tax purposes at $160,000 and the tax rate is 3 percent, the tax will be $4,800 ($160,000 × .03). (This assumes no equalization factor.)

Let's say the equalization factor is 120 percent. Thus, the equalized, assessed value is $192,000 ($160,000 × 1.20). From there, apply the tax rate of 3 percent (.03) to arrive at taxes of $5,760 ($192,000 × .03).

In Illinois   General real estate taxes are levied annually for the calendar year and become a *prior first lien,* superior to all other liens, on January 1 of that tax year. However, they are not due and payable until the following year.

General real estate taxes are payable in two equal installments in the year *after* they are levied: one-half by June 1 and the second half by September 1 (except in Cook County, as noted later). Taxes in Illinois, then, are said to be *paid in arrears*. The payment due dates are also called *penalty dates*, after which a 1.5 percent-per-month penalty is added to any unpaid amount. Because bills must be issued 30 days prior to a penalty date, the penalty date for an installment may be delayed if the county collector is late in preparing the bills.

In Cook County, the due date for the first installment of real estate taxes is the first business day in March. The second installment due date varies because the bill relies on the delivery of various sets of data by other state and county agencies. Unlike the first installment bill, the second installment bill reflects the new assessed values, assessment appeals, exemptions, the state equalization factor, and taxing district tax rates. The Cook County Treasurer's Office projects the second due date as soon as the process reaches the calculation of the tax rates.

Additional information on the Illinois tax code and specific tax situations can be found in Chapter 35 of the Illinois Compiled Statutes. ■

Enforcement of tax liens Real estate taxes must be valid to be enforceable. That means they must be levied properly, must be used for a legal purpose, and must be applied equitably to all property. Real estate taxes that have remained delinquent for the statutory period can be collected through a **tax sale.**

| In Illinois | The statutory requirements for enforcement of tax liens are complex. When a property owner fails to pay taxes on real estate in Illinois, the property ultimately may be sold in one of three ways:

- At an *annual tax sale*
- At a *forfeiture sale*
- At a *scavenger sale*

Annual sale If the taxes on a property have not been paid by the due date of the second installment, the county collector can enforce the tax lien and request that the circuit court order a tax sale. The county has notification requirements that are prescribed by statute. These requirements include publication in a newspaper of general circulation within the community and a certified or registered mailing to the last known address of the taxpayer. The court will render judgment in favor of the county if the taxes are shown to be delinquent and proper notice has been given. *The court order allows only the sale of the tax lien, not the property itself.*

Prior to the time of sale, the owner and any other party with a legal interest (except undisclosed beneficiaries of a land trust) may redeem the property and stop the sale by paying the delinquent taxes, applicable interest, and publication costs. Successful purchasers at the sale are those who offer to pay all outstanding taxes, interest, publication costs, processing charges, and the county treasurer's indemnity fund fee.

If competitive bidding results, the bid is for the lowest rate of interest that will be accepted by the bidder in case of redemption during the first six months of the redemption period. The only persons not allowed to bid at the sale are owners, persons with legal interest, and/or their agents. The successful bidder must pay with cash, cashier's check, or certified check. Upon payment, the purchaser receives a *certificate of purchase*. The certificate will ripen into a **tax deed** if no redemption is made within the statutorily prescribed period.

The statutory time period allowed for redemption on properties with six or fewer units is 2½ years from the date of sale. If the property is not redeemed by the owner within the period allowed, the tax sale purchaser is required to give notice to the delinquent owner and other parties who hold any interest in the property before applying for a tax deed.

Forfeiture sale If there are no bids on a property at the annual tax sale, the property is forfeited to the state, although title does not really change. The owner still may redeem the property after forfeiture by paying delinquencies, publication costs, and interest. On the other hand, anyone who wants to purchase the property for the outstanding taxes may make application to the county. If this happens and the owner does not claim the property within 30 days of notification, the applicant will be issued a certificate of purchase once she pays the outstanding taxes, interest, and other fees. If redemption is later made by the original owner, the certificate holder must be compensated based on 12 percent interest for each six months the certificate was held.

Scavenger sale   If the taxes have not been paid on a property for two years or more, the property may be sold at a *scavenger sale*. The county must go through the same court process as it would for tax sales and receive an order of sale. The property is sold to the highest bidder. The buyer is not required to pay the tax lien but must pay current taxes. In this case, former owners may not bid on their delinquent properties, either in person or through an agent, nor may individuals who are delinquent on their taxes by two or more years.

As noted earlier, redemption rights apply. However, the redemption period is only six months for vacant nonfarm real estate, commercial or industrial property, or property improved with seven or more residential units. For redemption to occur, all past-due taxes plus interest and penalties must be paid by the redeemer. In addition, the owner of the certificate of purchase must be paid back her bid price plus interest. ■

Special Assessments (Improvement Taxes)

Special assessments are taxes levied on real estate to fund public improvements to the property. Property owners living nearest to the improvements are required to pay for them because their properties benefit directly from the improvements. For example, the installation of paved streets, curbs, gutters, sidewalks, storm sewers, or street lighting increases the values of the affected properties. The owners, in effect, reimburse the levying authority. However, dollar-for-dollar increases in value are rarely the result.

Special assessments are always specific and statutory, but they can be either involuntary or voluntary liens. Improvements initiated by a public agency create involuntary liens. However, when property owners petition the local government to install a public improvement for which the owners agree to pay (such as a sidewalk or paved alley), the assessment lien is voluntary.

Whether the lien is voluntary or involuntary, each property in the improvement district is charged a prorated share of the total amount of the assessment. The share is determined either on a fractional basis (four houses may equally share the cost of one streetlight) or on a cost-per-front-foot basis (wider lots incur a greater cost than narrower lots for street paving and curb and sidewalk installation).

In Illinois

Special assessments usually are due in equal annual installments, plus interest, over a period of five to ten years, with the first installment usually due during the year following the public authority's approval of the assessment. The first bill includes one year's interest on the property owner's share of the entire assessment; subsequent bills include one year's interest on the unpaid balance. Property owners have the right to prepay any or all installments to avoid future interest charges. The annual due date for assessment payments in Illinois is generally January 2. ■

Special Service Areas

In Illinois

Special Service Areas (SSAs) are special taxing districts in municipalities that are established by ordinance, often at the request of developers of new housing subdivisions, in order to pass on the costs of the streets, landscaping, water lines, and sewer systems to homeowners who reside within the SSA. The SSA assessments pay off the municipal bonds that are issued to pay for the infrastructure. Assessments are billed annually on property tax bills, generally for a period of 20 to 30 years.

Even though these assessments appear on property tax bills, they are only tax-deductible if they are for the repairs or maintenance of existing infrastructure. The assessments are not tax-deductible if they are for new infrastructure. The interest portion of the assessment is tax-deductible only if the taxpayer has an itemized statement that clearly delineates or allocates the dollar amount of the interest from the principal, which is not done in most counties. ■

■ OTHER LIENS ON REAL PROPERTY

In addition to real estate tax and special assessment liens, a variety of other liens may be charged against real property.

Mortgage Liens (Deed of Trust Liens)

A **mortgage lien**, sometimes called a *deed of trust lien*, is a voluntary lien on real estate given to a lender by a borrower as security for a real estate loan. It becomes a lien on real property when the lender records the documents in the county where the property is located. Lenders generally require a preferred lien, referred to as a *first mortgage lien*. This means that no other liens against the property (aside from real estate taxes) would take priority over the mortgage lien. Subsequent liens are referred to as *junior liens*.

Mechanics' Liens

A **mechanic's lien** is a specific, involuntary lien that gives security to persons or companies that perform labor or furnish material to improve real property. A mechanic's lien is available to contractors, subcontractors, architects, equipment lessors, surveyors, laborers, and other providers. This type of lien is filed when the owner has not fully paid for the work or when the general contractor has been compensated but has not paid the subcontractors or material suppliers. Statutes in some states prohibit subcontractors from placing liens directly on certain types of property, such as owner-occupied residences. While laws regarding mechanics' liens vary from state to state, there are many similarities.

In Illinois

To be entitled to a mechanic's lien, the person who did the work must have had a contract (express or implied) with the owner or the owner's authorized representative. Releases of lien or lien waivers should be sought by the seller once work is paid, with signatures from the general contractor and the subcontractors. Also, a "no-lien contract" filed on the project precludes any liens. If improvements that were not ordered by the property owner have commenced, the property owner may execute a document called a *notice of nonresponsibility* to attempt to relieve herself from possible mechanics' liens. By posting this notice in some conspicuous place on the property and recording a verified copy of it in the public record, the owner gives notice that she is not responsible for the work done.

Contractors with unpaid bills who wish to enforce their lien rights against an owner must file their lien notices within four months after the work is completed. Subcontractors have the right in Illinois to file for their unpaid claims as well, even when the general contractor has been paid in full.

Under the Illinois Mechanic's Lien Act notice requirements, a contractor who makes improvements to an owner-occupied, single-family residence must give the owner written notice within ten days after recording a lien against any property of the owner. If timely notice is not given and, as a result, the owner suffers damages before notice is given, the lien is extinguished to the extent of the damages. The mere recording of the lien claim is not considered damages. The amendment specifically applies to contractors and not to subcontractors.

Mechanics' liens can take priority over a previously recorded lien if the work done has enhanced the value of the property. The lien attaches as of the date when the work was ordered or the contract was signed by the owner. The date of attachment establishes the lien's priority over other liens. From the point of view of the public or a prospective purchaser, an unpaid contractor has a "secret lien" until the notice is recorded. ■

Waiver and disclaimer   The names of all subcontractors must be listed by the general contractor in a sworn statement. This list is presented to the landowner who ordered the work. **Lien waivers** (or *waivers of lien*) should be collected by the landowner from each contractor and subcontractor to create a continuing record that all lien claimants have released their lien rights. Materials suppliers and property managers should also be approached for releases.

In Illinois   **Expiration of lien right and commencement of suit**   In Illinois, the contractor's lien right will expire two years after completion of that contractor's work, unless she files suit within that time to foreclose the lien. Suits to enforce mechanic's liens must be filed within two years after the last labor and/or materials were supplied. Under Section 34 of the Illinois Mechanic's Lien Act, a property owner can demand that the suit be commenced in 30 days. This suit can force the sale of the real estate through a court order to provide funds to pay the claimant's lien. ■

Judgments

A **judgment** is an order issued by a court that settles and defines the rights and obligations of the parties to a lawsuit. When the judgment establishes the amount a debtor owes and provides for money to be awarded, it is referred to as a *money judgment*.

A judgment is a general, involuntary, equitable lien on both real and personal property owned by the debtor. A judgment is not the same as a mortgage because no specific parcel of real estate was given as security at the time the debt was created. A lien usually covers only property located within the county in which the judgment is issued. As a result, a notice of the lien must be filed in any county to which a creditor wishes to extend the lien coverage.

A judgment becomes a general lien on all the defendant's real and personal property in a county at the time the judgment is recorded in the county recorder's office. For the lien to be effective in another county, a memorandum of judgment must be recorded in that county.

Judgment liens are effective in Illinois for seven years and may be renewed for another seven-year term.

To enforce an actual judgment, the creditor must obtain a *writ of execution* from the court. A writ of execution directs the sheriff to seize and sell as much of the debtor's property as is necessary to pay both the debt and the expenses of the sale. A judgment does not become a lien against *personal property* (as opposed to real property) of a debtor until the creditor orders the sheriff to levy the property and the levy actually is made. When property is sold, the debtor should demand a *satisfaction of judgment* (or *satisfaction piece*) to clear the record. ■

Lis pendens   There is often a considerable delay between the time a lawsuit is filed and the time final judgment is rendered. When any suit is filed that affects title to real estate, a special notice known as a **lis pendens** (Latin for "litigation pending") is recorded. A lis pendens is not itself a lien but rather notice of a possible future lien. Recording a lis pendens notifies prospective purchasers and lenders that there is a potential claim against the property. It also establishes a priority for the later lien: the lien is backdated to the recording date of the lis pendens.

Attachments   Special rules apply to realty that is not mortgaged or similarly encumbered. To prevent a debtor from conveying title to such previously unsecured real estate while a court suit is being decided, a creditor may seek a **writ of attachment**. By this writ, the court retains custody of the property until the suit concludes. First, the creditor must post a surety bond or deposit with the court. The bond must be sufficient to cover any possible loss or damage the debtor may suffer while the court has custody of the property. In the event the judgment is not awarded to the creditor, the debtor will be reimbursed from the bond.

Estate and Inheritance Tax Liens

Federal **estate taxes** and state **inheritance taxes** (as well as the debts of decedents) are *general, statutory, involuntary liens* that encumber a deceased person's real and personal property. These are normally paid or cleared in probate court proceedings.

Liens for Municipal Utilities

Municipalities often have the right to impose a *specific, equitable, involuntary lien* on the property of an owner who refuses to pay bills for municipal utility services.

Bail Bond Lien

A real estate owner who is charged with a crime for which she must face trial may post bail in the form of real estate rather than cash. The execution and recording of such a bail bond creates a *specific, statutory, voluntary lien* against the owner's real estate. If the accused fails to appear in court, the lien may be enforced by the sheriff or another court officer.

Corporation Franchise Tax Lien

State governments generally levy a *corporation franchise tax* on corporations as a condition of allowing them to do business in the state. Such a tax is a *general, statutory, involuntary lien* on all real and personal property owned by the corporation.

IRS Tax Lien

A *federal tax lien*, or Internal Revenue Service (IRS) tax lien, results from a person's failure to pay any portion of federal taxes, such as income and withholding taxes. A federal tax lien is a *general, statutory, involuntary lien* on all real and personal property held by the delinquent taxpayer. Its priority, however, is based on the date of filing or recording; it does not supersede previously recorded liens.

| In Illinois | The Commercial Real Estate Broker Lien Act permits commercial sponsoring brokers to place a lien on property in the amount of the commission they are entitled to receive for leasing as well as for a sale under a written brokerage agreement in the event they are not paid for their services. The lien applies to commercial property only, and it must be recorded before closing to be enforceable. ∎

A summary of the real estate-related liens discussed in this chapter appears in Table 10.1.

■ SUMMARY

Liens are claims of creditors or taxing authorities against the real and personal property of a debtor. A lien is a type of encumbrance. Liens are either general, covering all real and personal property of a debtor-owner, or specific, covering only identified property. They also are either voluntary, arising from an action of the debtor, or involuntary, created by statute (statutory) or based on the concept of fairness (equitable).

With the exception of tax liens and special assessment liens, which are always paid first, the priority of liens is generally determined by the order in which they are placed into the public record. The statutory requirements for enforcement of liens in Illinois are complex, vary from county to county, and depend on the type of property involved.

Real estate taxes are levied annually by local taxing authorities and are generally given priority over other liens when they are not paid.

TABLE 10.1

Real Estate–Related Liens

	General	Specific	Voluntary		Involuntary
General real estate tax (ad valorem tax) lien		•			•
Special assessment (improvement tax) lien		•	•	or	•
Mortgage lien		•	•		
Deed of trust lien		•	•		
Mechanic's lien		•			•
Judgment lien	•				•
Estate tax lien	•				•
Inheritance tax lien	•				•
Debts of a decedent	•				•
Municipal utilities lien		•			•
Bail bond lien		•	•		
Corporation franchise tax lien	•				•
Federal income tax lien	•				•

Taxes are determined by first determining total cost of public needs, then dividing the cost for these needs into the sum value of taxable property (equalized and adjusted) to determine a tax rate.

Payments for property taxes are required in each county before stated dates, after which penalties accrue. An owner may lose title to property for nonpayment of taxes because such tax-delinquent property can be sold at a tax sale. Some states allow a time period during which a defaulted owner can utilize right of redemption to save her real estate from tax sale.

Special assessments are levied to allocate the cost of public improvements to the specific parcels of real estate that benefit from them. Assessments usually are payable annually over a five- or ten-year period with interest due on the balance of the assessment.

Special service areas (SSAs) are special taxing districts in municipalities that are established by ordinance in order to pass on the costs of the streets, landscaping, water lines, and sewer systems to homeowners who reside within the SSA. They are billed annually, generally for a period of 20 to 30 years.

Mortgage liens (or deed of trust liens) are voluntary, specific liens given to lenders to secure payment for real estate loans.

Mechanics' liens protect general contractors, subcontractors, property managers, and material suppliers whose work enhances the value of real estate. Lien waivers protect property owners when these debts have been paid.

A judgment is a court decree obtained by a creditor, usually for a monetary award from a debtor. A judgment lien can be enforced by court issuance of a writ of execution and sale by the sheriff to pay the judgment amount and costs.

Attachment is a means of preventing a defendant from conveying property before completion of a suit in which a judgment is sought.

Lis pendens is a recorded notice of a lawsuit that is pending in court and that may result in a judgment affecting title to a parcel of real estate.

Federal estate taxes and state inheritance taxes are general liens against a deceased owner's property.

Liens for water charges or other municipal utilities and bail bond liens are specific liens, while corporation franchise tax liens are general liens.

IRS tax liens are general liens against the property of a person who is delinquent in paying IRS taxes.

In Illinois

The Homeowners' Exemption is an annual concession that reduces the assessed value of a property. The basic homeowners' exemption in many counties must be applied for every year. The Senior Citizen's Homestead Exemption is available to a homeowner over age 65 and renews automatically. The Seniors Citizen's Assessment Freeze Exemption, an even stronger alternative, freezes assessed valuation for the rest of a senior citizen's life if she applies and is over age 65. The Homestead Improvement Exemption gives any homeowner improving her home a four-year delay before the increased home value affects taxes.

General real estate taxes are payable in two equal installments in the year after they are levied—June 1 and September 1. Full reassessments for tax purposes take place every four years in Illinois.

When a property owner fails to pay taxes on her real estate, the property may be sold at an annual tax sale, a forfeiture sale, or a scavenger sale.

Mechanics' liens must be filed by contractors, electricians, plumbers, or other hired home improvement personnel within four months after work was completed. However, such liens are retroactive (making mechanics' liens the so-called secret liens). These liens attach (become legal and enforceable based on date) as of the time the work was ordered or when the contract was first signed by the owner.

Under the Illinois Mechanic's Lien Act notice requirements, a contractor who makes improvements to an owner-occupied, single-family residence must give the owner written notice within ten days after recording a lien against any property of the owner. If timely notice is not given and, as a result, the owner suffers damages before notice is given, the lien is extinguished to the extent of the damages. The mere recording of the lien claim is not considered damages. The amendment specifically applies to contractors and not to subcontractors.

A judgment becomes a general lien on all the defendant's real and personal property located in the county at the time the judgment was recorded. A judgment lien stays in effect in Illinois for seven years and is renewable for another seven. During such time, if the property is sold, the lien amount is usually paid from the proceeds. ∎

CHAPTER 10 QUIZ

1. Which lien affects all real and personal property of a debtor?
   - a. Specific
   - b. Voluntary
   - c. Statutory
   - d. General

2. Priority of liens refers to which of the following?
   - a. Order in which a debtor assumes responsibility for payment of obligations
   - b. Order in which liens will be paid if property is sold to satisfy a debt
   - c. Dates liens are filed for record
   - d. Fact that specific liens have greater priority than general liens

3. Which of the following is a lien on real estate made to secure payment for a specific municipal improvement project?
   - a. Mechanic's lien
   - b. Special assessment
   - c. Ad valorem
   - d. Utility lien

4. Which of the following would be classified as a general lien?
   - a. Mechanic's lien
   - b. Bail bond lien
   - c. Judgment
   - d. Real estate taxes

5. Which of the following liens would usually be given highest priority in disbursing funds from a foreclosure sale?
   - a. Mortgage dated last year
   - b. Real estate taxes due
   - c. Mechanic's lien for work started before the mortgage was made
   - d. Judgment rendered yesterday

6. A specific parcel of real estate has a market value of $160,000 and is assessed for tax purposes at 75 percent of market value. The tax rate for the county in which the property is located is 4 percent. The tax bill will be
   - a. $6,400.
   - b. $5,000.
   - c. $5,200.
   - d. $4,800.

   160,000 × 75% = 120K
   120K · 4% = 4800

7. Which of the following taxes targets homeowners in particular?
   - a. Personal property tax
   - b. Sales tax
   - c. Real property tax
   - d. Luxury tax

8. A homeowner decided to add a family room onto his house. An electrician was hired to wire the room and has not been paid. The electrician would have the right to
   - a. tear out his work.
   - b. record a notice of the lien.
   - c. record a notice of the lien and file a court suit within the time required by state law.
   - d. have personal property of the owner sold to satisfy the lien.

9. What is the annual real estate tax on a property valued at $135,000 and assessed for tax purposes at $47,250, with an equalization factor of 125 percent, when the tax rate is 2.5 percent?
   - a. $945
   - b. $1,181
   - c. $1,418
   - d. $1,477

   47,250 · 125.0% =
   59,062.50 · 2.5%
   = $1477

10. Which of the following is a voluntary, specific lien?
    - a. IRS tax lien
    - b. Mechanic's lien
    - c. Mortgage lien
    - d. Special assessment

11. In two weeks, a general contractor will file a suit against a homeowner for nonpayment. The contractor just learned that the homeowner has listed the property for sale with a real estate broker. In this situation, which of the following will the contractor's attorney use to protect the contractor's interest?

a. Seller's lien
b. Buyer's lien
c. Assessment
d. Lis pendens

12. Which of the following statements BEST describes special assessment liens?

a. They are general liens.
b. They are paid on a monthly basis.
c. They take priority over mechanics' liens.
d. They cannot be prepaid in full without penalty.

13. Which of the following creates a lien on real estate?

a. Easement running with the land
b. Unpaid mortgage loan
c. License
d. Encroachment

14. A mechanic's lien would be available to which of the following?

a. Seller's real estate agent
b. Buyer's real estate agent
c. Taxing authority
d. Contractor

15. A person owns a primary residence and two apartment buildings. He pays property taxes on two of the three properties. The delinquent taxes will result in a lien on

a. all three properties.
b. all real and personal property that he owns.
c. his primary residence only.
d. the property on which he has not paid the taxes.

16. General real estate taxes levied for the operation of the government are called

a. assessment taxes.
b. ad valorem taxes.
c. special taxes.
d. improvement taxes.

17. The equalization factor used in Illinois taxation is designed to

a. increase the tax revenues of the state.
b. correct discrepancies between the assessed values of similar parcels of land in various counties.
c. correct inequities in taxes for senior citizens and disabled persons.
d. decrease taxes for the poor and unemployed.

18. A person owns a condominium town house in Cook County and a weekend retreat in Sangamon County, both in Illinois. This person also owns investment property in Montana. If one of his creditors sues him in a Cook County court and a judgment is issued against him and is recorded in both Cook and Sangamon counties, which of the following is TRUE?

a. The judgment becomes a lien on the property located in both Cook and Sangamon counties.
b. The judgment becomes a lien on the weekend retreat, the person's speedboat, and all other items of real and personal property in Sangamon County.
c. The judgment becomes a lien on all the person's real and personal property, wherever located.
d. The judgment becomes a lien on the Cook County town house only.

19. Which of the following statements is TRUE of the successful bidder on property offered at an annual tax sale?

a. She owns the property after paying the outstanding taxes.
b. She bids the highest percentage of interest she will accept if the property is redeemed.
c. She may obtain a tax deed if the property is not redeemed within the redemption period.
d. She receives a tax deed at the time of the sale.

20. The first installment of the tax bill for all counties except Cook is due on

a. June 1.
b. September 1.
c. the first business day in March.
d. the day after the actual amount of the current year's tax is determined.

CHAPTER 11

Real Estate Contracts

■ **LEARNING OBJECTIVES**   *When you've finished reading this chapter, you should be able to*

- **identify** the requirements for a valid contract;

- **describe** the various types of contracts used in the real estate business;

- **explain** how contracts may be discharged;

- **distinguish** among bilateral and unilateral, executed and executory, and valid, void, and voidable contracts; and

- **define** the following *key terms*

assignment	executed contract	suit for specific
bilateral contract	executory contract	performance
breach of contract	express contract	time is of the essence
commingling	implied contract	unenforceable contract
consideration	installment contract	Uniform Vendor and
contingencies	land contract	Purchaser Risk Act
contract	liquidated damages	unilateral contract
conversion	novation	valid
counteroffer	offer and acceptance	void
earnest money	option	voidable
equitable title	statute of frauds	

■ CONTRACT LAW

> A contract is a voluntary, legally enforceable promise between two competent parties to perform some legal act in exchange for consideration.

The real estate market is driven by contracts. Both listing and buyer representation agreements are employment contracts. Options are contracts, and an offer is the first half of a sales contract. Leases and escrows are contracts. Wherever you go as a real estate professional, whatever aspect of the real estate business you find yourself in, you will be dealing with contracts. It is important for a licensee to know how a contract is created, what it means, what is required for the parties, and what kinds of actions can end it.

A **contract** is a voluntary agreement or promise between legally competent parties, supported by legal consideration, to perform (or refrain from performing) some legal act. That definition may be easier to understand if its various parts are examined separately. A contract must be

- *voluntary*—no one may be forced into a contract;
- *an agreement or a promise*—a contract is essentially a legally enforceable promise;
- made by *legally competent parties*—the parties must be viewed by the law as capable of making a legally binding promise;
- supported by *legal consideration*—a contract must be supported by something of value that induces a party to enter into the contract, and that something must be legally sufficient to support a contract; and
- having to do with a *legal act*—no one may legally contract to do something illegal.

Licensees use many types of contracts and agreements to carry out their responsibilities to sellers, buyers, and the general public. The general body of law that governs such agreements is known as *contract law*.

IN PRACTICE Real estate licensees are advised to use preprinted and preapproved forms provided by their sponsoring brokers or associations if they are members of a REALTOR® association. Also, remember that licensees cannot practice law without a license. Both the buyer and the seller have the option of seeking legal counsel for form preparation.

Express and Implied Contracts

Depending on how a contract is created, it is either express or implied. An **express contract** exists when the parties state the terms and show their intentions in *words*. An express contract may be oral or written. Under the **statute of frauds**, certain types of contracts (including those for the sale of real property) must be in writing to be enforceable in a court of law. (*Enforceable* means that the parties may be forced to comply with the contract's terms and conditions.) In an **implied contract**, the agreement of the parties is demonstrated by their *acts and conduct*.

■ FOR EXAMPLE When a buyer signs a contract to purchase a house for $350,000, and the seller signs the contract in agreement, this is an *express* contract. When a diner orders a meal in a restaurant, the diner has entered an *implied* contract with the restaurant to pay for the meal, even though payment was not mentioned before the meal was ordered.

In Illinois The Illinois Statute of Frauds requires that any contracts for the sale of land, or for leases that will not be fulfilled within one year from the date they are entered into, must be in writing to be enforceable in court. The Illinois Real Estate License Act of 2000 also indicates that certain contracts must be in writing, such as employment agreements between sponsoring brokers and their sponsored licensees. ■

Bilateral and Unilateral Contracts

Bilateral contract
Bi means two—must have two promises.
Unilateral contract
Uni means one—has only one promise.

Contracts may be classified as either *bilateral* or *unilateral*. In a **bilateral contract**, both parties promise to do something; one promise is given in exchange for another. A real estate sales contract is a bilateral contract because the seller promises to sell a parcel of real estate and convey property title to the buyer, who in turn promises to pay a certain sum of money for the property.

A **unilateral contract**, on the other hand, is a one-sided agreement. One party makes a promise to induce a second party to do something. The second party is not legally obligated to act. However, if the second party does comply, the first party is then obligated to keep the promise. An option contract to retain one's option to possibly make a purchase later is an example of a unilateral contract.

In Illinois Illinois case law supports the proposition that exclusive listing contracts are unilateral, not bilateral, contracts. If exclusive listing contracts were bilateral contracts, then the listing broker would be in breach of contract if he failed to produce a buyer. ■

■ **FOR EXAMPLE**   A homeowner offers to pay a commission to a broker to find a buyer for a property. The broker is not obligated to find a buyer. The property owner is only obligated to pay a commission to the broker who finds a buyer. This is a unilateral contract.

Executed and Executory Contracts

A contract may be classified as either *executed* or *executory*, depending on whether the agreement is performed. An **executed contract** is one in which all parties have fulfilled their promises: the contract has been performed. This sometimes can be confused with the word *execute*, which refers to the act of signing a contract. An **executory contract** exists when one or both parties still have an act to perform. A sales contract is an executory contract from the time it is signed until closing: ownership has not yet changed hands, and the seller has not received the sales price. At closing, the sales contract is executed.

Table 11.1 highlights the formation of a contract, which will be discussed in detail in this chapter.

Essential Elements of a Valid Contract

A contract must meet certain minimum requirements to be considered legally valid. The following are the basic essential elements of a contract.

T A B L E 11.1	**Preformation**	**Formation**	**Postformation**
Contract Formation	**Essential Elements**	**Classification**	**Discharge**
	Offer, Acceptance, Consideration, Legal Purpose, Legal Capacity	Valid, Void, Voidable, Enforceable, Unenforceable, Express, Implied, Unilateral, Bilateral, Executory, Executed	Performance, Breach, Remedies (Damages, Specific Performance, Rescission)

Elements of a Contract:

Offer and acceptance
Consideration
Legally competent parties
Consent
Legal purpose

Offer and acceptance (mutual assent)   There must be an offer by one party that is accepted by the other. The person who makes the offer is the *offeror*. The person who accepts the offer is the *offeree*. This requirement also is called *mutual assent*. It means that there must be a *meeting of the minds*, or complete agreement about the purpose and terms of the contract. Courts look to the objective intent of the parties to determine whether there was intent to enter into a binding agreement. In cases where the statute of frauds applies, the **offer and acceptance** must be in writing. The wording of the contract must express all the agreed-on terms and must be clearly understood by the parties.

An *offer* is a promise made by one party, requesting something in exchange for that promise. The offer is made with the intention that the offeror will be bound to the terms if the offer is accepted. The terms of the offer must be definite and specific and must be communicated to the offeree.

A *counteroffer* is a *new offer*; it voids the original offer.

Proposing any deviation from the terms of the offer constitutes a rejection of the original offer and creates a *new offer*. The original offer ceases to exist because the seller has rejected it. The buyer may accept or reject the seller's counteroffer. If the buyer desires, the process may continue by making another **counteroffer**. Any change in the last offer may result in a counteroffer until either party reached an agreement or one party walks away.

Any offer or counteroffer may be withdrawn at any time before it has been accepted, even if the person making the offer or counteroffer agreed to keep the offer open for a set period.

Acceptance   If the seller agrees to the original offer or a later counteroffer exactly as it is made and signs the document, the offer has been accepted and a contract is formed. The licensee must advise the buyer of the seller's acceptance and obtain the approval of the parties' attorneys if the contract calls for it. A copy of the contract must be provided to each party.

An offer is not considered accepted until the person making the offer has been notified of the other party's acceptance. When the parties communicate through a licensee or at a distance, questions may arise regarding whether an acceptance, rejection, or counteroffer has occurred. Though current technology allows for fast communication, a signed agreement that is faxed, for instance, would not necessarily constitute adequate communication. The licensee must transmit all offers, acceptances, or other responses as soon as possible to avoid questions of proper communication.

Under the REALTOR® Code of Ethics (Standard of Practice 1–6), "REALTORS® shall submit offers and counteroffers objectively and as quickly as possible."

Presenting and negotiating multiple offers on the same property has the potential for misunderstanding and legal issues for real estate licensees. Licensees must be very careful that the seller accepts only one offer. It is the duty of the licensee to protect his client while treating all parties honestly. It is also important to follow state license law dealing with duties to buyer clients and seller clients. (See Chapter 6)

IN PRACTICE The process of negotiating usually follows the same basic pattern and protocol. First, the buyer makes an offer. The seller then has three options: to accept the offer, reject it, or make a counteroffer. If the seller accepts or rejects the offer, the process is over; either there is a contract or there is not. If the seller makes a counteroffer, the seller is essentially starting the process over again. The buyer now has the same three options. Through this back-and-forth process, the parties hope to come to a mutual agreement. It's important that the licensees representing the parties keep them aware of where they are in the negotiating process to avoid confusion about what offers are (or are not) still active because each counteroffer negates the offer that preceded it.

Besides being terminated by a counteroffer, an offer may be terminated by the offeree's outright rejection of it. Alternatively, an offeree may fail to accept the offer before it expires if a time frame was attached to the offer. The offeror may *revoke* the offer at any time before receiving the acceptance. This revocation must be communicated to the offeree by the offeror, either directly or through the licensees who are the parties' agents. The offer also is considered revoked if the offeree learns of the revocation and observes the offeror acting in a manner that indicates that the offer no longer exists. (See Figure 11.1)

IN PRACTICE The licensee must transmit all offers, acceptances, or other responses *as soon as possible* to avoid charges of deliberate delay and possible communication problems. Such speed can be critical to the client's interests. Until a final offer is accepted, the property remains on the market, available to other buyers.

FIGURE 11.1

The Negotiation Process: Offer, Counteroffer, and Acceptance Flowchart

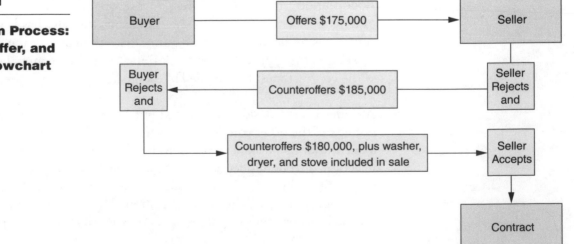

It is possible that the first buyer will lose the house to another buyer with a better offer or the price needed to acquire the property may escalate in a "multiple offer." When a sales contract hasn't been signed, a seller's prospective buyer may move to make an offer on a newly listed property down the block with a nicer kitchen and a lower asking price. These are real scenarios licenses want to avoid.

Consideration   The contract must be based on consideration. **Consideration** is something of legal value offered by one party and accepted by another as an inducement to perform or to refrain from performing some act. There must be a definite statement of consideration in a contract to show that something of value was given (or promised) in exchange for the other party's promise.

Consideration must be *good and valuable* between the parties. The courts do not inquire into the adequacy of consideration. Adequate consideration ranges from as little as a promise of "love and affection" to a substantial sum of money. Anything that has been bargained for and exchanged is legally sufficient to satisfy the requirement for consideration. The only requirements are that the parties agree to the consideration and that no undue influence or fraud occurred.

Reality of consent   Under the doctrine of *reality of consent*, a contract must be entered into as the free and voluntary act of each party. Each party must be able to make a prudent and knowledgeable decision without undue influence. A mistake, misrepresentation, fraud, undue influence, or duress deprives a person of that ability. If any of these circumstances is present, the contract is voidable by the injured party. If the other party were to sue for breach, as a defense, the injured party could say the agreement lacks reality of consent.

Legal purpose   A contract must be for a legal purpose—that is, even with all the other elements (consent, competent parties, consideration, and offer and acceptance). A contract for an illegal purpose or an act against public policies is not a valid contract.

Legally competent parties   All parties to the contract must have legal capacity. That is, they must be of legal age and have enough mental capacity to understand the nature or consequences of their actions in the contract. In most states, 18 is the age of contractual capacity.

Validity of Contracts

A contract can be described as *valid, void, voidable,* or *unenforceable,* depending on the circumstances.

A contract is **valid** when it meets all the essential elements that make it legally sufficient or enforceable.

A contract is **void** when it has no legal force or effect because it lacks some or all of the essential elements of a contract.

A contract that is **voidable** appears on the surface to be valid but may be rescinded or disaffirmed by one or both parties based on some legal principle. If it is not disaffirmed, a voidable contract may nevertheless end up being executed. A voidable

---

A Contract May Be

Valid—has all legal elements and is fully enforceable;
Void—lacks one or all legal elements;
Voidable—has all legal elements and may be rescinded or disaffirmed; or
Unenforceable—has all legal elements and is enforceable only between the parties.

contract is considered by the courts to be valid if the party who has the option to disaffirm the agreement does not do so within a period of time prescribed by state law. A contract entered into under duress or intoxication or as a result of fraud, mistake, or misrepresentation is always voidable by the compelled or defrauded party. A contract with a minor is also voidable; minors are permitted to disaffirm real estate contracts at any time while underage and for a certain period of time after reaching majority age. Finally, a contract entered into by a mentally ill person usually is voidable *during* the mental illness and for a reasonable period after recovery. On the other hand, a contract made by a person who has been adjudicated insane (that is, found to be insane by a court) is void at the outset based on insanity judgments being a matter of public record.

| In Illinois | Illinois law provides that all persons come of "legal age" on their 18th birthday. *Contracts entered into by a minor in Illinois are voidable until the minor reaches majority* and for a reasonable time afterward. There is no statutory period within which a person may void a contract after reaching majority in Illinois. What is considered "reasonable" depends on the circumstances of each case, although the courts tend to allow a maximum of six months. |

Contracts made by a minor for what the law terms *necessaries* are generally enforceable. "Necessaries" include items such as food, clothing, shelter, and medical expenses. While a real estate sales contract with a minor probably would not be enforceable in Illinois, *leases or rental agreements signed by minors generally are enforceable* because short-term housing is usually considered a necessity. ∎

IN PRACTICE   Mental capacity to enter into a contract is not the same as medical sanity. The test is whether the individual in question is capable of understanding what he is doing. A party may suffer from a mental illness but have a clear understanding of the significance of his actions. This is a thorny legal and psychological question that requires consultation with experts.

An **unenforceable contract** may seem on the surface to be valid; however, neither party can sue the other to force performance. A contract may be unenforceable because it is not in writing, as may be required under the statute of frauds.

∎ **FOR EXAMPLE**   An oral agreement for the sale of a parcel of real estate would be "unenforceable." An unenforceable contract is said to be "valid as between the parties." There is, however, a distinction between a suit to force performance and a suit for damages; *suits for damages are permissible in an oral agreement.* This means that once the agreement is fully executed and both parties are satisfied, neither has reason to initiate a lawsuit to force performance.

IN PRACTICE   If a contract contains any ambiguity, the courts generally interpret the agreement against the party who prepared it.

∎ DISCHARGE OF CONTRACTS

A contract is discharged when the agreement is terminated. The most desirable case is when a contract terminates because it has been completely performed, with all its terms carried out. However, a contract may be terminated for other reasons, such as a party's breach or a default.

Performance of a Contract

Each party has certain rights and duties to fulfill. The question of when a contract must be performed is an important factor. Many contracts call for a specific time by which the agreed-on acts must be completely performed. In addition, many contracts provide that **time is of the essence**. This means that the contract must be performed within the time limit specified. A party who fails to perform on time is liable for breach of contract.

When a contract does not specify a date for performance, the acts it requires should be performed within a reasonable time. The interpretation of what constitutes a reasonable time depends on the situation. Generally, unless the parties agree otherwise, if the act can be done immediately, it should be performed immediately. Courts sometimes have declared contracts to be invalid because they did not contain a time or date for performance.

| In Illinois |

In Illinois, a deed or contract executed on a Sunday or legal holiday is valid and enforceable. However, when the last day on which a deed or contract must be executed is a holiday or a Sunday, the deed or contract may be executed on the next regular business day. ∎

Assignment

Assignment is a transfer of rights or duties under a contract. Rights may be assigned to a third party (called the *assignee*) unless the contract forbids it. Obligations also may be assigned (or *delegated*), but the original party remains primarily liable unless specifically released. An assignment may be made without the consent of the other party unless the contract includes a clause that permits or forbids assignment.

∎ **FOR EXAMPLE**   A widower in his 80s wants to move closer to his children. His house has been on the market some time. The widower is in the hospital at the time a buyer makes an offer to purchase, so he assigns his contract rights to his son. This allows the property to be sold in a real estate closing transaction without him being present or signing documents.

Novation

Assignment = *substitution of parties*
Novation = *substitution of contracts*

Substitution of a new contract for an existing contract is called **novation**. The new agreement may be between the same parties, or a new party may be substituted for either (this is *novation of the parties*). The parties' intent must be to discharge the old obligation. For instance, when a real estate purchaser assumes the seller's existing mortgage loan, the lender may choose to release the seller and substitute the buyer as the party primarily liable for the mortgage debt. When there are many changes to a real estate contract and it is faxed several times, the contract may not be legible. Novation occurs when a new, clear contract with all the accepted changes is signed by all the parties.

Breach of Contract

A contract may be terminated if it is *breached* by one of the parties. A **breach of contract** is a violation of any of the terms or conditions of a contract without legal excuse. For instance, a seller who fails to deliver title to the buyer breaches a sales contract. The breaching or defaulting party assumes certain burdens, and the nondefaulting party has certain remedies.

Buyer Remedies
- Suit for specific performance
- Suit for damages
- Rescind contract

If the seller breaches a real estate sales contract, the buyer may sue for **specific performance** unless the contract specifically states otherwise. In a suit for specific performance, the buyer asks the court to force the seller to go through with the sale and convey the property as previously agreed. The buyer may choose to sue for damages, in which case the buyer asks that the seller pay for any costs and hardships suffered by the buyer as a result of the seller's breach. Alternatively, the buyer may *rescind* (cancel) the contract and the seller must return any earnest money deposit.

Seller Remedies
- Suit for specific performance
- Suit for damages
- Declare contract forfeited

If the buyer defaults, the seller can sue for damages or sue for the purchase price. A suit for the purchase price is essentially a suit for specific performance: The seller tenders the deed and asks that the buyer be compelled to pay the agreed price, or the seller may declare the contract forfeited. In this case, the contract usually permits the seller to retain the buyer's earnest money as *liquidated damages*. In addition, the seller may sue for *compensatory damages* if the buyer's breach resulted in further financial losses for the seller.

The contract may limit the remedies available to the parties. A *liquidated damages clause* permits the seller to keep the earnest money deposit and any other payments received from the buyer as the seller's sole remedy. The clause may limit the buyer's remedy to a return of the earnest money and other payments should the seller default.

Statute of limitations   Every state has laws that limit the time within which parties to a contract may bring legal suit to enforce their rights. The statute of limitations varies for different legal actions.

In Illinois

In Illinois, the statute of limitations for oral contracts is five years; for written contracts, ten years. Any rights not enforced within the applicable time period are lost. ■

Other Reasons for Termination

Contracts may also be discharged or terminated when any of the following occurs:

Partial performance of the terms, along with a written acceptance by the other party

- *Substantial performance*, in which one party has substantially performed on the contract but does not complete all the details exactly as the contract requires (Such performance may be enough to force payment, with certain adjustments for any damages suffered by the other party.) For instance, if a newly constructed addition to a home were finished except for polishing the brass doorknobs, the contractor would be entitled to the final payment.

■ *Impossibility of performance*, in which an act required by the contract cannot be legally accomplished

■ *Mutual agreement* of the parties to cancel

■ *Operation of law*—such as in the voiding of a contract by a minor—as a result of fraud, due to the expiration of the statute of limitations, or because a contract was altered without the *written consent of all parties involved*

■ *Rescission*—one party may cancel or terminate the contract as if it had never been made. Cancellation terminates a contract without a return to the original position. Rescission, however, returns the parties to their original positions before the contract, so any monies that have been exchanged must be returned. Rescission is normally a contractual remedy for a breach, but a contract may also be rescinded by the mutual agreement of the parties.

■ CONTRACTS USED IN THE REAL ESTATE BUSINESS

The written agreements most commonly used by brokers and managing brokers are

■ listing agreements and buyer agency agreements,

■ real estate sales contracts,

■ options agreements,

■ escrow agreements,

■ leases, and

■ land contracts or contracts for deed.

IN PRACTICE   Usually, the practice of law is interpreted as preparing legal documents, such as deeds and mortgages, and offering advice on legal matters. To avoid charges of unauthorized practice of law, real estate licensees should avoid offering legal advice and follow the guidelines created by state real estate officials, court decisions, or statutes in their states. Generally, licensees are permitted to fill in the blanks on certain approved preprinted documents, such as sales contracts, as directed by the client. No separate fee may be charged for completing the forms.

Contract forms   Because so many real estate transactions are similar in nature, preprinted forms are available for most kinds of contracts. The use of preprinted forms raises three problems: (1) what to write in the blanks, (2) what words and phrases should be ruled out by drawing lines through them because they don't apply, and (3) what additional clauses or agreements (called *riders* or *addenda*) should be added. All changes and additions are usually initialed in the margin or on the rider by both parties when a contract is signed.

IN PRACTICE   It is essential that both parties to a contract understand exactly what they are agreeing to. Poorly drafted documents, especially those containing extensive legal language, may be subject to various interpretations and lead to litigation. The parties in a real estate transaction should be advised to have sales contracts and other legal documents examined by their lawyers before they sign to ensure that the agreements accurately reflect their intentions. When preprinted forms do not sufficiently address the unique provisions of a transaction, the parties should have an attorney draft an appropriate contract.

In Illinois

The 1966 Illinois Supreme Court decision in the case of *Chicago Bar Association, et al. v. Quinlan and Tyson, Inc.*, placed certain limitations on real estate licensees in drafting a contract of sale. The court ruled that licensees are authorized only to fill in blanks on printed form contracts that are customarily used in the real estate community. Real estate sales contracts that fit the "customarily used" requirement typically have been drafted by local bar associations and approved by the local REALTOR® associations.

All insertions and deletions must be at the direction of the *principals*, based on the negotiations. Advising a buyer or seller of the legal significance of any part of the contract or writing any change to the form language constitutes the unauthorized practice of law.

A licensee may not request or encourage a party to sign a contract or document that contains blank spaces to be "filled in later," nor can the licensee make changes to a signed contract without the written consent of the parties. If changes are made by the agreement of all the principals, the buyers and sellers must initial any changes they agree to add. All licensees are required to give each person signing or initialing the contract an original "true copy" within 24 hours of the time of signing.

A licensee also must not prepare or complete any document subsequent to the sales contract or related to its implementation, such as a deed, bill of sale, affidavit of title, note, mortgage, or other legal instrument. ∎

Listing and Buyer Agency Agreements

Listing and buyer agency agreements are employment contracts. A *listing agreement* establishes the rights and obligations of the sponsoring broker as agent and the seller as principal. A buyer agency agreement establishes the relationship between a buyer as principal and sponsoring broker as agent. (Refer to Chapter 6 for a complete discussion.)

Customary Terms of Real Estate Sales Contracts

A real estate sales contract contains the complete agreement between the buyer of a parcel of real estate and the seller. Depending on the area, this agreement may be known as an *offer to purchase*, a *contract of purchase and sale*, a *purchase agreement*, an *earnest money agreement*, a *deposit receipt*, or a *sales contract*.

In Illinois

In Illinois, a licensee should not use any form titled "Offer to Purchase" if the form is intended to become a binding real estate contract. Illinois law requires that sales contracts indicate at the top **"Real Estate Sales Contract"** in bold type. ∎

Whatever the contract is called, it is an offer to purchase real estate as soon as it has been prepared and signed by the purchaser. If the document is accepted and signed by the seller, it becomes a contract of sale. This transformation is referred to as *ripening* the contract.

The *contract of sale* is the most important document in the sale of real estate. It establishes the legal rights and obligations of the buyer and seller. In effect, it dictates the contents of the deed.

Parts of a sales contract   All real estate sales contracts can be divided into a number of separate parts. Although each form of contract contains these divisions, their location within a particular contract may vary. Most sales contracts include the following information:

- The purchaser's name and a statement of the purchaser's obligation to purchase the property, including how the purchaser intends to take title
- An adequate description of the property, such as the street address (Note that while a street address may be adequate for a sales contract, it is not legally sufficient as a description of the real property being conveyed, as discussed in Chapter 12.)
- The seller's name and a statement of the type of deed a seller agrees to give, including any covenants, conditions, and restrictions that apply to the deed
- The purchase price and how the purchaser intends to pay for the property, including earnest money deposits, additional cash from the purchaser, and the conditions of any mortgage financing the purchaser intends to obtain or assume
- The amount and form of the down payment or earnest money deposit and whether it will be in the form of a check or promissory note
- A provision for the closing of the transaction and the transfer of possession of the property to the purchaser by a specific date
- A provision for title evidence (abstract and legal opinion, certificate of title, or title insurance policy)
- The method by which real estate taxes, rents, fuel costs, and other expenses are to be prorated
- A provision for the completion of the contract should the property be damaged or destroyed between the time of signing and the closing date
- A liquidated damages clause, a right-to-sue provision, or another statement of remedies available in the event of default
- Contingency clauses (such as the buyer's obtaining financing or selling a currently owned property or the seller's acquisition of another desired property or clearing of the title; attorney approval and home inspection are other commonly included contingencies)
- The dated signatures of all parties (the signature of a witness is not essential to a valid contract)—In some states, the seller's nonowning spouse may be required to release potential marital or homestead rights. An agent may sign for a principal if the agent has been expressly authorized to do so. When sellers are co-owners, all must sign if the entire ownership is being transferred.
- In most states, an agency disclosure statement

Additional provisions   Many sales contracts provide for the following:

- Any personal property to be left with the premises for the purchaser (such as major appliances or lawn and garden equipment)
- Any real property to be removed by the seller before the closing (such as a storage shed)

- The transfer of any applicable warranties on items such as heating and cooling systems or built-in appliances
- The identification of any leased equipment that must be transferred to the purchaser or returned to the lessor (such as security systems, cable television boxes, and water softeners)
- The appointment of a closing or settlement agent
- Closing or settlement instructions
- The transfer of any impound or escrow account funds
- The transfer or payment of any outstanding special assessments
- The purchaser's right to inspect the property shortly before the closing or settlement (often called the walk-through)
- The agreement as to what documents will be provided by each party and when and where they will be delivered

In Illinois

The sale of a residence often includes personal property, such as drapes, as well as items that are fixtures, such as screens and storm windows or a built-in range. In Illinois, any fixtures that might be questioned as fixtures are listed in the sales contract. This can help to eliminate possible arguments at the time of the final walk-through. Even attached bookcases and sometimes shrubbery have managed to disappear if they are not listed. Title to personal property usually is transferred by a *bill of sale*, prepared by the attorney. (A typical Illinois residential sales contract is reproduced in Figure 11.2.) ■

Earnest money deposits. It is customary (although not legally required) for a purchaser to provide a deposit when making an offer to purchase real estate. This deposit, usually in the form of a check, is referred to as **earnest money**. The earnest money deposit is evidence of the buyer's intention to carry out the terms of the contract in good faith. Usually the check is given to the listing sponsoring broker, who holds it for the parties in a special account. If the offer is not accepted, the earnest money deposit is returned immediately to the would-be buyer.

The amount of the deposit is a matter to be agreed on by the parties. Under the terms of most listing agreements, the sponsoring broker is required to accept a "reasonable amount" as earnest money. The deposit should be an amount sufficient to

- discourage the buyer from defaulting,
- help the seller feel comfortable in taking the property off the market, and
- cover any expenses the seller might incur if the buyer defaults.

In Illinois

Many contracts provide that the deposit becomes the seller's property as liquidated damages if the buyer defaults. To release earnest money in Illinois, for any reason, signatures of both parties are required.

Sponsoring brokers who are holding earnest money deposits in sales and security deposits in leasing must establish special trust (or escrow) accounts for the deposit of funds entrusted to them in connection with real estate transactions. A sponsoring broker need not open a special escrow account for *each* earnest money deposit received, however, but may deposit all earnest money funds in one account. The escrow account is noninterest bearing, unless both parties agree in writing. If interest is paid on the deposit, the disposition of any accrued interest must be

FIGURE 11.2

Typical Residential Real Estate Sales Contract

MULTI-BOARD RESIDENTIAL REAL ESTATE CONTRACT 5.0

1 **1. THE PARTIES:** Buyer and Seller are hereinafter referred to as the "Parties".

2 Buyer(s) (Please Print) _____

3 Seller(s) (Please Print) _____

4 **If Dual Agency applies, complete Optional Paragraph 41.**

5 **2. THE REAL ESTATE:** Real Estate shall be defined as the Property, all improvements, the fixtures and
6 Personal Property included therein. Seller agrees to convey to Buyer or to Buyer's designated grantee, the
7 Real Estate with the approximate lot size or acreage of _____ commonly known as:

8 _____
9 Address   City   State   Zip

10 _____
11 County   Unit # (if applicable)   Permanent Index Number(s) of Real Estate

12 **If Condo/Coop/Townhome Parking is Included**: # of space(s) ____; identified as Space(s) #_____;
13 *(check type)* ❏ deeded space ❏ limited common element ❏ assigned space.

14 **3. FIXTURES AND PERSONAL PROPERTY:** All of the fixtures and included Personal Property are owned by
15 Seller and to Seller's knowledge are in operating condition on the Date of Acceptance, unless otherwise
16 stated herein. Seller agrees to transfer to Buyer all fixtures, all heating, electrical, plumbing and well systems
17 together with the following items of Personal Property by Bill of Sale at Closing:
18 *[Check or enumerate applicable items]*

19 __ Refrigerator	__ Central Air Conditioning	__ Central Humidifier	__ Light Fixtures, as they exist
20 __ Oven/Range/Stove	__ Window Air Conditioners	__ Water Softener (owned)	__ Built-in or Attached Shelving
21 __ Microwave	__ Ceiling Fan(s)	__ Sump Pumps	__ All Window Treatments & Hardware
22 __ Dishwasher	__ Intercom System	__ Electronic or Media Air Filter	__ Existing Storms & Screens
23 __ Garbage Disposal	__ TV Antenna System	__ Central Vac & Equipment	__ Fireplace Screens/Doors/Grates
24 __ Trash Compactor	__ Satellite Dish	__ Security Systems (owned)	__ Fireplace Gas Logs
25 __ Washer	__ Outdoor Shed	__ Garage Door Openers	__ Invisible Fence System, Collars & Box
26 __ Dryer	__ Planted Vegetation	with all Transmitters	__ Smoke Detectors
27 __ Attached Gas Grill	__ Outdoor Playsets	__ All Tacked Down Carpeting	__ Carbon Monoxide Detectors

28 **Other items included:** _____
29 **Items NOT included:** _____
30 Seller warrants to Buyer that all fixtures, systems and Personal Property included in this Contract shall be in
31 operating condition at Possession, except: _____.
32 A system or item shall be deemed to be in operating condition if it performs the function for which it is
33 intended, regardless of age, and does not constitute a threat to health or safety.
34 **Home Warranty ❏ shall ❏ shall not be included at a Premium not to exceed $_____.**

35 **4. PURCHASE PRICE:** Purchase Price of $_____ shall be paid as follows: Initial earnest money
36 of $_____ by ❏ check, ❏ cash **OR** ❏ note due on _____, 20____ to be increased
37 to a total of $_____ by _____, 20____. The earnest money shall be held by the
38 *[check one]* ❏ Seller's Broker ❏ Buyer's Broker as "Escrowee", in trust for the mutual benefit of the Parties.
39 The balance of the Purchase Price, as adjusted by prorations, shall be paid at Closing by wire transfer of

Buyer Initial _____	*Buyer Initial* _____	*Seller Initial* _____	*Seller Initial* _____
Address _____			v5.0e

FIGURE 11.2

Typical Residential Real Estate Sales Contract (continued)

40 funds, or by certified, cashier's, mortgage lender's or title company's check (provided that the title company's
41 check is guaranteed by a licensed title insurance company).

42 **5. CLOSING:** Closing or escrow payout shall be on _____, 20____ or at such time as mutually
43 agreed by the Parties in writing. Closing shall take place at the escrow office of the title company (or its
44 issuing agent) that will issue the Owner's Policy of Title Insurance, situated nearest the Real Estate or as shall
45 be agreed mutually by the Parties.

46 **6. POSSESSION:** Unless otherwise provided in Paragraph 39, Seller shall deliver possession to Buyer at the
47 time of Closing. Possession shall be deemed to have been delivered when Seller has vacated the Real Estate
48 and delivered keys to the Real Estate to Buyer or to the office of the Seller's Broker.

49 **7. STATUTORY DISCLOSURES:** If applicable, prior to signing this Contract, Buyer *[check one]* ❏ has ❏ has
50 not received a completed Illinois Residential Real Property Disclosure Report; *[check one]* ❏ has ❏ has not
51 received the EPA Pamphlet, "Protect Your Family From Lead in Your Home"; *[check one]* ❏ has ❏ has not
52 received a Lead-Based Paint Disclosure; *[check one]* ❏ has ❏ has not received the IEMA Pamphlet "Radon
53 Testing Guidelines for Real Estate Transactions"; *[check one]* ❏ has ❏ has not received the Disclosure of
54 Information on Radon Hazards.

55 **8. PRORATIONS:** Proratable items shall include, without limitation, rents and deposits (if any) from tenants;
56 Special Service Area or Special Assessment Area tax for the year of Closing only; utilities, water and sewer;
57 and Homeowner or Condominium Association fees (and Master/Umbrella Association fees, if applicable).
58 Accumulated reserves of a Homeowner/Condominium Association(s) are not a proratable item. Seller
59 represents that as of the Date of Acceptance Homeowner/Condominium Association(s) fees are $_____
60 per _____ (and, if applicable, Master/Umbrella Association fees are $_____ per _____). Seller agrees
61 to pay prior to or at Closing any special assessments (by any association or governmental entity) confirmed
62 prior to the Date of Acceptance. Installments due after the year of Closing for a Special Assessment Area or
63 Special Service Area shall not be a proratable item and shall be payable by Buyer. The general Real Estate
64 taxes shall be prorated as of the date of Closing based on _____% of the most recent ascertainable full year
65 tax bill. All prorations shall be final as of Closing, except as provided in Paragraph 20. If the amount of the
66 most recent ascertainable full year tax bill reflects a homeowner, senior citizen or other exemption, a senior
67 freeze or senior deferral, then Seller has submitted or will submit in a timely manner all necessary
68 documentation to the appropriate governmental entity, before or after Closing, to preserve said exemption(s).

69 **9. ATTORNEY REVIEW:** Within five (5) Business Days after the Date of Acceptance, the attorneys for the
70 respective Parties, by Notice, may:
71 (a) Approve this Contract; or
72 (b) Disapprove this Contract, which disapproval shall not be based solely upon the Purchase Price; or
73 (c) Propose modifications except for the Purchase Price. If within ten (10) Business Days after the Date of
74   Acceptance written agreement is not reached by the Parties with respect to resolution of the proposed
75   modifications, then either Party may terminate this Contract by serving Notice, whereupon this Contract
76   shall be null and void; or
77 (d) Propose suggested changes to this Contract. If such suggestions are not agreed upon, neither Party may
78   declare this Contract null and void and this Contract shall remain in full force and effect.
79 **Unless otherwise specified, all Notices shall be deemed made pursuant to Paragraph 9(c). If Notice is not**
80 **served within the time specified herein, the provisions of this paragraph shall be deemed waived by the**
81 **Parties and this Contract shall remain in full force and effect.**

Buyer Initial _____ *Buyer Initial* _____ *Seller Initial* _____ *Seller Initial* _____

Address _____ v5.0e

F I G U R E   11.2

Typical Residential Real Estate Sales Contract (continued)

82 **10. PROFESSIONAL INSPECTIONS AND INSPECTION NOTICES:** Buyer may conduct at Buyer's expense
83 (unless otherwise provided by governmental regulations) a home, radon, environmental, lead-based paint
84 and/or lead-based paint hazards (unless separately waived), and/or wood destroying insect infestation
85 inspection of the Real Estate by one or more licensed or certified inspection service(s).
86 (a) Buyer agrees that minor repairs and routine maintenance items of the Real Estate do not constitute
87 defects and are not a part of this contingency. **The fact that a functioning major component may be at**
88 **the end of its useful life shall not render such component defective for purposes of this paragraph.**
89 Buyer shall indemnify Seller and hold Seller harmless from and against any loss or damage caused by the
90 acts or negligence of Buyer or any person performing any inspection. The home inspection shall cover
91 only the major components of the Real Estate, including but not limited to central heating system(s),
92 central cooling system(s), plumbing and well system, electrical system, roof, walls, windows, ceilings,
93 floors, appliances and foundation. A major component shall be deemed to be in operating condition if it
94 performs the function for which it is intended, regardless of age, and does not constitute a threat to health
95 or safety. If radon mitigation is performed, Seller shall pay for any retest.
96 (b) Buyer shall serve Notice upon Seller or Seller's attorney of any defects disclosed by any inspection for
97 which Buyer requests resolution by Seller, together with a copy of the pertinent pages of the inspection
98 reports within five (5) Business Days (ten (10) calendar days for a lead-based paint and/or lead-based
99 paint hazard inspection) after the Date of Acceptance. If within ten (10) Business Days after the Date of
100 Acceptance written agreement is not reached by the Parties with respect to resolution of all inspection
101 issues, then either Party may terminate this Contract by serving Notice to the other Party, whereupon this
102 Contract shall be null and void.
103 (c) Notwithstanding anything to the contrary set forth above in this paragraph, in the event the inspection
104 reveals that the condition of the Real Estate is unacceptable to Buyer and Buyer serves Notice to Seller
105 within five (5) Business Days after the Date of Acceptance, this Contract shall be null and void.
106 (d) Failure of Buyer to conduct said inspection(s) and notify Seller within the time specified operates as a
107 waiver of Buyer's right to terminate this Contract under this Paragraph 10 and this Contract shall remain
108 in full force and effect.

109 **11. MORTGAGE CONTINGENCY:** This Contract is contingent upon Buyer obtaining a firm written mortgage
110 commitment (except for matters of title and survey or matters totally within Buyer's control) on or before
111 _____, 20____ for a *[check one]* ❑ fixed ❑ adjustable; *[check one]* ❑ conventional ❑ FHA/VA
112 (if FHA/VA is chosen, complete Paragraph 35) ❑ other_____ loan of _____% of Purchase
113 Price, plus private mortgage insurance (PMI), if required. The interest rate (initial rate, if applicable) shall not
114 exceed _____% per annum, amortized over not less than _____ years. Buyer shall pay loan origination fee
115 and/or discount points not to exceed _____% of the loan amount. Buyer shall pay the cost of application,
116 usual and customary processing fees and closing costs charged by lender. (Complete Paragraph 33 if closing
117 cost credits apply.) Buyer shall make written loan application within five (5) Business Days after the Date of
118 Acceptance. **Failure to do so shall constitute an act of Default under this Contract. If Buyer, having applied**
119 **for the loan specified above, is unable to obtain such loan commitment and serves Notice to Seller within**
120 **the time specified, this Contract shall be null and void. If Notice of inability to obtain such loan**
121 **commitment is not served within the time specified, Buyer shall be deemed to have waived this**
122 **contingency and this Contract shall remain in full force and effect. Unless otherwise provided in**
123 **Paragraph 31, this Contract shall not be contingent upon the sale and/or closing of Buyer's existing real**
124 **estate.** Buyer shall be deemed to have satisfied the financing conditions of this paragraph if Buyer obtains a
125 loan commitment in accordance with the terms of this paragraph even though the loan is conditioned on the
126 sale and/or closing of Buyer's existing real estate. If Seller at Seller's option and expense, within thirty (30)
127 days after Buyer's Notice, procures for Buyer such commitment or notifies Buyer that Seller will accept a

Buyer Initial _____ *Buyer Initial* _____ *Seller Initial* _____ *Seller Initial* _____

Address _____ v5.0e

FIGURE 11.2

Typical Residential Real Estate Sales Contract (continued)

128 purchase money mortgage upon the same terms, this Contract shall remain in full force and effect. In such
129 event, Seller shall notify Buyer within five (5) Business Days after Buyer's Notice of Seller's election to
130 provide or obtain such financing, and Buyer shall furnish to Seller or lender all requested information and
131 shall sign all papers necessary to obtain the mortgage commitment and to close the loan.

132 **12. HOMEOWNER INSURANCE:** This Contract is contingent upon Buyer obtaining evidence of insurability for
133 an Insurance Service Organization HO-3 or equivalent policy at standard premium rates within ten (10)
134 Business Days after the Date of Acceptance. **If Buyer is unable to obtain evidence of insurability and serves**
135 **Notice with proof of same to Seller within the time specified, this Contract shall be null and void. If**
136 **Notice is not served within the time specified, Buyer shall be deemed to have waived this contingency**
137 **and this Contract shall remain in full force and effect.**

138 **13. FLOOD INSURANCE:** Unless previously disclosed in the Illinois Residential Real Property Disclosure
139 Report, Buyer shall have the option to declare this Contract null and void if the Real Estate is located in a
140 special flood hazard area which requires Buyer to carry flood insurance. **If Notice of the option to declare**
141 **this Contract null and void is not given to Seller within ten (10) Business Days after the Date of**
142 **Acceptance or by the Mortgage Contingency deadline date described in Paragraph 11 (whichever is later),**
143 **Buyer shall be deemed to have waived such option and this Contract shall remain in full force and effect.**
144 Nothing herein shall be deemed to affect any rights afforded by the Residential Real Property Disclosure Act.

145 **14. CONDOMINIUM/COMMON INTEREST ASSOCIATIONS:** (If applicable) The Parties agree that the terms
146 contained in this paragraph, which may be contrary to other terms of this Contract, shall supersede any
147 conflicting terms.
148 (a) Title when conveyed shall be good and merchantable, subject to terms, provisions, covenants and
149   conditions of the Declaration of Condominium/Covenants, Conditions and Restrictions and all
150   amendments; public and utility easements including any easements established by or implied from the
151   Declaration of Condominium/Covenants, Conditions and Restrictions or amendments thereto; party wall
152   rights and agreements; limitations and conditions imposed by the Condominium Property Act;
153   installments due after the date of Closing of general assessments established pursuant to the Declaration
154   of Condominium/Covenants, Conditions and Restrictions.
155 (b) Seller shall be responsible for payment of all regular assessments due and levied prior to Closing and for
156   all special assessments confirmed prior to the Date of Acceptance.
157 (c) Buyer has, within five (5) Business Days from the Date of Acceptance, the right to demand from Seller
158   items as stipulated by the Illinois Condominium Property Act, if applicable, and Seller shall diligently
159   apply for same. This Contract is subject to the condition that Seller be able to procure and provide to
160   Buyer, a release or waiver of any option of first refusal or other pre-emptive rights of purchase created by
161   the Declaration of Condominium/Covenants, Conditions and Restrictions within the time established by
162   the Declaration of Condominium/Covenants, Conditions and Restrictions. In the event the
163   Condominium Association requires the personal appearance of Buyer and/or additional documentation,
164   Buyer agrees to comply with same.
165 (d) In the event the documents and information provided by Seller to Buyer disclose that the existing
166   improvements are in violation of existing rules, regulations or other restrictions or that the terms and
167   conditions contained within the documents would unreasonably restrict Buyer's use of the premises or
168   would result in financial obligations unacceptable to Buyer in connection with owning the Real Estate,
169   then Buyer may declare this Contract null and void by giving Seller Notice within five (5) Business Days
170   after the receipt of the documents and information required by Paragraph 14(c), listing those deficiencies
171   which are unacceptable to Buyer. If Notice is not served within the time specified, Buyer shall be deemed
172   to have waived this contingency, and this Contract shall remain in full force and effect.

Buyer Initial _____ *Buyer Initial* _____ *Seller Initial* _____ *Seller Initial* _____

Address _____ v5.0e

FIGURE 11.2

Typical Residential Real Estate Sales Contract (continued)

173 (e) Seller shall not be obligated to provide a condominium survey.

174 (f) Seller shall provide a certificate of insurance showing Buyer and Buyer's mortgagee, if any, as an insured.

175 **15. THE DEED:** Seller shall convey or cause to be conveyed to Buyer or Buyer's designated grantee good and
176 merchantable title to the Real Estate by recordable general Warranty Deed, with release of homestead rights,
177 (or the appropriate deed if title is in trust or in an estate), and with real estate transfer stamps to be paid by
178 Seller (unless otherwise designated by local ordinance). Title when conveyed will be good and merchantable,
179 subject only to: general real estate taxes not due and payable at the time of Closing; covenants, conditions
180 and restrictions of record; and building lines and easements, if any, provided they do not interfere with the
181 current use and enjoyment of the Real Estate.

182 **16. TITLE:** At Seller's expense, Seller will deliver or cause to be delivered to Buyer or Buyer's attorney within
183 customary time limitations and sufficiently in advance of Closing, as evidence of title in Seller or Grantor, a
184 title commitment for an ALTA title insurance policy in the amount of the Purchase Price with extended
185 coverage by a title company licensed to operate in the State of Illinois, issued on or subsequent to the Date of
186 Acceptance, subject only to items listed in Paragraph 15. The requirement to provide extended coverage shall
187 not apply if the Real Estate is vacant land. The commitment for title insurance furnished by Seller will be
188 conclusive evidence of good and merchantable title as therein shown, subject only to the exceptions therein
189 stated. **If the title commitment discloses any unpermitted exceptions or if the Plat of Survey shows any**
190 **encroachments or other survey matters that are not acceptable to Buyer, then Seller shall have said**
191 **exceptions, survey matters or encroachments removed, or have the title insurer commit to either insure**
192 **against loss or damage that may result from such exceptions or survey matters or insure against any court-**
193 **ordered removal of the encroachments.** If Seller fails to have such exceptions waived or insured over prior to
194 Closing, Buyer may elect to take the title as it then is with the right to deduct from the Purchase Price prior
195 encumbrances of a definite or ascertainable amount. Seller shall furnish Buyer at Closing an Affidavit of Title
196 covering the date of Closing, and shall sign any other customary forms required for issuance of an ALTA
197 Insurance Policy.

198 **17. PLAT OF SURVEY:** Not less than one (1) Business Day prior to Closing, except where the Real Estate is a
199 condominium (see Paragraph 14) Seller shall, at Seller's expense, furnish to Buyer or Buyer's attorney a Plat
200 of Survey that conforms to the current Minimum Standards of Practice for boundary surveys, is dated not
201 more than six (6) months prior to the date of Closing, and is prepared by a professional land surveyor
202 licensed to practice land surveying under the laws of the State of Illinois. The Plat of Survey shall show
203 visible evidence of improvements, rights of way, easements, use and measurements of all parcel lines. The
204 land surveyor shall set monuments or witness corners at all accessible corners of the land. All such corners
205 shall also be visibly staked or flagged. The Plat of Survey shall include the following statement placed near
206 the professional land surveyor seal and signature: "This professional service conforms to the current Illinois
207 Minimum Standards for a boundary survey." A Mortgage Inspection, as defined, is not a boundary survey
208 and is not acceptable.

209 **18. ESCROW CLOSING:** At the election of either Party, not less than five (5) Business Days prior to Closing,
210 this sale shall be closed through an escrow with the lending institution or the title company in accordance
211 with the provisions of the usual form of Deed and Money Escrow Agreement, as agreed upon between the
212 Parties, with provisions inserted in the Escrow Agreement as may be required to conform with this Contract.
213 The cost of the escrow shall be paid by the Party requesting the escrow. If this transaction is a cash purchase
214 (no mortgage is secured by Buyer), the Parties shall share the title company escrow closing fee equally.

215 **19. DAMAGE TO REAL ESTATE OR CONDEMNATION PRIOR TO CLOSING:** If prior to delivery of the deed the
216 Real Estate shall be destroyed or materially damaged by fire or other casualty, or the Real Estate is taken by

| *Buyer Initial* _____ | *Buyer Initial* _____ | *Seller Initial* _____ | *Seller Initial* _____ |

Address _____   v5.0e

Typical Residential Real Estate Sales Contract (continued)

217 condemnation, then Buyer shall have the option of either terminating this Contract (and receiving a refund of
218 earnest money) or accepting the Real Estate as damaged or destroyed, together with the proceeds of the
219 condemnation award or any insurance payable as a result of the destruction or damage, which gross
220 proceeds Seller agrees to assign to Buyer and deliver to Buyer at Closing. Seller shall not be obligated to
221 repair or replace damaged improvements. The provisions of the Uniform Vendor and Purchaser Risk Act of
222 the State of Illinois shall be applicable to this Contract, except as modified by this paragraph.

223 **20. REAL ESTATE TAX ESCROW:** In the event the Real Estate is improved, but has not been previously taxed
224 for the entire year as currently improved, the sum of three percent (3%) of the Purchase Price shall be
225 deposited in escrow with the title company with the cost of the escrow to be divided equally by Buyer and
226 Seller and paid at Closing. When the exact amount of the taxes to be prorated under this Contract can be
227 ascertained, the taxes shall be prorated by Seller's attorney at the request of either Party and Seller's share of
228 such tax liability after proration shall be paid to Buyer from the escrow funds and the balance, if any, shall be
229 paid to Seller. If Seller's obligation after such proration exceeds the amount of the escrow funds, Seller agrees
230 to pay such excess promptly upon demand.

231 **21. SELLER REPRESENTATIONS:** Seller represents that with respect to the Real Estate Seller has no
232 knowledge of nor has Seller received written notice from any governmental body regarding:
233 (a) zoning, building, fire or health code violations that have not been corrected;
234 (b) any pending rezoning;
235 (c) boundary line disputes;
236 (d) any pending condemnation or Eminent Domain proceeding;
237 (e) easements or claims of easements not shown on the public records;
238 (f) any hazardous waste on the Real Estate;
239 (g) any improvements to the Real Estate for which the required permits were not obtained;
240 (h) any improvements to the Real Estate which are not included in full in the determination of the most
241   recent tax assessment; or
242 (i) any improvements to the Real Estate which are eligible for the home improvement tax exemption.

243 Seller further represents that:
244 1. There *[check one]* ❏ is ❏ is not a pending or unconfirmed special assessment affecting the Real Estate by
245   any association or governmental entity payable by Buyer after date of Closing.
246 2. The Real Estate *[check one]* ❏ is ❏ is not located within a Special Assessment Area or Special Service
247   Area, payments for which will not be the obligation of Seller after the year in which the Closing occurs.
248 **If any of the representations contained herein regarding a Special Assessment Area or Special Service**
249 **Area are unacceptable to Buyer, Buyer shall have the option to declare this Contract null and void. If**
250 **Notice of the option to declare this Contract null and void is not given to Seller within ten (10) Business**
251 **Days after the Date of Acceptance or by the Mortgage Contingency deadline date described in Paragraph**
252 **11 (whichever is later), Buyer shall be deemed to have waived such option and this Contract shall remain**
253 **in full force and effect. Seller's representations contained in this paragraph shall survive the Closing.**

254 **22. CONDITION OF REAL ESTATE AND INSPECTION:** Seller agrees to leave the Real Estate in broom clean
255 condition. All refuse and personal property that is not to be conveyed to Buyer shall be removed from the
256 Real Estate at Seller's expense prior to delivery of Possession. Buyer shall have the right to inspect the Real
257 Estate, fixtures and included Personal Property prior to Possession to verify that the Real Estate,
258 improvements and included Personal Property are in substantially the same condition as of the Date of
259 Acceptance, normal wear and tear excepted.

Buyer Initial _____ *Buyer Initial* _____ *Seller Initial* _____ *Seller Initial* _____

Address _____ v5.0

FIGURE 11.2

Typical Residential Real Estate Sales Contract (continued)

260 **23. MUNICIPAL ORDINANCE, TRANSFER TAX, AND GOVERNMENTAL COMPLIANCE:**
261 (a) Parties are cautioned that the Real Estate may be situated in a municipality that has adopted a pre-closing
262   inspection requirement, municipal Transfer Tax or other similar ordinances. Transfer taxes required by
263   municipal ordinance shall be paid by the party designated in such ordinance.
264 (b) Parties agree to comply with the reporting requirements of the applicable sections of the Internal
265   Revenue Code and the Real Estate Settlement Procedures Act of 1974, as amended.

266 **24. BUSINESS DAYS/HOURS:** Business Days are defined as Monday through Friday, excluding Federal
267 holidays. Business Hours are defined as 8:00 A.M. to 6:00 P.M. Chicago time.

268 **25. FACSIMILE OR DIGITAL SIGNATURES:** Facsimile or digital signatures shall be sufficient for purposes of
269 executing, negotiating, and finalizing this Contract.

270 **26. DIRECTION TO ESCROWEE:** In every instance where this Contract shall be deemed null and void or if this
271 Contract may be terminated by either Party, the following shall be deemed incorporated: "and earnest money
272 refunded to Buyer upon written direction of the Parties to Escrowee or upon entry of an order by a court of
273 competent jurisdiction". There shall be no disbursement of earnest money unless Escrowee has been
274 provided written direction from Seller and Buyer. Absent a direction relative to the disbursement of earnest
275 money within a reasonable period of time, Escrowee may deposit funds with the Clerk of the Circuit Court
276 by the filing of an action in the nature of Interpleader. Escrowee shall be reimbursed from the earnest money
277 for all costs, including reasonable attorney fees, related to the filing of the Interpleader action. Seller and
278 Buyer shall indemnify and hold Escrowee harmless from any and all conflicting claims and demands arising
279 under this paragraph.

280 **27. NOTICE:** Except as provided in Paragraph 31(C)(2) regarding the manner of service for "kick-out"
281 Notices, all Notices shall be in writing and shall be served by one Party or attorney to the other Party or
282 attorney. Notice to any one of a multiple person Party shall be sufficient Notice to all. Notice shall be given in
283 the following manner:
284 (a) By personal delivery; or
285 (b) By mailing to the addresses recited herein by regular mail and by certified mail, return receipt requested.
286   Except as otherwise provided herein, Notice served by certified mail shall be effective on the date of
287   mailing; or
288 (c) By facsimile transmission. Notice shall be effective as of date and time of the transmission, provided that
289   the Notice transmitted shall be sent on Business Days during Business Hours. In the event Notice is
290   transmitted during non-business hours, the effective date and time of Notice is the first hour of the next
291   Business Day after transmission; or
292 (d) By e-mail transmission if an e-mail address has been furnished by the recipient Party or the recipient
293   Party's attorney to the sending Party or is shown on this Contract. Notice shall be effective as of date and
294   time of e-mail transmission, provided that, in the event e-mail Notice is transmitted during non-business
295   hours, the effective date and time of Notice is the first hour of the next Business Day after transmission.
296   An attorney or Party may opt out of future e-mail Notice by any form of Notice provided by this
297   Contract; or
298 (e) By commercial overnight delivery (e.g., FedEx). Such Notice shall be effective on the next Business Day
299   following deposit with the overnight delivery company.

300 **28. PERFORMANCE: Time is of the essence of this Contract.** In any action with respect to this Contract, the
301 Parties are free to pursue any legal remedies at law or in equity and the prevailing Party in litigation shall be
302 entitled to collect reasonable attorney fees and costs from the non-Prevailing Party as ordered by a court of
303 competent jurisdiction.

Buyer Initial _____ *Buyer Initial* _____ *Seller Initial* _____ *Seller Initial* _____		
Address _____ v5.0		

FIGURE 11.2

Typical Residential Real Estate Sales Contract (continued)

304 **29. CHOICE OF LAW/GOOD FAITH:** All terms and provisions of this Contract including but not limited to the
305 Attorney Review and Professional Inspection Paragraphs shall be governed by the laws of the State of Illinois
306 and are subject to the covenant of good faith and fair dealing implied in all Illinois contracts.

307 **30. OTHER PROVISIONS:** This Contract is also subject to those OPTIONAL PROVISIONS initialed by the
308 Parties and the following attachments, if any: _____
309 _____.

310   **OPTIONAL PROVISIONS (Applicable ONLY if initialed by all Parties)**

311 ____ ____ ____ ____ **31. SALE OF BUYER'S REAL ESTATE:**
312 [Initials]
313 **(A) REPRESENTATIONS ABOUT BUYER'S REAL ESTATE:** Buyer represents to Seller as follows:
314   (1) Buyer owns real estate commonly known as (address):
315   _____.
316   (2) Buyer *[check one]* ❏ has ❏ has not entered into a contract to sell said real estate.
317   If Buyer has entered into a contract to sell said real estate, that contract:
318   (a) *[check one]* ❏ is ❏ is not subject to a mortgage contingency.
319   (b) *[check one]* ❏ is ❏ is not subject to a real estate sale contingency.
320   (c) *[check one]* ❏ is ❏ is not subject to a real estate closing contingency.
321   (3) Buyer *[check one]* ❏ has ❏ has not listed said real estate for sale with a licensed real estate broker and
322   in a local multiple listing service.
323   (4) If Buyer's real estate is not listed for sale with a licensed real estate broker and in a local multiple
324   listing service, Buyer *[check one]*
325   (a) ❏ Shall list said real estate for sale with a licensed real estate broker who will place it in a local
326   multiple listing service within five (5) Business Days after the Date of Acceptance.
327   [For information only] Broker: _____
328   Broker's Address: _____ Phone: _____.
329   (b) ❏ Does not intend to list said real estate for sale.
330 **(B) CONTINGENCIES BASED UPON SALE AND/OR CLOSE OF BUYER'S REAL ESTATE:**
331   (1) This Contract is contingent upon Buyer having entered into a contract for the sale of Buyer's real
332   estate that is in full force and effect as of _____, 20____. Such contract should provide
333   for a closing date not later than the Closing Date set forth in this Contract. **If Notice is served on or**
334   **before the date set forth in this subparagraph that Buyer has not procured a contract for the sale of**
335   **Buyer's real estate, this Contract shall be null and void. If Notice that Buyer has not procured a**
336   **contract for the sale of Buyer's real estate is not served on or before the close of business on the**
337   **date set forth in this subparagraph, Buyer shall be deemed to have waived all contingencies**
338   **contained in this Paragraph 31, and this Contract shall remain in full force and effect.** (If this
339   paragraph is used, then the following paragraph **must** be completed.)
340   (2) In the event Buyer has entered into a contract for the sale of Buyer's real estate as set forth in
341   Paragraph 31(B)(1) and that contract is in full force and effect, or has entered into a contract for the
342   sale of Buyer's real estate prior to the execution of this Contract, this Contract is contingent upon
343   Buyer closing the sale of Buyer's real estate on or before _____, 20____. **If Notice that**
344   **Buyer has not closed the sale of Buyer's real estate is served before the close of business on the**
345   **next Business Day after the date set forth in the preceding sentence, this Contract shall be null and**
346   **void. If Notice is not served as described in the preceding sentence, Buyer shall be deemed to have**
347   **waived all contingencies contained in this Paragraph 31, and this Contract shall remain in full**
348   **force and effect.**

Buyer Initial _____ *Buyer Initial* _____ *Seller Initial* _____ *Seller Initial* _____

Address _____ v5.0

Typical Residential Real Estate Sales Contract (continued)

349   (3) If the contract for the sale of Buyer's real estate is terminated for any reason after the date set forth in
350   Paragraph 31(B)(1) (or after the date of this Contract if no date is set forth in Paragraph 31(B)(1)),
351   Buyer shall, within three (3) Business Days of such termination, notify Seller of said termination.
352   **Unless Buyer, as part of said Notice, waives all contingencies in Paragraph 31 and complies with**
353   **Paragraph 31(D), this Contract shall be null and void as of the date of Notice. If Notice as required**
354   **by this subparagraph is not served within the time specified, Buyer shall be in default under the**
355   **terms of this Contract.**
356 **(C) SELLER'S RIGHT TO CONTINUE TO OFFER REAL ESTATE FOR SALE:** During the time of this contingency,
357 Seller has the right to continue to show the Real Estate and offer it for sale subject to the following:
358   (1) If Seller accepts another bona fide offer to purchase the Real Estate while the contingencies expressed
359   in Paragraph 31(B) are in effect, Seller shall notify Buyer in writing of same. Buyer shall then have
360   _____ hours after Seller gives such Notice to waive the contingencies set forth in Paragraph
361   31(B), subject to Paragraph 31(D).
362   (2) Seller's Notice to Buyer (commonly referred to as a 'kick-out' Notice) shall be in writing and shall be
363   served on Buyer, not Buyer's attorney or Buyer's real estate agent. Courtesy copies of such "kick-out"
364   Notice should be sent to Buyer's attorney and Buyer's real estate agent, if known. Failure to provide
365   such courtesy copies shall not render Notice invalid. Notice to any one of a multiple-person Buyer
366   shall be sufficient Notice to all Buyers. Notice for the purpose of this subparagraph only shall be
367   served upon Buyer in the following manner:
368   (a) By personal delivery effective at the time and date of personal delivery; or
369   (b) By mailing to the addresses recited herein for Buyer by regular mail and by certified mail. Notice
370   shall be effective at 10:00 A.M. on the morning of the second day following deposit of Notice in
371   the U.S. Mail; or
372   (c) By commercial overnight delivery (e.g., FedEx). Notice shall be effective upon delivery or at 4:00
373   P.M. Chicago time on the next delivery day following deposit with the overnight delivery
374   company, whichever first occurs.
375   (3) If Buyer complies with the provisions of Paragraph 31(D) then this Contract shall remain in full force
376   and effect.
377   (4) If the contingencies set forth in Paragraph 31(B) are NOT waived in writing within said time period
378   by Buyer, this Contract shall be null and void.
379   (5) Except as provided in Paragraph 31(C)(2) above, all Notices shall be made in the manner provided by
380   Paragraph 27 of this Contract.
381   (6) Buyer waives any ethical objection to the delivery of Notice under this paragraph by Seller's attorney
382   or representative.
383 **(D) WAIVER OF PARAGRAPH 31 CONTINGENCIES:** Buyer shall be deemed to have waived the contingencies in
384 Paragraph 31(B) when Buyer has delivered written waiver and deposited with the Escrowee additional
385 earnest money in the amount of $_____ in the form of a cashier's or certified check within the
386 time specified. **If Buyer fails to deposit the additional earnest money within the time specified, the waiver**
387 **shall be deemed ineffective and this Contract shall be null and void.**
388 **(E) BUYER COOPERATION REQUIRED:** Buyer authorizes Seller or Seller's agent to verify representations
389 contained in Paragraph 31 at any time, and Buyer agrees to cooperate in providing relevant information.

390 ____ ____ ____ ____ **32. CANCELLATION OF PRIOR REAL ESTATE CONTRACT:** In the event either Party has
391 entered into a prior real estate contract, this Contract shall be subject to written cancellation of the prior
392 contract on or before _____, 20____. **In the event the prior contract is not cancelled within the**
393 **time specified, this Contract shall be null and void. Seller's notice to the purchaser under the prior**

Buyer Initial _____   *Buyer Initial* _____   *Seller Initial* _____   *Seller Initial* _____

Address _____ v5.0

FIGURE 11.2

Typical Residential Real Estate Sales Contract (continued)

394 contract should not be served until after Attorney Review and Professional Inspections provisions of this
395 Contract have expired, been satisfied or waived.

396 ___ ___ ___ ___ **33. CREDIT AT CLOSING:** Provided Buyer's lender permits such credit to show on the
397 HUD-1 Settlement Statement, **and if not, such lesser amount as the lender permits,** Seller agrees to credit to
398 Buyer at Closing $_____ to be applied to prepaid expenses, closing costs or both.

399 ___ ___ ___ ___ **34. INTEREST BEARING ACCOUNT:** Earnest money (with a completed W-9 and other
400 required forms), shall be held in a federally insured interest bearing account at a financial institution
401 designated by Escrowee. All interest earned on the earnest money shall accrue to the benefit of and be paid to
402 Buyer. **Buyer shall be responsible for any administrative fee (not to exceed $100) charged for setting up the
403 account.** In anticipation of Closing, the Parties direct Escrowee to close the account no sooner than ten (10)
404 Business Days prior to the anticipated Closing date.

405 ___ ___ ___ ___ **35. VA OR FHA FINANCING:** If Buyer is seeking VA or FHA financing, this provision shall
406 be applicable: **Required FHA or VA amendments and disclosures shall be attached to this Contract.** If VA,
407 the Funding Fee, or if FHA, the Mortgage Insurance Premium (MIP) shall be paid by Buyer and *[check one]*
408 ❑ shall ❑ shall not be added to the mortgage loan amount.

409 ___ ___ ___ ___ **36. INTERIM FINANCING:** This Contract is contingent upon Buyer obtaining a written
410 commitment for interim financing on or before _____, 20___ in the amount of $_____.
411 **If Buyer is unable to secure the interim financing commitment and gives Notice to Seller within the time
412 specified, this Contract shall be null and void. If Notice is not served within the time specified, this
413 provision shall be deemed waived by the Parties and this Contract shall remain in full force and effect.**

414 ___ ___ ___ ___ **37. WELL AND/OR SEPTIC/SANITARY INSPECTIONS:** Seller shall obtain at Seller's
415 expense a well water test stating that the well delivers not less than five (5) gallons of water per minute and
416 including a bacteria and nitrate test (and lead test for FHA loans) and/or a septic report from the applicable
417 County Health Department, a Licensed Environmental Health Practitioner, or a licensed well and septic
418 inspector, each dated not more than ninety (90) days prior to Closing, stating that the well and water supply
419 and the private sanitary system are in proper operating condition with no defects noted. Seller shall remedy
420 any defect or deficiency disclosed by said report(s) prior to Closing, provided that if the cost of remedying a
421 defect or deficiency and the cost of landscaping together exceed $3,000.00, and if the Parties cannot reach
422 agreement regarding payment of such additional cost, this Contract may be terminated by either Party.
423 Additional testing recommended by the report shall be obtained at Seller's expense. If the report
424 recommends additional testing after Closing, the Parties shall have the option of establishing an escrow with
425 a mutual cost allocation for necessary repairs or replacements, or either Party may terminate this Contract
426 prior to Closing. Seller shall deliver a copy of such evaluation(s) to Buyer not less than one (1) Business Day
427 prior to Closing.

428 ___ ___ ___ ___ **38. WOOD DESTROYING INFESTATION:** Notwithstanding the provisions of Paragraph 10,
429 within ten (10) Business Days after the Date of Acceptance, Seller at Seller's expense shall deliver to Buyer a
430 written report, dated not more than six (6) months prior to the date of Closing, by a licensed inspector
431 certified by the appropriate state regulatory authority in the subcategory of termites, stating that there is no
432 visible evidence of active infestation by termites or other wood destroying insects. Unless otherwise agreed
433 between the Parties, if the report discloses evidence of active infestation or structural damage, Buyer has the
434 option within five (5) Business Days of receipt of the report to proceed with the purchase or declare this
435 Contract null and void.

Buyer Initial _____ *Buyer Initial* _____ *Seller Initial* _____ *Seller Initial* _____

Address _____ v5.0

FIGURE 11.2

Typical Residential Real Estate Sales Contract (continued)

436 ____ ____ ____ ____ **39. POST-CLOSING POSSESSION:** Possession shall be delivered no later than 11:59 P.M.
437 on the date that is _____ days after the date of Closing ("the Possession Date"). Seller shall be responsible
438 for all utilities, contents and liability insurance, and home maintenance expenses until delivery of possession.
439 Seller shall deposit in escrow at Closing with _____, *[check one]* ❑ one percent (1%) of the
440 Purchase Price or ❑ the sum of $_____ to be paid by Escrowee as follows:
441 (a) The sum of $_____ per day for use and occupancy from and including the day after
442   Closing to and including the day of delivery of Possession, if on or before the Possession Date;
443 (b) The amount per day equal to three (3) times the daily amount set forth herein shall be paid for each day
444   after the Possession Date specified in this paragraph that Seller remains in possession of the Real Estate;
445   and
446 (c) The balance, if any, to Seller after delivery of Possession and provided that the terms of Paragraph 22
447   have been satisfied. Seller's liability under this paragraph shall not be limited to the amount of the
448   possession escrow deposit referred to above. Nothing herein shall be deemed to create a
449   Landlord/Tenant relationship between the Parties.

450 ____ ____ ____ ____ **40. "AS IS" CONDITION:** This Contract is for the sale and purchase of the Real Estate in its
451 "As Is" condition as of the Date of Offer. Buyer acknowledges that no representations, warranties or
452 guarantees with respect to the condition of the Real Estate have been made by Seller or Seller's Designated
453 Agent other than those known defects, if any, disclosed by Seller. Buyer may conduct an inspection at
454 Buyer's expense. In that event, Seller shall make the Real Estate available to Buyer's inspector at reasonable
455 times. Buyer shall indemnify Seller and hold Seller harmless from and against any loss or damage caused by
456 the acts or negligence of Buyer or any person performing any inspection. **In the event the inspection reveals**
457 **that the condition of the Real Estate is unacceptable to Buyer and Buyer so notifies Seller within five (5)**
458 **Business Days after the Date of Acceptance, this Contract shall be null and void. Failure of Buyer to notify**
459 **Seller or to conduct said inspection operates as a waiver of Buyer's right to terminate this Contract under**
460 **this paragraph and this Contract shall remain in full force and effect.** Buyer acknowledges that the
461 provisions of Paragraph 10 and the warranty provisions of Paragraph 3 do not apply to this Contract.

462 ____ ____ ____ ____ **41. CONFIRMATION OF DUAL AGENCY:** The Parties confirm that they have previously
463 consented to _____
464 (Licensee) acting as a Dual Agent in providing brokerage services on their behalf and specifically consent to
465 Licensee acting as a Dual Agent with regard to the transaction referred to in this Contract.

466 ____ ____ ____ ____ **42. SPECIFIED PARTY APPROVAL:** This Contract is contingent upon the approval of the
467 Real Estate by _____
468 Buyer's Specified Party, within five (5) Business Days after the Date of Acceptance. In the event Buyer's
469 Specified Party does not approve of the Real Estate and Notice is given to Seller within the time specified,
470 this Contract shall be null and void. If Notice is not served within the time specified, this provision shall be
471 deemed waived by the Parties and this Contract shall remain in full force and effect.

472 ____ ____ ____ ____ **43. MISCELLANEOUS PROVISIONS:** Buyer's and Seller's obligations are contingent upon
473 the Parties entering into a separate written agreement consistent with the terms and conditions set forth
474 herein, and with such additional terms as either Party may deem necessary, providing for one or more of the
475 following: *(check applicable boxes)*
476 ❑ Articles of Agreement for Deed or   ❑ Assumption of Seller's Mortgage   ❑ Commercial/Investment
477   Purchase Money Mortgage   ❑ Cooperative Apartment   ❑ New Construction
478 ❑ Short Sale   ❑ Tax-Deferred Exchange   ❑ Vacant Land

Buyer Initial _____   *Buyer Initial* _____   *Seller Initial* _____   *Seller Initial* _____

Address _____   v5.0

FIGURE 11.2

Typical Residential Real Estate Sales Contract (continued)

479 **THIS DOCUMENT WILL BECOME A LEGALLY BINDING CONTRACT WHEN SIGNED BY ALL PARTIES AND**
480 **DELIVERED TO THE PARTIES OR THEIR AGENTS.**

481 The Parties represent that the text of this form has not been altered and is identical to the official Multi-Board
482 Residential Real Estate Contract 5.0.

483 _____   _____
484 Date of Offer   DATE OF ACCEPTANCE

485 _____   _____
486 Buyer Signature   Seller Signature

487 _____   _____
488 Buyer Signature   Seller Signature

489 _____   _____
490 Print Buyer(s) Name(s) *[Required]*   Print Seller(s) Name(s) *[Required]*

491 _____   _____
492 Address   Address

493 _____   _____
494 City   State   Zip   City   State   Zip

495 _____   _____
496 Phone   E-mail   Phone   E-mail

497   *FOR INFORMATION ONLY*

498 _____   _____
499 Buyer's Broker   MLS #   Seller's Broker   MLS #

500 _____   _____
501 Buyer's Designated Agent   MLS #   Seller's Designated Agent   MLS #

502 _____   _____
503 Phone   Fax   Phone   Fax

504 _____   _____
505 E-mail   E-mail

506 _____   _____
507 Buyer's Attorney   E-mail   Seller's Attorney   E-mail

508 _____   _____
509 Phone   Fax   Phone   Fax

510 _____   _____
511 Mortgage Company   Phone   Homeowner's/Condo Association (if any)   Phone

512 _____   _____
513 Loan Officer   Phone/Fax   Management Co. /Other Contact   Phone

517 Approved by the following organizations as of July 20, 2009
517 Illinois Real Estate Lawyers Association · DuPage County Bar Association · Will County Bar Association
518 Northwest Suburban Bar Association · Chicago Association of REALTORS®
519 Mainstreet Organization of REALTORS® · Aurora-Tri County Association of REALTORS® · West Towns Board of REALTORS®
520 REALTOR® Association of Northwest Chicagoland · REALTOR® Association of the Fox Valley
521 Oak Park Area Association of REALTORS® · McHenry Association of REALTORS® · Three Rivers Association of REALTORS®
522 North Shore–Barrington Association of REALTORS®

523 **Seller Rejection:** This offer was presented to Seller on _____, 20____ at ____:____ AM/PM
524 and rejected on _____, 20____ at ____:____ AM/PM ____ ____ (Seller initials).

Buyer Initial _____ *Buyer Initial* _____ *Seller Initial* _____ *Seller Initial* _____

Address, _____ v5.0

F I G U R E   11.2

Typical Residential Real Estate Sales Contract (continued)

Loan Status Disclosure
Recommended Form - To Be Completed By Loan Officer

Borrowers/Buyers Name(s): _____

Current Address: _____
      Street Address

_____
City or Town   State   Zip

Purchase Price dollar amount prequalified, pre-approved, or approved for:

$_____. Loan Amount $_____ with a total monthly payment not to exceed $_____.

The current status of prequalification or application status of the borrowers/buyers is:

❑ **Prequalification, WITHOUT credit review*:**

The borrowers/buyers listed on this form have **INQUIRED** with our firm about financing to purchase a home and the documentation they provided regarding income and down payment has been reviewed by the loan originator listed below. It is the opinion of said loan originator that the borrowers/buyers should/would qualify for the terms listed in the attached letter.

❑ **Prequalification, WITH credit review*:**

The borrowers/buyers listed on this form have **INQUIRED** with our firm about financing to purchase a home and the documentation of income, down payment and credit report have been reviewed by the loan originator listed below. After careful review, it is the opinion of said loan originator that the borrowers/buyers should/would qualify for the terms listed in the attached letter.
This Prequalification is ❑ **WITH or** ❑ **WITHOUT** Automated Underwriting approval.

❑ **Pre-Approval*:**

The borrowers/buyers have **APPLIED** with our firm for a mortgage loan to purchase a home and the loan application has been approved by an Automated Underwriting System issued or accepted by FNMA, FHLMC, HUD or Nationally recognized purchaser/pooler of mortgage loans, and a conditional commitment has been issued. See attached commitment.

❑ **Approval*:**

The borrowers/buyers have **APPLIED** with our firm for a mortgage loan to purchase a home and the loan application has been reviewed by the actual lender's underwriter and conditional commitment has been issued. See attached commitment.

*Please note that nothing contained herein constitutes a loan commitment or guarantee of financing and is used for disclosure purposes only. See actual commitment letter for specific conditions/requirements of the lender. All approvals are subject to satisfactory appraisal, title, and no material change to borrower(s) financial status.

Information on mortgage company issuing the prequalification, pre-approval or approval:

Originating Company's Name: _____

Company Address: _____
      Street address   City or Town   State   Zip Code

Company Phone: _____ Fax: _____

Loan Originator's name: _____ Date: _____

Loan Originator's signature: _____

Use Recommended by: Illinois Association of Mortgage Professionals;
Illinois Association of REALTORS® and Illinois Real Estate Lawyers Association

designated by the parties in writing, and a separate interest bearing account must be set up for that deposit.

Each sponsoring broker must maintain a complete journal and ledger of all earnest money transactions and notify the IDFPR of the name of the federally insured institution where the money is deposited. All funds must be deposited to that account no later than the end of the next business day following the acceptance of the real estate contract or lease agreement. Both the account itself and sponsoring broker records are subject to inspection at any time. Sponsoring broker records need to be produced within 24 hours upon official request. Escrow reconciliations must be completed within ten days after receipt of the monthly bank statement and must be kept for a minimum of five years.

Only the sponsoring broker or an authorized agent may withdraw funds from the account. Fees and/or commissions earned by the sponsoring broker that are to be paid from the funds in this account are to be disbursed by the sponsoring broker from the account no earlier than the day the transaction is consummated or terminated and no later than the next business day after consummation or termination of the transaction.

Sponsoring brokers are strictly prohibited from **commingling,** that is, mixing their own funds with funds in special escrow accounts except for the purpose of maintaining a minimum running balance required by the depository. If a sponsoring broker uses his own funds to avoid incurring service charges, scrupulous records must be kept. Sponsoring brokers may never use escrow funds for personal use; this illegal act is known as **conversion.** ■

Equitable title   When a buyer signs a contract to purchase real estate, the buyer does not receive legal title to the land. Legal title transfers only on delivery and acceptance of a deed. However, after both buyer and seller have executed a sales contract, the buyer acquires an interest in the land. This interest is known as **equitable title**. Equitable title may give the buyer an insurable interest in the property.

Destruction of the premises   Under the common law of contracts, the buyer always bore the risk of loss in the event the property was damaged or destroyed prior to closing. A few states still adhere to this common-law principle. The laws and court decisions of most states, however, have increasingly placed the risk of loss on the seller. Many of these states have adopted the **Uniform Vendor and Purchaser Risk Act**, which specifically states that the seller bears any loss that occurs before the title passes or the buyer takes possession. As a practical matter, the seller should be certain the property is fully insured for sale price value up until the closing is completed and possession has been given.

| In Illinois | Illinois law subscribes to the Uniform Vendor and Purchaser Risk Act. If the entire premises or a material part of it is destroyed, the seller cannot enforce the contract against the buyer. Any earnest money must be returned. On the other hand, if title or possession has been transferred to the buyer, he must pay the full contract price, even in the event of partially or totally destroyed premises (e.g., the house burns while both parties are at the closing). ■

Liquidated damages To avoid a lawsuit if one party breaches the contract, the parties may agree on a certain amount of money that will compensate the nonbreaching party. That money is called **liquidated damages**. If a sales contract specifies that the earnest money deposit is to serve as liquidated damages in case the buyer defaults, the seller will be entitled to keep the deposit if the buyer refuses to perform without good reason. The seller who keeps the deposit as liquidated damages may not sue for any further damages if the contract provides that the deposit is the seller's sole remedy.

Contingencies Additional conditions that must be satisfied before a sales contract is fully enforceable are called **contingencies**. A contingency includes the following three elements:

1. The specific actions necessary to satisfy the contingency
2. The time frame within which the actions must occur
3. Who is responsible for paying any costs involved

The most common contingencies include:

- *Mortgage contingency*—The buyer's earnest money is protected until a lender commits the mortgage loan funds. (This is sometimes called a financing contingency.)
- *Inspection contingency*—A sales contract may be contingent on the buyer obtaining certain inspections of the property within a set time frame. Inspections may include a basic home inspection or special inspections for radon, wood-boring insects, lead-based paint, structural and mechanical systems, sewage facilities, or various toxic materials.
- *Property sale contingency*—Buyers may make the sales contract contingent on the sale of their current home by a certain date. This protects the buyer from owning two homes at the same time and also helps ensure the availability of cash for the purchase.
- A seller may insist on an *escape clause*, which permits the seller to continue to market the property until all the buyer's contingencies have been satisfied or removed. The buyer may retain the right to eliminate the contingencies if the seller receives a more favorable offer. (Note that contingencies create a *voidable contract*; if the contingencies are rejected or not satisfied, the contract is void.)

Amendment = Change
Addendum = Addition

Amendments and addendums An *amendment* is a change to an existing contract. For instance, the parties may agree to change a closing date or alter a list of personal property items included in the sale. Any time words or provisions are added to or deleted from the body of the contract, the contract has been amended. Amendments *must be signed or initialed by all parties*.

On the other hand, an *addendum* is any provision added to an existing contract *without* altering the content of the original. An addendum is essentially a new contract between the parties that includes the original contract's provisions "by reference"; that is, the addendum mentions the original contract. An addendum must be signed by both parties. For example, an addendum might be an agreement to split the cost of repairing certain flaws discovered in a home inspection. Such an addendum would be handled by the attorneys as a part of attorney modification.

| In Illinois | Illinois requires several mandatory disclosures by sellers and licensees acting as their agents, such as disclosure of property conditions and agency relationships. These disclosures are included in the sales contract by physical attachment or by reference. ■ |

Options

An **option** is a contract by which an optionor (generally an owner) gives an optionee (a prospective purchaser or lessee) the right to buy or lease the owner's property at a fixed price within a certain period of time. The optionee pays a fee (agreed-on consideration) for this option right. The optionee has no other obligation until he decides to either exercise the option right or allow the option to expire. An option is enforceable by only one party—the optionee.

An option contract is *not* a sales contract. At the time the option is signed by the parties, the owner does not sell and the optionee does not buy. The parties merely agree that the optionee has the right to buy and the owner is obligated to sell if the optionee decides to exercise his right of option. Options must contain all the terms and provisions required for a valid contract.

The option agreement (which is a *unilateral contract*) requires that the optionor act only after the optionee gives notice that he elects to execute the option. If the option is not exercised within the time specified in the contract, both the optionor's obligation and the optionee's right expire. An option contract may provide for renewal, which often requires additional consideration. The optionee cannot recover the consideration paid for the option right. The contract may state whether the money paid for the option is to be applied to the purchase price of the real estate if the option is exercised.

A common application of an option is a lease that includes an option for the tenant to purchase the property. Options on commercial real estate frequently depend on some specific conditions being fulfilled, such as obtaining a zoning change or a building permit. The optionee may be obligated to exercise the option if the conditions are met. Similar terms could also be included in a sales contract.

Land Contracts

A real estate sale can be made by a **land contract**, also called a *contract for deed*, an **installment contract**, or *articles of agreement for warranty deed*. Under a typical land contract, the seller (also known as the *vendor*) retains legal title. The buyer (called the *vendee*) takes possession and gets **equitable title** to the property. The buyer agrees to give the seller a down payment and pay regular monthly installments of principal and interest over a number of years. The buyer also agrees to pay real estate taxes, insurance premiums, repairs, and upkeep on the property.

Although the buyer obtains possession under the initial land contract, the seller is *not* obligated to execute and deliver a deed to the buyer until the terms of the contract have been satisfied. Also, a land contract usually is assumable by subsequent purchasers, but this must be approved and agreed to by the seller.

IN PRACTICE Legislatures and courts have not looked favorably on the harsh provisions of some real estate installment contracts. A seller and buyer contemplating such a sale should first consult an attorney to make sure that the agreement meets all legal requirements.

In Illinois

Installment contracts (or *articles of agreement* or *land contracts*) are commonly used in Illinois when creative seller financing is needed to consummate a sale. Real estate licensees may suggest an installment contract to assist buyers who are having trouble getting a loan or for sellers who have a hard-to-sell property or who wish to retain ties to their property for some reason. While a real estate licensee may assist in negotiating basic terms, in Illinois, the actual articles of agreement must be drawn up by an attorney owing to the legal complexities involved.

Any provision in an installment contract or land contract is void if the document

- forbids the contract buyer to record the contract,
- provides that recording shall not constitute notice, or
- provides any penalty for recording.

Any installment contract for the sale of a dwelling that consists of 12 or fewer units is voidable at the option of the buyer unless either a certificate of compliance or an express warranty that no notice of a building code violation has been received within the past ten years is attached to or incorporated into the contract. If notice has been received within the past ten years and not complied with, each notice must be listed with a detailed explanation. Neither buyer nor seller may waive this requirement.

A buyer who, under an installment contract, purchases residential property containing six or fewer units (which includes one unit) from a land trust must be told the names of all beneficiaries of the trust at the time the contract is executed. The buyer has the option to void the contract if the names are not revealed. ■

■ SUMMARY

A contract is a legally enforceable promise or set of promises that must be performed; if a breach occurs, the law provides a remedy.

Contracts may be classified according to whether the parties' intentions are express (i.e., expressed, stated) or merely implied by their actions. They may also be classified as bilateral (when both parties have obligated themselves to act) or unilateral (when one party is obligated to perform only if the other party acts). In addition, contracts may be classified according to their legal enforceability as valid, void, voidable, or unenforceable.

Many contracts specify a time for performance. In any case, all contracts must be performed within a reasonable time. An executed contract is one that has been fully performed. An executory contract is one in which some act remains to be performed.

The essentials of a valid contract are legally competent parties, offer and acceptance, consent, consideration, and legal purpose. A valid real estate contract must include a description of the property. It must be in writing and signed by all parties to be enforceable in court.

In many types of contracts, either of the parties may transfer his rights and obligations under the agreement by assignment or novation (substitution of a new contract).

Contracts usually provide that the seller has the right to declare a sale canceled if the buyer defaults. If either party suffers a loss because of the other's default, he may sue for damages to cover the loss. If one party insists on completing the transaction, he may sue the defaulter for specific performance of the terms of the contract; a court can order the other party to comply with the agreement if it was in writing.

Contracts frequently used in the real estate business include listing agreements, sales contracts, options, land contracts (often called installment contracts or articles of agreement), and leases.

A real estate sales contract binds a buyer and a seller to a definite transaction as described in detail within the contract. The buyer is bound to purchase the property for the amount stated in the agreement and to perform by the various dates stipulated (financing, closing). The seller is bound to deliver title free from liens and encumbrances (except those identified and agreed to in the contract).

Under an option agreement, the optionee purchases from the optionor, for a limited time period, the exclusive right to purchase or lease the optionor's property. A land contract or installment contract (articles of agreement for deed) is a seller financing agreement under which a buyer purchases a seller's real estate over time. The buyer takes possession of and responsibility for the property but does not receive the deed until all payments have been made in full. Instead, he receives equitable title.

In Illinois

The Illinois Statute of Frauds requires that all contracts for the sale of land and rental agreements that will not be fulfilled within one year be in writing to be enforceable in court. Additionally, under the Real Estate License Act of 2000, any exclusive brokerage agreement must be in writing.

Real estate contracts undertaken prior to the legal age of 18 are usually voidable; however, leases by minors in Illinois are often enforceable if they may be classified as "necessaries" (food, water, shelter). Contracts made under duress or undertaken while intoxicated are also voidable. Those with mistakes, misrepresentations, or fraud are voidable by the damaged party. Contracts by legally adjudicated insane persons are void.

Brokers and managing brokers may only fill in blanks on preprinted contract forms that are customarily used in the real estate industry. They may not write addendums or qualifying clauses. (*Chicago Bar Association, et al. v. Quinlan and Tyson, Inc.* is the famous Illinois real estate case dealing with this issue.)

Land contracts and options are used with some frequency in Illinois to facilitate transactions that might not otherwise occur. Licensees may negotiate basic terms in a land contract, but attorneys must prepare the articles of agreement.

Earnest money must be deposited in a special escrow or trust account, which bears interest only if all parties agree in writing. It is assumed this money will go to the seller as liquidated damages in the event of a buyer default unless some other arrangement is indicated in a typeface larger than the rest of the contract. ■

CHAPTER 11 QUIZ

1. A legally enforceable agreement under which two parties agree to do something for each other is known as a(n)
   a. escrow agreement.
   b. legal promise.
   c. valid contract.
   d. option agreement.

2. A buyer approaches a seller and says, "I'd like to buy your house." The seller says, "Sure," and they agree on a price. What kind of contract is this?
   a. Implied
   b. Unenforceable
   c. Void
   d. There is no contract.

3. A contract is said to be bilateral if
   a. one of the parties is a minor.
   b. the contract has yet to be fully performed.
   c. only one party to the agreement is bound to act.
   d. all parties to the contract are bound to act.

4. During the period of time after a real estate sales contract is signed but before title actually passes, the status of the contract is
   a. voidable.
   b. executory.
   c. unilateral.
   d. implied.

5. A man and a woman sign a contract under which the man will convey the property to the woman. The man changes his mind, and the woman sues for specific performance. What is the woman seeking in this lawsuit?
   a. Money damages
   b. New contract
   c. Deficiency judgment
   d. Conveyance of the property

6. In a standard sales contract, several words were crossed out; others were inserted. To eliminate future controversy as to whether the changes were made before or after the contract was signed, the usual procedure is to
   a. write a letter to each party listing the changes.
   b. have each party write a letter to the other approving the changes.
   c. redraw the entire contract.
   d. have both parties initial or sign in the margin, along with date, near each change.

7. A buyer makes an offer on a seller's house, and the seller accepts. Both parties sign the sales contract. At this point, the buyer has what type of title to the property?
   a. Equitable
   b. Voidable
   c. Escrow
   d. Contract

8. The sales contract says a man will purchase only if his wife approves the sale by the following Saturday. His wife's approval is a
   a. contingency.
   b. reservation.
   c. warranty.
   d. consideration.

9. A buyer verbally offers to buy a seller's house for $150,000. No written real estate sales contract is drawn up, but the seller agrees to the offer. What kind of contract is this?
   a. Unilateral
   b. Option
   c. Implied
   d. Unenforceable

10. A man and woman enter into a real estate sales contract. Under the contract's terms, the man will pay the woman $500 a month for ten years. The woman will continue to hold legal title to the property. The man will live on the property and pay all real estate taxes, insurance premiums, and regular upkeep costs. What kind of contract do these two people have?

    a. Option contract
    b. Contract for mortgage
    c. Unilateral contract
    d. Land or installment contract

11. Under the statute of frauds, all contracts for the sale of real estate must be

    a. originated by a real estate broker.
    b. on preprinted forms.
    c. in writing to be enforceable.
    d. accompanied by earnest money deposits.

12. A buyer makes an offer in writing to purchase a house for $220,000, including its draperies, with the offer set to expire on Saturday at noon. The seller replies in writing on Thursday, accepting the $220,000 offer, but excluding the draperies. On Friday while the buyer considers this counteroffer, the seller decides to accept the original offer, draperies included, and state that in writing. At this point, which of the following statements is *TRUE*?

    a. The buyer is legally bound to buy the house although the buyer has the right to insist that the draperies be included.
    b. The buyer is not bound to buy.
    c. The buyer must buy the house and are not entitled to the draperies.
    d. The buyer must buy the house but may deduct the value of the draperies from the $220,000.

13. A broker has found a buyer for a seller's home. The buyer has indicated in writing his willingness to buy the property for $1,000 less than the asking price and has deposited $5,000 in earnest money with the broker. The seller is out of town for the weekend, and the broker has been unable to inform him of the signed document. At this point, the buyer has signed a(n)

    a. voidable contract.
    b. offer.
    c. executory agreement.
    d. implied contract.

14. A buyer and seller agree to the purchase of a house for $200,000. The contract contains a clause stating that "time is of the essence." Which of the following statements is *TRUE*?

    a. The closing may take place within a reasonable period after the stated date.
    b. A "time is of the essence" clause is not binding on either party.
    c. The closing date must be stated as a particular calendar date and not simply as a formula, such as "two weeks after loan approval."
    d. If the closing date passes and no closing takes place, the contract may have been breached.

15. A buyer signs a contract allowing her to purchase the property for $230,000 any time in the next three months. The buyer pays the owner $5,000 at the time the contract is signed. Which of the following *BEST* describes this contract?

    a. Contingency
    b. Option
    c. Installment
    d. Sales

16. In preparing a sales contract, an Illinois licensee may
    a. fill in factual and business details in the blank spaces of a customary preprinted form.
    b. draft riders to alter a preprinted contract to fit the transaction.
    c. fill out and sign an offer to purchase for the customer.
    d. advise a buyer or seller of the legal significance of certain parts of the contract.

17. On Tuesday, a sponsoring broker received $1,750 in earnest money from a buyer. The seller accepted the offer on Thursday. Where and when must the sponsoring broker deposit the buyer's money?
    a. In the sponsoring broker's personal checking account by Wednesday
    b. In a special trust account no later than midnight on Thursday
    c. In a special noninterest-bearing trust account by Friday.
    d. In a special noninterest-bearing trust account by Wednesday

18. An Illinois broker does not need written consent of both parties to a transaction to do which of the following?
    a. Disburse interest accrued on an earnest money account
    b. Fill in the blanks on a sales offer as directed by principals
    c. Make changes in the terms of a signed sales contract
    d. Change the commission payment terms designated in the listing agreement

19. The unauthorized practice of law was dealt with in which Illinois Supreme Court case?
    a. *Illinois State Bar Association v. Illinois Board of REALTORS®*
    b. *Chicago Bar Association, et al. v. Quinlan and Tyson, Inc.*
    c. *Attorney Registration and Disciplinary Commission v. Illinois State Department of Professional Regulation*
    d. *Quinlan Associates, Inc. v. Illinois Real Estate Commission*

20. Which provision could legally be placed in an Illinois installment contract?
    a. "Buyer may not record this contract."
    b. "Seller will retain legal title."
    c. "Recording shall not constitute notice."
    d. "Buyer will forfeit $1,000 for recording."

CHAPTER 12

Transfer of Title

■ **LEARNING OBJECTIVES** *When you've finished reading this chapter, you should be able to*

- **identify** the basic requirements for a valid deed;

- **describe** the seven fundamental types of deeds;

- **explain** how property may be transferred through involuntary alienation;

- **distinguish** transfers of title by will from transfers by intestacy; and

- **define** the following *key terms*

acknowledgment	grantee	quitclaim deed
adverse possession	granting clause	special warranty deed
bargain and sale deed	grantor	testate
beneficiary	habendum clause	testator
bequest	heir	title
deed	intestate	transfer tax
deed in trust	involuntary alienation	trustee's deed
devise	legacy	voluntary alienation
devisee	legatee	will
general warranty deed	probate	

■ TITLE

Transfer of title is an aspect of the real estate transaction generally handled by lawyers and title companies, rarely by real estate licensees. Nonetheless, as with other legal aspects of the transaction, a licensee who is aware of the fundamentals of deeds and title issues will know what kind of questions to ask. An informed licensee will know how to direct consumers to professionals to avoid potential title problems.

→ TITLE INSURANCE

Title Transfer Occurs
- Voluntarily
- Involuntarily
- Will
- Descent

The term *title* has two meanings. **Title** to real estate means the right to ownership or actual ownership of the land; it represents the owner's bundle of rights. Title also serves as evidence of that ownership. A person who holds the title would, if challenged in court, be able to recover or retain ownership or possession of a parcel of real estate. Title is a way of referring to ownership; it is not an actual printed document. The document by which the owner transfers the title to another is the **deed**. The deed must be recorded to give public notice of new ownership.

Real estate may be transferred *voluntarily* by sale or gift. Alternatively, it may be transferred *involuntarily* by operation of law. Real estate may be transferred at any time while the owner lives or by will or descent after the owner dies. Title transfers or *passes* as a symbol of ownership.

■ VOLUNTARY ALIENATION

Voluntary alienation is the legal term for the voluntary transfer of title. The owner may voluntarily transfer title by either making a gift or selling the property. To transfer during one's lifetime, the owner must use some form of deed of conveyance.

- A **grantor** conveys property to a grantee.
- A **grantee** receives property from a grantor.
- A **deed** is the instrument that conveys property from a grantor to a grantee.

A deed is the written instrument by which an owner of real estate intentionally conveys the right, title, or interest in a parcel of real estate to someone else. The statute of frauds requires that all deeds be in writing. The owner who transfers the title is referred to as the **grantor.** The person who acquires the title is called the **grantee.** A deed is executed *only* by the grantor, or seller.

The formal requirements for a deed are established by state law and vary from state to state.

Requirements for a Valid Deed

In Illinois

The following are the minimum requirements for a valid deed in Illinois:

- *Grantor*, who has the legal capacity to execute (sign) the deed
- *Grantee* named with reasonable certainty to be identified
- Recital of *consideration*
- *Granting clause* (words of conveyance, together with any words of limitation)
- Accurate *legal description* of the property conveyed
- Any relevant *exceptions* or *reservations*
- *Signature of the grantor*, sometimes with a seal, witness, or acknowledgment
- *Delivery* of the deed and *acceptance* by the grantee to pass title ■

Some states require a **habendum clause** to define ownership taken by the grantee. The habendum clause begins with the words to *have and to hold*. Its provisions must agree with those stated in the granting clause. If there is a discrepancy, the granting clause prevails.

Grantor   A grantor must be of lawful age, at least 18 years old. A deed executed by a minor is usually voidable.

A grantor also must be of *sound mind*. Generally, any grantor who can understand the action is viewed as mentally capable of executing a valid deed. A deed executed by someone who was mentally impaired at the time is voidable but not automatically *void*. If, however, the grantor has been *judged* legally incompetent, the deed will be *void*. Real estate owned by someone who is legally incompetent can be conveyed only with a court's approval.

The grantor's name must be spelled correctly and consistently throughout the deed. If the grantor's name has been changed since the title was acquired, as when a person changes her name by marriage, both names should be shown—for example, "Mary Smith, formerly Mary Jones."

Grantee   To be valid, a deed must name a grantee. The grantee must be specifically named so that the person to whom the property is being conveyed can be readily identified from the deed itself. However, the grantee (new owner) is not required to sign the deed.

■   **FOR EXAMPLE**   Phil wanted to convey Napa Ranch to his nephew, James Christian. In the deed, Phil wrote the following words of conveyance: "I, Phil, hereby convey to James all my interest in Napa Ranch." The only problem was that Phil also had a son named James, a cousin James, and a neighbor James. The grantee's identity could not be discerned from the deed itself. Phil should have conveyed Napa Ranch "to my nephew, James Christian."

If more than one grantee is involved, the granting clause should specify their rights in the property. The clause might state, for instance, that the grantees will take title as "joint tenants," "tenants in common," or "tenants by the entirety." This is especially important when specific wording is necessary to create a joint tenancy or tenancy by the entirety.

| In Illinois |

The purchaser's or grantee's present address is required in Illinois as an element of a valid deed. Also, if no specific form of ownership is selected, tenancy in common is assumed in Illinois. One can determine, then, how ownership is held by consulting the deed language. ■

Consideration   A valid deed must contain a clause acknowledging that the grantor has received *consideration*. Generally, the amount of consideration is stated in dollars. When a deed conveys real estate as a gift to a relative, "love and affection" may be sufficient consideration. In most states, however, it is customary to recite at least a *nominal consideration*, such as "$10 and other good and valuable consideration."

Granting clause (words of conveyance)   A deed must contain a **granting clause** that states the grantor's intention to convey the property. Depending on the type of deed and the obligations agreed to by the grantor (discussed later in this chapter), the wording would be similar to one of the following:

- "I, Kent Long, *convey and warrant . . .*" (creates a warranty deed)
- "I, Kent Long, *remise, release, alienate, and convey. . .*" (creates a special warranty deed)
- "I, Kent Long, *grant, bargain, and sell . . .*" (creates a bargain and sale deed)
- "I, Kent Long, *remise, release, and quitclaim . . .*" (creates a quitclaim deed)

A deed that conveys the grantor's entire fee simple absolute interest usually contains wording such as "to ABC *and to her heirs and assigns forever.*" If the grantor conveys less than her complete interest, such as a life estate, the wording must indicate this limitation—for example, "to ABC for the duration of her natural life."

Legal description of real estate   To be valid, a deed must contain an accurate *legal description* of the real estate conveyed. Land is considered adequately described if a competent surveyor can locate the property using the description.

Exceptions and reservations   A valid deed must specifically note any encumbrances, reservations, or limitations that affect the title being conveyed. This might include such things as restrictions and easements that run with the land. In addition to citing existing encumbrances, a grantor may reserve some right to the land, such as an easement, for the grantor's use. A grantor may also place certain restrictions on a grantee's use of the property. Developers often restrict the number of houses that may be built on each lot in a subdivision. Such private restrictions must be stated in the deed or contained in a previously recorded document, such as the subdivider's master deed, that is expressly referred to in the deed. Many of these deed restrictions have time limits and often include renewal clauses.

Signature of grantor   To be valid, a deed must be signed by all grantors named in the deed. Some states also require witnesses to the grantor's signature.

Most states permit an attorney-in-fact to sign for a grantor. The attorney-in-fact must act under a *power of attorney*—the specific written authority to execute and sign one or more legal instruments for another person. Usually, the power of attorney is recorded in the county where the property is located. The power of attorney terminates when the person on whose behalf it is exercised dies. As a result, adequate evidence must be submitted that the grantor was alive at the time the attorney-in-fact signed the deed.

In some states a grantor's spouse is expected to sign any deed of conveyance to waive any marital or homestead rights. This requirement varies according to state law and depends on the manner in which title to real estate is held and whether the property is used as a homestead (residence).

Many states still require a seal (or simply the word *seal*) to be written or printed after an individual grantor's signature. The corporate seal may be required of a corporate grantor.

In Illinois Seals are not required in Illinois for individual grantor's signatures. Also, corporations need not affix their official corporate seals to validate a deed when they are grantors. ■

Acknowledgment/notarization   An **acknowledgment** (also called *notarization*) is a formal declaration that the person who signs a written document does so voluntarily and that her signature is genuine. The declaration is made before a notary public or an authorized public officer, such as a judge, a justice of the peace, or some other person as prescribed by state law. An acknowledgment usually states that the person signing the deed or other document is known to the officer or has produced sufficient identification to prevent a forgery. The form of acknowledgment required by the state where the property is located should be used even if the signing individual is a resident of another ("foreign") state.

In Illinois In Illinois, acknowledgment is not essential to the validity of the deed. However, unless the deed is acknowledged, it may not be introduced as evidence in a court of law without some further proof of its execution. As a result, it is customary that virtually all documents conveying title are acknowledged/notarized. Recording offices, as a rule, also expect deeds to be notarized before they will record them. Most title insurance companies require acknowledgment/notarization for deeds covered by their policies. ■

Transfer of title requires both delivery and acceptance of deed.

Delivery and acceptance   A title is not considered transferred until the deed is actually *delivered* to and *accepted* by the grantee. The grantor may deliver the deed to the grantee either personally or through a third party. The third party, commonly known as a *settlement agent* or *escrow agent*, will deliver the deed to the grantee as soon as certain requirements have been satisfied. In an arm's-length transaction, the title must be delivered during the grantor's lifetime and accepted during the grantee's lifetime. The effective date of the transfer of title from the grantor to the grantee is the date of delivery of the deed itself. When a deed is delivered in escrow, the date of delivery generally relates back to the date of deposit with the escrow agent.

Execution of Corporate Deeds

The laws governing a corporation's right to convey real estate vary from state to state. However, two basic rules must be followed:

■ A corporation can convey real estate only by authority granted in its bylaws or upon resolution passed by its board of directors. If all or a substantial portion of a corporation's real estate is being conveyed, a resolution authorizing the sale must usually be secured from the shareholders.
■ Deeds to corporate real estate can be signed only by an *authorized officer*.

Rules pertaining to religious corporations and not-for-profit corporations are complex and vary even more widely. Because the legal requirements must be followed exactly, an attorney should be consulted for all corporate conveyances.

Types of Deeds

A deed can take several forms, depending on the extent of the grantor's pledges to the grantee. Regardless of any guarantees the deed offers, however, the grantee will want additional assurance that the grantor has the right to offer what the deed conveys. To obtain this protection, grantees commonly seek evidence of title.

The most common deed forms are the

- general warranty deed,
- special warranty deed,
- bargain and sale deed,
- quitclaim deed,
- deed in trust,
- trustee's deed, and
- deed executed pursuant to a court order.

General warranty deed A **general warranty deed** provides the greatest protection of any deed. It is called a general warranty deed because the grantor is legally bound by certain covenants or warranties (promises). In most states, the warranties are implied by the use of certain words specified by statute. The basic warranties are as follows:

> **General Warranty Deed**
>
> *Five covenants:*
> - Covenant of seisin
> - Covenant against encumbrances
> - Covenant of quiet enjoyment
> - Covenant of further assurance
> - Covenant of warranty forever

- *Covenant of seisin*—The grantor warrants that she owns the property and has the right to convey title to it. (*Seisin* simply means "possession.") The grantee may recover damages up to the full purchase price if this covenant is broken.
- *Covenant against encumbrances*—The grantor warrants that the property is free from liens or encumbrances, except for any specifically stated in the deed. Encumbrances generally include mortgages, mechanics' liens, and easements. If this covenant is breached, the grantee may sue for the cost of removing the encumbrances.
- *Covenant of quiet enjoyment*—The grantor guarantees that the grantee's title will be good against third parties who might bring court actions to establish superior title to the property. If the grantee's title is found to be inferior, the grantor is liable for damages.
- *Covenant of further assurance*—The grantor promises to obtain and deliver any instrument needed to make the title good. For example, if the grantor's spouse has failed to sign away dower rights, the grantor must deliver a quitclaim deed (discussed later) to clear the title.
- *Covenant of warranty forever*—The grantor promises to compensate the grantee for the loss sustained if the title fails at any time in the future.

In Illinois

Illinois law provides that a deed using the *words "convey and warrant"* implies and includes all covenants of general warranty, which are as binding on the grantor, her heirs, and personal representatives as if written at length in the deed. These covenants in a general warranty deed are not limited to matters that occurred during the time the grantor owned the property; they extend back to its origins. The grantor defends the title against herself and against all others as predecessors in title.

In addition, it is sufficient for a general warranty deed to recite only nominal consideration. ∎

Special Warranty Deed

Two warranties:
- Warranty that grantor received title
- Warranty that property was unencumbered by grantor

Special warranty deed A **special warranty deed** contains two basic warranties:

1. Warranty that the grantor received title
2. Warranty that the property was not encumbered during the time the grantor held title, except as otherwise noted in the deed

In effect, the grantor defends the title against herself but not against previous encumbrances. The granting clause generally contains the words "grantor remises, releases, alienates, and conveys." The grantor may include additional warranties, but they must be specifically stated in the deed. In areas where a special warranty deed is more commonly used, the purchase of title insurance is viewed as providing adequate protection to the grantee.

A special warranty deed may be used by fiduciaries such as trustees, executors, and corporations. A special warranty deed is appropriate for a fiduciary because she lacks the authority to warrant against acts of predecessors in title. A fiduciary may hold title for a limited time without having a personal interest in the proceeds. Sometimes a special warranty deed may be used by a grantor who has acquired title at a tax sale.

Bargain and sale deed In some states, a **bargain and sale deed** contains no express warranties against encumbrances. It does, however, imply that the grantor holds title and possession of the property.

In Illinois

Bargain and Sale Deed

No express warranties:
- Implication that grantor holds title and possession

The words in the granting clause are "grant, bargain, and sell." A grant, bargain, and sale deed conveys a simple title with the following covenants: (1) the grantor holds a fee simple estate, (2) the title is free from encumbrances made by the grantor except those listed in the deed, and (3) the grantor warrants quiet enjoyment. An Illinois bargain and sale deed is similar to a warranty deed but less complete in its warranties. The buyer should purchase title insurance for protection. ■

Quitclaim Deed

No express or implied covenants or warranties:
- Used primarily to convey less than fee simple or to cure a title defect

Quitclaim deed A **quitclaim deed** provides the grantee with the least protection of any deed. It carries no covenants or warranties and generally conveys only whatever interest the grantor may have when the deed is delivered. If the grantor has no interest, the grantee will acquire nothing. Nor will the grantee acquire any right of warranty claim against the grantor. A quitclaim deed can convey title as effectively as a warranty deed if the grantor has good title when she delivers the deed, but it provides none of the guarantees that a warranty deed does. Through a quitclaim deed, the grantor only "remises, releases, and quitclaims" her interest in the property, if any.

A quitclaim deed is the only type of deed that may be used to convey less than a fee simple estate. This is because a quitclaim deed conveys only the grantor's right, title, or interest without giving any kind of guarantee as to the quality or nature of title being conveyed.

A quitclaim deed frequently is used to cure a defect, called a *cloud on the title*. For example, if the name of the grantee is misspelled on a warranty deed filed in the public record, a quitclaim deed with the correct spelling may be executed to the grantee to perfect the title.

A quitclaim deed also is used when a grantor allegedly inherits property but is not certain that the decedent's title was valid. A warranty deed in such an instance could carry with it obligations of warranty, while a quitclaim deed would convey only the grantor's interest.

In Illinois   A quitclaim deed uses the words "convey and quit claim," and conveys in fee all the grantor's existing legal and equitable rights held at the time of delivery. ■

Deed in Trust
Conveyance from trustor to trustee.

Deed in trust   A deed in trust is the means by which a trustor conveys real estate to a trustee for the benefit of a beneficiary. The real estate is held by the trustee to fulfill the purpose of the trust. (See Figure 12.1.)

Trustee's Deed
Conveyance from trustee to third party.

Trustee's deed   A deed executed by a trustee is a **trustee's deed**. It is used when a trustee conveys real estate held in the trust to the beneficiary. The trustee's deed must state that the trustee is executing the instrument in accordance with the powers and authority granted by the trust instrument.

Deed executed pursuant to court order   Executors' and administrators' deeds, masters' deeds, sheriffs' deeds, and many other types are all deeds executed pursuant to a court order. These deeds are established by state statute and are used to convey title to property that is transferred by court order or by will. The form of such a deed must conform to the laws of the state in which the property is located.

One common characteristic of deeds executed pursuant to court order is that the full consideration is usually stated in the deed. Instead of "$10 and other valuable consideration," for example, the deed lists the actual sales price.

Transfer Tax Stamps

Many states have enacted laws providing for a state transfer tax on conveyances of real estate. Many municipalities have local transfer stamps as well.

In Illinois   The Illinois Real Estate Transfer Act imposes a tax on conveying title to real estate in the amount of $0.50 per $500, and in all Illinois counties, there is an additional transfer tax of $0.25 per $500. Total transfer tax to state and county combined is $0.75 per $500 or fraction thereof. Fifty percent of the state tax

FIGURE   12.1

Deed in Trust

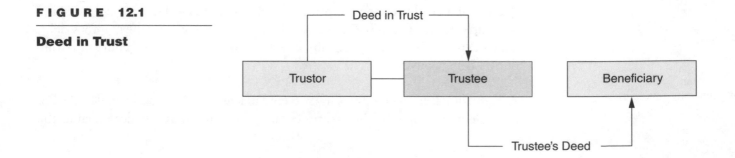

collected is deposited into the Illinois Affordable Housing Trust Fund (under the Illinois Affordable Housing Act of 1989), 35 percent is deposited into the Open Space Land Acquisition and Development Fund, and the remaining 15 percent goes to the Natural Areas Acquisition Fund. The seller generally pays the state and county transfer tax.

The **transfer tax** must be paid before the recording of the deed (or before transferring the beneficial interest in a land trust). This is done by purchasing *tax stamps* from the county recorder or the city offices if there are local stamps required. These stamps are literally affixed to the deed. ■

Local transfer tax   Many local municipalities have their own tax as well. Charts indicating these local transfer tax amounts are available from counties and individual municipalities. Local transfer tax can be paid by either buyer or seller, so it is important to check each municipality.

IN PRACTICE   Real estate professionals have an important role to play in letting buyers or sellers know about transfer taxes early on. For the *sellers*, this comes at listing presentation time when an approximate estimate of total selling costs for sellers is usually given—commission cost, mortgage payoff, attorney fee, survey, title insurance, and transfer tax (if payable by seller). For the *buyers' real estate agents*, it may mean mentioning transfer taxes any time the agent notes that the buyer has an interest in homes located where buyer-paid taxes apply.

In Illinois

Tax formula   The formula used in Illinois to determine the exact taxable consideration is as follows:

Full actual consideration (sales price)	$ _____
Less value of personal property included in purchase	– _____
Less amount of mortgage to which property remains subject	– _____
Equals net TOTAL taxable consideration to be covered by stamps	= _____
Amount of Illinois state tax stamps ($.50 per $500 or taxable amount)	$ _____
Amount of county tax ($.25 per $500)	+ $ _____
Total transfer tax	= $ _____

■ **FOR EXAMPLE**   A parcel of real estate sold for $350,000. The purchaser agreed to assume the seller's existing mortgage of $128,000 and to pay $222,000 in cash upon receipt of the seller's deed. The purchase price includes $25,000 of personal property. What amount of county and state stamps must the seller affix to the deed?

The total transfer tax would be computed as follows:

Sales price	$350,000
Less personal property	– $ 25,000
Less assumable mortgage	– $128,000
Equals net total taxable consideration	$197,000

To be covered by stamps

$197,000 divided by $500 = 394 stamps × $.50 (State) =	$197.00
$197,000 divided by $500 = 394 stamps × $.25 (County) =	$ 98.50
$197.00 + $98.50 = $295.50 Total transfer tax ■	

In Illinois

Real Estate Transfer Declaration   The amount of consideration used for determining transfer taxes must be shown on the Real Estate Transfer Declaration form. The form must be signed by the buyer and seller or their agents, and it provides for the inclusion of the property description, manner of conveyance, and type of financing used. The financing data helps the Department of Revenue accurately determine equalization factors between different counties and eliminate inconsistencies caused by the use of nonconventional or creative financing.

A completed declaration must accompany every deed presented to the recorder for recording. (The Cook County Recorder's office has its own separate transfer form, which also must be presented with every deed.) A willful falsification or omission of any of the required data constitutes a Class B misdemeanor and is punishable by up to six months in jail. The information contained on the form is *not* confidential and is available for inspection by the public.

Exempted from the transfer tax are deeds such as those conveying real estate from or between any governmental bodies; those held by charitable, religious, or educational institutions; those securing debts or releasing property as security for a debt; partitions; tax deeds; deeds pursuant to mergers of corporations; deeds from subsidiary to parent corporations for cancellation of stock; and deeds subject to federal documentary stamp tax. When the actual consideration for conveyance is less than $100, the transfer is considered a gift and is exempt from tax. An exemption statement is usually typed on an exempted deed and signed before the deed is recorded.

Tax stamps and land trusts   Under the Land Trust Recordation and Transfer Tax Act, a land trustee has the obligation to record a facsimile of the assignment of beneficial interest. The names of the beneficiaries need not be disclosed, and privacy is maintained. The tax rate and the exemptions are the same for the assignment as for the transfer of real property. ■

■ INVOLUNTARY ALIENATION

Title to property may be transferred without the owner's consent by **involuntary alienation.** (See Figure 12.2.) Involuntary transfers are usually carried out by operation of law—such as by condemnation or a sale to satisfy delinquent tax or mortgage liens. When a person dies intestate and leaves no heirs, the title to the real estate passes to the county (in Illinois) by the state's power of escheat. Additional land may be acquired through the process of accretion or lost through erosion, and other acts of nature, such as earthquakes, hurricanes, sinkholes, and mudslides, may add to or eliminate a landowner's holdings.

Involuntary Alienation

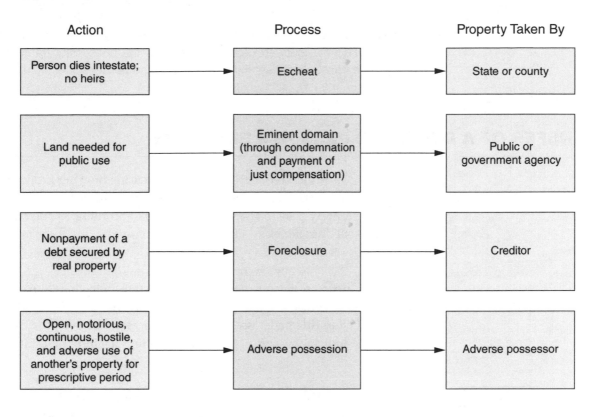

Transfer by Adverse Possession

Adverse possession, sometimes referred to as *squatter's rights,* is another means of involuntary transfer. An individual who makes a claim to certain property, takes possession of it, and *uses* it may take title away from an owner who fails to use or inspect the property for a period of years. The law recognizes that the use of land is an important function of its ownership. Usually, the possession by the claimant must be

- open,
- notorious,
- continuous and uninterrupted,
- hostile, and
- adverse to the true owner's possession.

In Illinois   The period of uninterrupted possession required to claim title by adverse possession is 20 years. However, if the party whose property is being claimed has *color of title* (that is, if her apparently good title actually is invalidated by some flaw) and if the real estate taxes on the property are paid while satisfying the other statutory requirements, the possessory period may be shortened to seven years. ■

Through the principle of *tacking,* successive periods of different adverse possession by different adverse possessors can be combined, enabling a person who is not in possession for the entire required time to establish a claim. For instance, if a woman held a property in adverse possession for five years, then Daughter A held the same property for ten years, then Daughter B held the property for five more years, Daughter B would be able to claim the property by adverse possession even though she had not *personally* possessed the property for the full statutory 20 years.

IN PRACTICE   The right of adverse possession is a statutory right. State requirements must be followed carefully to ensure the successful transfer of title. The parties to a transaction that might involve adverse possession should seek legal counsel.

■ TRANSFER OF A DECEASED PERSON'S PROPERTY

A person who dies **testate** has prepared a will indicating how her property should be handled. In contrast, when a person dies **intestate** (without a will), real estate and personal property pass to the decedent's heirs according to the state's statute of *descent and distribution*. In effect, the state provides a will for an intestate decedent.

Legally, when a person dies, ownership of real estate immediately passes either to the heirs by descent or to the persons named in the will. Before these individuals can take full title and possession of the property, however, the estate must go through the judicial process of *probate*, and claims against the estate must be satisfied.

In Illinois   When the owner of real estate dies, how title to the property was held (rather than the laws of descent and distribution or the presence of a will) may dictate who the new owners will be:

- If the property was owned by a husband and wife in *tenancy by the entirety* or was held in *joint tenancy*, the surviving spouse (or other owner) will automatically be the new owner. If the property was held as a *life estate*, it automatically reverts to the former owner or passes to a remainderman. In any case, no probate is required.
- If the property was not held in joint tenancy, tenancy by the entirety, or as a life estate, and the owner left a valid will (died testate), the devisees named in the will own the real estate.
- If the owner died without a will (intestate), relatives will inherit the property according to the Illinois Law of Descent. (In effect, the state makes a will for such decedents.)
- If the owner died without a will (intestate) and left no heirs, the real property will *escheat* to the Illinois county it lies in. ■

Transfer of Title by Will

A **will** is an instrument made by an owner to convey title to real or personal property after the owner's death. A will is a testamentary instrument; that is, it takes effect only after death. This differs from a deed, which must be delivered during the lifetime of the grantor and conveys a present interest in property. While the **testator** (the person who makes a will) is alive, any property included in the will can still be conveyed by the owner. The parties named in a will have no rights or interests as long as the party who made the will lives; they acquire interest or title only after the owner's death.

Only property owned by the testator at the time of her death may be transferred by will. The gift of real property by will is known as a **devise**, and a person who receives property by will is known as a **devisee**. The gift of personal property by will is known as a **legacy** or a **bequest**, and a person who receives the personal property by will is known as a **legatee** or **beneficiary**.

For title to pass to the devisee(s), state laws require that upon the death of a testator, the will must be filed with the court and probated. Probate is a legal procedure for verifying the validity of a will and accounting for the decedent's assets. The process can take several months to complete.

| In Illinois | **Legal requirements for making a will**   Any person 18 or older, who is of sound mind and memory, may make a will. A will must be in writing and signed and declared by the maker (the *testator*) in the presence of two or more witnesses to be her last will and testament. Witnesses cannot be beneficiaries under the will because their gifts will likely be voided by the probate court. |

A modification of, an amendment of, or an addition to a previously executed will may be set forth in a separate document called a *codicil.*

A *holographic will* is written in the testator's own handwriting. A *nuncupative will*, such as a deathbed bequest, is given orally by a testator and is for personal property. Illinois courts recognize neither holographic wills nor noncupative wills unless also witnessed by two people in each case.

Upon the death of a testator, the will must be filed and a petition for probate initiated in the circuit court of the county in which the decedent resided. For six months after the executor has been appointed and the decedent's property has been inventoried, claims may be presented to the executor for debts owed by the deceased. On completion of probate, the executor's final account is filed with the court and the executor is discharged. The real estate is considered free from debts, claims, or taxes of the decedent.

While an individual may freely disinherit children or other previously named heirs, in Illinois, a surviving spouse may not be disinherited by the decedent spouse. A surviving spouse who is disinherited by the decedent has a statutory right to renounce the will and claim a share of the estate as follows:

- If the deceased left no child or descendant(s) of a child, *one-half of the personal estate* and *one-half of each parcel of real estate* goes to the spouse if claimed.
- If the deceased left spouse and descendants, *one-third of the personal estate* and *one-third of each parcel of real estate* goes to the spouse if claimed.
- The will remains operative with respect to the balance of the estate. ◾

Transfer of Title by Descent

When a person dies *intestate* (without leaving a valid will), her state's law of descent governs how and to whom her property will be distributed.

In Illinois

The Illinois Law of Descent and Distribution (in the Illinois Probate Act) provides that real estate located in Illinois owned by a deceased resident or nonresident who did not leave a valid will is distributed as indicated in Figure 12.3.

The estate of an intestate decedent must be probated to determine which statutory heirs will inherit, as well as to inventory the assets of and claims against the estate. Any **heir** or other interested person may petition the circuit court of the county in which the decedent last resided to probate the estate. Proof of heirship must be presented to the court. Probate generally proceeds as if the decedent had left a valid will. ■

Probate Proceedings

Probate is a formal judicial process that

- proves or confirms the validity of a will,
- determines the precise assets of the deceased person, and
- identifies the persons to whom the assets are to pass.

The purpose of probate is to see that the assets are distributed correctly. All assets must be accounted for, and the decedent's debts must be satisfied before any property is distributed to the heirs. In addition, estate taxes must be paid before any distribution. The laws of each state govern the probate proceedings in that state and the functions of the individuals appointed to administer the decedent's affairs.

FIGURE 12.3

Statutory Distributions Under the Illinois Law of Descent and Distribution

Descendent Status	Family Status	Property Passes . . .
Married, with surviving spouse	No children No other relatives	100% to surviving spouse
Married, with surviving spouse	Children	50% to surviving spouse; 50% shared by children or descendants of deceased child
Married, no surviving spouse	Children	Children share equally, with descendants of a deceased child taking their parent's share
Unmarried, no children	Relatives	100% to parents, brothers, or sisters equally; however, if there is one surviving parent, that parent takes two shares and all others share equal portions; if no parents or brothers or sisters survive, the estate passes to other relatives as determined by the probate court.
	No other relatives or heirs as defined by state law	100% to the county in which the real estate is located, by escheat

Assets that are distributed through probate are those that do not otherwise distribute themselves. For instance, property held in joint tenancy or tenancy by the entirety passes immediately. Any probate proceedings will take place in the county in which the decedent resided. If the decedent owned real estate in another county, probate would occur in that county as well.

The person who has possession of the will—normally the person designated in the will as *executor*—presents it for filing with the court. The court is responsible for determining that the will meets the statutory requirements for its form and execution. If a codicil or more than one will exists, the court will decide how these documents should be probated.

The court must rule on a challenge if a will is contested. Once the will is upheld, the assets can be distributed according to its provisions. Probate courts distribute assets according to statute only when no other reasonable alternative exists.

When a person dies intestate, the court determines who inherits the assets by reviewing proof from relatives of the decedent and their entitlement under the statute of descent and distribution. Once the heirs have been determined, the court appoints an *administrator* or a personal representative to administer the affairs of the estate—the role usually taken by an executor.

Whether or not a will is involved, the administrator or executor is responsible for having the estate's assets appraised and for ensuring that all the decedent's debts are satisfied. She is also responsible for paying federal estate taxes and state inheritance taxes out of the assets. Once all obligations have been satisfied, the representative distributes the remaining property according to the terms of the will or the state's law of descent.

IN PRACTICE A sponsoring broker entering into a listing agreement with the executor or administrator of an estate in probate should be aware that a commission amount is fixed by the court and a commission is payable only from the proceeds of the sale. The sponsoring broker will not be able to collect a commission unless the court approves the sale.

■ SUMMARY

Title to real estate is the right to and evidence of ownership of the land. It may be transferred by voluntary alienation, involuntary alienation, will, and descent.

The voluntary transfer of an owner's title is made by a deed executed (signed) by the owner (the grantor) to the purchaser (or donee) as grantee.

Among the most common requirements for a valid deed are a grantor with legal capacity to contract, a readily identifiable grantee, a granting clause, a legal description of the property, a recital of consideration, exceptions and reservations on the title, and the signature of the grantor. In addition, the deed should be properly witnessed and acknowledged/notarized before a notary public to provide evidence of a genuine signature and to facilitate recording. Title to the property passes when the grantor delivers a deed to the grantee and it is accepted. The level of guarantee a grantor offers is determined by the form of the deed.

A general warranty deed provides the greatest protection of any deed by binding the grantor to certain covenants or warranties. A special warranty deed warrants only that the real estate is not encumbered except as stated in the deed. A bargain and sale deed carries with it no warranties but implies that the grantor holds title to the property. A quitclaim deed carries with it no warranties whatsoever and conveys only the interest, if any, the grantor possesses in the property. The language of each deed is a key as to its type.

An owner's title may be transferred by her permission or without her permission by a court action or by death. The real estate of an owner who makes a valid will (who dies testate) passes to the devisees through the probating of the will. The title of an owner who dies without a will (intestate or intestatory) passes according to the provisions of the laws of descent and distribution of the state in which the real estate is located.

In Illinois

In Illinois, the requirements for a valid deed are a grantor with legal capacity to contract, a readily identifiable grantee, a granting clause, a legal description of the property, a recital of consideration, and the signature of the grantor. Title to the property passes when the grantor delivers a deed to the grantee and it is accepted. The obligation of a grantor is determined by the form of the deed. The specific words of conveyance in the granting clause are critical in determining the form of deed.

Acknowledgment and notarization are standard in county recorders' offices. Recording is required for tax deeds and if a deed is to be used as evidence in a court of law.

In Illinois, a bargain and sale deed includes covenants that make it similar to a special warranty deed. A quitclaim deed carries with it no warranties whatsoever and conveys only the interest, if any, the grantor possesses in the property.

Generally, state and county transfer tax stamps are paid for by the seller. This money goes to the state and county for affordable housing and land preservation. Many municipalities have their own transfer tax as well, which can be paid by either the seller or the buyer.

The title of an owner who dies without a will (intestate) passes to the decedent's statutory heirs, according to the provisions of the Illinois Law of Descent and Distribution. Property conveyed by devise is property conveyed by will. Where a decedent leaves no statutory heirs, the real property escheats to the county in Illinois where it is located. ∎

CHAPTER 12 QUIZ

1. The basic requirements for a valid conveyance are governed by
   a. state law.
   b. local custom.
   c. national law.
   d. the law of descent.

2. Every deed must be signed by the
   a. grantor.
   b. grantee.
   c. grantor and grantee.
   d. devisee.

3. A 15-year-old boy recently inherited many parcels of real estate from his late father and has decided to sell one of the parcels. If the boy enters into a deed conveying his interest in the property to a purchaser, such a conveyance will be
   a. valid.
   b. void.
   c. invalid.
   d. voidable.

4. A husband who works for an international corporation has already moved to Germany. To authorize his wife to act on his behalf, he signed a(n)
   a. power of attorney.
   b. release deed.
   c. quitclaim deed.
   d. acknowledgment.

5. What is the major difference between a general warranty deed and a quitclaim deed?
   a. A general warranty deed provides the least protection for the buyer; a quitclaim deed provides the most protection for the buyer.
   b. A general warranty deed can be used only in foreclosure sales; a quitclaim deed is used only in residential sales.
   c. A general warranty deed provides the most protection for the buyer; a quitclaim deed provides the least protection for the buyer.
   d. A general warranty deed creates an indefeasible title; a quitclaim deed creates a defeasible title.

6. Under the covenant of quiet enjoyment, the grantor
   a. promises to obtain and deliver any instrument needed to make the title good.
   b. guarantees that if the title fails in the future, she will compensate the grantee.
   c. warrants that she is the owner and has the right to convey title to the property.
   d. guarantees that the title will be good against the title claims of third parties.

7. Which of the following types of deeds merely implies, but does not specifically warrant, that the grantor holds good title to the property?
   a. Special warranty
   b. Bargain and sale
   c. Quitclaim
   d. Trustee's

8. Step 1: A decided to convey his property to B. Step 2: A signed a deed transferring title to B. Step 3: A gave the signed deed to B, who accepted it. Step 4: B took the deed to the county recorder's office and had it recorded. At which step did title to the property actually transfer or pass to B?
   a. Step 1
   b. Step 2
   c. Step 3
   d. Step 4

9. A woman signed a deed transferring ownership of her property to a man. To provide evidence that the woman's signature was genuine, she executed a declaration before a notary. This declaration is known as an
   a. affidavit.
   b. acknowledgment.
   c. affirmation.
   d. estoppel.

10. A woman bought acreage in a distant county, never went to see the acreage, and did not use the ground. A man moved his mobile home onto the land, had a well drilled for water, and lived there for 22 years. The man may become the owner of the land if he has complied with the state law regarding

    a. requirements for a valid conveyance.
    b. adverse possession.
    c. avulsion.
    d. voluntary alienation.

11. What do the terms *condemnation* and *escheat* have in common?

    a. They are examples of voluntary alienation.
    b. They are processes used in adverse possession claims.
    c. They are methods of transferring title by descent.
    d. They are examples of involuntary alienation.

12. A deed contains a guarantee that the grantor will compensate the grantee for any loss resulting from the title's failure in the future. This is an example of which type of covenant?

    a. Warranty forever
    b. Further assurance
    c. Quiet enjoyment
    d. Seisin

13. Which of the following documents transfers title to real estate at the death of the owner?

    a. Warranty deed
    b. Special warranty deed
    c. Trustee's deed
    d. Will

In Illinois

14. For Illinois courts to recognize a holographic will, the will must

    a. be handwritten.
    b. have no amendments.
    c. have two witnesses.
    d. be modified by codicil.

15. In Illinois, how many years are required to acquire title by adverse possession?

    a. 5
    b. 7
    c. 20
    d. 30

16. Which of the following statements is *TRUE* regarding the execution of a valid will in Illinois?

    a. The testator must be at least 21 years old and of sound mind.
    b. The will must be in writing, signed, and witnessed by two people.
    c. The will must be witnessed by three people.
    d. The will must be notarized.

17. In Illinois, the transfer tax is

    a. customarily paid by the buyer.
    b. computed on the sales price less the amount of any existing mortgage to which the property remains subject.
    c. not required if the actual total consideration is less than $500.
    d. assessed at the rate of $1 per $1,000 of sales price.

18. Which deed requires the Illinois transfer tax?

    a. A deed conveying a property owned by a charitable institution
    b. A deed conveying a property owned by a government body
    c. Deeds for property valued at less than $100
    d. Deeds between relatives

19. A longtime Illinois resident who owned considerable real and personal property died testate, leaving only $1 to his wife who was his sole survivor. The balance of his estate was left to his trusted real estate broker. The wife renounced the will. Which of the following is *TRUE*?

    a. The entire will is invalid.
    b. The wife is entitled to a one-quarter share of all property.
    c. The wife is entitled to one-half of the personal estate and one-half of each parcel of real estate.
    d. Because the man left no descendants, the wife is entitled to the entire estate by the law of descent.

20. An Illinois resident died intestate. The man was survived by a mother and brother. Under these facts, which of the following correctly states how the man's estate will be distributed?

  a. The man's estate will be left entirely to his mother.

  b. The estate will be divided equally between the mother and brother.

  ✓ c. The estate will be divided so that the man's mother receives two-thirds and the brother receives one-third.

  d. The man's mother receives one-third and his brother receives two-thirds.

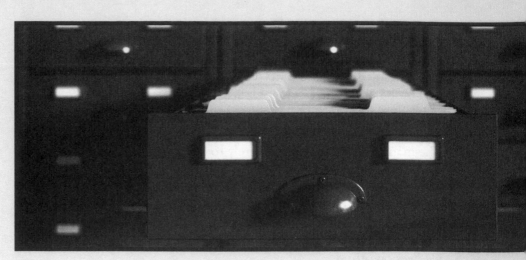

13

CHAPTER

Title Records

■ **LEARNING OBJECTIVES** *When you've finished reading this chapter, you should be able to*

- **identify** the various proofs of ownership;

- **describe** recording, notice, and chain of title issues;

- **explain** the process and purpose of a title search;

- **distinguish** constructive and actual notice; and

- **define** the following *key terms*

abstract and attorney's opinion of title	chain of title	subrogation
abstract of title	constructive notice	suit to quiet title
actual notice	marketable title	title insurance
certificate of title	priority	title search
	recording	

■ PUBLIC RECORDS

Public records contain detailed information about each parcel of real estate in a city or county. These records are crucial in establishing ownership, giving notice of encumbrances, and establishing priority of liens. They protect the interests of real estate owners, taxing bodies, creditors, and the general public. The real estate recording system includes written documents that affect title, such as deeds and mortgages. Public records regarding taxes, judgments, probate, and marriage also may offer important information about the title to a particular property. In most states, written documents must be recorded in the county where the land is located.

Public records are maintained by

- recorders of deeds,
- county clerks,
- county treasurers,
- city clerks,
- collectors, and
- clerks of court.

In Illinois The recorder of deeds, county clerk, county treasurer, city clerk and collector, and clerks of various courts maintain these records. In Illinois, a recorder of deeds must be elected in each county with a population of 60,000 or more. In counties with a population of fewer than 60,000, the county clerk serves as the recorder of deeds. ∎

Public records are just that: open to the public. This means that anyone interested in a particular property can review the records to learn about the documents, claims, and other issues that affect its ownership. A prospective purchaser, for example, needs to be sure that the seller can convey title to the property. If the property is subject to any liens or other encumbrances, a prospective buyer or lender will want to know.

IN PRACTICE Although we speak of prospective purchasers conducting title searches, purchasers themselves rarely search the public records for evidence of title or encumbrances. Instead, title companies conduct searches before providing title insurance. An attorney also may search the title.

Recording

Recording is the act of placing documents in the public record. The specific rules for recording documents are a matter of state law. However, although the details may vary, recording essentially provides that any written document that affects any estate, right, title, or interest in land must be recorded in the county where the land is located to serve as public notice. That way, anyone interested in the title to a parcel of property will know where to look to discover the various interests of all other parties. Recording acts also generally give legal priority to those interests recorded first—the *first in time, first in right* or *first come, first served* principle.

To be eligible for recording, a document must be drawn and executed as stipulated in the recording acts of the state in which the real estate is located.

In Illinois Illinois law does not require that most documents be filed or recorded within a specified period of time. However, when creditors and subsequent purchasers do not actually know the content of the documents affecting certain real estate interests, the courts will hold these creditors and purchasers responsible for "discovering" (knowing) that information only as of the date on which the documents are recorded. Tax deeds, by law, must be recorded within one year after the redemption period expires. A tax deed that is not recorded or filed within one year becomes null and void. No instrument affecting title to real property may include any provision prohibiting recording. Any such prohibiting provision is void as a matter of law.

The original document must be filed with the county recorder of deeds and must meet specific requirements (in addition to the nine requirements of a valid deed):

- Grantor's name typed or printed below his signature
- Full address of the grantee
- Name and address of the person who prepared the deed
- Permanent tax index number (required only in some counties)
- Common address of the property (required only in some counties)
- 3½" × 5" blank space for use by the recorder
- Completed real estate transfer declaration
- Proof of payment of the state and county transfer taxes or indication of an applicable exemption
- Proof of payment of the municipal transfer tax (if applicable)

When the parcel of land being transferred is a division of a larger parcel and smaller than five acres, the recording provisions of the Illinois Plat Act apply. If the conveyance is exempt, an affidavit stating the reason for the exemption may be required by the recorder.

In some municipalities, the water department must declare, by way of an endorsement stamp on the municipal transfer declaration, that all outstanding water bills have been paid.

A deed in any language other than English, although valid between the parties, does not give constructive notice unless an official English translation of the document is attached at the time of recording. The translation must be prepared by a credible source, such as the local consulate of a country in which the language is used. ■

Notice

Anyone who has an interest in a parcel of real estate can take certain steps, called *giving notice*, to ensure that others know about the individual's interest. There are two basic types of notice: *constructive notice* and *actual notice*.

Constructive notice is the legal presumption that information may be obtained by an individual through due diligence. Properly recording documents in the public record serves as constructive notice to the world of an individual's rights or interest, as does the physical possession of a property. Because the information or evidence is readily available to the world, a prospective purchaser or lender is responsible for discovering the interest.

Actual notice means not only that the information is available but also that someone has been given the information and actually knows it. An individual who has searched the public records and inspected the property has actual notice, also known as *direct knowledge*. If it can be proved that an individual has had actual notice of information, that person cannot use a lack of constructive notice (such as an unrecorded deed) to justify a claim.

Priority   **Priority** refers to the order of rights in time. Many complicated situations can affect the priority of rights in a parcel of real estate—who recorded first, which party was in possession first, who had actual or constructive notice. How the courts rule in any situation depends, of course, on the specific facts of the case. These are strictly legal questions that should be referred to the parties' attorneys.

■ **FOR EXAMPLE**   In May, Buyer A purchased a property from Seller B and received a deed. Buyer A did not record the deed but took possession of the property in June. In November, Seller B sold the same property to Buyer C who received a deed, which Buyer C promptly recorded. Buyer C never inspected the property to determine if someone was in possession of it. By taking possession of the property, Buyer A has the superior right to the property even though Buyer A did not record the deed.

Unrecorded Documents

Certain types of liens are not recorded. Real estate taxes and special assessments are liens on specific parcels of real estate and usually are not recorded until some time after the taxes or assessments are past due. Inheritance taxes and franchise taxes are statutory liens. They are placed against all real estate owned by a decedent at the time of death or by a corporation at the time the franchise taxes became a lien. Like real estate taxes, they are not recorded.

Notice of these liens must be gained from sources other than the recorder's office. Evidence of the payment of real estate taxes, special assessments, municipal utilities, and other taxes can be gathered from paid tax receipts and letters from municipalities. Creative measures are often required to get information about these "off the record" liens.

In Illinois

A *mechanic's lien* that has not been recorded may nonetheless still have priority over other liens that have been recorded. ■

Chain of Title

A **chain of title** is the record of a property's ownership. Beginning with the earliest owner, title may pass to many individuals. Each owner is linked to the next so that a chain is formed. An unbroken chain of title can be traced through linking conveyances from the present owner back to the earliest recorded owner. Chain of title does not include liens and encumbrances or any other document not directly related to ownership.

If ownership cannot be traced through an unbroken chain, a gap or cloud in the chain of title is said to exist. In these cases, the cloud on the title makes it necessary to establish ownership by a court action called a **suit to quiet title**. For instance, a suit might be required when a grantor acquired title under one name and conveyed it under another name, or there may be a forged deed in the chain, after which no subsequent grantee acquired legal title. All possible claimants are allowed to present evidence during a court proceeding; then the court's judgment is filed. Often, the simple procedure of obtaining any relevant quitclaim deeds is used to clear title and establish ownership.

Title Search and Abstract of Title

A **title search** is an examination of all of the public records to determine whether any defects exist in the chain of title. The records of the conveyances of ownership are examined, beginning with the present owner. Then the title is traced backward to its origin. The time back to which the title must be searched is limited in states that have adopted the Marketable Title Act. This law extinguishes certain interests and cures certain defects arising before the *root of the title*—the conveyance that establishes the source of the chain of title. Normally, the root is considered to be 40 years. Under most circumstances, then, it is necessary to search only from the current owner to the root.

In Illinois For normal title searches in Illinois, the search goes back 40 years under the Illinois Marketable Title Act. When the possibility of litigation exists, the search must go back 75 years. Interestingly, in Cook and Du Page counties, title searches cannot go back beyond 1871. In that year, most records were destroyed in the Great Chicago Fire.

Other public records are examined to identify wills, judicial proceedings, and other encumbrances that may affect title. These include a variety of taxes, special assessments, and other recorded liens.

A title search usually is not ordered until after the major contingencies in a sales contract have been cleared—for instance, after a loan commitment has been secured. Before providing money for a loan, a lender or the attorney orders a title search to ensure that no lien is superior to its mortgage lien. In most cases, the cost of the title search in Illinois is paid by the seller. ■

An **abstract of title** is a summary report of what the title search found in the public record. The person who prepares this report is called an *abstractor*. The abstractor searches all the public records and then summarizes the various events and proceedings that affected the title throughout its history. The report begins with the original grant (or root), then provides a chronological list of recorded instruments. All recorded liens and encumbrances are included, along with their current statuses. A list of all of the public records examined is also provided as evidence of the scope of the search.

IN PRACTICE An abstract of title is a condensed history of those items that can be found in public records. It does not reveal such items as encroachments, forgeries, or any interests or conveyances that have not been recorded.

Marketable Title

Under the terms of the typical real estate sales contract, the seller is required to deliver **marketable title** to the buyer at the closing. To be marketable, a title must

■ disclose no serious defects and not depend on doubtful questions of law or fact to prove its validity;

- not expose a purchaser to the hazard of litigation or threaten the *quiet enjoyment* of the property; and
- convince a reasonably well-informed and prudent purchaser, acting on business principles and with knowledge of the facts and their legal significance, that he could sell or mortgage the property at a later time.

Although a title that does not meet these requirements still could be transferred, it contains certain defects that may limit or restrict its ownership. A buyer cannot be forced to accept a conveyance that is materially different from the one bargained for in the sales contract. However, questions of marketable title must be raised by a buyer before acceptance of the deed. Once a buyer has accepted a deed with an unmarketable title, the only available legal recourse is to sue the seller under any covenants of warranty contained in the deed.

■ PROOF OF OWNERSHIP

Proof of ownership is evidence that title is marketable. A deed by itself is not considered sufficient evidence of ownership in Illinois. Even though a warranty deed conveys the grantor's interest, it contains no proof of the condition of the grantor's title at the time of the conveyance. The grantee needs some assurance that he actually is acquiring ownership and that the title is marketable. A certificate of title, title insurance, or a Torrens certificate is commonly used to prove ownership.

Certificate of Title

A **certificate of title** is a statement of opinion regarding title status on the date the certificate is issued. A certificate of title is not a full guarantee of ownership. Rather, it certifies the condition of the title's history based on an actual examination of the public records—a title search. The certificate may be prepared by a title company, a licensed abstractor, or an attorney. An owner, a mortgage lender, or a buyer may request the certificate.

Although a certificate of title is used as evidence of ownership, it is not perfect. Unrecorded liens or rights of parties in possession cannot be discovered by a search of the public records. Hidden defects, such as transfers involving forged documents, incorrect marital information, incompetent parties, minors, or fraud cannot be detected. A certificate offers no defense against these defects because they are unknown. The person who prepares the certificate is liable only for negligence in preparing the certificate.

Abstract and Attorney's Opinion of Title

An **abstract and attorney's opinion of title** are used in some areas, including Illinois, as evidence of title. This is an opinion of title status based on a review of the abstract by an attorney. Similar to a certificate of title, the opinion of title does not protect against defects that cannot be discovered from the public records. Many buyers purchase title insurance to defend the title from these defects.

Title Insurance

Title insurance is a contract under which the policyholder is protected from losses arising from defects in the title. A title insurance company determines whether the title is insurable based on a review of the public records. If so, a policy is issued. Unlike other insurance policies that insure against future losses, title insurance protects the insured from an event that occurred *before* the policy was issued. Title insurance is considered the best defense of title; the title insurance company will defend any lawsuit based on an insurable defect and pay claims if the title proves to be defective.

After examining the public records, the title company usually issues what may be called a *preliminary report of title* or a *commitment to issue a title policy*. This describes the type of policy that will be issued and includes

- the name of the insured party;
- the legal description of the real estate;
- the estate or interest covered;
- conditions and stipulations under which the policy is issued; and
- a schedule of all exceptions, including encumbrances and defects found in the public records and any known unrecorded defects.

The *premium* for the policy is paid once, at closing. The maximum loss for which the company may be liable cannot exceed the face amount of the policy. When a title company makes a payment to settle a claim covered by a policy, the company generally acquires the right to any remedy or damages available to the insured. This right is called **subrogation**. An exception or defect noted in the title commitment may be waived or endorsed by the title company with the submission of credible supporting evidence. The title company may charge additional fees for the waiver or endorsement.

In Illinois

A title insurance policy is the most commonly used evidence that an owner of Illinois real property tenders to a prospective purchaser or lender as proof of good title. Careful listing agents often request a copy of the first page of a title insurance policy for their files so as to be certain those selling a property have the right to do so.

The Illinois Title Insurance Act requires that parties to a "contract for the sale of residential real property who are obligated to provide and pay for title insurance have the right to choose the title insurance company and title insurance agent that will provide the title insurance."

"No lender or producer of title business, as a condition of making the loan or providing services of any kind, require a party to a residential sales contract and who is obligated by that contract to furnish and pay for title insurance at their expense, to procure title insurance from a title insurance company that is not chosen by the party paying for the insurance." *Statute ILCS 155/3* ∎

TABLE 13.1

Owner's Title Insurance Policy

Standard Coverage	Extended Coverage	Not Covered by Either Policy
1. Defects found in public records 2. Forged documents 3. Incompetent grantors 4. Incorrect marital statements 5. Improperly delivered deeds	Standard coverage plus defects discoverable through the following: 1. Property inspection, including unrecorded rights of persons in possession 2. Examination of survey 3. Unrecorded liens not known by policyholder	1. Defects and liens listed in policy 2. Defects known to buyer 3. Changes in land use brought about by zoning ordinances

Coverage   Exactly which defects the title company will defend depends on the type of policy. (See Table 13.1.) A *standard coverage policy* normally insures the title as it is known from the public records. In addition, the standard policy insures against such hidden defects as forged documents, conveyances by incompetent grantors, incorrect marital statements, and improperly delivered deeds.

Extended coverage, as provided by an American Land Title Association (ALTA) policy, includes the protections of a standard policy plus additional protections. An extended or ALTA policy protects a homeowner against defects that may be discovered by inspection of the property (i.e., rights of parties in possession, examination of a survey, and certain unrecorded liens). Most lenders require extended coverage title policies.

In Illinois   An extended title insurance policy would offer the buyer protection against "secret liens," such as unrecorded mechanics' liens, and also is required by most lenders. ■

Title insurance does not offer guaranteed protection against all defects. A title company will not insure a bad title or offer protection against defects that clearly appear in a title search. The policy generally names certain uninsurable losses, called *exclusions*. These include zoning ordinances, restrictive covenants, easements, certain water rights, and current taxes and special assessments.

Types of policies   The different types of policies depend on who is named as the insured. An owner's policy is issued for the benefit of the owner (new buyer) and the owner's heirs or devisees. This policy is almost always paid for by the seller at the closing. A lender's policy is issued for the benefit of the mortgage company. This policy is usually paid for by the buyer at the closing. The amount of the coverage depends on the amount of the mortgage loan. As the loan balance is reduced, the coverage decreases.

A lessee's interest can be insured with a leasehold policy. Certificate of sale policies are available to insure the title to property purchased in a court sale.

■ SUMMARY

The purpose of the recording acts is to give legal, public, and constructive notice to the world of parties' interests in real estate. The recording provisions have been adopted to create an orderly system for real estate transfer. Without them, it would be virtually impossible to transfer real estate from one party to another. The interests and rights of the various parties in a particular parcel of land must be recorded so that such rights are legally effective against third parties who do not have knowledge or notice of the rights. If a transfer of real estate title is taking place, any provision in the transfer documents intended to prevent recording is void.

Recording is generally interpreted as constructive notice. Actual notice is knowledge acquired through personal service or by visiting the property.

Title evidence shows whether a seller conveys marketable title. A deed of conveyance is evidence that a grantor has conveyed his interest in land, but it is not evidence of the title's kind or condition. A marketable title is generally one that is so free from significant defects that the purchaser can be insured against having to defend the title.

Three forms of providing title evidence are commonly used throughout the United States: abstract and attorney's opinion of title, certificate of title, and title insurance policy. Each form reveals the history of a title. Title evidence must be revisited or dated as a continuation whenever title evidence is reissued.

Title searches prior to closing are done in some detail to assure the new homeowner that the title was clear at the time of conveyance. A deed shows that the previous owner's interest was conveyed, but it does not by itself provide assurance of the condition of the title.

In Illinois

In Illinois, the title insurance policy is the most commonly used indication of ownership and clear title. ■

CHAPTER 13 QUIZ

1. A title search in the public records may be conducted by
   a. anyone.
   b. attorneys and abstractors only.
   c. attorneys, abstractors, and real estate licensees only.
   d. anyone who obtains a court order under the Freedom of Information Act.

2. Which of the following statements *BEST* explains why instruments affecting real estate are recorded?
   a. Recording gives constructive notice to the world of the rights and interests of a party in a particular parcel of real estate.
   b. Failing to record will void the transfer.
   c. The instruments must be recorded to comply with the terms of the statute of frauds.
   d. Recording proves the execution of the instrument.

3. A purchaser went to the county building to check the recorder's records. She found that the seller was the grantee in the last recorded deed, and no mortgage was on record against the property. The purchaser may assume which of the following?
   a. All taxes are paid, and no judgments are outstanding.
   b. The seller has good title.
   c. The seller did not mortgage the property.
   d. No one else is occupying the property.

4. The date and time a document was recorded establish which of the following?
   a. Priority
   b. Abstract of title
   c. Subrogation
   d. Marketable title

5. X sold her home to Y. Y moved into the home but did not record the deed. A few weeks later, X died. X's heirs in another city were unaware that X had sold the home. The heirs conveyed title to Z, who actually recorded the deed. Who owns the property?
   a. Y
   b. Z
   c. X's heirs
   d. Both Y and Z

6. If a property has encumbrances that will outlast the closing, the property
   a. cannot be sold.
   b. can be sold only if title insurance is provided.
   c. cannot have a deed recorded without a survey.
   d. can be sold if a buyer agrees to take it subject to the encumbrances.

7. Which would *NOT* be an acceptable proof of ownership?
   a. ALTA policy
   b. Title insurance policy
   c. Abstract and attorney's opinion
   d. Deed signed by the last seller

8. Chain of title refers to which of the following?
   a. Summary or history of all documents and legal proceedings affecting a specific parcel of land
   b. Report of the contents of the public record regarding a particular property
   c. Instrument or document that protects the insured parties (subject to specific exceptions) against defects in the examination of the record and hidden risks such as forgeries, undisclosed heirs, and errors in the public records
   d. Record of a property's ownership

9. The seller delivered a deed to the buyer at the closing. A title search disclosed no serious defects, and the title did not appear to be based on doubtful questions of law or fact nor did it appear to expose the buyer to possible litigation. The seller's title did not appear to present a threat to the buyer's quiet enjoyment, and the title policy was sufficient to convince a reasonably well-informed person that the property could be resold. The title conveyed would commonly be referred to as a(n)
   a. certificate of title.
   b. abstract of title.
   c. marketable title.
   d. attorney's opinion of title.

10. The person who prepares an abstract of title for a parcel of real estate
   a. searches the public records and then summarizes the events and proceedings that affect title.
   b. insures the condition of the title.
   c. inspects the property.
   d. issues a certificate of title.

11. A homeowner wants to sell her property but cannot find her deed. In this situation, the homeowner
   a. may need a suit to quiet title.
   b. must buy title insurance.
   c. does not need the deed to sell if it was recorded.
   d. should execute a replacement deed to herself.

12. Mortgage title policies protect which parties from loss?
   a. Buyers
   b. Sellers
   c. Mortgagees
   d. Buyers and lenders

13. Which statement is TRUE regarding the lender's title insurance?
   a. The lender's protection increases with each principal payment that is made.
   b. The seller is usually required to purchase the lender's policy.
   c. The mortgagee's policy covers only the mortgagee.
   d. The mortgagee's premium is paid monthly with the mortgage payment.

14. Which of the following are traditionally covered by a standard title insurance policy?
   a. Unrecorded rights of persons in possession
   b. Improperly delivered deeds
   c. Changes in land use due to zoning ordinances
   d. Unrecorded liens not known of by the policyholder

15. The documents referred to as title evidence include
   a. title insurance.
   b. warranty deeds.
   c. security agreements.
   d. a deed.

16. The legal presumption that information can be obtained through diligent inquiry is referred to as
   a. actual notice.
   b. constructive notice.
   c. priority.
   d. subrogation.

In Illinois

17. What is necessary for a deed to be recorded in Illinois?
   a. The names of the grantor and grantee typed or printed below their signatures
   b. The full address of the grantee
   c. An escrow exemption statement
   d. Permanent tax index number

18. Which of the following statements correctly describes the requirements for recording a tax deed?
    a. A tax deed must be recorded within 30 days after expiration of the redemption period.
    b. A tax deed may be recorded at any time before or after the redemption period.
    c. Tax deeds are specifically exempted from recording deadlines and are effective regardless of whether or not they have been recorded.
    d. A tax deed must be recorded within one year after expiration of the redemption period or it will become null and void.

19. A Chicago resident purchases farmland in southern Illinois as an investment. The deed to the Chicago resident should be recorded
    a. in the county recorder's office of Cook County, where the individual's permanent residence is located.
    b. in the statewide land registry located in Springfield.
    c. in the recorder's office of the county in which the farmland is located.
    d. in the tax records of the city of Chicago.

20. The population of Outlet County is 54,000. In Outlet County, the recorder of deeds
    a. must be elected.
    b. is the county clerk.
    c. is the county treasurer.
    d. is appointed by the secretary of state.

Illinois Real Estate License Law

When you've finished reading this chapter, you should be able to

- ■ **identify** the various categories of licensure;

- ■ **describe** the actions which result in discipline against a licensee;

- ■ **explain** the statutory duties of the agency relationship;

- ■ **distinguish** the processes involved in sponsoring and terminating a license; and

- ■ **define** the following *key terms*

Advisory Council
blind ads
branch office license
broker
designated agency
disclosure of
 compensation
Division of Professional
 Regulation
Illinois Department
 of Financial and
 Professional Regulation
 (IDFPR, or the
 Department)

informed written consent
inoperative status
laws of agency
leasing agent
licenses
managing broker
pocket card
Real Estate Administration
 and Disciplinary Board
Real Estate Audit Fund
Real Estate License
 Administration Fund

Real Estate Recovery
 Fund
Real Estate Research and
 Education Fund
regular employees
sponsoring broker
sponsor card

Since 1921, Illinois has had a real estate license law. This body of law is intended to regulate the real estate industry for the *protection of the public*. Today, the law is called the Real Estate License Act of 2000. The real estate industry in Illinois is regulated by the Division of Professional Regulation (PDR), a branch of the Illinois Department of Financial and Professional Regulation (IDFPR)—also known as the Department, which is charged with protecting and improving the lives of Illinois consumers. A piece of legislation that helps to accomplish this goal is the Illinois Real Estate License Act of 2000. This act regulates the real estate industry and aims to ensure that real estate practitioners in Illinois are competent to practice.

The Department is responsible for administering and enforcing the Illinois Real Estate License Act of 2000. In addition, the Department administers all licenses for Illinois real estate brokers, managing brokers, leasing agents, real estate corporations, partnerships, limited liability companies, real estate branch offices, real estate schools, and real estate instructors.

The Department promulgates rules for the Act's implementation and enforcement. These are often referred to as "the rules," and they supply explanatory detail and guidelines for the Act. The Act, rules, and other significant legislation are available online at *www.ilga.gov* (click on Illinois Compiled Statutes, Chapter 225; ILCS 454). These are essential for any real estate licensee to know.

References to article and section numbers in the Real Estate License Act of 2000 will be displayed throughout so that you can reference the Act itself for more detail on any topic.

■ ADMINISTRATION OF THE ILLINOIS REAL ESTATE LICENSE ACT

There are four major funds administered through the Department: the **Real Estate License Administration Fund** (to which license fees and other funds initially go), the **Real Estate Research and Education Fund** (for research and scholarships), the **Real Estate Recovery Fund** (a consumer-oriented fund for compensating consumers harmed by licensees' actions), and the **Real Estate Audit Fund** (for conducting audits of special accounts).

Division of Professional Regulation

The Department, through the Division of Professional Regulation (DPR) has primary authority to administer the Illinois Real Estate License Act of 2000. It is also empowered to issue rules and regulations that implement and interpret the Act. The rules accompanying the Act are important to a full understanding of the Act's implications and applications. The Department has the authority to contract with third parties for any services deemed necessary for proper administration of the Act, such as the Applied Measurement Professionals, Inc. (AMP) testing service for Illinois state testing.

The Department is responsible for administrative activities such as these:

■ Conducting license examinations
■ Issuing and renewing licenses

■ Preparing all forms, including applications, licenses, and sponsor cards
■ Collecting fees from applicants and licensees

The Department has the following additional functions, which may be exercised only on the initiative and approval of the Real Estate Administration and Disciplinary Board:

■ Conducting hearings that may result in the revocation or suspension of licenses or in the refusal to issue or renew licenses
■ Imposing penalties for violations of the Act
■ Restoring suspended or revoked licenses

Real Estate Coordinator (Section 25-15)

A licensed broker is appointed to the position of Real Estate Coordinator by the Secretary of the IDFPR after the recommendations of real estate professionals and organizations are considered. This individual's license is surrendered to the Department during the appointment.

The Real Estate Coordinator's duties include:

■ acting as ex officio Chairperson of the Real Estate Administration and Disciplinary Board (without a vote);
■ being the direct liaison between the Department, the real estate profession, and real estate organizations and associations;
■ preparing and circulating educational and informational material for licensees;
■ appointing any committees necessary to assist the Department in carrying out its duties;
■ supervising real estate activities; and
■ serving as ex officio Chairman of the Advisory Council without a vote.

Real Estate Administration and Disciplinary Board (Section 25-10)

The Real Estate Administration and Disciplinary Board ("the Board") acts in an advisory capacity to the Real Estate Coordinator regarding matters involving standards of professional conduct, discipline, and examination. In addition to its advisory functions, the Board conducts hearings on disciplinary actions against persons accused of violating the Act or the rules.

Composition of the Board   The Board is composed of nine members appointed by the governor, all of whom must have been residents and citizens of Illinois for at least six years before their appointment date. Six of the nine must have been active real estate managing brokers, brokers or salespeople for at least ten years prior to the appointment. The remaining three must be unlicensed, unconnected with the real estate profession, and represent consumer interests. None of the consumer members (or their spouses) or a person who has an ownership interest in a real estate brokerage business may hold licenses. The Board itself should reasonably reflect representation from all the various geographic areas of Illinois.

Members are appointed to four-year staggered terms. Appointments to fill vacancies are for the unexpired portion of the replaced member's term. Board members may be reappointed, but no individual may serve more than a total of 12 years in a lifetime. Missing more than four board meetings annually is grounds for termination. The governor may also terminate board members on the basis of their own judgment if there is cause. According to Section 25-10 of the Act,

> *The Board makes recommendations to the Secretary regarding professional conduct and discipline of licensees as well as testing of license seekers. Board members are reimbursed through the Real Estate License Administration Fund for expenses incurred in carrying out their duties; they may also receive per diem stipends at the Secretary's discretion. The IFDPR develops forms and issues rules pertaining to real estate licensing after considering the requirements of the Illinois Real Estate License Act and any recommendations made by the Board. A quorum of five board members is required to make board decisions official.*

The Real Estate Coordinator is the nonvoting, ex officio board chairperson.

Advisory Council (Section 30-10)

Matters related to real estate education are handled by the Advisory Council, another governor-appointed body. This five-member council is charged with considering applications for real estate licensing schools and instructors. Prelicensing and continuing education (CE) course content is also supervised by this body. Members are appointed for four-year staggered terms, with a 12-year lifetime limit.

The purpose of the Advisory Council is to approve and regulate schools, curricula, sponsors, and programs and to suggest administrative rules to the Department. Two of the five members must be current members of the Real Estate Administration and Disciplinary Board, one must be a representative of an Illinois real estate trade organization (someone who is not a member of the disciplinary board), one must be a representative of an approved prelicense school or CE school, and one must be from an institution of higher education that offers prelicense and CE courses. The Real Estate Coordinator serves as the ex officio chairperson of the Advisory Council without a vote. Section 13-10 of the Act states

> *The Advisory Council makes recommendations for the requirements that prelicensing and continuing education schools and instructors must meet to obtain or renew their licenses; reviews license applications from these schools and instructors to verify that license seekers meet the requirements set out by law and by rule; approve the curricula for prelicensing and continuing education providers; and advise the Board concerning rules to govern these schools and instructors and administer the portions of the Illinois Real Estate License Act that pertain to education. A quorum of three Advisory Council members is required for all council decisions.*

The Real Estate Research and Education Fund (Section 25-25)

According to Section 25-25 of the act,

> *The Real Estate Research and Education Fund is administered by the Department and held in trust by the Illinois Treasury. On September 15 of each year, the*

treasurer transfers $125,000 from the Real Estate Research and Education Fund to the Real Estate License Administration Fund, primarily to be used to promote real estate research and education at Illinois organizations and institutions of higher learning. Of this sum, $15,000 is set aside for a scholarship program, administered by the Department or a designee of the Department, to support the real estate education of minority real estate professionals. The scholarship money must go toward courses meant to increase the recipients' knowledge or expertise in the real estate field, including Department-approved broker and managing broker licensing courses, courses necessary to secure the Graduate REALTORS® Institute designation, and courses at accredited Illinois institutions of higher learning.

The guidelines for investment and use of money in the Real Estate Research and Education Fund are the same as for funds in the Real Estate Recovery Fund. As per Section 2105-300 of the Department of Professional Regulation Law of the Civil Administrative Code of Illinois, these funds can also be allocated to the Professions Indirect Cost Fund.

■ OBTAINING AND KEEPING A REAL ESTATE LICENSE

Determining who can obtain a real estate license, the purposes of a license, and the types of licenses available are all covered in Article 5 of the Real Estate License Act of 2000, with supportive definitions found in Article 1. Educational requirements such as the prelicensing coursework needed, testing requirements, and continuing education requirements for all Illinois licenses are covered in Article 5 of the Act.

Who Needs to Be Licensed? (Section 1-10)

It is illegal for anyone to act as a broker, managing broker, salesperson, or leasing agent without a real estate license issued by the Department. Any broker who performs any of the following services, either directly or indirectly, whether in or through any media or technology, for another and for compensation must have a real estate license:

- Sells, exchanges, purchases, rents, or leases real estate
- Offers to sell, exchange, purchase, rent, or lease real estate
- Negotiates, offers, attempts, or agrees to negotiate the sale, exchange, purchase, rental, or leasing of real estate
- Lists, offers, attempts, or agrees to list real estate for sale, lease, or exchange
- Buys, sells, offers to buy or sell, or otherwise deals in options on real estate or improvements thereon
- Supervises the collection, offer, attempt, or agreement to collect rent for the use of real estate
- Advertises or represents herself as being engaged in the business of buying, selling, exchanging, renting, or leasing real estate
- Assists or directs in the procuring or referring of leads or prospects intended to result in the sale, exchange, lease, or rental of real estate
- Assists or directs in the negotiation of any transaction intended to result in the sale, exchange, lease, or rental of real estate
- Opens real estate to the public for marketing purposes
- Sells, leases, or offers for sale or lease real estate at auction

License Requirement Exemptions (Section 5-20)

The requirement for holding a broker, managing broker, salesperson, or leasing agent license does not apply to the following:

- Owners or lessors (whether individuals or business entities) or their regular employees who sell, lease, or otherwise deal with *their own property* in the ways described under Article 1 definitions (This applies in the course of the management, the sale, or other disposition of their own [or their employer's] property.)
- Attorneys-in-fact acting under duly executed and recorded power of attorney to convey real estate from the owner or lessor
- The services rendered by an attorney at law in the performance of her duties as an attorney at law
- Any person acting as receiver, trustee in bankruptcy, administrator, executor, or guardian, or while acting under a court order or under the authority of a will or a testamentary trust
- A resident apartment manager working for an owner or working for a broker managing the property, if the apartment is her primary residence and if she is engaged in leasing activities of the managed property
- State and federal officers and employees or state government or political subdivision representatives performing official duties
- Multiple listing services or other similar information exchange
- Railroads and other public utilities regulated by the state of Illinois or their subsidiaries or affiliates and the employees of such organizations
- Any advertising medium that routinely sells or publishes real estate advertising but provides no other real estate-related services
- Any tenant of a residential dwelling unit who refers no more than three tenants in any 12-month period, who receives no more than $1,500 or one month's rent (whichever is less) in any 12-month period, who limits activities to referring prospective tenants to the owner, and who does not engage in actually showing the properties or discussing terms
- An exchange company and its regular employees registered under the Real Estate Timeshare Act of 1999 only when conducting an exchange program as defined in the act
- An existing time-share owner who, for compensation, refers prospective purchasers but only if the existing time-share owner refers no more than 20 prospective purchasers in any calendar year, receives no more than $1,000 for referrals in any calendar year, and limits activities to referring prospective purchasers of time-share interests to the developer
- Any person who is licensed without examination under Section 10-25 of the Auction License Act for the limited purpose of selling or leasing real estate at auction subject to restrictions
- A hotel operator who is registered with the Illinois Department of Revenue and pays taxes under the Hotel Operator's Occupation Tax Act and rents rooms for a period of not more than 30 consecutive days and not more than 60 days in a calendar year

Civil Penalty for the Unlicensed Practice of Real Estate (Section 20-10)

It is illegal in Illinois for any person to practice, offer, or attempt to practice, or to hold oneself out to practice as a real estate broker, managing broker, salesperson, or leasing agent without being licensed. Anyone who does so is subject to a civil fine (in addition to any other penalties provided by law) of up to $25,000 for each offense as determined by the Department. The civil fine is assessed by and payable to the Department after a disciplinary hearing. The Department has the authority to investigate any and all unlicensed activity. The civil fine must be paid within 60 days after the effective date of the order. The order constitutes a judgment and may be filed and execution had thereon in the same manner from any court of record.

■ LICENSE CATEGORIES AND REQUIREMENTS (ARTICLE 5)

The Real Estate License Act of 2000 designates four categories of real estate licensees: broker, managing broker, and leasing agent. The law provides requirements and limitations specific to each type of licensee. (Note that salesperson licenses are no longer being issued by the Department and will end on April 30, 2012.)

General requirements   All individual license applicants must pass a written examination administered by an independent testing service, which currently is Applied Measurement Professionals, Inc. (AMP). Anyone who wishes to take the exam must apply to AMP. AMP acts as the agent of the Department and is empowered to screen potential license candidates to ensure that they meet the statutory requirements as established in the Act. For a detailed content outline of the AMP examination, visit the AMP Web site at *www.goamp.com*.

Once licensed, each licensee must carry a pocket card indicating the license held. This pocket card must be shown to anyone requesting it. The Department maintains a list of all active licensees. Should a sponsoring broker's license be revoked or rendered inoperative, all licensees under that sponsoring broker will be considered inoperative until such time as the sponsoring broker's license is reinstated or renewed or the licensee changes employment. Expiration dates and renewal periods for each license are set by rule, and licenses can be renewed within 90 days prior to expiration upon completion of CE and payment of the required fees.

Broker's License (Article 5)

A **broker** is defined as any individual, partnership, limited liability company (LLC), corporation, or registered limited liability partnership other than or leasing agent who, for another and for compensation, whether in person or through any media or technology, or with the intention or expectation of receiving compensation, either directly or indirectly, performs any of the services for which a real estate license is required (Section 1-10).

Broker requirements   Applicants for a broker's license must meet the following requirements, as discussed in Section 5-27:

- Be at least 21 years of age and willing to supply a Social Security number. (The minimum age of 21 years will be waived for anyone seeking a broker's license who has attained the age of 18 and has four semesters of college credit emphasizing real estate completed in a school approved by the Department)
- Be of good moral character
- Have graduated from high school or obtained the equivalent of a high school diploma verified under oath by the applicant
- Have completed a minimum of 15 of the previous required hours of prelicense education in brokerage administration
- Provide satisfactory evidence of having completed 90 hours of instruction, 15 hours of which must consist of situational and case studies presented in the classroom or by other interactive delivery method presenting instruction and real time discussion between the instructor and the students, provide satisfactory completion of the 30 hour post-license course for the prerenewal period in which the course is taken
- Satisfactorily pass a state-sponsored written examination

Managing Broker's License (Article 5)

Managing broker requirements   As of May 1, 2012, all applicants for managing broker licenses in Illinois must:

- be 21 years old or older;
- be of good moral character;
- have been licensed as a real estate salesperson or broker for at least two of the previous three years;
- have completed four years of study at a high school or secondary school, approved by the Illinois board of education, or the equivalent to four years of study as determined by an Illinois Board of Education-administered exam and verified by the applicant under oath;
- have completed at least 165 hours of education as follows: 120 pre- and post-licensure hours, as required to obtain a broker's license, and, in the year before the application for managing broker is filed, 45 additional hours on brokerage administration and management (Of these 45 hours, 15 must consist of classroom instruction or some other means of interactive, real-time instruction and discussion between student and instructor);
- take and pass a Department-authorized written examination for licensure; and
- submit a valid application for a managing broker license along with a sponsor card, a managing broker appointment, and the required fees.

An applicant is permitted to act as managing broker after filing her application with the Department and prior to receiving her license but must not continue in this role past the term of 90 days after filing unless her license has been obtained within that period. Applicants who are authorized to practice law by the Supreme Court of Illinois and who are in active standing are exempt from the requirements set out in item (5) of Subsection (a) of the Illinois Real Estate License Act of 2000.

Each application for a license (new or renewal) must include the applicant's social security number or tax identification number, in addition to the other required information.

Education exemptions: broker, managing broker, and salesperson   If an applicant for a broker's or salesperson's license is currently an attorney admitted to the practice of law by the Illinois Supreme Court, she is exempt from the education requirements. The attorney still must take and pass the state exam.

Salesperson's License (Article 5)

A **salesperson** is defined as any individual, other than a real estate broker or leasing agent, who is employed by a real estate broker or is associated with a real estate broker as an independent contractor and participates in any activity described in the definition of *broker* (Section 1-10).

No new salesperson licenses will be issued after April 30, 2011, and all existing salesperson licenses will terminate on May 1, 2012.

Salesperson Transition

To transition to a broker's license, a salesperson will have to complete 30 hours of post-license education, pass a written examination approved by the Department and administered by a licensed prelicense school or pass a proficiency examination administered by a licensed prelicense school, which can be taken only one time by any one individual salesperson, and present a valid application for a broker's license no later than April 30, 2012, accompanied by a sponsor card and the fees specified by rule.

Continued eligibility—brokers and salespersons (Section 5-35)   Approved education for potential salespersons and brokers is valid for purposes of licensure for four years after date of satisfactory course completion. An official uniform transcript is needed for taking the state exam except for persons exempt from the educational requirements.

The salesperson, broker, or managing broker license must be applied for within one year of passing the state test. Failure to do so means retaking the test. Failing the state test (either broker or managing broker) four times requires one to retake the educational coursework.

Corporations, Limited Liability Companies, and Partnerships (Section 5-15)

A corporation, partnership, or limited liability company (LLC) may receive a broker's license under the following conditions:

- In a *corporation*, every corporate officer who actively participates in the organization's real estate activities must hold a managing broker license. In addition, every employee of the corporation who acts as a licensee on the corporation's behalf also must hold a license as a real estate broker, managing broker, or leasing agent.

- In a *partnership*, every general partner must hold a managing broker license. Every employee of the partnership who acts as a licensee on the partnership's behalf also must hold a license as a real estate broker, managing broker, or leasing agent.
- In a *limited liability company* (LLC) or *limited liability partnership* (LLP), every manager must hold a managing broker's license. Additionally, every employee of the LLC/LLP who acts as a licensee on the LLC/LLP's behalf also must hold a license as a broker, managing broker, or leasing agent.

No corporation, partnership, LLC, or LLP may be licensed to conduct a brokerage business if any individual broker, leasing agent, or group of brokers and/or leasing agents owns—or directly or indirectly controls—more than 49 percent of the shares of stock or ownership interest in the business entity.

Affidavit of non participation

Leasing Agent's License (Article 5)

The Real Estate License Act of 2000 provides for a limited scope **leasing agent license** for persons who wish to engage only in activities limited to the leasing of residential real property in which a license is required. This license allows such activities as "leasing or renting residential real property; attempting, offering, or negotiating to lease or rent residential real property; or supervising the collection, offer, attempt, or agreement to collect rent for the use of residential real property." Licensed brokers and managing brokers do not need a leasing agent license for these activities.

A limited leasing agent license applicant must meet the following requirements:

- Be at least 18 years of age
- Be of good moral character
- Have a high school diploma or its equivalent
- Successfully complete a 15-hour leasing agent prelicense course
- Pass the state's written leasing license examination

Persons who hold leasing agent licenses must comply with qualification requirements, standards of practice, and disciplinary guidelines established and enforced by the Department. A leasing agent must be sponsored by a licensed real estate broker.

Note: A person may engage in residential leasing activities for a period of 120 consecutive days without being licensed, so long as the person is acting under the supervision of a licensed real estate broker and that broker has notified the Department that the person is pursuing licensure.

All education, examination, and fee requirements must be met during the 120-day period. The Department may establish additional criteria to ensure that no unlicensed person is permitted to repeatedly or continually carry out any activities that, by law, require a license.

■ THE LICENSING EXAMINATION

Applicants are eligible to take the licensing examination only after they have met the education and age requirements; they must also be able to demonstrate that they have met the other requirements set out by the Illinois Real Estate License Act of 2000 and any associated rules. The content of the licensing examinations relate directly to the skills and knowledge required of a qualified licensee may be administered only at times and places approved by the Department. Each test taker must pay the required fee to the appropriate testing center but will forfeit the fee if failing to appear at the scheduled time, date, and place to take the exam following receipt and acknowledgment of one's application by the Department or testing center.

Candidates must register with the testing service in advance of the test and pay any fees to reserve a spot at one of many convenient locations throughout Illinois on a day that is convenient to them.

All candidates must bring to the testing center two pieces of current identification. The first MUST be a driver's license with photograph, a passport or military identification with photograph, or an official state identification card with photograph. The second form of identification must display the name and signature of the candidate for signature verification. All examinations are given on a computer that displays all the test questions on a monitor and records all the answers. No special knowledge of computers is necessary.

After completing the test, candidates are immediately informed if they passed or failed. Passing candidates will be given a *score report*, which will let them know they passed, but will not be given an actual score unless they fail. Passing candidates also receive a license application, including directions for applying for a real estate license, and an applicant sponsor card. Passing candidates have one year in which to apply for a license, after which time a new examination will be required.

Candidates who fail the examination will be told their score and be given diagnostic information in addition to directions on how to apply for a future test. Candidates who fail only one portion (either the state or national portion) of the exam are required to retake only the failed portion.

After four failures, the applicant must successfully repeat all prelicense education before further testing. The fifth attempt to pass the exam is then treated by the Department as if it were a first attempt (Section 5-35c).

■ THE REAL ESTATE LICENSE

After passing the state exam, a formal application for licensure needs to be made to the state.

Prior to receiving the actual license and pocket card in the mail, a person who has just passed the licensing exam still may practice real estate as long as that person has a sponsor card. After passing the state exam, the person is given a blank **sponsor card** at the testing site with her picture on it. When completed by a sponsoring broker, this sponsor card is valid for 45 days while the wall license and pocket card are being processed.

Once a brokerage company has been selected, the sponsoring broker signs the card, makes a copy for the new licensee and for office records, and sends the original to the Department within 24 hours of issuing the sponsor card. The sponsor card certifies the bearer's relationship with the sponsoring broker and serves as a temporary permit to practice real estate.

The license will specify whether the individual is authorized to act as a broker, managing broker, salesperson, or leasing agent. In addition to the license, the Department issues a **pocket card** to each licensee. This card authorizes the bearer to engage in appropriate licensed activities for the current license period. *Licensees must carry this card when engaging in any of the activities for which a license is required by Illinois law.* The pocket card must be displayed on request.

What Happens to Your License When You Change or Leave Firms? (Section 5-40)

When a licensee or the sponsoring broker terminates employment with the sponsoring broker or a managing broker for any reason, the licensee must obtain her license from the employing broker at whose firm it has been kept. The employing broker signs the license, which indicates that the relationship has been terminated. The broker must send the Department a copy of the signed license *within two days of the termination.* The signed license automatically becomes inoperative, as does the licensee's ability to practice real estate, unless she accepts employment with a new sponsoring broker. If the licensee is simply changing brokers, the new sponsoring broker will immediately complete a sponsor card for the licensee to carry until a new license and pocket card (with the new firm's name indicated as sponsor) arrives. The sponsoring broker prepares and sends a duplicate sponsor card to the Department for this transition period within 24 hours of sponsorship, along with the original signed or terminated license from the previous sponsoring broker and the required fee.

Change of Address, Name, or Business Information (Section 5-41)

It is the licensee's responsibility to promptly notify the Department of any change of name, address, or office location. When a licensee acquires or transfers any interest in a corporation, LLC, partnership, or LLP that is licensed under the Real Estate License Act of 2000, appropriate change of business information must be filed with the Department. Additionally, any changes in managing brokers, branch managers, or principal officers must be reported in writing to the Department within 15 days after the change.

Expiration and Renewal

License expiration and renewal dates are established by rule, consistent with the Act; Licenses may be renewed—by paying required fees and meeting CE requirements—up to 90 days prior to expiration of the license.

Newly licensed brokers are required to complete and provide evidence of completing 30 hours of Advisory Council–approved post-license education. Fifteen of these 30 hours must consist of classroom instruction or some other means of interactive, real-time instruction and discussion between student(s) and instructor and must cover situational and case studies. These individuals must also take and pass a Department examination before their licenses can be renewed.

Brokers, managing brokers, and leasing agents may renew their licenses (provided they pay the necessary fees and meet the continuing education and other requirements) for up to two years following license expiration. Beyond this two-year period, licensees will be required to meet the qualifications for *new* licenses set out by the Act.

Nonresidents and License by Reciprocity (Section 5-60)

A managing broker or broker who lives in a state that has a reciprocal licensing agreement with Illinois may be issued an Illinois license if the following conditions are met. For a reciprocal managing broker's license:

- the broker or managing broker holds a *broker* or *managing broker's license* in her home state;
- the licensing standards of that state are substantially equivalent to or greater than the minimum standards required in Illinois;
- the managing broker or broker has been actively practicing as a managing broker or broker for at least two years immediately prior to the application date;
- the managing broker or broker furnishes the Department with an official statement, under seal, from her home state's licensing authority that the managing broker or broker has an active managing broker's or broker's license, is in good standing, and has no complaints pending;
- the managing broker's or broker's home state grants reciprocal privileges to Illinois licensees; and
- the managing broker or broker completes a course of education and passes a test on Illinois-specific real estate brokerage laws.

Currently, Illinois has reciprocity with the following states under the Real Estate License Act of 2000: Nebraska, South Dakota, Colorado, Connecticut, Indiana, Iowa, Georgia, and Wisconsin. Always check the Department Web site for the latest update on reciprocal states.

Before a nonresident managing broker or broker will be issued a license, the applicant must file a designation in writing to act as her agent in Illinois. Additionally, she must agree that all judicial or other process or legal notices directed to the nonresident may be served on the designee. Service upon the agent so designated is equivalent to personal service on the nonresident licensee.

Nonresidents applying for an Illinois license must furnish the Department with proof of active licensure in their home state. They also must pay the same license fees that are required of resident brokers and managing brokers. Prospective nonresident licensees must agree in writing to abide by all provisions of the Act and to submit to the Department's jurisdiction.

However, once acquired, the reciprocal license allows a new resident who has recently been working under a nonresident license to obtain a valid resident's license without examination. Licenses previously granted under reciprocal agreements with other states shall remain in force "so long as the Department has a reciprocal agreement with that state."

Renewal without Fee (Section 5-50)

Licensees whose licenses have expired may renew without paying any lapsed renewal or reinstatement fees if the license expired within two years after the termination of the service, training, or education while the licensee was performing any of the following functions:

- On active duty with the U.S. armed services or called into the service or training by the state militia
- Engaged in training or education under supervision of the United States prior to induction into military service
- Serving as the Coordinator of Real Estate in Illinois or as an employee of the Department

■ LICENSE FEES

Applicants for real estate licenses are subject to appropriate fees in addition to the testing fee paid to AMP when applying for the examination. The Illinois Real Estate License Act of 2000 provides for predetermined licensing fees.

The leasing license initial fee is $75. When applying for a broker license, the applicant must submit an initial license fee of $125. The initial broker's license fee for a partnership, LLC, or corporation is $125. Included in the initial license fees are a Real Estate Recovery Fund fee of $10 and a Real Estate Research and Education fee of $5. Other licensing fees are indicated in the rules and are set according to actual cost incurred by the Department and may vary.

Returned check penalties and failure to pay (Section 20-25)   Anyone who delivers a check or other payment to the Department that is returned for insufficient funds must pay a returned check fine of $50, plus the amount originally owed. If the licensee fails to make full payment of all fees and fines owed within 30 calendar days of the notification that payment is due, the Department will automatically terminate the license or deny the application without a hearing. The licensee may apply for restoration or issuance of the license and pay all fees and fines due the Department.

License Renewals

Broker: April 30, even years
Salesperson: April 30, odd years
Leasing agent: July 31, even years
Real estate businesses: October 31, even years

Expiration and Renewal of Licenses

Managing broker's licenses expire on April 30 of every odd-numbered year, and broker's licenses expire on April 30 of every even-numbered year. Licensees may renew their licenses preceding the expiration date by paying a renewal fee of $150. Sponsoring brokers will also submit a completed "consent to audit and examine special accounts" form.

Salespersons' licenses in Illinois will expire on April 30, 2012, at which time they must have completed the transition requirements to a broker's license. Every leasing agent license expires on July 31 of each even-numbered year. A leasing agent license is renewable by paying the renewal fee of $100. Licenses issued to business entities or branch offices expire on October 31 of every even-numbered year.

■ CONTINUING EDUCATION

Each managing broker and broker who applies for renewal of her license must successfully complete six hours *per year* (or its equivalent) of real estate CE courses approved by the Advisory Council.

Managing brokers seeking to renew their licenses, beginning with the first pre-renewal period following this act's effective date, must complete a 12-hour Department-approved CE course on broker management during each pre-renewal period and, at the conclusion of the course, take and pass a test developed and administered according to Department specifications. The 12-hour course must be delivered in a classroom or by some other interactive means that features real-time teaching and discussion between students and instructors.

All brokers and managing brokers must complete the required courses or equivalent before their licenses may be renewed. Exceptions to this rule are:

■ licensees who have had the requirements waived for good cause by the Secretary as recommended by the Advisory Council;
■ licensees who serve in the U.S. armed services;
■ licensees who are employed full-time by the Department; and
■ licensees who, by Illinois Supreme Court rule, are authorized to practice law in the state.

A person who receives her *initial* license less than 90 days prior to the April 30, 2012, renewal date is exempt from the CE course requirement for this first renewal.

Only schools approved by the Advisory Council may provide real estate CE courses. Instructors and course materials also must be approved for both the pre-licensing schools and the CE schools. The license law includes strict criteria for obtaining and renewing approvals.

Course Content

The CE requirement may be satisfied by successfully completing coursework consisting of three hours per year from core courses and three hours per year of electives. The goal of the Advisory Council in setting core curriculum guidelines is to instruct licensees on new laws and changes to existing laws as well as to offer a refresher on aspects of license law and Department policy that the council considers key to keeping licensees in compliance with the Illinois Real Estate License Act of 2000, thereby protecting the people of Illinois. The elective curriculum established by the council is intended to deal with various areas of real estate practice addressed by the Act.

Core requirements   The core CE requirement, now the same for both managing brokers and brokers requires three hours in each of the following mandatory topic areas:

- Core A, which consists of license law and escrow
- Core B, which consists of agency and fair housing

Electives   A maximum of six hours of coursework also must be completed from among such elective topics as appraisal; property management; residential brokerage; farm property management; rights and duties of sellers, buyers, and brokers; commercial brokerage and leasing; financing; or any other currently approved CE courses.

Courses that may *not* be used for CE   Exam-prep courses such as typing, office and business skills, speed reading, memory improvement, advertising, or sales psychology; sales promotion; time management; or standard real estate company training will not satisfy CE requirements.

Instructors   Real estate CE credit may be earned by serving as an approved instructor in an approved course. The amount of credit earned matches the amount of credit given to the course.

Credit hours may be earned for self-study programs   A broker or managing broker may earn credit for a specific CE course only once during the pre-renewal period.

No more than six hours of courses may be taken in any one day   Pre- and post-licensing course hours may not be counted toward the CE credit-hour requirements unless specifically permitted by the Illinois Real Estate License Act of 2000. The CE requirement for brokers can be met during a given pre-renewal period by successfully completing a Department-approved, 30-hour, post-licensing course for broker licensees or a 45-hour brokerage administration and management course during that period.

Exempt from the CE requirement are licensees who, during the pre-renewal period, served in the armed services of the United States, served as elected state or federal officials, served as a full-time employee of the Department, and licensees who are licensed attorneys admitted to practice law in Illinois.

If a renewal applicant has earned CE hours in another state, the Advisory Council may approve the credit at its discretion based upon whether the course is one that would be approved under the Act.

YOUR REAL ESTATE BUSINESS AND THE ACT

Place of Business (Section 5-45)

Any sponsoring broker actively engaged in the real estate business must maintain a definite office or place of business within Illinois. The sponsoring broker must display a visible, conspicuous identification sign outside the office. Inside, the sponsoring broker must conspicuously display the branch office license she sponsors.

The sponsoring broker's office or place of business may not be located in any retail or financial establishment, unless it is set apart as a clearly separate and distinct area within that establishment.

Branch offices   Any sponsoring broker who wants to establish branch offices must apply for a **branch office license** for each branch office maintained. The sponsoring broker names a managing broker for each branch office and is responsible for supervising all managing brokers. The managing broker, who must be a licensed Illinois managing broker, oversees the branch's operations.

The name of the branch office must be the same as the primary real estate office or closely linked to it. The Department must be notified immediately in writing of any change of a primary or branch office location and within 15 days of a change of a managing broker for any branch.

Exceptions to required place of business   A broker licensed in Illinois by reciprocity with another state may be exempt from the requirement of maintaining a definite place of business in Illinois if the broker

- maintains an active broker's license in the home state;
- maintains an office in the home state; and
- has filed a written statement with the Department appointing the Secretary to act as the broker's agent for service of process and other legal notices, agreeing to abide by all the provisions of the Illinois Real Estate License Act of 2000 and submitting to the jurisdiction of the Department.

Loss of a Branch Office Manager (Section 5-45e)

In the event a sponsoring broker dies or a managing broker leaves a branch office unexpectedly, a request may be made to the Department within 15 days of the loss to grant an extension for continued office operations. The extension may be granted for up to 60 days unless extended by the Department for good cause shown and upon written request by the broker or representative.

Employment Agreements (Section 10-20)

Who Needs a Written Agreement with Their Sponsoring Brokers?

- *All* salespersons, brokers, or leasing agents
- *All* licensed personal assistants in the firm

A licensee must have only one sponsoring broker at any given time and may perform real estate activities only for that sponsoring broker. In turn, a sponsoring broker must have a written agreement with any managing brokers or brokers she employs. The agreement must describe the significant aspects of their professional relationship, such as supervision, duties, compensation, and grounds for termination, and must address the employment or independent contractor relationship terms. A sponsoring broker must also have a written agreement with any licensed personal assistants of licensees sponsored by the broker.

Agency Relationships (Article 15)

Once a relationship has been formed between a licensee and a sponsoring broker, the next set of relationships that dominate the real estate business falls under **law of agency**. Article 15 deals with the licensee's relationships with the public. This article indicates specific standards to be held to in agency relationships. It clearly indicates that "the law of agency under this Act . . . primarily governs the actions of licensees, not common law." Note that Article 15 of the Real Estate License Act of 2000 is the only section of the Act that has private right of action.

Section 15-10 sets out the basic relationship with consumers by saying "licensees shall be considered to be representing the consumer they are working with as a designated agent for the consumer unless (1) there is a written agreement between the sponsoring broker and the consumer providing that there is a different relationship or (2) the licensee is performing only ministerial acts [see earlier definition] on behalf of the consumer."

> **Who Is a Client?**
>
> Any consumer with whom a licensee works is presumed to be a client unless parties agree in writing.

Replacing common law, **Section 15-15** notes the statutory duties a licensee has toward her client. The statutory duties are fulfilled by

- performing the terms of the brokerage agreement between a sponsoring broker and a client;
- promoting the best interest of the client (e.g., timely offer presentation, material facts disclosure, best interests of the client prevail over any self-interest);
- obeying any directions that are not contrary to public policy or law;
- exercising skill and care in performing brokerage services;
- timely accounting for all money and property received in which the client has, may have, or should have had an interest;
- keeping confidential information confidential; and
- complying with the Act and applicable statutes.

The Act also clarifies certain often misunderstood situations that occur when one is an agent. Under the Act the following apply:

- It is considered reasonable to show available properties to various prospects without being viewed as breaching duty to a given client.
- A licensee must provide written disclosure to all clients for whom the licensee is preparing or making contemporaneous offers or contract to purchase or lease the same property and must refer any client that requests a referral to another designated agent.
- It is *not* considered a conflict for a buyer's agent to show homes wherein the commission is based on the ultimate sales price (in other words, where a higher price creates a higher commission).
- Unless a licensee "knew or should have known the information was false," a licensee is not considered responsible or liable for false information passed on to the client from a customer via the licensee, or vice versa.
- The licensee remains responsible under common law "for negligent or fraudulent misrepresentation of material information."

Section 15-25 deals with a licensee's treatment of *customers*. A licensee shall "treat all customers honestly and shall not negligently or knowingly give them false information." Ministerial acts are permitted.

Section 15-40 clearly states that compensation does not determine agency.

Informed written consent is required of both buyer and seller for dual agency under Section 15-45 of the Act. Also, a licensee may not serve as dual agent in any transaction in which she has an ownership interest, whether direct or indirect.

Designated agency is highlighted in **Section 15-50**. This allows the sponsoring broker to appoint or designate one agent for the buyer and one agent for the seller, even within the same firm, without legally being construed as a dual agent. The broker is obligated to protect any confidential information. Because of this, "a designated agent may disclose to his or her sponsoring broker (or persons specified by the sponsoring broker) confidential information of a client for the purpose of seeking advice or assistance for the benefit of the client in regard to a possible transaction."

Article 15 (Agency) also clearly notes the following:

- Offers of subagency through the multiple listing service (MLS) are not permitted in Illinois.
- A consumer cannot be held "vicariously liable" for the acts or omissions of a licensee in providing licensed activities for or on behalf of the consumer.
- The Department may further amplify anything in Article 15 by way of promulgating additional rules at any time.
- There is a time limit on legal actions. Legal actions under Article 15 may be forever barred "unless commenced within two years after the person bringing the action knew or should reasonably have known of such act or omission." In no case may actions be brought after more than five years.

Disclosure

Disclosure issues go hand in hand with agency, and consequently, they are heavily addressed in Article 15. Real estate disclosure means an acknowledgment, stated clearly and usually in writing, of certain key facts that the law holds might, if left unknown or if unclear, unfairly influence the course of events. Disclosures have to do with who has clear and full representation in a transaction and who does not. They may have to do with one's interest as a licensee in a property that one is selling. Matters of structure, surroundings, client representation, dual agency, previous agency, or agent interest in a property all may demand disclosure. Failure to disclose is an increasingly serious issue in a consumer-based society and under consumer-driven laws.

What Must Be Disclosed:

- Material facts of a property
- Known latent physical defects
- Agency relationships
- Designated agency
- Dual agency
- Lack of agency (to a purchasing customer)
- Compensation sources

Article 15, material facts disclosure A licensee must disclose to the client "material facts concerning the transaction of which the licensee has actual knowledge, unless that information is confidential information. Material facts do not include physical conditions with little or no adverse effect on the value of the real estate."

Material facts must also be disclosed to customers. A listing agent must disclose to prospective buyer customers "all latent, material, adverse facts pertaining to the physical condition of the property that are actually known by the licensee and that could not be discovered by a reasonably diligent inspection of the property by the customer." A licensee is not to be held liable for false information provided to the customer that the licensee did not actually know was false (15-25a).

Non-required disclosure items are HIV, AIDS, or "any other medical condition"; the fact that a property was "the site of an act or occurrence that had no effect on the physical condition of the property or its environment or the structures located thereon"; factual situations for properties other than the "subject of the transaction"; and physical conditions on nearby properties that "do not have a substantial adverse effect on the value of the real estate that is the subject of the transaction." (It is illegal under federal law to disclose that a property's occupant has or had HIV or AIDS.)

Section 15-35, agency relationship disclosure   Before a listing agreement, buyer agency agreement, or any other brokerage agreement may be created, a consumer must be told in writing

- that a designated agency exists;
- the sponsoring broker's compensation policy insofar as cooperating with brokers who represent other parties in a transaction;
- the name or names of designated agent(s); and
- that licensee is not acting as the agent of the customer at a time intended to prevent disclosure of confidential information.

Section 10-5, disclosure of compensation   The Act holds that clients must be made aware of compensation, source of compensation, and the sponsoring broker's policy on sharing commission with cooperating brokers.

Handling Client Funds (Section 20-20)

A critical area of the real estate business involves handling the funds of others. Licensees should immediately provide any earnest money checks to their sponsoring broker for proper deposit in a special account. The Act states that the sponsoring broker's escrow account is to be noninterest bearing, "unless the character of the deposit is such that payment of interest thereon is otherwise required by law or unless the principals to the transaction specifically require, in writing, that the deposit be placed in an interest-bearing account and who the recipient of the interest is."

The sponsoring broker must "maintain and deposit in a special account, separate and apart from personal and other business accounts, all escrow monies belonging to others entrusted to a licensee while acting as a real estate agent, escrow agent, or temporary custodian of the funds of others." Receipts must be made, and a duplicate kept by the sponsoring broker for any escrow monies received. Earnest money and security deposits must be deposited within *one business day* of contract or lease acceptance or, if a holiday, the next available business day. The escrow must be in a federally insured depository. The Act does not limit the number of escrow accounts one sponsoring broker may maintain. Commingling of personal and business funds is prohibited.

If there should be disputes between parties regarding escrow money, the sponsoring broker "shall continue to hold the deposit." The sponsoring broker must wait for all parties to signal agreement on the escrow disposition by signing a definite agreement; otherwise she should not disburse funds until such an agreement or a court decision is reached or deemed abandoned and transferred to the Office of the State Treasurer to be handled as unclaimed pursuant to the Uniform Disposition of Unclaimed Property Act. Each sponsoring broker who accepts earnest money shall maintain, in her office or place of business, a bookkeeping system in accordance with sound accounting principles, and such system shall consist of at least the following escrow records:

■ **Journal.** A journal must be maintained for each escrow account. The journal shall show the chronological sequence in which funds are received and disbursed. For funds received, the journal shall include the date the funds were received, the name of the person on whose behalf the funds are delivered to that sponsoring broker, and the amount of the funds delivered. For fund disbursement, the journal shall include the date, the payee, the check number, and the amount disbursed. A running balance shall be shown after each entry (receipt of disbursement).

■ **Ledger.** A ledger shall be maintained for each transaction. The ledger shall show the receipt and the disbursement of funds affecting a single particular transaction such as between buyer and seller, or landlord and tenant, or the respective parties to any other relationship. The ledger shall include the names of all parties to a transaction, the amount of such funds received by the sponsoring broker, and the date of such receipt. The ledger shall show, in connection with the disbursements of such funds, the date, the payee, the check number, and the amount disbursed. The ledger shall segregate one transaction from another transaction. There shall be a separate ledger or separate section of each ledger, as the sponsoring broker shall elect, for each of the various kinds of real estate transactions. If the ledger is computer generated, the sponsoring broker must maintain copies of the bank deposit slips, bank disbursement slips, or other bank receipts to account for the data on the ledger.

■ **Monthly Reconciliation Statement.** Each sponsoring broker shall reconcile, within ten days after receipt of the monthly bank statement, each escrow account maintained by the sponsoring broker except where there has been no transactional activity during the previous month. Such reconciliation shall include a written work sheet comparing the balances as shown on the bank statement, the journal, and the ledger, respectively, in order to insure agreement between the escrow account and the journal and the ledger entries with respect to such escrow account. Each reconciliation shall be kept for at least five years from the last day of the month covered by the reconciliation.

■ **Master Escrow Account Log.** Each sponsoring broker shall maintain a master escrow account log identifying all escrow bank account numbers and the name and address of the bank where the escrow accounts are located. The master escrow account log must specifically include all bank account numbers opened for the individual transactions, even if such account numbers fall under another umbrella account number.

The sponsoring broker must always be able to account for client or escrow funds and any pertinent documents. If the Department requests to view or audit escrow records, they must be supplied within *24 hours* of the request to the Department personnel. Escrow records must be maintained for five years. The escrow records for the immediate prior two years shall be maintained in the office location, and the balance of the records can be maintained at another location.

The License Act and Personal Assistants

As a real estate business grows, it is not uncommon for a licensee to hire a personal assistant. The Real Estate License Act of 2000 has addressed this issue. Illinois provides that personal assistants may either be licensed or unlicensed.

Unlicensed assistants can legally perform only limited tasks (typing, filing, answering phones). However, the actual employment agreement for a licensed assistant is made with the sponsoring broker of the firm.

This same pattern applies to compensation. "Any person who is a licensed personal assistant for another licensee may only be compensated in her capacity as a personal assistant by the sponsoring broker for that licensed personal assistant" (Section 10-5c).

Advertising Regulations (Section 10-30)

A sponsoring broker must include her business name and franchise affiliation in all advertisements. **Blind ads** are prohibited (that is, those not indicating the brokerage firm name; not indicating that the advertiser is a licensee; and offering only a box number, street address, or telephone number for responses). No blind advertisements may be used by a licensee regarding the sale or lease of any real estate, other real estate activities, or the hiring of other licensees.

Managing brokers must advertise as managing brokers. In addition, pursuant to Section 10-40, every brokerage company or entity, other than a sole proprietorship with no other sponsored licensees, must adopt a company or office policy covering certain topics including advertising,

Ads prepared by licensees should at least include

- licensee name,
- company name (as registered with the Department) and company city/state, and
- the city or area of the advertised property.

Licensees must disclose to consumers their intent to share or sell consumer information that has been collected via the Internet or any other means of electronic communication. This disclosure must be conspicuous and timely.

Licensees advertising via the Internet or other forms of electronic media are forbidden to:

- employ deceptive or misleading URLs or domain names;
- frame the Web site of another real estate brokerage or multiple listing service without permission or with the intent or effect of deceiving the consumer; and
- use keywords or other such tools to mislead consumers or deceptively guide or engage Internet traffic.

A licensee must
- NEVER advertise in only her name;
- ALWAYS include the firm's name;
- NEVER advertise another sponsoring broker's listings without permission; and
- ALWAYS keep advertisements up-to-date and clear.

Advertising on the Internet   Ads prepared for the Internet must adhere to the following:

- An Internet ad must include proper identification—licensee name, company name, company location, and geographic location of property.
- E-correspondence, bulletin boards, or e-commerce discussion groups require licensee name, company name, and company location.
- Links to listing information from other Internet sites are permitted without approval unless the Web site owner requires approval for links to be added. Any such link must not "mislead or deceive the public as to the ownership of any listing information."
- As with other advertising, Internet sites are to be updated periodically and kept current.

In Internet advertising situations, the rules do not allow

- "advertising a property that is subject to an exclusive listing agreement with a sponsoring broker other than the licensee's own without the permission of and identifying that listing broker," and
- "failing to remove advertising of a listed property within a reasonable time, given the nature of the advertising, after the earlier of the closing of a sale on the listed property or the expiration or termination of the listing agreement."

Advertising must contain all the information necessary to communicate to the public in an accurate, direct, and readily comprehensible manner.

Selling your own property   Selling or leasing your own property or a property in which you have an interest means you, as a licensee, must use the term "broker-owned" or "**agent**-owned" in all advertising and on listing sheets.

If the real estate firm's sign is used in the yard, and the firm's services are being used, then having the "**agent**-owned" or "broker-owned" notation on the sign itself is deemed not necessary. However, all written materials (listing sheets, ads, Internet ads) still must carry the "broker-owned" or "**agent**-owned" notation. The Illinois Real Estate License Act of 2000 provides that no matter how one lists an agent-owned property—by owner or through a real estate firm—the agent must take care not to confuse the public.

Finally, it *is* possible and permitted by the Department to list your own personal real estate with a firm other than the one at which you work if you so desire and if your sponsoring broker approves.

If a licensee advertises to personally purchase or lease real estate, disclosure of licensee status is required.

Phone book listings   Licensees must not place their own names under the heading "Real Estate" in a telephone directory or otherwise advertise their services to the public through any media without also listing the business name of the sponsoring broker with whom they are affiliated. This rule is consistent throughout all advertising media.

> **A licensee must**
> - ALWAYS disclose "agent-owned"
> - Place "agent-owned" on the sign if FSBO

Print size restriction changes   There no longer is a print size restriction "as between the broker's business name and the name of the licensee" [Article 10, Section 30 (f)].

Collecting Your Paycheck

While collecting your paycheck may seem like a simple proposition, experience has proven that issues surrounding compensation can become confusing and sometimes may pose ethical questions. Compensation procedures, therefore, are strictly covered by the Act. Real estate checks always go to and come from the sponsoring broker. The check at the closing will be in the sponsoring broker's name only.

Compensation and Business Practice (Article 10)

- **Section 10-5**—A licensee may not receive compensation from anyone other than her sponsoring broker. In turn, brokers may compensate only licensees whom they personally sponsor (including licensed personal assistants). The one exception is a former licensee now working for another sponsoring broker but who is due a commission from work completed while still at the first firm.

Sponsoring brokers may directly compensate other sponsoring brokers (as in a cooperative commission arrangement for the listing broker to pay commission to the firm with the buyer).

- **Section 10-10**—Disclosure of compensation is a significant issue. The Act holds that clients must be made aware of compensation, source of compensation, and the sponsoring broker's policy on sharing commission with cooperating sponsoring brokers.

If compensation is being issued to an agent from both buyer and seller in one transaction, this must be disclosed. Any third-party compensation must also be disclosed.

If a licensee refers a client to a service in which the licensee has greater than 1 percent interest (title, legal, mortgage), the interest must be disclosed.

- **Section 10-15**—It is illegal to compensate unlicensed persons or anyone being held in violation of the Act.

To sue for commission in Illinois, one must be a licensed real estate sponsoring broker.

Funds from sellers or buyers always go through the sponsoring broker. She is the only one who issues compensation to salespersons, brokers, managing brokers, leasing agents, or licensed personal assistants working under her.

No licensee may pay a referral fee to an unlicensed person who is not a principal to the transaction. A licensee may not request a referral fee unless *reasonable cause* for payment of the fee exists (a contractual referral fee arrangement).

- Section 10-15 also states that a licensee "may offer cash, gifts, prizes, awards, coupons, merchandise, rebates or chances to win a game of chance, if not prohibited by any other law" to consumers as a legitimate approach to garnering business. Additionally, it is perfectly legal to share commission compensation with a principal to a given transaction.

■ It now is legal for a sponsoring broker to pay a corporation set up by the licensee, rather than the licensee directly, if desired.

■ DISCIPLINARY PROVISIONS AND LOSS OF LICENSE

The Real Estate License Act of 2000 lists specific violations for which licensees may be subject to discipline. The Department is authorized to impose the following disciplinary penalties:

■ Refuse to issue or renew any license
■ Suspend or revoke any license
■ Censure or reprimand a licensee
■ Place a licensee on probation
■ Impose a civil penalty of not more than $25,000 for any one cause or any combination of causes

Causes for Discipline

The Department may take disciplinary action against a licensee for any one cause or a combination of causes. Specifically, a licensee may be subject to disciplinary action or fines if the licensee

■ makes a false or fraudulent representation in attempting to obtain or renew a license;
■ has been convicted of a felony or of a crime involving dishonesty, fraud, larceny, embezzlement, or obtaining money, property, or credit by false pretenses or by means of a confidence game;
■ is unable to practice the profession with reasonable judgment, skill, or safety as a result of a physical illness;
■ practices as a licensee in a retail sales establishment from an office, desk, or space that is not separated from the main retail business and in a separate and distinct area;
■ has been subjected to disciplinary action by another state, the District of Columbia, a territory, a foreign nation, a government agency, or any other entity authorized to impose discipline if at least one of the grounds for that discipline is the same as or equivalent to a cause for discipline in Illinois;
■ has engaged in real estate brokerage without a license or with an expired or inoperative license;
■ attempts to subvert or cheat on the licensing exam or assists someone else in doing so; or
■ advertising that is inaccurate, misleading, or contrary to provisions of the act.

A licensee also is subject to disciplinary action if the licensee is found guilty of any of the following activities:

■ Making any substantial misrepresentation or untruthful advertising
■ Making any false promises to influence, persuade, or induce
■ Pursuing a continued and flagrant course of misrepresentation or making false promises through licensee, employees, agents, advertising, or otherwise

- Using any misleading or untruthful advertising
- Using any trade name or insignia of membership in any real estate organization of which the licensee is not a member
- Acting for more than one party in a transaction without providing written agency disclosure
- Representing or attempting to represent a broker other than the sponsoring broker
- Failing to account for or remit any monies or documents belonging to others that come into the licensee's possession
- Failing to properly maintain and deposit escrow monies in a separate account
- Failing to make all escrow records maintained in connection with the practice of real estate available during normal business hours and within 24 hours of submitted request
- Failing to furnish, on request, copies of all documents relating to a real estate transaction to all parties executing them
- Failure of the sponsoring broker to provide appropriate licensing documents (sponsor cards, license termination information) in a timely way
- Engaging in dishonorable, unethical, or unprofessional conduct of a character likely to deceive, defraud, or harm the public
- Commingling the money or property of others with one's own
- Employing any person on a purely temporary or single-deal basis as a means of evading the law regarding illegal payment of fees to nonlicensees
- Permitting the use of one's managing broker's license by another person in order to operate a real estate office
- Engaging in any dishonest dealing, whether specifically mentioned by the act or not
- Displaying a *For Rent* or *For Sale* sign on any property, or advertising in any fashion, without the written consent of the owner
- Failing to provide information requested within 30 days of the request as related to audits or complaints made against the licensee based on the Act
- Utilizing blind advertising
- Offering an improperly constructed guaranteed sales plan, one that does not meet the Act's requirements for such plans
- Intending to promote racial or religious segregation by use of actions or words or behaving or speaking in such a way as to discourage integration
- Violating the Illinois Human Rights Act
- Inducing any individual to break out of an existing contract to enter into a new one, whether a sales contract or a listing contract
- Negotiating directly with the client of another agent
- Acting as an attorney in the same transaction in which one acts as a real estate licensee
- If merchandise or services are advertised for free, any conditions or obligations necessary for receiving the merchandise or services must appear in the same ad or offer
- Disregarding or violating any provisions of the Land Sales Registration Act or the Time-Share Act
- Violating a disciplinary order
- Paying or failing to disclose compensation that violates the Act

■ Disregarding or violating any provision of this act or the published rules or any regulations promulgated to enforce the Act

■ Failing to provide the minimum services required under an exclusive brokerage agreement

■ Violating the terms of a disciplinary order issued by the Department

■ Forcing any party to a transaction to compensate the licensee as a requirement for releasing earnest money

■ Habitual use or addiction to alcohol, narcotics, stimulants, or any other chemical agent that results in licensee's inability to practice with skill and safety

Nonpayment of child support, income tax, student loans   Specifically highlighted in the Illinois Real Estate License Act of 2000, the Department will refuse to issue or renew (or may revoke or suspend) the licenses of individuals who are more than 30 days delinquent in child support payments.

> To keep your license, be sure to pay
> ■ all Illinois taxes,
> ■ student loans, and
> ■ child support.

Anyone who fails to file a tax return or to pay any tax, penalty, interest, or final assessment required by the Illinois Department of Revenue may have her license withheld or suspended until any such tax requirements are met (Section 20-35).

Failure to repay Illinois student loans is also emphasized. If student loans were provided or guaranteed by the Illinois Student Assistance Commission or any governmental agency of the state, and not paid back, the Department will not grant a real estate license to that individual. For an existing licensee, a hearing is made available, after which, if no satisfactory repayment plan has been made, the license may be suspended or revoked.

Licensee guilty of discrimination (Section 20-50)   If there has been a civil or criminal trial in which a licensee has been found to have engaged in illegal discrimination in the course of a licensed activity, the Department must suspend or revoke the licensee's license unless the adjudication is in appeal. Similarly, if an administrative agency finds that a licensee has engaged in illegal discriminatory activities, the Department must take disciplinary action against the licensee unless the administrative order is in appeal.

Guaranteed sales plans   One of the areas noted for discipline is the offering of an improperly constructed guaranteed sales plan. A licensee is subject to disciplinary action if she offers a guaranteed sales plan without complying with the Act's requirements for such agreements. A *guaranteed sales plan* is any real estate purchase or sales plan in which a sponsoring broker enters into an unconditional written contract with a seller, promising to purchase the seller's property for a specified price if the property has not sold within an agreed period of time on terms acceptable to the seller.

The Act indicates how such a plan can be constructed so as to comply with Illinois law. An Illinois sponsoring broker who offers a guaranteed sales plan in compliance with the Act must

■ provide the details and conditions of the plan in writing to the seller;

■ offer evidence of sufficient financial resources to satisfy the agreement's purchase commitment;

- market the listing in the same manner in which she would market any other property, unless the agreement with the seller provides otherwise; and
- not purchase the seller's property until the brokerage agreement has ended or is otherwise terminated.

A sponsoring broker who fails to perform on a guaranteed sales plan in strict accordance with its terms is subject to all the penalties for violating the Act, plus a civil penalty of up to $25,000, payable to the injured party.

Unlawful actions by associates if no sponsoring broker knowledge
A sponsoring broker will not have her license revoked because of an unlawful act or violation by any managing broke or broker employed by or associated with the sponsoring broker, or by any unlicensed employee, unless the sponsoring broker had knowledge of the unlawful act or violation. The sponsoring broker could possibly be held liable for the employee's actions under *vicarious responsibility*.

Any person providing or offering to provide real estate services, or who is licensed or claims to be licensed under the Act, may be investigated by the Department. At least 30 days before the date of a hearing set for examination of such an issue, and prior to taking any disciplinary action (including but not limited to reprimand, probation, or revocation or suspension of license), the Department will do the following:

- In writing, inform the person under investigation of the charges being brought against her and the location and time of the hearing; this notification may be sent by personal delivery or certified mail to the address given by the individual in her last communication with the Department
- Instruct the accused individual to respond to the charges, under oath and in writing, within 20 days of being informed of the charges and hearing
- Notify the individual that unless she responds as instructed, default will be taken against her and disciplinary action, such as imposition of a fine or license suspension, revocation, or probation, may be instituted.

At the hearing, the charges will be presented to the Board, and the accused individual and her counsel will be allowed to offer a defense via statements, arguments, testimony, and evidence. The Board may continue the hearing from time to time. When an individual fails to respond to the notice and the charges are deemed sufficient, the Department may institute disciplinary action without a hearing.

The Department is required to keep a record of all formal hearing proceedings, at the Department's expense. According to the same guidelines (concerning fees, mileage, and manner) provided for civil cases for state court, the Department is empowered to subpoena materials, such as books, documents, and records, and bring people before it to testify orally or give depositions, or both. All members of the Board as well as the Secretary, the designated hearing officer, may place witnesses under oath in any authorized Department hearing or in other contexts in which the Department is authorized to do so by this act.

The Department will present the licensee with a copy of the Board's report following the conclusion of the hearing. The licensee may request a rehearing, via a motion in writing, which indicates the reasons justifying a new hearing. This request must be made within 20 days after the licensee has been served with the

Department's report. If the motion for rehearing is denied, the Secretary is empowered to enter an order as recommended by the Board.

If the Secretary determines that emergency action is required to protect the public interest, welfare, or safety, she may move to suspend the accused individual's license without a hearing first. However, a hearing must be scheduled for within 30 days of the suspension. The licensee may seek a continuance to postpone the hearing, but in such a case, the suspension will remain in effect.

In any action intended to discipline a license holder or to refuse to issue, restore, or renew a license, the Secretary may appoint an Illinois-licensed attorney to serve in her place as the hearing officer, with complete authority to direct the proceedings. The officer must establish findings pertaining to the allegations, the licensee's conduct, and the law, and present these conclusions to the Board, along with her recommendations. Board members may attend hearings, if they wish, and are required to review the hearing officer's report and then present the board findings to the Secretary and all parties to the hearing. The Secretary is permitted to enter an order that is inconsistent with the board or hearing officer's recommendations if she disagrees with either party.

Once the order to suspend or revoke a license has been put through, the licensee is required to immediately hand over her license. If the licensee fails to surrender her license, the Department is empowered to seize it. If the Board so recommends (in writing), the Department can restore the suspended or revoked license at any time following the event. The exception to this is any instance in which the Board further investigates the issue, holds a hearing, and decides that restoring the license would not serve the public interest.

The Secretary may order that another hearing be held (before the same examiners or a different set) in the event that she believes that the disciplinary action taken was unjust.

Right to Petition Administrative/Judicial Review (Section 20-75)

All final administrative decisions are subject to judicial review under the provisions of the Administrative Review Law and its rules. The accused may request a judicial review by petitioning the circuit court of the county of her residence. If the party is not a resident of Illinois, the venue will be in Sangamon County.

Good Moral Character (Section 5-25)

The Board may revoke licenses or refuse to grant licenses to applicants who make false statements on their licensure applications. In evaluating an applicant's moral character and deciding whether to grant a license, the Board may take into account facts and events from the applicant's past, including prior conduct; revocation of her license; conviction for a felony that involved moral turpitude; or a conviction or plea of guilty or nolo contendere in cases involving "forgery, embezzlement, obtaining money under false pretenses, larceny, extortion, or conspiracy to defraud."

In evaluating past conduct, the Board will consider the particular details of the behavior or violation, how long ago the event(s) took place, whether the applicant has made restitution or been rehabilitated, and other factors as the Board desires.

Violations (Section 20-22)

Any person who is found working or acting as a managing broker, broker, or leasing agent without being issued a valid existing license is guilty of a Class A misdemeanor and, on conviction of a second or subsequent offense, the violator is guilty of a Class 4 felony.

Injunctions

In addition to criminal prosecutions, the Department has the duty and authority to originate an injunction to prevent or stop a violation or to prevent an unlicensed person from acting as a broker, managing broker, or leasing agent.

A violation of the Illinois Real Estate License Act of 2000 is specifically declared to be harmful to the public welfare and a public nuisance. The attorney general of Illinois, a county state's attorney, the Department, and even private citizens may seek an injunction to stop or prevent a violation.

Disciplinary Statute of Limitations (Section 20-115)

No action may be taken by the Department against any person for violation of the terms of this act or its rules unless the action is commenced within five years after the occurrence of the alleged violation.

Index of Decisions (Section 20-5)

The Department is required to maintain an index of all its licensee-related formal decisions. This includes all refusals to issue, all renewals or refusals to renew, all revocations or suspensions of licenses, and all probationary and other disciplinary actions. The index is available for public inspection during normal business hours.

■ THE REAL ESTATE RECOVERY FUND

The Real Estate Recovery Fund provides a means of compensation for actual monetary losses (as opposed to losses in market value) suffered by any person as a result of

- a violation of the Real Estate License Act of 2000, its rules and regulations; or
- act of embezzlement of money or property, obtaining money or property by false pretenses, artifice, trickery, forgery, fraud, misrepresentation, deceit, or discrimination by a licensee or a licensee's unlicensed employee.

People who have been harmed through certain actions, statements, or other behavior of a licensee or a licensee's employee may recover damages from the Real Estate Recovery Fund, which is maintained by the Department. This applies in instances where these actions and statements violated the Act or the accompanying rules, amounted to embezzling money or property, or resulted in the acquisition of money from someone through tricks, forgery, lies, misrepresentations, fraud, discrimination, or the like, causing cash losses (rather than the loss of market value) to the harmed party. The fund may pay out a maximum sum of $25,000 to the wronged person, as ordered by the relevant county's circuit court. This amount can include payment for legal costs and attorneys' fees of up to 15 percent of the total amount ordered as recovery for the improper conduct. Interest is not paid on the recovery amount. Licensees can receive payments from the fund only in cases of intentional misconduct that resulted in losses. The maximum fund liability of $100,000 must be spread equally among all co-owners. Recovery sums will only be paid out in cases where valid judgments have been made and will *not* be paid out for violations of the Land Sales Act or the Time-Share Act. If the licensee wishes to have their license reinstated, the licensee must reimburse the fund all fees plus interest. The interest rate is established by state statute.

Collection from the Recovery Fund (Section 20-90)

When a lawsuit may result in a claim against the Real Estate Recovery Fund, the Department must be notified in writing by the aggrieved person at the time the action is commenced—specifically, within seven days of filing. Failure to notify the Department of the potential liability precludes any recovery from the fund. If the plaintiff is unable to serve the defendant with a summons, the Secretary may be served instead, and this service will be valid and binding on the defendant. Additionally, legal action must have commenced no later than two years after the aggrieved person knew of the acts or omissions that gave rise to possible right of recovery from the fund.

If a claimant recovers a valid judgment in any court against any licensee or unlicensed employee for damages resulting from an act or omission qualifying for coverage under the fund, the Department must receive written notice of the judgment within 30 days. The Department is also entitled to 20 days' written notice of any supplementary proceedings, in order to permit the Department to participate in all efforts to collect on the judgment.

For a claimant to obtain recovery from the fund, all proceedings (including all reviews and appeals) must be completed. In addition, the claimant must show that she has attempted to recover the judgment amount from the licensee or unlicensed employee's real or personal property or other assets and was either unable to do so or the amount recovered was insufficient to satisfy the judgment. The names of all licensees and other parties that are in any way responsible for the loss must have been named in the suit. If they were not, it may preclude recovery from the fund. Finally, the claimant must show that the amount of attorney's fees being sought is reasonable.

When a judgment amount is paid from the Recovery Fund, the Department takes over the rights of the aggrieved party on this issue. She is required to assign all right, title, and interest in judgment to the Department. By this *subrogation*, any funds recovered on the judgment will be deposited back in the Recovery Fund.

Fund Losses Held Against the Licensee (Section 20–90)

When payment is made from the recovery fund to settle a claim or satisfy a judgment against a licensed broker, managing broker, or unlicensed employee, the license of the offending broker or managing broker is automatically terminated. The broker, or managing broker, may not petition for the restoration of her license until she has made repayment in full to the recovery fund of all awards made due to her actions, plus interest at the statutory annual rate. A discharge in bankruptcy does not relieve a person from the liabilities and penalties provided for in the Illinois Real Estate License Act of 2000.

Statute of Limitations (Sections 20–90 and 20–115)

A suit that may ultimately result in collection from the fund must be commenced within two years after the date the alleged violation occurred. The Department must initiate any action it plans to take against an individual licensee within five years of the violation.

Financing the Recovery Fund (Sections 25–35)

If at any time during the year the fund slips below $750,000, the Real Estate License Administration Fund is utilized to upgrade the level to a minimum balance of $800,000.

All recovery fund monies received from applications, renewals, and fines and penalties are deposited into the Real Estate Recovery Fund, and its sums may be invested and reinvested. Any interest or dividends returned from the investment efforts are deposited into the License Administration Fund.

■ SUMMARY

The Illinois Department of Financial and Professional Regulation (the Department) is the key governing authority for real estate activity in Illinois. The Department, through the Division of Professional Regulation, has the responsibility for administering and enforcing the Illinois Real Estate License Act of 2000 and its rules.

It is vital that all licensees and prospective licensees have a clear understanding of all facets of the Act and rules to ensure that their activities are ethical, legal, and responsible. No summary of reasonable length could do justice to the critical details of the Act. The Act also lists a long series of specific definitions designed to give a clear understanding of real estate as it is practiced in Illinois and as legally defined by the Act. These can be found in Article 1 General Provisions.

You can reach the Department directly at:

Financial Institutions	Professional Regulation
320 W. Washington	320 W. Washington
Springfield, IL 62786	Springfield, IL 62786
Phone: (217) 782-2831	Phone: (217) 785-0800
Toll Free: 1-888-298-8089	TDD: (217) 524-6735
TDD: (217) 785-3022	Fax: (217) 782-7645
Fax: (217) 785-6157	
100 W Randolph	100 W. Randolph
9th Floor	9th Floor
Chicago, IL 60601	Chicago, IL 60601
Phone: (312) 814-2000	Phone: (312) 814-4500
Toll Free: 1-877-710-5331	TDD: (312) 814-2603
TDD: (312) 814-7138	Fax: (312) 814-3145
Fax: (312) 814-5168	

CHAPTER 14 QUIZ

1. In Illinois, which of the following would need to hold a real estate license?
   a. A person who employs fewer than three apartment leasing agents
   b. A licensed attorney acting under a power of attorney to convey real estate
   c. A resident apartment manager working for an owner, if the manager's primary residence is the apartment building being managed
   d. A partnership selling a building owned by the partners

2. An unlicensed individual who has been found twice to be engaging in activities for which a real estate license is required is subject to which of the following penalties?
   a. A fine not to exceed $1,000
   b. A fine not to exceed $5,000 and one year imprisonment
   c. A civil penalty not to exceed $25,000 in addition to other penalties provided by law
   d. A civil penalty not to exceed $25,000 and a mandatory prison term not to exceed five years

3. Which statement is *TRUE* of a corporation that wishes to receive a managing broker's license in Illinois?
   a. Every officer actively engaged in the real estate business must hold at a minimum a broker's license.
   b. No more than 50 percent of the shares of the company may be held by brokers.
   c. The initial license fee is $125.
   d. The business must submit a $55 license processing fee.

4. To meet the continuing education requirement in Illinois, brokers must obtain how many hours of continuing education per year?
   a. 4
   b. 6
   c. 10
   d. 18

5. The Department has revoked a sponsoring broker's license. The sponsoring broker may
   a. appeal the license revocation to the local circuit court.
   b. have the license reinstated by signing an irrevocable release of liability and filing it within 60 days of the disciplinary action.
   c. continue to conduct business for 90 days after the revocation by posting a bond with the recovery fund.
   d. allow her sponsored licensees to continue in business for 90 days because they were not found guilty of any offense.

6. If an aggrieved person is awarded a judgment against a real estate licensee for violations of the Illinois Real Estate License Act of 2000, under the license law, the aggrieved party has the right
   a. to immediately apply for payment from the recovery fund for the full judgment amount, plus court costs and attorney's fees.
   b. to a maximum award amount of $100,000 from the recovery fund, including court costs and attorney's fees.
   c. to seek satisfaction from the licensee in a private civil action after being compensated from the recovery fund.
   d. to a $25,000 maximum recovery from the recovery fund, plus limited court costs and attorney's fees.

7. Under what conditions may a sponsoring broker who lives in a state that has a reciprocal licensing agreement with Illinois be issued an Illinois license?
   a. The sponsoring broker maintains an office in Illinois.
   b. The sponsoring broker passes the Illinois managing broker's license exam.
   c. The sponsoring broker's home state has a reciprocal licensing agreement with Illinois.
   d. The sponsoring broker's sponsored licensees have reciprocal licenses in Illinois.

8. When a broker passes the license examination, the first proof of eligibility to engage in real estate activities in Illinois is a
   a. sponsor card.
   b. pocket card.
   c. license.
   d. pass card.

9. A sponsoring broker licensed in Illinois by reciprocity with another state may be exempt from the requirement of maintaining a definite place of business in Illinois if the sponsoring broker
   a. employs no sponsored licensees.
   b. has been licensed for at least ten years.
   c. does not plan on engaging in any real estate activities.
   d. maintains an office in her home state.

10. If a sponsored broker is found guilty of violating the Illinois Real Estate License Act of 2000, her sponsoring broker also may be disciplined if the
    a. sponsored broker was a convicted criminal.
    b. sponsoring broker had prior knowledge of the violation.
    c. sponsoring broker failed to conduct the four-step, pre-employment investigation of the sponsored broker's background and character required by the license law.
    d. sponsoring broker failed to keep all local business licenses current.

11. Which of the following activities requires a real estate license?
    a. A resident manager who collects rent on behalf of a building owner
    b. A service that, for a fee (not a commission), matches individuals from different parts of the country who want to exchange properties and assists them in doing so
    c. A multiple listing service providing listing information to members
    d. An executor selling a decedent's building

12. An Illinois real estate broker's license can be revoked for
    a. agreeing with a seller to accept a listing for more than the normal commission rate.
    b. disclosing her agency relationship.
    c. showing buyers with the same specifications the same properties.
    d. depositing escrow money in her personal checking account.

13. A broker has violated the license law, resulting in monetary damages to a consumer. What is the latest date on which the injured party may file a lawsuit that may result in a collection from the Real Estate Recovery Fund?
    a. One year after the alleged violation occurred
    b. Two years after the alleged violation occurred
    c. Three years after the alleged violation occurred
    d. Three years after the date on which a professional relationship of trust and accountability commenced

14. A sponsoring broker offers the seller the following inducement to sign his listing agreement: "I'll buy your property if it doesn't sell in 90 days." Under these facts, the sponsoring broker may NOT
    a. buy the property at the agreed figure at any time during the 90 days.
    b. market the property as if no special agreement existed.
    c. show the seller evidence of the sponsoring broker's financial ability to buy the property.
    d. show the seller written details of the plan before any contract of guaranty is executed.

15. Which action is legal under Illinois law?

    a. Encouraging a seller to reject an offer because the prospective buyer is a Methodist
    b. Placing a *For Sale* sign in front of a house after asking the seller's permission and receiving written permission to do so
    c. Advertising that individuals who attend a promotional presentation will receive a prize without mentioning that they will also have to take a day trip to a new subdivision site
    d. Standing in the hallway outside the testing room and offering employment to new licensees as soon as they receive their passing score at the testing center

16. All advertising by an affiliated licensee must include the

    a. licensee's license number.
    b. expiration date of the license.
    c. licensee's home address.
    d. name of the licensee's sponsoring broker.

17. In Illinois, all real estate broker's licenses expire on

    a. April 30 of every even-numbered year.
    b. March 31 of every even-numbered year.
    c. January 31 of every odd-numbered year.
    d. January 31 of every even-numbered year.

18. In Illinois, an individual who wishes to engage only in activities related to the leasing of residential real property

    a. must obtain a broker's license and associate with a sponsoring broker who specializes in residential leases.
    b. may obtain a certified leasing agent designation by completing a 20-hour training course and passing a written examination.
    c. may obtain a limited leasing agent license by completing 15 hours of instruction and passing a written examination.
    d. may engage in residential leasing activities without obtaining a license or other certification.

19. What is the purpose of the Illinois Real Estate Recovery Fund?

    a. To ensure that Illinois real estate licensees have adequate funds available to pay their licensing and continuing education fees
    b. To provide a means of compensation for actual monetary losses suffered by individuals as a result of the acts of a licensee who violated the license law or committed other illegal acts related to a real estate transaction
    c. To protect the Department from claims by individuals that they have suffered a monetary loss as the result of the action of a licensee who violated the license law or committed other illegal acts related to a real estate transaction
    d. To provide an interest-generating source of revenue to fund the activities of the Department

20. Under what circumstances can a limited liability company (LLC) obtain a real estate managing broker's license?

    a. Only if every managing member holds a managing broker's license
    b. Only if at least 50 percent of the ownership interest in the LLC is controlled by individuals who are licensed real estate brokers
    c. Only if no licensed brokers holds stock or any other ownership interest in the entity
    d. Only if the LLC has engaged in real estate sales activities for three of the past five years

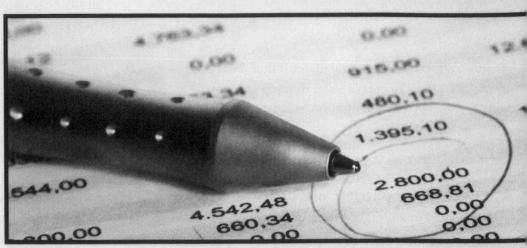

15

Real Estate Financing: Principles

■ **LEARNING OBJECTIVES** *When you've finished reading this chapter, you should be able to*

■ **identify** the basic provisions of security and debt instruments: promissory notes, mortgage documents, deeds of trust, and land contracts;

■ **describe** the effect of discount points on yield;

■ **explain** the procedures involved in a foreclosure;

■ **distinguish** between lien, title, and intermediate theories; and

■ **define** the following *key terms*

acceleration	hypothecation	note
acceleration clause	impound account	prepayment penalty
alienation clause	interest	promissory note
beneficiary	intermediate mortgage	release deed
certificate of sale	theory	satisfaction of mortgage
deed in lieu of foreclosure	judicial foreclosure	sheriff's deed
deed of reconveyance	judicial sale	sheriff's sale
deed of trust	land contract	statutory right of
defeasance clause	lien theory	redemption
deficiency judgment	loan amount	statutory right of
discount points	loan origination fee	reinstatement
equitable right of	mortgage	strict foreclosure
redemption	mortgagee	title theory
equitable title	mortgagor	trust account
escrow account	negotiable instrument	usury
foreclosure	non-judicial foreclosure	

■ REAL ESTATE FINANCING PRINCIPLES

Perhaps the most important investment decision your clients will ever make is the one you help them with: buying a home. In the United States, relatively few homes are purchased for cash. Most homes are bought with borrowed money, and a huge lending industry has been built to service the financial requirements of homebuyers. Knowing how real estate financing works, then, is especially important to become a successful licensee. If the buyer can't get funding to purchase the property, there can be no transaction.

Chapters 15 and 16 will help you understand how to guide your buyer or seller clients through a process that enables them to buy or sell their property. A borrower and a lender can tailor financing instruments to suit the type of transaction and the financial needs of both parties.

IN PRACTICE   Although it is best for licensees to refer consumers to a lender to be preapproved for a loan prior to writing a real estate sales contract, it is important for the licensee to be knowledgeable about real estate financing programs and products in order to provide quality service, especially when serving buyers.

■ MORTGAGE LAW

> The *mortgagor* is the *borrower*.
> The *mortgagee* is the *lender*.

A **mortgage** is a *voluntary lien* on real estate. The person who borrows money to buy a piece of property voluntarily gives the lender the right to take that property if the borrower fails to repay the loan. The borrower, or **mortgagor,** pledges the land to the lender, or **mortgagee,** as security for the debt. Exactly what rights the mortgagor gives the mortgagee vary from state to state.

In **title-theory states**, the mortgagor actually gives *legal title* to the mortgagee (or some other designated individual) and retains **equitable title**. Legal title is returned to the mortgagor when the debt is paid in full (or some other obligation is performed). In theory, the lender actually owns the property until the debt is paid. The lender allows the borrower all the usual rights of ownership, such as possession and use. Because the lender holds legal title, the lender has the right to immediate possession of the real estate and rents from the mortgaged property if the mortgagor defaults.

In **lien-theory** states, the mortgagor/borrower holds both legal and equitable title. The mortgagee/lender simply has a lien on the property as security for the mortgage debt. The mortgage is nothing more than collateral for the loan. If the mortgagor defaults, the mortgagee must go through a formal *foreclosure* proceeding to obtain legal title. The property is offered for sale, and sale proceeds are used to pay all or part of the remaining debt. In some states, a defaulting mortgagor may redeem the property during a certain period after the sale. A borrower who fails to redeem the property during that time loses the property irrevocably.

A number of states have adopted an **intermediate mortgage theory** based on the principles of title-theory states but still requiring the mortgagee to formally foreclose to obtain legal title.

| In Illinois | Illinois does not adhere strictly to either the title or lien theory. As a result, Illinois often is referred to as an intermediate mortgage theory state. Mortgages and deeds of trust in Illinois convey only qualified title to the lender as security for the loan during the existence of the debt. The mortgagor/borrower remains the owner of the mortgaged property for all beneficial purposes, subject to the lien created by the mortgage or deed of trust. The qualified title held by the lender is subject to the **defeasance clause**, which stipulates that such title must be fully reconveyed, or released back, to the mortgagor at the time the debt is repaid in full. ■ |

In reality, the differences between the parties' rights in a lien-theory state and those in a title-theory state are more technical than actual. A typical procedure before any foreclosure is to *accelerate* the loan based on the original agreement made with the borrower. **Acceleration** means asking for the loan to be paid in full based on the borrower's having broken the original promise to repay with regular payments.

■ SECURITY AND DEBT

A basic principle of property law is that no one can convey more than he actually owns. This principle also applies to mortgages. The owner of a fee simple estate can mortgage the fee. The owner of a leasehold or subleasehold can mortgage that leasehold interest. The owner of a condominium unit can mortgage the fee interest in the condominium. The owner of a cooperative interest may be able to offer that personal property *interest* as collateral for a loan.

Mortgage Loans

A mortgage loan, like all loans, creates a relationship between a debtor and a creditor. In the relationship, the creditor loans the debtor money for some purpose, and the debtor agrees to pay or pledges to pay the principal and interest according to an agreed schedule. The debtor agrees to offer some property or collateral to the creditor if the loan is not repaid.

Mortgage loans are secured loans. Mortgage loans have two parts: the debt itself and the security for the debt. When a property is mortgaged, the owner must *execute* (sign) two separate instruments—a promissory note stating the amount owed and a security document.

Hypothecation In mortgage lending practice, a borrower is required to pledge specific real property as security (collateral) for the loan. The debtor retains the right of possession and control, while the creditor receives an underlying equitable right in the pledged property. This type of pledging is termed **hypothecation**. The right to foreclose on the pledged property in the event a borrower defaults is contained in a security agreement, such as a mortgage or a deed of trust.

■ PROMISSORY NOTES

The **promissory note**, referred to as the *note* or *financing instrument*, is the borrower's personal promise to repay a debt according to agreed terms. The note exposes all the borrower's assets to claims by secured creditors. The mortgagor executes one or more promissory notes to total the amount of the debt.

A promissory note executed by a borrower (known as the *maker* or *payor*) is a contract complete in itself. It generally states the amount of the debt, the time and method of payment, and the rate of interest. When signed by the borrowers and other necessary parties, the note becomes a legally enforceable and fully negotiable instrument of debt. When the terms of the note are satisfied, the debt is discharged. If the terms of the note are not met, the lender may choose to sue to collect on the note or to foreclose.

A note need not be tied to a mortgage or a deed of trust. A note used as a debt instrument without any related collateral is called an *unsecured note*. Unsecured notes are used by banks and other lenders to extend short-term personal loans.

A **note** is a **negotiable instrument** like a check or bank draft. The lender who holds the note is referred to as the *payee* and may transfer the right to receive payment to a third party in one of two ways:

- By signing the instrument over (that is, by *assigning* it) to the third party
- By delivering the instrument to the third party

IN PRACTICE   All notes should be clearly dated. Accurate dates are essential because time is of the essence in every real estate contract. Also, the dates of the notes may be necessary to determine the chronological order of priority rights.

Interest

Interest is a charge for the use of money. Interest may be due at either the end or the beginning of each payment period. Payment made at the beginning of each period is *payment in advance*. When payments are made at the end of a period, it is known as *payment in arrears*. Whether interest is charged in arrears or in advance is specified in the note. This distinction is important if the property is sold before the debt is repaid in full. Most mortgages have interest in arrears.

Usury   Charging interest in excess of the maximum rate allowed by law is called **usury**. To protect consumers from unscrupulous lenders, many states have enacted laws limiting the interest rate that may be charged on loans. In some states, the legal maximum rate is a fixed amount. In others, it is a floating interest rate that is adjusted up or down at specific intervals based on a certain economic standard such as the prime lending rate or the rate of return on government bonds.

Whichever approach is taken, lenders are penalized for making usurious loans. In some states, a lender that makes a usurious loan is permitted to collect the borrowed money but only at the legal rate of interest. In others, a usurious lender may lose the right to collect any interest or may lose the entire amount of the loan in addition to the interest.

Technically, there is no legal limit specifically imposed by Illinois on the rate of interest that a lender may charge a borrower *when the loan is secured by real estate.*

There is, however, exemption from these state laws. *Residential first mortgage loans made by federally chartered institutions, or loans made by lenders insured or guaranteed by federal agencies, are exempt from state interest regulations,* and consequently are subject to federal limits.

Included in the federal law's definition of "residential loans" are loans for purchasing houses, condominiums, manufactured housing, and loans to buy stock in a cooperative. *The overall effect in Illinois is to apply federal usury limits to many if not most residential loans, thereby protecting the consumer.* ■

Loan origination fee The processing of a mortgage application is known as *loan origination.* When a mortgage loan is originated, a **loan origination fee** is charged by most lenders to cover the expenses involved in generating the loan. These include the loan officer's salary, paperwork, and the lender's other costs of doing business. A loan origination fee is not prepaid interest; rather, it is a charge that must be paid to the lender. While a loan origination fee serves a different purpose from discount points, both increase the lender's yield. Therefore, the federal government treats the fee like discount points. It is included in the annual percentage rate of *Regulation Z,* and the IRS lets a buyer deduct the loan origination fee as interest paid up front.

Discount points A lender may sell a mortgage to investors (discussed later in this chapter). However, the interest rate that a lender charges the borrower for a loan might be less than the yield (true rate of return) an investor demands. To make up the difference, the lender charges the borrower **discount points.** The number of points charged depends on two factors:

■ The difference between the interest rate and the required investor yield
■ How long the lender expects it will take the borrower to pay off the loan

A point is 1 percent of the loan amount.

For the borrowers, one discount point equals 1 percent of the **loan amount** and is charged as prepaid interest at the closing. For instance, three discount points charged on a $100,000 loan would be $3,000 ($100,000 × 3%, or .03). If a house sells for $100,000 and the borrower seeks an $80,000 loan, each point would be $800. In some cases, however, the points in a new acquisition may be paid in cash at closing rather than being financed as part of the total loan amount.

■ **FOR EXAMPLE** To determine how many points are charged on a loan, divide the total dollar amount of the points by the amount of the loan. For example, if the loan amount is $350,000 and the charge for points is $9,275, how many points are being charged?

$$\$9,275 \div \$350,000 = 0.0265 \text{ or } 2.65\% \text{ or } 2.65 \text{ points}$$

Prepayment

Most mortgage loans are paid in installments over a long period of time. As a result, the total interest paid by the borrower may add up to more than the principal amount of the loan. That does not come as a surprise to the lender; the total amount of accrued interest is carefully calculated during the origination phase to determine the profitability of each loan. If the borrower repays the loan before the end of the term, the lender collects less than the anticipated interest. For this reason, some mortgage notes contain a prepayment clause. This clause requires that the borrower pay a **prepayment penalty** against the unearned portion of the interest for any payments made ahead of schedule.

The penalty may be as little as 1 percent of the balance due at the time of prepayment or as much as all the interest due for the first ten years of the loan. Some lenders allow the borrower to pay off a certain percentage of the original loan without paying a penalty. However, if the loan is paid off in full, the borrower may be charged a percentage of the principal paid in excess of that allowance. **Note:** Lenders may not charge prepayment penalties on mortgage loans insured or guaranteed by the federal government or on those loans that have been sold to Fannie Mae or Freddie Mac.

| In Illinois | Lenders in Illinois are prohibited from charging a borrower a *prepayment penalty* on a fixed rate loan secured by residential real estate when the loan's interest rate is greater than 8 percent per year. However, they can charge a prepayment penalty on an adjustable rate loan. ∎ |

■ MORTGAGE DOCUMENT OR DEED OF TRUST

As previously stated, a note does need to be tied to either a mortgage or a deed of trust. In Illinois, the note used to obtain money to purchase real property is usually secured by a mortgage.

The mortgage document or deed of trust clearly establishes that the property is security for a debt, identifies the lender and the borrower, and includes an accurate legal description of the property. Both the mortgage document and deed of trust incorporate the terms of the note by reference. They should be signed by all parties who have an interest in the real estate. Common provisions of both instruments are discussed here.

Deed of Trust

In some situations, lenders may prefer to use a three-party instrument known as a **deed of trust**, or trust deed, rather than a mortgage. A deed of trust conveys naked title or bare legal title—that is, title without the right of possession. The deed is given as security for the loan to a third party, called the trustee. The trustee holds title on behalf of the lender, who is known as the **beneficiary**. The beneficiary is the holder of the note. The conveyance establishes the actions that the trustee may take if the borrower (the *trustor*) defaults under any of the deed of trust terms. (See Figure 15.1 and Figure 15.2 for a comparison of mortgages and deeds of trust.) In states where a deed of trust is generally preferred, foreclosure procedures for default are usually simpler and faster than for mortgage loans.

FIGURE 15.1

Mortgages

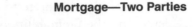
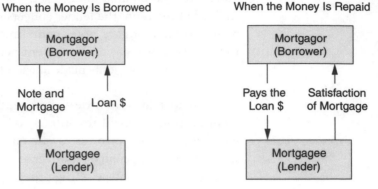

Mortgage—Two Parties

| When the Money Is Borrowed | When the Money Is Repaid |

In Illinois

In Illinois, a deed of trust is treated like a mortgage and is subject to the same rules including foreclosure. In Illinois, the trustor (borrower) in a deed of trust holds the title to the real estate. ■

Duties of the Mortgagor or Trustor

The borrower is required to fulfill certain obligations created by the mortgage or deed of trust. These usually include the following:

- Payment of the debt in accordance with the terms of the note
- Payment of all real estate taxes on the property given as security
- Maintenance of adequate insurance to protect the lender if the property is destroyed or damaged by fire, windstorm, or other hazard
- Maintenance of the property in good repair at all times
- Receipt of lender authorization before making any major alterations on the property

Failure to meet any of these obligations can result in a borrower's default. The loan documents may, however, provide for a grace period (such as 30 days) during which the borrower can meet the obligation and cure the default. If the borrower does not do so, the lender has the right to foreclose on the mortgage or deed of trust and collect on the note.

FIGURE 15.2

Deeds of Trust

Deed of Trust—Three Parties

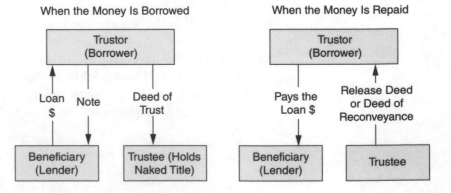

Provisions for Default

The mortgage or deed of trust typically includes an **acceleration clause** to assist the lender in foreclosure. If a borrower defaults, the lender has the right to "accelerate the maturity of the debt." This means the lender may declare the entire debt due and payable immediately. Without an acceleration clause, the lender would have to sue the borrower every time a payment was overdue.

Other clauses in a mortgage or deed of trust enable the lender to take care of the property in the event of the borrower's negligence or default. If the borrower does not pay taxes or insurance premiums or fails to make necessary repairs on the property, the lender may step in and do so. The lender has the power to protect the security (the real estate). Any money advanced by the lender to cure a default may be either added to the unpaid debt or declared immediately due from the borrower.

MATH CONCEPTS

DISCOUNT POINTS AND INVESTOR YIELD

Lenders use computers or prepared tables to determine the number of discount points that must be paid. However, as a general guideline, each discount point paid to the lender will increase the lender's yield (return) by approximately ⅛ of 1 percent (.00125). In using the guideline, for each discount point charged by a lender, add ⅛ to the stated (contract) mortgage interest rate to estimate the lender's real return (and cost to the borrower) from the loan.

Note: This guideline calculation is designed to estimate the real (or effective) mortgage interest rate expressed as an annual percentage rate (APR), not as a dollar amount. The stated interest rate, as such, will not change.

To determine the actual cost, in dollars, added by discount points, each discount point is equal to 1% of the mortgage balance (1 point = 1%). The mortgage balance (loan amount) is multiplied by this discount percent to find the dollar amount of the discount being charged.

For example, assume the market rate of interest is 10¼% and the FHA rate of interest is 9½%. The following steps should be used to approximate the discount points required to equal the market rate of interest and determine the amount of discount charged on a $60,000 FHA mortgage.

A. Estimating the discount points required to raise the yield to the lender's required return:
   1. Calculate the difference in the two rates.
      Current market rate – Stated (contract) interest rate = Difference
      10¼% – 9½% = ¾%
   2. Convert the difference to eighths of a percent.
      ¾% = 6/8%
   3. Convert the eighths into discount points.
      6/8% ÷ ⅛% = 6 discount points required

B. Amount of discount charged
   1. Convert discount points to discount rate.
      6 points × 1% per point = 6%
   2. Calculate the amount of discount.
      Total loan amount × Discount rate = Amount of discount
      $60,000 × .06 = $3,600 (cost of discount)

MATH CONCEPTS

DISCOUNT POINTS AND INVESTOR YIELD (CONTINUED)

With most loans, a borrower usually is not familiar with the above information. Commonly, the borrower or his agent is told that a loan will require payment of 4 discount points, or 3, or 5, and so forth. The problem then is not only to calculate the amount of discount cost (step B above) but also to determine the real yield to the lender.

For example, using the same situation as above, assume that the need is to find the amount of yield to the lender if 6 discount points are charged for an FHA loan showing a contract rate of 9½% interest.

1. Convert discount points to percent of increase (1 point results in ⅛ of 1% increase)

    6 points × ⅛% per point = ⅝% increase
2. Add to the contract rate the percent of increase

    9½% + ⅝% = 10¼% (approximate yield to lender)

When solving mortgage discount problems, remember that the cost of discount points is figured on the amount of the loan (1 discount point = 1% of the loan amount).

Used with permission: *Real Estate Math*, Fifth Edition, by George Gaines, Jr., David S. Coleman, and Linda L. Crawford. Copyright by Dearborn Financial Publishing, Inc.® Published by Dearborn Real Estate Education™, a division of Dearborn Financial Publishing, Inc.®, Chicago. All rights reserved.

Assignment of the Mortgage

Without changing the provisions of a contract, a note may be sold to a third party, such as an investor or another mortgage company. The original mortgagee endorses the note to the third party and executes an assignment of mortgage. The assignee becomes the new owner of the debt and security instrument. When the debt is paid in full (or satisfied), the assignee is required to execute the *satisfaction* (or release) of the security instrument.

Release of the Mortgage Lien

When all mortgage loan payments have been made and the note has been paid in full, the borrower will want the public record to show that the debt has been satisfied and that the lender is divested of all rights conveyed under the mortgage. By the provisions of the *defeasance clause* in most mortgage documents, the lender is required to execute a **satisfaction of mortgage** (also known as a *release of mortgage* or *mortgage discharge*) when the note has been fully paid. This document returns to the borrower all interest in the real estate originally conveyed to the lender. Entering this release in the public record shows that the mortgage lien has been removed from the property.

If a mortgage has been assigned by a recorded assignment, the release must be executed by the assignee or mortgagee.

When a real estate loan secured by a deed of trust has been completely repaid, the beneficiary must make a written request that the *trustee* convey the property back to the *grantor*. The trustee executes and delivers a **release deed**, sometimes called a **deed of reconveyance**, to the trustor. The release deed conveys the same rights and powers that the trustee was given under the deed of trust. The release deed should be acknowledged and recorded in the public records of the county in which the property is located.

In Illinois

Any mortgagee, or his assigns or agents, who fails to deliver a release to the mortgagor or the grantor of a deed of trust within one month after full payment and satisfaction will be liable to pay the mortgagor or grantor a $200 penalty. The release also must state the following on its face in bold letters: **FOR THE PROTECTION OF THE OWNER, THIS RELEASE SHALL BE FILED WITH THE RECORDER OR THE REGISTRAR OF TITLES IN WHOSE OFFICE THE MORTGAGE OR DEED OF TRUST WAS FILED.** It is then the mortgagor's responsibility to record the release. ■

Tax and Insurance Reserves

> The basic recurring components of a borrower's monthly loan payment may be remembered as **PITI**: *Principal, Interest, Taxes,* and *Insurance*.

Many lenders require that borrowers provide a reserve fund to meet future real estate taxes and property insurance premiums. This fund is called an **impound account**, a **trust account,** or an **escrow account**. When the mortgage or deed of trust loan is made, the borrower starts the reserve by depositing funds to cover the amount of unpaid real estate taxes. If a new insurance policy has just been purchased, the insurance premium reserve will be started with the deposit of one-twelfth of the insurance premium liability. The borrower's monthly loan payments will include PITI: principal, interest, tax, and insurance. Other costs such as private mortgage insurance premiums (PMI), flood insurance, or homeowners' association dues may also be included.

In Illinois

Illinois law prescribes additional guidelines that must be followed by lenders who require escrow accounts for mortgage loans on single-family, owner-occupied residential properties. The Illinois Mortgage Tax Escrow Account Act at 765 ILCS 915/ provides that except during the first year of the loan, a lender may not require an escrow accumulation of more than 150 percent of the previous year's real estate taxes. Lenders must give borrowers written notice of the act's provisions at closing. The Illinois Mortgage Escrow Account Act at 765 ILCS 910/ states that when the principal loan balance has been reduced to 65 percent of its original amount, the borrower may terminate his escrow account. The latter does not apply to loans insured, guaranteed, supplemented, or assisted by the state of Illinois or agencies of the federal government such as FHA and VA.

Also, borrowers have the right to pledge an interest-bearing deposit in an amount sufficient to cover the entire amount of anticipated future tax bills and insurance premiums instead of establishing an escrow account. ■

Flood insurance reserves   The National Flood Insurance Reform Act of 1994 imposes certain mandatory obligations on lenders and loan servicers to set aside (escrow) funds for flood insurance on new loans. The act also applies to any loan still outstanding on September 23, 1994. This means that if a lender or servicer discovers that a secured property is in a flood hazard area, it must notify the borrower. The borrower then has 45 days to purchase flood insurance. If the borrower fails to procure flood insurance, the lender must purchase the insurance on the borrower's behalf. The cost of the insurance may be charged to the borrower.

Assignment of Rents — Non disturbance clause

If the property involved includes rental units, the borrower may provide for rents to be assigned to the lender in the event of the borrower's default. The assignment may be included in the mortgage or deed of trust, or it may be a separate document. In either case, the assignment should clearly indicate that the borrower intends to assign the rents, not merely pledge them as security for the loan. In title-theory states, lenders are automatically entitled to any rents if the borrower defaults.

Buying Property "Subject to" or "Assuming" Existing Financing

When a person purchases real estate that is subject to an outstanding mortgage or deed of trust, the buyer may take the property in one of two ways. The property may be purchased *subject* to the mortgage or the buyer may *assume* the mortgage or deed of trust and agree to pay the debt. This technical distinction becomes important if the buyer defaults and the mortgage or deed of trust is foreclosed.

When the property is sold *subject* to the mortgage, the buyer is not personally obligated to pay the debt in full. The buyer takes title to the real estate knowing that he must make payments on the existing loan. Upon default, the lender forecloses and the property is sold by court order to pay the debt. If the sale does not pay off the entire debt, the purchaser is not liable for the difference. In some circumstances, however, the original seller might continue to be liable.

■ **FOR EXAMPLE** A man owns an investment rental property that is mortgaged. For health reasons, he wants to sell the property to the woman who has been managing the property and who also wants to use the rental property as an investment. The owner sells the property to the woman *subject to* the mortgage. In the sale, the buyer takes title and assumes responsibilities for the loan, but after two months she can no longer make payments on the loan. There is a foreclosure sale and because the owner sold the property *subject to* the mortgage, he (not the buyer) is personally liable if proceeds from the foreclosure sale do not meet the obligations.

In contrast, a buyer who purchases the property and assumes the seller's debt becomes *personally obligated* for the payment of the entire debt, and the seller (original mortgagor) is still liable until the mortgagee releases the seller. This release generally occurs when the buyer establishes a seasoned payment history (a stable and consistent history of payments under the terms of the loan). If the mortgage is foreclosed and the court sale does not bring enough money to pay the debt in full, a deficiency judgment against the assumer and the original borrower may be obtained for the unpaid balance of the note. If the lender has released the original borrower, only the assumer is liable.

If a seller wants to be completely free of the original mortgage loan, the seller(s), buyer(s), and lender must execute a **novation** agreement in writing. The novation makes the buyer solely responsible for any default on the loan. The original borrower (seller) is freed of any liability for the loan.

The existence of a lien does not prevent the transfer of property; however, when a secured loan is assumed, the mortgagee or beneficiary must approve the assumption and any release of liability of the original mortgagor or trustor. Because a loan may not be assumed without lender approval, the lending institution would require the assumer to qualify financially, and many lending institutions charge a transfer fee to cover the costs of changing the records. This charge can be paid by either the buyer or the seller.

Alienation clause   The lender may want to prevent a future purchaser of the property from being able to assume the loan, particularly if the original interest rate is low. For this reason, some lenders include an **alienation clause**, also known as a *resale clause*, *due-on-sale clause*, or *call clause*, in the note. An alienation clause provides that when the property is sold, the lender may either declare the entire debt due immediately or permit the buyer to assume the loan at the current market interest rate.

Recording a Mortgage or Deed of Trust

The mortgage document or deed of trust must be recorded in the recorder's office of the county in which the real estate is located. Recording gives constructive notice to the world of the borrower's obligations. Recording also establishes the lien's priority.

Priority of a Mortgage or Deed of Trust

Priority of mortgages and other liens normally is determined by the order in which they were recorded. A mortgage or deed of trust on land that has no prior mortgage lien is a *first mortgage* or *deed of trust*. If the owner later executes another loan for additional funds, the new loan becomes a *second mortgage* or *deed of trust* (or a *junior lien*) when it is recorded. The second lien is *subject to* the first lien; the first has prior claim to the value of the land pledged as security. Because second loans represent greater risk to the lender, they are usually issued at higher interest rates.

The priority of mortgage or deed of trust liens may be changed by a *subordination agreement*, in which the first lender *subordinates* its lien to that of the second lender. To be valid, such an agreement must be signed by both lenders.

■ PROVISIONS OF LAND CONTRACTS AND OTHER OWNER FINANCING

Real estate can be purchased under a land contract, also known as a *contract for deed* or an *installment contract* (See Chapter 11). Real estate is usually sold on contract for specific financial reasons. For instance, mortgage financing may be unavailable to a borrower for some reason. High interest rates may make borrowing too expensive, or the purchaser may not have a sufficient down payment to cover the difference between a mortgage loan and the selling price.

Under a **land contract,** the buyer (called the *vendee*) agrees to make a down payment and a monthly loan payment that includes interest and principal directly to the seller. The payment also may include real estate tax and insurance reserves.

The seller (called the *vendor*) retains legal title to the property during the contract term, and the buyer is granted *equitable title* and possession. At the end of the loan term, the seller delivers clear title. In the event the seller fails to deliver clear title, the buyer (vendee) would file a vendee's lien. The contract usually permits the seller to evict the buyer in the event of default. In that case, the seller may keep any money the buyer has already paid. If, however, the buyer has 20 percent equity in the property and a contract in excess of five years, judicial foreclosure would be necessary.

While land contracts or **owner financing** can occur with residential or commercial properties, they are more common with unimproved acreage and farmland sales. Sometimes the seller is the primary lender, and at other times, the seller may be in a secondary position. In either case, the sellers would want to secure their interest either by the use of a deed, note and mortgage, deed of trust, or perhaps the use of a contract for deed instrument.

■ FORECLOSURE

Because of job losses and economic uncertainty over the last several years, borrowers defaulting on mortgage payments have forced lenders to exercise their rights to foreclose against properties used as security for their loans. **Foreclosure** is a legal procedure in which property pledged as security is sold to satisfy the debt. The foreclosure procedure brings the rights of the parties and all junior lienholders to a conclusion. It passes title either to the person holding the mortgage document or deed of trust or to a third party who purchases the realty at a *foreclosure sale*. The purchaser could be the mortgagee. At the foreclosure sale, the property is sold free of the foreclosing mortgage and all junior liens.

Methods of Foreclosure

There are three general types of foreclosure proceedings—nonjudicial, judicial, and strict foreclosure. One, two, or all three may be available. The specific provisions and procedures for each vary from state to state.

Nonjudicial foreclosure Some states allow **nonjudicial foreclosure** procedures to be used when the security instrument contains a *power-of-sale* clause. In nonjudicial foreclosure, no court action is required.

Judicial foreclosure Judicial foreclosure allows the property to be sold by court order after the mortgagee has given sufficient public notice. When a borrower defaults, the lender may accelerate the due date of the remaining principal balance, along with all overdue interest, penalties, and administrative costs. The lender's attorney then can file a suit to foreclose the lien. After presentation of the facts in court, the property is ordered sold. A public sale is advertised and held, and the real estate is sold to the highest bidder.

| In Illinois | By statute, mortgage foreclosures may be brought about only through a court proceeding. As a result, Illinois is classified as a *judicial foreclosure state*. Under the Illinois 1987 Mortgage Foreclosure Law, the term *mortgage* includes |

- deeds of trust,
- installment contracts payable over a period in *excess* of five years (when the unpaid balance is less than 80 percent of the purchase price),
- certain collateral assignments of the beneficial interest in land trusts used as security for lenders, and
- traditional mortgage instruments. ■

Strict foreclosure   Although judicial foreclosure is the prevalent practice, it is still possible in some states for a lender to acquire mortgaged property through a **strict foreclosure** process. First, appropriate notice must be given to the delinquent borrower. Second, once the proper papers have been prepared and recorded, the court establishes a deadline by which time the balance of the defaulted debt must be paid in full. If the borrower does not pay off the loan by that date, the court simply awards full legal title to the lender. No sale takes place.

Deed in Lieu of Foreclosure

As an alternative to foreclosure, a lender may accept a **deed in lieu of foreclosure** from the borrower. This is sometimes known as a *friendly foreclosure* because it is carried out by mutual agreement rather than by lawsuit. The major disadvantage of the "deed in lieu" is that the mortgagee takes the real estate *subject to all junior liens*. In a foreclosure action, all junior liens are eliminated. Also, by accepting a deed in lieu of foreclosure, the lender usually loses any rights pertaining to FHA or private mortgage insurance or VA guarantees. Finally, a deed in lieu of foreclosure is still considered an adverse element in the borrower's credit history.

Today, many property owners are unable to meet their mortgage payments, in part because they may have lost their jobs and/or their adjustable rate mortgage (ARM) payments became more than they could afford. When these owners put their home on the market, they find that values have declined that they now owe more money than they can realize from the sale of their home.

Short Sales

A short sale is the process by which a lender accepts less than the amount owed on the property. Although not always the case, a short sale request most often occurs when the owner/borrower is unable to make the mortgage payments and cannot sell the house for what is owed on the property. The lender agrees to accept less because the lender may lose more money by acquiring the property through a foreclosure process and then holding the property until the lender can find another buyer.

Lenders are leery of short sales due to the potential for several different types of fraud. The first type is when the buyers are not actually buying for themselves. The buyers might actually be friends or relatives of the delinquent borrower who are helping the borrower gain back the house for a lower amount. In other situations, the buyers are investors using "straw buyers" to buy the house for a low amount expecting to quickly sell it at a profit shortly thereafter.

Still another variation of a fraudulent short sale is when payments are made to someone (e.g., seller, other mortgage holders) in order to get them to agree to the sale. For example, when the holder of a second (junior) mortgage is unwilling to accept the amount that the senior lien holder (the one agreeing to the sale) an arrangement is privately agreed to for additional payments that are not shown on the HUD-1 closing statement and remain unknown to the senior lien holder. This is a violation of RESPA.

For these reasons, fewer delinquent borrowers have been able to benefit from a short sale. Still another issue arises when lenders typically reserve the right to file suit to acquire the missing amount, called a *deficiency*. Although few lenders actually file suit to recover the missing amount, they can. Because the borrower has received the money and has not repaid it, the borrower generally owes income tax on the deficient amount (i.e., the amount forgiven in the short sale and then receiving an IRS Form 1099). Under the Mortgage Debt Relief Act of 2007, however, taxpayers are permitted to exclude from taxable income the amount of debt reduced through mortgage restructuring as well as mortgage debt forgiven through foreclosure. The act applies to debt forgiven in the years 2007 through 2012. For specific details, be sure to consult a competent accountant.

Lenders take their time agreeing to a short sale. Licensees working in this field should expect the process to be long and tedious and likely to fail before closing or a foreclosure takes place.

Government Programs

The "Making Home Affordable" programs (2009), part of President Obama's approach to help the housing market, are available to assist delinquent borrowers and consist of several components: the Home Affordable Modification Program (HAMP), the Home Affordable Refinance Program (HARP), and the Home Affordable Foreclosure Alternatives Program (HAFA). All programs are voluntary, and not all lenders participate.

HAMP The goal of HAMP is to help delinquent borrowers modify the terms of their home mortgage loan to an affordable level (i.e., no more than 31 percent of the borrower's pretax monthly income using a combination of three factors: reduce the interest rate, increase the term up to 40 years, and reduce the principal on which interest is charged until the loan is repaid). Modifications are only available to owner occupants of one- to four-family dwellings with loan amounts not exceeding $729,750 for a single-family dwelling (amounts increase for 2, 3, or 4 units). HAMP is a voluntary program and is set to expire December 31, 2012.

HARP The HARP program is designed to help property owners refinance their properties who are not yet delinquent or more than 30 days overdue in the past 12 months. Lenders will scrutinize all financial information from a HARP applicant, requiring previous income taxes statements and more. This program expires June 10, 2011.

HAFA   The HAFA program provides alternatives to foreclosures by encouraging lenders and delinquent borrowers to enter into a short sale or a deed-in-lieu of foreclosure.

Redemption

Most states give defaulting borrowers a chance to redeem their property through the **equitable right of redemption**. If, after default but *before* the foreclosure sale, the borrower (or any other person who has an interest in the real estate, such as another creditor) pays the lender the amount in default, plus costs, the debt will be reinstated and regular payments may be resumed. In some cases, the person who redeems may be required to repay the accelerated loan in full. If some person other than the mortgagor or trustor redeems the real estate, the borrower becomes responsible to that person for the amount of the redemption.

Some states also allow defaulted borrowers a period in which to redeem their real estate after the sale. During this period (which may be as long as one year), the borrower has a **statutory right of redemption.** The mortgagor who can raise the necessary funds to redeem the property within the statutory period pays the redemption money to the court. Because the debt was paid from the proceeds of the sale, the borrower can take possession free and clear of the former defaulted loan. The court may appoint a receiver to take charge of the property, collect rents, and pay operating expenses during the redemption period.

In Illinois

There is no statutory right of redemption in Illinois. In Illinois, a mortgagor in default who wishes to exercise the equitable right of redemption to avoid loss of the mortgaged real estate may do so for a period of *seven months after the date of service* on the mortgagor or after first publication date, whichever is later. This time period can currently be *shortened to as little as 30 days after a judgment is entered if the property has been abandoned or is vacant.* When a property is redeemed in this way, the foreclosure sale does not occur. Otherwise, the foreclosure sale is held as soon as possible after the equitable right of redemption expires.

The mortgagor generally has a right to remain in possession of the property from the time of service of summons until the entry of a judgment of foreclosure. After judgment and through the 30th day after confirmation of the sale, the mortgagor can still retain possession, but he may be required to pay rent to the holder of the certificate of sale. Thirty-one days after judgment, the mortgagor must have vacated the property or be subject to eviction. The owner of the certificate of sale receives a **sheriff's deed** and gains the right to possession.

While Illinois does not have statutory right of redemption, it does offer a **statutory right of reinstatement.** This option is applicable when the defaulting mortgagor wishes to cure the default and reinstate the loan as if no acceleration had occurred. The mortgagor has the right to exercise this statutory right *for a period of 90 days after service of summons or publication date.* At the lender's discretion, expressed through an attorney, the right of reinstatement may be extended to run as long as the equitable right of redemption.

The reinstatement right usually may be exercised only *once every five years*. After reinstatement occurs, the suit must be dismissed by the lender, and the mortgage loan remains in effect just as before. (See the Illinois Code of Civil Procedure, Article 15; 735 ILCS 5/.)

When a default is not cured by redemption or reinstatement, the entry of a decree of foreclosure will lead to a **judicial sale** of the property, usually called a **sheriff's sale**. Each defendant to the suit must be given written personal notice of the sale, and public notice of the sale must be published in a newspaper of general circulation. The successful bidder at the sale receives a **certificate of sale**, not a deed. Only after the sale is confirmed by the court will the certificate holder receive a *sheriff's deed*. ■

Deficiency Judgment

The foreclosure sale may not produce enough cash to pay the loan balance in full after deducting expenses and accrued unpaid interest. In this case, where permitted by law, the mortgagee may be entitled to a *personal judgment* against the borrower for the unpaid balance. Such a judgment is a **deficiency judgment.** It also may be obtained against any endorsers or guarantors of the note and against any owners of the mortgaged property who assumed the debt by written agreement. However, if any money remains from the foreclosure sale after paying the debt and any other liens (such as a second mortgage or mechanic's lien), expenses, and interest, these proceeds are paid to the borrower. Strict foreclosure does not always provide for a deficiency judgment.

■ SUMMARY

Some states, known as title-theory states, recognize the lender as the owner of mortgaged property. Others, known as lien-theory states, recognize the borrower as the primary owner of mortgaged property.

In Illinois

A few intermediate mortgage theory states, such as Illinois, recognize modified, compromised versions of these theories. In Illinois, required court procedures protect consumers in the event of possible foreclosure. ■

Loans secured by a mortgage or deed of trust provide the principal sources of financing for real estate operations. Mortgage loans involve a borrower (the mortgagor) and a lender (the mortgagee). Deed of trust loans involve a third party "manager" (the trustee), in addition to a borrower (the trustor) and a lender (the beneficiary). Often the trustee/manager and the beneficiary in this type of loan have close interaction.

After a lending institution has received, investigated, and approved a loan application, it issues a commitment to make the mortgage loan. The borrower is required to execute a note agreeing to repay the debt and a mortgage or deed of trust placing a lien on the real estate to secure the note. The security instrument is recorded to give constructive notice to the world of the lender's interest.

The mortgage document or deed of trust secures the debt and sets forth the obligations of the borrower and the rights of the lender. Full payment of the note by its terms entitles the borrower to a satisfaction, or release, which is recorded to clear the lien from the public records. Default by the borrower may result in acceleration of payments, a foreclosure sale, and, after the redemption period (if provided by state law), loss of title.

Lenders may accept a deed in lieu of foreclosure from the borrower instead of pursuing a formal foreclosure. This does not eliminate junior liens and is still an adverse element in the borrower's credit history.

Another alternative to foreclosure is the short sale. As previously stated, a short sale occurs when the lender agrees to accept less than the outstanding loan balance when the property is sold. The lender must agree to accept the lesser amount and may or may not forgive the resulting deficiency. Under the Mortgage Debt Relief Act of 2007, delinquent borrowers do not have to pay tax on the delinquent amount if it was obtained through mortgage restructuring or foreclosure.

In Illinois

Illinois is an intermediate mortgage theory state. There is no state-imposed usury limit in Illinois on the rate that may be charged for a loan secured by real estate and made by private lenders. However, federal anti-usury laws supersede state laws on first-time residential mortgages and on federally insured or guaranteed loans. The Illinois Mortgage Escrow Account Act gives borrowers certain protections by limiting the size of escrow accounts and permitting alternatives to escrow.

Illinois is also classified as a judicial foreclosure state. There is no statutory right of redemption in Illinois, but there is equitable right of redemption and statutory right of reinstatement. When property is purchased at a sheriff's sale, the successful bidder receives a certificate of sale until the sale is confirmed by a court. After confirmation, the certificate holder receives a quitclaim deed, which in this situation is also called a sheriff's deed. ■

CHAPTER 15 QUIZ

1. A charge of three discount points on a $120,000 loan equals
   a. $450.   *120k × 3%.*
   b. $3,600.
   c. $4,500.
   d. $116,400.

2. A prospective buyer needs to borrow money to buy a house. The buyer applies for and obtains a real estate loan from a mortgage company. The buyer then signs a note and a mortgage. In this example, the buyer is referred to as the
   a. mortgagor.
   b. beneficiary.
   c. mortgagee.
   d. vendor.

3. In the previous question, the mortgage company is the
   a. mortgagor.
   b. beneficiary.
   c. mortgagee.
   d. vendor.

4. The borrower under a deed of trust is known as the
   a. trustor.
   b. trustee.
   c. beneficiary.
   d. vendee.

5. In a land contract, the vendee
   a. is not responsible for the real estate taxes on the property.
   b. does not pay interest and principal.
   c. obtains legal title at closing.
   d. has possession during the term of the contract.

6. A borrower has defaulted on a loan. Which of the following would BEST describe the rights of the lender in this situation?
   a. The escalation clause in the note allows the lender to collect all future interest due on the loan should a buyer default.
   b. The defeasance clause in the note stipulates that the lender may begin foreclosure proceedings to collect the remaining mortgage balance.
   c. The alienation clause in the note allows the lender to convey the mortgage to a buyer at the foreclosure sale.
   d. The acceleration clause in the note gives the lender the right to have all future installments due and payable immediately on default.

7. What is MOST likely to occur after a mortgagor makes her final payment to the mortgagee?
   a. The mortgagee would give the mortgagor a satisfaction of mortgage.
   b. The mortgagee would give the mortgagor a release deed.
   c. The mortgagee would give the mortgagor a deed of trust.
   d. The mortgagee would give the mortgagor a mortgage estoppel.

8. Under a typical land contract, when does the vendor give the deed to the vendee?
   a. When the contract is fulfilled and all payments have been made
   b. At the closing
   c. When the contract for deed is approved by the parties
   d. After the first year's real estate taxes are paid

9. If a borrower must pay $2,700 for points on a $90,000 loan, how many points is the lender charging for this loan?
   a. 2
   b. 3
   c. 5
   d. 6

10. Pledging property for a loan without giving up possession of the property itself is referred to as
   a. hypothecation.
   b. defeasance.
   c. alienation.
   d. novation.

11. Although the homeowners have located a buyer for their home, the buyer's offer is less than what the homeowners owe. In this situation, if the lender agrees to accept an amount less than owed, the lender has agreed to a
   a. friendly foreclosure.
   b. short sale.
   c. deed in lieu of foreclosure.
   d. waiver of redemption.

12. Discount points on a mortgage are computed as a percentage of the
   a. selling price.
   b. loan amount.
   c. closing costs.
   d. down payment.

In Illinois

13. In Illinois, mortgage foreclosures may be obtained only through a court proceeding. This means Illinois is characterized as a
   a. strict foreclosure state.
   b. judicial foreclosure state.
   c. foreclosure-by-lawsuit state.
   d. intermediate mortgage theory state.

14. In Illinois, when may a mortgagor in default exercise his right of reinstatement?
   a. At any time prior to the foreclosure sale
   b. Up to six months after the foreclosure sale
   c. Up to 90 days after service of summons
   d. Up to 90 days after the payments become delinquent but before summons

15. In Illinois, when must a release be delivered to a mortgagor or trustor once the mortgage or deed of trust has been fully satisfied?
   a. Within 48 hours of full payment and satisfaction
   b. Within five business days after full payment and satisfaction
   c. Within one month after full payment and satisfaction
   d. Within 90 days after full payment and satisfaction

16. The successful bidder at a foreclosure sale in Illinois immediately receives a
   a. sheriff's deed.
   b. certificate of sale.
   c. deed of foreclosure.
   d. certificate of foreclosure.

17. According to the Illinois Mortgage Escrow Act, an individual who has owned his home for 12 years and reduced his mortgage balance to 65 percent of its original amount may
   a. receive a 50 percent rebate from the lender on his escrow account.
   b. earn the statutory interest rate on his escrow account deposit.
   c. terminate his escrow account.
   d. obtain a second loan with only a token down payment.

18. What is the Illinois usury ceiling for loans secured by real property?
   a. 8 percent
   b. 9½ percent
   c. A fluctuating rate based on the quarterly federal reserve rate
   d. There is no usury ceiling for such loans in Illinois

19. Which of the following is included in the definition of mortgage contained in the Illinois Mortgage Foreclosure Law?
   a. Installment contracts payable over a maximum of five years
   b. Assignments of beneficial interests in living trusts
   c. Deeds in trust
   d. Installment contracts payable over at least five years, with a 20 percent down payment

20. Which of the following describes the theory of the mortgagor/mortgagee relationship in Illinois?

    a. Title theory
    b. Lien theory
    c. Intermediate mortgage theory
    d. Conventional theory

CHAPTER 16

Real Estate Financing: Practice

■ **LEARNING OBJECTIVES** *When you've finished reading this chapter, you should be able to*

■ **identify** the types of institutions in the primary and secondary mortgage markets;

■ **describe** the various types of financing techniques available to real estate purchasers and the role of government financing regulations;

■ **explain** the requirements and qualifications for conventional, FHA, and VA loan programs;

■ **distinguish** among the different types of financing techniques; and

■ **define** the following *key terms*

adjustable-rate mortgage (ARM)	Fannie Mae	interest-only loan
amortized loans	Federal Deposit Insurance Corporation (FDIC)	loan-to-value ratios (LTV)
balloon payment		margin
blanket loan	Federal Reserve System (the Fed)	mortgage insurance premium (MIP)
buydown	FHA loan	mortgage loan originators (MLOs)
certificate of reasonable value (CRV)	Freddie Mac	open-end loan
Community Reinvestment Act (CRA)	Ginnie Mae	package loan
construction loan	growing equity mortgage	primary mortgage market
conventional loans	home equity loan	private mortgage insurance (PMI)
Equal Credit Opportunity Act (ECOA)	Homeowners Protection Act of 1998	
	index	

purchase-money mortgage (PMM)	sale-leaseback	straight loan
Real Estate Settlement Procedures Act (RESPA)	secondary mortgage market	term loan
Regulation Z	Secure and Fair Enforcement for Mortgage Licensing Act of 2008 (SAFE Act)	trigger terms
reverse mortgage		Truth in Lending Act (TILA)
		VA loan
		wraparound loan

■ REAL ESTATE FINANCING: PRACTICE

Most real estate transactions require some form of financing. The real estate lending and borrowing environment is complex. As economic conditions change, the forces of supply and demand create a rapidly evolving mortgage market. The challenge for today's real estate licensees is to maintain a working knowledge of the various financing options. By understanding financing techniques and payment options, real estate licensees can be valuable participants in helping buyers reach their real estate goals.

■ INTRODUCTION TO THE REAL ESTATE FINANCING MARKET

The real estate financing market has the following three basic components:

■ Government influences, primarily the Federal Reserve System, but also the Home Loan Bank System and the Office of Thrift Supervision
■ The primary mortgage market
■ The secondary mortgage market

Under the umbrella of the financial policies set by the Federal Reserve System, the primary mortgage market originates loans that are bought, sold, and traded in the secondary mortgage market. Before turning to the specific types of mortgage options available to consumers, it is important to have a clear understanding of the bigger picture: the market in which those mortgages exist.

The Federal Reserve System

The role of the **Federal Reserve System** (the Fed) is to maintain sound credit conditions, help counteract inflationary and deflationary trends, and create a favorable economic climate. The Fed divides the country into 12 federal reserve districts, each served by a federal reserve bank. All nationally chartered banks must join the Fed and purchase stock in its district reserve banks. The Federal Reserve System regulates the flow of money and interest rates in the marketplace through its member banks by controlling *reserve requirements* and *discount rates*.

Reserve requirements   The Federal Reserve System requires that each member bank keep a certain level of assets on hand as reserve funds. These reserves are unavailable for loans or any other use. This requirement not only protects customer deposits but also provides a means of manipulating the flow of cash in the money market.

Fed Controls

Decreasing reserve requirements lowers rates
■ Increases money for loans
■ Stimulates market
■ Increases inflation
Increasing reserve requirements raises rates
■ Decreases money flow
■ Slows economy and purchases
■ Slows inflation

By increasing its reserve requirements, the Federal Reserve System in effect limits the amount of money that member banks can use to make loans. When the amount of money available for lending decreases, interest rates (the amount lenders charge for the use of their money) rise. By causing interest rates to rise, the Fed can slow down an overactive economy; higher rates limit the number of loans that would have been directed toward major purchases of goods and services. The opposite is also true: By decreasing the reserve requirements, the Fed can encourage more lending. Increased lending causes the amount of money circulated in the marketplace to rise while simultaneously causing interest rates to drop.

Discount rate   Federal Reserve member banks are permitted to borrow money from the district reserve banks to expand their lending operations. The discount rate is the rate charged by the Federal Reserve when it lends money to its member banks. The *prime rate* (the short-term interest rate charged to a bank's largest, most creditworthy customers) is strongly influenced by the Fed's discount rate. In turn, the prime rate is often the basis for determining a bank's interest rate on other loans, including home mortgages. When the Federal Reserve System discount rate is high, bank interest rates are high. When bank interest rates are high, fewer loans are made and less money circulates in the marketplace. A lower discount rate results in lower interest rates, more bank loans, and more money in circulation.

The Primary Mortgage Market

The **primary mortgage market** is made up of the lenders that originate mortgage loans. These lenders make money available directly to borrowers. From a borrower's point of view, a loan is a means of financing an expenditure; from a lender's point of view, a loan is an investment. All investors look for profitable returns on their investments. Income on the loan is realized from two sources:

- *Finance charges*—collected at closing, such as loan origination fees and discount points
- *Recurring income*—the interest collected during the term of the loan

In addition to the income directly related to loans, some lenders derive income from *servicing* loans for other mortgage lenders or the investors who have purchased the loans. Servicing loans involves such activities as

- collecting payments (including insurance and taxes),
- accounting,
- bookkeeping,
- preparing insurance and tax records,
- processing payments of taxes and insurance, and
- following up on loan payment and delinquency.

Some of the major lenders in the primary market include the following:

- *Thrifts, savings associations, and commercial banks:* These institutions are known as *fiduciary lenders* because of their fiduciary obligations to protect and preserve their depositors' funds. *Thrifts* is a generic term for the savings associations. Mortgage loans are perceived as secure investments for generating income and enable these institutions to pay interest to their depositors. Fiduciary lenders are subject to standards and regulations established by

Primary Mortgage Market

- Thrifts
- Savings associations
- Commercial banks
- Insurance companies
- Credit unions
- Pension funds
- Endowment funds
- Investment group financing
- Mortgage banking companies

government agencies such as the **Federal Deposit Insurance Corporation (FDIC)**. The various government regulations (which include reserve fund, reporting, and insurance requirements) are intended to protect depositors against the reckless lending that characterized the savings and loan industry in the 1980s.

- *Insurance companies:* Insurance companies accumulate large sums of money from the premiums paid by their policyholders. While part of this money is held in reserve to satisfy claims and cover operating expenses, much of it is free to be invested in profit-earning enterprises such as long-term real estate loans.

- *Credit unions:* Credit unions are cooperative organizations whose members place money in savings accounts. In the past, credit unions made only short-term consumer and home improvement loans. Now, they routinely originate longer-term first and second mortgage and deed of trust loans.

- *Pension funds:* Pension funds usually have large amounts of money available for investment. Because of the comparatively high yields and low risks offered by mortgages, pension funds have begun to participate actively in financing real estate projects. Most real estate activities for pension funds are handled through mortgage bankers and mortgage brokers.

- *Endowment funds:* Many commercial banks and mortgage bankers handle investments for endowment funds. The endowments of hospitals, universities, colleges, charitable foundations, and other institutions provide a good source of financing for low-risk commercial and industrial properties.

- *Investment group financing:* Large real estate projects, such as highrise apartment buildings, office complexes, and shopping centers, are often financed as joint ventures through group financing arrangements like syndicates, limited partnerships, and real estate investment trusts.

- *Mortgage banking companies:* Mortgage banking companies originate mortgage loans with money belonging to insurance companies, pension funds, and individuals with funds of their own. They make real estate loans with the intention of selling them to investors and receiving a fee for servicing the loans. Mortgage banking companies generally are organized as stock companies. As a source of real estate financing, they are subject to fewer lending restrictions than are commercial banks or savings associations.

- *Mortgage brokers:* Mortgage brokers are not lenders. They are intermediaries who bring borrowers and lenders together. Mortgage brokers locate potential borrowers, process preliminary loan applications, and submit the applications to lenders for final approval. They do not service loans once they are made. Mortgage brokers also may be real estate licensees who offer these financing services in addition to their regular brokerage activities. Many state governments are establishing separate licensure requirements for mortgage brokers to regulate their activities.

In Illinois

The federal **Secure and Fair Enforcement for Mortgage Licensing Act of 2008 (SAFE Act)** requires that each individual state must license and register **mortgage loan originators (MLOs)**. A MLO is defined as anyone who, for compensation or expectation of compensation, takes a residential mortgage loan by phone or in person. Among those exempt from license requirements are those who perform only clerical or administrative tasks and real estate licensees unless compensated by a loan originator. The SAFE Act suggests, but does not require, participation in the Nationwide Mortgage Licensing System (NMLS). Because Illinois is a participant, all Illinois MLOs are required to register. Illinois also requires an eight-hour continuing education course. ■

IN PRACTICE   A growing number of consumers apply for mortgage loans via the Internet. Many major lenders have Web sites that offer information to potential borrowers regarding their current loan programs and requirements. In addition, online brokerage or matchmaking organizations link lenders with potential borrowers. Some borrowers prefer the Internet for its convenience in shopping for the best rates and terms, accessing a wide variety of loan programs, and speeding up the loan approval process.

The Secondary Mortgage Market

In addition to the primary mortgage market where loans are originated, there is a **secondary mortgage market**. The secondary mortgage market helps lenders raise capital to continue making mortgage loans. Furthermore, the secondary market is especially useful when money is in short supply; it stimulates both the housing construction market and the mortgage market by expanding the types of loans available.

In the secondary mortgage market, loans are bought and sold only after they have been funded. Lenders routinely sell loans to avoid interest rate risks and to realize profits on the sales. This secondary market activity helps lenders raise capital to continue making mortgage loans. Secondary market activity is especially desirable when money is in short supply; it stimulates both the housing construction market and the mortgage market by expanding the types of loans available. Growth in the use of secondary markets has greatly increased the standardization of loans. When a loan is sold, the original lender may continue to collect the payments from the borrower. The lender then passes the payments along to the investor who purchased the loan. The investor is charged a fee for servicing of the loan.

In the secondary market, various agencies purchase a number of mortgage loans and assemble them into packages (called *pools*). These agencies purchase the mortgages from banks and savings associations. Securities that represent shares in these pooled mortgages are then sold to investors or other agencies (See Table 16.1).

Fannie Mae   In September 2008, the Federal National Mortgage Association (**Fannie Mae**) became a government-owned enterprise. Until that time, it was organized as a completely privately owned corporation that issued its own stock. Then, as now, it provides a secondary market for mortgage loans. Fannie Mae deals in conventional and Federal Housing Administration (FHA) and Department of

T A B L E 16.1 **Secondary Mortgage Market**	Institution	Secondary Market Function
	Fannie Mae	Conventional, VA, FHA Loans
	Feddie Mac	Mostly conventional loans
	Ginnie Mae	Special assistance loans

Veterans Affairs (VA) loans. Fannie Mae buys from a lender a *block* or *pool* of mortgages that may then be used as collateral for *mortgage-backed securities* that are sold on the global market. The Fannie Mae loan limits shown in Table 16.2 define loans that are conforming.

Ginnie Mae   The Government National Mortgage Association (**Ginnie Mae**) has always been a governmental agency. Ginnie Mae is a division of the Department of Housing and Urban Development (HUD), organized as a corporation without capital stock. Ginnie Mae administers special-assistance programs and guarantees mortgage backed securities using FHA and VA loans as collateral.

Ginnie Mae guarantees investment securities issued by private offerors (such as banks, mortgage companies, and savings and loan associations) and backed by pools of FHA and VA mortgage loans. The Ginnie Mae *pass-through certificate* is a security interest in a pool of mortgages that provides for a monthly pass-through of principal and interest payments directly to the certificate holder. Such certificates are guaranteed by Ginnie Mae.

Freddie Mac   The Federal Home Loan Mortgage Corporation (**Freddie Mac**) is also now a government-owned enterprise, similar to Fannie Mae, which provides a secondary market primarily for conventional loans.

Many lenders use the standardized forms and follow the guidelines issued by Fannie Mae and Freddie Mac. In fact, the use of such forms is mandatory for lenders wishing to sell mortgages in the agencies' secondary mortgage market. The standardized documents include loan applications, credit reports, and appraisal forms.

■ FINANCING TECHNIQUES

Real estate financing comes in a wide variety of forms. While the payment plans described in the following sections are commonly referred to as *mortgages*, they are really loans secured by either a mortgage or a deed of trust.

Straight Loans

A **straight loan** or **interest-only loan** (also known as a *term loan*) is a nonamortized loan that essentially divides the loan into two amounts to be paid off separately.

TABLE   16.2

Fannie Mae/Freddie Mac Conforming Loan Limits (2011)

Fannie Mae/Freddie Mac Conforming Loan Limits (2011)	
One-family unit	$417,000
Two-family unit	$533,850
Three-family unit	$645,300
Four-family unit	$801,950
Second mortgages	$208,500
Maximum loan limits are 50 percent higher in Alaska, Hawaii, the U.S. Virgin Islands, and Guam.	

The borrower makes periodic payments of interest only, followed by the payment of the principal in full at the end of the term.

Amortized Loans

Unlike a straight loan payment, the payment in an **amortized loan** partially pays off both principal and interest. Most mortgage and deed of trust loans are amortized loans. Regular periodic payments are made over a term of years, generally 15 or 30 years, although 40- and 50-year mortgages are available. Each payment is applied first to the interest owed; the balance of the payment is then applied to the principal amount.

At the end of the term, the full amount of the principal and all interest due is reduced to zero. Such loans are also called *direct reduction loans*. Most amortized mortgage and deed of trust loans are paid in monthly installments.

MATH CONCEPTS

INTEREST AND PRINCIPAL CREDITED FROM AMORTIZED PAYMENTS

Lenders charge borrowers a certain percentage of the principal as interest for each year a debt is outstanding. The amount of interest due on any one payment date is calculated by computing the total yearly interest (based on the unpaid balance) and dividing that figure by the number of payments made each year.

For example, assume the current outstanding balance of a loan is $70,000. The interest rate is 7.5 percent per year, and the monthly payment is $489.30. Based on these facts, the interest and principal due on the next payment would be computed as shown:

$70,000 loan balance × .075 annual interest rate = $5,250 annual interest
$5,250 annual interest ÷ 12 months = $437.50 monthly interest
$489.30 monthly payment – $437.50 monthly interest = $51.80 monthly principal
$70,000 loan balance – $51.80 monthly principal = $69,948.20

This process is followed with each payment over the term of the loan. The same calculations are made each month, starting with the declining new balance figure from the previous month.

Different payment plans alternately tend to gain and lose favor with lenders and borrowers as the cost and availability of mortgage money fluctuates. The most frequently used plan is the *fully amortized loan*, or *level-payment loan*. The mortgagor pays a constant amount, usually monthly. The lender credits each payment first to the interest due, then to the principal amount of the loan. As a result, while each payment remains the same, the portion applied to repayment of the principal grows and the interest due declines as the unpaid balance of the loan is reduced. (See Figure 16.1.) If the borrower pays additional amounts that are applied directly to the principal, the loan will amortize more quickly. This benefits the borrower because she will pay less interest if the loan is paid off before the end of its term.

FIGURE 16.1

Level-Payment Amortized Loan

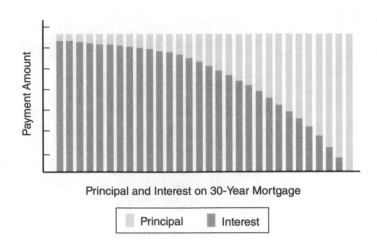

Principal and Interest on 30-Year Mortgage

☐ Principal   ■ Interest

The amount of the constant payment is determined from a mortgage factor chart. (See Table 16.3.) The mortgage factor chart indicates the amount of monthly payment per $1,000 of a loan, depending on the term and interest rate. The factor is multiplied by the number of thousands (and fractions of thousands) of the amount borrowed.

IN PRACTICE Of course, there are relatively inexpensive calculators that will accurately perform most of the standard mortgage lending calculations. Also, most commercial lenders provide mortgage calculators on their Web sites. Nonetheless, it's valuable both to know what the calculator is doing and to be able to perform the calculations manually if the calculator breaks or no calculator is available.

Adjustable-Rate Mortgages (ARMs)

Adjustable-rate mortgages (ARMs) generally originate at one rate of interest, then fluctuate up or down during the loan term, based on some objective economic indicator. Because the interest rate on ARMs may change, the mortgagor's loan repayments also may change. Details of how and when the interest rate will change are included in the note. Common components of an ARM include the following:

- The **index** is an undeterminable economic indicator that is used to adjust the interest rate in the loan. Most indexes are tied to U.S. Treasury securities.
- Usually, the interest rate is the interest rate is the index rate plus a premium, called the *margin*. The margin represents the lender's cost of doing business.
- *Rate caps* limit the amount the interest rate may change. Most ARMs have two types of rate caps—periodic and aggregate. A *periodic rate cap* limits the amount the rate may increase at any one time. An *aggregate rate cap* limits the amount the rate may increase over the entire life of the loan.
- The mortgagor is protected from unaffordable individual payments by the payment cap. The payment cap sets a maximum amount for payments.
- The adjustment period establishes how often the rate may be changed, whether it is monthly, quarterly, or annually.
- Lenders may offer a conversion option, which permits the mortgagor to convert from an adjustable-rate to a fixed-rate loan at certain intervals during the life of the mortgage.

TABLE 16.3

Mortgage Factor Chart

How To Use This Chart

To use this chart, start by finding the appropriate interest rate. Then follow that row over to the column for the appropriate loan term. This number is the *interest rate factor* required each month to amortize a $1,000 loan.

To calculate the principal and interest (PI) payment, multiply the interest rate factor by the number of 1,000s in the total loan. For example, if the interest rate is 4 percent for a term of 30 years, the interest rate factor is 4.78. If the total loan is $100,000, the loan contains 100 1,000s. Therefore, 100 × 4.78 = $478 PI only.

To estimate a mortgage loan amount using the amortization chart, divide the PI payment by the appropriate interest rate factor. Using the same facts as in the first example:

$478 ÷ 4.78 = $100 1,000s or $100,000

Rate	Term 10 Years	Term 15 Years	Term 20 Years	Term 25 Years	Term 30 Years
3	9.66	6.91	5.55	4.74	4.22
3⅛	9.71	6.97	5.61	4.81	4.28
3¼	9.77	7.03	5.67	4.87	4.35
3⅜	9.83	7.09	5.74	4.94	4.42
3½	9.89	7.15	5.80	5.01	4.49
3⅝	9.95	7.21	5.86	5.07	4.56
3¾	10.01	7.27	5.93	5.14	4.63
3⅞	10.07	7.33	5.99	5.21	4.70
4	10.13	7.40	6.06	5.28	4.78
4⅛	10.19	7.46	6.13	5.35	4.85
4¼	10.25	7.53	6.20	5.42	4.92
4⅜	10.31	7.59	6.26	5.49	5.00
4½	10.37	7.65	6.33	5.56	5.07
4⅝	10.43	7.72	6.40	5.63	5.15
4¾	10.49	7.78	6.47	5.71	5.22
4⅞	10.55	7.85	6.54	5.78	5.30
5	10.61	7.91	6.60	5.85	5.37
5⅛	10.67	7.98	6.67	5.92	5.45
5¼	10.73	8.04	6.74	6.00	5.53
5⅜	10.80	8.11	6.81	6.07	5.60
5½	10.86	8.18	6.88	6.15	5.68
5⅝	10.92	8.24	6.95	6.22	5.76
5¾	10.98	8.31	7.03	6.30	5.84
5⅞	11.04	8.38	7.10	6.37	5.92
6	11.10	8.44	7.16	6.44	6.00
6⅛	11.16	8.51	7.24	6.52	6.08
6¼	11.23	8.57	7.31	6.60	6.16
6⅜	11.29	8.64	7.38	6.67	6.24
6½	11.35	8.71	7.46	6.75	6.32
6⅝	11.42	8.78	7.53	6.83	6.40
6¾	11.48	8.85	7.60	6.91	6.49
6⅞	11.55	8.92	7.68	6.99	6.57
7	11.61	8.98	7.75	7.06	6.65
7⅛	11.68	9.06	7.83	7.15	6.74
7¼	11.74	9.12	7.90	7.22	6.82
7⅜	11.81	9.20	7.98	7.31	6.91
7½	11.87	9.27	8.05	7.38	6.99
7⅝	11.94	9.34	8.13	7.47	7.08
7¾	12.00	9.41	8.20	7.55	7.16
7⅞	12.07	9.48	8.29	7.64	7.25
8	12.14	9.56	8.37	7.72	7.34

Figure 16.2 illustrates the effect interest rate fluctuations and periodic caps have on an adjustable-rate mortgage. Obviously, without rate caps and payment caps, a single mortgage's interest rate could fluctuate wildly over several adjustment periods, depending on the behavior of the index to which it is tied. In Figure 16.2, the borrower's rate changes from a low of 5.9 percent to a high of 9.5 percent. Such unpredictability makes personal financial planning difficult. On the other hand, if the loan had a periodic rate cap of 7.5 percent, the borrower's rate would never go above that level, regardless of the index's behavior. Similarly, a lender would want a floor to keep the rate from falling below a certain rate (here, 6.5 percent). The shaded area in the figure shows how caps and floors protect against dramatic changes in interest rates.

Balloon Payment Loan

When the periodic payments are not enough to fully amortize the loan by the time the final payment is due, the final payment is larger than the others. This is called a **balloon payment.** A balloon loan is a *partially amortized loan* because principal is still owed at the end of the term. It is frequently assumed that if payments are made promptly, the lender will extend the balloon payment for another limited term. The lender, however, is not legally obligated to grant this extension and can require payment in full when the note is due.

Growing Equity Mortgage (GEM)

A **growing equity mortgage** (GEM) is also known as a *rapid-payoff mortgage.* The GEM uses a fixed interest rate, but payments of principal are increased according to an index or a schedule. Thus, the total payment increases, and the loan is paid off more quickly. A GEM is most frequently used when the borrower's income is expected to keep pace with the increasing loan payments.

Reverse Mortgage — for SENIORS

A **reverse mortgage** allows people 62 or older to borrow money against the equity they have built in their home. Reverse mortgages are the opposite of conventional mortgages in that the homeowner's equity diminishes as the loan amount increases. The money may be used for any purpose, and the borrowers decide if they want to receive the money in a lump sum, fixed monthly payments, an open line of credit, or other options. The borrower is charged a fixed rate of interest, and no payments are due until the property is sold or the borrow defaults, moves, or dies. Though reverse mortgages have been available for almost 30 years, they

FIGURE 16.2

Adjustable-Rate Mortgage

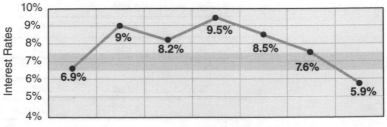

Adjustment Periods

have become more widespread as people live longer and need more money. The FHA home equity conversion mortgage (HECM) is one of the more common reverse mortgages.

Nonrecourse Loan

A *nonrecourse loan* is one in which the borrower is not held personally responsible for the loan. The lender has no recourse against the borrower personally in the event of a default. Nonrecourse loans are common in those situations in which the lender is highly confident that the value of the property involved is itself sufficient security. Nonrecourse loans are more common in commercial and investment real estate transactions than in residential situations.

■ LOAN PROGRAMS

Mortgage loans are generally classified based on their **loan-to-value ratios,** or LTVs. The LTV is the ratio of debt to value of the property. *Value* is the sale price or the appraisal value, whichever is less. The *lower* the ratio of debt to value, the *higher* the down payment by the borrower. For the lender, the higher down payment means a more secure loan, which minimizes the lender's risk.

MATH CONCEPTS

DETERMINING LTV

If a property has an appraised value of $100,000, secured by a $90,000 loan, the LTV is 90 percent:

$$\$90{,}000 \div \$100{,}000 = 90\%$$

Conventional Loans

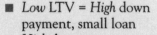

- *Low* LTV = *High* down payment, small loan
- *High* down payment = *Low* lender risk

Conventional loans are viewed as the most secure loans because their loan-to-value ratios are often lowest. Usually, the ratio is 80 percent of the value of the property or less because the borrower makes a down payment of at least 20 percent. The security for the loan is provided solely by the mortgage; the payment of the debt rests on the ability of the borrower to pay. In making such a loan, the lender relies primarily on its appraisal of the property. Information from credit reports that indicates the reliability of the prospective borrower is also important. No additional insurance or guarantee on the loan is necessary to protect the lender's interest. In conventional loans, the government is not involved.

Lenders can set criteria by which a borrower and the collateral are evaluated to qualify for a loan. Today, the secondary mortgage market has a significant impact on borrower qualifications, standards for the collateral, and documentation procedures followed by lenders. Loans must meet strict criteria to be sold to Fannie Mae and Freddie Mac. Lenders still can be flexible in their lending decisions, but they may not be able to sell unusual loans in the secondary market.

Importance of credit scores The creditworthiness of buyers also is a key element in qualifying for a conventional loan today. Underwriters consider several factors known about the applicant before determining whether to make the loan (e.g., credit scores and payment history). Today, with the exception of FHA loans and a few nonconforming loans, the interest rate available to borrowers is largely based on credit scores, which can range from 300 to 850. The higher the credit score, the lower the risk to the lender. Lenders offer these borrowers lower interest rates and may permit a smaller down payment. Lenders almost always require a higher interest rate and/or a larger down payment for those with lower scores. Today, the FHA is the best source for a mortgage loan for a borrower with a lower credit score.

The nonconforming market accepts loans that do not meet Fannie Mae and Freddie Mac requirements. Examples of such loans include loan amounts that exceed the limits set by Fannie Mae and Freddie Mac, loans secured by a property that does not qualify (e.g., commercial, more than four family units), and factors specific to the individual borrower (e.g., no down payment, high debt-to-income ratios, or the self-employed borrower does not show enough income to qualify).

Importance of credit history In addition to credit scores, underwriters consider two years in detail and up to seven years of repayment history, whether or not the applicant has made timely payments, especially for rent and/or mortgage loans. A payment is considered late if more than 30 days past due. Underwriters especially look for bankruptcies, judgments, and foreclosures. Underwriters may make exceptions if the applicant can show specific reasons for the late payments (e.g., a death, divorce, medical reasons). Applicants who are consistently more than 30 days late for rent or mortgage payments will most likely be ineligible for VA and FHA loans and others that are sold to Fannie Mae and Freddie Mac.

Judgments, foreclosures, bankruptcies Fannie Mae, Freddie Mac, FHA, and the VA require that all judgments be paid in full, and they prefer that the judgments be at least two years old. Generally, the nonconforming market is open to funding and buying loans even if the judgment has paid so long as the judgment does not impact title.

For most bankruptcy actions, both Fannie Mae and Freddie Mac require four years to re-establish credit. Fannie Mae and Freddie Mac may purchase loans made to someone who was in foreclosure. However, they require that the foreclosure of the borrower's primary residence was at least three years prior and caused by circumstances out of the borrower's control, such as the death of the primary wage earner, job layoff, or long-term serious illness. Although the nonconforming market may purchase a loan, it often requires a substantial down payment if the foreclosure is less than three years old.

To qualify for a conventional loan under Fannie Mae guidelines, the borrower's monthly housing expenses, including PITI, must not exceed 28 percent of total monthly gross income. Also, the borrower's total monthly obligations, including housing costs plus other regular monthly payments, must not exceed 36 percent of her total monthly gross income (33 percent in the case of 95 percent LTV loans). Loans that meet these criteria are called *conforming loans* and are eligible to be sold in the secondary market. Loans that exceed the limits are referred to as *nonconforming loans* and are not marketable in the secondary market but, instead, are generally held in the lender's investment portfolio.

Conforming loans with larger ratios may be available in certain situations. Both Fannie Mae and Freddie Mac currently have a variety of conforming affordable loan products with qualifying ratios of 33 percent for housing expense and up to 38 percent for total debt. These loans only require a 3 percent down payment but are subject to certain income limitations and may require the borrowers to attend homeownership classes.

Private Mortgage Insurance

One way a borrower can obtain a mortgage loan with a lower down payment is by obtaining **private mortgage insurance** (PMI). In a PMI program, the borrower purchases an insurance policy that provides the lender with funds in the event the borrower defaults on the loan. This allows the lender to assume more risk so that the loan-to-value ratio is higher than for other conventional loans. The borrower purchases insurance from a private mortgage insurance company as additional security to insure the lender against borrower default. In 2010, LTVs of up to 95 percent of the appraised value of the property are possible with mortgage insurance, although these percentages change.

PMI protects the top 20 to 30 percent of the loan against borrower default. The borrower pays a monthly fee, which can be financed in with the loan, while the insurance is in force. Because only a portion of the loan is insured, the lender must allow the borrower to terminate the coverage once the loan is repaid to a certain level.

Under the **Homeowners' Protection Act of 1998** (implemented in 1999), PMI must terminate automatically when the borrower reaches a 22 percent equity position based on the original value of the property at the time the loan was originated with no allowance for appreciation or depreciation if the loan was written after July 29, 1999, and the borrower is current on mortgage payments.

FHA-Insured Loans

The Federal Housing Administration (FHA), which operates under HUD, neither builds homes nor lends money. The common term **FHA loan** refers to a loan that is *insured* by the agency. These loans must be made by FHA-approved lending institutions. The FHA insurance provides security to the lender in addition to the real estate. As with private mortgage insurance, the FHA insures lenders against loss from borrower default.

The most popular FHA program is Title II, Section 203(b), fixed-interest-rate loans for 10 years to 30 years on one- to four-family residences. Rates are competitive with other types of loans, even though they are high LTV loans. According to the FHA Web site (in 2010), the borrower is eligible for approximately 96.5 percent financing for one- to four-unit structures. Certain technical requirements must be met before the FHA will insure the loans. These requirements include the following:

- The borrower must pay a down payment of at least 3.5 percent of the purchase price, but most of the closing costs and fees can be included in the loan.
- The borrower is charged a **mortgage insurance premium (MIP)** for all FHA loans. The *up-front premium* is charged at closing and can be financed into the mortgage loan. The borrower is also responsible for paying an annual premium that is usually charged monthly. The up-front premium is charged on all FHA loans, except those for the purchase of a condominium, that require only a monthly MIP.
- The mortgaged real estate must be appraised by an *approved* FHA appraiser.
- The FHA sets maximum mortgage limits for various regions of the country.
- The borrower must meet standard FHA credit qualifications.
- Financing for manufactured homes and factory-built housing is also available, both for those who own the land that the home is on and also for manufactured homes that are, or will be, located on another plot of land.

If the purchase price exceeds the FHA-appraised value, the buyer may pay the difference in cash as part of the down payment. Some exceptions are made for special programs, such as the Good Neighbor Program.

Other types of FHA loans are available, including one-year adjustable-rate mortgages, home improvement and rehabilitation loans, and loans for the purchase of condominiums. Specific standards for condominium complexes and the ratio of owner-occupants to renters must be met for a loan on a condominium unit to be financed through the FHA insurance programs.

A qualified buyer may assume an existing FHA-insured loan. The application consists of a credit check to demonstrate that the person assuming the loan is financially qualified. The process is quicker and less expensive than applying for a new loan. Sometimes, the older loan has a lower interest rate and no appraisal is required.

IN PRACTICE The FHA sets lending limits for single-unit and multiple-unit properties. The limits vary significantly depending on the average cost of housing in different regions of the country. In addition, the FHA changes its regulations for various programs from time to time. Contact your local FHA office or mortgage lender for loan amounts in your area and for specific loan requirements, or visit *www.hud.gov/ buying/loans.cfm*.

Assumption rules The assumption rules for FHA-insured loans vary, depending on the dates the loans were originated, as follows:

- FHA loans originating before December 1986 generally have no restrictions on their assumptions.
- For an FHA loan originating between December 1, 1986, and December 15, 1989, a creditworthiness review of the prospective assumer is required. If the original loan was for the purchase of a principal residence, this review is required during the first 12 months of the loan's existence. If the original

loan was for the purchase of an investment property, the review is required during the first 24 months of the loan.

■ For FHA loans originating on December 15, 1989, and later, no assumptions are permitted without complete buyer qualification.

Discount points The lender of an FHA-insured loan may charge discount points in addition to a loan origination fee. The payment of points is a matter of negotiation between the seller and the buyer. As of November 2009, if the seller pays more than 6 percent of the costs normally paid by the buyer (such as discount points, the loan origination fee, the mortgage insurance premium, buy-down fees, prepaid items, and impound or escrow amounts), the lender will treat the payments as a reduction in sales price and recalculate the mortgage amount accordingly.

VA-Guaranteed Loans

The Department of Veterans Affairs (VA) is authorized to guarantee loans to purchase or construct homes for eligible veterans and their spouses (including unremarried spouses of veterans whose deaths were service-related). The VA also guarantees loans to purchase mobile homes and plots on which to place them. Eligibility is defined as veterans who served on active duty and have some form of honorable discharge after a minimum of 90 days of service during wartime and a minimum of 181 continuous days in times of peace. Two years are required for veterans who enlisted and began service after September 7, 1980, or for officers who began service after October 16, 1981. Six years are required for reservists and members of the National Guard. There are specific rules regarding the eligibility of surviving spouses.

With over 25.5 million veterans and service personnel eligible, a VA loan is desirable and has many benefits. The VA assists veterans in financing the purchase of homes with little or no down payments at market interest rates. The VA issues rules and regulations that set forth the qualifications, limitations, and conditions under which a loan may be guaranteed.

Like the FHA loan, *VA loan* is something of a misnomer. The VA does not normally lend money; it guarantees loans made by lending institutions approved by the agency. The term *VA loan* refers to a loan that is not made by the agency but is guaranteed by it.

There is no VA dollar limit on the amount of the loan a veteran can obtain; this limit is determined by the lender and qualification of the buyer. The VA limits the amount of the loan it will guarantee.

IN PRACTICE The VA loan guarantee is tied to the current conforming loan limit for Fannie Mae and Freddie Mac. Typically, lenders will loan four times the guarantee (for example, a conforming loan of $417,000 ÷ 4 = $104,250 VA guarantee).

To determine what portion of a mortgage loan the VA will guarantee, the veteran must apply for a *certificate of eligibility*. This certificate does not mean that the veteran automatically receives a mortgage. It merely sets forth the maximum guarantee to which the veteran is entitled. For individuals with full eligibility, no down payment is required for a loan up to the maximum guarantee limit.

The VA also issues a **certificate of reasonable value (CRV)** for the property being purchased. The CRV states the property's current market value based on a VA-approved appraisal. The CRV places a ceiling on the amount of a VA loan allowed for the property. If the purchase price is greater than the amount cited in the CRV, the veteran may pay the difference in cash. The CRV is based on an appraisal. New VA regulations allow only one active VA loan at a time, and a veteran may own only two properties that were acquired using VA loan benefits. VA benefits will never expire as long as the previous benefit use has been paid.

The VA borrower pays a loan origination fee to the lender, as well as a funding fee to the Department of Veterans Affairs. The funding fee depends on whether it is first-time use (2.15 percent) or a subsequent use (3.15 percent). The funding fee drops with down payments of 5 percent or more. Reservists and National Guard veterans pay higher funding fees. Reasonable discount points may be charged on a VA-guaranteed loan, and either the veteran or the seller may pay them.

Prepayment privileges   As with an FHA loan, the borrower under a VA loan can prepay the debt at any time without penalty.

Assumption rules   VA loans made before March 1, 1988, are freely assumable, although an assumption processing fee will be charged. For loans made on or after March 1, 1988, the VA must approve the buyer and assumption agreement. The original veteran borrower remains personally liable for the repayment of the loan unless the VA approves a *release of liability*. The release of liability will be issued by the VA only if

- the buyer assumes all of the veteran's liabilities on the loan, and
- the VA or the lender approves both the buyer and the assumption agreement.

Releases are also possible if veterans use their own entitlement in assuming another veteran's loan.

IN PRACTICE   A release of liability issued by the VA does not release the veteran's liability to the lender. This must be obtained separately from the lender. Real estate licensees should contact their local VA offices or mortgage lenders for specific requirements for obtaining or assuming VA-insured loans. The programs change from time to time.

VA legislation   The **Veterans Millennium Health Care and Benefits Act of 1999**, Public Law 106-117, authorized the VA to restore the home loan eligibility of surviving spouses who lost such eligibility as a result of remarriage if the remarriage has been terminated by death or divorce. More on eligibility, including that of individuals who are not otherwise eligible and who have completed a total of at least six years of honorable service in the Selected Reserves, including the National Guard, is available on the VA's Internet loan information site.

Agricultural Loan Programs

The Farm Service Agency (FSA) is a federal agency of the Department of Agriculture. The FSA offers programs to help families purchase or operate family farms. Through the rural Housing and Community Development Service (RHCDS), it also provides loans to help families purchase or improve single-family homes in rural areas. FSA loan programs fall into two categories: guaranteed loans, made and serviced by private lenders and guaranteed for a specific percentage by the FSA, and loans made directly by the FSA.

The Farm Credit System (Farm Credit) provides loans to farmers, ranchers, rural homeowners, agricultural cooperatives, rural utility systems, and agribusinesses. Unlike commercial banks, Farm Credit System banks and associations do not take deposits. Instead, loanable funds are raised through the system-wide sale of bonds and notes in the nation's capital markets.

Farmer Mac (formerly the Federal Agricultural Mortgage Corporation, or FAMC) is another government-sponsored enterprise (GSE) that operates similarly to Fannie Mae and Freddie Mac but in a context of agricultural loans. It was created to improve the availability of long-term credit at stable interest rates to America's farmers, ranchers, and rural homeowners, businesses, and communities. Farmer Mac pools or bundles agricultural loans from lenders for sale as mortgage-backed securities.

■ OTHER FINANCING TECHNIQUES

Because borrowers often have different needs, a variety of other financing techniques have been created.

Purchase-Money Mortgages

A **purchase-money mortgage** (PMM) is a note and mortgage created at the time of purchase when the seller agrees to finance all or part of the purchase price and consists of a first or junior lien depending on whether prior mortgage liens exist. Often referred to as seller financing or owner financing, a PMM is often used when the buyer does not qualify for a typical lender loan. The buyer/borrower executes a note and mortgage at the time of purchase; the seller records the mortgage against the property. Payments are made to the seller, according to the terms of the note. If the buyer stops making payments, the seller has recourse to foreclose on the property.

■ **FOR EXAMPLE** A man wants to buy a farm for $200,000. He has a $40,000 down payment and agrees to assume an existing mortgage of $80,000. Because the buyer might not qualify for a new mortgage under the circumstances, the owner agrees to take back a purchase-money second mortgage in the amount of $80,000. At the closing, the buyer will execute a mortgage and note in favor of the owner, who will convey title to the buyer.

Package Loans

A **package loan** includes real and personal property. In recent years, these kinds of loans have been very popular with developers and purchasers of unfurnished condominiums. Package loans usually include furniture, drapes, the kitchen range, refrigerator, dishwasher, washer, dryer, food freezer, and other appliances as part of the sales price of the home.

Blanket Loans

A **blanket loan** covers more than one parcel or lot. It is usually used to finance subdivision developments. However, it can be used to finance the purchase of improved properties or to consolidate loans as well. A blanket loan usually includes a provision known as a *partial release clause*. This clause permits the borrower to obtain the release of any one lot or parcel from the lien by repaying a certain amount of the loan. The lender issues a partial release for each parcel released from the mortgage lien. The release form includes a provision that the lien will continue to cover all other unreleased lots.

Wraparound Loans

A **wraparound loan** enables a borrower with an existing mortgage or deed of trust loan to obtain additional financing from a second lender without paying off the first loan. The second lender gives the borrower a new, increased loan at a higher interest rate and assumes payment of the existing loan. The total amount of the new loan includes the existing loan as well as the additional loan taken out by the borrower. The borrower makes payments to the new lender based on the total amount, and the new lender in turn makes payments on the original loan out of the borrowers' payments.

A wraparound mortgage can be used to refinance real property or to finance the purchase of real property when an existing mortgage cannot be prepaid. The buyer executes a wraparound mortgage to the seller or lender, who collects payments based on the terms of the new loan and continues to make payments on the old loan.

A wraparound loan is only possible if the original loan permits it. An **alienation clause** or a **due-on-sale clause** in the original loan documents may prevent a sale under a wraparound loan. *Due-on-sale* means that if a property is sold, full payment must be made to the lender and the loan ends.

IN PRACTICE To protect themselves against a seller's default on a previous loan, buyers should require protective clauses to be included in any wraparound document to grant them the right to make payments directly to the original lender.

Open-End Loans

An **open-end loan** secures a note executed by the borrower to the lender. It also secures any future advances of funds made by the lender to the borrower. The interest rate on the initial amount borrowed is fixed, but interest on future advances may be charged at the market rate in effect. An open-end loan is often a less costly alternative to a home improvement loan. It allows the borrower to "open" the mortgage or deed of trust to increase the debt to its original amount, or the amount stated in the note, after the debt has been reduced by payments over a period of time. The mortgage usually states a maximum amount that can be secured, the terms and conditions under which the loan can be opened, and the provisions for repayment.

Construction Loans (Interim Financing)

A **construction loan** is made to finance the construction of improvements on real estate such as homes, apartments, and office buildings. The lender commits to the full amount of the loan but disburses the funds in payments during construction. These payments also are known as *draws*. Draws are made to the general contractor for that part of the construction work that has been completed since the previous payment. Before each payment, the lender has the right to inspect the work. The general contractor must provide the lender with adequate waivers that release all mechanic's lien rights for the work covered by the payment.

Construction loans are generally *short-term* or *interim financing*. The borrower pays interest only on the monies that have actually been disbursed. The borrower is expected to arrange for a permanent loan, also known as an *end loan* or *take-out loan*, which will repay or take out the construction financing lender when the work is completed.

Sale-Leaseback

Sale-leaseback arrangements are used to finance large commercial or industrial properties. The land and building, usually used by the seller for business purposes, are sold to an investor. The real estate is then leased back by the investor to the seller, who continues to conduct business on the property as a tenant. The buyer becomes the landlord (lessor), and the original owner becomes the tenant (lessee). This enables a business to free money tied up in real estate to use as working capital.

Buydowns

A **buydown** is a way to temporarily (or permanently) lower the initial interest rate on a mortgage or deed of trust loan. Perhaps a homebuilder wishes to stimulate sales by offering a lower-than-market rate, or a first-time residential buyer may have trouble qualifying for a loan at the prevailing rates. Relatives of the sellers might want to help the buyer qualify. In any case, a lump sum is paid in cash to the lender at the closing. The payment offsets (and so reduces) the interest rate and monthly payments during the mortgage's first few years.

Typical buydown arrangements reduce the interest rate by 1 to 2 percent over the first one to two years of the loan term. After that, the rate rises. The assumption is that the borrower's income will also increase, making it more likely that the borrower will be able to pay the increased monthly payments. In a permanent buydown, a larger up-front payment reduces the effective interest rate for the life of the loan.

Home Equity Loans

Home equity loans are a source of funds using the equity built up in a home. The original mortgage loan remains in place; the home equity loan is junior to the original lien. It is an alternative to refinancing and can be used for a variety of financial needs, such as to

- finance the purchase of expensive items;
- consolidate existing installment loans on credit card debt; and
- pay medical, education, home improvement, or other expenses.

The original mortgage loan remains in place, and the home equity loan is junior to the original lien. If the homeowner refinances, the original mortgage loan is paid off and replaced by a new loan.

A home equity loan can be taken out as a fixed loan amount or as an equity line of credit. With the home equity line of credit, referred to as a HELOC, lenders extend a line of credit that borrowers can use at will. Borrowers receive their money by checks sent to them, deposits made into checking or savings accounts, or a book of drafts they can use up to their credit limits.

IN PRACTICE   The homeowner must consider a number of factors before deciding to secure a home equity loan, including

- the costs involved in obtaining a new mortgage loan or a home equity loan,
- current interest rates,
- total monthly payments, and
- income tax consequences.

■ FINANCING LEGISLATION

The federal government regulates the lending practices of mortgage lenders through the Truth in Lending Act, the Equal Credit Opportunity Act, the Community Reinvestment Act of 1977, and the Real Estate Settlement Procedures Act.

Truth in Lending Act and Regulation Z

Regulation Z, which was enacted pursuant to the **Truth in Lending Act,** by the Federal Trade Commission (FTC), requires that credit institutions inform borrowers of the *true cost of obtaining credit*. With proper disclosures, borrowers can compare the costs of various lenders to avoid the uninformed use of credit. Regardless of the amount, however, Regulation Z applies when a credit transaction is secured by a residence. The regulation does *not* apply to business or commercial loans or to agricultural loans of any amount.

Under the Truth-in-Lending Act, Regulation Z, a consumer must be fully informed of all finance charges and the true interest rate before a transaction is completed. The finance charge disclosure must include any loan fees, finder's fees, service charges, and points, as well as interest. In the case of a mortgage loan made to finance the purchase of a dwelling, the lender must compute and disclose the annual percentage rate (APR).

Creditor A *creditor*, for purposes of Regulation Z, is any person who extends consumer credit more than 25 times each year or more than 5 times each year if the transactions involve dwellings as security. The credit must be subject to a finance charge or payable in more than four installments by written agreement.

Three-day right of rescission In the case of many consumer credit transactions covered by Regulation Z, the borrower has three days in which to rescind the transaction by merely notifying the lender. However, this right of rescission does *not* apply to owner-occupied residential purchase-money, first mortgage, or deed of trust loans. It does, however, apply to refinancing a home mortgage or to a home equity loan.

Advertising Regulation Z provides strict regulation of real estate advertisements in all media (e.g., newspapers, flyers, signs, billboards, Web sites, radio or television ads, direct mailings) that refer to mortgage financing terms. General phrases like "flexible terms available" may be used, but if details are given, they must comply with the act. The APR—which is calculated based on all charges rather than the interest rate alone—must be stated.

Advertisements for buydowns or reduced-rate mortgages must show both the limited term to which the interest rate applies and the annual percentage rate. If a variable-rate mortgage is advertised, the advertisement must include

■ the number and timing of payments;
■ the amount of the largest and smallest payments; and
■ a statement of the fact that the actual payments will vary between these two extremes.

Specific credit terms, such as *down payment, monthly payment, dollar amount of the finance charge,* or *term of the loan* are referred to as **trigger terms**. These terms may not be advertised unless the advertisement includes the following information:

■ Cash price
■ Required down payment
■ Number, amounts, and due dates of all payments
■ Annual percentage rate
■ Total of all payments to be made over the term of the mortgage (unless the advertised credit refers to a first mortgage or deed of trust to finance the acquisition of a dwelling)

Penalties Regulation Z provides penalties for noncompliance. The penalty for violation of an administrative order enforcing Regulation Z is $10,000 for each day the violation continues. A fine of up to $10,000 may be imposed for engaging in an unfair or a deceptive practice. In addition, a creditor may be liable to a consumer for twice the amount of the finance charge, for a minimum of $100 and a maximum of $1,000, plus court costs, attorneys' fees, and any actual damages. Willful violation is a misdemeanor punishable by a fine of up to $5,000, one year's imprisonment, or both.

Equal Credit Opportunity Act (ECOA)

The federal **Equal Credit Opportunity Act (ECOA)** prohibits lenders and others who grant or arrange credit to consumers from discriminating against credit applicants on the basis of

- race,
- color,
- religion,
- national origin,
- sex,
- marital status,
- age (provided the applicant is of legal age), or
- dependence on public assistance.

Furthermore, lenders and other creditors must inform all rejected credit applicants of the principal reasons for the denial or termination of credit. The notice must be provided in writing within 30 days. The ECOA also provides that a borrower is entitled to a copy of the appraisal report if the borrower paid for the appraisal.

Community Reinvestment Act (CRA)

Community reinvestment refers to the responsibility of financial institutions to help meet their communities' needs for low-income and moderate-income housing. In 1977, Congress passed the **Community Reinvestment Act (CRA)**. Under the CRA, financial institutions are expected to meet the deposit and credit needs of their communities; participate and invest in local community development and rehabilitation projects; and participate in loan programs for housing, small businesses, and small farms.

The law requires any federally supervised financial institution to prepare a statement containing

- a definition of the geographic boundaries of its community;
- an identification of the types of community reinvestment credit offered (such as residential housing loans, housing rehabilitation loans, small-business loans, commercial loans, and consumer loans); and
- comments from the public about the institution's performance in meeting its community's needs.

Financial institutions are periodically reviewed by one of three federal financial supervisory agencies: the Comptroller of the Currency, the Federal Reserve's Board of Governors, or the **Federal Deposit Insurance Corporation** (FDIC). The institutions must post a public notice that their community reinvestment activities are subject to federal review, and they must make the results of these reviews public.

Real Estate Settlement Procedures Act (RESPA)

The federal **Real Estate Settlement Procedures Act** (RESPA) applies to any residential real estate transaction involving a new first mortgage loan. RESPA is designed to ensure that buyer and seller are fully informed of all settlement costs.

■ SCORING AND AUTOMATED UNDERWRITING

Automated underwriting procedures can shorten loan approvals from weeks to minutes because once the information is entered, the loan officer can quickly determine what documentation is necessary for that particular loan. Automated underwriting also tends to lower the cost of loan application and approval by reducing lenders' time spent on the approval process. Freddie Mac uses a system called *Loan Prospector*; Fannie Mae's is *Desktop Underwriter*. These systems rely on the borrower's credit report, a paycheck stub, and a drive-by appraisal of the property. Documentation is still required.

Lenders have been using credit scoring systems to predict prospective borrowers' likelihood of default for many years. When used as part of traditional manual evaluation of applicants, credit scoring provides a useful objective standard against which to balance the loan officer's more subjective professional judgment. When used in automated underwriting systems, however, the application of credit scores has become somewhat controversial. Critics of scoring are concerned that they may not be accurate or fair, and in the absence of human discretion, they could result in making it more difficult for low-income and minority borrowers to obtain mortgages.

Freddie Mac has the following to say about automated underwriting:

> *Whether using traditional or automated methods, underwriters must consider all three areas of underwriting—collateral, credit reputation, and capacity. When reviewing collateral, underwriters look at house value, down payment, and property type. Income, debt, cash reserves, and product type are considered when underwriters are looking at capacity. Credit scores are simply one consideration when underwriters are reviewing credit reputation. Even lenders who use an automated underwriting system such as Loan Prospector, still rely on human judgment when the scoring system indicates that the loan application is a higher risk.*

■ SUMMARY

The federal government affects real estate financing money and interest rates through the Federal Reserve Board's discount rate and reserve requirements; it also participates in the secondary mortgage market. The secondary market purchases and holds the loans as investments.

Types of loans available are almost infinite with today's creative lenders. The common ones include fully amortized and straight loans as well as adjustable-rate mortgages, growing-equity mortgages (GEMS), balloon payment mortgages, and reverse mortgages.

Many mortgage and deed of trust loan programs exist, including conventional loans, those insured by the FHA or private mortgage insurance companies, or those guaranteed by the VA. FHA and VA loans must meet certain requirements for the borrower to obtain the benefits of government backing. It is this backing that induces the lender to lend its funds at the good rates FHA and VA purchasers typically enjoy. The interest rates for these loans are often lower than those charged for conventional loans, and other requirements may be less stringent. Consequently, FHA and VA loans are usually very advantageous for those who qualify.

The Farm Service Agency (FSA), formerly Farmers Home Administration, is part of the Department of Agriculture and has the following programs to help families purchase or operate family farms: Rural Housing and Community Development Service (RHCDS), Farm Credit System (Farm Credit), and Farmer Mac (formerly Federal Agricultural Mortgage Corporation).

Other types of real estate financing include seller-financed purchase-money mortgages or deeds of trust, blanket mortgages, package mortgages, wraparound mortgages, open-end mortgages, construction loans, sale-leasebacks, and home equity loans.

Regulation Z implements the federal Truth in Lending Act. This act requires that lenders inform prospective borrowers of all finance charges involved in a loan if real estate is the security. Severe penalties are provided for noncompliance. The federal Equal Credit Opportunity Act prohibits creditors from discriminating against credit applicants on the basis of race, color, religion, national origin, sex, marital status, age, or dependence on public assistance. The Real Estate Settlement Procedures Act requires that lenders inform both buyers and sellers of all fees and charges required for the settlement or closing of residential real estate transactions.

CHAPTER 16 QUIZ

1. The buyers purchased a residence for $195,000. They made a down payment of $25,000 and agreed to assume the seller's existing mortgage, which had a current balance of $123,000. The buyers financed the remaining $47,000 of the purchase price by executing a mortgage and note to the seller. This type of loan by which the seller becomes the mortgagee is called a
   a. wraparound mortgage.
   b. package mortgage.
   c. balloon note.
   d. purchase-money mortgage.

2. A buyer purchased a new residence for $175,000. The buyer made a down payment of $15,000 and obtained a $160,000 mortgage loan. The builder of the house paid the lender 3 percent of the loan balance for the first year and 2 percent for the second year. This represented a total savings for the buyer of $8,000. What type of mortgage arrangement is this?
   a. Wraparound
   b. Package
   c. Blanket
   d. Buydown

3. Which of the following is *NOT* a participant in the secondary market?
   a. Fannie Mae
   b. Ginnie Mae
   c. Credit union
   d. Freddie Mac

4. A buyer purchased a home for cash 30 years ago. Today, the buyer receives monthly checks from a mortgage lender that supplements her income. The buyer *MOST* likely has obtained a(n)
   a. shared-appreciation mortgage.
   b. adjustable-rate mortgage.
   c. reverse mortgage.
   d. overriding deed of trust.

5. Which characteristic of a fixed-rate home loan that is amortized according to the original payment schedule is *TRUE*?
   a. The amount of interest to be paid is predetermined.
   b. The loan cannot be sold in the secondary market.
   c. The monthly payment amount will fluctuate each month.
   d. The interest rate change may be based on an index.

6. When the Federal Reserve Board raises its discount rate, which is likely to happen?
   a. The buyer's points will decrease.
   b. Interest rates will rise.
   c. Mortgage money will become plentiful.
   d. The percentage of ARMs will decrease.

7. In a loan that requires periodic payments that do not fully amortize the loan balance by the final payment, what term *BEST* describes the final payment?
   a. Adjustment
   b. Acceleration
   c. Balloon
   d. Variable

8. A developer received a loan that covers five parcels of real estate and provides for the release of the mortgage lien on each parcel when certain payments are made on the loan. This type of loan arrangement is called a
   a. purchase-money loan.
   b. blanket loan.
   c. package loan.
   d. wraparound loan.

9. Funds for Federal Housing Administration (FHA) loans are usually provided by
   a. the Federal Housing Administration.
   b. the Federal Reserve System.
   c. qualified lenders.
   d. the seller.

373

10. A home is purchased using a fixed-rate, fully amortized mortgage loan. Which statement regarding this mortgage is *TRUE*?
    a. A balloon payment will be made at the end of the loan.
    b. Each mortgage payment amount is the same.
    c. Each mortgage payment reduces the principal by the same amount.
    d. The principal amount in each payment is greater than the interest amount.

11. Which of the following *BEST* defines the secondary market?
    a. Lenders who deal exclusively in second mortgages
    b. Where loans are bought and sold after they have been originated
    c. The major lender of residential mortgages and deeds of trust
    d. The major lender of FHA and VA loans

12. The primary activity of Freddie Mac is to
    a. guarantee mortgages with the full faith and credit of the federal government.
    b. buy and pool blocks of conventional mortgages.
    c. act in tandem with Ginnie Mae to provide special assistance in times of tight money.
    d. buy and sell VA and FHA mortgages.

. 13. A borrower obtains a $100,000 mortgage loan for 30 years at 7.5 percent interest. If the monthly payments of $902.77 are credited first to interest and then to principal, what will be the balance of the principal after the borrower makes the first payment?
    a. $99,772.00
    b. $99,722.23
    c. $99,097.32
    d. $100,000.00

. 14. A buyer borrowed $85,000 to be repaid in monthly installments of $823.76 at 11½ percent annual interest. How much of the buyer's first month's payment was applied to reducing the principal amount of the loan?
    a. $8.15
    b. $9.18
    c. $91.80
    d. $814.58

. 15. If a lender agrees to make a loan based on an 80 percent LTV, what is the amount of the loan if the property appraises for $114,500 and the sales price is $116,900?
    a. $83,200
    b. $91,300
    c. $91,600
    d. $92,900

16. A borrower wanted to negotiate a $113,000 loan. Different lenders in his town offered him the following loans. Which loan would he need to accept to pay the least amount of interest over the life of the loan?
    a. 7 percent amortized over a period of 30 years
    b. 8 percent amortized over a period of 20 years
    c. 9 percent amortized over a period of 15 years
    d. 10 percent amortized over a period of 25 years

17. The difference between the market value and any mortgages the borrower has on the property is *BEST* described by the word
    a. equity.
    b. equitable interest.
    c. equitable title.
    d. equitable lien.

18. Which law requires that all advertising that references mortgage financing terms contain certain disclosures?
    a. Equal Credit Opportunity Act
    b. Truth in Lending Act (Regulation Z)
    c. Community Reinvestment Act
    d. Fair Housing Act

19. Which statement is *TRUE* regarding truth in lending (Regulation Z)?

    a. Finance charges that must be disclosed include loan fees, service charges, and discount points.

    b. If a borrower is refinancing, Regulation Z states that the borrower has five days to rescind the transaction by merely notifying the lender.

    c. If an advertisement discloses the interest rate, then it has met truth-in-lending requirements.

    d. For the purposes of Regulation Z, a creditor is a person who extends consumer credit more than five times each year.

20. In order to assist a prospective buyer who lacked a down payment on their property, Mr. and Mrs. Seller agreed to "take back paper" at the closing for a part of the purchase price. The document *MOST* likely used would be a

    a. reverse annuity mortgage.

    b. package mortgage.

    c. purchase-money mortgage.

    d. shared appreciation mortgage.

(14) 85K × 11.5 = 9775/12 = 814.58   823.76 - 814.58 = $9.18

Leases

■ **LEARNING OBJECTIVES** *When you've finished reading this chapter, you should be able to*

■ **identify** the four types of leasehold estates;

■ **describe** the requirements and general conditions of a valid lease and how a lease may be discharged;

■ **explain** the rights of landlords and tenants in an eviction proceeding and the effect of pro-tenant legislation and civil rights laws on the landlord-tenant relationship;

■ **distinguish** the various types of leases; and

■ **define** the following *key terms*

actual eviction	holdover tenancy	nondisturbance clause
assignment	implied warranty of	percentage lease
cash rent	habitability	rental-finding service
constructive eviction	lease	renewal option
estate at sufferance	leasehold estate	reversionary right
estate at will	lease purchase	right of first refusal
estate for years	lessee	security deposit
estate from period to	lessor	sharecropping
period	letter of intent	sublease
gross lease	month-to-month tenancy	
ground lease	net lease	

LEASES

By the end of 2009, more than 36 million occupied residential units were rentals. Although some owners manage their own properties (a real estate license is not required to do so), most are professionally managed. In many states, property managers are required to hold a real estate or property manager license. Real estate licensees should be aware of their local rental market to better assist buyers who may not qualify to buy their own property, to locate an appropriate property for an investor-buyer, or to manage their own portfolios. In any case, real estate licensees should be aware of leases, management agreements, landlord-tenant issues, and more.

LEASING REAL ESTATE

A **lease** is a contract between an owner of real estate (the **lessor**) and a tenant (the **lessee**). It is a contract to transfer the lessor's rights to exclusive possession and use of the property to the tenant for a specified period of time. The lease establishes the length of time the contract is to run and the amount the lessee is to pay for use of the property. Other rights and obligations of the parties may be set forth as well.

In effect, the lease agreement combines two contracts. It is a conveyance of an interest in the real estate and a contract to pay rent and assume other obligations. The lessor grants the lessee the right to occupy the real estate and use it for purposes stated in the lease. In return, the landlord receives payment for use of the premises and retains a **reversionary right** to possession after the lease term expires. The lessor's interest is called a *leased fee estate plus reversionary right*.

| In Illinois | The statute of frauds in Illinois requires that lease agreements be in writing to be enforceable if they are for *more than one year*. The written rule also applies to leases for one year or less that will not be performed within one year of the contract date. Verbal leases for one year or less that *can* be performed within a year of their making are enforceable. Written leases should be signed by both lessor and lessee. ∎

LEASEHOLD ESTATES

A tenant's right to possess real estate for the term of the lease is called a **leasehold** (less-than-freehold) **estate.** A leasehold is generally considered personal property. Just as there are several types of freehold (ownership) estates, there are different kinds of leasehold estates. (See Figure 17.1.)

Estate for Years

An **estate** (tenancy) **for years** is a leasehold estate that continues for a *definite period of time*. That period may be years, months, weeks, or even days. An estate for years (sometimes referred to as fixed term tenancy) always has specific beginning and ending dates.

FIGURE   17.1

Leasehold Estates

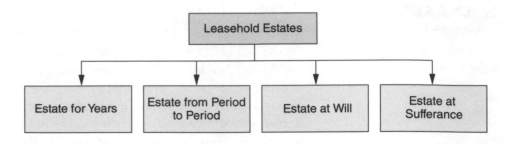

When the estate expires, the lessee is required to vacate the premises and surrender possession to the lessor. No notice is required to terminate the estate for years because the lease agreement states a specific expiration date. When the expiration date comes, the lease expires, and the tenant's rights are extinguished.

Tenancy for years = Any definite period

If both parties agree, the estate for years may be terminated before the expiration date. Otherwise, neither party may terminate without showing that the lease agreement has been breached. Any extension of the tenancy requires that a new contract be negotiated.

As is characteristic of all leases, a tenancy for years gives the lessee the right to occupy and use the leased property according to the terms and covenants contained in the lease agreement. It must be remembered that a lessee has the right to use the premises for the entire lease term. That right is unaffected by the original lessor's death or sale of the property unless the lease states otherwise. If the original lease provides for an option to renew, no further negotiation is required; the tenant merely exercises his option.

Estate from Period to Period

Periodic tenancy = *Indefinite term; automatically renewing*

An **estate from period to period,** or *periodic tenancy,* is created when the landlord and tenant enter into an agreement for an indefinite time. That is, the lease does not contain a specific expiration date. Such a tenancy is created for a specific payment period—for instance, month to month, week to week, or year to year—but continues *indefinitely* until proper notice of termination is given. Rent is payable at *definite* intervals. A periodic tenancy is characterized by continuity because it is *automatically renewable under the original terms of the agreement until one of the parties gives notice to terminate.* In effect, the payment and acceptance of rent extend the lease for another period. A **month-to-month tenancy,** for example, is created when a tenant takes possession with no definite termination date and pays monthly rent.

An estate from period to period also might be created when a tenant with an estate for years remains in possession, or holds over, after the lease term expires. If no new lease agreement has been made, a **holdover tenancy** is created. The landlord's acceptance of rent usually is considered conclusive proof of acceptance of the periodic (holdover) tenancy. The courts customarily rule that a tenant who holds over can do so for a term equal to the term of the original lease, provided the period is for one year or less. For example, a tenant with a lease for six months would be entitled to a new six-month tenancy. However, if the original lease were for five years, the holdover tenancy could not exceed one year. Some leases stipulate that in the absence of a renewal agreement, a tenant who holds over does so as a month-to-month tenant.

| In Illinois |

In Illinois, a holdover tenancy is for the same term as the estate from period to period. ■

To *terminate* a periodic estate, either the landlord or the tenant must give proper notice. The form and timing of the notice are usually established by state statute. Normally, the notice must be given *one period in advance*. That is, to terminate an estate from week to week, one week's notice is required; to terminate an estate from month to month, one month's notice is required. For an estate from year to year, however, the requirements vary from two to six months' notice.

| In Illinois |

The following notices are required by Illinois statute:

- *Tenancy from year to year*—At least 60 days' written notice is required at any time within the four-month period prior to the last 60 days of the lease period.
- *Tenancy from month to month*—In any periodic estate having a term of less than year to year but greater than week to week, 30 days' written notice is required.
- *Tenancy from week to week*—Seven days' written notice is required.
- *Farm tenancies from year to year*—Parties must give at least four months' written notice to terminate and may do so only at the end of the period. To vacate March 1, farm tenancy notice must be given by November 1. ■

Estate at Will

> **Tenancy at will** = *Indefinite term; possession with landlord's consent*

An **estate (tenancy) at will** gives the tenant the right to possess property *with the landlord's consent* for an unspecified or uncertain term. An estate at will is a tenancy of indefinite duration; it continues until it is terminated by either party giving proper notice. No definite initial period is specified, as is the case in a periodic tenancy. An estate at will is automatically terminated by the death of either the landlord or the tenant. It may be created by express agreement or by operation of law. During the existence of a tenancy at will, the tenant has all the rights and obligations of a lessor-lessee relationship, including the duty to pay rent at regular intervals.

As a practical matter, tenancy at will is rarely used in a written agreement and is viewed skeptically by the courts. It is usually interpreted as a periodic tenancy, with the period being defined by the interval of rental payments.

Estate at Sufferance

> **Tenancy at sufferance** = Tenant's previously lawful possession continued without landlord's consent

An **estate (tenancy) at sufferance** arises when a tenant who lawfully possessed real property continues in possession of the premises *without* the landlord's consent after the rights expire. This is also known as a holdover. This estate can arise when a tenant for years fails to surrender possession at the lease's expiration and continues until the landlord completes the eviction process, or when a tenant is in breach of the lease. A tenancy at sufferance also can occur by operation of law when a borrower continues in possession after a foreclosure sale and beyond the redemption period's expiration.

In Illinois	A landlord has the option of considering an estate at sufferance (a holdover tenant's action) as being a willful withholding of possession, in which case the landlord is entitled to charge double rent. ■

■ LEASE AGREEMENTS

Most states require no special wording to establish the landlord-tenant relationship. The lease may be written, oral, or implied, depending on the circumstances and the requirements of the statute of frauds. The law of the state where the real estate is located must be followed to ensure the validity of the lease.

Requirements of a Valid Lease

A lease is a form of contract. To be valid, a lease must meet essentially the same requirements as any other contract:

The elements of a valid lease can be remembered by the acronym **CLOAC**: **C**apacity, **L**egal objective, **O**ffer and **A**cceptance, and **C**onsideration

- *Capacity to contract*—The parties must have the legal capacity to contract.
- *Legal objectives*—The objectives of the lease must be legal.
- *Offer and acceptance*—The parties must reach a mutual agreement on all the terms of the contract.
- *Consideration*—The lease must be supported by valid consideration. Rent is the normal consideration given for the right to occupy the leased premises. However, the payment of rent is not essential as long as consideration was granted in creating the lease itself. Sometimes, for instance, this consideration is labor performed on the property. Because a lease is a contract, it is not subject to subsequent changes in the rent or other terms unless these changes are in writing and executed in the same manner as the original lease.

The leased premises should be clearly described. The legal description of the real estate should be used if the lease covers land, such as a ground lease. If the lease is for a part of a building, such as an apartment, the space itself or the apartment designation should be described specifically. If supplemental space is to be included, the lease should clearly identify it.

IN PRACTICE   Preprinted lease agreements are usually better suited to residential leases. Commercial leases are generally more complex, have different legal requirements, and may include complicated calculations of rent and maintenance costs. **Letters of intent** are often prepared in advance of a commercial lease by the licensees representing the respective parties. This letter of intent generally sets forth the basic agreement between the parties that both parties' attorneys can then use to prepare the lease from. Drafting a commercial lease or a complex residential lease should be done by a licensed attorney.

F I G U R E 17.2

Sample Lease Agreement

This lease form is intended for properties to which the Chicago Residential Landlord and Tenant Ordinance is applicable. However, the Chicago Association of Realtors© recommends that the Ordinance be carefully reviewed and that an attorney be consulted before using this or any other standard lease form for properties in the City of Chicago.

INSTRUCTIONS TO TENANT: Please sign and return both copies to Landlord. Your copy will be mailed back to you.

REV. 2008 CHICAGO ASSOCIATION OF REALTORS©
ALL RIGHTS RESERVED

NOT FURNISHED **CHICAGO APARTMENT LEASE**

DATE OF LEASE	TERM OF LEASE		MONTHLY RENT	SECURITY DEPOSIT*
	BEGINNING	ENDING		

*IF NONE, WRITE "NONE" and Section 5 of Lease Agreements and Covenants shall then be INAPPLICABLE.

ADDITIONAL CHARGES AND FEES*			
Late Charge $ _____	Returned Check Charge $_____	Reletting Charge $ _____	Monthly Parking Fee $_____
Monthly Condominium Association Fee $_____	Monthly Storage Fee $_____	Property Management Administrative Fee $ _____	Monthly Rent Due Upon Lease Execution $ _____

*IF NONE, WRITE "NONE".

TENANT:	LANDLORD:
NAME(S):	NAME:
ADDRESS: STREET: UNIT #: CITY: STATE: ZIP:	ADDRESS: STREET: UNIT #: CITY: STATE: ZIP:
TELEPHONE #:	TELEPHONE #:
NAMES OF PERSONS AUTHORIZED TO OCCUPY PREMISES:	PERSON AUTHORIZED TO ACT ON BEHALF OF LANDLORD FOR PURPOSE OF SERVICE OR PROCESS AND RECEIPT OF NOTICES: ☐ Check box if same address as above
	NAME:
ADDRESS OF LEASED APARTMENT (the "Premises"):	ADDRESS: STREET: UNIT #: CITY: STATE: ZIP:
ADDRESS: STREET: UNIT #: CITY: STATE: ZIP:	TELEPHONE #:

ADDITIONAL AGREEMENTS AND COVENANTS (INCLUDING DECORATING, REPAIRS AND CONDOMINIUM BYLAWS, IF ANY)

* IF NONE, WRITE "NONE".

NOTICE OF CONDITIONS AFFECTING HABITABILITY

I hereby acknowledge that Landlord has disclosed any code violations, code enforcement litigation and/or compliance board proceedings during the previous 12 months for the Premises and the Building and any notice from utility providers of intent to terminate utility services, copies of which, if any, are attached to this Lease.

_____(Tenant(s) Initials)

FURTHER ACKNOWLEDGMENTS BY TENANT

Tenant hereby acknowledges that as of the Date of Lease, Tenant has received from Landlord the following documents:

☐ Security Deposit Receipt _____ (Tenant(s) initials)

☐ Heating Cost Disclosure Statement _____ (Tenant(s) initials)

☐ Rules of Building from Property Manager and/or Condominium Association _____ (Tenant(s) initials)

☐ Lead-Based Paint Brochure: *Protect Your Family From Lead in Your Home* _____ (Tenant(s) initials)

In consideration of the mutual agreements and covenants set forth in this Lease, and in further consideration of the statements made by Tenant in the application for Lease and all supporting documents thereto, including Tenant's financial statements (if any), the truth and accuracy thereof being attested to by Tenant and the information therein contained being incorporated into this Lease as if set forth herein in full, Landlord hereby leases to Tenant, and Tenant hereby leases from Landlord, for use as a private dwelling unit only, the Premises, together with the fixtures and appliances belonging thereto, for the Term. If there is more than one undersigned Tenant, the term "Tenant", as used herein, shall include all of such undersigned persons and each and every provision of this Lease shall be binding on each and every one of the undersigned persons and they shall be jointly and severally liable hereunder and Landlord shall have the right to join one or all of them in any proceeding or to proceed against them in any order.

TENANT:		LANDLORD:	
Name	Date	Name	Date
Name	Date	Name	Date

FIGURE 17.2

Sample Lease Agreement (continued)

LEASE AGREEMENTS AND COVENANTS

1. **RENT**: Tenant shall pay to Landlord at the above address (or such other address as Landlord may designate in writing) the Monthly Rent set forth above on or before the first day of each month of the Term in advance. The Monthly Rent, Monthly Storage Fee and Monthly Parking Fee, and all other rental fees due and payable under this Lease, if any, shall hereinafter be referred to collectively as "Rent". The time of each and every payment of Rent is deemed to be of the essence of this Lease. To cover Landlord's added costs resulting from late payments, the Rent set forth above shall be increased by the amount set forth above as "Late Charge" if paid after the 5th day of the month. To cover Landlord's added costs for processing of checks that are dishonored or are returned due to insufficient funds in the account, Rent shall be increased by the amount set forth above as "Returned Check Charge." Rent mailed in shall be deemed paid on date of receipt by Landlord. If Tenant fails to pay Rent within 5 days after receipt of written notice from Landlord that such Rent is overdue, Landlord may terminate this Lease or pursue any other rights and remedies of Landlord at law or in equity.

2. **POSSESSION**: On or prior to the Beginning Date of this Lease, Landlord shall deliver possession of the Premises to Tenant. Possession shall be deemed to have been delivered to Tenant on the day that Landlord either (A) actually delivers to Tenant keys to the Premises or (B) makes available to Tenant at the office of the Building or at such other place as designated by Landlord keys to the Premises. If Landlord cannot deliver possession of the Premises to Tenant on or prior to the Beginning Date of the Term, this Lease shall remain in full force and effect with Rent abated until such time as the Premises is available for Tenant's occupancy, unless Tenant elects to maintain an action for possession of the Premises, or, upon written notice to Landlord, elects to terminate this Lease.

3. **APPLICATION**: The application for this Lease and all representations and promises contained therein are hereby made a part of this Lease. Tenant warrants that the information given by Tenant in the application is true. If such information is false, Landlord may at Landlord's option terminate this Lease by giving Tenant not less than 10 days prior written notice, which shall be Landlord's sole remedy. Tenant shall be responsible for any and all Rent which accrues under this Lease prior to the termination date.

4. **PROMISES OF THE PARTIES**: The terms and conditions contained herein shall be conclusively deemed the agreement between Tenant and Landlord and no modification, waiver or amendment of this Lease or any of its terms, conditions or covenants shall be binding upon the parties unless made in writing and signed by the party sought to be bound.

5. **SECURITY DEPOSIT**: Tenant has deposited with Landlord the Security Deposit in the amount set forth above for the performance of each and every covenant and agreement to be performed by Tenant under this Lease. Landlord shall have the right, but not the obligation, to apply the Security Deposit in whole or in part as payment of such amounts as are covenants or agreements contained herein. Landlord's right to possession of the Premises for non-payment of Rent by Tenant or any other reason shall not be affected by the fact that Landlord is holding the Security Deposit. Tenant's liability is not limited to the amount of the Security Deposit. Within 30 days after Landlord's application of the Security Deposit, or any part thereof, Landlord shall give Tenant written notice of such application. If the application is on account of maintenance, repairs or replacements necessitated by Tenant, Landlord's notice shall include the estimated or actual cost of the same, attaching estimates or paid receipts. Upon receipt of Landlord's notice, Tenant shall at once pay to Landlord an amount sufficient to restore the Security Deposit in full. Upon termination of this Lease, full payment of all amounts due and performance of all Tenant's covenants and agreements (including surrender of the Premises in accordance with Section 15), the Security Deposit or any portion thereof remaining unapplied shall be returned to Tenant in accordance with applicable law. The Security Deposit shall not be deemed, construed or allocated by Tenant as payment of Rent for any month of the Term.

6. **LANDLORD'S MAINTENANCE OBLIGATIONS**:

A. Tenant hereby declares that Tenant has inspected the Premises, the Building and all related areas and grounds and that Tenant is satisfied with the physical condition thereof. Tenant agrees that no representations, warranties (expressed or Implied) or covenants with respect to the condition, maintenance or improvements of the Premises, the Building, or other areas have been made to Tenant except (1) those contained In this Lease or otherwise In writing signed by Landlord and (2) those provided under applicable law.

B. Landlord agrees that Landlord will perform work required to be performed by Landlord under this Lease within a reasonable time not to exceed 30 days from the Beginning Date hereof.

C. Landlord covenants that all times during the Term, Landlord shall maintain the Premises and the Building (if Landlord owns and/or has control over the owners of the Building) to the following minimum standards:

(1) Effective weather protection, including unbroken windows and doors;
(2) Plumbing facilities in good working order;
(3) A water supply which either under the control of Tenant is capable of producing hot and cold running water, or under the control of Landlord produces hot and cold running water, furnished to appropriate fixtures, and connected to a sewerage system;
(4) Heating (and, if furnished, air cond'tioning and ventilation) facilities in good working order which, if under the control of Tenant, are capable of producing, or, if under the control of Landlord, produce heat (and, if furnished, air conditioning and ventilation) in fixtures provided (and no others) within reasonable accepted tolerances and during reasonable hours. (In the case of heat, minimum tolerances shall be those established by the governing municipal code or ordinance);
(5) Gas and/or electrical appliances which are supplied by Landlord in good working order, and appropriate gas piping and electrical wiring system to the extent existing in the Building maintained in good working order and sale condition;
(6) Building, grounds and areas under the control of Landlord in clean, sanitary and safe condition free from all accumulations of debris, filth, rubbish, garbage, rodents and vermin;
(7) Adequate and appropriate receptacle(s) for garbage and rubbish, and, if under the control of Landlord, in clean condition and good repair;
(8) Floors, stairways, and railings and common areas in good repair;
(9) Apartment floors, walls and ceilings in good repair and safe condition; and
(10) Elevators (it existing) in good repair and safe condition.

D. It is, however understood and agreed that the Building is a physical structure subject to aging, wear, tear, abuse, inherent defects, and numerous forces causing disrepair or breakdown beyond Landlord's reasonable control, and that components and skilled workmen are not always immediately available. Landlords costs of operation are fixed and unavoidable and to permit rent abatement or damages to Tenant would create an intolerable burden on Landlord, other tenants and the surrounding neighborhood. It is, therefore, understood and agreed that breakdowns of equipment or disrepair caused by (1) conditions caused by Tenant, members of Tenant's household, guests or other persons who enter or occupy the Premises with Tenant's consent; (2) Tenant's unreasonable refusal of or other interference with entry of Landlord or Landlord's workmen or contractors into the Premises or the Building for purposes of correcting defective conditions; (3) lack of reasonable opportunity for Landlord to correct defective conditions; or (4) conditions beyond Landlord's reasonable control, including strikes or lockouts. In any action against Landlord for breach of the Lease or the covenants contained herein with respect to Landlord's obligations to maintain the Building and/or the Premises, Landlord may assert, as a defense to such claim, that Landlord did not have actual knowledge of such defective conditions.

7. **UTILITIES**: Unless otherwise agreed in writing, if the Premises is separately metered for utilities, Tenant shall pay the utility company or authorized metering agency directly for all applicable charges for gas, electricity, water and other utilities serving the Premises, including, if applicable, telephone, internet, cable, and current used for electric heating, ventilation, air conditioning, hot water, etc., as such charges become due and payable. If Tenant fails to timely pay the utility companies for the use of such utilities, Landlord shall have the right, but not the obligation, to pay such utility companies directly, in which event Tenant shall reimburse Landlord for such costs, including any late fees, upon demand. Unless otherwise agreed in writing, if the Premises are not separately metered for utilities, Tenant shall reimburse Landlord, no more than once per month, for all utilities consumed by Tenant in the Premises during the Term within 10 days after Landlord delivers a statement to Tenant setting forth Tenant's share of the costs for such utilities, which statement shall include invoices, receipts or other documentation setting forth such costs in reasonable detail.

8. **TENANT'S USE OF PREMISES**: The Premises shall be occupied solely for residential purposes by Tenant, those other persons specifically listed on the first page of this Lease, if any, and any children which may be born to or legally adopted by Tenant during the Term. Neither Tenant nor any of those persons shall perform nor permit any practice that may damage the reputation of or otherwise be injurious to the Premises, the Building or the neighborhood, or be disturbing to other tenants, be illegal, or increase the rate of insurance on the Premises or the Building.

9. **TENANT'S MAINTENANCE OBLIGATIONS**: Tenant covenants and agrees to perform the following obligations during the Term: (A) maintain the Premises and appurtenances in a clean, sanitary and safe condition; (B) dispose of all rubbish, garbage and other waste in a clean, sanitary and timely manner from the Premises into the refuse receptacles provided; (C) properly use and operate all appliances, electrical, gas and plumbing fixtures within the Premises; (0) not place in the Premises or the Building any furniture, plants, animals, or any other things which harbor insects, rodents, or other pests; (E) keep out of the Premises and the Building materials which cause a fire hazard or safety hazard and comply with all reasonable requirements of Landlord's fire insurance carrier; (F) not destroy, deface, damage, impair nor remove any part of the Building, the Premises or facilities, equipment or appurtenances thereto; (G) maintain the smoke detector and carbon monoxide detector, if any, in the Premises in accordance with applicable law, and (H) prevent any person in the Premises or the Building with Tenant's permission from violating any of the foregoing obligations of Tenant. Tenant shall not suffer or commit any waste in or about the Premises or the Building and shall, at Tenant's expense, keep the Premises in good order and repair (except with respect to the maintenance obligations of Landlord under this Lease). On termination of this Lease, Tenant shall return the Premises to Landlord in the condition that the Premises was in as of the Beginning Date, reasonable wear excepted.

10. **ALTERATIONS, ADDITIONS, FIXTURES, APPLIANCES, PERSONAL PROPERTY**: Tenant shall make no alterations or additions nor install, attach, connect or construct in the Premises or any part of the Building, interior or exterior, major appliances or devices of any kind without, in each and every instance, first receiving the written consent of Landlord, and then, if such consent is granted, only upon the terms and conditions specified in such written consent. All alterations, additions and fixtures (including security devices) whether temporary or permanent in character, made by Landlord or Tenant, in or upon the Premises shall, unless otherwise agreed to in writing or unless Landlord requests their removal prior to the Ending Date, become Landlord's properly and shall remain in the Premises at the termination of the Lease without compensation to Tenant. The foregoing notwithstanding, neither Landlord's nor Tenant's insurance carriers shall be liable to Tenant for the replacement of such alterations, additions, or fixtures in the event of casualty loss unless Tenant notifies Landlord of the replacement value and pays, as additional rent, the resultant premium increase, if any. If Landlord shall permit or demand removal, Tenant shall put that part of the Premises into the same condition as existed prior to the installation of such alteration, addition, or fixture.

11. **ACCESS**: Landlord reserves the right in accordance herewith to enter the Premises in order to inspect same, make necessary or agreed repairs, decorations, alterations, or improvements, supply necessary or agreed services, or exhibit the Premises to prospective or actual purchasers, mortgagees, tenants, workmen, or contractors, or as is otherwise necessary in the operation and/or protection of the Premises, the Building, its components or persons therein. At Landlord's discretion, Landlord shall be provided with and may retain and use copies of any keys necessary for access to the Premises. In the event of apparent or actual emergency, Landlord may enter the Premises at any time without notice. At any time within 90 days prior to the end of the Term, after a single general written notice, Landlord may as often as necessary show the Premises for rent any day between the hours of 9 AM and 8 PM on not less than 15-minute verbal or written specific notice to Tenant or other occupant of the Premises. At other times, Landlord shall only enter the Premises at times mutually agreed upon between Landlord and Tenant; however, if entry at such times is impractical or refused, Landlord may enter the Premises after 24 hours' notice and only during the period of 7 AM to 7 PM Monday through Saturday. In the event of the willful or negligent breach of this Section 11, the non-breaching party shall at once be entitled to actual damages or liquidated damages in the amount of 2 months of the then-current Monthly Rent and an injunction, if necessary, to prevent continuation of such breach.

12. **SUBLETTING AND RE-LETTING**:

A. In no event shall Tenant assign this Lease or sublet the Premises without, in each instance, first receiving the prior written consent of Landlord. Tenant may only assign this Lease or sublet the Premises if all of the following conditions are met: (1) Tenant is not then in default under the terms of this Lease, (2) Landlord consents to the prospective new tenant in writing, and (3) Tenant upon demand pays, in advance, (a) the deficiency, if any, that exists between the aggregate rent being paid as a result of such assignment or subletting and the Rent that is due and owing Landlord under this Lease for the balance of the Term, and (b) ell permissible expenses of Landlord on account of such assignment or subletting, if any, including, but not limited to, decorating, repairs, replacements, commissions and/or administrative fees for performing the details attendant to such a transaction in the amount set forth above as the 'Reletting Charge.' Landlord, at Landlord's option, shall determine whether Tenant's transfer of interest in the Lease or the Premises shall be treated as a subletting, assignment or re-letting. In the event of a subletting or assignment, Tenant shall still be liable for all of the terms and conditions required of Tenant to be performed under this Lease. In the event of a re-letting, this Lease shall terminate as of the date of such re-letting and Tenant shall have no further obligations hereunder, except for those obligations that expressly survive termination of this Lease.

B. Landlord may at any time and for any reason reject any prospective new tenant offered by Tenant or by others; provided, however, that if Landlord shall do so without cause, Tenant shall be liable to Landlord only for the deficiency and/or actual or estimated expenses described in A(2) (a) and (b) of this Section 12 which would have been due from Tenant had the prospective new tenant been accepted. Cause shall be deemed to be the failure, based on information and data made available to Landlord (or lack thereof), of such prospective new tenant to meet the criteria customarily employed by Landlord to evaluate the acceptability of prospects as tenants for similar apartments in the Building. During the last 3 months of the Term, Landlord shall be obligated to accept an otherwise qualified prospective new tenant only If said prospective new tenant enters into a direct lease with Landlord for a term for which leases are customarily offered for similar apartments in the Building. Landlord may fill other vacancies in the Building first before re-letting or subletting or attempting to re-let or sublet the Premises.

C. Tenant shall neither sublet the Premises nor any part thereof nor assign this Lease nor permit by any act or default or any transfer of Tenant's interest in the Premises or this Lease by operation of law or otherwise, nor offer the Premises or any part thereof for lease or sublease except in accordance with the terms and conditions of this Section 12. Any attempted transfer by Tenant in violation of the terms of this Section 12 shall be voidable by Landlord.

13. **ABANDONMENT**: Tenant shall not abandon the Premises, nor permit the Premises to remain vacant or unoccupied for a period of time which could be construed as abandonment under state or local law or ordinance. Tenant shall not allow persons other than those authorized by this Lease to occupy the Premises as guests for periods in excess of 7 consecutive days during the Term for any reason.

14. **FIRE AND CASUALTY**:

A. If the Premises and/or the Building is damaged or destroyed by fire or casualty, and the Premises is only partially damaged and is inhabitable, and Landlord makes full repairs within 90 days, this Lease shall continue without abatement or apportionment of rent; or

B. If the Premises is damaged or destroyed by fire or casualty and (1) the Premises is rendered uninhabitable, (2) continued occupancy would be illegal, or (3) Landlord cannot or does not repair within 90 days, then Landlord may. at Landlord's option, (1) terminate this Lease or (2) relocate Tenant to another comparable apartment in the Building until repair and restoration of the Premises is completed. If Landlord cannot or does not repair within 90 days, Tenant's sole remedy shall be to vacate the Premises (or substitute premises) and notify Landlord in writing within 5 days thereafter of Tenant's intent to terminate this Lease, in which event this Lease shell terminate as of the date Tenant vacates the Premises and all prepaid rent and unapplied Security Deposit shall be returned to Tenant.

C. In the event that a fire or casualty causes damage or destruction to the Premises, nothing in this Section 14 shall be construed to limit the rights and remedies available to Tenant under state and local laws and ordinances governing fire and casualty damage in buildings like the Building.

15. **TERMINATION AND RETURN OF POSSESSION**:

A. Upon the termination of this Lease, whether by lapse of time or otherwise, or upon termination of Tenant's right of possession without termination of this Lease, Tenant shall immediately vacate and surrender possession of the Premises to Landlord and deliver all keys to Landlord at the place where Rent is payable, or as otherwise directed by Landlord. The mere retention of possession of the Premises after termination of this Lease or termination of Tenant's right of possession of the Premises shall constitute a forcible detainer, and Landlord shall have the right and license with process of law (and if Tenant abandons the Premises, Tenant grants Landlord and Landlord shall have such right and license without process of law) to enter into the Premises, to have the Premises returned to Landlord as Landlord's former estate and to take possession of the Premises and to expel and remove Tenant, and any others who may be occupying or within the Premises, and any personal property within the Premises from the Premises without relinquishing Landlord's right to Rent or any other right given to Landlord under this Lease or by operation of law. If Tenant abandons the Premises and Landlord exercises the right and license to enter without process of law, Landlord r may use such force as may be necessary without being deemed in any manner guilty of trespass, eviction, or forcible entry or detainer.

B. Tenant agrees that in the event Tenant fails to vacate and surrender the Premises upon termination of this Lease or Tenant's right of possession of the Premises that:

(1) Tenant shall pay as liquidated damages for the entire time that possession is withheld a sum equal to the greater of (i) three times the amount of rent herein reserved, pro rated per day of such withholding, or (ii) Landlord's actual damages if same are ascertainable; or

(2) Landlord, at its sole option, may, upon giving Tenant written notice, extend the Term of this Lease for a like period of time not to exceed one year at such rent as Landlord has stated prior to said termination date; or

(3) If Landlord fails to notify Tenant or Landlord's election under either (1) or (2) of this Section 15 within 45 days of the termination of this Lease or the termination of Tenant's right of possession, Tenant's continued occupancy shall be for a month-to-month term.

C. No action or non-action by Landlord except as expressly provided herein shall operate as a waiver of Landlord's right to terminate this Lease or Tenant's right of possession, nor operate to extend the Term.

16. **EMINENT DOMAIN (CONDEMNATION)**: If the whole or any substantial part of the Building is taken or condemned by any competent authority for any public use or purpose, or if any adjacent property or street shall be so condemned or improved in such a manner as to require the use of any part of the Building, the Term of this Lease shall, at the option of Landlord or the condemning authority, be terminated upon, and not before, the date when possession of the part so taken shall be required for such use or purpose, and Landlord shell be entitled to receive the entire award without apportionment with Tenant. Rent shall be apportioned as of the date when Tenant vacates the Premises and possession of the part of the Building so taken is transferred to the condemning authority.

17. **LANDLORD'S MORTGAGE**: This Lease is not to be recorded and is, and shall hereafter be deemed to be, subordinate to any present or future mortgages on the real estate (or any part of It) upon which the Building is situated and to all advances upon the security of such mortgages.

18. LEASE BINDING ON HEIRS, ETC: All the covenants and agreements of this Lease shall be binding upon and inure to the benefit of the heirs, executors, administrators, successors, and assigns of Landlord and Tenant, subject to the restrictions set forth in Section 12 hereof, except that where there are only one or two persons named or remaining as Tenant herein, then, in the event of the death of one or both Tenants, the surviving Tenant and/or the heirs or legal representatives of the deceased Tenant may terminate this Lease effective as of the last day any calendar month within 120 days of said occurrence by delivering to Landlord not less than 45 days prior written notice.

19. **NOTICES**: Except as herein provided, any demand to be made or notice to be served, including those provided by statute, shall be construed to mean notice in writing signed by or on behalf of the party giving same, and served upon the other party (A) in person, or (B) by certified or registered mail, return receipt requested, postage prepaid, al the address herein set forth or at such other address as either party may designate by written notice to the other. Notice by mail shall be deemed given, served and effective at the time deposited Into the United Slates Mail, regardless of when received. Notice served in person on Tenant may be served if left with some person residing in or in possession of the Premises above the age of 12 years, and in the event of an apparent abandonment, notice may be served by posting same on the door of the Premises in addition to service by mail in accordance herewith, Notices served in person on Landlord may be served on any office employee of Landlord, or, if Landlord receives Rent at Landlord's home, in the same manner as on Tenant.

20. **RULES AND REGULATIONS**: The rules and regulations at the end of this Lease shall be a part of this Lease. Tenant covenants and agrees to keep and observe these rules and regulations. Tenant also covenants and agrees to keep and observe such further reasonable rules and regulations as may later be promulgated by Landlord or Landlord's agent for the necessary, proper and orderly care of the Building (provided such later rules do not materially change the terms contained in the body of this Lease).

FIGURE 17.2

Sample Lease Agreement (continued)

21. TENANT TO INSURE POSSESSIONS / LIMITATIONS OF LANDLORD LIABILITY: Landlord is not an insurer of Tenant's person or possessions. Tenant agrees that all of Tenant's person and property in the Premises or elsewhere in the Building shall be at the risk of Tenant only and that Tenant will carry such insurance as Tenant deems necessary therefor. Tenant further agrees that except for instances of negligence or willful misconduct of Landlord, Landlord's agents or employees (collectively, the "Landlord Parties"), the Landlord Parties shall not be liable for any damage to the person or property of Tenant or any other person occupying, visiting or entering the Premises or the Building, sustained due to the Premises or the Building or any part thereof or any appurtenances thereof becoming out of repair (as example and not by way of limitation), due to damage caused by water, snow, ice, frost, steam, fire, sewer gas or odors; heating, cooling, and ventilating equipment, bursting leaking pipes, faucets, and plumbing fixtures; mechanical breakdown or failure; electrical failure; the misuse or non operation of observation cameras or devices (if any), master or central television equipment and antennas (if any), cable television equipment (If any) or mailboxes; or due to the happening of any accident in or about the Building; or due to any act or neglect of any other tenant or occupant of the Building or any other person. Further, Landlord shall not be liable to Tenant for any damage to the person or property of Tenant sustained due to, arising out of, or caused by, the acts or omissions of any third party whether or not such third party Is a tenant of the Building.

22. REMEDIES CUMULATIVE, NON-WAIVER: All rights and remedies given to Tenant or to Landlord shall be distinct, separate and cumulative, and the use of one or more thereof shall not exclude or waive any other right or remedy allowed by law, unless specifically limited or waived in this Lease. No waiver of any breach or default of either party hereunder shall be implied from any omission by the other party to take any action on account of a similar or different breach or default. The payment or acceptance of money after it falls due after knowledge of any breach of this Lease by Landlord or Tenant, or after the termination in any way of the Term or of Tenant's right of possession hereunder, or after the service of any notice, or after the commencement of any suit, or after final judgment for possession of the Premises shall not reinstate, continue or extend the Term of this Lease nor affect any such notice, demand or suit or any right hereunder not expressly waived. No express waiver shall affect any breach other than the breach specified in the express waiver and then only for the time and to the extent therein stated. Tenant's obligation to pay Rent during the Term or any extension thereof or any holdover tenancy shall not be waived, released or terminated by the service of any 5-day notice, demand for possession, notice of termination of tenancy, institution of any action or forcible detainer, ejectment or for any judgment for possession, or any other act or acts resulting in termination of Tenant's right of possession.

23. TENANT'S REMEDIES: If Landlord defaults in (i) Landlord's duty to maintain the Premises or the Building or to perform repairs, remodeling, or decorating as set forth in Section 6 and such default is not cured by Landlord within 30 days after written notice from Tenant to Landlord (unless such default involves a hazardous condition or failure to furnish heat, hot water or essential services, which shall be cured forthwith); and provided Landlord's failure to cure is not excused on account of one or more of the defenses set forth in Section 6, in which case Landlord shall notify Tenant of specific facts constituting such excuse within said 30-day period (or in the case of a hazardous condition, or failure to furnish heat, hot water or essential services, within 5 days of Tenant's notice); or (ii) the performance of any other covenant or agreement of this Lease and such default is not cured by Landlord within 10 days after written notice from Tenant to Landlord, Tenant may (A) treat such event as a breach of this Lease and, in addition to all other rights and remedies provided at law or in equity (including without limitation those provided in the Illinois Revised Statutes relating to building code violations) may, by giving Landlord not less than 10 days prior written notice, terminate this Lease by setting forth the date of said termination In the 10 days' notice and vacating the Premises on or before said date, with Rent paid up to and including said termination date. Prepaid rent and the security deposit, if any, shall be promptly refunded to Tenant in accordance with the terms and conditions of this Lease.

24. TENANT'S WAIVER: Tenant's covenant to pay Rent is and shall be independent of each and every other covenant of this Lease. Tenant agrees that Tenant's damages for Landlord's breach of this Lease shall in no event be deducted from Rent nor set off for purposes of determining whether any Rent is due in a forcible detainer action brought on the basis of unpaid Rent.

25. LANDLORD'S REMEDIES: If Tenant defaults (i) in the payment of any single installment of Rent or In the payment of any other sum required to be paid under this Lease or under the terms of any other agreement between Tenant and Landlord and such default is not cured within 5 days of Tenant's receipt of written notice of such default from Landlord, or (ii) in the performance of any other covenant or agreement hereof, and such default is not cured by Tenant within 10 days after written notice to Tenant from Landlord (unless the default involves a hazardous condition which shall be cured forthwith), Landlord may treat such default as a breach of this Lease and Landlord shall have any one or more of the following described remedies in addition to all other rights and remedies provided at law or in equity:

A. Landlord may terminate this Lease, in which event Landlord may forthwith repossess the Premises in accordance with Section 15 hereof and Tenant agrees to pay to Landlord damages in an amount equal to the amount of Rent provided in this Lease to be paid by Tenant for the balance of the Term, less the fair rental value of the Premises for said period, and, in addition, any other sum of money and damages owed by Tenant to Landlord;

B. Landlord may terminate Tenant's right of possession and may repossess the Premises in accordance with Section 15 hereof without further demand or notice of any kind to Tenant and without such entry and possession terminating this Lease or releasing Tenant in whole or in part from Tenant's obligation to pay Rent hereunder for the full Term. Upon and after such entry into and possession of the Premises without termination of this Lease, Landlord may, but need not, re-let the Premises as Tenant's agent and may, but need not, make repairs, alterations and additions in or to the Premises and redecorate, as necessary, all under the same terms and conditions as set forth in Section 12 hereof. Tenant shall on demand pay to Landlord damages and all of Landlord's expenses of re-letting as set forth and described in Section 12 hereof. If the consideration collected by Landlord from any such re-letting for Tenant's account is not sufficient to pay the amount provided in the Lease to be paid monthly by Tenant together with all such expenses, Tenant shall pay to Landlord, as damages, the amount of each monthly deficiency for the remainder of the Term. Tenant agrees that Landlord may from time to time file suit to recover any such sums falling due under the terms of this Section and that no suit or recovery of any portion due Landlord hereunder shall be a defense to any subsequent action brought for any amount not theretofore reduced to judgment in favor of Landlord except that Landlord shall not be permitted more than one recovery In the aggregate amount so due.

C. Tenant shall pay Landlord all of Landlord's costs, expenses and attorney's fees incurred by Landlord in the enforcement of the covenants and agreements of this Lease.

26. OTHER AGREEMENTS:

A. The headings or captions of Sections in this Lease are for identification purposes only and do not limit or construe the contents of the Sections.

B. "Landlord" as used herein shall refer to the person, partnership, corporation or trust hereinabove set forth in that capacity, and if such person be designated an agent, Landlord shall also refer to and Include the principal. Obligations and duties to be performed by Landlord may be performed by any of the Landlord Parties, Landlord's agents, employees or Independent contractors. Only Landlord or Landlord's designated agent may amend or modify this Lease or Landlord's obligations hereunder.

C. All rights and remedies of Landlord under this Lease, or that may be provided by law, may be exercised by Landlord in Landlord's own name individually, or in Landlord's name by Landlord's agent, and all legal proceedings for the enforcement of any such rights or remedies, including distress for Rent, forcible detainer, and any other legal or equitable proceedings may be commenced and prosecuted to final judgment and execution by Landlord in Landlord's own name individually, or by agent of any Landlord who is a principal.

D. Tenant agrees that Landlord may at any lime and as often as desired assign or re-assign all of its rights as Landlord under this Lease.

E. The words 'Landlord" and "Tenant" as used herein shall be construed to mean plural where necessary and the necessary grammatical changes required to make the provisions hereof apply to corporations or persons, women or men, shall in at cases be assumed as though in each case fully expressed.

F. The obligations of two or more persons designated Tenant in this Lease shall be joint end several. If there be more than one party named as Tenant, other than children in a family, all must execute this Lease and any modification or amendment hereto.

G. "Premises" used herein shall refer to the dwelling unit leased to Tenant.

H. Tenant's occupancy or use of any storeroom, storage area, laundry room or parking space in or about the Building shall be as licensee only and, unless specifically provided otherwise in this Lease, such license is granted without charge to Tenant and may be revoked by Landlord at any time. Tenant understands and agrees that due to the construction, location and use of such storeroom, storage area, laundry room or parking spaces, Landlord cannot and shall not be liable for any loss or damage of or to any property placed therein. Tenant should not store or leave valuable items in such areas. The termination of this Lease for any reason shall also serve to automatically terminate Tenant's right to use such storeroom, storage area, laundry room or parking spaces.

I. "Building" as used herein shall include the entire physical structure located at and about the address hereinabove slated, including machinery, equipment end appurtenances which are a part thereof, grounds, recreational areas and facilities, garages and out-buildings, and other apartment buildings which form a complex owned an operated as a single entity.

J. The invalidity or unenforceability of any provision hereof shall not effect or impact any other provision.

RULES AND REGULATIONS

These rules are for the mutual benefit of all tenants. Please cooperate. Violations of the Rules and Regulations may cause termination of your Lease.

1. Tenant cannot have any pets or animals in the Premises without written consent of Landlord or Landlord's agent (which consent may be revoked upon 10 days prior written notice at any time). No animals without leash are allowed in any public area of the Building.

2. Passages, public halls, stairways, landings, elevators and elevator vestibules shall not be obstructed or be used for play or for any other purpose than for ingress to and egress from the Building or apartments, nor shall any person be permitted to congregate or play In or around the common interior areas of the Building. All personal possessions must be kept in the Premises or in other storage areas if provided.

3. All furniture, supplies, goods and packages of every kind shall be delivered through the rear or service entrance, stairway or elevator.

4. Carriages, velocipedes, bicycles, sleds and the like shall not be allowed in the lobbies, public halls, passageways, courts or elevators of the Building and are to be stored only in places designated for their storage by Landlord or Landlord's agent.

5. Laundry and drying apparatus shall be used in such a manner and at such times as Landlord may clearly post in such area. Clothes washers and dryers, and dishwashers, unless installed by Landlord cannot be kept or installed in the Premises or the Building.

6. The use of garbage receptacles **or** Incinerators shall be in accordance with posted signs and only garbage and refuse wrapped in small, tight parcels, may be placed in garbage receptacles or incinerator hoppers. Aerosol cans or inflammable materials shall be placed **in** garbage receptacles or dropped into the incinerator only as so posted. They are highly explosive.

7. No sign, signal, illumination, advertisement, notice or any other lettering, or equipment shall be exhibited, inscribed, painted, affixed or exposed on or at any window or on any part of the outside or inside of the Premises or the Building without the prior written consent of Landlord.

8. No awnings or other projections including air conditioners, television or radio antennas or wiring shall be attached to or extend from or beyond the outside walls of the Building.

9. Tenant shall not alter any lock or install a new lock or a knocker or other attachment on any door of the Premises without the written consent of Landlord.

10. No noise, music or other sounds shall be permitted et any time In such manner as to disturb or annoy other occupants of the Building.

11. No waste receptacles, supplies, footwear, umbrellas or other articles shall be placed In the halls, on the staircase landings, nor shall anything be hung or shaken from the windows or balconies or placed upon the outside window sills.

12. The water closets, basins and other plumbing fixtures shall not be used for any purpose other than for those for which they were designed; no sweepings, rubbish, rags or any other improper articles shall be thrown into them. Any damage resulting from misuse of such facilities shall be paid for by Tenant.

13. There shall be no cooking or baking done in or about the Premises except in the kitchen. Cooking on a barbeque or other similar equipment on a porch, terrace, or balcony is expressly forbidden.

14. If Landlord provides television master antenna hookup, at the option of Landlord, only Landlord's authorized agent shall install Tenant's television set to master antenna and Tenant agrees to pay installation cost and annual maintenance fee. Tenant shall permit access to disconnect hookup for nonpayment. Tenant agrees to pay $100.00 as liquidated damages to Landlord's authorized agent for each illegal hookup in the Premises.

15. No furniture filled with a liquid or semi-liquid shall be brought in or used in the Premises unless contained in proper frame and liner.

16. Except as otherwise required by applicable law, Landlord shall have no obligation to cause or allow cable television service or internet to be installed in the Building or the Premises. In the event that cable television service is provided in the Building or the Premises, Tenant understands end agrees that (a) Landlord cannot and shall not be liable to Tenant for any damage suffered by or to the person or property of Tenant due to improper or inadequate cable television or internet installation or reception, (b) Landlord shall have no obligation or responsibility to collect any fee on behalf of any provider of cable television service or internet, and (c) Tenant shall provide access to the Premises at all reasonable hours to allow the installation, repair or maintenance of the cable television or internet equipment in the Building or the Premises.

17. If the Premises is part of a condominium building or co-op, the rules and regulations of the condominium association and/or co-op board shall apply to the Premises as if fully set forth in this Lease.

GUARANTY

In consideration of One Dollar ($1.00) to the undersigned in hand paid, and other good and valuable consideration, the receipt and sufficiency of which is hereby acknowledged, the undersigned Guarantor hereby guarantees the payment of Rent and the performance by Tenant, Tenant's heirs, executors, administrators, successors and assigns of all covenants and agreements of this Lease. Any assignment of the Lease or subletting of the Premises shall not release the undersigned Guarantor from any obligations hereunder, unless Landlord expressly consents to such release of the undersigned Guarantor in writing at the time Landlord consents to such assignment or subletting. If more than one party executes this Guaranty, then each undersigned Guarantor shall be joint and severally liable for all obligations of Tenant hereunder.

______________________________ ______________________________

Name Date Name Date

FIGURE 17.3

Sample Letter of Intent

November 16, 2010

Mr. Robert Smith, Broker
The Smith Group
123 Appleton Way
Tinseltown, Illinois 12345

RE: Parkway Ventures

Dear Mr. Smith:

On behalf of ABC Development, we are pleased to present the following Letter of Intent to Parkway Ventures (referred to hereafter as Tenant) for your review and analysis.

BUILDING:	Mitchell Towers
LANDLORD:	ABC Development owners and operators of Mitchell Towers since 2000.
PREMISES:	Suite 1000 approximately 950 rentable square feet.
LEASE TERM:	Two years (2 years).
RENT & LEASE COMMENCEMENT:	January 1, 2011, or upon substantial completion. Rent shall escalate on every 12-month anniversary.
GROSS RENTAL RATE:	$19.00 per rentable square foot.
GROSS RENTAL RATE ESCALATION:	The gross rental rate shall escalate by $.50 annually per year cumulative commencing Year 2 of the lease term.
SECURITY DEPOSIT:	Tenant shall provide 1 month's gross rent at the time of lease execution.
REAL ESTATE TAXES & OPERATING EXPENSES:	Tenant shall pay its proportionate share of annual real estate taxes and annual operating expenses in excess of a 2011 base year. Current operating and tax estimates for the 2011 year are $12.00. The 2010 actual operating and taxes were $11.60.
ELECTRICITY:	The premises are separately metered for lights and outlets. Tenant shall receive a monthly electricity invoice from the building.
TENANT IMPROVEMENT:	Tenant shall accept the premises in "AS IS" condition. Tenant shall be responsible for all phone and data work.
AMENITIES:	The building is equipped with many amenities including but not limited to fiber optics, indoor parking, and a conference center.
AFTER-HOURS HVAC SUPPLEMENTAL SYSTEM:	Landlord currently provides heating, ventilation, and air-conditioning (HVAC) during regular business hours, which is from 6:00 am to 6:00 pm weekdays and from 6:00 am to 2:00 pm on Saturdays. HVAC required at times other than these mentioned shall be provided at an extra cost to the tenant.
SECURITY:	Landlord provides 24-hour manned security 365 days per year.
JANITORIAL:	The building provides office cleaning by a professional cleaning company five nights per week. The building shall provide cleaning to the levels provided in Class "A" properties.
TELECOMMUNICATIONS FACILITIES:	Landlord shall allow Tenant the right to choose its own telephone and data vendor and will allow said vendor reasonable access to the Tenant premises.
LEASE COMMISSION:	Landlord recognizes that Tenant is represented by The Smith Group, a real estate company. In addition, Landlord shall not be subject to any outside claim presented by any other "real estate company" on this transaction. Tenant shall indemnify Landlord from any such claim. A separate leasing commission agreement shall be executed as part of this transaction at the appropriate time.
CONFIDENTIALITY:	The information contained herein is for the express purpose of consummating a lease transaction with Tenant.
EXPIRATION:	This Lease proposal shall be null and void in the event that the Landlord has not entered into a lease with Tenant within thirty (30) days from the date hereof.
EXCULPATION:	This Letter of Intent is non-binding and is subject to prior leasing, the approval of Landlord, and the mutual execution and delivery of a fully executed lease satisfactory to both Landlord and Tenant. This Letter of Intent shall supersede previous Letters of Intent submitted.

Best Regards,
John Doe
ABC Development

Possession of Premises

The lessor, as the owner of the real estate, is usually bound by the implied covenant of quiet enjoyment. The covenant of quiet enjoyment is a presumed promise by the lessor that the lessee may take possession of the premises. The landlord further guarantees that he will not interfere in the tenant's possession or use of the property.

The lease may allow the landlord to enter the property to perform maintenance, to make repairs, or for other stated purposes. The tenant's permission is usually required.

If the premises are occupied by a holdover tenant or an adverse claimant at the beginning of the new lease period, most states require that the landlord take whatever measures are necessary to recover actual possession. In a few states, however, the landlord is bound to give the tenant only the right of possession; it is the tenant who must bring a court action to secure actual possession.

Use of Premises

A lessor may restrict a lessee's use of the premises through provisions included in the lease.

Use restrictions are particularly common in leases for stores or commercial space. For example, a lease may provide that the leased premises are to be used "only as a real estate office and for no other purpose." In the absence of such clear limitations, a lessee may use the premises for any lawful purpose.

Term of Lease

The term of a lease is the period for which the lease will run. It should be stated precisely, including the beginning and ending dates, together with a statement of the total period of the lease. For instance, a lease might run "for a term of 30 years beginning June 1, 2011, and ending May 31, 2041." A perpetual lease for an inordinate amount of time or an indefinite term usually will be ruled invalid. However, if the language of the lease and the surrounding circumstances clearly indicate that the parties intended such a term, the lease will be binding on the parties. Some states prohibit leases that run for 100 years or more.

Security Deposit

Most leases require that the tenant provide some form of **security deposit** to be held by the landlord during the lease term. If the tenant defaults on payment of rent or destroys the premises, the lessor may keep all or part of the deposit to compensate for the loss. Some state laws set maximum amounts for security deposits and specify how they must be handled. Some prohibit security deposits from being used for both nonpayment of rent and property damage. Some require that lessees receive annual interest on their security deposits.

Other safeguards against nonpayment of rent may include an advance rental payment, contracting for a lien on the tenant's property, or requiring that the tenant have a third person guarantee payment.

In Illinois Landlords who receive security deposits on residential leases of units in properties containing *five or more units* may not withhold any part of a security deposit as compensation for property damage unless they give the tenant an itemized statement listing the alleged damage. This statement must be delivered within 30 days of the date on which the premises are vacated. If the statement is not furnished, the landlord must return the entire security deposit within 45 days of the premises being vacated. Any landlord who is found by a court to have failed to comply with this requirement, or who has done so in bad faith, must pay the tenant double the security deposit due plus court costs and attorney's fees.

Illinois lessees are entitled to receive annual interest on their security deposits. Landlords who receive security deposits on residential leases of units in properties of 25 or more units, on deposits held for more than six months, are required to pay interest from the date of the deposit at a rate equal to the interest paid on a minimum deposit passbook savings account of the state's largest commercial bank (measured by total assets) with its main banking facilities located in Illinois. Any landlord who is found by a court to have willfully withheld interest on a tenant's security deposit must pay the tenant an amount equal to the security deposit plus the tenant's court costs and attorney's fees. Note: Chicago security deposit rules and rates for residential landlords differ under the Chicago Residential Landlord and Tenant Ordinance. ■

IN PRACTICE A lease should specify whether a payment is a security deposit or an advance rental. If it is a security deposit, the tenant is usually not entitled to apply it to the final month's rent. If it is an advance rental, the landlord must treat it as income for tax purposes.

Improvements

Neither the landlord nor the tenant is required to make any improvements to the leased property. The tenant may, however, make improvements with the landlord's permission. In most residential properties, any alterations become the property of the landlord. However in many commercial leases, tenants are permitted to install trade fixtures, those articles attached to a rental space that are required by tenants to conduct their businesses. Trade fixtures may be removed before the lease expires, provided the tenant restores the premises to their previous condition, with allowance for the wear and tear of normal use.

Accessibility The federal Fair Housing Act makes it illegal to discriminate against prospective tenants on the basis of physical disability. Tenants with disabilities must be permitted to make reasonable modifications to a property at their own expense. However, if the modifications would interfere with a future tenant's use, the landlord may require that the premises be restored to their original condition at the end of the lease term at the tenant's expense.

FIGURE 17.4

Residential Landlord and Tenant Ordinance

City of Chicago
Richard M. Daley
Mayor

RESIDENTIAL LANDLORD AND TENANT ORDINANCE
Rate of Interest on Security Deposits

Municipal Code Chapters 5-12-080, 5-12-081 and 5-12-170

- A landlord must give a tenant a receipt for a security deposit that includes the owner's name, the date it was received and a description of the dwelling unit. The receipt must be signed by the person accepting the security deposit.
- A landlord must pay interest each year on security deposits (eff. 11-6-86) and prepaid rent (eff.1-1-92) held more than six months.
- The rate of interest that a landlord must pay is set each year by the City Comptroller. (eff. 7-1-97)
- Before a landlord can deduct expenses for damages from the security deposit, the landlord must provide the tenant with an itemized statement of the damages within 30 days of the date the tenant vacates the dwelling unit.
- Within 45 days of the date the tenant vacates the dwelling unit, a landlord must return all security deposit and required interest, if any, minus unpaid rent and expenses for damages.
- In the event of fire, a landlord must return all security deposit and required interest, if any, minus unpaid rent and expenses for damages, within seven days from the date that the tenant provides notice of termination of the rental agreement. (eff. 1-1-92).

Under Chapter 5-12 of the Municipal Code of Chicago sections 5-12-081 and 5-12-082, the City Comptroller shall calculate and announce on the first business day of each year, the rate of interest to be paid on security deposits. As of **January 1, 2010**, based on information from the City Comptroller's Office, the interest rate to be paid on security deposits is **0.073%**. The rate is based upon the average of the rates of interest of the following types of accounts at Chase Bank, which is the commercial bank having the most branches located in the City of Chicago: savings account 0.01 percent, insured Money Market 0.01 percent and six-month Certificate of Deposit (based on a deposit of $1,000) 0.20 percent.

Security Deposit Interest Rate	
Current rate — January 1, 2010 through December 31, 2010:	.073%
January 1, 2009 through December 31, 2009	0.12%
January 1, 2008 through December 31, 2008:	1.26%
January 1, 2007 through December 31, 2007:	1.68%
January 1, 2006 through December 31, 2006:	1.71%
January 1, 2005 through December 31, 2005:	1.01%
January 1, 2004 through December 31, 2004:	0.42%
January 1, 2003 through December 31, 2003:	0.52%
January 1, 2002 through December 31, 2002:	0.83%
January 1, 2001 through December 31, 2001:	3.10 %
January 1, 2000 through December 31, 2000:	2.71%
January 1, 1999 through December 31, 1999:	2.63%
January 1, 1998 through December 31, 1998:	3.38%
July 1, 1997 through December 31, 1997:	3.42%
Before July 1, 1997:	5.00%

For a copy of the complete Residential Landlord and Tenant Ordinance, visit the Office of the City Clerk, Room 107, City Hall, 121 N. LaSalle St. For a copy of the Residential Landlord and Tenant Ordinance Summary, visit the Department of Community Development at 121 N. LaSalle St., 10th Floor.

IN PRACTICE The Americans with Disabilities Act (ADA) applies to commercial, nonresidential property in which public goods or services are provided. The ADA requires that such properties either be free of architectural barriers or provide reasonable accommodations for people with disabilities.

Maintenance of Premises

Many states require a lessor of residential property to maintain dwelling units in a habitable condition. Landlords must make any necessary repairs to common areas such as hallways, stairs, and elevators, and they must maintain safety features such as fire sprinklers and smoke alarms. The tenant does not have to make any repairs but must return the premises in the same condition they were received, with allowances for ordinary wear and tear. Lessees of commercial and industrial properties, however, usually maintain the premises and are often responsible for making their own repairs.

In Illinois

The Illinois Supreme Court first confirmed the concept of an **implied warranty of habitability** in residential tenancies in 1972. Since then, Illinois courts have repeatedly confirmed and amplified the warranty. A landlord must deliver and maintain throughout the duration of the lease any residential leasehold free from defects that would render the use of the dwelling "unsafe or unsanitary" and unfit for human occupancy. Nothing may be present on the premises that could seriously endanger the life, health, or safety of the tenant.

The conditions that violate the implied warranty of habitability vary depending on the state and jurisdiction where the premises are located. Generally, a landlord can be in violation by failing to provide access to

- drinkable water and hot water,
- heat during cold weather,
- working electricity,
- a smoke detector,
- a working bathroom and toilet;
- removal of rodent or insect infestation; or
- building code violations.

A tenant must give the landlord notice of a defect and reasonable time in which to cure it. As a remedy, the tenant may choose to

- move out and terminate the lease if repairs are not made within a reasonable time;
- stay and repair the problem himself and deduct the repair costs from the next month's rent (repair costs cannot exceed one month's rent); or
- sue for any damages resulting from the defective condition. ■

The obligation to pay rent for damaged or destroyed premises differs depending on the type of property and the lease. Usually, residential tenants are permitted to reduce their rent payments in proportion to the amount of space they are unable to use. Likewise, tenants who lease only part of a building, such as office or commercial space, generally are not required to continue to pay rent after the leased premises are destroyed. In fact, in some states, if the property was destroyed as a result of the landlord's negligence, the tenant can recover damages.

Destruction of Premises

On the other hand, tenants who have constructed buildings on leased land, often agricultural or industrial land, are still obligated for the payment of rent if the improvements are damaged or destroyed. If the buildings are destroyed, these tenants must turn to their insurance companies to deal with their loss of the improvement.

Assignment and Subleasing

When a tenant transfers all of his leasehold interests to another person, the lease has been *assigned*. The new tenant is legally obligated for all the promises the original tenant made in the lease.

On the other hand, when a tenant transfers less than all the leasehold interests by leasing them to a new tenant, the original tenant has **subleased** (or sublet) the property. The original tenant remains responsible for rent being paid by the new tenant and for any damage done to the rental during the lease term. The new tenant is responsible only to the original tenant to pay the rent due. **Assignment** and **subleasing** are only allowed when a lease specifically permits them. In both assignments and subleases, details of the new arrangement should be in writing.

In most cases, the sublease or assignment of a lease does not relieve the original lessee of the obligation to pay rent. The landlord may, however, agree to waive the former tenant's liability. Most leases prohibit a lessee from assigning or subletting without the lessor's consent. This permits the lessor to retain control over the occupancy of the leased premises. As a rule, the lessor must not unreasonably withhold consent. The sublessor's (original lessee's) interest in the real estate is known as a *sandwich lease*. (See Figure 17.5.)

Recording a Lease

Anyone who inspects the property receives actual notice. For these reasons, it is usually considered unnecessary to record a lease. However, most states do allow a lease to be recorded in the county in which the property is located. Furthermore,

FIGURE   17.5

Assignment versus Subletting

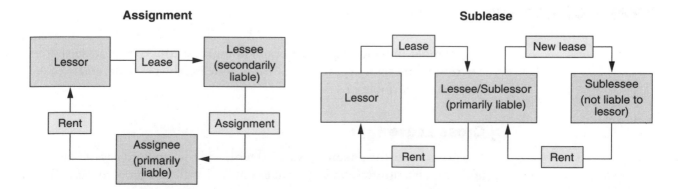

leases of three years or longer often are recorded as a matter of course. Some states require that long-term leases be recorded, especially when the lessee intends to mortgage the leasehold interest.

In some states, only a memorandum of lease is filed. A *memorandum of lease* gives notice of the interest but does not disclose the terms of the lease. Only the names of the parties and a description of the property are included.

Creditors of the property owner and purchasers who do not have actual notice of a leasehold interest are considered to have legal notice of a lease if the lease, or a memorandum of it, is recorded with the recorder or registrar of the county in which the property is located.

Nondisturbance Clause

A **nondisturbance clause** is a mortgage clause stating that the mortgagee agrees not to terminate the tenancies of lessees who pay their rent should the mortgagee foreclose on the mortgagor-lessor's building.

Options

A lease may contain an *option* that grants the lessee the privilege of renewing the lease (called a renewal option). The lessee must, however, give notice of his intention to exercise the option. Some leases grant the lessee the option to purchase the leased premises (called a purchase option). This option normally allows the tenant the right to purchase the property at a predetermined price within a certain time period, possibly the lease term. The lease might also contain a **right of first refusal** clause, allowing the tenant the opportunity to buy the property before the owner accepts an offer from another party. Although it is not required, the owner may give the tenant credit toward the purchase price for some percentage of the rent paid. The lease agreement is a primary contract over the option to purchase.

IN PRACTICE   All of these general statements concerning provisions of a lease are controlled largely by the terms of the agreement and state law. Great care must be exercised in reading the entire lease document before signing it because every clause in the lease has an economic and a legal impact on either the landlord or the tenant. While preprinted lease forms are available, there is no such thing as a standard lease. When complicated lease situations arise, legal counsel should be sought.

■ TYPES OF LEASES

The manner in which rent is determined indicates the type of lease that exists. There are three basic types of leases: the gross lease, the net lease, and the percentage lease. (See Table 17.1.)

Gross Lease

In a **gross lease**, the tenant pays a fixed rent, and the landlord pays all taxes, insurance, repairs, utilities, and the like connected with the property (usually called

Type of Lease	Lessee
Gross lease	Pays basic rent
Net lease	Pays basic rent plus all or some property charges
Percentage lease	Pays basic rent plus percent of gross sales (may pay property charges)

TABLE 17.1

Types of Leases

property charges or *operating expenses*). This is typically the type of rent structure involved in apartment rentals.

Net Lease

In a **net lease,** the tenant pays *all or some* of the property charges in addition to the rent. The monthly rental is net income for the landlord after operating costs have been paid. Leases for entire commercial or industrial buildings and the land on which they are located, ground leases, and long-term leases, are usually net leases.

In a **triple-net lease,** or *net-net-net lease*, the tenant pays *all operating and other expenses* in addition to rent. These expenses include taxes, insurance, assessments, maintenance, utilities, and other charges related to the premises.

Percentage Lease

Either a gross lease or a net lease may be a **percentage lease.** The rent is based on a minimum fixed rental fee plus a *percentage* of the gross income received by the tenant doing business on the leased property. This type of lease is usually used for retail businesses and restaurants. The percentage charged is negotiable and varies depending on the nature of the business, the location of the property, and general economic conditions.

Variable Lease

Several types of leases allow for increases in the rental charges during the lease periods. One of the more common is the **graduated lease**, which provides for specified rent increases at set future dates. Another is the **index lease**, which allows rent to be increased or decreased periodically, based on changes in the consumer price index or some other indicator.

Ground Lease

When a landowner leases unimproved land to a tenant who agrees to erect a building on the land, the lease is usually referred to as a **ground lease**. Ground leases usually involve *separate ownership* of the land and buildings. These leases must be for a long enough term to make the transaction desirable to the tenant investing in the building and often run for terms of 50 years up to 99 years. Ground leases are generally net leases. The lessee must pay rent on the ground as well as real estate taxes, insurance, upkeep, and repairs.

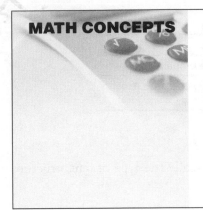

MATH CONCEPTS

CALCULATING PERCENTAGE LEASE RENTS

Percentage leases usually call for a minimum monthly rent plus a percentage of gross sales income exceeding a stated annual amount. For example, a lease might require minimum rent of $1,300 per month plus 5 percent of the business's sales exceeding $160,000. On an annual sales volume of $250,000, the annual rent would be calculated as follows:

$1,300 per month	× 12 months	= $15,600
$250,000	− $160,000	= $90,000
$90,000	× .05 (5%)	= $4,500
$15,600 base rent	+ $4,500 percentage rent	= $20,100 total rent

Oil and Gas Lease

When an oil company leases land to explore for oil and gas, a special lease agreement must be negotiated. Usually, the landowner receives a cash payment for executing the lease. If no well is drilled within the period stated in the lease, the lease expires. However, most oil and gas leases permit the oil company to continue its rights for another year by paying another flat rental fee. Such rentals may be paid annually until a well is produced. If oil or gas is found, the landowner usually receives a percentage of its value as a royalty. As long as oil or gas is obtained in significant quantities, the lease continues indefinitely.

Lease Purchase

A **lease purchase** is used when a tenant wants to purchase the property but is unable to do so. Perhaps the tenant cannot obtain favorable financing or clear title, or the tax consequences of a current purchase would be unfavorable. In this arrangement, the purchase agreement is the primary consideration, and the lease is secondary. Part of the periodic rent is applied toward the purchase price of the property until that price is reduced to an amount for which the tenant can obtain financing or purchase the property outright, depending on the terms of the lease-purchase agreement.

Agricultural landowners often lease their land to tenant farmers, who provide the labor to produce and bring in the crop. An owner can be paid by a tenant in one of two ways: as an agreed-on rental amount in cash in advance **(cash rents),** or as a percentage of the profits or losses from the sale of the crop when it is sold **(sharecropping).**

Sale-and-leaseback

A **sale-and-leaseback** is the arrangement whereby the owners of property sell the property and then lease it back again for an agreed period and rental. A sale-and-leaseback is often used when extra capital is needed on a construction project. The original owners pull out their equity to use on other projects and reduce their taxable income when they pay rent to the new owner. The new owner now has a reliable source of rental income for an extended time.

■ DISCHARGE OF LEASES

As with any contract, a lease is discharged when the contract terminates. Termination can occur when all parties have fully performed their obligations under the agreement. In addition, the parties may agree to cancel the lease. If the tenant, for instance, offers to surrender the leasehold interest and the landlord accepts the tenant's offer, the lease is terminated. A tenant who simply abandons leased property remains liable for the terms of the lease—including the rent. The terms of the lease will usually indicate whether the landlord is obligated to try to re-rent the space. If the landlord intends to sue for unpaid rent, most states require an attempt to mitigate damages by re-renting the premises to limit the amount owed.

The lease does not terminate if the parties die or if the property is sold. There are two exceptions to this general rule:

- ■ A lease from the owner of a *life estate* ends when the tenant's life ends.
- ■ The death of either party terminates a *tenancy at will.*

In all other cases, the heirs of a deceased landlord are bound by the terms of existing leases.

If leased real estate is sold or otherwise conveyed, the new landlord takes the property subject to the rights of the tenants. A lease agreement may, however, contain language that permits a new landlord to terminate existing leases. The clause, commonly known as a *sale clause,* requires that the tenants be given some period of notice before the termination. Because the new owner has taken title subject to the rights of the tenants, the sale clause enables the new landlord to claim possession and negotiate new leases under his own terms and conditions.

A tenancy may also be terminated by operation of law, as in a bankruptcy or condemnation proceeding.

Breach of Lease

When a tenant breaches any lease provision, the landlord may sue the tenant to obtain a judgment to cover past-due rent, damages to the premises, or other defaults. Likewise, when a landlord breaches any lease provision, the tenant is entitled to certain remedies. The rights and responsibilities of the landlord-tenant relationship are usually governed by state law.

If a tenant defaults on the payment of rent, the landlord has two options:

- ■ He may elect to serve the tenant with five days' written notice, demanding payment of the delinquent rent within five days after the notice is received. If the tenant fails to pay the rent, the landlord may terminate the lease automatically and sue for possession without further notice. If the tenant pays the past-due rent, the lease continues in full force.
- ■ Alternatively (and in cases in which the tenant's breach is other than nonpayment of rent), the landlord may terminate the tenancy by serving the tenant with ten days' written notice, including a demand for possession. After the ten-day period expires, the landlord may sue for possession without further notice, even if the default is cured.

Landlord's remedies—actual eviction   When a tenant breaches a lease or improperly retains leased premises, the landlord may regain possession through a legal process known as **actual eviction**. The landlord must serve notice on the tenant before commencing the lawsuit. Most lease terms require at least a ten-day notice in the case of default. In many states, however, only a five-day notice is necessary when the tenant defaults in the payment of rent. When a court issues a judgment for possession to a landlord, the tenant must vacate the property. If the tenant fails to leave, the landlord can have the judgment enforced by a court officer, who forcibly removes the tenant and the tenant's possessions. The landlord then has the right to re-enter and regain possession of the property.

In Illinois

In Illinois, a landlord seeking actual eviction of a tenant must file an action called a *forcible entry and detainer*. It can be used when a tenancy has expired by default, by its terms, by operation of law, or by proper notice. The suit should be filed in the circuit court of the county in which the property is located.

If the court rules in favor of the landlord, a *judgment for possession* (and money damages) will be entered, and an *order of possession* will be issued by the clerk of the court. The tenant must then leave peaceably, removing all of his property from the premises. Traditionally, however, if a residential tenant personally appears in court and the landlord prevails, the court will delay issuing the order for a reasonable period of time to allow the tenant to find alternative housing.

When a tenant refuses to vacate peaceably after a judgment for possession has been entered, the landlord must deliver the order to the sheriff, who will forcibly evict the tenant. The landlord then has the right to re-enter and regain possession of the property.

Until a judgment for possession is issued, the landlord must be careful not to harass the tenant in any manner, such as locking the tenant out of the property, impounding the tenant's possessions, or disconnecting the utilities (such as electricity and natural gas). Illinois landlords have no right to *self-help*; that is, they may not forcibly remove a tenant without following the proper legal procedures. ■

Tenants' remedies—constructive eviction   If a landlord breaches any clause of a lease agreement, the tenant has the right to sue and recover damages against the landlord. If the leased premises become unusable for the purpose stated in the lease, the tenant may have the right to abandon them. This action, called **constructive eviction**, terminates the lease agreement. The tenant must prove that the premises have become unusable because of the conscious neglect of the landlord. To claim constructive eviction, the tenant must leave the premises while the conditions that made the premises uninhabitable exist.

■ CIVIL RIGHTS LAWS

The fair housing and civil rights laws affect landlords and tenants just as they do sellers and purchasers. All persons must have access to housing of their choice without any differentiation in the terms and conditions because of their race, color, religion, familial status (the presence of children under the age of 18), disability, or gender. State and local municipalities may have their own fair housing laws that add protected classes such as age and sexual orientation. Withholding an apartment that is available for rent, segregating certain persons in separate sections of an apartment complex or parts of a building, and charging different amounts for rent or security deposits to persons in the protected classes all constitute violations of the law.

It is important that landlords realize that changes in the laws stemming from the federal Fair Housing Amendments Act of 1988 significantly alter past practices, particularly as they affect individuals with disabilities and families with children. The fair housing laws require that the same tenant criteria be applied to families with children that are applied to adults. A landlord cannot charge a different amount of rent or security deposit because one of the tenants is a child. While landlords have historically argued that children are noisy and destructive, the fact is that many adults are noisy and destructive as well.

> **In Illinois**   The Illinois Human Rights Act extends the list of protected classes for Illinois. It states as the public policy of Illinois and purpose of the act: "Freedom from unlawful discrimination. To secure for all individuals within Illinois the freedom from discrimination against an individual because of his or her race, color, religion, sex, national origin, ancestry, age, marital status, physical or mental disability, familial status, military status, unfavorable discharge from military service, or sexual orientation and order of protection status in connection with employment, real estate transactions, access to financial credit, and the availability of public accommodations." Article 3 of this act deals with real estate transactions. ■

■ LEAD-BASED PAINT

The 1996 federal Lead-Based Paint Hazard Reduction Act—Title X focused more strongly on disclosure and REALTOR® liability. This federal law supersedes any state laws that are not as strong. Real estate licensees leasing properties built before 1978 must ensure that landlords disclose any possible lead-based paint or related hazards. This disclosure form must be completed even in the case of an oral lease agreement. Once an offer for lease is received, the licensee representing the lessor (landlord) must make certain a completed Disclosure of Information (from landlord) and Acknowledgment Form (from tenant) are attached, showing that the disclosure requirements were met. Finally, a federal lead hazard information pamphlet, obtained through the National Lead Information Clearinghouse at 800-424-LEAD (5323), must be distributed before leasing the property. (See Chapter 22 for more detail.)

> **In Illinois**   The Illinois Lead Poisoning Prevention Act requires that the owner of any residential building cited by the state as a lead paint hazard give prospective tenants written notice of the danger unless the owners have a certificate of compliance. This act is bolstered in its scope by the federal legislation noted earlier. When a mitigation order is issued to an owner of a building containing lead hazards, the owner has 90 days to eliminate the hazard in a manner prescribed by state law, or 30 days if occupied by a child under age six or by a pregnant woman. ■

■ REGULATION OF THE RENTAL INDUSTRY

Rental-Finding Services

Because of the nationwide demand for rental housing, caused in part by the increased mobility of the U.S. population, there has been a rapid growth in the rental-finding service industry.

In Illinois A **rental-finding service** is any business that finds, attempts to find, or offers to find for any person for consideration a unit of rental real estate or a lessee for a unit of rental real estate not owned or leased by the business. Any person or business entity that operates a rental-finding service must obtain a real estate license and comply with all provisions of the Illinois Real Estate License Act of 2000. General-circulation newspapers that advertise rental property and listing contracts between owners or lessors of real estate and registrants are exempt from this requirement. ■

Rental-finding services are required to enter into written contracts with the parties for whom their services are to be performed. The contract must clearly disclose

- the term of the contract;
- the total amount to be paid for the services;
- the service's policy regarding the refunding of fees paid in advance, and the conditions under which refunds may or may not be paid (printed in a larger typeface than the rest of the contract);
- the type of rental unit, geographic area, and price range the prospective tenant desires;
- a detailed statement of the services to be performed;
- a statement that the contract shall be void, and all fees paid in advance shall be refunded, if the information provided regarding possible rental units available is not current or accurate (that is, if a rental unit is listed that has not been available for more than two days); and
- a disclosure that information regarding possible rental units may be up to two days old.

With regard to any individual rental unit, a prospective tenant must be provided with the name, address, and telephone number of the owner; a description of the unit, monthly rent, and security deposit required; a description of the utilities available and included in the rent; the occupancy date and lease term; a statement describing the source of the information; and any other information the prospective tenant may reasonably be expected to need.

A rental-finding service may not list or advertise any rental unit without the express written authority of the unit's owner or agent.

A real estate licensee who violates any of these requirements will be construed to have demonstrated unworthiness or incompetence and will be subject to the appropriate disciplinary measures.

Leasing Agents

The Illinois Real Estate License Act of 2000 (Section 5-5 through Section 5-10) provides for a limited-scope license for individuals who wish to engage *solely* in activities related to the leasing of residential real property. For instance, the following activities would appropriately fall under this limited license, if the licensee did not engage in any other real estate activities (such as marketing single-family homes):

- Leasing or renting residential real property
- Collecting rent for residential real property
- Attempting, offering, or negotiating to lease, rent, or collect rent for the use of residential real property

The Act establishes specific qualifications and educational requirements for leasing agents, including a written examination. (See Chapter 14 for requirements.)

Referral Fees

In Illinois

The Illinois Real Estate License Act of 2000 (Section 5-20) allows landlords to pay a referral fee to tenants. A resident tenant of a unit who refers a prospective tenant for a unit in the same building or complex may be paid a referral fee if he

- refers no more than three prospective lessees in any 12-month period;
- receives compensation of no more than $1,500 or the equivalent of one month's rent, whichever is less, in any 12-month period; and
- limits his activities to referring prospective lessees to the owner (or the owner's agent) and does not show units, discuss lease terms, or otherwise participate in the negotiation of a lease. ■

■ SUMMARY

A lease is an agreement that grants one person the right to use the property of another in return for consideration.

A leasehold estate that runs for a specific length of time creates an estate for years; one that runs for an indefinite period creates an estate from period to period (e.g., year to year, month to month). An estate at will runs as long as the landlord permits. An estate at sufferance is possession without the consent of the landlord. A leasehold estate is classified as a personal property interest.

The requirements of a valid lease include capacity to contract, legal objectives, offer and acceptance, and consideration. In addition, state statutes of frauds generally require that any lease that will not be completed within one year of the date of its making must be in writing to be enforceable in court. Most leases also include clauses relating to rights and obligations of the landlord and tenant, such as the use of the premises, subletting, judgments, maintenance of the premises, and termination of the lease period.

A lease may be terminated by the expiration of the lease period, the mutual agreement of the parties, or a breach of the lease by either the landlord or tenant. In most cases, neither the death of the tenant nor the landlord's sale of the rental property terminates a lease.

If a tenant defaults on any lease provision, the landlord may sue for a money judgment, actual eviction, or both. If the premises have become uninhabitable due to the landlord's negligence or failure to correct within a reasonable time, the tenant may have the remedy of constructive eviction—that is, the right to abandon the premises and refuse to pay rent until the premises are repaired.

The rental industry is highly regulated. Fair housing laws protect the rights of tenants. Besides prohibiting discrimination based on race, color, religion, familial status, national origin, and sex, the laws address the rights of individuals with disabilities and families with children.

In Illinois   The Illinois Real Estate License Act of 2000 (Section 5-5 through Section 5-10) provides for a limited-scope license for individuals who wish to engage solely in activities related to the leasing of residential real property. Article 5 contains particulars on the leasing agent license.

The Illinois Human Rights Act defines fair housing in this state as including freedom from discrimination against an individual due to race, color, religion, sex, national origin, ancestry, age, marital status, physical or mental disability, familial status, military status, unfavorable discharge from military service, or sexual orientation and order of protection status in connection with employment, real estate transactions, access to financial credit, and the availability of public accommodations.

The Illinois Statute of Frauds requires that leases for more than one year or that cannot be performed within one year be in writing to be enforceable. Oral leases for less than one year are enforceable. Illinois law establishes specific notice requirements for termination of leases and for the withholding or payment of interest on security deposits. Federal lead-based-paint laws are strictly enforced in Illinois. Even a short oral lease requires that a lead paint disclosure be supplied. ∎

CHAPTER 17 QUIZ

1. A ground lease is usually
    a. short term.
    b. for 100 years or longer.
    c. long term.
    d. a gross lease.

2. A tenant enters into a commercial lease that requires a monthly rent based on a minimum set amount plus an additional amount determined by the tenant's gross receipts exceeding $5,000. This type of lease is called a
    a. standard lease.
    b. gross lease.
    c. percentage lease.
    d. net lease.

3. If a tenant moved out of a rented store building because access to the building was blocked as a result of the landlord's negligence, the
    a. tenant would have no legal recourse against the landlord.
    b. landlord would be liable for the rent until the expiration date of the lease.
    c. landlord would have to provide substitute space.
    d. tenant would be entitled to recover damages from the landlord.

4. A tenant signs a lease that includes a schedule of rent increases on specific dates over the course of the lease term. What kind of lease has the tenant signed?
    a. Percentage
    b. Net
    c. Graduated
    d. Index

5. A tenant still has five months remaining on a one-year apartment lease. When the tenant moves to another city, she transfers possession of the apartment to a friend for the entire remaining term of the lease. The friend pays rent directly to the tenant. In this situation, the tenant has become a(n)
    a. assignor.
    b. sublessor.
    c. sublessee.
    d. lessor.

6. A tenant's lease has expired. The tenant has neither vacated nor negotiated a renewal lease, and the landlord has declared that she does not want the tenant to remain in the building. This form of possession is called a(n)
    a. estate for years.
    b. periodic estate.
    c. estate at will.
    d. estate at sufferance.

7. A tenant's tenancy for years will expire in two weeks. The tenant plans to move to a larger apartment across town when the current tenancy expires. What must the tenant do to terminate this agreement?
    a. The tenant must give the landlord two weeks' prior notice.
    b. The tenant must give the landlord one week's prior notice.
    c. The tenant needs to do nothing; the agreement will terminate automatically.
    d. The agreement will terminate only after the tenant signs a lease for the new apartment.

8. When a tenant holds possession of a landlord's property without a current lease agreement and without the landlord's approval, the
    a. tenant is maintaining a gross lease.
    b. landlord can file suit for possession.
    c. tenant has no obligation to pay rent.
    d. landlord may be subject to a constructive eviction.

9. Under the negotiated terms of a certain residential lease, the landlord is required to maintain the water heater. If the tenant is unable to get hot water because of a faulty water heater that the landlord has failed to repair after repeated notification, which remedy would be available to the tenant?

a. Suing the tenant for damages
b. Abandoning the premises under constructive eviction
c. Refunding the tenant back rent
d. Assigning the lease agreement

10. A person has a one-year leasehold interest in a house. The interest automatically renews itself at the end of each year. The person's interest is referred to as a tenancy

a. for years.
b. from period to period.
c. at will.
d. at sufferance.

11. What is rent?

a. Contractual consideration to a third party
b. Consideration for the use of real property
c. All monies paid by the lessor to the lessee
d. Total balance owed under the terms of a lease

12. Which of the following describes a net lease?

a. An agreement in which the tenant pays a fixed rent and the landlord pays all taxes, insurance, and other charges on the property
b. A lease in which the tenant pays rent plus maintenance and property charges
c. A lease in which the tenant pays the landlord a percentage of the monthly profits derived from the tenant's commercial use of the property
d. A lease-purchase agreement in which the landlord agrees to apply part of the monthly rent toward the ultimate purchase price of the property

13. A commercial lease calls for a minimum rent of $1,200 per month plus 4 percent of the annual gross business exceeding $150,000. If the total rent paid at the end of one year was $19,200, how much business did the tenant do during the year?

a. $159,800
b. $250,200
c. $270,000
d. $279,200

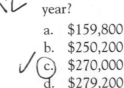 19,200 - 14400 = 4800

In Illinois

14. In Illinois, which of the following statements is *TRUE* regarding a lease for more than one year?

a. The lease must be in writing and signed to be enforceable in court.
b. The lease must include a provision for interest to be paid on all security deposits.
c. The lease must be recorded to give actual notice of the resident tenant's right of possession.
d. The lease may be terminated only by written notice to the tenant, even if it contains a definite expiration date.

15. A tenant rents an apartment in a 100-unit highrise in a Chicago suburb for $900 per month. The tenant decides to move when she learns that her rent will be raised by 25 percent at the expiration of her one-year lease. When she moved in, the tenant deposited $1,200 as a security deposit. How will the interest paid on the tenant's deposit be determined?

a. The interest paid should be based on the prime rate as of December 31 of the calendar year preceding the rental agreement.
b. The interest paid should be 5 percent per year, from the date of deposit.
c. The interest rate should be computed at a rate equal to that paid on a minimum deposit passbook savings account at the state's largest commercial bank.
d. Under these facts, the tenant is not entitled to receive interest on her security deposit.

16. How many days' advance notice is required to terminate a month-to-month tenancy in Illinois?
    a. 5
    b. 15
    c. 30
    d. 60

17. A landlord who owns a 20-unit apartment building in Decatur, Illinois, has held a tenant's security deposit for three months. The tenant, who is on a month-to-month lease, informs the landlord that he will be vacating the apartment in 30 days. Based on these facts, which of the following statements is *TRUE*?
    a. The landlord must pay the tenant four months' interest on the security deposit.
    b. The landlord owes the tenant no interest on the security deposit.
    c. The tenant is entitled to three months' interest on the security deposit.
    d. If the tenant vacates the premises in these circumstances, the landlord is entitled to retain the security deposit as statutory damages.

18. A tenant has a one-year lease on an apartment. If the tenant fails to pay his rent when it is due, the landlord may
    a. serve notice on the tenant to pay the delinquent rent within five days.
    b. terminate the tenant's lease without notice when the rent is more than ten days past due.
    c. hire a moving company to remove the tenant's furniture and personal property from the premises.
    d. serve notice on the tenant to pay the rent within five days and proceed with a suit for possession regardless of whether or not the tenant pays the past-due rent.

19. In Illinois, a landlord must give a tenant at least 60 days' written notice to terminate which of the following tenancies?
    a. Tenancy at will
    b. Tenancy for years
    c. Tenancy from year to year
    d. Tenancy at sufferance

20. Before entering into a service relationship with a prospective tenant, a rental-finding service must provide the prospective tenant with a written contract that discloses what information?
    a. The total amount to be paid over the lease term
    b. A statement that the contract will be invalid if information about a rental unit is provided when the unit has been unavailable for more than five days
    c. A statement that information about rental units may be up to two days old
    d. A copy of the brokerage agreement between the owner and the rental-finding service

18 CHAPTER

Property Management

■ **LEARNING OBJECTIVES** *When you've finished reading this chapter, you should be able to*

- ■ **identify** the basic elements of a management agreement;

- ■ **describe** a property manager's functions;

- ■ **explain** the role of environmental regulations and the Americans with Disabilities Act in the property manager's job;

- ■ **distinguish** the various types of insurance alternatives; and

- ■ **define** the following *key terms*

Americans with Disabilities Act	management agreement	surety bonds
construction	multiperil policies	tenant improvements
life cycle costing	property manager	workers' compensation acts
	risk management	

■ THE PROPERTY MANAGER

As a specialized field, property management is one of the fastest growing areas of real estate. Many mortgage lenders require that investors hire a professional property manager to manage their properties. Property management involves the leasing, managing, marketing, and overall maintenance of real estate owned by others.

The role of the **property manager** is complex, requiring the manager to wear many hats. It is not unusual for a property manager to be a market analyst, leasing agent, accountant, advertising specialist, and maintenance person—all in the same day. In addition, the property manager frequently interacts with people in various professions, including lawyers, environmental engineers, and accountants. The property manager has three principal responsibilities:

- Achieve the objectives of the property owners
- Generate income for the owners
- Preserve and/or increase the value of the investment property

A property manager

- maintains the owner's investment, and
- ensures that the property produces income.

The property manager carries out the goals of the property owners by making sure the property earns income. This can be done in several ways. The physical property must be maintained in good condition. Suitable tenants must be found, rent must be collected, and employees must be hired and supervised. The property manager is responsible for budgeting and controlling expenses, keeping proper accounts, and making periodic reports to the owner. In all of these activities, the manager's primary goal is to operate and maintain the physical property in such a way as to preserve and enhance the owner's capital investment.

Some property managers work for property management companies. These firms manage properties for a number of owners under management agreements (discussed later). Other property managers are independent. The property manager has an agency relationship with the owner, which involves greater authority and discretion over management decisions than an employee would have. A property manager or an owner may employ building managers to supervise the daily operations of a building. In some cases, these individuals may be residents of the building.

In Illinois

Illinois property managers must be licensed real estate brokers or managing brokers because they engage in collecting rent, negotiating leases and rentals, and procuring tenants, among other functions. However, the Illinois Real Estate License Act of 2000 specifically exempts resident managers of apartment buildings, duplexes, and apartment complexes from licensure requirements when their primary residence is on the premises being managed.

Illinois permits individuals whose real estate practice is limited to leasing or renting residential property, collecting rent, negotiating leases, and similar activities to obtain a limited scope leasing-agent license instead of the broader-scope broker or managing broker license. An individual with a leasing-agent license must be sponsored by a sponsoring broker. ■

Securing Management Business

Possible sources of a property management business include

- corporate owners,
- apartment buildings,
- owners of small rental residential properties,
- homeowners' associations,
- investment syndicates,
- trusts, and
- owners of office buildings.

A good reputation is often the manager's best advertising. A manager who consistently demonstrates the ability to increase property income over previous levels should have little difficulty finding new business.

Before contracting to manage any property, however, the professional property manager should be certain that the building owner has realistic income expectations. Necessary maintenance, unexpected repairs, and effective marketing all take time and money. In addition, most states have landlord-tenant laws that require the landlord-owner to keep the property repaired and make sure it complies with building codes. Through the agency relationship with the owner, the property manager becomes responsible for repairs and the building's condition.

New Opportunities

Specialization has opened a range of new opportunities. Well-trained specialists are needed to manage shopping centers, commercial buildings, and industrial parks in addition to the more visible management of residential properties. Here are just a few of the specialties looking for a few good people.

Community association management   The prevalence of homeowners' and condominium associations, combined with complex planning and development codes, have placed new demands on property managers. Working as part of a team, property managers assist in providing a comprehensive array of services to volunteer boards. Many states now require at least a real estate license or an association management license for those who specialize in managing associations.

| In Illinois |

The Community Association Manager Licensing and Disciplinary Act was created to provide for the regulation of managers of community associations, to ensure that managers are qualified to engage in community association management, and to provide for high standards of professional conduct by those licensed. Anyone acting under this license cannot perform any activities for which a real estate broker's license is required under the Illinois Real Estate License Act of 2000. ■

Housing for the near-elderly and elderly   Opportunities abound in managing housing for the near-elderly and elderly, many of which are federally assisted housing programs. In addition to marketing, these property managers are often responsible for the operations of the facility, as well as housekeeping, meal service, social event planning, and medical emergency planning. Since subsidized housing is involved, these property managers need to be familiar with state and federal rules pertaining to eligibility requirements and income verification.

Manufactured homes (i.e., mobile home parks)   Homes built in factories meeting HUD specifications are called manufactured homes (incorrectly, mobile homes). These homes may be placed on individually owned land, but more than a third are sited in communities. The tenants may be renting only the "pad," the land on which the home is sited, or the home itself. Many manufactured home communities are geared toward the near-elderly and elderly, so managers of these communities must be effective at building community spirit.

Resort housing   Managing second-home and resort rentals presents specific challenges. These managers must be able to care for and maintain often-vacant properties and be able to attract and manage short-term tenants. Many of these properties are located in high-risk areas for natural disasters such as hurricanes, so the manager must be ready to work with insurance adjusters as well.

Concierge services   A new area for property managers to specialize in is the training and managing of concierge staff for office buildings and other settings. Concierge staff is responsible for anything from arranging for taxi rides to assisting with visual aids equipment for a conference.

Asset management   Asset managers monitor a portfolio of properties similar to a securities portfolio by analyzing the performance of the properties and making recommendations to the owners of the properties. Real property asset management helps clients decide what type of real estate to invest in (commercial or residential), which property is best to purchase, the best financial sources for a real estate purchase, and when to dispose of property.

Corporate property managers   Corporate property managers manage properties for corporations that invest in real estate. Because these corporations do not usually deal in real estate, they are not necessarily knowledgeable about property management. Hiring a corporate property manager allows a corporation to invest in real estate and increase its capital without needing the specialized knowledge of property management. Typically, corporate property managers are employees of the corporation and not independent contractors.

Leasing agents   Leasing agents are usually independent contractors working on a commission basis and are in high demand because of their skill in securing lessees.

■ THE MANAGEMENT PLAN AND AGREEMENT

The Management Plan

Property management begins with a **management plan** prepared by the property manager. A management plan outlines the details of the owner's objectives with the property, as well as what the property manager expects to accomplish and how, including all financial objectives. In preparing a management plan, a property manager analyzes three factors: the owner's objectives, the regional and neighborhood market, and the specific property. Occupancy, absorption rates, and new starts are critical indicators. The plan also includes a budgetary section on sources of revenue and anticipated expenses. While the management plan is a document for the present, it is forward-looking in determining the feasibility of a property owner's long-term goals for a specific property.

The Management Agreement

The first step in taking over the management of any property is to enter into a **management agreement** with the owner. This agreement creates a general *agency relationship* between the owner and the property manager. It defines the duties and responsibilities of each party. It is also a guide used in operating the property as well as a reference in case of future disputes.

Like any other contract involving real estate, the management agreement should be in writing. It should include the following:

- *Description* of the property. This should include the street address of the property as well as the legal description.
- *Time period* the agreement covers. This would include specific provisions for termination.
- Definition of the *management's responsibilities*. All the manager's duties should be specifically stated in the contract. Any limitations or restrictions on what the manager may do should be included.
- Statement of the *owner's purpose*. The owner should clearly state what the manager is to accomplish. One owner may want to maximize net income, while another will want to increase the capital value of the investment. Long-term goals are often key.
- Extent of the *manager's authority*. This provision should state what authority the manager is to have in matters such as hiring, firing, and supervising employees; fixing rental rates for space; and making expenditures and authorizing repairs. Repairs that exceed a certain expense limit may require the owner's written approval.
- *Reporting.* The frequency and detail of the manager's periodic reports on operations and financial position should be agreed on. These reports serve as a means for the owner to monitor the manager's work and operational trends; they form a basis for shaping management policy.
- *Management fee.* The fee may be based on a percentage of gross or net income, a fixed fee, or some combination of these and other factors. Management fees are subject to the same antitrust considerations as sales commissions and cannot be standardized in the marketplace (e.g., price-fixing). The fee must be negotiated between the property manager and the principal. In addition, the property manager may be entitled to a commission on new rentals and renewed leases.
- *Allocation of costs.* The agreement should state which of the property manager's expenses—such as office rent, office help, telephone, advertising, and association fees—will be paid by the manager. Other costs will be paid by the owner.
- *Antitrust provisions.* Management fees are subject to the same antitrust considerations as sales commissions.
- *Equal opportunity statement.* Residential property management agreements should include a statement that the property will be shown, rented, and otherwise made available to all persons protected by state or federal law.

■ PROPERTY MANAGER'S RESPONSIBILITIES

A property manager's specific responsibilities are determined by the management agreement. Certain duties, however, are found in most agreements. Basic management duties include budgeting, capital expenditures, setting rental rates, selecting tenants, collecting rent, maintaining the property, and complying with legal requirements.

Financial Reports

One of the primary responsibilities of a property manager is maintaining financial reports, including an operating budget, cash flow report, workew and loss statement, and budget comparison statement. While there are no standard formats for these reports, there is some similarity among the reports, and it is important for the property manager to adapt a report to meet an owner's needs.

Operating budget   An operating budget is the projection of income and expense for the operation of a property over a one-year period. This budget, developed before attempting to rent property, is based on anticipated revenues and expenses and provides the owner the amount of anticipated profit. The property uses the operating budget as a guide for the property's financial performance in the present and future.

MATH CONCEPTS

RENTAL COMMISSIONS

Residential property managers often earn commissions when they find tenants for a property. Rental commissions usually are based on the annual rent from a property. For example, if an apartment unit rents for $1,200 per month and the commission payable is 8 percent, the commission is calculated as follows:

$$\$1,200 \text{ per month} \times 12 \text{ months} = \$14,400$$
$$\$14,400 \times .08 \ (8\%) = \$1,152$$

Once a property manager has managed a property for a length of time, an operating budget may be developed based on the results of the profit and loss statement in comparison to the original budget (actual versus projected). After making the comparison, a new operating budget is prepared for a new time period in the future.

Cash flow report   A cash flow report is a monthly statement that details the financial status of the property. Sources of income and expenses are noted, as well as net operating income and net cash flow. The cash flow report is the most important financial report because it provides a picture of the current financial status of a property.

Income   Income includes gross rentals collected, delinquent rental payments, utilities, vending, contracts, late fees, and storage charges. Any losses from uncollected rental payments or evictions are deducted from the total gross to arrive at the total adjusted income.

In some properties, there is space that is not income producing, such as the property manager's office. The rental value of the property that is not producing income is subtracted from the gross rental income to equal the gross collectible, or billable, rental income.

Expenses   Fixed and variable expenses include administrative costs (including building personnel), operating expenses, and maintenance costs. Fixed expenses that remain constant and do not change include employee wages, utilities, and other basic operating costs. Variable expenses may be recurring or nonrecurring and can include capital improvements, building repairs, and landscaping.

Cash flow report A cash flow report is a monthly statement that details the financial status of the property. Sources of income and expenses are noted, as well as net operating income, and net cash flow. The cash flow report is the most important financial report because it provides a picture of the current financial status of a property.

The formula for arriving at cash flow is as follows:

Gross rental income + Other income − Losses incurred = Total income

Total income − Operating expenses = Net operating income before debt service (e.g., mortgage payments)

Net operating income before debt service − Debt service − Reserves = Cash flow

A profit and loss statement is a financial picture of the revenues and expenses used to determine whether the business has made money or suffered a loss. It may be prepared monthly, quarterly, semiannually, or annually. The statement is created from the monthly cash flow reports and does not include itemized information. A formula for profit and loss statement looks like this:

Gross receipts − Operating expenses − Total mortgage payment + Mortgage loan principal = Net profit

Budget comparison statement The budget comparison statement compares the actual results with the original budget, often giving either percentages or a numerical variance of actual versus projected income and expenses. Budget comparisons are especially helpful in identifying trends in order to help with future budget planning.

Renting the Property

Effective rental of the property is essential to ensure the long-term financial health of the property. The property manager sometimes makes use of a leasing agent as one part of property management.

Setting rental rates Rental rates are influenced primarily by supply and demand. The property manager should conduct a detailed survey of the competitive space available in the neighborhood, emphasizing similar properties. In establishing rental rates, the property manager has four long-term considerations:

- The rental income must be *sufficient to cover the property's fixed charges and operating expenses*.
- The rental income must *provide a fair return on the owner's investment*.
- The rental rate should be *in line with prevailing rates in comparable buildings in the area*. It may be slightly higher or slightly lower, depending on the strength of the property.
- The *current vacancy rate in the property* is a good indicator of how much of a rent increase is advisable. A building with a low vacancy rate is a better candidate for an increase than one with a high vacancy rate.

A rental rate for residential space is usually stated as the monthly rate per unit. Commercial leases—including office, retail, and industrial space rentals—are usually stated according to either annual or monthly rates *per square foot.*

An elevated level of vacancy may indicate poor management or a defective or an undesirable property. On the other hand, a high occupancy rate may mean that rental rates are too low. Whenever the occupancy level of an apartment house or office building exceeds 95 percent, consideration should be given to raising rents. First, however, the manager should investigate the rental market to determine whether a rent increase is warranted.

Selecting Tenants

Proper selection is the first step in establishing and maintaining sound, long-term relationships with tenants. The manager should be sure that the premises are suitable for a tenant in size, location, and amenities and that the tenant is able to pay for the space.

A commercial tenant's business should be compatible with the building and the other tenants. The manager must consider how all tenants mesh. The types of businesses or services should be complementary, and the introduction of competitors (sometimes precluded in the lease) should be undertaken only with care. This not only pleases existing tenants but helps diversify the owner's investment and increases the likelihood of profitability.

If a commercial tenant is likely to expand in the future, the manager should consider the property's potential for expansion.

The residential property manager must always comply with fair housing laws in selecting tenants. Although fair housing laws do not apply to commercial properties, commercial property managers need to be aware of federal, state, and local antidiscrimination and equal opportunity laws that may govern industrial or retail properties.

Collecting rents   A property manager should accept only those tenants who can be expected to meet their financial obligations. In addition to contacting credit bureaus, the selection process involves calling financial references and, if possible, interviewing the former landlord.

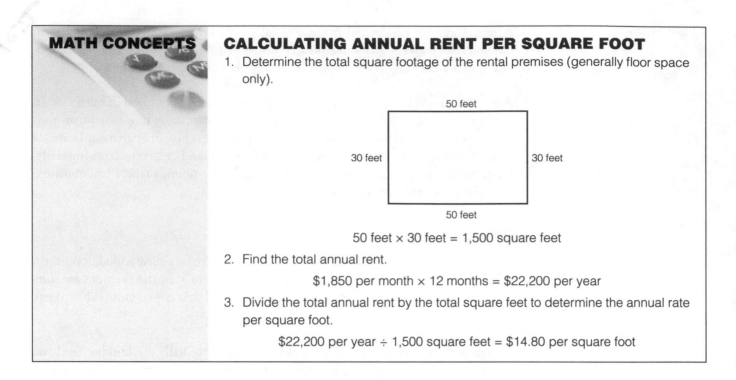

MATH CONCEPTS

CALCULATING ANNUAL RENT PER SQUARE FOOT

1. Determine the total square footage of the rental premises (generally floor space only).

50 feet

30 feet   30 feet

50 feet

50 feet × 30 feet = 1,500 square feet

2. Find the total annual rent.

$1,850 per month × 12 months = $22,200 per year

3. Divide the total annual rent by the total square feet to determine the annual rate per square foot.

$22,200 per year ÷ 1,500 square feet = $14.80 per square foot

The terms of rental payment should be spelled out in the lease agreement, including

■ time and place of payment,
■ provisions and penalties for late payment and returned checks, and
■ provisions for cancellation and damages in case of nonpayment.

The property manager should establish a firm and consistent collection plan. The plan should include a system of notices and records that complies with state and local law.

Every attempt must be made to collect rent without resorting to legal action. Legal action is costly and time-consuming and does not contribute to good tenant relations. When it is unavoidable, legal action must be taken in cooperation with the property owner's or management firm's legal counsel.

In Illinois

Specific legal procedures must be followed in taking legal action against a tenant. In addition, Illinois law has specific provisions regarding the maintenance and payment of interest on security deposits. Property managers (who must have broker or managing broker licenses) must put security deposits in a special escrow account, in the same way that real estate licensees must handle earnest money. The security deposits must be deposited in the escrow account by the *next business day* after a lease is signed, and this must be recorded in the journal and ledger. This escrow account is a non-interest-bearing account unless the property is residential with 25 or more units, in which case interest must be paid to the tenants. ■

Maintaining Good Relations with Tenants

The ultimate success of a property manager depends on the ability of the manager to maintain good relations with tenants. Dissatisfied tenants eventually vacate the property. A high tenant turnover rate results in greater expenses for advertising and redecorating as well as lowered profits from rents.

An effective property manager establishes a good communication system with tenants. Regular newsletters or posted memoranda help keep tenants informed and involved. Maintenance and service requests must be attended to promptly, and all lease terms and building rules must be enforced consistently and fairly. A good manager is tactful and decisive and acts to the benefit of both owner and occupants.

The property manager must be able to handle residents who do not pay their rents on time or who break building regulations. When one tenant fails to follow the rules, the other tenants often become frustrated and dissatisfied. Careful record keeping shows whether rent is remitted promptly and in the proper amount. Records of all lease renewal dates should be kept so that the manager can anticipate expiration and retain good tenants who otherwise might move when their leases end.

Maintaining the Property

One of the most important functions of a property manager is the supervision of property maintenance. A manager must learn to balance services provided with their costs—that is, to satisfy tenants' needs while minimizing operating expenses.

To maintain the property efficiently, the manager must be able to assess the building's needs and how best to meet them. Staffing requirements vary with the type, size, and geographic location of the property, so the owner and manager usually agree in advance on maintenance objectives. In some cases, the best plan may be to operate a low-rental property with minimal expenditures for services and maintenance. Another property may be more lucrative if kept in top condition and operated with all possible tenant services. A well-maintained, high-service property can command premium rental rates.

A primary maintenance objective is to protect the physical integrity of the property over the long term. For example, preserving the property by repainting the exterior or replacing the heating system helps decrease long-term maintenance costs. Keeping the property in good condition involves the following four types of maintenance:

- Preventive maintenance
- Repair or corrective maintenance
- Routine maintenance
- Construction

Preventive maintenance
helps prevent problems
and expenses.
Corrective maintenance
corrects problems after
they've occurred.
Routine maintenance keeps
up with everyday wear and
tear.

Preventive maintenance includes regularly scheduled activities such as painting and seasonal servicing of appliances and systems. Preventive maintenance preserves the long-range value and physical integrity of the building. This is both the most critical and the most neglected maintenance responsibility. Failure to perform preventive maintenance invariably leads to greater expense in other areas of maintenance.

Repair or *corrective maintenance* involves the actual repairs that keep the building's equipment, utilities, and amenities functioning. Repairing a boiler, fixing a leaky faucet, or mending a broken air-conditioning unit are acts of corrective maintenance.

A property manager must also supervise the *routine maintenance* of the building. Routine maintenance includes such day-to-day duties as cleaning common areas, performing minor carpentry and plumbing adjustments, and providing regularly scheduled upkeep of landscaping. Good routine maintenance is similar to good preventive maintenance. Both head off problems before they become expensive.

IN PRACTICE   One of the major decisions a property manager faces is whether to contract for maintenance services from an outside firm or hire on-site employees to perform such tasks. This decision should be based on a number of factors, including

- size of the building,
- complexity of the tenants' requirements, and
- availability of suitable labor.

> **Construction** involves making a property meet a tenant's needs.

A commercial or an industrial property manager often is called on to make **tenant improvements**. These are alterations to the interior of the building to meet a tenant's particular space needs. Such *construction* alterations range from simply repainting or recarpeting to completely gutting the interior and redesigning the space by erecting new walls, adding partitions, and revamping electrical systems. In new construction, especially, the interiors are usually left incomplete so that they can be adapted to the needs of individual tenants. One matter that must be clarified is which improvements will be considered *trade fixtures* (personal property belonging to the tenant) and which will belong to the owner of the real estate.

Modernization or renovation of buildings that have become functionally obsolete and thus unsuited to today's building needs is also important. The renovation of a building often enhances marketability and potential income.

Handling Environmental Concerns

Property managers must be able to respond to a variety of environmental problems because they have become increasingly important issues. Managers may manage structures containing asbestos or radon or be called on to arrange an environmental audit of a property. Managers must see that any hazardous wastes produced by their employers or tenants are properly disposed of. Even nonhazardous waste of an office building must be controlled to avoid violation of laws requiring segregation and recycling of types of wastes. Of course, property managers may want to provide recycling facilities for tenants even if not required by law to do so. On-site recycling creates an image of good citizenship that enhances the reputation (and value) of a commercial or residential property.

Air quality issues are a key concern for those involved in property management and design. Building related illness (BRI) and sick building syndrome (SBS) are illnesses that are more prevalent today because of energy and efficiency standards used in construction that make buildings more airtight with less ventilation. SBS is more typical in an office building.

The Americans with Disabilities Act

The **Americans with Disabilities Act** (ADA) has had a significant impact on the responsibilities of the property manager, both in building amenities and in employment issues.

Title I of the ADA provides for the employment of qualified job applicants regardless of their disability. Any employer with 15 or more employees must adopt nondiscriminatory employment procedures. In addition, employers must make reasonable accommodations to enable individuals with disabilities to perform essential job functions.

Property managers must also be familiar with Title III of the ADA, which prohibits discrimination in commercial properties and public accommodations. The ADA requires that managers ensure that people with disabilities have full and equal access to facilities and services. The property manager typically is responsible for determining whether a building meets the ADA's accessibility requirements. The property manager must also prepare and execute a plan for restructuring or retrofitting a building that is not in compliance. ADA experts and architectural designers may need to be consulted.

To protect owners of existing structures from the massive expense of extensive remodeling, the ADA recommends *reasonably achievable accommodations* to provide access to the facilities and services. New construction and remodeling, however, must meet higher standards because new design costs less than retrofitting. An unexpected benefit to new owners is that many of the accessible design features and accommodations benefit everyone.

Existing barriers must be removed when this can be accomplished in a readily achievable manner—that is, with little difficulty and at low cost. (See Figure 18.1.) The following are typical examples of readily achievable modifications:

- Ramping or removing an obstacle from an otherwise accessible entrance
- Lowering wall-mounted public telephones
- Adding raised letters and Braille markings on elevator buttons
- Installing auditory signals in elevators
- Reversing the direction in which doors open (for wheelchair accessibility)
- Providing doors that have mechanisms that will open and close the doors automatically

Alternative methods can be used to provide reasonable accommodations if extensive restructuring is impractical or if retrofitting is unduly expensive. For instance, installing a cup dispenser at a water fountain that is too high for an individual in a wheelchair may be more practical than installing a lower unit.

IN PRACTICE   Federal, state, and local laws may provide additional requirements for accommodating people with disabilities. Real estate licensees should be aware of the full range of laws to ensure that their practices are in compliance.

F I G U R E   18.1

Reasonable Modifications to Public Facilities or Services

Provide doors with automatic opening mechanisms	Provide menus (and real estate listings) in a large-print or braille format.
Install an intercom so customers can contact a second-floor business in a building without an elevator	Lower public telephones
Add grab bars to public restroom stalls	Permit service animals to accompany customers
Provide a shopper's assistant to help disabled customers	Provide ramps in addition to entry stairs

■ RISK MANAGEMENT

Enormous monetary losses can result from certain unexpected or catastrophic events. As a result, one of the most critical areas of responsibility for a property manager is risk management. **Risk management** involves answering the question "What happens if something goes wrong?"

The perils of any risk must be evaluated in terms of options. In considering the possibility of a loss, the property manager must decide whether it is better to

The four alternative risk management techniques may be remembered by the acronym **ACTOR**: *Avoid, Control, Transfer, or Retain.*

- *avoid* risk, by removing the source of risk (for instance, a swimming pool may pose an unacceptable risk if a day care center is located in the building);
- *control* risk, by preparing for an emergency before it happens (e.g., by installing sprinklers, fire doors, and security systems);
- *transfer* risk, by shifting the risk onto another party (that is, by taking out an insurance policy); or
- *retain* risk, by deciding that the chances of the event occurring are too small to justify the expense of any other response (an alternative might be to take out an insurance policy with a large deductible, which is usually considerably less expensive).

Security of Tenants

The physical safety of tenants of the leased premises is an important issue for property managers and owners. Recent court decisions in several parts of the country have held owners and their agents responsible for physical harm that was inflicted on tenants by intruders. These decisions have prompted property managers and owners to think about how to protect tenants and secure apartments from intruders.

Types of Insurance

Insurance is one way to protect against losses. Many types of insurance are available. An insurance audit should be performed by a competent, reliable insurance agent who is familiar with insurance issues for the type of property involved. The audit will indicate areas in which greater or lesser coverage is recommended and will highlight particular risks. The final decision, however, must be made by the property owner.

Some common types of coverage available to income property owners and managers include the following:

■ *Fire and hazard:* Fire insurance policies provide coverage against direct loss or damage to property from a fire on the premises. Standard fire coverage can be extended to include other hazards such as windstorm, hail, smoke damage, or civil insurrection.

■ *Consequential loss, use, and occupancy:* Consequential loss insurance covers the results, or consequences, of a disaster. Consequential loss can include the loss of rent or revenue to a business that occurs if the business's property cannot be used.

■ *Contents and personal property:* This type of insurance covers building contents and personal property during periods when they are not actually located on the business premises.

■ *Liability:* Public liability insurance covers the risks an owner assumes whenever the public enters the building. A claim paid under this coverage is used for medical expenses by a person who is injured in the building as a result of the owner's negligence. Claims for those hurt in the course of their employment are covered by state laws known as **workers' compensation acts.** (A building owner who is an employer must obtain a workers' compensation policy from a private insurance company.)

■ *Casualty:* Casualty insurance policies include coverage against theft, burglary, vandalism, and machinery damage as well as health and accident insurance. Casualty policies are usually written on specific risks, such as theft, rather than being all-inclusive.

■ *Surety bonds:* **Surety bonds** cover an owner against financial losses resulting from an employee's criminal acts or negligence while performing assigned duties.

Many insurance companies offer **multiperil policies** for apartment and commercial buildings. Such a policy offers the property manager a "package" of standard commercial coverages, such as fire, hazard, public liability, and casualty. Special coverage for earthquakes and floods is also available.

Insurance for the personal property of tenants is also available to tenants. Many tenants do not realize that if a property burns, their personal property is usually not covered by the landlord's policy. (In Illinois, the policy type tenants should ask for is HO-4, designed specifically to cover renters' personal property.)

Claims

Two possible methods can be used to determine the amount of a claim under an insurance policy. One is the *depreciated*, or *actual, cash value* of the damaged property. That is, the property is not insured for what it would cost to replace it but rather for what it was originally worth, *less the depreciation in value* that results from use and the passage of time. The other method is *current replacement cost*. In this sort of policy, the building or property is insured for what it would cost to rebuild or replace it today.

When purchasing insurance, a manager must decide whether a property should be insured at full replacement cost or at a depreciated cost. Full replacement cost coverage is generally more expensive than depreciated cost. As with homeowners' policies, commercial policies include coinsurance clauses that require the insured to carry fire coverage, usually in an amount equal to 80 percent of a building's replacement value. If the coinsured amount is met on a policy guaranteeing replacement cost, it may mean that if a property is destroyed, the insured can collect more than the stated appraised value on the property.

■ THE MANAGEMENT PROFESSION

Most metropolitan areas have local associations of building and property owners and managers that are affiliates of regional and national associations. of these professional organizations provide information and contacts for all aspects of property management. Here is a list of some well-known associations:

- Building Owners and Managers Association International (BOMA): commercial real estate
- Building Owners and Managers Institute International (BOMI): education programs for commercial property and facility management industries
- Community Associations Institute (CAI): homeowners' associations, condominiums, and other planned communities
- Institute of Real Estate Management (IREM): multifamily and commercial real estate designation
- International Council of Shopping Centers (ICSC): shopping centers worldwide
- National Apartment Association (NAA): multifamily housing industry
- National Association of Home Builders (NAHB): all aspects of home building
- National Association of Residential Property Managers (NARPM): single-family and small residential properties

■ SUMMARY

Property management is a specialized service provided to owners of income-producing properties. The owner's managerial function may be delegated to an individual or a firm with particular expertise in the field. The property manager, as agent of the owner, becomes the administrator of the project and assumes the executive functions required for the care and operation of the property.

A management agreement establishes the agency relationship between owner and manager. It must be prepared carefully to define and authorize the manager's duties and responsibilities, and it should be in writing.

Projected expenses, the manager's analysis of the building's condition, and local rent patterns form the basis for determining rental rates for the property. Once a rent schedule is established, the property manager is responsible for soliciting financially responsible tenants whose needs are suited to the available space. The manager collects rents, maintains the building, hires necessary employees, pays taxes for the building, and deals with tenant problems.

Maintenance includes safeguarding the physical integrity of the property and performing routine cleaning and repairs. It also includes making tenant improvements, such as adapting the interior space and overall design of the property to suit tenants' needs.

The manager is expected to secure adequate insurance coverage for the premises. Fire and hazard insurance cover the property and fixtures against catastrophes. Consequential loss, use, and occupancy insurance protects the owner against revenue losses. Casualty insurance provides coverage against losses such as theft, vandalism, and destruction of machinery. The manager should also secure public liability insurance to insure the owner against claims made by people injured on the premises. Workers' compensation policies cover the claims of employees injured on the job.

Increasing needs for safety and security awareness, knowledge of environmental issues, and concern for the federal and state fair housing laws round out the potpourri of issues that a property manager must often address.

This growing real estate specialty is supported by many regional and national organizations that help property managers maintain high professional standards. A few of the most important ones are the Building Owners and Managers Association (BOMA), the Building Owners and Managers Institute (BOMI), and the Institute of Real Estate Management (IREM).

In Illinois

Property managers must be licensed real estate brokers or managing brokers. Resident managers are exempt under certain circumstances.

Community association managers are now regulated under the Community Association Manager Licensing and Disciplinary Act. ■

CHAPTER 18 QUIZ

1. Which type of insurance coverage insures an employer against MOST claims for job-related injuries?
   a. Consequential loss
   b. Workers' compensation
   c. Casualty
   d. Surety bond

2. Residential leases are usually expressed as a(n)
   a. annual or monthly rate per square foot.
   b. percentage of total space available.
   c. monthly rate per unit.
   d. annual rate per room.

3. Avoid, control, transfer, or retain are the four alternative techniques of
   a. tenant relations.
   b. acquiring insurance.
   c. risk management
   d. property management.

4. From a management point of view, apartment building occupancy that reaches as high as 98 percent would tend to indicate that the
   a. building is poorly managed.
   b. building has reached its maximum potential.
   c. building is a desirable place to live.
   d. rents could be raised.

5. A guest slips on an icy apartment building stair and is hospitalized. A claim against the building owner for medical expenses may be paid under which of the following policies held by the owner?
   a. Workers' compensation
   b. Casualty
   c. Liability
   d. Fire and hazard

6. When a property manager is establishing a budget for the building, what should be included as an operating expense?
   a. Replacement reserves
   b. Debt service
   c. Utilities
   d. Depreciation

7. A property manager is offered a choice of three insurance policies with different deductibles. If the property manager selects the policy with the highest deductible, which risk management technique is being used?
   a. Avoiding risk
   b. Retaining risk
   c. Controlling risk
   d. Transferring risk

8. Contaminated groundwater, toxic fumes from paint and carpeting, and lack of proper ventilation are all examples of
   a. issues beyond the scope of a property manager's job description.
   b. problems faced only in newly constructed properties.
   c. issues that arise under the Americans with Disabilities Act.
   d. environmental concerns that a property manager may have to address.

9. Tenant improvements are
   a. always construed to be fixtures.
   b. adaptations of space to suit tenants' needs.
   c. removable by the tenant.
   d. paid for by the landlord.

10. Which of the following would be considered a variable expense when a manager develops an operating budget?
    a. Employee wages
    b. Utilities
    c. Building repairs
    d. Basic operating costs

11. In MOST market areas, rents are determined by
    a. supply-and-demand factors.
    b. the local apartment owners' association.
    c. HUD's annually published rental guidelines.
    d. a tenants' union.

12. A highrise apartment building burns to the ground. What type of insurance covers the landlord against the resulting loss of rent?
    a. Fire and hazard
    b. Liability
    c. Consequential loss, use, and occupancy
    d. Casualty

13. A property manager hires a full-time maintenance person. While repairing a faucet in one of the apartments, the maintenance person steals a television set, and the tenant sues the owner. The property manager could protect the owner against this type of loss by purchasing
    a. liability insurance.
    b. workers' compensation insurance.
    c. a surety bond.
    d. casualty insurance.

14. Which of the following might indicate rents are too low?
    a. A poorly maintained building
    b. Many *For Lease* signs in the area
    c. High building occupancy
    d. High tenant turnover rates

15. A property manager repairs a malfunctioning boiler in the building. This is classified as which type of maintenance?
    a. Preventive
    b. Corrective
    c. Routine
    d. Construction

16. A property manager who enters into a management agreement with an owner is usually a
    a. special agent.
    b. a general agent.
    c. universal agent.
    d. designated agent.

17. Which law requires removing existing barriers when readily achievable in public buildings and adding Braille markings to elevator buttons?
    a. Fair Housing Act
    b. Equal Credit Opportunity Act
    c. Americans with Disabilities Act
    d. Regulation Z

18. Which action by a property manager would be a breach of her fiduciary relationship to the owner?
    a. Checking the credit history of minority applicants only
    b. Generating a high net operating income by maintaining the property
    c. Maintaining good relations with the tenants
    d. Scrutinizing property expenses

In Illinois

19. A property manager's total compensation consists of a monthly salary, a 12 percent commission based on annual rental for each vacant unit the property manager fills, and the free use of one of the apartments as the property manager's personal primary residence. Based on these facts, is the property manager required by Illinois law to obtain a real estate broker or managing broker license?
    a. Yes. Any person who is compensated for performing real estate activities for a commission must have a broker or managing broker license, regardless of any other form of compensation.
    b. Yes. Because the property manager's compensation is based in part on recruiting new tenants rather than simply collecting rents, the property manager must have a broker or managing broker license.
    c. No. Property managers are not required to have real estate licenses in Illinois.
    d. No. Persons acting as resident managers, who live in the managed property, are specifically exempt from the general licensing requirements.

20. The manager of a small (20 units) apartment building requires a security deposit. In this case, the manager
    a. must pay interest on the security deposit.
    b. is not required to pay interest on the security deposit.
    c. is not required to deposit the security deposit into an escrow account.
    d. may deposit the security deposit into the general operating fund.

Real Estate Appraisal

■ **LEARNING OBJECTIVES**   *When you've finished reading this chapter, you should be able to*

- ■ **identify** the different types and basic principles of value;

- ■ **describe** the three basic valuation approaches used by appraisers;

- ■ **explain** the steps in the appraisal process;

- ■ **distinguish** the four methods of determining reproduction or replacement cost; and

- ■ **define** the following *key terms*

anticipation	gross income multiplier (GIM)	reconciliation
appraisal		regression
appraiser	gross rent multiplier (GRM)	replacement cost
assemblage		reproduction cost
broker's price opinion (BPO)	highest and best use	sales comparison approach
	income approach	
capitalization rate (cap)	index method	square-foot method
change	law of increasing returns	straight-line method
competition	law of diminishing returns	substitution
conformity	market value	supply and demand
contribution	net operating income (NOI)	Uniform Standards of Professional Appraisal Practice (USPAP)
cost approach		
depreciation	physical deterioration	unit-in-place method
economic life	plottage	value
external obsolescence	progression	
functional obsolescence	quantity-survey method	

■ REAL ESTATE APPRAISAL

Appraisal is a distinct area of specialization within the world of real estate professionals. Appraisal provides a clearer understanding about the market's response to a subject property. Real estate licensees must be aware of the fundamental principles of valuation in order to complete an accurate and effective competitive market analysis (CMA) that assists seller clients in arriving at a reasonable asking price and buyer clients to make appropriate offers based on current market conditions. Furthermore, knowledge of the appraisal process allows the licensee to recognize an unacceptable appraisal.

■ APPRAISING

An **appraisal** is an opinion of value based on supportable evidence and approved methods. An *appraisal* report is an opinion of market value on a property given to a lender or client with detailed and accurate information. An **appraiser** is an independent person trained to provide an *unbiased* opinion of value in an impartial and objective manner, according to the appraisal process. Appraising is a professional service performed for a fee.

Regulation of Appraisal Activities

Title XI of the federal Financial Institutions Reform, Recovery, and Enforcement Act of 1989 (FIRREA) requires that most appraisals used in connection with a federally related transaction be performed by someone licensed or certified by law. A *federally related transaction* is any real estate-related financial transaction in which a federal financial institution or regulatory agency engages in, contracts for, or regulates and requires the services of an appraiser. This includes transactions involving the sale, lease, purchase, investment, or exchange of real property. It also includes the financing, refinancing, or the use of real property as security for a loan or an investment, including mortgage-backed securities.

Federal law requires that appraisers be licensed or certified according to individual state law. State qualifications must conform to the federal requirements that, in turn, follow the criteria for certification established by the Appraiser Qualifications Board of the Appraisal Foundation. The Appraisal Foundation is a national body composed of representatives of the major appraisal and related organizations. Appraisers are also expected to follow the **Uniform Standards of Professional Appraisal Practice (USPAP)** established by the foundation's Appraisal Standards Board.

In Illinois | The Real Estate Appraiser Licensing Act of 2002, as amended in 2009, provides for mandatory licensure with limited exceptions of Illinois appraisers. It is located under Illinois Compiled Statutes, Chapter 225, 225 ILCS 458, at *www.ilga.gov*.

Illinois recognizes three categories of appraisers:

■ *Associate real estate trainee appraiser*—entry level appraiser; all reports must be cosigned by a state certified residential real estate appraiser or state certified general real estate appraiser.

- *Certified residential real estate appraiser*—qualified to appraise residential property of one unit to four units without regard to transaction value or complexity, but with restrictions in accordance with Title XI, USPAP, and criteria established by the Appraisal Qualifications Board (AQB).
- *Certified general real estate appraiser*—qualified to appraise all types of real property without restrictions as to the scope of practice subject to USPAP requirements.

Only individuals (not corporations, partnerships, firms, or groups) may be certified as appraisers or act as associate real estate appraisers. A certified appraiser may, however, sign appraisal reports on behalf of a business entity. ■

An appraisal report prepared by an appraiser recognized under the act must identify on the report, by name, the individual who ordered or originated the appraisal assignment. The appraiser must retain the original copy of all contracts engaging his services as an appraiser and all appraisal reports, including any supporting data used to develop the appraisal report, for a period of not less than five years, or two years after the final disposition of any judicial proceeding in which testimony was given, whichever is longer. In addition, the appraiser must retain contracts, logs, and appraisal reports used in meeting prelicense experience requirements for a period of five years.

The Real Estate Appraiser Licensing Act of 2002 established a fee structure and disciplinary and enforcement mechanism for appraisers. Associate real estate trainee and certification candidates also must meet strict competency, educational, examination, and experience requirements. The appraisal profession itself maintains rigorous standards requiring all Illinois associate trainees to become certified residential appraisers within two years of initial licensure. An individual appraiser may *not* use the titles "state certified" or "associate real estate trainee appraiser" unless he is recognized as such by the state.

Competitive Market Analysis

Not all estimates of value are made by professional appraisers. Real estate licensees often must help a seller arrive at a listing price or assist a buyer in determining an offering price for property without the aid of a formal appraisal report. In such a case, the licensee would use a comparative market analysis (CMA). A CMA is distinctly different from an appraisal report offered by a licensed appraiser. An appraisal is based on an analysis of properties that have actually sold; the CMA, in contrast, features properties similar to the subject property in size, location, and amenities. The CMA is based on

- recently closed properties (solds),
- properties currently on the market (competition for the subject property), and
- properties that did not sell (expired listings in the area).

Broker's Price Opinion (BPO)

A broker's price opinion (BPO) is a less-expensive alternative of valuating properties often used by lenders working with home equity lines, refinancing, portfolio management, loss mitigation, and collections. Both Fannie Mae and Freddie

Mac provide forms that are used by real estate licensees who perform BPOs for a fee. Although some BPOs are more extensive, including information about the neighborhood and interior analysis, many are simply "drive bys" that verify the existence of the property, along with a listing of comparable sales. A BPO should not be confused with an appraisal, which consists of more in-depth analysis of gathered information and which may be performed only by a licensed appraiser. A BPO cannot be used if the matter involves a federally related transaction that requires an appraisal and/or the transaction occurs in a state that requires an appraiser's license.

■ VALUE

Memory Tip

The four characteristics of value can be remembered by the acronym **DUST**:
- Demand
- Utility
- Scarcity
- Transferability

To have **value** in the real estate market—that is, to have monetary worth based on desirability—a property must have the following four characteristics:

- *Demand*—The need or desire for possession or ownership backed by the financial means to satisfy that need
- *Utility*—The property's usefulness for its intended purposes
- *Scarcity*—A finite supply
- *Transferability*—The relative ease with which ownership rights are transferred from one person to another

Market Value

The goal of an appraiser is to estimate or express an opinion of market value. The **market value** of real estate is the most probable price that a property should bring in a fair sale. This definition makes three assumptions. First, it presumes a competitive and open market. Second, the buyer and seller are both assumed to be acting prudently and knowledgeably. Finally, market value depends on the price not being affected by unusual circumstances.

The following are essential factors in rendering an opinion of value:

- The most probable price is *not* the average or highest price.
- The buyer and seller must be unrelated and acting without undue pressure.
- Both buyer and seller must be well informed about the property's use and potential, including both its defects and its advantages.
- A reasonable time must be allowed for exposure in the open market.
- Payment must be made in cash or its equivalent.
- The price must represent a normal consideration for the property sold, unaffected by special financing amounts or terms, services, fees, costs, or credits incurred in the market transaction.

Market value is a reasonable opinion of a property's value.
Market price is the actual selling price of a property.
Cost may not equal either market value or market price.

Market value versus market price   *Market value* is an opinion of value based on an analysis of data. The data may include not only an analysis of comparable sales but also an analysis of potential income, expenses, and replacement costs (less any depreciation). *Market price*, on the other hand, is what a property *actually* sells for—its sales price.

Market value versus cost   An important distinction can be made between market value and cost. One of the most common misconceptions about valuing property is that cost represents market value. Cost and market value may be the same. In fact, when the improvements on a property are new, cost and value are likely to be equal. But more often, cost does not equal market value. For example, a homeowner may install a swimming pool for a cost of $15,000; however, the cost of the improvement may not add $15,000 to the value of the property.

Basic Principles of Value

A number of economic principles can affect the value of real estate. The most important are defined in the text that follows.

Anticipation   According to the principle of **anticipation**, value is created by the expectation that certain events will occur. Value can increase or decrease in anticipation of some future benefit or detriment. For instance, the value of a house may be affected if rumors circulate that an adjacent property may be converted to commercial use in the near future. If a property is neglected, it is possible that the neighboring home's value will increase. If a vacant property was perceived as a park or playground that added to the neighborhood's quiet atmosphere, the news of commercial use might cause a home's value to decline. The principle of anticipation is the foundation on which the income approach to value is based.

Change   No physical or economic condition remains constant. This is the principle of **change**. Real estate is subject to natural phenomena such as tornadoes, fires, and routine wear and tear. The real estate business is subject to market demands, as is any other business. An appraiser must be knowledgeable about both the past and perhaps the predictable future effects of natural phenomena and the changeable behavior of the marketplace.

Competition   **Competition** is the *interaction* of supply and demand. Excess profits tend to attract competition. For example, the success of a retail store may cause investors to open similar stores in the area. This tends to mean less profit for all the stores concerned unless the purchasing power in the area increases substantially.

Conformity   The principle of **conformity** means that maximum value is created when a property is in harmony with its surroundings. Maximum value is realized if the use of land conforms to existing neighborhood standards. In single-family residential neighborhoods, for instance, buildings should be similar in design, construction, size, and age.

Contribution   Under the principle of **contribution**, the value of any part of a property is measured by its effect on the value of the whole. Installing a swimming pool, greenhouse, or private bowling alley may not add value to the property equal to the cost, but remodeling an outdated kitchen or bathroom might.

Highest and best use   The most profitable single use to which a property may be put, or the use that is most likely to be in demand in the near future, is the property's **highest and best use**. The use must be

■ legally permitted,
■ economically or financially feasible,
■ physically possible, and
■ the most profitable or maximally productive.

The highest and best use of a site can change with social, political, and economic forces. A parking lot in a busy downtown area, for example, may not maximize the land's profitability to the same extent an office would. Highest and best use is noted in every appraisal.

Increasing and diminishing returns   The addition of more improvements to land and structures increases total value only to the asset's *maximum value*. Beyond that point, additional improvements no longer affect a property's value. As long as money spent on improvements produces an increase in income or value, the **law of increasing returns** applies. At the point where additional improvements do not increase income or value, the **law of diminishing returns** applies. No matter how much money is spent on the property, the property's value will not keep pace with the expenditures. A remodeled kitchen or bathroom might increase the value of a house; adding restaurant-quality appliances and gold faucets, however, would be a cost that the owner probably would not be able to recover.

Plottage: The total value of two adjacent properties may be greater if they are combined than the sum of their individual values if each is sold separately.

Plottage   The principle of **plottage** holds that merging or consolidating adjacent lots into a single larger one produces a greater total land value than the sum of the two sites valued separately. For example, two adjacent lots valued at $35,000 each might have a combined value of $90,000 if consolidated. The process of merging two separately owned lots under one owner is known as **assemblage**. *Plottage* is the amount that value is increased by successful assemblage.

Regression: The lowering of a property's value due to its neighbors.
Progression: The increasing of a property's value due to its neighbors.

Regression and progression   In general, the worth of a better-quality property is adversely affected by the presence of a lesser-quality property. This is known as the principle of **regression**. Thus, in a neighborhood of modest homes, a structure that is larger, better maintained, or more luxurious would tend to be valued in the same range as the less-lavish homes. Conversely, under the principle of **progression**, the value of a modest home would be higher if it were located among larger, fancier properties.

Substitution   Under the principle of **substitution**, the maximum value of a property tends to be set by how much it would cost to purchase an equally desirable and valuable substitute property. Substitution is the foundation of the sales comparison approach.

Supply and demand   The principle of **supply and demand** holds that the value of a property depends on the number of properties available in the marketplace—the supply of the product. When supply increases, value decreases and when demand increases, value increases. Other factors include the prices of other properties, the number of prospective purchasers, and the price buyers will pay.

■ THE THREE APPROACHES TO VALUE

To arrive at an accurate opinion of value, appraisers traditionally use three basic valuation techniques: the *sales comparison approach*, the *cost approach*, and the *income approach*. The three methods serve as checks against each other. Using them narrows the range within which the final estimate of value falls. Each method addresses a specific type of property.

The Sales Comparison Approach

In the **sales comparison approach** (also known as the *market data approach*), an estimate of value is obtained by comparing the property being appraised (the *subject property*) with recently sold *comparable properties* (properties similar to the subject, called *comps*). Because no two parcels of real estate are exactly alike, each comparable property must be analyzed for differences and similarities between it and the subject property. This approach is a good example of the principle of substitution, discussed previously. The elements of comparison for which adjustments must be made include the following:

■ *Property rights:* An adjustment must be made when less than fee simple, the full legal bundle of rights, is involved. This includes land leases, ground rents, life estates, easements, deed restrictions, and encroachments.
■ *Financing concessions:* The financing terms must be considered, including adjustments for differences such as mortgage loan terms and owner financing.
■ *Market conditions:* Interest rates, supply and demand, and other economic indicators must be analyzed.
■ *Conditions of sale:* Adjustments must be made for motivational factors that would affect the sale, such as foreclosure, a sale between family members, or some nonmonetary incentive.
■ *Market conditions since the date of sale:* An adjustment must be made if economic changes occur between the date of sale of the comparable property and the date of the appraisal.
■ *Location or area preference:* Similar properties might differ in price from neighborhood to neighborhood or even between locations within the same neighborhood.
■ *Physical features and amenities:* Physical features, such as the structure's age, size, and condition, may require adjustments.

■ **FOR EXAMPLE** Two condos in the same neighborhood, one that sold and one that is the subject of an appraisal, are very similar. The comp sold for $145,000 and has a garage valued at $9,000. The subject property has no garage, but it has a fireplace valued at $5,000. What is the indicated value of the property?

$145,000	The comp sale price
−9,000	(The Comp is Better, Subtract—CBS)
+5,000	(The Comp is Poorer, Add—CPA)
$141,000	The indicated value of the subject property

Memory Tip

Take the selling price of the comp and add or subtract for any differences, one at a time, from the subject property. The rules are CBS and CPA. **CBS** = if the **C**omp is **B**etter, **S**ubtract. **CPA** = if the **C**omp is **P**oorer, **A**dd

Memory Tip

6 month/1 mile rule

The sales comparison approach is considered the most reliable of the three approaches in appraising single-family homes, where the intangible benefits might be difficult to measure otherwise. Most appraisals include a minimum of three comparable sales reflective of the subject property. Whenever possible, the comparables should be recent (less than six months) and close by (less than a mile) to the subject property. An example of the sales comparison approach is shown in Table 19.1.

TABLE   19.1

Sales Comparison Approach to Value

	Subject Property:	Comparables		
		A	B	C
Sales price		**$260,000**	**$252,000**	**$265,000**
Financing concessions Date of sale	none	none current	none current	none current
Location Age	good 6 years	same same	poorer +6,500 same	same same
Size of lot Landscaping	60' × 135' good	same same	same same	larger –5,000 same
Construction	brick	same	same	same
Style	ranch	same	same	same
No. of rooms	6	same	same	same
No. of bedrooms	3	same	poorer +500	same
No. of baths	1½	same	same	better –500
Sq. ft. of living	1,500	same	same	better –1,000
space	full basement	same	same	same
Other space (basement)	average	better –1,500	poorer +1,000	better –1,500
Condition—	good	same	same	better –500
exterior	2-car attached	same	same	same
Condition—interior	none	none	none	none
Garage				
Other improvements				
Net adjustments		–1,500	+8,000	–8,500
Adjusted value		$258,500	$260,000	$256,500

Note: The value of a feature that is present in the subject but not in the comparable property is *added* to the sales price of the comparable. Likewise, the value of a feature that is present in the comparable but not in the subject property is *subtracted*. A good way to remember this is: CBS stands for "comp better subtract"; and CPA stands for "comp poor add." The adjusted sales prices of the comparables represent the probable range of value of the subject property. From this range, a single market value estimate can be selected.

The Cost Approach

The **cost approach** to value also is based on the principle of substitution. The cost approach consists of five steps:

1. Estimate the *value of the land* as if it were vacant and available to be put to its highest and best use.
2. Estimate the *current cost* of constructing the buildings and improvements.
3. Estimate the amount of *accrued depreciation* resulting from the property's physical deterioration, functional obsolescence, and external depreciation.
4. *Deduct* the accrued depreciation (Step 3) from the current construction cost (Step 2).
5. *Add* the estimated land value (Step 1) to the depreciated cost of the building and site improvements (Step 4) to arrive at the total property value.

■ **FOR EXAMPLE**

> Current cost of construction = $185,000
> Accrued depreciation = $30,000
> Value of the land = $55,000
> $185,000 – $30,000 + 55,000 = $210,000

In this example, the total property value is $210,000.

There are two ways to look at the construction cost of a building for appraisal purposes: reproduction cost and replacement cost. **Reproduction cost** is the construction cost at current prices of an exact duplicate of the subject improvement, including both the benefits and the drawbacks of the property. **Replacement cost** is the cost to construct an improvement similar to the subject property using current construction methods and materials, but not necessarily an exact duplicate. **Replacement cost** is more frequently used in appraising older structures because it eliminates obsolete features and takes advantage of current construction materials and techniques.

An example of the cost approach to value, applied to the same property as in Table 19.1, is shown in Table 19.2.

Determining reproduction or replacement cost new An appraiser using the cost approach computes the reproduction or replacement cost of a building using one of the following four methods:

■ **Square-foot method.** The cost per square foot of a recently built comparable structure is multiplied by the number of square feet (using exterior dimensions) in the subject building. This is the most common and easiest method of cost estimation. Table 19.2 uses the square-foot method, also referred to as the *comparison method.* For some properties, the cost per cubic foot of a recently built comparable structure is multiplied by the number of cubic feet in the subject structure.

■ **Unit-in-place method.** In the unit-in-place method, the replacement cost of a structure is estimated based on the construction cost per unit of measure of individual building components, including material, labor, overhead, and builder's profit. Most components are measured in square feet, although

TABLE 19.2	Subject Property	
Cost Approach to Value	Land valuation: Size 60' × 135' @ $450 per front foot	= $27,000
	Plus site improvements: driveway, walks, landscaping, etc.	= 8,000
	Total	$35,000
	Building valuation: Replacement cost	
	1,500 sq. ft. @ $85 per sq. ft.	= $127,500
	Less depreciation:	
	Physical depreciation	
	Curable	
	(items of deferred maintenance)	
	exterior painting	$4,000
	Incurable (structural deterioration)	9,750
	Functional obsolescence	2,000
	External depreciation	-0-
	Total depreciation	$15,750
	Depreciated value of building	$111,750
	Indicated value by cost approach	$146,750

items such as plumbing fixtures are estimated by cost. The sum of the components is the cost of the new structure.

■ **Quantity-survey method.** The quantity and quality of all materials (such as lumber, brick, and plaster) and the labor are estimated on a unit cost basis. These factors are added to indirect costs (e.g., building permit, survey, payroll, taxes, and builder's profit) to arrive at the total cost of the structure. Because it is so detailed and time-consuming, this method is usually used only in appraising historical properties. It is, however, the most accurate method of appraising new construction.

■ **Index method.** A factor representing the percentage increase of construction costs up to the present time is applied to the original cost of the subject property. Because it fails to take into account individual property variables, this method is useful only as a check of the estimate reached by one of the other methods.

Depreciation   In a real estate appraisal, **depreciation** is a loss in value due to any cause compared with today's cost of replacement. It refers to a condition that adversely affects the value of an improvement to real property. *Land does not depreciate*—it retains its value indefinitely, except in such rare cases as downzoned urban parcels, improperly developed land, or misused farmland. Depreciation is the result of a negative condition that affects real property.

Depreciation is considered to be *curable* or *incurable*, depending on the contribution of the expenditure to the value of the property. For appraisal purposes, depreciation is divided into three classes, according to its cause:

■ **Physical deterioration.** A *curable* item is one in need of repair, such as painting (deferred maintenance), that is economically feasible and would result in an increase in value equal to or exceeding the cost. An item is *incurable* if it is a defect caused by physical wear and tear if its correction would not be economically feasible or contribute a comparable value to the building, such as a crack in the foundation. The cost of a major repair may not warrant the financial investment.

- **Functional obsolescence.** *Obsolescence* means a loss in value from the market's response to the item. Outmoded or unacceptable physical or design features that are no longer considered desirable by purchasers are considered curable. Such features could be replaced or redesigned at a cost that would be offset by the anticipated increase in ultimate value. Outmoded plumbing, for instance, is usually easily replaced. Room function may be redefined at no cost if the basic room layout allows for it. A bedroom adjacent to a kitchen, for example, may be converted to a family room. Incurable obsolescence includes undesirable physical or design features that cannot be easily remedied because the cost of cure would be greater than its resulting increase in value. For example, an office building that cannot be economically air-conditioned suffers from incurable functional obsolescence if the cost of adding air-conditioning is greater than its contribution to the building's value.

- **External obsolescence.** If caused by negative factors not on the subject property, such as zoning, environmental, social, or economic forces, the depreciation is always incurable. The loss in value cannot be reversed by spending money on the property. For example, proximity to a nuisance, such as a polluting factory or a deteriorating neighborhood, is one factor that could not be cured by the owner of the subject property.

The easiest but least precise way to determine depreciation is the **straight-line method,** also called the *economic age-life method.* Depreciation is assumed to occur at an even rate over a structure's **economic life,** the period during which it is expected to remain useful for its original intended purpose. The property's cost is divided by the number of years of its expected economic life to derive the amount of annual depreciation.

■ **FOR EXAMPLE**   A $300,000 property may have a land value of $75,000 and an improvement value of $225,000. If the improvement is expected to last 60 years, the annual straight-line depreciation would be $3,750 ($225,000 divided by 60 years). Such depreciation can be calculated as an annual dollar amount or as a percentage of a property's improvements.

The cost approach is most helpful in the appraisal of newer or special-purpose buildings such as schools, churches, and public buildings. Such properties are difficult to appraise using other methods because there are seldom enough local sales to use as comparables and because the properties do not ordinarily generate income.

Much of the functional obsolescence and all of the external depreciation can be evaluated only by considering the actions of buyers in the marketplace.

The Income Approach

The **income approach** to value is based on the present value of the rights to future income. It assumes that the income generated by a property will determine the

TABLE 19.3	Potential gross annual income	$60,000
	Market rent (100% capacity)	
Income Capitalization Approach to Value	Income from other sources (vending machines and pay phones)	+ 600
		$60,600
	Less vacancy and collection losses (estimated) @4%	−2,424
	Effective gross income	$58,176
	Expenses:	
	Real estate taxes	$9,000
	Insurance	1,000
	Heat	2,500
	Maintenance	6,400
	Utilities	800
	Repairs	1,200
	Decorating	1,400
	Replacement of equipment	800
	Legal and accounting	600
	Advertising	300
	Management	3,000
	Total	$27,000
	Annual net operating income	$31,176

Capitalization rate = 10% (overall rate)

Capitalization of annual net income: $31,176 ÷ 0.10 = $311,760

Indicated Value by Income Approach = $311,760

property's value. The income approach is used for valuation of income-producing properties such as apartment buildings, office buildings, and shopping centers. In estimating value using the income approach, an appraiser must take five steps, illustrated in Table 19.3.

1. Estimate annual *potential gross income*. An estimate of economic rental income must be made based on market studies. Current rental income may not reflect the current market rental rates, especially in the case of short-term leases or leases about to terminate. Potential income includes other income to the property from such sources as vending machines, parking fees, and laundry machines.
2. Deduct an appropriate allowance for vacancy and rent loss, based on the appraiser's experience, and arrive at *effective gross income*.
3. Deduct the annual operating expenses, enumerated in Table 19.3, from the effective gross income to arrive at the annual *net operating income* (NOI). Management costs are always included, even if the current owner manages the property. Mortgage payments (principal and interest) are *debt service* and not considered operating expenses. Capital expenditures are not considered expenses; however, an allowance can be calculated representing the annual usage of each major capital item.
4. Estimate the price a typical investor would pay for the income produced by this particular type and class of property. This is done by estimating the rate of return (or yield) that an investor will demand for the investment of capital in this type of building. This rate of return is called the **capitalization** (or

"cap") **rate** and is determined by comparing the relationship of net operating income to the sales prices of similar properties that have sold in the current market. For example, a comparable property that is producing an annual net income of $15,000 is sold for $187,500. The capitalization rate is $15,000 divided by $187,500, or 8 percent. If other comparable properties sold at prices that yielded substantially the same rate, it may be concluded that 8 percent is the rate that the appraiser should apply to the subject property.

5. Apply the capitalization rate to the property's annual net operating income to arrive at the estimate of the property's value.

With the appropriate capitalization rate and the projected annual net operating income, the appraiser can obtain an indication of value by the income approach.

This formula and its variations are important in dealing with income property:

Income ÷ Rate = Value   Income ÷ Value = Rate   Value × Rate = Income

These formulas may be illustrated graphically as

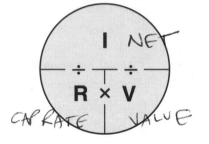

Annual net operating income ÷ Capitalization rate = Value

Example: $72,000 income ÷ 9% cap rate = $800,000 value, or
$72,000 income ÷ 8% cap rate = $900,000 value

Note the relationship between the rate and value. As the rate goes down, the value increases.

A very simplified version of the computations used in applying the income approach is illustrated in Table 19.3.

Gross rent or gross income multipliers   If a buyer is interested in purchasing a one-to-four-unit residential rental property, the **gross rent multiplier** (GRM) would be used for the appraisal value. If the buyer is interested in purchasing five or more units, a commercial **gross income multiplier** (GIM) is often used in the appraisal process.

Because single-family residences usually produce only rental incomes, the gross rent multiplier is used. This relates a sales price to monthly rental income. However, commercial and industrial properties generate income from many other sources (rent, concessions, escalator clause income, and so forth), and they are valued using their annual income from all sources.

The formulas are as follows:

For five or more residential units, commercial, or industrial property:
Sales price ÷ Gross annual income = Gross income multiplier (GIM)

or

For one to four residential units:
Sales price ÷ Gross monthly rent = Gross rent multiplier (GRM)

[handwritten notes: Duplex / GRM 125k / monthly rent 1000 per / Duplex = 2 individual units]

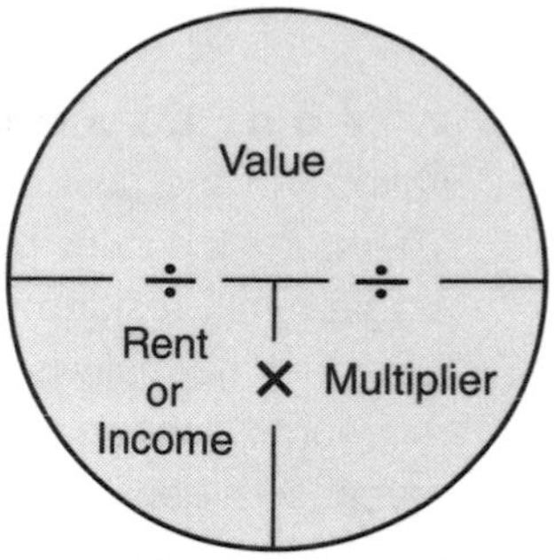

[diagram: circle divided with "Value" on top, "Rent or Income" ÷ and "× Multiplier" below]

■ **FOR EXAMPLE**   If a home recently sold for $382,000 and its monthly rental income was $2,650, the GRM for the property would be computed

$$\$382,000 \div \$2,650 = 144.15 \text{ GRM}$$

To establish an accurate GRM, an appraiser must have recent sales and rental data from at least four properties that are similar to the subject property. The resulting GRM then can be applied to the estimated fair market rental of the subject property to arrive at its market value. The formula would be

Rental income × GRM = Estimated market value

Table 19.4 shows some examples of GRM comparisons.

Reconciliation

When the three approaches to value are applied to the same property, they normally produce three separate indications of value. (For instance, compare Table 19.1 with Table 19.2.) **Reconciliation** is the act of analyzing and effectively weighing the findings from the three approaches. In reconciliation, an appraiser explains not only the appropriateness of each approach but also the relative reliability of

TABLE 19.4	Comparable No.	Sales Price	Monthly Rent	GRM
Gross Rent Multiplier	1	$193,600	$1,650	117
	2	178,500	1,450	123
	3	195,500	1,675	117
	4	182,000	1,565	116
	Subject	*187,400?*	1,625	?

Note: Based on an analysis of these comparisons, a GRM of 117 seems reasonable for homes in this area. In the opinion of an appraiser, then, the estimated value of the subject property would be $1,625 × 117, or $190,125.

the data within each approach in line with the type of value. The appraiser should also explain how the data reflect the market functions.

The process of reconciliation is not simply taking the average of the three estimates of value. An average implies that the data and logic applied in each of the approaches are equally valid and reliable and should therefore be given equal weight. In fact, however, certain approaches are more valid and reliable with some kinds of properties than with others.

■ **FOR EXAMPLE** In appraising a home, the income approach is rarely valid, and the cost approach is of limited value unless the home is relatively new. Therefore, the sales comparison approach is usually given greatest weight in valuing single-family residences. In the appraisal of income or investment property, the income approach normally is given the greatest weight. In the appraisal of churches, libraries, museums, schools, and other special-use properties where little or no income or sales revenue is generated, the cost approach usually is assigned the greatest weight. From this analysis, or reconciliation, a single estimate of market value is produced.

■ THE APPRAISAL PROCESS

Although appraising is not an exact or a precise science, the key to an accurate appraisal lies in the methodical collection and analysis of data. The appraisal process is an orderly set of procedures used to collect and analyze data to arrive at an ultimate value conclusion. The data are divided into two basic classes:

■ *General data*, which covers the nation, region, city, and neighborhood. Of particular importance is the neighborhood, where an appraiser finds the physical, economic, social, and political influences that directly affect the value and potential of the subject property.
■ *Specific data*, which covers details of the subject property as well as comparative data relating to costs, sales, and income and expenses of properties similar to and competitive with the subject property.

Figure 19.1 outlines the steps an appraiser takes in carrying out an appraisal assignment.

Once the approaches have been reconciled and an opinion of value has been reached, the appraiser prepares a report for the client. The report should

■ identify the real estate and real property interest being appraised;
■ state the purpose and intended use of the appraisal;
■ define the value to be estimated;
■ state the effective date of the value and the date of the report;
■ state the extent of the process of collecting, confirming, and reporting the data;
■ list all assumptions and limiting conditions that affect the analysis, opinion, and conclusions of value;
■ describe the information considered, the appraisal procedures followed, and the reasoning that supports the report's conclusions; if an approach was excluded, the report should explain why;

- describe (if necessary or appropriate) the appraiser's opinion of the highest and best use of the real estate;
- describe any additional information that may be appropriate to show compliance with the specific guidelines established in the USPAP or to clearly identify and explain any departures from these guidelines; and
- include signed certification, as required by the USPAP.

Figure 19.2 shows the Uniform Residential Appraisal Report, the form required by many government agencies. It illustrates the types of detailed information required of an appraisal of residential property.

IN PRACTICE   While the appraiser does not determine value, neither is value determined by what the seller wants to get, what the buyer wants to pay, or what the real estate licensee recommends. The appraiser, relying on experience and expertise in valuation theories, develops a supportable and objective report called an appraisal that verifies the value indicated by the market. Sellers and real estate licensees may not agree with the appraiser's value and may argue that it is lower than they think that it should be. However, since most appraisals are ordered by lenders who base their loan on this value, the appraiser must be able to back up the appraisal report with quantifiable conclusions; in the event of a loan default, at what value can the property most probably be sold for the lender to recover the remaining loan balance?

FIGURE   19.1

The Appraisal Process

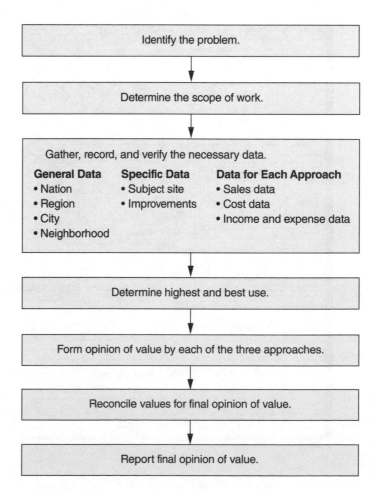

F I G U R E   19.2

Uniform Residential Appraisal Report

Uniform Residential Appraisal Report   File

The purpose of this summary appraisal report is to provide the lender/client with an accurate, and adequately supported, opinion of the market value of the subject property.

SUBJECT

Property Address	City	State	Zip Code
Borrower	Owner of Public Record	County	
Legal Description			
Assessor's Parcel #	Tax Year	R.E. Taxes $	
Neighborhood Name	Map Reference	Census Tract	

Occupant ☐ Owner ☐ Tenant ☐ Vacant   Special Assessments $ ☐ PUD   HOA $ ☐ per year ☐ per month
Property Rights Appraised ☐ Fee Simple ☐ Leasehold ☐ Other (describe)
Assignment Type ☐ Purchase Transaction ☐ Refinance Transaction ☐ Other (describe)
Lender/Client   Address
Is the subject property currently offered for sale or has it been offered for sale in the twelve months prior to the effective date of this appraisal? ☐ Yes ☐ No
Report data source(s) used, offering price(s), and date(s).

CONTRACT

I ☐ did ☐ did not analyze the contract for sale for the subject purchase transaction. Explain the results of the analysis of the contract for sale or why the analysis was not performed.

Contract Price $ Date of Contract   Is the property seller the owner of public record? ☐ Yes ☐ No   Data Source(s)
Is there any financial assistance (loan charges, sale concessions, gift or downpayment assistance, etc.) to be paid by any party on behalf of the borrower? ☐ Yes ☐ No
If Yes, report the total dollar amount and describe the items to be paid.

NEIGHBORHOOD

Note: Race and the racial composition of the neighborhood are not appraisal factors.

Neighborhood Characteristics	One-Unit Housing Trends	One-Unit Housing	Present Land Use %
Location ☐ Urban ☐ Suburban ☐ Rural	Property Values ☐ Increasing ☐ Stable ☐ Declining	PRICE AGE	One-Unit %
Built-Up ☐ Over 75% ☐ 25-75% ☐ Under 25%	Demand/Supply ☐ Shortage ☐ In Balance ☐ Over Supply	$ (000) (yrs)	2-4 Unit %
Growth ☐ Rapid ☐ Stable ☐ Slow	Marketing Time ☐ Under 3 mths ☐ 3–6 mths ☐ Over 6 mths	Low	Multi-Family %
Neighborhood Boundaries		High	Commercial %
		Pred.	Other %

Neighborhood Description

Market Conditions (including support for the above conclusions)

SITE

Dimensions   Area   Shape   View
Specific Zoning Classification   Zoning Description
Zoning Compliance ☐ Legal ☐ Legal Nonconforming (Grandfathered Use) ☐ No Zoning ☐ Illegal (describe)
Is the highest and best use of the subject property as improved (or as proposed per plans and specifications) the present use? ☐ Yes ☐ No   If No, describe

Utilities	Public	Other (describe)		Public	Other (describe)	Off-site Improvements—Type	Public	Private
Electricity	☐	☐	Water	☐	☐	Street	☐	☐
Gas	☐	☐	Sanitary Sewer	☐	☐	Alley	☐	☐

FEMA Special Flood Hazard Area ☐ Yes ☐ No   FEMA Flood Zone   FEMA Map #   FEMA Map Date
Are the utilities and off-site improvements typical for the market area? ☐ Yes ☐ No   If No, describe
Are there any adverse site conditions or external factors (easements, encroachments, environmental conditions, land uses, etc.)? ☐ Yes ☐ No   If Yes, describe

IMPROVEMENTS

General Description	Foundation	Exterior Description materials/condition	Interior materials/condition
Units ☐ One ☐ One with Accessory Unit	☐ Concrete Slab ☐ Crawl Space	Foundation Walls	Floors
# of Stories	☐ Full Basement ☐ Partial Basement	Exterior Walls	Walls
Type ☐ Det. ☐ Att. ☐ S-Det./End Unit	Basement Area sq. ft.	Roof Surface	Trim/Finish
☐ Existing ☐ Proposed ☐ Under Const.	Basement Finish %	Gutters & Downspouts	Bath Floor
Design (Style)	☐ Outside Entry/Exit ☐ Sump Pump	Window Type	Bath Wainscot
Year Built	Evidence of ☐ Infestation	Storm Sash/Insulated	Car Storage ☐ None
Effective Age (Yrs)	☐ Dampness ☐ Settlement	Screens	☐ Driveway # of Cars
Attic ☐ None	Heating ☐ FWA ☐ HWBB ☐ Radiant	Amenities ☐ Woodstove(s) #	Driveway Surface
☐ Drop Stair ☐ Stairs	☐ Other Fuel	☐ Fireplace(s) # ☐ Fence	☐ Garage # of Cars
☐ Floor ☐ Scuttle	Cooling ☐ Central Air Conditioning	☐ Patio/Deck ☐ Porch	☐ Carport # of Cars
☐ Finished ☐ Heated	☐ Individual ☐ Other	☐ Pool ☐ Other	☐ Att. ☐ Det. ☐ Built-in

Appliances ☐ Refrigerator ☐ Range/Oven ☐ Dishwasher ☐ Disposal ☐ Microwave ☐ Washer/Dryer ☐ Other (describe)
Finished area above grade contains: Rooms   Bedrooms   Bath(s)   Square Feet of Gross Living Area Above Grade
Additional features (special energy efficient items, etc.)

Describe the condition of the property (including needed repairs, deterioration, renovations, remodeling, etc.).

Are there any physical deficiencies or adverse conditions that affect the livability, soundness, or structural integrity of the property? ☐ Yes ☐ No   If Yes, describe

Does the property generally conform to the neighborhood (functional utility, style, condition, use, construction, etc.)? ☐ Yes ☐ No   If No, describe

Freddie Mac Form 70 March 2005   Page 1 of 6   Fannie Mae Form 1004 March 2005

FIGURE   19.2

Uniform Residential Appraisal Report (continued)

Uniform Residential Appraisal Report   File

| There are | comparable properties currently offered for sale in the subject neighborhood ranging in price from $ | to $ | |

| There are | comparable sales in the subject neighborhood within the past twelve months ranging in sale price from $ | to $ | |

FEATURE	SUBJECT	COMPARABLE SALE # 1		COMPARABLE SALE # 2		COMPARABLE SALE # 3	
Address							
Proximity to Subject							
Sale Price	$		$		$		$
Sale Price/Gross Liv. Area	$ sq. ft.	$ sq. ft.		$ sq. ft.		$ sq. ft.	
Data Source(s)							
Verification Source(s)							
VALUE ADJUSTMENTS	DESCRIPTION	DESCRIPTION	+(-) $ Adjustment	DESCRIPTION	+(-) $ Adjustment	DESCRIPTION	+(-) $ Adjustment
Sale or Financing Concessions							
Date of Sale/Time							
Location							
Leasehold/Fee Simple							
Site							
View							
Design (Style)							
Quality of Construction							
Actual Age							
Condition							
Above Grade	Total Bdrms. Baths	Total Bdrms. Baths		Total Bdrms. Baths		Total Bdrms. Baths	
Room Count							
Gross Living Area	sq. ft.	sq. ft.		sq. ft.		sq. ft.	
Basement & Finished Rooms Below Grade							
Functional Utility							
Heating/Cooling							
Energy Efficient Items							
Garage/Carport							
Porch/Patio/Deck							
Net Adjustment (Total)		☐ + ☐ -	$	☐ + ☐ -	$	☐ + ☐ -	$
Adjusted Sale Price of Comparables		Net Adj. % Gross Adj. % $		Net Adj. % Gross Adj. % $		Net Adj. % Gross Adj. % $	

I ☐ did ☐ did not research the sale or transfer history of the subject property and comparable sales. If not, explain

My research ☐ did ☐ did not reveal any prior sales or transfers of the subject property for the three years prior to the effective date of this appraisal.

Data source(s)

My research ☐ did ☐ did not reveal any prior sales or transfers of the comparable sales for the year prior to the date of sale of the comparable sale.

Data source(s)

Report the results of the research and analysis of the prior sale or transfer history of the subject property and comparable sales (report additional prior sales on page 3).

ITEM	SUBJECT	COMPARABLE SALE # 1	COMPARABLE SALE # 2	COMPARABLE SALE # 3
Date of Prior Sale/Transfer				
Price of Prior Sale/Transfer				
Data Source(s)				
Effective Date of Data Source(s)				

Analysis of prior sale or transfer history of the subject property and comparable sales

Summary of Sales Comparison Approach

Indicated Value by Sales Comparison Approach $

Indicated Value by: **Sales Comparison Approach** $ Cost Approach (if developed) $ Income Approach (if developed) $

This appraisal is made ☐ "as is", ☐ subject to completion per plans and specifications on the basis of a hypothetical condition that the improvements have been completed, ☐ subject to the following repairs or alterations on the basis of a hypothetical condition that the repairs or alterations have been completed, or ☐ subject to the following required inspection based on the extraordinary assumption that the condition or deficiency does not require alteration or repair:

Based on a complete visual inspection of the interior and exterior areas of the subject property, defined scope of work, statement of assumptions and limiting conditions, and appraiser's certification, my (our) opinion of the market value, as defined, of the real property that is the subject of this report is $, as of   , which is the date of inspection and the effective date of this appraisal.

Freddie Mac Form 70 March 2005   Page 2 of 6   Fannie Mae Form 1004 March 2005

FIGURE 19.2

Uniform Residential Appraisal Report (continued)

Uniform Residential Appraisal Report   File #

ADDITIONAL COMMENTS

COST APPROACH TO VALUE (not required by Fannie Mae)

Provide adequate information for the lender/client to replicate the below cost figures and calculations.

Support for the opinion of site value (summary of comparable land sales or other methods for estimating site value)

ESTIMATED ☐ REPRODUCTION OR ☐ REPLACEMENT COST NEW	OPINION OF SITE VALUE	= $
Source of cost data	Dwelling Sq. Ft. @ $	=$
Quality rating from cost service Effective date of cost data	Sq. Ft. @ $	=$
Comments on Cost Approach (gross living area calculations, depreciation, etc.)		
	Garage/Carport Sq. Ft. @ $	=$
	Total Estimate of Cost-New	= $
	Less Physical Functional External	
	Depreciation	=$( )
	Depreciated Cost of Improvements	=$
	"As-Is" Value of Site Improvements	=$
Estimated Remaining Economic Life (HUD and VA only) Years	Indicated Value By Cost Approach	=$

INCOME APPROACH TO VALUE (not required by Fannie Mae)

Estimated Monthly Market Rent $ X Gross Rent Multiplier   = $ Indicated Value by Income Approach

Summary of Income Approach (including support for market rent and GRM)

PROJECT INFORMATION FOR PUDs (if applicable)

Is the developer/builder in control of the Homeowners' Association (HOA)? ☐ Yes ☐ No Unit type(s) ☐ Detached ☐ Attached

Provide the following information for PUDs ONLY if the developer/builder is in control of the HOA and the subject property is an attached dwelling unit.

Legal name of project

Total number of phases   Total number of units   Total number of units sold

Total number of units rented   Total number of units for sale   Data source(s)

Was the project created by the conversion of an existing building(s) into a PUD? ☐ Yes ☐ No If Yes, date of conversion

Does the project contain any multi-dwelling units? ☐ Yes ☐ No Data source(s)

Are the units, common elements, and recreation facilities complete? ☐ Yes ☐ No If No, describe the status of completion.

Are the common elements leased to or by the Homeowners' Association? ☐ Yes ☐ No If Yes, describe the rental terms and options.

Describe common elements and recreational facilities

Freddie Mac Form 70 March 2005   Page 3 of 6   Fannie Mae Form 1004 March 2005

FIGURE   19.2

Uniform Residential Appraisal Report (continued)

Uniform Residential Appraisal Report   File

This report form is designed to report an appraisal of a one-unit property or a one-unit property with an accessory unit; including a unit in a planned unit development (PUD). This report form is not designed to report an appraisal of a manufactured home or a unit in a condominium or cooperative project.

This appraisal report is subject to the following scope of work, intended use, intended user, definition of market value, statement of assumptions and limiting conditions, and certifications. Modifications, additions, or deletions to the intended use, intended user, definition of market value, or assumptions and limiting conditions are not permitted. The appraiser may expand the scope of work to include any additional research or analysis necessary based on the complexity of this appraisal assignment. Modifications or deletions to the certifications are also not permitted. However, additional certifications that do not constitute material alterations to this appraisal report, such as those required by law or those related to the appraiser's continuing education or membership in an appraisal organization, are permitted.

SCOPE OF WORK: The scope of work for this appraisal is defined by the complexity of this appraisal assignment and the reporting requirements of this appraisal report form, including the following definition of market value, statement of assumptions and limiting conditions, and certifications. The appraiser must, at a minimum: (1) perform a complete visual inspection of the interior and exterior areas of the subject property, (2) inspect the neighborhood, (3) inspect each of the comparable sales from at least the street, (4) research, verify, and analyze data from reliable public and/or private sources, and (5) report his or her analysis, opinions, and conclusions in this appraisal report.

INTENDED USE: The intended use of this appraisal report is for the lender/client to evaluate the property that is the subject of this appraisal for a mortgage finance transaction.

INTENDED USER: The intended user of this appraisal report is the lender/client.

DEFINITION OF MARKET VALUE: The most probable price which a property should bring in a competitive and open market under all conditions requisite to a fair sale, the buyer and seller, each acting prudently, knowledgeably and assuming the price is not affected by undue stimulus. Implicit in this definition is the consummation of a sale as of a specified date and the passing of title from seller to buyer under conditions whereby: (1) buyer and seller are typically motivated; (2) both parties are well informed or well advised, and each acting in what he or she considers his or her own best interest; (3) a reasonable time is allowed for exposure in the open market; (4) payment is made in terms of cash in U. S. dollars or in terms of financial arrangements comparable thereto; and (5) the price represents the normal consideration for the property sold unaffected by special or creative financing or sales concessions* granted by anyone associated with the sale.

*Adjustments to the comparables must be made for special or creative financing or sales concessions. No adjustments are necessary for those costs which are normally paid by sellers as a result of tradition or law in a market area; these costs are readily identifiable since the seller pays these costs in virtually all sales transactions. Special or creative financing adjustments can be made to the comparable property by comparisons to financing terms offered by a third party institutional lender that is not already involved in the property or transaction. Any adjustment should not be calculated on a mechanical dollar for dollar cost of the financing or concession but the dollar amount of any adjustment should approximate the market's reaction to the financing or concessions based on the appraiser's judgment.

STATEMENT OF ASSUMPTIONS AND LIMITING CONDITIONS: The appraiser's certification in this report is subject to the following assumptions and limiting conditions:

1. The appraiser will not be responsible for matters of a legal nature that affect either the property being appraised or the title to it, except for information that he or she became aware of during the research involved in performing this appraisal. The appraiser assumes that the title is good and marketable and will not render any opinions about the title.

2. The appraiser has provided a sketch in this appraisal report to show the approximate dimensions of the improvements. The sketch is included only to assist the reader in visualizing the property and understanding the appraiser's determination of its size.

3. The appraiser has examined the available flood maps that are provided by the Federal Emergency Management Agency (or other data sources) and has noted in this appraisal report whether any portion of the subject site is located in an identified Special Flood Hazard Area. Because the appraiser is not a surveyor, he or she makes no guarantees, express or implied, regarding this determination.

4. The appraiser will not give testimony or appear in court because he or she made an appraisal of the property in question, unless specific arrangements to do so have been made beforehand, or as otherwise required by law.

5. The appraiser has noted in this appraisal report any adverse conditions (such as needed repairs, deterioration, the presence of hazardous wastes, toxic substances, etc.) observed during the inspection of the subject property or that he or she became aware of during the research involved in performing this appraisal. Unless otherwise stated in this appraisal report, the appraiser has no knowledge of any hidden or unapparent physical deficiencies or adverse conditions of the property (such as, but not limited to, needed repairs, deterioration, the presence of hazardous wastes, toxic substances, adverse environmental conditions, etc.) that would make the property less valuable, and has assumed that there are no such conditions and makes no guarantees or warranties, express or implied. The appraiser will not be responsible for any such conditions that do exist or for any engineering or testing that might be required to discover whether such conditions exist. Because the appraiser is not an expert in the field of environmental hazards, this appraisal report must not be considered as an environmental assessment of the property.

6. The appraiser has based his or her appraisal report and valuation conclusion for an appraisal that is subject to satisfactory completion, repairs, or alterations on the assumption that the completion, repairs, or alterations of the subject property will be performed in a professional manner.

Uniform Residential Appraisal Report (continued)

Uniform Residential Appraisal Report   File

APPRAISER'S CERTIFICATION: The Appraiser certifies and agrees that:

1. I have, at a minimum, developed and reported this appraisal in accordance with the scope of work requirements stated in this appraisal report.

2. I performed a complete visual inspection of the interior and exterior areas of the subject property. I reported the condition of the improvements in factual, specific terms. I identified and reported the physical deficiencies that could affect the livability, soundness, or structural integrity of the property.

3. I performed this appraisal in accordance with the requirements of the Uniform Standards of Professional Appraisal Practice that were adopted and promulgated by the Appraisal Standards Board of The Appraisal Foundation and that were in place at the time this appraisal report was prepared.

4. I developed my opinion of the market value of the real property that is the subject of this report based on the sales comparison approach to value. I have adequate comparable market data to develop a reliable sales comparison approach for this appraisal assignment. I further certify that I considered the cost and income approaches to value but did not develop them, unless otherwise indicated in this report.

5. I researched, verified, analyzed, and reported on any current agreement for sale for the subject property, any offering for sale of the subject property in the twelve months prior to the effective date of this appraisal, and the prior sales of the subject property for a minimum of three years prior to the effective date of this appraisal, unless otherwise indicated in this report.

6. I researched, verified, analyzed, and reported on the prior sales of the comparable sales for a minimum of one year prior to the date of sale of the comparable sale, unless otherwise indicated in this report.

7. I selected and used comparable sales that are locationally, physically, and functionally the most similar to the subject property.

8. I have not used comparable sales that were the result of combining a land sale with the contract purchase price of a home that has been built or will be built on the land.

9. I have reported adjustments to the comparable sales that reflect the market's reaction to the differences between the subject property and the comparable sales.

10. I verified, from a disinterested source, all information in this report that was provided by parties who have a financial interest in the sale or financing of the subject property.

11. I have knowledge and experience in appraising this type of property in this market area.

12. I am aware of, and have access to, the necessary and appropriate public and private data sources, such as multiple listing services, tax assessment records, public land records and other such data sources for the area in which the property is located.

13. I obtained the information, estimates, and opinions furnished by other parties and expressed in this appraisal report from reliable sources that I believe to be true and correct.

14. I have taken into consideration the factors that have an impact on value with respect to the subject neighborhood, subject property, and the proximity of the subject property to adverse influences in the development of my opinion of market value. I have noted in this appraisal report any adverse conditions (such as, but not limited to, needed repairs, deterioration, the presence of hazardous wastes, toxic substances, adverse environmental conditions, etc.) observed during the inspection of the subject property or that I became aware of during the research involved in performing this appraisal. I have considered these adverse conditions in my analysis of the property value, and have reported on the effect of the conditions on the value and marketability of the subject property.

15. I have not knowingly withheld any significant information from this appraisal report and, to the best of my knowledge, all statements and information in this appraisal report are true and correct.

16. I stated in this appraisal report my own personal, unbiased, and professional analysis, opinions, and conclusions, which are subject only to the assumptions and limiting conditions in this appraisal report.

17. I have no present or prospective interest in the property that is the subject of this report, and I have no present or prospective personal interest or bias with respect to the participants in the transaction. I did not base, either partially or completely, my analysis and/or opinion of market value in this appraisal report on the race, color, religion, sex, age, marital status, handicap, familial status, or national origin of either the prospective owners or occupants of the subject property or of the present owners or occupants of the properties in the vicinity of the subject property or on any other basis prohibited by law.

18. My employment and/or compensation for performing this appraisal or any future or anticipated appraisals was not conditioned on any agreement or understanding, written or otherwise, that I would report (or present analysis supporting) a predetermined specific value, a predetermined minimum value, a range or direction in value, a value that favors the cause of any party, or the attainment of a specific result or occurrence of a specific subsequent event (such as approval of a pending mortgage loan application).

19. I personally prepared all conclusions and opinions about the real estate that were set forth in this appraisal report. If I relied on significant real property appraisal assistance from any individual or individuals in the performance of this appraisal or the preparation of this appraisal report, I have named such individual(s) and disclosed the specific tasks performed in this appraisal report. I certify that any individual so named is qualified to perform the tasks. I have not authorized anyone to make a change to any item in this appraisal report; therefore, any change made to this appraisal is unauthorized and I will take no responsibility for it.

20. I identified the lender/client in this appraisal report who is the individual, organization, or agent for the organization that ordered and will receive this appraisal report.

Freddie Mac Form 70   March 2005   Page 5 of 6   Fannie Mae Form 1004   March 2005

F I G U R E   19.2

Uniform Residential Appraisal Report (continued)

Uniform Residential Appraisal Report   File

21. The lender/client may disclose or distribute this appraisal report to: the borrower; another lender at the request of the borrower; the mortgagee or its successors and assigns; mortgage insurers; government sponsored enterprises; other secondary market participants; data collection or reporting services; professional appraisal organizations; any department, agency, or instrumentality of the United States; and any state, the District of Columbia, or other jurisdictions; without having to obtain the appraiser's or supervisory appraiser's (if applicable) consent. Such consent must be obtained before this appraisal report may be disclosed or distributed to any other party (including, but not limited to, the public through advertising, public relations, news, sales, or other media).

22. I am aware that any disclosure or distribution of this appraisal report by me or the lender/client may be subject to certain laws and regulations. Further, I am also subject to the provisions of the Uniform Standards of Professional Appraisal Practice that pertain to disclosure or distribution by me.

23. The borrower, another lender at the request of the borrower, the mortgagee or its successors and assigns, mortgage insurers, government sponsored enterprises, and other secondary market participants may rely on this appraisal report as part of any mortgage finance transaction that involves any one or more of these parties.

24. If this appraisal report was transmitted as an "electronic record" containing my "electronic signature," as those terms are defined in applicable federal and/or state laws (excluding audio and video recordings), or a facsimile transmission of this appraisal report containing a copy or representation of my signature, the appraisal report shall be as effective, enforceable and valid as if a paper version of this appraisal report were delivered containing my original hand written signature.

25. Any intentional or negligent misrepresentation(s) contained in this appraisal report may result in civil liability and/or criminal penalties including, but not limited to, fine or imprisonment or both under the provisions of Title 18, United States Code, Section 1001, et seq., or similar state laws.

SUPERVISORY APPRAISER'S CERTIFICATION: The Supervisory Appraiser certifies and agrees that:

1. I directly supervised the appraiser for this appraisal assignment, have read the appraisal report, and agree with the appraiser's analysis, opinions, statements, conclusions, and the appraiser's certification.

2. I accept full responsibility for the contents of this appraisal report including, but not limited to, the appraiser's analysis, opinions, statements, conclusions, and the appraiser's certification.

3. The appraiser identified in this appraisal report is either a sub-contractor or an employee of the supervisory appraiser (or the appraisal firm), is qualified to perform this appraisal, and is acceptable to perform this appraisal under the applicable state law.

4. This appraisal report complies with the Uniform Standards of Professional Appraisal Practice that were adopted and promulgated by the Appraisal Standards Board of The Appraisal Foundation and that were in place at the time this appraisal report was prepared.

5. If this appraisal report was transmitted as an "electronic record" containing my "electronic signature," as those terms are defined in applicable federal and/or state laws (excluding audio and video recordings), or a facsimile transmission of this appraisal report containing a copy or representation of my signature, the appraisal report shall be as effective, enforceable and valid as if a paper version of this appraisal report were delivered containing my original hand written signature.

APPRAISER	SUPERVISORY APPRAISER (ONLY IF REQUIRED)
Signature_____	Signature_____
Name _____	Name_____
Company Name _____	Company Name _____
Company Address_____	Company Address_____
_____	_____
Telephone Number _____	Telephone Number _____
Email Address_____	Email Address _____
Date of Signature and Report _____	Date of Signature _____
Effective Date of Appraisal _____	State Certification # _____
State Certification # _____	or State License # _____
or State License # _____	State _____
or Other (describe) _____ State # _____	Expiration Date of Certification or License _____
State _____	
Expiration Date of Certification or License _____	SUBJECT PROPERTY

ADDRESS OF PROPERTY APPRAISED

_____

APPRAISED VALUE OF SUBJECT PROPERTY $ _____

LENDER/CLIENT

Name _____

Company Name _____

Company Address_____

_____

Email Address_____

SUBJECT PROPERTY

☐ Did not inspect subject property

☐ Did inspect exterior of subject property from street
Date of Inspection _____

☐ Did inspect interior and exterior of subject property
Date of Inspection _____

COMPARABLE SALES

☐ Did not inspect exterior of comparable sales from street

☐ Did inspect exterior of comparable sales from street
Date of Inspection _____

Freddie Mac Form 70   March 2005   Page 6 of 6   Fannie Mae Form 1004   March 2005

■ SUMMARY

An appraisal is an estimate or opinion of value based on supportable evidence and appraisal methods, defined by the Uniform Standards of Appraisal Practice (USPAP). An appraiser must be state-licensed or certified for an appraisal performed as part of a federally related transaction.

Real estate licensees also compile data. A comparative market analysis (CMA) is a report of market statistics that assists consumers in the listing and buying process, but it is not an appraisal. A broker's price opinion (BPO) may be used in a non-federally related transaction: home equity lines, refinancing, portfolio management loss mitigation, and collections.

Basic to appraising are certain underlying economic principles, such as highest and best use, substitution, supply and demand, conformity, anticipation, increasing and diminishing returns, regression, progression, plottage, contribution, competition, and change.

Value is created by demand, utility, scarcity, and transferability of property (DUST). Market value is the most probable price that property should bring in a fair sale, but market value is not necessarily the same as price paid or cost to construct.

A sales comparison approach (market data approach) makes use of sales of properties comparable (referred to as comps) to the property that is the subject of the appraisal by adding or subtracting the value of a feature present or absent in the subject property versus the comparable.

The cost approach estimates current reproduction or replacement cost of constructing building and other property improvements using the square-foot method, the unit-in-place method, the quantity-survey method, or the index method. The cost approach also estimates accrued depreciation using the straight-line method (economic age-life method) or by estimating items of physical deterioration, functional obsolescence, or external obsolescence.

The income approach is based on the present value of the right to future income and uses the following five steps:

1. Estimate annual potential gross income.
2. Deduct allowance for vacancy and rent loss to find effective gross income.
3. Deduct annual operating expenses to find net operating income (NOI).
4. Estimate rate of return (capitalization rate or cap rate) for subject analyzing cap rates of similar properties.
5. Derive estimate of subject's market value by applying cap rate to annual NOI using this formula: Net operating income divided by capitalization rate equals value.

The gross rent multiplier (GRM) may be used to estimate the value of single-family residential rental properties; a gross income multiplier (GIM), based on gross annual income from all sources, may be used for larger residential and commercial properties.

| In Illinois | The Illinois Real Estate Appraiser Licensing Act of 2002, as amended in 2009, requires mandatory licensure, with limited exceptions, of Illinois appraisers. Only individuals (not corporations, partnerships, firms, or groups) may be certified as appraisers or act as associate real estate trainee appraisers. ∎ |

CHAPTER 19 QUIZ

1. Which of the following appraisal methods uses a rate of investment return?
   a. Sales comparison approach
   b. Cost approach
   c. Income approach
   d. Gross income multiplier method

2. The characteristics of value include which of the following?
   a. Competition
   b. Scarcity
   c. Anticipation
   d. Balance

3. There are two adjacent vacant lots, each worth approximately $50,000. If their owner sells them as a single lot, however, the combined parcel will be worth $120,000. What principle does this illustrate?
   a. Substitution
   b. Plottage
   c. Regression
   d. Progression

4. The amount of money a property commands in the marketplace is its
   a. intrinsic value.
   b. market value.
   c. subjective value.
   d. book value.

5. A homeowner constructs an eight-bedroom brick house with a tennis court, a greenhouse, and an indoor pool in a neighborhood of modest two-bedroom and three-bedroom frame houses on narrow lots. The value of this house is MOST likely to be affected by what principle?
   a. Progression
   b. Assemblage
   c. Change
   d. Regression

6. In Question 5, the owners of the lesser-valued houses in the neighborhood may find that the values of their homes are affected by what principle?
   a. Progression
   b. Increasing returns
   c. Competition
   d. Regression

7. For appraisal purposes, depreciation is NOT caused by
   a. functional obsolescence.
   b. physical deterioration.
   c. external obsolescence.
   d. accelerated capitalization.

8. The term *reconciliation* refers to which of the following?
   a. Loss of value due to any cause
   b. Separating the value of the land from the total value of the property to compute depreciation
   c. Analyzing the results obtained by the different approaches to value to determine a final estimate of value
   d. The process by which an appraiser determines the highest and best use for a parcel of land

9. If a property's annual net income is $24,000 and it is valued at $300,000, what is its capitalization rate?
   a. 8 percent
   b. 10.5 percent
   c. 12.5 percent
   d. 15 percent

10. Certain figures must be determined by an appraiser before value can be computed by the income approach. Which of the following is NOT used by an appraiser applying the income approach to value?
    a. Annual net operating income
    b. Capitalization rate
    c. Accrued depreciation
    d. Annual gross income

444

11. An appraiser, asked to determine the value of an existing strip shopping center, would probably give the MOST weight to which approach to value?

   a. Cost approach
   b. Sales comparison approach
   c. Income approach
   d. Index method

12. The market value of a parcel of real estate is

   a. an estimate of its future benefits.
   b. the amount of money paid for the property.
   c. an estimate of the most probable price it should bring.
   d. its value without improvements.

13. Capitalization is the process by which annual net operating income is used to

   a. determine cost.
   b. estimate value.
   c. establish depreciation.
   d. determine potential tax value.

14. From the reproduction or replacement cost of a building, the appraiser deducts depreciation, which represents

   a. the remaining economic life of the building.
   b. remodeling costs to increase rentals.
   c. loss of value due to any cause.
   d. costs to modernize the building.

15. The effective gross annual income from a property is $112,000. Total expenses for this year are $53,700. What capitalization rate was used to obtain a valuation of $542,325?

   a. 9.75 percent
   b. 10.25 percent
   c. 10.50 percent
   d. 10.75 percent

16. Which factor would be important in comparing properties under the sales comparison approach to value?

   a. Active listings
   b. Property rent roll
   c. Depreciation
   d. Date of sale

17. A building was purchased five years ago for $240,000. It currently has an estimated remaining useful life of 60 years. What is the property's total depreciation to date?

   a. $14,364
   b. $18,462
   c. $20,000
   d. $54,000

18. In Question 17, what is the current value of the building?

   a. $235,636
   b. $221,538
   c. $220,000
   d. $186,000

19. The appraised value of a residence with four bedrooms and one bathroom would probably be reduced because of

   a. external obsolescence.
   b. functional obsolescence.
   c. curable physical deterioration.
   d. incurable physical deterioration.

In Illinois

20. An individual wants to be an appraiser in the northwest suburbs of Chicago. While she would be willing to appraise residential properties, her real interest is in appraising commercial properties. If she wants to be qualified to conduct appraisals under FIRREA, this individual must

   a. become a licensed real estate appraiser.
   b. become a certified appraiser.
   c. become a certified general appraiser.
   d. do nothing because individuals who wish to conduct appraisals under FIRREA must receive federal appraisal certification rather than state licensing.

CHAPTER 20

Land-Use Controls and Property Development

■ **LEARNING OBJECTIVES** *When you've finished reading this chapter, you should be able to*

- ■ **identify** the various types of public and private land-use controls;

- ■ **describe** how a comprehensive plan influences local real estate development;

- ■ **explain** the various issues involved in subdivision;

- ■ **distinguish** the function and characteristics of building codes and zoning ordinances; and

- ■ **define** the following *key terms*

buffer zones	developer	percolation test
building codes	enabling acts	plat
clustering	Illinois Human Rights Act	restrictive covenants
comprehensive plan	Illinois Land Sales	subdivider
conditional-use permit	Registration Act	subdivision
covenants, conditions,	Interstate Land Sales Full	taking
and restrictions	Disclosure Act	variance
(CC&Rs)	inverse condemnation	zoning ordinances
deed restriction	master plan	
density zoning	nonconforming use	

■ LAND-USE CONTROLS

Broad though they may be, the rights of real estate ownership are not absolute. Land use is regulated by public and private restrictions and through the public ownership of land by federal, state, and local governments.

Over the years, the government's policy has been to encourage private ownership of land, but this does not always mean that owners can do whatever they want with their properties. It is necessary for a certain amount of land to be owned by the government for such uses as municipal buildings, state government buildings, schools, and military bases. Government ownership may also serve the public interest through urban renewal efforts, public housing, and streets and highways. Often, the only way to ensure that enough land is set aside for recreational and conservation purposes is through direct government ownership in the form of national and state parks and forest preserves. Beyond this sort of direct ownership of land, most government controls on property occur at the local level.

The states' *police power* is their inherent authority to create regulations needed to protect the public health, safety, and welfare. Through enabling acts, states delegate to counties and local municipalities the authority to enact ordinances in keeping with general laws. (See Chapter 2.) The increasing demands placed on finite natural resources have made it necessary for cities, towns, and villages to increase their limitations on the private use of real estate. There are now controls over noise, air, and water pollution as well as population density.

In Illinois   *Article VII of the Illinois Constitution* allows for *home rule* units of government. Any municipality with a population in excess of 25,000 and any county that has a chief executive officer elected by the people are automatically home rule units. However, a home rule unit may elect by referendum not to be one. On the other hand, a municipality of fewer than 25,000 people may elect by referendum to become a home rule unit of government. *Townships are not allowed to be home rule units.*

Constitutionally, a home rule unit of government may exercise any power and perform any function pertaining to its government, including the exercise of *police power* by way of laws that control the use of land. Home rule units also have greater freedom to enforce their laws, including the power to jail offenders for up to six months. Non-home rule units derive their authority to pass land-use controls from the state government through *enabling statutes*.

Occasionally, the laws of one unit of government conflict with another's. If any ordinance of a home rule county conflicts with any ordinance of a home rule municipality, the *municipal ordinance prevails*. Township zoning ordinances must give way to county zoning ordinances, and townships are not empowered to pass subdivision controls or building codes. ■

■ THE COMPREHENSIVE PLAN

Local governments, municipalities, and counties establish development goals by creating a **comprehensive plan.** The comprehensive plan, also known as a **master plan,** is not a regulatory document but rather a guide to planning for change rather than reacting to proposals. The comprehensive plan usually is long term, perhaps 20 years or longer, and often includes (1) a general plan that can be revised and updated more frequently, (2) plans for specific areas, and (3) strategic plans. Systematic planning for orderly growth consists of the following basic elements:

- Land use—that is, a determination of how much land may be proposed for residence, industry, business, agriculture, traffic and transit facilities, utilities, community facilities, parks and recreational facilities, floodplains, and areas of special hazards
- Housing needs of present and anticipated residents—rehabilitation of declining neighborhoods as well as new residential developments
- Movement of people and goods—highways and public transit, parking facilities, and pedestrian and bikeway systems
- Community facilities and utilities—schools, libraries, hospitals, recreational facilities, fire and police stations, water resources, sewage and waste treatment and disposal, storm drainage, and flood management
- Energy conservation to reduce energy consumption and promote the use of renewable energy sources

The preparation of a comprehensive plan involves surveys, studies, and analyses of housing, demographic, and economic characteristics and trends. A given municipality's planning activities may be coordinated with other government bodies and private interests to achieve orderly growth and development.

■ **FOR EXAMPLE**   After the Great Chicago Fire of 1871 reduced most of the city's downtown to rubble and ash, the city engaged planner Daniel Burnham to lay out a design for Chicago's future. The resulting Burnham Plan of orderly boulevards, linking a park along Lake Michigan with other large parks and public spaces throughout the city, established an ideal urban space. This master plan is still being implemented today.

■ ZONING

Zoning is a regulatory tool that helps communities regulate and control how land is used for the protection of public health, safety, and welfare. **Zoning ordinances** are local laws that implement the comprehensive plan and regulate and control the use of land and structures within designated land-use districts. If the comprehensive or master plan is the big picture, zoning makes up the details.

No nationwide or statewide zoning ordinances exist. Rather, zoning powers are conferred on municipal governments by state **enabling acts.** State and federal governments may, however, regulate land use through special legislation, such as scenic easement, coastal management, and environmental laws.

Zoning affects such matters as

- permitted uses of each parcel of land,
- lot sizes,
- types of structures,
- building heights,
- setbacks (the minimum distance away from streets or sidewalks that structures may be built),
- style and appearance of structures,
- density (the ratio of land area to structure area), and
- protection of natural resources.

Zoning ordinances cannot be static; they must remain flexible to meet the changing needs of society.

■ **FOR EXAMPLE**   In many cities, factories and warehouses sit empty. Some cities have begun changing the zoning ordinances for such properties to permit new residential or commercial developments in areas once zoned strictly for heavy industrial use. Coupled with tax incentives, the changes lure developers back into the cities. The resulting housing is modern, conveniently located, and affordable. Simple zoning changes can help revitalize whole neighborhoods in big cities.

Zoning Objectives

Land is divided into zones. The zones are identified by a coding system that outlines how the land may be used according to the code. Common zoning classifications include "C" for commercial, "R" for residential, and "A" for agricultural. There are subcategories in the classifications, and some land may be zoned for mixed use.

A planned unit development (PUD) is a development where land is set aside for mixed-use purposes, such as residential, commercial, and public areas. Zoning regulations may be modified for PUDs.

Zoning ordinances have traditionally classified land use into residential, commercial, industrial, and agricultural. These land-use areas are further divided into subclasses. For example, residential areas may be subdivided to provide for detached single-family dwellings, semi-detached structures containing not more than four dwelling units, walk-up apartments, highrise apartments, and so forth.

To meet both the growing demand for a variety of housing types and the need for innovative residential and nonresidential development, municipalities are adopting ordinances for subdivisions and planned residential developments. Some municipalities also use buffer zones to ease transition from one use to another. A **buffer zone** is typically a strip of land separating land dedicated to one use from land dedicated to another use. For example, landscaped parks and playgrounds and hiking trails are used to screen residential areas from nonresidential zones. Certain types of zoning that focus on special land-use objectives are used in some areas. These include

- *bulk zoning* (or *density zoning*) to control density and avoid overcrowding by imposing restrictions such as setbacks, building heights, and percentage of open area or by restricting new construction projects;

■ *aesthetic zoning* to specify certain types of architecture for new buildings; and

■ *incentive zoning* to ensure that certain uses are incorporated into developments, such as requiring the street floor of an office building to house retail establishments.

Constitutional issues and zoning ordinances   Zoning can be a highly controversial issue and often raises questions of constitutional law. The preamble of the U.S. Constitution provides for the promotion of the general welfare. More specifically, the Fourteenth Amendment prevents the states from depriving "any person of life, liberty, or property, without due process of law." The ongoing question is how a local government can enact zoning ordinances that protect public safety and welfare without violating the constitutional rights of property owners. The government provides a forum for the citizens to discuss zoning ordinances before they are enacted; these are called *public hearings*.

Any land-use legislation that is destructive, unreasonable, arbitrary, or confiscatory usually is considered void. Furthermore, zoning ordinances must not violate the various provisions of the state's constitution. Commonly applied tests in determining the validity of ordinances require that

■ power be exercised in a reasonable manner;

■ provisions be clear and specific;

■ ordinances be nondiscriminatory;

■ ordinances promote public health, safety, and general welfare under the police power concept; and

■ ordinances apply to all property in a similar manner.

Taking   The concept of **taking** is similar to eminent domain in that it comes from the takings clause of the Fifth Amendment to the U.S. Constitution. The clause reads, "nor shall private property be taken for public use, without just compensation." This means that when land is taken for public use through the government's power of eminent domain or condemnation, the owner must be compensated. This payment is referred to as *just compensation*—compensation that is just and fair. The compensation may be negotiated between the owner and the government, or the owner may seek a court judgment setting an amount based on appraisals. In general, no land is exempt from government seizure.

Inverse condemnation is an action brought by a property owner seeking just compensation for land taken for a public use where it appears that the taker of the property does not intend to bring eminent domain proceedings. The property is condemned because its use and value have been diminished due to an adjacent property's public use. For example, property along a newly constructed highway may be inversely condemned. While the property itself was not used in constructing the highway, the property value may be significantly diminished due to the construction of the highway close to the property. The property owner may bring an inverse condemnation action to be compensated for the loss.

It is sometimes very difficult to determine what level of compensation is fair in any particular situation. The compensation may be negotiated between the owner and the government, or the owner may seek a court judgment setting the amount.

IN PRACTICE   One method used to determine just compensation is the before-and-after method. This method is used primarily where a portion of an owner's property is seized for public use. The value of the owner's remaining property after the taking is subtracted from the value of the whole parcel before the taking. The result is the total amount of compensation due to the owner.

Zoning Permits

Compliance with zoning can be monitored by requiring that property owners obtain permits before they begin any development. A permit will not be issued unless a proposed development conforms to the permitted zoning, among other requirements. Zoning permits are usually required before building permits can be issued.

Zoning hearing board   Zoning hearing boards (or zoning boards of appeal) have been established in most communities to hear complaints about the effects a zoning ordinance may have on specific parcels of property. Petitions for variances or exceptions to the zoning law may be presented to an appeal board.

Nonconforming use   Frequently, a lot or an improvement does not conform to the zoning law because it existed before the enactment or amendment of the zoning ordinance. Such a **nonconforming use** may be allowed to continue legally as long as it complies with the regulations governing nonconformities in the local ordinance or until the improvement is destroyed or torn down or the current use is abandoned. If the nonconforming use is allowed to continue indefinitely, it is grandfathered into the new zoning.

Real estate licensees should never assume, nor allow their clients to assume, that the existing nonconforming use will be allowed to continue. Buyers should verify with the local zoning authorities the conditions under which the use is allowed to remain or whether changes are permitted.

■ **FOR EXAMPLE**   Under a city's old zoning ordinances, a grocery store was well within a commercial zone. When the zoning map was changed to accommodate an increased need for residential housing, the grocery store was *grandfathered* into the new zoning; that is, it was allowed to continue its successful operations even though it did not fit the new zoning rules.

Variances and conditional-use permits   Once a plan or zoning ordinance is enacted, property owners and developers know what they can and cannot do on their property. However, they may want to propose changes to the existing zoning in order to use their property somewhat differently. Generally these owners may appeal for either a **conditional-use permit** or a variance to allow a use that does not meet current zoning requirements.

Conditional-use permits allow nonconforming but related land uses. *Variances* permit prohibited land uses to avoid undue hardship.

A conditional-use permit (also known as a *special-use permit*) is usually granted to a property owner to allow a special use of property, defined as an allowable conditional use, within that zone, such as a house of worship or day care center in a residential district. For a conditional-use permit to be appropriate, the intended use must meet certain standards set by the municipality.

A **variance** (or *exception*), on the other hand, provides relief if zoning regulations deprive an owner of the reasonable use of the property. To qualify for a variance, the owner must demonstrate the unique circumstances that make the variance necessary. In addition, the owner must prove that she is harmed and burdened by the regulations. Any such variance is said to "run with the land," meaning the exception is passed on to any later owners after a change has been made.

A variance might also be sought to provide relief if existing zoning regulations create a physical hardship for the development of a specific property. For example, if an owner's lot is level next to a road but slopes steeply 30 feet away from the road, the zoning board may allow a variance so the owner can build closer to the road than the setback allows.

Both variances and conditional-use permits are issued by zoning boards only after public hearings. The neighbors of a proposed use must be given an opportunity to voice their opinions.

A property owner also can seek a complete change in the zoning classification of a parcel of real estate by obtaining an amendment to the district map or a zoning ordinance for that area, but this is significantly more involved and requires approval by the governing body of the community. Local zoning laws and maps are increasingly available on the Internet for the specific communities involved (*keyword search: zoning, [community name]*).

■ BUILDING CODES AND CERTIFICATES OF OCCUPANCY

Most municipalities have enacted ordinances to specify construction standards that must be met when repairing or erecting buildings. These are called **building codes,** and they set the requirements for kinds of materials and standards of workmanship, sanitary equipment, electrical wiring, fire prevention, and similar issues. The International Code Council (ICC) offers Internet support to professionals in keeping track of these numerous codes.

In addition to adhering to building codes, a property owner who wants to build a structure or alter or repair an existing building usually must obtain a *building permit*. Through the permit requirement, municipal officials are made aware of new construction or alterations and can verify compliance with building codes and zoning ordinances. Inspectors will closely examine the plans and conduct periodic inspections of the work. Once the completed structure has been inspected and found satisfactory, the municipal inspector issues a **certificate of occupancy** or *occupancy permit*.

If a building has been converted from another use to residential use or a new home has been constructed, the municipal inspector must ensure that the construction complies with relevant ordinances and codes. A certificate of occupancy or occupancy permit indicating that the property is suitable for habitation by meeting certain safety and health standards must be issued before anyone moves in and often before a lender will allow closing.

If the construction of a building or an alteration violates a deed restriction, the issuance of a building permit will not cure this violation. A building permit is merely evidence of the applicant's compliance with municipal regulations.

Similarly, communities with historic districts, or those that are interested in maintaining a particular "look" or character, may have aesthetic ordinances. These laws require that all new construction or restorations be approved by a special board. The board ensures that the new structures will "blend in" with existing building styles. Owners of existing properties may need to obtain approval to have their homes painted or remodeled.

IN PRACTICE   The subject of planning, zoning, and restricting the use of real estate is extremely technical, and the interpretation of the law is not always clear. Questions concerning any of these subjects in relation to real estate transactions should be referred to legal counsel. Furthermore, the landowner should be aware of the costs for various permits.

■ SUBDIVISION

Subdividers split up land into parcels.
Developers construct improvements on the subdivided parcels.

Most communities have adopted **subdivision** and land development ordinances as part of their comprehensive plans. An ordinance includes provisions for submitting and processing *subdivision plats*. A major advantage of subdivision ordinances is that they encourage flexibility, economy, and ingenuity in the use of land. A **subdivider** is a person who buys undeveloped acreage and divides it into smaller lots for sale to individuals or developers or for the subdivider's own use. A **developer** (who also may be a subdivider) improves the land, constructs homes or other buildings on the lots, and sells them. In a new residential subdivision, developers usually pay the costs to provide new water, sewer, streets, curbs, and sidewalks. Developing is generally a much more extensive activity than subdividing.

Regulation of Land Development

Just as no national zoning ordinance exists, no uniform planning and land development legislation affects the entire country. Laws governing subdividing and land planning are controlled by the state and local governing bodies where the land is located. Rules and regulations developed by government agencies have, however, provided certain minimum standards. Many local governments have established standards that are higher than minimum standards.

Land development plan   Before the actual subdividing can begin, the subdivider must go through the process of land planning. The resulting land development plan must comply with the municipality's comprehensive plan. Although comprehensive plans and zoning ordinances are not necessarily inflexible, a plan that requires them to be changed must undergo more complicated hearings.

Plats   From the land development and subdivision plans, the subdivider draws plats. A **plat** is a detailed map that illustrates the geographic boundaries of individual lots. It shows the blocks, sections, streets, public easements, and monuments in the prospective subdivision. A plat also may include engineering data and restrictive covenants. The plats must be approved by the municipality before they can be recorded. Once a plat is properly recorded, it may be used as an adequate description of real property. A developer is often required to submit an environmental impact report with the application for subdivision approval. This report explains what effect the proposed development will have on the surrounding area. Plat maps are increasingly available for viewing on the Internet.

Subdivision Plans

In plotting out a subdivision according to local planning and zoning controls, a subdivider usually determines the size as well as the location of the individual lots. The maximum or minimum size of a lot generally is regulated by local ordinances and must be considered carefully.

The land itself must be studied, usually in cooperation with a surveyor, so that the subdivision takes advantage of natural drainage and land contours. In addition, a percolation test of the soil is done to determine the ability of the ground to absorb and drain water. This information helps to determine the suitability of a site for certain kinds of development and for the installation of septic tanks or injection wells for sewage treatment plants. A subdivider registering her development with the U.S. Housing and Urban Development (HUD) must include a percolation report in the application. A subdivider should provide for utility easements as well as easements for water and sewer mains.

Most subdivisions are laid out by use of lots and blocks. An area of land is designated as a block, and the area making up this block is divided into lots.

One negative aspect of subdivision development is the potential for increased tax burdens on all residents, both inside and outside the subdivision. To protect local taxpayers against the costs of a heightened demand for public services, many local governments strictly regulate nearly all aspects of subdivision development and may impose impact fees. *Impact fees* are charges made in advance to cover anticipated expenses involving off-site capital improvements such as expanding water and sewer facilities, additional roads, and school expansions.

Subdivision Density

Zoning ordinances control land use. Such controls often include minimum lot sizes and population density requirements for subdivisions. For example, a typical zoning restriction may set the minimum lot area on which a subdivider can build a single-family housing unit at 10,000 square feet. This means that the subdivider can build four houses per acre. Many zoning authorities establish special **density zoning** (or *bulk zoning*) ordinances for certain subdivisions, which restrict the average maximum number of houses per acre that may be built within a particular subdivision. In such cases, the subdivider may choose to cluster building lots to achieve an open effect. Regardless of lot size or number of units, the subdivider will be consistent with the ordinance as long as the average number of units in the development remains at or below the maximum density. This average is called *gross density*.

F I G U R E   20.1

Street Patterns

Gridiron   **Curvilinear**

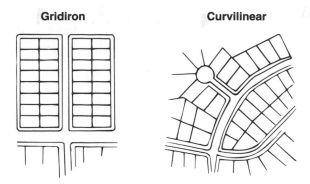

Street patterns   By varying street patterns and clustering housing units, a sub-divider can dramatically increase the amount of open or recreational space in a development. Two possible patterns are the *gridiron* and *curvilinear* patterns. (See Figure 20.1.)

The gridiron pattern evolved out of the government rectangular survey system. Curvilinear developments avoid the uniformity of the gridiron and are quieter and more secure. However, getting from place to place may be more challenging.

Clustering for open space   By slightly reducing lot sizes and **clustering** them around varying street patterns, a divider can house as many people in the same area as could be done using traditional subdividing plans but with substantially increased tracts of open space.

For example, compare the two subdivisions illustrated in Figure 20.2. Both subdivisions are equal in size and terrain. But when lots are reduced in size and clustered around limited-access cul-de-sacs, the number of housing units remains nearly the same (366), with less street area (17,700 linear feet) and dramatically increased open space (23.5 acres).

■ PRIVATE LAND-USE CONTROLS

Not all restrictions on the use of land are imposed by government bodies. Certain restrictions to control and to maintain the desirable quality and character of a property or subdivision may be created by private entities, including the property owners themselves. These restrictions are separate from and in addition to the land-use controls exercised by the government. However, no private restriction can violate a local, state, or federal law.

Restrictive covenants   Restrictive **covenants** are limitations to the use of property imposed by a past owner or the current owner and are binding on future grantees.

On the other hand, **covenants, conditions, and restrictions (CC&Rs)** are private rules set up by the developer that set standards for all the parcels within the defined subdivision. The developer's restrictions may be imposed through a covenant in the deed or by a separate recorded declaration. CC&Rs typically govern

FIGURE 20.2

Subdivision Styles

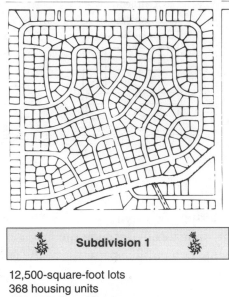

Subdivision 1	Subdivision 2

12,500-square-foot lots
368 housing units
1.6 acres of parkland
23,200 linear feet of street

7,500-square-foot lots
366 housing units
23.5 acres of parkland
17,700 linear feet of street

the type, height, and size of buildings that individual owners can erect, as well as land use, architectural style, construction methods, setbacks, and square footage. CC&Rs are enforced by the homeowners' association.

Unlike most deed restrictions, many CC&Rs have time limitations; for example, a restriction might state that it is "effective for a period of 25 years from this date." After this time, it becomes inoperative or it may be extended if approved by the required number of owners. Many developers also include methods by which a required number of homeowners may change a CC&R.

Restrictive covenants are usually considered valid if they are reasonable restraints that benefit all property owners in the subdivision; that is, they protect property values or safety. If the terms of the restrictions are too broad, they may be construed as preventing the free transfer of property. If a restrictive covenant or condition is judged unenforceable by a court, the estate will stand free from the invalid covenant or condition. Restrictive covenants cannot be used for illegal purposes, such as for the exclusion of members of certain races, nationalities, or religions.

Private land-use controls may be more restrictive of an owner's use than the local zoning ordinances. The rule is that the more restrictive of the two takes precedence.

Private restrictions can be enforced in court when one lot owner applies to the court for an injunction to prevent a neighboring lot owner from violating the recorded restrictions. The court injunction will direct the violator to stop or remove the violation. The court retains the power to punish the violator for failing to obey. If adjoining lot owners stand idly by while a violation is committed, they can lose the right to an injunction by their inaction. The court might claim their right was lost through laches—that is, the legal principle that a right may be lost through undue delay or failure to assert it.

| In Illinois | Any restrictive covenant that forbids or restricts conveyance, encumbrance, occupancy, or lease on the basis of race, color, religion, or national origin is void. Exceptions to this section of the **Illinois Human Rights Act** are allowed for religious and charitable organizations. ∎

■ REGULATION OF LAND SALES

Just as the sale and use of property within a state are controlled by state and local governments, the sale of property in one state to buyers in another is subject to strict federal and state regulations.

Interstate Land Sales Full Disclosure Act

The U.S. Congress created the federal **Interstate Land Sales Full Disclosure Act** to facilitate regulation of interstate land sales and to protect consumers from fraud and abuse in the sale or lease of land. The act required land developers to register subdivisions of 100 or more non-exempt lots with HUD and to provide each purchaser with a disclosure document called a property report. The property report contains relevant information about the subdivision and must be delivered to each purchaser before the signing of the contract or agreement.

The report must disclose specific information about the land, including

- the type of title being transferred to the buyer,
- the number of homes currently occupied on the site,
- the availability of recreation facilities,
- the distance to nearby communities,
- utility services and charges, and
- soil conditions and foundation or construction problems.

Under the act, the purchaser has the right to revoke any contract to purchase a regulated lot until midnight on the seventh day after the contract was signed. If the purchaser or lessee does not receive a copy of the property report before signing the purchase contract or lease, she may bring an action to void the contract within two years after signing it.

The act provides a number of exceptions. For instance, it does not apply to subdivisions consisting of fewer than 25 lots or to those in which the lots are of 20 acres or more. Lots offered for sale solely to developers also are exempt from the act's requirements, as are lots on which buildings exist or where a seller is obligated to construct a building within two years. Misrepresentation or failure to comply with the act's requirements subjects a seller to criminal penalties (fines and imprisonment) as well as to civil damages.

State "Subdivided Land" Sales Laws

Many state legislatures have enacted their own subdivided-land sales laws. Some affect only the sale of land located outside the state to state residents. Other states' laws regulate sales of land located both inside and outside the state. These state land sales laws tend to be stricter and more detailed than the federal law. Real estate licensees should be aware of the laws in their state and how they compare with federal law.

| In Illinois |

The sale or promotion within Illinois of subdivided land is regulated by the **Illinois Land Sales Registration Act of 1999.** This act regulates the offering, sale, lease, or assignment of any improved or unimproved land divided into 25 or more lots and offered as a part of a common promotional plan.

Under this legislation, subdividers must register with the state and file a full disclosure report containing information on the land, location, tax status, financial arrangements, and liens associated with the offering. As in the federal statute, a purchaser who receives the report prior to signing a contract or agreement may cancel the contract or agreement by giving notice to the seller any time before midnight of the seventh day following the signing of the contract or agreement. A purchaser who does not receive this report before a contract or agreement is signed may cancel the contract or agreement anytime within two years from the date of signing. ■

■ SUMMARY

Land use is controlled and regulated through public restrictions, private (or nongovernmental) restrictions, and direct public ownership of land.

The police power of the state is the state's authority to create regulations to protect the public health, safety, and welfare. State enabling acts allow the power to enact laws authorized by the state's police power to be passed down to municipalities and other local governing authorities. Such regulations must be exercised in a reasonable manner, clear and specific, nondiscriminatory, and applicable to all property in a similar manner.

Land may be taken for public use through the government's power of eminent domain or condemnation. The owner must be given just (fair) compensation. A property owner may claim compensation under inverse condemnation if an adjacent public land use diminishes the value of the owner's property but the property has not been condemned for public use.

A comprehensive plan or master plan sets forth the development goals and objectives for the community. Zoning ordinances are local laws implementing the land uses designated in the comprehensive plan and typically cover items such as permitted uses, lot sizes, types of structures, building heights, setbacks, style and appearance of structures, density, and protection of natural resources. Zoning classifies property by uses and types, such as commercial, industrial, residential, agricultural, and planned unit developments (PUDs).

Other ways in which zoning is used include

- buffer zones separating residential from nonresidential areas,
- bulk zoning to control density,
- aesthetic zoning to specify certain types of architecture for new buildings, and
- incentive zoning to require certain uses in developments.

Zoning is enforced through the use of permits, and an individual case may be considered by a zoning hearing board (or zoning board of appeals), which may decide to allow a nonconforming use to continue, grant a variance from a zoning ordinance to permit a prohibited land use to avoid undue hardship, or grant a conditional-use (special-use permit).

Building codes specify standards for construction, plumbing, sewers, electrical wiring, and fire prevention equipment. A certificate of occupancy (occupancy permit) is used upon satisfactory completion of work for which the permit was issued.

Subdivision and land development regulations are adopted to maintain control of the development of expanding community areas so that growth is harmonious with community standards.

A subdivider buys undeveloped acreage, divides it into smaller parcels, and develops or sells it. A developer builds homes on the lots and sells them through the developer's own sales organization or through local real estate brokerage firms. City planners and land developers, working together, plan whole communities that are later incorporated into cities, towns, or villages.

Land development must comply with the master plans adopted by counties, cities, villages, or towns. This may entail approval of land-use plans by local planning committees or commissioners.

The process of subdivision includes dividing the tract of land into lots and blocks and providing for utility easements, as well as laying out street patterns and widths. A subdivider generally must record a completed plat of subdivision (including the necessary approvals from public officials) in the county where the land is located. Subdividers usually place restrictions on the use of all lots in a subdivision as a general plan for the benefit of all future owners.

By varying street patterns and housing density and clustering housing units, a subdivider can dramatically increase the amount of open and recreational space within a development.

Private land-use controls are exercised by owners through deed restrictions and restrictive covenants. These private restrictions may be enforced by obtaining a court injunction to stop a violator.

Subdivided land sales are regulated on the federal level by the Interstate Land Sales Full Disclosure Act. This law requires that developers engaged in certain interstate land sales or leases register the details of the land with HUD. Developers also must provide prospective purchasers or lessees with property reports containing all essential information about the property in any development that exceeds 100 lots.

In Illinois

The Illinois Constitution provides for certain units of government to exercise home rule authority. When a county's ordinance conflicts with a municipality's, the municipal ordinance prevails.

The Illinois Human Rights Act prohibits restrictive covenants that discriminate on the basis of race, color, religion, or national origin.

The sale or promotion within Illinois of subdivided land is regulated by the Illinois Land Sales Registration Act of 1999. Additional property-related statutes are located in Chapter 765 of the Illinois Compiled Statutes. ■

CHAPTER 20 QUIZ

1. A subdivision declaration reads, "No property within this subdivision may be further subdivided for sale or otherwise, and no property may be used for other than single-family housing." This is an example of
   a. a restrictive covenant.
   b. an illegal reverter clause.
   c. R-1 zoning.
   d. a conditional-use clause.

2. A landowner who wants to use property in a manner that is prohibited by a local zoning ordinance but would benefit the community can apply for which of the following?
   a. Conditional-use permit
   b. Prescriptive easement
   c. Occupancy permit
   d. Property dedication

3. What is NOT included in public land use controls?
   a. Subdivision regulations
   b. Restrictive covenants
   c. Environmental protection laws
   d. Comprehensive plan specifications

4. Under its zoning, a town may legally regulate which of the following?
   a. Building ownership
   b. Business ownership
   c. The number of buildings
   d. Enabling acts

5. The purpose of a building permit is to
   a. assert a deed's restrictive covenant.
   b. maintain municipal control over the volume of building.
   c. provide evidence of compliance with municipal regulations.
   d. show compliance with restrictive covenants.

6. Zoning powers are conferred on municipal governments in which of the following ways?
   a. By state enabling acts
   b. Through the master plan
   c. By popular local vote
   d. Through city charters

7. A town enacts a new zoning code. Under the new code, commercial buildings are not permitted within 1,000 feet of the lake. A commercial building that is permitted to continue in its former use even though it is built on the lakeshore is an example of
   a. nonconforming use.
   b. variance.
   c. special use.
   d. adverse possession.

8. To determine whether a location can be put to future use as a retail store, one would examine the
   a. building code.
   b. list of permitted nonconforming uses.
   c. housing code.
   d. zoning ordinance.

9. All of the following are legal deed restrictions EXCEPT
   a. the types of buildings that may be constructed.
   b. the allowable ethnic origins of purchasers.
   c. the activities that are not to be conducted at the site.
   d. the minimum size of buildings to be constructed.

10. A restriction in a seller's deed may be enforced by which of the following?
    a. Court injunction
    b. Zoning board of appeal
    c. City building commission
    d. State legislature

11. A man owns a large tract of land. After an adequate study of all the relevant facts, the man legally divides the land into 30 lots suitable for the construction of residences. In this situation, the man is acting as a(n)
    a. subdivider.
    b. developer.
    c. land planner.
    d. urban planner.

12. A map illustrating the sizes and locations of streets and lots in a subdivision is called a
    a. gridiron plan.
    b. survey.
    c. plat of subdivision.
    d. property report.

13. In one city, developers are limited by law to constructing no more than an average of three houses per acre in any subdivision. What does this restriction regulate?
    a. Clustering
    b. Gross density
    c. Out-lots
    d. Covenants

14. A city is laid out in a pattern of intersecting streets and avenues. All streets run north and south; all avenues run east and west. This city is an example of which street pattern style?
    a. Block plan
    b. Gridiron system
    c. Radial streets plan
    d. Intersecting system

15. Permitted land uses and set-asides, housing projections, transportation issues, and objectives for implementing future controlled development would all be found in a community's
    a. zoning ordinance.
    b. comprehensive plan.
    c. enabling act.
    d. land-control law.

16. A subdivider can increase the amount of open or recreational space in a development by
    a. varying street patterns.
    b. meeting local housing standards.
    c. scattering housing units.
    d. eliminating multistory dwellings.

17. Under the federal law designed to protect the public from fraudulent interstate land sales, a developer involved in interstate land sales of 100 or more lots must
    a. provide each purchaser with a printed report disclosing details of the property.
    b. pay the prospective buyer's expenses to see the property involved.
    c. provide preferential financing.
    d. allow a 30-day cancellation period.

---

18. Which of the following statements BEST describes enabling statutes in Illinois?
    a. They grant counties, cities, and villages the power to make and enforce local zoning ordinances.
    b. They make all counties, cities, and villages subject to Illinois state zoning laws.
    c. They require all Illinois counties, cities, and villages to adopt the requirements of the federal municipal planning commission.
    d. They set environmental controls on current land use.

19. A person feels that video game arcades are a bad influence on the city's young people and wants the city zoned to prohibit all arcades and other public video gaming facilities. Which of the following would be the person's BEST course of action?
    a. Try to get the Illinois legislature to amend the state zoning laws
    b. File suit to force the city to conform with existing Illinois zoning laws
    c. Try to persuade the town government to change the local zoning laws
    d. Ask HUD to force the city to zone against video arcades under its Fifth Amendment powers

20. A zoning law passed by a village conflicts with an existing county zoning law. Both the village and the county are home rule units of government. In this situation, which of the following statements is *TRUE*?

a. Under the Illinois constitution, the county law will prevail because its zoning laws affect a larger geographic area.

b. The village's law will prevail because municipal ordinances supersede county ordinances under the Illinois Constitution.

c. The Illinois Constitution provides that a conflict between the laws of two home rule units must be resolved in the appropriate circuit court.

d. Whichever law is most restrictive will prevail, unless the issue involves a constitutional question, in which case the law least restrictive of private property rights will supersede the more restrictive law.

Fair Housing and Ethical Practices

■ FAIR HOUSING AND ETHICAL PRACTICES

Licensees and their clients and customers today reflect the changing diversity in American society: those for whom English is a second language, people from a wide range of cultural backgrounds, people of various age and religious preferences; and people with disabilities, to name just a few. Although some differences are protected by state and federal laws, others are not. Understanding and working within the context of equal opportunity is critical to creating and maintaining a more diverse, vibrant, and ultimately profitable real estate market for everyone. When challenged to meet consumers on their terms, successful licensees recognize that embracing diversity is a good business practice and builds bridges.

■ EQUAL OPPORTUNITY IN HOUSING

"All citizens of the United States shall have the same right in every state and territory as is enjoyed by white citizens thereof to inherit, purchase, lease, sell, hold, and convey real and personal property."
—Civil Rights Act of 1866

The civil rights laws that affect the real estate industry ensure that everyone has the opportunity to live where they choose. Federal, state, and local fair housing or equal opportunity laws affect every phase of a real estate transaction, from listing to closing. U.S. Congress and the Supreme Court have created a legal framework that preserves the constitutional rights of all citizens. However, while the passage of laws may establish a code for public conduct, damaging attitudes reinforced by centuries of discrimination are not so easily eliminated. Real estate licensees *must* eliminate actions or words that create discrimination (or the appearance of discrimination) if they wish to conduct an ethical and legal business. Similarly, any discriminatory attitudes of property owners or property seekers *must* be addressed by the licensee if these attitudes affect compliance with fair housing laws.

Working with clients who may have discriminatory attitudes is not easy, and the pressure to avoid offending a seller client or buyer client can be intense. However, ethics and the law demand that licensees comply with fair housing laws. Failure to comply with fair housing laws is both a civil and criminal violation and constitutes grounds for disciplinary action against a licensee.

In Illinois

The Illinois Real Estate License Act of 2000 and the general rules require that licensees fully adhere to the principles of equal housing opportunity. A licensee is prohibited from taking any listing or participating in any transaction in which the property owner seeks to discriminate based on race, color, ancestry, religion, national origin, sex, handicap, or familial status. Breaking fair housing laws in Illinois is a criminal act and grounds for discipline. Violating provisions or restrictions of the Illinois Real Estate License Act of 2000 (or the rules) can result in suspension, nonrenewal, or revocation of the violator's license or censure, reprimand, or fine imposed by IDFPR.

The Real Estate License Act of 2000 requires that when a judgment in either a civil or criminal proceeding has been made against a licensee for illegally discriminating, his license must be suspended or revoked unless an appeal is active. Finally, if there has already been an order by an administrative agency finding discrimination by a licensee, the board must penalize the licensee.

In addition to state and federal laws, many cities and villages in Illinois have their own fair housing laws. These laws are enforced on the local level and may take precedence over federal laws when the local law has been ruled substantially equivalent to the federal statute. Many local fair housing laws are stricter than state or federal laws. Licensees should be familiar with local regulations as well as with state and federal law. ■

Federal Laws

The federal government's effort to guarantee equal housing opportunities to all U.S. citizens began with the passage of the **Civil Rights Act of 1866.** This law prohibits any type of discrimination based on race.

The U.S. Supreme Court's 1896 decision in *Plessy v. Ferguson* established the "separate but equal" doctrine of "legalized" racial segregation. A series of court decisions and federal laws in the 20 years between 1948 and 1968 attempted to address housing inequities resulting from *Plessy*. Those efforts, however, often addressed only specific aspects of the housing market (such as federally funded housing programs). As a result, their impact was limited. Title VIII of the Civil Rights Act of 1968, however, prohibited specific discriminatory practices throughout the real estate industry.

■ FAIR HOUSING ACT

The Fair Housing Act prohibits discrimination based on
■ race,
■ color,
■ religion,
■ sex,
■ disability,
■ familial status, and
■ national origin.

Title VIII of the Civil Rights Act of 1968 prohibits discrimination in housing based on race, color, religion, and national origin. In 1974, the Housing and Community Development Act added sex to the list of protected classes. In 1988, the Fair Housing Amendments Act added *disability* and *familial status* (that is, the presence of children). Today, these laws together are known as the federal **Fair Housing Act.** (See Figure 21.1.) The Fair Housing Act prohibits discrimination on the basis of race, color, religion, sex, disability, familial status, or national origin. The act also prohibits discrimination against individuals because of their association with persons in the protected classes.

The **Department of Housing and Urban Development (HUD)** administers the Fair Housing Act. HUD has established rules and regulations that further interpret impacted housing practices. In addition, HUD distributes the equal housing opportunity poster. (See Figure 21.2.) This poster declares that the office in which it is displayed promises to adhere to the Fair Housing Act and pledges support for affirmative marketing and advertising programs. The fair housing poster should be displayed in every real estate office.

In 1988, Congress passed the Fair Housing Amendments Act that expanded federal civil rights protections. In addition to race, color, religion, and national origin being protected classes, the act extended coverage to include families with children and persons with physical or mental disabilities. The act also made the penalties more severe and added damages for noneconomic injuries (e.g., humiliation, embarrassment, inconvenience, and mental anguish).

FIGURE 21.1

Federal and State Fair Housing Laws

HUD

Legislation	Race	Color	Religion	National Origin	Sex	Age	Marital Status	Disability	Familial Status	Public Assistance Income
Civil Rights Act of 1866	•									
Fair Housing Act of 1968 (Title VIII)	•	•	•	•						
Housing and Community Development Act of 1974	•	•	•	•	•					
Fair Housing Amendments Act of 1988								•	•	
Equal Credit Opportunity Act of 1974 (lending)	•	•	•	•	•	•	•			•
* Illinois Human Rights Act	•	•	•	•	•	•	•	•	•	

* The Illinois Human Rights Act specifies both "physical and mental" disability. It also adds as a protected class: ancestry, military status, unfavorable military discharge, sexual orientation, and order of protection status as it impacts employment, real estate transactions, financial credit, or availability of public accommodations.

In 1995, Congress passed the Housing for Older Persons Act (HOPA), which repealed the requirement that 55-and-older housing have "significant facilities and services" designed for seniors. HOPA still requires that at least 80 percent of occupied units have one person age 55 or older living there. The act prohibits the awarding of monetary damages against those who, in good faith, reasonably believed that property designated as housing for older persons was exempt from familial status provisions of the Fair Housing Act.

IN PRACTICE   When HUD investigates a licensee for discriminatory practices, it may consider failure to prominently display the equal housing opportunity poster in the licensee's place of business as evidence of discrimination.

Definitions

HUD's regulations provide specific definitions that clarify the scope of the Fair Housing Act.

Housing   The regulations define *housing* as a *dwelling* that includes ing or part of a building designed for occupancy as a residence by o families. This includes a single-family house, a condominium, a coope manufactured housing, as well as vacant land on which any of these str be built.

FIGURE 21.2

Equal Opportunity Housing Poster

U.S. Department of Housing and Urban Development

EQUAL HOUSING
OPPORTUNITY

We Do Business in Accordance With the Federal Fair Housing Law

(The Fair Housing Amendments Act of 1988)

> ## It is Illegal to Discriminate Against Any Person Because of Race, Color, Religion, Sex, Handicap, Familial Status, or National Origin

- ■ In the sale or rental of housing or residential lots
- ■ In advertising the sale or rental of housing
- ■ In the financing of housing

- ■ In the provision of real estate brokerage services
- ■ In the appraisal of housing
- ■ Blockbusting is also illegal

Anyone who feels he or she has been discriminated against may file a complaint of housing discrimination:
   1-800-669-9777 (Toll Free)
   1-800-927-9275 (TDD)

U.S. Department of Housing and Urban Development Assistant Secretary for Fair Housing and Equal Opportunity Washington, D.C. 20410

Previous editions are obsolete

form HUD-928.1A (2/2003)

Familial status   *Familial status* refers to the presence of one or more individuals who have not reached the age of 18 and who live with either a parent or guardian. In effect, the familial status reference means that the act's protections extend to families with children. The term includes a woman who is pregnant. Unless a property qualifies as housing for older persons, all properties must be made available to families with children under the same terms and conditions as to anyone else. It is illegal to advertise properties as being for "adults only" or to indicate preferred number of children. Occupancy standards (the number of persons permitted to reside in a property) must be based on objective factors such as sanitation or safety. Landlords cannot restrict the number of occupants to eliminate families with children.

■ **FOR EXAMPLE**   A man owned an apartment building. One of his elderly tenants was terminally ill. The tenant requested that no children be allowed in the vacant apartment next door because the noise would be difficult for her to bear. The owner of the apartment building agreed and refused to rent to families with children. Even though the intent was to make things easier for a dying tenant, the owner was nonetheless found to have violated the Fair Housing Act by discriminating on the basis of familial status.

Disability   A *disability* is a physical or mental impairment. It is unlawful to discriminate against prospective buyers or tenants on the basis of disability. The term includes having a history of, or being regarded as having, an impairment that limits one or more of an individual's major life activities. Persons who have AIDS are protected by the fair housing laws under this classification.

IN PRACTICE   The federal fair housing laws do not extend to defining current users of illegal or controlled substances as persons with disabilities. Nor is anyone who has been convicted of the illegal manufacture or distribution of a controlled substance protected under this law. However, the law does prohibit discrimination against those who are participating in addiction recovery programs. For instance, a landlord could lawfully discriminate against a cocaine addict but not against a member of Alcoholics Anonymous.

Landlords must make reasonable accommodations to existing policies, practices, or services to permit persons with disabilities to have equal enjoyment of the premises. For instance, it would be reasonable for a landlord to permit service animals (such as guide dogs) in a normally "no-pets" building or to provide designated parking spaces for persons with disabilities.

People with disabilities must be permitted to make reasonable modifications to the premises at their own expense. Such modifications might include lowering door handles or installing bath rails for a person in a wheelchair. *Failure to permit reasonable modification constitutes discrimination.* However, the law recognizes that certain reasonable modifications might make a rental property undesirable to the general population. In such a case, the landlord is allowed to require that the property be restored to its previous condition when the lease period ends.

The landlord may not increase the customarily required security deposit for persons with disabilities. However, where it is necessary in order to ensure with reasonable certainty that funds will be available to pay for the restorations at the end of the tenancy, the landlord may negotiate as part of such a restoration agreement a provision requiring that the tenant pay into an interest bearing escrow account, over a reasonable period, a reasonable amount of money not to exceed the cost of the restorations. The interest in the account accrues to the benefit of the tenant. A landlord may condition permission for a modification on the renter providing a reasonable description of the proposed modifications as well as reasonable assurances that the work will be done in a workmanlike manner and that any required building permits will be obtained.

The law does not prohibit restricting occupancy to persons with disabilities in dwellings that are designed specifically for their accommodation.

In newly constructed multifamily buildings with an elevator and four or more units, the public and common areas must be accessible to persons with disabilities, and doors and hallways must be wide enough for wheelchairs. The entrance

TABLE 21.1

Fair Housing Act Restrictions

Prohibited by Federal Fair Housing Act	Example
Refusing to sell, rent, or negotiate the sale or rental of housing	An apartment building has several vacant units. When an Asian family asks to see one of the units, the owner tells them to go away.
Changing terms, conditions, or services for different individuals as a means of discriminating	A landlord tells a Roman Catholic prospective tenant that the rent for a duplex is $500 per month. However, when talking with the other tenants, the prospective tenant learns that all the Lutherans in the complex pay only $425 per month.
Advertising any discriminatory preference or limitation in housing or making any inquiry or reference that is discriminatory in nature	A real estate licensee places the following advertisement in a newspaper: "Just Listed! Perfect home for white family, near excellent parochial school!" A developer places this ad in an urban newspaper: "Sunset River Hollow—Dream Homes Just For You!" The ad is accompanied by a photo of several African-American families.
Representing that a property is not available for sale or rent when in fact it is	A man who uses a wheelchair is told that the house he wants to rent is no longer available. The next day, however, the For Rent sign is still in the window.
Profiting by inducing property owners to sell or rent on the basis of the prospective entry into the neighborhood of persons of a protected class	A real estate licensee sends brochures to homeowners in the predominantly white Ridgewood neighborhood. The brochures, which feature the licensee's past success selling homes, include photos of racial minorities, population statistics, and the caption, "The Changing Face of Ridgewood."
Altering the terms or conditions of a home loan, or denying a loan, as a means of discrimination	A lender requires a divorced mother of two young children to pay for a credit report. In addition, her father must cosign her application. After talking to a single male friend, the woman learns that he was not required to do either of those things, despite his lower income and poor credit history.
Denying membership or participation in a multiple listing service, a real estate organization, or another facility related to the sale or rental of housing as a means of discrimination	The County Real Estate Practitioners' Association meets every week to discuss available properties and buyers. None of the county's black or female licensees is allowed to be a member of the association.

to each unit must be accessible, as well as the light switches, electrical outlets, thermostats, and other environmental controls. People in wheelchairs should be able to use the kitchen and bathrooms; bathroom walls should be reinforced to accommodate later installation of grab bars. Ground-floor units must meet these requirements in buildings that do not have an elevator. Licensees should be aware that state and local law may require stricter standards.

Exemptions to the Fair Housing Act

The federal Fair Housing Act provides for certain exemptions. It is important for licensees to know in what situations the exemptions apply. However, licensees should be aware that no exemptions involve race and no exemptions apply when a real estate licensee is involved in a transaction (including when selling or leasing his own property).

The Fair Housing Act exempts

- owner-occupied buildings with no more than four units,
- single-family housing sold or rented without the use of a real state licensee, and
- housing operated by organizations and private clubs that limit occupancy to members.

The sale or rental of a single-family home is exempt when

- the home is owned by an individual who does not own more than three such homes at one time (and who does not sell more than one every two years),
- a real estate licensee is *not* involved in the transaction, and
- discriminatory advertising is not used.

The rental of rooms or units is exempt in an owner-occupied one- to four-family dwelling.

Note that dwelling units owned by religious organizations may be restricted to people of the same religion if membership in the organization is not restricted on the basis of race, color, or national origin. A private club that is not open to the public may restrict the rental or occupancy of lodgings that it owns to its members as long as the lodgings are not operated commercially.

The Fair Housing Act does not require that housing be made available to any individual whose tenancy would constitute a direct threat to the health or safety of other individuals or that would result in substantial physical damage to the property of others.

Housing for older persons While the Fair Housing Act protects families with children, certain properties can be restricted to occupancy by elderly persons. Housing intended for persons age 62 or older or housing occupied by at least one person 55 years of age or older (where 80 percent of the units are occupied by individuals 55 or older) is exempt from the familial status protection.

Jones v. Mayer In 1968, the Supreme Court heard the case of *Jones v. Alfred H. Mayer Company*, 392 U.S. 409 (1968). In its decision, the court upheld the Civil Rights Act of 1866. This decision is important because although the federal law exempts individual homeowners and certain groups, the 1866 law prohibits all racial discrimination without exception. A person who is discriminated against on the basis of race may still recover damages under the 1866 law. Where race is involved, no exceptions apply.

The U.S. Supreme Court has expanded the definition of the term race to include ancestral and ethnic characteristics, including certain physical, cultural, or linguistic characteristics that are shared by a group with a common national origin. These rulings are significant because discrimination on the basis of race, as it is now defined, affords due process of complaints under the provisions of the Civil Rights Act of 1866.

Megan's Law   Federal legislation, known as Megan's Law, promotes the establishment of state registration systems to maintain residential information on every person who kidnaps children, commits sexual crimes against children, or commits sexually violent crimes. Upon release from prison, offenders must register their name with state authorities and indicate where they will be residing. Local law enforcement agencies may release relevant information about such an offender upon request if they deem it necessary for the protection of the public.

Megan's Law affects a licensee's duty of disclosure. In accordance with state law, a licensee may need to request that a customer sign a form indicating where the customer may obtain information about the sex offender registry. An index to sex offender registries in all 50 states can be found at *www.prevent-abuse-now. com/register.htm.* Depending on the state, a licensee may be required to disclose information regarding a released offender if the licensee is aware that officials have informed individuals, groups, or the public that a sex offender resides in a particular area. Megan's Law, in effect, creates another category of stigmatized property. (See Chapter 4.)

Equal Credit Opportunity Act

The Equal Credit Opportunity Act prohibits discrimination in granting credit based on
- race,
- color,
- religion,
- national origin,
- sex,
- marital status,
- age, and
- public assistance.

The federal **Equal Credit Opportunity Act** (ECOA) prohibits discrimination based on race, color, religion, national origin, sex, marital status, or age in the granting of credit. Note that ECOA protects more classes of persons than the Fair Housing Act. The ECOA bars discrimination on the basis of marital status and age. It also prevents lenders from discriminating against recipients of public assistance programs, food stamps, or Social Security. The ECOA requires that credit applications be considered only on the basis of income, net worth, job stability, and credit rating.

A creditor may not consider age unless the applicant is too young to legally sign a contract, which is usually 18, although the creditor may consider age when determining if income will drop due to retirement. Lenders are prohibited from discriminating against recipients of public assistance programs such as food stamps and Social Security. Lenders may not ask questions about a spouse unless the spouse is also applying for credit (e.g., lenders may not discount a woman's income or assume that she will leave the workforce to raise children).

The agency that enforces ECOA depends on the type of financial institution. In general, the ECOA is enforced by the Federal Trade Commission (FTC) and the Department of Justice as well as other agencies.

Americans with Disabilities Act

The Americans with Disabilities Act requires reasonable accommodations in employment and access to goods, services, and public buildings.

Although the **Americans with Disabilities Act (ADA)** is not a housing or credit law, it still has a significant effect on the real estate industry. The ADA is important to licensees because it addresses the rights of individuals with disabilities in employment and public accommodations. Real estate licensees are often employers, and real estate brokerage offices are public spaces. The ADA's goal is to enable individuals with disabilities to become part of the economic and social mainstream of society.

Title 1 of the ADA requires that employers (including real estate licensees) make *reasonable accommodations* that enable an individual with a disability to perform essential job functions. Reasonable accommodations include making the work site accessible, restructuring a job, providing part-time or flexible work schedules, and modifying equipment used on the job. The provisions of ADA apply to any employer with 15 or more employees.

Title III of the ADA requires that individuals with disabilities have full accessibility to businesses, goods, and public services. While the federal civil rights laws have traditionally been seen as focused on residential housing, business and commercial real estate are fully covered by Title III. Because people with disabilities have the right to full and equal access to businesses and public services under the ADA, building owners and managers must ensure that any obstacle restricting this right is eliminated. The Americans with Disabilities Act Accessibility Guidelines (ADAAG) contain detailed specifications for designing parking spaces, curb ramps, elevators, drinking fountains, toilet facilities, and directional signs to ensure maximum accessibility. Unless the licensee is a qualified ADA expert, it is best to advise commercial clients to seek the services of an attorney, an architect, or a consultant who specializes in ADA issues.

IN PRACTICE   In 1999, the U.S. Supreme Court strictly limited the definition of *persons with disabilities* protected by the ADA. The decision excludes individuals whose disability, such as nearsightedness, can be corrected. In 2002, the U.S. Supreme Court narrowed the definition even further by stating that in determining whether or not a person is disabled, you may ask whether the impairment(s) prevent or restrict the person from performing tasks that are of central importance to most people's daily lives.

ADA and the Fair Housing Act   The ADA exempts the following two types of property from its requirements:

- Property that is covered by the Fair Housing Act
- Property that is exempt from coverage by the Fair Housing Act

Some properties are subject to both laws. For example, in an apartment complex, the rental office is a place of public accommodation. As such, it is covered by the ADA and must be accessible to persons with disabilities at the owner's expense.

Individual rental units would be covered by the Fair Housing Act. A tenant who wished to modify the unit to make it accessible would be responsible for the cost.

Issues of housing and disability discrimination are often litigated in the courts. For example, in the 2005 case of, *Wells v. State Manufactured Homes*, the landlord ordered the owner of a manufactured housing unit to move from the community because he claimed she violated the no-pets provision of her rental agreement. The landlord refused to make a reasonable accommodation for the owner's emotional disability by not permitting her to keep a dog. She filed suit under the ADA and Fair Housing Act. The court held that there was no violation of the Fair Housing Act or the ADA. The court said she failed to establish that her mental impairment substantially limited a major life activity and that she was not disabled under the ADA.

IN PRACTICE   Real estate licensees need a general knowledge of the ADA's provisions. It is necessary for a licensee's workplace and employment policies to comply with the law. Amendments to the ADA are periodically introduced in the U.S. Congress, and it is important to be aware of changes in the law. Also, licensees who are building managers must ensure that the properties are legally accessible. However, ADA compliance questions may arise with regard to a client's property, too. Unless the licensee is a qualified ADA expert, it is best to advise commercial clients to seek the services of an attorney, an architect, or a consultant who specializes in ADA issues. It is possible that an appraiser may be liable for failing to identify and account for a property's noncompliance.

■ FAIR HOUSING PRACTICES

For the civil rights laws to accomplish their goal of eliminating discrimination, licensees must apply them routinely. Of course, compliance also means that licensees consistently represent the ethical standards of the profession. The following discussion examines certain ethical and legal issues that may confront real estate licensees in their day-to-day practice.

Blockbusting

Blockbusting: encouraging the sale or renting of property by claiming that the entry of a protected class of people into the neighborhood will negatively affect property values.

Blockbusting is the act of encouraging people to sell or rent their homes by claiming that the entry of a protected class of people into the neighborhood will have some sort of negative impact on property values. Any message, however subtle or accidental, that property should be sold or rented because the neighborhood is "undergoing changes" is considered blockbusting. It is illegal to suggest that the presence of certain persons will cause property values to decline, crime or antisocial behavior to increase, or the quality of schools to suffer.

A critical element in defining blockbusting, according to HUD, is the profit motive. A property owner may be intimidated into selling his property at a depressed price to the blockbuster, who in turn sells the property to another person at a higher price. Blockbusting is also called *panic selling*. To avoid accusations of blockbusting, licensees should use good judgment when choosing locations and methods for marketing their services and soliciting listings.

Steering

Steering: channeling homebuyers to particular neighborhoods based on race, religion, nationality, or other consideration.

Steering is the channeling of homeseekers to particular neighborhoods. It also includes discouraging potential buyers from considering some areas. In either case, it is an illegal limitation of a purchaser's options. In the rental process, steering occurs when the landlord puts members of a protected class on a certain floor or building. Another form of steering occurs when the landlord tells a prospective tenant that no vacancy exists when, in fact, there is a vacancy. When the misstatement is made on the basis of a protected class, the prospect is steered away from that building. Many cases of steering are subtle, motivated by assumptions or perceptions about a homebuyer's preferences, and based on some stereotype. Such assumptions about a buyer's preferences may be legally dangerous. The licensee should never assume that prospective buyers "expect" to be directed to neighborhoods or properties. Steering anyone is illegal.

In Illinois

The Illinois Real Estate License Act of 2000 expressly prohibits "Influencing or attempting to influence by any words or acts a prospective seller, purchaser, occupant, landlord, or tenant of real estate, in connection with viewing, buying or leasing of real estate, so as to promote, or tend to promote, the continuance or maintenance of racially and religiously segregated housing, or so as to retard, obstruct or discourage racially integrated housing on or in any street, block, neighborhood, or community." ■

Advertising

Advertisements of property for sale or rent may not include language indicating a preference or limitation. No exception to this rule exists, regardless of subtle or "accidental" wordings. HUD's regulations cite numerous examples that are considered discriminatory. (See Figure 21.3.) However, an advertisement that is gender specific, such as "female roommate sought," is allowed as long as the advertiser seeks to share living quarters with someone of the same gender. The media used for promoting property or real estate services must not target any one population to the exclusion of others. The use of media that targets only certain groups based on, for example, language or geography, is also viewed as being potentially discriminatory. For instance, limiting advertising to a cable television channel viewed mostly by one demographic group might be construed as discriminatory. The best rule is never to advertise using only one group of narrowly focused media. Running ads in several locales *or* in general-circulation media as a standard rule is good practice.

Positive language in the ads, too, may be a factor in determining the legitimacy of a discrimination charge. Many licensees choose to run a small version of the equal housing opportunity symbol in all of the materials that represent them, along with the words "equal housing opportunity" underneath. Repeating the HUD poster statement, "We do business in accordance with the Federal Fair Housing Law" may go a long way toward assisting a licensee whose integrity on such issues is ever incorrectly questioned. The fair housing symbol signals the world that one is open for business to anyone who is of age and financially able to purchase real estate.

FIGURE   21.3

HUD's Advertising Guidelines

Category	Rule	Permitted	Not Permitted
Race Color National origin	No discrimination limitation/preference may be expressed	"master bedroom" "good neighborhood"	"white neighborhood "no French"
Religion	No religious preference/limitation	"chapel on premises" "kosher meals available" "Merry Christmas"	"no Muslims" "nice Christian family" "near great Catholic school"
Sex	No explicit preference based on sex	"mother-in-law suite" "master bedroom" "female roommate sought"	"great house for a man" "wife's dream kitchen"
Disability	No exclusions or limitations based on disability	"wheelchair ramp" "walk to shopping"	"no wheelchairs" "able-bodied tenants only"
Familial status	No preference or limitations based on family size or nature	"two-bedroom" "family room" "quiet neighborhood"	"married couple only" "no more than two children" "retiree's dream house"
Photographs or illustrations of people	People should be clearly representative and nonexclusive	Illustrations showing ethnic races, family groups, singles, and so forth	Illustrations showing only singles, African American families, elderly white adults, and so forth

Appraising

Those who prepare appraisals or any statements of valuation—whether they are formal or informal, oral or written (including a competitive market analysis)—may consider any normal qualifying factors that affect value. However, race, color, religion, national origin, sex, disability, and familial status are *not* factors that may be considered.

Redlining

The practice of refusing to make mortgage loans or issue insurance policies in specific areas for reasons other than the applicant's financial qualifications is known as **redlining**. Redlining refers to literally or figuratively drawing a line around particular areas. Such practices contribute to the deterioration of older neighborhoods. Redlining is often based on racial grounds rather than on any real objection to an applicant's creditworthiness. Redlining means that the lender has made a policy decision that no property in a certain area will qualify for a loan, no matter who wants to buy it. The federal Fair Housing Act prohibits discrimination in mortgage lending and covers not only the actions of primary lenders but also activities in the secondary mortgage market. A lending institution can, however, refuse a loan solely on sound, documentable financial grounds.

The **Home Mortgage Disclosure Act** requires that all institutional mortgage lenders with assets in excess of $36 million and one or more offices in a given geographic area make annual reports. The reports must detail all mortgage loans the institution has made or purchased, broken down by census tract. This law enables the government to detect patterns of lending behavior that might constitute redlining.

Intent and Effect

If an owner or real estate licensee purposely sets out to engage in blockbusting, steering, or other unfair activities, the intent to discriminate is obvious. However, owners and licensees must examine their activities and policies carefully to determine whether they unintentionally appear to engage in discriminatory actions. Whenever policies or practices result in unequal treatment of persons in a protected class, they are considered discriminatory, regardless of intent. This "effects test" is applied by regulatory agencies to determine whether discrimination has occurred.

Response to Concerns of Terrorism

In response to the concern of future terrorist attacks, landlords and property managers have been developing new security procedures. These procedures have focused on protecting buildings and residents. Landlords and property managers are also educating residents on signs of possible terrorist activity and how and where to report it. At the same time, landlords and property managers need to ensure that their procedures and education do not infringe on the fair housing rights of others.

For screening and rental procedures, it is unlawful to screen housing applicants on the basis of race, color, religion, sex, national origin, disability, or familial status. According to HUD, landlords and property managers have been inquiring about whether they can screen applicants on the basis of citizenship status. The Fair Housing Act does not specifically prohibit discrimination based solely on a person's citizenship status. Therefore, asking applicants for citizenship documentation or immigration status papers during the screening process does not violate the Fair Housing Act. For many years, the federal government has been asking for these documents in screening applicants for federally assisted housing. There is, however, a specific procedure for collecting and verifying citizenship papers provided by HUD.

■ **FOR EXAMPLE**   In an interview with a landlord, a woman mentions that she left her native country to study at the local university. The landlord is concerned about the woman's visa and whether it will expire during the lease term. The landlord asks the woman for documentation to determine how long she can legally live in the United States. The landlord asks for this information, regardless of her race or national origin. The landlord has not violated the Fair Housing Act.

■ ENFORCEMENT OF THE FAIR HOUSING ACT

The federal Fair Housing Act is administered by the Office of Fair Housing and Equal Opportunity (OFHEO) under the direction of the secretary of HUD. Any aggrieved person who believes illegal discrimination has occurred may file a complaint with HUD within one year of the alleged act. HUD may also initiate its own complaint. Complaints may be reported to the Office of Fair Housing and

Equal Opportunity, Department of Housing and Urban Development, Washington, DC 20410, or to the Office of Fair Housing and Equal Opportunity in care of the nearest HUD regional office. Complaints may also be submitted directly to HUD using an online form available on the HUD Web site.

On receiving a complaint, HUD initiates an investigation. Within 100 days of the filing of the complaint, HUD either determines that reasonable cause exists to bring a charge of illegal discrimination or dismisses the complaint. During this investigation period, HUD can attempt to resolve the dispute informally through conciliation. Conciliation is the resolution of a complaint by obtaining assurance that the person against whom the complaint was filed (the respondent) will remedy any violation that may have occurred. The respondent further agrees to take steps to eliminate or prevent discriminatory practices in the future. If necessary, these agreements can be enforced through civil action.

Once a formal charge of discrimination has been filed, a formal hearing is required. Either the complainant or the respondent may force the hearing to district court by means of what is called an election, which must be made within 20 days after charges are issued. If no election is made, the case will be heard before a **U.S. administrative law judge (ALJ)** who is an expert in housing discrimination. If either party prefers, then, by election, the case goes to a **U.S. district court judge** (no fair housing specialization, under the Department of Justice, and a jury trial may be requested). Cases under the ALJs normally proceed much more quickly than if they were heard in district court, and the fair housing expertise may be higher. The judge has the authority to award actual damages to the aggrieved person or persons and, if it is believed the public interest will be served, to impose monetary penalties. The penalties range from up to $16,000 for a first offense to $65,000 for a third violation within seven years. An ALJ also has the authority to issue an injunction to order the offender to either take action (such as rent an apartment to the complaining party) or refrain from an action (such as continuing to rent to only one group).

Errors and Omissions Insurance

May not cover fair housing violations!

The parties may elect civil action in federal court at any time within two years of the discriminatory act. For cases heard in federal court, unlimited punitive damages can be awarded in addition to actual damages. The court also can issue injunctions. *Errors and omissions insurance carried by licensees may not cover violations of the fair housing laws.*

Whenever the attorney general has reasonable cause to believe that any person or group is engaged in a pattern or practice of resistance to the full enjoyment of any of the rights granted by the federal fair housing laws, he may file a civil action in any federal district court. The district court may award actual and punitive damages along with attorney's fees and costs.

Complaints brought under the Civil Rights Act of 1866 are taken directly to federal courts. The only time limit for action is a state's statute of limitations for torts.

The Illinois Human Rights Act   The Illinois Real Estate License Act of 2000 prohibits any action that constitutes a violation of the Illinois Human Rights Act. This is true regardless of whether a complaint has been filed with or adjudicated by the Human Rights Commission. The Illinois Human Rights Act includes some prohibitions that also are specifically addressed by the Real Estate License Act of 2000.

Under the Illinois Human Rights Act, it is a civil rights violation for any licensee to engage in any of the following acts of discrimination based on race, color, religion, national origin, ancestry, age, sex, marital status, physical or mental disability, military service or unfavorable discharge from military service, familial status, or sexual orientation and order of protection status in connection with employment, real estate transactions, access to financial credit, and the availability of public accommodations:

- Refuse to engage in a real estate transaction with a person
- Alter the terms, conditions, or privileges of a real estate transaction
- Refuse to receive or fail to transmit an offer
- Refuse to negotiate
- Represent that real property is not available for inspection, sale, rental, or lease when in fact it is available; or fail to bring a property listing to an individual's attention; or refuse to permit him to inspect real estate
- Publicize, through any means or use, an application form that indicates an intent to engage in unlawful discrimination
- Offer, solicit, accept, use, or retain a listing of real property with knowledge that unlawful discrimination is intended

It is a civil rights violation for the owner or agent of any housing accommodation to engage in any of the following discriminatory acts against children:

- Require, as a condition to the rental of a housing accommodation, that the prospective tenant shall not have one or more children under 18 residing in his family at the time the application for rental is made
- Insert a condition in any lease that terminates the lease if one or more children younger than age 18 are ever in the family occupying the housing
  Any agreement or lease that contains a condition such as "the above is legally void as to that condition"; the lease itself remains in force, but the clause is void and unenforceable

It is also a civil rights violation in Illinois to discriminate against any person who is blind, hearing-impaired, or physically disabled in the terms, conditions, or privileges of sale or rental property. Similarly, it is a civil rights violation to refuse to sell or rent to a prospective buyer or tenant because he has a service animal. Neither may a seller or landlord require the inclusion of any additional charge in a lease, rental agreement, or contract of purchase or sale because a person who is blind, hearing-impaired, or physically disabled has a service animal. Of course, the tenant may be liable for any actual damage done to the premises by the animal.

The Illinois Human Rights Act defines elderly person as "the chronological age of a person who is at least 40 years old."

Exemptions Certain individuals, property types, and transactions are exempt from the anti-discriminatory provisions of the Illinois Human Rights Act:

- Private owners of single-family homes if (1) they own fewer than three single-family homes (including beneficial interests); (2) they were (or a member of their family was) the last current resident of the home; (3) the home was sold without the use of a real estate licensee; and (4) the home was sold without the use of discriminatory advertising
- Owner-occupied apartment buildings of five units or less
- Private rooms in a private home occupied by an owner or owner's family member
- Reasonable local, state, or federal restrictions regarding the maximum number of occupants permitted to occupy a dwelling
- A religious organization, association, or society (or any nonprofit institution or organization operated, controlled, or supervised by or in conjunction with a religious organization, association, or society) may limit the sale, rental, or occupancy of dwellings owned or operated by it (for other than commercial reasons) to persons of the same religion or give preference to persons of the same religion. This exemption is limited; it does not apply if membership in the religion is restricted on account of race, color, or national origin.
- Restricting the rental of rooms in a housing accommodation to persons of one sex
- Appraisers may take into consideration any factors other than those based on unlawful discrimination or familial status in furnishing appraisals
- Individuals who have been convicted by any court of illegally manufacturing or distributing controlled substances
- Housing for older persons on the basis of familial status. "Housing for older persons" means housing that is intended for and occupied solely by persons 62 years of age or older, or intended and operated for occupancy by persons 55 years of age or older and at least 80 percent of the occupied units are occupied by at least one person who is 55 or older
- A child sex offender who owns residential real estate, in which the offender lives and rents, is exempt from renting a unit in that property to a person who is the parent or guardian of a child or children under 18 years of age. (P.A. 95-42, eff. 8-10-07; 95-820, eff. 1-1-09.) ■

Threats or Acts of Violence

It is possible that licensees may find themselves the targets of threats, verbal abuse, or intimidation merely for complying with fair housing laws. The federal Fair Housing Act of 1968 protects the rights of those who seek the benefits of the open housing law. It also protects owners and licensees who aid or encourage the enjoyment of open housing rights. Threats or coercion are punishable as criminal actions. In such a case, the victim should report the incident immediately to law enforcement officials.

■ IMPLICATIONS FOR REAL ESTATE LICENSEES

The real estate industry is largely responsible for creating and maintaining an open housing market. Licensees are a community's real estate experts. Along with the privilege of profiting from real estate transactions comes the social and legal responsibilities to ensure that everyone's civil rights are protected. Establishing relationships with community and fair housing groups to discuss common concerns and develop solutions to problems is a constructive activity. Moreover, a licensee who is active in helping to improve his community will earn a reputation for being a concerned citizen, which may well translate into a larger client base.

Fair housing is the law. The consequences for anyone who violates the law are serious. In addition to the financial penalties, a licensee's livelihood will be in danger if his license is suspended or revoked. That the offense was unintentional is no defense. Licensees must scrutinize their practices with care and not fall victim to clients or customers who maneuver to discriminate.

All parties deserve the same standard of service. Every future homeowner has the right to expect fair and equal treatment, with house showings based only on his stated needs and financial capability. A good test is to answer the question, "Are we providing this service for everyone?" If an act is not performed consistently, or if an act affects individuals in a less than standard way, it could be construed as discriminatory. Standardized inventories of property listings, standardized criteria for financial qualification, and written documentation of activities and conversations (especially if the licensee senses a client wishes to act in a discriminatory way) are three effective means of self-protection for licensees.

HUD requires that its fair housing posters be displayed in any place of business where real estate is offered for sale or rent. Following HUD's advertising procedures and using the fair housing slogan and logo bolsters public awareness of the licensee's commitment to equal opportunity.

Beyond being the law, fair housing is good business. It ensures the greatest number of properties available for sale and rent and the largest possible pool of potential purchasers and tenants.

■ PROFESSIONAL ETHICS

Professional conduct involves more than compliance with the law. The letter of the law is not always enough; every day licensees perform legally but unethically.

Ethics refers to a high moral system of principles, rules, and standards based on conduct and values. The ethical system of a profession establishes guidelines that reach to the higher principles of what is "right." Those principles may form the law, but they exist apart from the law. Professional ethics in business usually focus on two main aspects of the profession:

- They establish standards for integrity and competence in dealing with consumers of an industry's services.
- They define a code of conduct for relations within the industry and among its professionals.

Code of Ethics

A copy of the *Code of Ethics and Standards of Practice* may be obtained by writing the National Association of REALTORS® at 430 North Michigan Avenue, Chicago, Illinois 60611, or on the Internet at *www.realtor.org*.

One way that many organizations address ethics among their members or in their respective businesses is by adopting specific, written codes of ethical conduct. A **code of ethics** is a written system of standards for professional, values-based conduct. The code contains statements designed to advise, guide, and regulate job behavior. To be effective, a code of ethics must be specific by creating rules that either prohibit or encourage certain behaviors. By including sanctions for violators, a code of ethics becomes more effective.

The National Association of REALTORS® (NAR), the largest trade association in the country with over one million members, adopted a code of ethics for its members in 1913. REALTORS® are expected to subscribe to this strict code of conduct. Not all licensees are REALTORS®—only those who are members of NAR. NAR has established procedures for professional standards committees at the local, state, and national levels of the organization to administer compliance. Practical applications of the articles of the code are known as Standards of Practice. The NAR Code of Ethics has proved helpful because it contains practical applications of business ethics. Many other professional organizations in the real estate industry have codes of ethics as well. In addition, many state real estate commissions are required by law to establish codes or canons of ethical behavior for their states' licensees. (See Appendix B for the complete Code of Ethics and Standards of Practice of the National Association of REALTORS®.)

■ SUMMARY

The federal regulations regarding equal opportunity in housing are contained principally in two laws. The Civil Rights Act of 1866 prohibits all racial discrimination, and the Fair Housing Act (Title VIII of the Civil Rights Act of 1968), as amended, prohibits discrimination on the basis of race, color, religion, sex, disability, familial status, or national origin in the sale, rental, or financing of residential property. Discriminatory actions include refusing to deal with an individual or a specific group, changing any terms of a real estate or loan transaction, changing the services offered for any individual or group, creating statements or advertisements that indicate discriminatory restrictions, or otherwise attempting to make a dwelling unavailable to any person or group because of race, color, religion, sex, disability, familial status, or national origin. The law also prohibits steering, blockbusting, and redlining.

Complaints under the Fair Housing Act may be reported to and investigated by the Department of Housing and Urban Development (HUD). Such complaints also may be taken directly to U.S. district courts. In states and localities that have enacted fair housing legislation that is substantially equivalent to the federal law, complaints are handled by state and local agencies and state courts. Complaints under the Civil Rights Act of 1866 must be taken to federal courts.

A real estate business is only as good as its reputation. Real estate licensees can maintain good reputations by demonstrating good business ability and adhering to ethical standards of business practices. Many licensees subscribe to a code of ethics as members of professional real estate organizations, such as the National Association of REALTORS®, with its various state and local chapters.

In Illinois   Licensees are required by various statutes and the Real Estate License Act of 2000 to adhere to all principles of equal opportunity in housing. Failure to comply with state and federal equal housing laws is grounds for license revocation in addition to other civil or criminal penalties.

The Illinois Human Rights Act amplifies federal legislation for Illinois. It bars discrimination on the basis of race, color, religion, national origin, ancestry, age, sex, marital status, physical and mental disability, military service, unfavorable military discharge, familial status, sexual orientation, and order of protection status. ■

CHAPTER 21 QUIZ

1. Under the Fair Housing Act, which action is legally permitted?
    a. Advertising property for sale only to a special group
    b. Altering the terms of a loan for a member of a minority group
    c. Refusing to make a mortgage loan to a minority individual because of a poor credit history
    d. Telling a minority individual that an apartment has been rented when in fact it has not

2. Complaints relating to the Civil Rights Act of 1866
    a. must be taken directly to federal courts.
    b. are no longer reviewed in the courts.
    c. are handled by HUD.
    d. are handled by state enforcement agencies.

3. Why is the Civil Rights Act of 1866 unique?
    a. It has been broadened to protect the aged.
    b. It adds welfare recipients as a protected class.
    c. It contains "choose your neighbor" provisions.
    d. It provides no exceptions that would permit racial discrimination.

4. On a listing presentation a real estate licensee said to the seller, who owned two residential properties, "I hear they are moving in, and you'd better put your house on the market before values drop!" Has the licensee violated fair housing law?
    a. Yes, and this example represents steering.
    b. Yes, and this example represents blockbusting.
    c. No, because the seller owns fewer than three houses.
    d. No, because the licensee does not intend to publicly advertise the property.

5. A licensee entered into a buyer agency agreement with a person from Japan who was moving to America. The licensee showed him only properties where it was obvious that other Japanese people lived. Has the licensee violated fair housing law?
    a. Yes, and this example represents blockbusting.
    b. Yes, and this example represents steering.
    c. No, because a buyer from Japan would want to live in a Japanese neighborhood.
    d. No, because as a buyer agent it is the licensee's responsibility to make decisions for the buyer.

6. A lender's refusal to lend money to potential homeowners attempting to purchase properties located in predominantly African American neighborhoods is known as
    a. redlining.
    b. blockbusting.
    c. steering.
    d. prequalifying.

7. All of the following would be permitted under the federal Fair Housing Act EXCEPT
    a. an expensive club in New York rents rooms only to members who are graduates of a particular university.
    b. the owner of a 20-unit residential apartment building rents to white men only.
    c. a Catholic convent refuses to furnish housing for a Jewish man.
    d. an owner refuses to rent the other side of her duplex to a family with children.

8. A sponsoring broker wants to end racial segregation. As an office policy, the sponsoring broker requires that sponsored licensees show prospective buyers from racial or ethnic minority groups only properties that are in certain areas of town where few members of their groups currently live. The sponsoring broker prepares a map illustrating the appropriate neighborhoods for each racial or ethnic group. Through this policy, the sponsoring broker hopes to achieve racial balance in residential housing. Which of the following statements is *TRUE* regarding the sponsoring broker's policy?

   a. While the sponsoring broker's policy may appear to constitute blockbusting, application of the effects test proves its legality.
   b. Because the effect of the sponsoring broker's policy is discriminatory, it constitutes illegal steering regardless of his intentions.
   c. The sponsoring broker's policy clearly shows the intent to discriminate.
   d. While the sponsoring broker's policy may appear to constitute steering, application of the intent test proves its legality.

9. If a mortgage lender discriminates against a loan applicant on the basis of marital status, what law is violated?

   a. ADA
   b. Civil Rights Act of 1866
   c. ECOA
   d. Fair Housing Act

10. A Lithuanian American real estate broker offers a special discount to Lithuanian American clients. This practice is

    a. legal in certain circumstances.
    b. illegal.
    c. legal but ill-advised.
    d. an example of steering.

11. Which of the following statements describes the Supreme Court's decision in the case of *Jones v. Alfred H. Mayer Company*?

    a. Racial discrimination is prohibited by any party in the sale or rental of real estate.
    b. Sales by individual residential homeowners are exempted, provided the owners do not use real estate licensees.
    c. Laws against discrimination apply only to federally related transactions.
    d. Persons with disabilities are a protected class.

12. After a broker takes a listing of a residence, the owners specify that they will not sell their home to any Asian family. The broker should do which of the following?

    a. Advertise the property exclusively in Asian-language newspapers
    b. Explain to the owner that the instruction violates federal law and that the broker cannot comply with it
    c. Abide by the principal's directions despite the fact that they conflict with the fair housing laws
    d. Require that the owner sign a separate legal document stating the additional instruction as an amendment to the listing agreement

13. The fine for a first violation of the federal Fair Housing Act could be as much as

    a. $8,000.
    b. $9,500.
    c. $10,000.
    d. $16,000.

14. A single man with two small children has been told by a real estate licensee that homes for sale in a condominium complex are available only to married couples with no children. Which statement is *TRUE*?

    a. Because a single-parent family can be disruptive if the parent provides little supervision of the children, the condominium is permitted to discriminate against the family under the principle of rational basis.

    b. Condominium complexes are exempt from the fair housing laws and can therefore restrict children.

    c. The man may file a complaint alleging discrimination on the basis of familial status.

    d. Restrictive covenants in a condominium take precedence over the fair housing laws.

15. The following ad appeared in the newspaper: "For sale: 4 BR brick home; Redwood School District; excellent Elm Street location; next door to St. John's Church and right on the bus line. Move-in condition; priced to sell." Which of the following statements is *TRUE*?

    a. The ad describes the property for sale and is very appropriate.

    b. The fair housing laws do not apply to newspaper advertising.

    c. The ad should state that the property is available to families with children.

    d. The ad should not mention St. John's Church.

16. A landlord rented an apartment to a person with a disability. The tenant wants to make certain changes to the unit to accommodate her disability. Which of the following would *NOT* constitute a reasonable modification?

    a. Widen the doorways.
    b. Lower the kitchen cabinets.
    c. Lower the light switches.
    d. Equip the elevator lobby with a dog run.

17. Which of the following would be considered legal?

    a. Charging a family with children a higher security deposit that those with no children

    b. Requiring a person with a disability to establish an escrow account for the cost to restore a property after it has been modified

    c. Picturing only white people in a brochure as the "happy residents" in a housing community

    d. Refusing to sell a house to a person who has a history of mental illness

---

In Illinois

18. The Illinois Human Rights Act defines an elderly person as being how old?

    a. 40
    b. 65
    c. 68
    d. 70

19. When a landlord rented an apartment in his six-unit building to a young couple, he didn't notice that the woman was pregnant. After the baby was born, the landlord canceled their lease, citing the no-children clause that had been inserted in it. Based on these facts, which of the following statements is *TRUE*?

    a. The landlord is violating the Illinois Human Rights Act regarding the exclusion of children.

    b. The landlord is acting legally under an exemption to the Illinois Human Rights Act.

    c. The landlord must give the tenants 60 days in which to find a new apartment.

    d. The landlord may refuse to rent to families with children only if he lives in the building.

20. A woman owns two multiunit apartment buildings: a two-flat on Oak Street and a 12-unit building on Main Street. She lives in an apartment in the Main Street property. Which of her properties, if any, is exempt from the Illinois Human Rights Act?

a. The Oak Street property only
b. The Main Street property only
c. Neither property
d. Both properties

CHAPTER 22

Environmental Issues and the Real Estate Transaction

■ **LEARNING OBJECTIVES** *When you've finished reading this chapter, you should be able to*

- **identify** the basic environmental hazards a real estate agent should be aware of in order to protect her client's interests;

- **describe** the warning signs, characteristics, causes, and solutions for the various environmental hazards most commonly found in real estate transactions;

- **explain** the fundamental liability issues arising under environmental protection laws;

- **distinguish** lead-based paint issues from other environmental issues; and

- **define** the following *key terms*

asbestos	environmental impact statement (EIS)	radon
brownfields		retroactive liability
capping	environmental site assessment (ESA)	Small Business Liability Relief and Brownfields Revitalization Act
carbon monoxide		
chlorofluorocarbons	formaldehyde	
Comprehensive Environmental Response, Compensation, and Liability Act (CERCLA)	groundwater	strict liability
	innocent landowner immunity	Superfund Amendments and Reauthorization Act (SARA)
	joint and several liability	
	landfill	underground storage tanks (USTs)
electromagnetic fields (EMFs)	lead	
	mold	urea-formaldehyde foam insulation (UFFI)
encapsulation	polychlorinated biphenyls (PCBs)	
		water table

■ ENVIRONMENTAL ISSUES

Most states, including Illinois, have recognized the need to balance commercial use of land with the need to preserve vital resources and to protect our air, water, and soil. A growing number of homebuyers base their decisions in part on the desire for fresh air, clean water, and outdoor recreational opportunities. Preservation of a state's environment both enhances the quality of life and helps strengthen property values. Preventing environmental problems and cleaning up existent pollutants revitalizes the land while creating greater opportunities for responsible development.

| In Illinois | The Illinois Environmental Protection Agency (IEPA) is charged with maintaining and enhancing the state's air, land, and water quality through education, inspection, regulation, enforcement, recycling, and prevention activities. The Pollution Control Board and Hazardous Waste Advisory Council are two of the many bodies created to assist the IEPA in specific areas. Most Illinois environmental regulations are required by statute to be "identical in substance" to environmental protection regulations established by the U.S. Environmental Protection Agency (EPA). ■ |

Environmental issues are health issues, and health issues based on environmental hazards have become real estate issues. For this reason, it is extremely important that licensees not only make property disclosures but also see that prospective purchasers get authoritative information about hazardous substances so that they can make informed decisions.

IN PRACTICE   It is important that licensees are aware of local environmental issues and practice proper disclosure, encouraging buyer clients to seek outside expertise for testing and information whenever appropriate. Licensees must also encourage their seller clients to make full, honest disclosures and assist any buyer clients to locate authoritative information about hazardous substances. Licensees are expected to be aware of environmental issues and to ensure that the safety interests of all parties involved in real estate transactions are protected. Licensees should be familiar with state and federal environmental laws and the regulatory agencies that enforce them.

■ HAZARDOUS SUBSTANCES

Pollution and hazardous substances in the environment can affect the desirability and market value of entire neighborhoods and towns. No one wants to live in a toxic environment. When showing properties, each possible living structure should be studied with an eye to red flags that may suggest problems. (See Figure 22.1.)

Asbestos

Asbestos is a fire-resistant mineral that was once used extensively as insulation and to strengthen other materials. A component of more than 3,000 types of building materials, asbestos was found in most construction, including residential,

Environmental Hazards

until 1978 when its use was banned. The EPA estimates that, even today, about 20 percent of the nation's commercial and public buildings have asbestos-containing materials (ACMs).

> *Asbestos* insulation can create airborne contaminants that may result in respiratory diseases.

Asbestos was used to cover pipes, ducts, and heating and hot water units. Its fire-resistant properties made it a popular material for use in floor tile, exterior siding, roofing products, linoleum flooring materials, joint compounds, wallboard material, backing, and mastics. Though some ACMs are easy to identify (e.g., insulation around heating and water pipes), identifying asbestos may be more difficult when it is behind walls or under floors.

Asbestos is highly friable, meaning that as it ages, asbestos fibers break down easily into tiny filaments and particles. This makes asbestos especially harmful when it is disturbed or exposed and becomes airborne, as often occurs during renovation or remodeling. Those who have inhaled asbestos fibers often develop serious and deadly respiratory diseases decades later. While federal regulations establish guidelines for owners of public and commercial buildings to test for asbestos-containing materials, there are no guidelines regarding the presence of asbestos in residential properties.

Because improper removal procedures may further contaminate the air within the structure, the process requires state-licensed technicians and specially sealed environments. The waste generated must be disposed of at a licensed facility, which further adds to the cost of removal. **Encapsulation,** or the sealing off of disintegrating asbestos, is an alternate method of asbestos control that may be preferable to removal in certain circumstances. However, an owner must periodically monitor the condition of the encapsulated asbestos to make sure it is not disintegrating.

Only a certified asbestos inspector should perform an asbestos inspection of a structure to identify which building materials may contain asbestos. The inspector can also provide recommendations and costs associated with remediation. It is vital that a buyer knows where asbestos-containing materials are located so that they are not disturbed during any repair, remodeling, demolition, or even routine use. Appraisers also should be aware of the possible presence of asbestos.

More information on asbestos-related issues is available from the EPA at 202-554-1404. The EPA has numerous publications that provide guidance, information, and assistance with asbestos issues.

Lead-Based Paint and Other Lead Hazards

Lead was used as a pigment and drying agent in alkyd oil-based paint. Lead-based paint may be on any interior or exterior surface, but it is particularly common on doors, windows, and other woodwork. The federal government estimates that lead is present in about 75 percent of all private housing built before 1978, or approximately 57 million homes, ranging from low-income apartments to million-dollar mansions.

Lead from paint or other sources can result in damage to the brain, nervous system, kidneys, and blood. Children under the age of six are particularly vulnerable.

Children younger than six are the most vulnerable to damage from excessive lead levels. Elevated levels of lead in children cause learning disabilities, developmental delays, reduced height, and poor hearing, and the effects are generally irreversible. Excessive exposure in adults can induce anemia and hypertension, trigger gallbladder problems, and cause reproductive problems in both men and women.

Lead dust can be ingested from the hands by a crawling infant; inhaled by any occupant of a structure, or ingested from the water supply because of lead pipes or lead solder. Soil and groundwater may be contaminated by everything from lead plumbing in leaking landfills to discarded skeets and bullets from an old shooting range. High levels of lead have been found in soil located near waste-to-energy incinerators.

In 1996, the EPA and the Department of Housing and Urban Development (HUD) issued final regulations, known as the Lead-Based Paint Hazard Reduction Act (LBPHRA) of 1992, which requiring the disclosure of the presence of any known lead-based paint hazards to potential buyers or renters. The federal law does not require that anyone test for the presence of lead-based paint.

LBPHRA requires the following from sellers and landlords of residential dwellings built before 1978:

- Landlords must disclose known information on lead-based paint and hazards before leases take effect. Leases must include a disclosure form regarding lead-based paint.
- Sellers have to disclose known information on lead-based paint and hazards prior to an execution of a contract for sale. Sales contracts must include a completed disclosure form about lead-based paint. (See Figure 22.2.) This is the form for sellers and is slightly different from the form for landlords. Licensees should use EPA-written disclosure forms rather than creating their own forms.
- Buyers have up to ten days to conduct a risk assessment or an inspection for the presence of lead-based paint hazards.
- Licensees provide buyers and lessees with "Protect Your Family from Lead in Your Home," the pamphlet created by the EPA, HUD, and the U.S. Consumer Product Safety Commission.
- Renovators must give homeowners the "Protect Your Family from Lead in Your Home" pamphlet before starting any renovation work.
- Beginning April 2010, federal law requires anyone who is paid to perform work that disturbs paint in housing and child-occupied facilities to be trained and certified in the EPA's new lead-based work practices. This includes residential rental property owners/managers, general contractors, and special trade contractors (e.g., painters, plumbers, carpenters, electricians). The Renovation, Repair, and Painting (RR&P) program involves pre-renovation education. This education includes distribution of the pamphlet "Renovate Right" to the property owners before work commences.
- Licensees must ensure that all parties comply with the law.
- Sellers, lessors, and renovators are required to disclose any prior test results or any knowledge of lead-based paint hazards. With only a very narrow exception, all real estate licensees (subagent, buyer's agent, and facilitator) are required to advise sellers to make the required disclosures. Only buyer's agents who are paid entirely by the buyer are exempt.

IN PRACTICE   Nearly 20 years after the law took effect, serious problems with notifications still exist. However, the EPA and HUD are serious about enforcement. In early 2008, a Boston property management company agreed to pay a $28,000 penalty and spend nearly $290,000 to replace windows containing lead-based paint. A year later, a large, nonprofit corporation that develops, finances, and manages affordable, mixed-income housing and nearly two dozen associated property owners agreed to pay a $200,000 penalty and to spend more than $2 million in lead paint abatement at their residential properties. In the fall of 2009, a New York City property management company and 20 affiliated owners of federally assisted multifamily properties in Brooklyn agreed to pay a $20,000 penalty and to perform lead-based paint hazard reduction work in 639 units in 17 properties.

FIGURE 22.2

Disclosure of Lead-Based Paint and Lead-Based Paint Hazards Forms

CHICAGO ASSOCIATION OF REALTORS©

**DISCLOSURE OF INFORMATION AND ACKNOWLEDGEMENT
LEAD-BASED PAINT AND/OR LEAD-BASED PAINT HAZARDS**

Lead Warning Statement

Every purchaser of any interest in residential real property on which a residential dwelling was built prior to 1978 is notified that such property may present exposure to lead from lead-based paint that may place young children at risk of developing lead poisoning. Lead poisoning in young children may produce permanent neurological damage, including learning disabilities, reduced intelligence quotient, behavioral problems, and impaired memory. Lead poisoning also poses a particular risk to pregnant women. The seller of any interest in residential real property is required to provide the buyer with any information on lead-based paint hazards from risk assessments or inspections in the seller's possession and notify the buyer of any known lead-based paint hazards. A risk assessment or inspection for possible lead-based paint hazards is recommended prior to purchase.

Seller's Disclosure (initial) (All Sellers should initial)

_____ (a) Presence of lead-based paint and/or lead-based paint hazards (check one below):

_____ ☐ Known lead-based paint and/or lead-based paint hazards are present in the housing (explain):

_____

_____ ☐ Seller has no knowledge of lead-based paint and/or lead-based paint hazards in the housing.

_____ (b) Records and Reports available to the seller (check one below):

_____ ☐ Seller has provided the purchaser with all available records and reports pertaining to lead-based paint and/or lead-based hazards in the housing (list documents below):

_____

_____ ☐ Seller has no reports or records pertaining to lead-based paint and/or lead-based paint hazards in the housing.

Purchaser's Acknowledgement (initial) (All Purchasers should initial)

_____ (c) Purchaser has received copies of all information listed above.

_____

_____ (d) Purchaser has received the pamphlet *Protect Your Family From Lead in Your Home.*

_____

_____ (e) Purchaser has (check one below):

_____

_____ ☐ Received a 10-day opportunity (or mutually agreed upon period) to conduct a risk assessment or inspection of the presence of lead-based paint or lead-based paint hazards; or

_____ ☐ Waived the opportunity to conduct a risk assessment or inspection for the presence of lead-based paint and/or lead-based paint hazards.

Agent's Acknowledgement (initial) (Seller's Designated Agent)

_____ (f) Agent has informed the seller of the seller's obligations under 42 U.S.C. 4852 d and is aware of his/her responsibility to ensure compliance.

Certification of Accuracy

The following parties have reviewed the information above and certify, to the best of their knowledge, that the information they have provided is true and accurate.

Seller_____ Date _____   Seller_____ Date _____

Purchaser _____ Date _____   Purchaser _____ Date _____

Agent _____ Date _____   Agent _____ Date _____

Location of Property _____ City _____ State ___ Zip Code _____

Keep a fully executed copy of this document for three (3) years from the date hereof.
This Disclosure From should be attached to the Real Estate Sale Contract.

Source: Published with Permission, Chicago Association of REALTORS®

The regulations apply to housing built prior to 1978 with the following six exceptions:

- Property sold at foreclosure, although the disclosure must be made at resale time
- Rental property that is certified "lead-based paint free" by an inspector who is certified under a federal program or federally authorized state certification program
- Property leased for 100 days or less, with no lease renewal or extension
- Renewals of existing leases if disclosure was made at the time of the initial lease
- Units with no bedrooms or with no separation between sleeping and living areas
- Housing for the elderly or disabled if children under the age of six are not expected to live there

> 1978 is a year to remember. Lead paint *and* asbestos were both banned.

There is considerable controversy about practical approaches for handling the presence of lead-based paint. Removal or encapsulation is sometimes utilized. Federal law requires that only licensed lead inspectors, abatement contractors, risk assessors, abatement project designers, and abatement workers may deal with the removal or encapsulation of lead in a structure.

In Illinois

Anyone who performs lead abatement or mitigation activities without a license is guilty of a Class A misdemeanor. The Department of Public Health (DPH) oversees the qualifying, training, and licensing of lead abatement contractors and lead abatement workers in Illinois.

EPA guidance pamphlets and other information about lead-based hazards are available from the National Lead Information Center at (800) 424-5323.

The Illinois Lead Poisoning Prevention Act (410 ILCS 45) requires that physicians screen children younger than six years old for lead poisoning when the child lives in an area considered by the state to be at "high risk" for lead exposure. High-risk areas include slum and blighted housing; proximity to highway or heavy local traffic; proximity to a lead-using or lead-generating industry; and incidence of elevated blood lead levels, poverty, and the number of young children in the area.

When a child is diagnosed as having an elevated level of lead in her bloodstream, the physician must report the condition to the Department of Public Health (DPH). After notification, the DPH may inspect the child's residence for the existence of exposed lead-bearing substances (including dust, paint, and lead pipes). If the inspection identifies a lead hazard, the property owner is required to mitigate the condition within 90 days (30 days if a child under six or a pregnant woman is at risk). Licensed lead abatement contractors must be used for lead removal. The owner will receive a certificate of compliance once the DPH is satisfied that the lead hazard has been removed.

An owner who has received a lead mitigation notice must provide any p[...] lessees for the affected unit with a written notice of the existence of an[...] lead hazard. In addition, all owners of residential buildings or units must give current and prospective lessees information on the potential health hazards posed by lead and a copy of an informational brochure. ■

Radon

Radon is a naturally occurring, colorless, odorless, tasteless, radioactive gas produced by the decay of other radioactive substances. Radon is measured in picocuries (a unit of radiation) contained in a liter of air (i.e., pCi/L). Radon is found in every state and territory, with radon levels in the outdoor air averaging 0.4 pCi/L. Fans and thermal "stack effects" (i.e., rising hot air draws cooler air in from the ground through cracks in the basement and foundation walls) pulls radon into buildings.

> **Radon** is a naturally occurring gas that is a suspected cause of lung cancer.

The potential for developing lung cancer from exposure to radon is a function of the extent and the length of a person's exposure to radon. Radon has been classified as a "Class A" known human carcinogen. Furthermore, smokers have a risk factor 15 times greater than nonsmokers.

Because neither the EPA nor current scientific consensus has been able to establish a "threshold" safe level of radon exposure, the EPA suggests an "action" level of 4 pCi/L. The action level of 4 was chosen because 95 percent of the time, current technology can bring the level below 4, and 75 percent of the time, levels can be reduced to 2 pCi/L. Radon mitigation is less expensive when the system is installed during construction; mitigation consists of removing the radon before it seeps into the house. A fan is installed in a pipe running from the basement to the attic to draw the radon up and out.

Home testing may be done with passive devices, such as alpha track detectors and a charcoal canister. Continuous monitors require electrical power and usually a trained technician. Test results are normally received within 10 days or so when using a passive device (immediately when using an electric continuous monitor). Although a 90-day testing period is most accurate, the EPA developed a 48-hour procedure that can be used in a real estate transaction. The 48-hour test can satisfactorily predict whether a home's annual average is at or above 4 pCi/L in 94 percent of cases.

Because one out of every 15 homes probably needs mitigation, before looking at properties, licensees should discuss radon concerns with their buyers. Licensees can direct buyers to the EPA Web site for the pamphlet "A Citizen's Guide to Radon" and for additional information about testing and mitigation methods.

> **In Illinois**

The Illinois Radon Awareness Act requires a seller to provide to a buyer, before the buyer is obligated under any contract to purchase residential real property, a Disclosure of Information on Radon Hazards along with a pamphlet entitled "Radon Testing Guidelines for Real Estate Transactions" stating that the property may present the potential for exposure to radon. (See Figure 22.3.)

FIGURE 22.3

Radon Disclosure Form

Illinois Association of REALTORS®

DISCLOSURE OF INFORMATION ON RADON HAZARDS
(For Residential Real Property Sales or Purchases)

Radon Warning Statement

Every buyer of any interest in residential real property is notified that the property may present exposure to dangerous levels of indoor radon gas that may place the occupants at risk of developing radon-induced lung cancer. Radon, a Class-A human carcinogen, is the leading cause of lung cancer in non-smokers and the second leading cause overall. The seller of any interest in residential real property is required to provide the buyer with any information on radon test results of the dwelling showing elevated levels of radon in the seller's possession.

The Illinois Emergency Management Agency (IEMA) strongly recommends ALL homebuyers have an indoor radon test performed prior to purchase or taking occupancy, and mitigated if elevated levels are found. Elevated radon concentrations can easily be reduced by a qualified, licensed radon mitigator.

Seller's Disclosure (initial each of the following which applies)

_____(a) Elevated radon concentrations (above EPA or IEMA recommended Radon Action Level) are known to be present within the dwelling. (Explain)

_____(b) Seller has provided the purchaser with all available records and reports pertaining to elevated radon concentrations within the dwelling.

_____(c) Seller either has no knowledge of elevated radon concentrations in the dwelling or prior elevated radon concentrations have been mitigated or remediated.

_____(d) Seller has no records or reports pertaining to elevated radon concentrations within the dwelling.

Purchaser's Acknowledgment (initial each of the following which applies)

_____(e) Purchaser has received copies of all information listed above.

_____(f) Purchaser has received the IEMA approved Radon Disclosure Pamphlet.

Agent's Acknowledgement (initial IF APPLICABLE)

_____(g) Agent has informed the seller of the seller's obligations under Illinois law.

Certification of Accuracy

The following parties have reviewed the information above and each party certifies, to the best of his or her knowledge, that the information he or she has provided is true and accurate.

Seller _____	**Date** _____
Seller _____	**Date** _____
Purchaser _____	**Date** _____
Purchaser _____	**Date** _____
Agent _____	**Date** _____
Agent _____	**Date** _____
Property Address _____	**City, State, Zip Code** _____

FORM 422 Revised 08-09   COPYRIGHT ILLINOIS ASSOCIATION OF REALTORS

Source: Published with Permission, Illinois Association of REALTORS®

In short, the act requires a separate disclosure document for radon to be included in the majority of residential real estate transactions. The disclosure document

■ has a radon warning statement advising buyers that the home may pose a threat to their health if it has elevated levels of radon and that all homes should be tested for radon;

■ requires that a seller provide an Illinois Emergency Management Agency (IEMA)-approved pamphlet about general radon information to a buyer and disclose all information along with any available documentation of the radon levels in the home;

■ requires that real estate agents sign the disclosure to confirm that seller has been made aware of her obligations;

■ requires that all parties involved sign the disclosure acknowledging the transfer of the above information; and

■ requires that sellers must disclose that they have no knowledge of elevated radon concentrations or that prior elevated radon concentrations have been mitigated or remediated.

The act does not require that all homes in a real estate transaction be tested or that the home be mitigated if the test results are elevated. It also does not apply to the transfer of any residential dwelling unit located three stories (or higher) above ground level in any structure.

If any of the required disclosures occur after the buyer has made an offer to purchase the residential real property, the seller shall complete the required disclosure activities prior to accepting the buyer's offer and allow the buyer an opportunity to review the information and possibly amend the offer.

The provisions of this act do not apply to

■ transfers pursuant to court order;

■ transfers from a mortgagor to a mortgagee by deed in lieu of foreclosure or consent judgment, transfer by judicial deed issued pursuant to a foreclosure sale, transfer by a collateral assignment of a beneficial interest of a land trust, or a transfer by a mortgagee or a successor in interest to the mortgagee's secured position;

■ transfers by a fiduciary in the course of the administration of a decedent's estate, guardianship, conservatorship, or trust;

■ transfers from one co-owner to one or more other co-owners;

■ transfers pursuant to testate or intestate succession;

■ transfers made to a spouse or to a person or persons in the lineal line of consanguinity of one or more of the sellers;

■ transfers from an entity that has taken title to residential real property from a seller for the purpose of assisting in the relocation of the seller, so long as the entity makes available to all prospective buyers a copy of the disclosure form furnished to the entity by the seller;

■ transfers to or from any governmental entity; and

■ transfers of any residential dwelling unit located three stories (or higher) above ground level in any structure. ■

Formaldehyde

Formaldehyde, a colorless chemical with a strong, pronounced odor, is used widely in the manufacture of building materials and many household products because of its preservative characteristics. Often emitted as a gas, formaldehyde is one of the most common and problematic volatile organic compounds (VOCs) and is one of the few indoor air pollutants that can be measured. Formaldehyde was listed as a hazardous air pollutant in the Clean Air Act Amendments of 1990.

Formaldehyde is classified as a "probable human carcinogen" (i.e., causing cancer in animals and probably in humans). For the 10 to 20 percent of the population that is "sensitive" to formaldehyde, formaldehyde may trigger respiratory problems (e.g., shortness of breath, wheezing, chest tightness, asthma) as well as eye and skin irritations (burning sensations in the eyes and throat). It is a major contributor to sick building syndrome (SBS) in commercial properties. (See Chapter 17.)

The largest source of formaldehyde in any building is likely to be the off-gassing from pressed-wood products made from using adhesives that contain urea-formaldehyde (UF) resins. Pressed-wood products include particleboard, hardwood plywood paneling, and medium-density fiberboard. It is also used in carpeting and ceiling tiles. Since 1985, the Department of Housing and Urban Development (HUD) has regulated the use of plywood and particleboard so that they conform to specified formaldehyde-emission levels in the construction of prefabricated homes and manufactured housing (mobile homes).

UFFI is an insulating foam that can release harmful formaldehyde gases.

Urea-formaldehyde foam insulation (UFFI), once popular, then banned, and now legal again, is rarely used. When incorrectly mixed, UFFI never properly cures, resulting in strong emissions shortly after installation. Studies have shown that formaldehyde emissions generally decrease over time, so homes where UFFI was installed many years ago are unlikely to have high levels of formaldehyde now unless the insulation is exposed to extreme heat or moisture. Still, licensees should check their state's property disclosure form to see if UFFI must be disclosed. Appraisers should also be aware of the presence of formaldehyde.

IN PRACTICE   Licensees should be careful that any conditions in an agreement of sale that require tests for formaldehyde are worded properly to identify the purpose for which the tests are being conducted, such as to determine the presence of the insulation or to identify some other source. Appraisers should also be aware of the presence of UFFI.

Carbon Monoxide

Carbon monoxide is a by-product of fuel combustion that may result in death in poorly ventilated areas.

Carbon monoxide (CO) is a colorless, odorless gas that occurs due to incomplete combustion as a by-product of burning such fuels as wood, oil, and natural gas. Furnaces, water heaters, space heaters, fireplaces, and wood stoves all produce CO as a natural result of combustion. When these appliances function properly and are properly ventilated, CO emissions are not a problem. However, when improper ventilation or equipment malfunctions permit large quantities of CO to be released into a residence or commercial structure, it poses a significant health hazard. The effects of CO are compounded by the fact that it is so difficult to detect. CO is quickly absorbed by the body, where it inhibits the blood's ability to transport oxygen and results in dizziness and nausea. As the concentrations of CO increase, the symptoms become more severe. More than 300 deaths from carbon monoxide poisoning occur each year, with thousands of others requiring hospital emergency room care.

CO detectors are available, and their use is mandatory in some areas. Annual maintenance of heating systems also helps avoid CO exposure.

In Illinois

Illinois requires that all residences be equipped with working carbon monoxide detectors. ■

Polychlorinated Biphenyls

Polychlorinated biphenyls (PCBs) linger in the environment for long periods of time and can cause health problems.

Polychlorinated biphenyls (PCBs) consist of more than 200 chemical compounds that are not found naturally in nature. Flame resistant, they were often used in electrical equipment such as transformers, electrical motors in refrigerators, caulking compounds, and hydraulic oil in older equipment. The EPA has classified PCBs as reasonably carcinogenic, and they have been implicated in lower fertility and shortened life spans. Although the commercial distribution of PCBs was banned in 1979, PCBs remain in the environment because burning them at more than 2,400 degrees in a closed environment is the only known way to destroy them.

PCBs are most likely a concern for commercial and industrial property managers. These managers should ask the local utility company to identify and remove any type of transformer that might be a source of PCBs. If the PCBs leak into the environment, penalties and removal methods are expensive.

Chlorofluorocarbons

Chlorofluorocarbons (CFCs) are nontoxic, nonflammable chemicals containing atoms of carbon, chlorine, and fluorine. CFCs are most often used in air conditioners, refrigerators, aerosol sprays, paints, solvents, and foam blowing applications. Although CFCs are safe in most applications and are inert in the lower atmosphere, once CFC vapors rise to the upper atmosphere, where they may survive from 2 to 150 years, they are broken down by ultraviolet light into chemicals that deplete the ozone layer.

Global treaties have sought to reduce the production levels of CFCs. The manufacture of these chemicals ended for the most part in 1996, with exceptions for production in developing countries, medical products (for example, asthma inhalers), and research.

Although newer air conditioners use a different product, older appliances may leak CFCs and should be properly disposed of to prevent further leakage. Licensees may wish to advise their buyers to consider upgrading to newer, more energy-efficient and environmentally safe appliances.

Only EPA-certified technicians should do any work on a refrigeration system, especially the larger systems found in commercial and industrial buildings. Approved equipment should carry a label reading "This equipment has been certified by ARI/UL to meet EPA's minimum requirements for recycling and recovery equipment."

Electromagnetic Fields

EMFs are produced by electrical currents and may be related to a variety of health complaints.

Electromagnetic fields (EMFs) are generated by the movement of electrical currents. The use of any electrical appliance creates a small field of electromagnetic radiation; clock radios, blow-dryers, televisions, and computers all produce EMFs. The major concern regarding EMFs involves high-tension power lines. The EMFs produced by these high-voltage lines, as well as by secondary distribution lines and transformers, are suspected of causing cancer, hormonal changes, and behavioral abnormalities. There is considerable controversy (and much conflicting evidence) about whether EMFs pose a health hazard.

IN PRACTICE Buyers who are aware of the controversy may, however, be unwilling to purchase property near power lines or transformers. Real estate licensees should stay informed about current findings and are cautioned to remain neutral, letting buyers draw their own conclusions.

Mold

Mold can be found almost anywhere and can grow on almost any organic substance, so long as moisture, oxygen, and an organic food source are present. Moisture feeds mold growth. If a moisture problem is not discovered or addressed, mold growth can gradually destroy what it is growing on.

In addition, some molds can cause serious health problems. They can trigger allergic reactions and asthma attacks. Some molds are known to produce potent toxins and/or irritants.

Some moisture problems in homes and buildings have been directly linked to recent changes in construction practices. Some of these practices have resulted in buildings that are too tightly sealed, preventing adequate ventilation. Building materials, such as drywall, may not allow moisture to escape easily. The material used in drywall *wicks* moisture to the nutrition source of glue and paper. Vinyl wallpaper and exterior insulation finish systems (EIFS), also known as synthetic stucco, do not allow moisture to escape. Other moisture problems include roof leaks, unvented combustion appliances, and landscaping or gutters that direct water to the building.

The EPA has published guidelines for the remediation and/or cleanup of mold and moisture problems in schools and commercial buildings.

IN PRACTICE Mold is an important issue for licensees. Initially, lawsuits were brought against construction and insurance companies until the insurance companies started amending their homeowner's insurance policies to exclude mold from coverage. Now, plaintiffs name sellers, landlords, property management companies, and real estate licensees as defendants, in addition to construction and insurance companies.

■ **FOR EXAMPLE** In a 2005 case, *Eddy v. B.S.T.V.*, Inc, a couple sued a real estate company for failing to disclose mold contamination in the home they purchased. The real estate company's insurers refused to provide coverage stating that the insurance policies had specific exclusion clauses that would not cover property damage arising out of a real estate agent's failure to render professional services. The issue in the case was whether the professional-services exclusion clause in the insurance policy issued to the real estate company applied to the couple's claims. The couple alleged that the real estate agents breached the real estate company's professional-service responsibilities and, therefore, the exclusions applied. The real estate company tried to argue that because its real estate agents were trained in identifying mold-related hazards, the claim did not fit the exclusion clause. The court did not agree, and the real estate company was held liable. The court held the exclusion clauses in the policies prevented insurance coverage for the injuries.

In light of this case and other court decisions on this topic, it can be difficult for real estate companies and licensees to know what to do when mold is suspected or found on a property. There are no federal requirements to disclose mold contamination at this time, and only a few states require disclosure. Licensees should remind buyers that sellers cannot disclose what they do not know. Also, licensees should advise buyers that they not only have the right but the burden to discover.

Statutory, regulatory, and case law addressing the duties of real estate licensees regarding mold concerns is currently evolving. Real estate licensees should consider adopting practices intended to help their clients and customers become aware of and familiar with mold concerns.

IN PRACTICE HUD now requires mold disclosure on all HUD sales contracts. Mold disclosure forms are available through your state or local REALTOR® association. (See Figure 22.4.)

■ GROUNDWATER PROTECTION

Groundwater is the water that exists under the earth's surface within the tiny spaces or crevices in geological formations. Groundwater forms the **water table,** the natural level at which the ground is saturated. The water table may be several hundred feet underground or near the surface. When the earth's natural filtering systems are inadequate to ensure the availability of pure water, any contamination of underground water threatens the supply of pure, clean water for private wells or public water systems. Numerous state and federal laws have been enacted to preserve and protect the water supply.

If groundwater is not protected from contamination, the earth's natural filtering systems may be inadequate to ensure the availability of pure water. Numerous state and federal laws have been enacted to preserve and protect the water supply, led by the Safe Drinking Water Act (SDWA) and its 1996 and 2000 amendments. The SDWA authorizes the EPA to set national health-based standards for drinking water. Later amendments strengthened the law by increasing source water protection, operator training, and funding for water system improvements and public information. For example, the EPA now requires that water suppliers

FIGURE 22.4

Mold Disclosure Form

MOLD DISCLOSURE
(Buyer and Seller)

Printed Name(s) of Seller(s): _____

Printed Name(s) of Buyer(s): _____

Property Address: _____

1. Seller's Disclosure: To the best of Seller's actual knowledge, Seller represents:

    A. The Property described above _____ has _____ has not been previously tested for molds:

        (If the answer for 1.A. is "has not", then skip 1.B and 1.C and go to Section 2.)

    B. The molds found _____ were _____ were not identified as toxic molds;

    C. With regard to any molds that were found, measures _____ were _____ were not taken to remove those molds.

2. Mold Inspection: Molds, fungus, mildew, and similar organisms ("Mold Conditions") may exist in the Property of which the Seller is unaware and has not actual knowledge. The Mold Conditions generally grow in places where there is excessive moisture, such as where leakage may have occurred in roofs, pipes, walls, plant pots, or where there has been flooding. A professional home inspection may not disclose Mold Conditions. As a result, Buyer may wish to obtain an inspection specifically for Mold Conditions to more fully determine the condition of the Property and this environmental status. Neither Seller's nor Buyer's agents are experts in the field of Mold Conditions and other related conditions and Buyer and Seller shall not rely on Broker or it's agents for information relating to such conditions. Buyer is strongly encouraged to satisfy itself as to the condition of the property.

3. Hold Harmless: Buyer's decision to purchase the Property is independent of representation of the Broker or Broker's agents involved in the transaction regarding Mold Conditions. Accordingly, Buyer agrees to indemnify and hold _____

    _____ (print name of Broker(s) and Designated Agent(s)) harmless in the event any Mold Conditions are present on the Property.

4. Receipt of Copy: Seller and Buyer have read and acknowledge receipt of a copy of this Mold Disclosure.

Professional Advice: Seller and Buyer acknowledge that they have been advised to consult with a professional of their choice regarding any questions or concerns relating to Mold Conditions or this Mold Disclosure.

_____ _____   _____ _____
Buyer   Date   Seller   Date

_____ _____   _____ _____
Buyer   Date   Seller   Date

REV 01/03

report any health risk situation within 24 hours instead of the 72 hours mandated in the past.

Water can be contaminated from a number of sources. Runoff from waste disposal sites, leaking underground storage tanks, and pesticides and herbicides are some of the main culprits. Because water flows naturally, contamination can spread far from its source. Once contamination has been identified, its source can usually be eliminated, and the water may eventually become or be made clean. However, the process can be time-consuming and expensive.

Many property disclosure forms require sellers to identify the property's water source, such as well water, municipal water supply, or some other source. Anything other than a municipal water supply should be tested. Also, sellers are generally required to identify the type of septic system because an incorrectly placed or poorly functioning system can contaminate the water source.

IN PRACTICE   Real estate licensees should educate their sellers about full and honest disclosure concerning the property's water supply and septic systems. Buyers should be educated about potential groundwater contamination sources both on and off a property. Licensees should always recommend testing the water supply when it is not part of a municipal source.

■ UNDERGROUND STORAGE TANKS

Underground storage tanks (USTs) are commonly found on sites where petroleum products are used or where gas stations and auto repair shops are located. They also may be found in a number of other commercial and industrial establishments—including printing and chemical plants, wood treatment plants, paper mills, paint manufacturers, dry cleaners, and food-processing plants—for storing chemicals or process wastes. Military bases and airports are also common sites for underground tanks. In residential areas, they are used to store heating oil.

Some tanks are currently in use, but many are long forgotten. Over time, neglected tanks may leak hazardous substances into the environment, permitting contaminants to pollute not only the soil around the tank but also adjacent parcels and groundwater. Licensees should be particularly alert to the presence of fill pipes, vent lines, stained soil, and fumes or odors, any of which may indicate the presence of a UST.

State and federal laws impose strict requirements on landowners to detect and correct leaks in an effort to protect the groundwater. The federal UST program is regulated by the EPA. The regulations apply to tanks that contain hazardous substances or liquid petroleum products and that store at least 10 percent of their volume underground. UST owners are required to register their tanks and adhere to strict technical and administrative requirements that govern

■ installation,
■ maintenance,
■ corrosion prevention,
■ overspill prevention,

■ monitoring, and

■ record keeping.

Owners are also required to demonstrate that they have sufficient financial resources to cover any damage that might result from leaks.

The following types of tanks are among those that are exempt from the federal regulations:

■ Tanks that hold less than 110 gallons
■ Farm and residential tanks that hold 1,100 gallons or less of motor fuel used for noncommercial purposes
■ Tanks that store heating oil burned on the premises
■ Tanks on or above the floor of underground areas such as basements or tunnels
■ Septic tanks and systems for collecting stormwater and wastewater

Some states have adopted laws regulating underground storage tanks that are more stringent than the federal laws.

In addition to being aware of possible noncompliance with state and federal regulations, the parties to a real estate transaction should be aware that many older tanks have never been registered. There may be no visible sign of their presence.

| In Illinois |

The Leaking Underground Storage Tank (LUST) program governs the detection, identification, monitoring, mitigation, and removal of buried underground storage tanks (particularly those containing petroleum products). The program is administered by the state fire marshal and the IEPA and is authorized to disburse money from a special fund to assist property owners in complying with mandatory remediation activities. ■

■ WASTE DISPOSAL SITES

Federal, state, and local regulations govern the location, construction, content, and maintenance of landfill sites built to accommodate the vast quantities of garbage produced every day in America. A **landfill** is an enormous hole, either excavated for the purpose of waste disposal or left over from surface mining operations. The hole is lined with clay or a synthetic liner to prevent leakage of waste material into the water supply. A system of underground drainage pipes permits the monitoring of leaks and leaching. Waste is laid on the liner at the bottom of the excavation, and a layer of topsoil is then compacted onto the waste. The layering procedure is repeated until the landfill is full, with the layers mounded up sometimes as high as several hundred feet.

Capping is the process of laying two to four feet of soil over the top of the site and then planting grass on it to enhance the landfill's aesthetic value and prevent erosion. A ventilation pipe runs from the landfill's base through the cap to vent off accumulated natural gases created by the decomposing waste. Test wells around landfill operations are installed to constantly monitor the groundwater in the surrounding area, and soil analyses test for contamination.

Capped landfills have been used as parks and golf courses. Rapid suburban growth has resulted in many housing developments and office campuses being built on landfill sites. Most newer landfill sites are well documented, but the locations of many older landfill sites are no longer known.

Special hazardous waste disposal sites contain radioactive waste from nuclear power plants, toxic chemicals, and waste materials produced by medical, scientific, and industrial processes. Additional waste disposal sites used as on-site garbage dumps are located on rural property, such as farms, ranches, and residences. Some materials, such as radioactive waste, are sealed in containers buried deep underground and placed in *tombs* designed to last thousands of years. These disposal sites are usually limited to extremely remote locations, well away from populated areas or farmland.

Hazardous and radioactive waste disposal sites are subject to strict state and federal regulation to prevent the escape of toxic substances.

| In Illinois | The construction and maintenance of waste disposal sites in Illinois are regulated by statute (415 ILCS 5/20 et seq.). ■

■ BROWNFIELDS

Brownfields are defunct, derelict, or abandoned commercial or industrial sites, many of which are suspected to contain toxic wastes. According to the U.S. General Accounting Office, several hundred thousand brownfields plague communities as eyesores and potentially dangerous and hazardous properties, often contributing to the decline of urban property values.

The **Small Business Liability Relief and Brownfields Revitalization Act** (or Brownfields Law) was signed into law in 2002. The Brownfields Law provides funds to assess and clean up brownfields, clarifies liability protections, and provides tax incentives toward enhancing state and tribal response programs. The law is also important for property owners and developers because it shields innocent developers from liability for toxic wastes that existed at a site prior to the purchase of property. In effect, a property owner who neither caused nor contributed to the contamination is not liable for the cleanup.

Significantly, the law encourages the development of abandoned properties, some of which are located in prime real estate areas.

IN PRACTICE Since 1979, the U.S Department of Energy has attempted to gain approval to store spent nuclear fuel and high-level radioactive wastes, currently stored at 121 sites around the nation, in one repository built on Yucca Mountain, Nye County, Nevada. These materials are a result of nuclear power generation and national defense programs. The proposal has been challenged repeatedly by environmentalists and nearby residents as well as by the communities through which the waste material would be transported. Approval, which seemed certain in 2002, is less sure today.

■ ENVIRONMENTAL PROTECTION

The majority of legislation dealing with environmental problems has been enacted within the past four decades. Although the Environmental Protection Agency (EPA) was created in 1970 at the federal level to oversee such problems, several other federal agencies' areas of concern generally overlap. The federal laws were created to encourage state and local governments to enact their own legislation.

CERCLA

The **Comprehensive Environmental Response, Compensation, and Liability Act (CERCLA)** was created in 1980. It established a fund of $9 billion, called the Superfund, to clean up uncontrolled hazardous waste sites and to respond to spills. It created a process for identifying potentially responsible parties (PRPs) and ordering them to take responsibility for the cleanup action. CERCLA is administered and enforced by the EPA.

Liability   Landowners are liable under CERCLA when a release (or a threat of release) of a hazardous substance has occurred on their property. Regardless of whether the contamination is the result of the landowner's actions or those of others, the owner can be held responsible for the cleanup. This liability includes the cleanup not only of the landowner's property but also of any neighboring property that has been contaminated. A landowner who is not responsible for the contamination can seek recovery reimbursement for the cleanup cost from previous landowners, any other responsible party, or the Superfund. However, if other parties are not available, even a landowner who did not cause the problem could be solely responsible for the costs.

Once the EPA determines that hazardous material has been released into the environment, it is authorized to begin remedial action. First, it attempts to identify the PRPs. If the PRPs agree to cooperate in the cleanup, they must agree about how to divide the cost. If the PRPs do not voluntarily undertake the cleanup, the EPA may hire its own contractors to do the necessary work. The EPA then bills the PRPs for the cost. If the PRPs refuse to pay, the EPA can seek damages in court for up to three times the actual cost of the cleanup.

Liability under the Superfund is considered to be strict, joint and several, and retroactive. Strict liability means that the owner is responsible to the injured party without excuse. Joint and several liability means that each of the individual owners is personally responsible for the total damages. If only one of the owners is financially able to handle the total damages, that owner must pay the total and collect the proportionate shares from the other owners whenever possible. Retroactive liability means that the liability is not limited to the current owner but includes people who have owned the site in the past.

Superfund Amendments and Reauthorization Act

In 1986, the U.S. Congress reauthorized the **Superfund Amendments and Reauthorization Act (SARA)**. The amended statute contains stronger cleanup standards for contaminated sites and five times the funding of the original Superfund, which expired in September 1985.

The amended act also sought to clarify the obligations of lenders. As mentioned, liability under the Superfund extends to both the present and all previous owners of the contaminated site. Real estate lenders found themselves either as present owners or somewhere in the chain of ownership through foreclosure proceedings.

The amendments created a concept called **innocent landowner immunity**. It was recognized that in certain cases, a landowner in the chain of ownership was completely innocent of all wrongdoing and therefore should not be held liable. The innocent landowner immunity clause established the criteria by which to judge whether a person or business could be exempted from liability. The criteria included the following:

- The pollution was caused by a third party.
- The property was acquired after the fact.
- The landowner had no actual or constructive knowledge of the damage.
- Due care was exercised when the property was purchased (the landowner made a reasonable search, called an *environmental site assessment*) to determine that no damage to the property existed.
- Reasonable precautions were taken in the exercise of ownership rights.

IN PRACTICE The EPA has conducted a number of studies to determine the impact on surrounding property values with regard to proximity to landfills and hazardous waste sites. In the report "Challenges in Applying Property Value Studies to Assess the Benefits of the Superfund Program," released January 2009, the EPA concluded the following:

- Impacts on surrounding residential property values vary in size and direction.
- Expected declines have been found, but increases in property values around Superfund sites have also been found.
- The direction of the price effect on surrounding home values appears to vary significantly with individual sites.
- Remedial action can reverse the decline at some sites.
- Delays in cleanup result in a more permanent decline in value.

The most serious problems associated with value involve the presence of undisclosed landfills and hazardous waste sites. Licensees can encourage buyers to consult *www.epa.gov/superfund/sites/index.htm* to determine whether a property of interest is located near a Superfund site. Buyers should also speak with neighbors. Many buyers of commercial and industrial properties hire an environmental engineer to conduct detailed studies prior to closing. In other words, the parties should do everything possible to avoid surprises.

■ LIABILITY OF REAL ESTATE LICENSEES

Environmental law is relatively new. Although federal and state laws have defined many of the liabilities involved, common law is being used for further interpretation. Real estate licensees and all others involved in a real estate transaction must be aware of both actual and potential liability.

Sellers often carry the most legal liability exposure. Innocent landowners might be held responsible, even though they did not know about the presence of environmental hazards. Purchasers may be held liable, even if they didn't cause the contamination. Lenders may end up owning worthless assets if owners default on the loans rather than undertaking expensive cleanup efforts. Real estate licensees could be held liable for improper disclosure; therefore, it is necessary to be aware of the potential environmental risks from neighboring properties such as gas stations, manufacturing plants, or even funeral homes.

> **Real estate licensees can avoid liability with environmental issues by**
> - becoming familiar with common environmental problems in their area;
> - looking for signs of environmental contamination;
> - advising (and including as a contingency) an environmental audit if you suspect contamination; and
> - not giving advice on environmental issues.

Additional exposure is created for individuals involved in other aspects of real estate transactions. For example, real estate appraisers must identify and adjust for environmental problems. Adjustments to market value typically reflect the cleanup cost plus a factor of the degree of panic and suspicion that exist in the current market. Although the sales price can be affected dramatically, it is possible that the underlying market value would remain relatively equal to others in the neighborhood. The real estate appraiser's greatest responsibility is to the lender, who depends on the appraiser to identify environmental hazards. Although the lender may be protected under certain conditions through the 1986 amendments to the Superfund Act, the lender must be aware of any potential problems and may require additional environmental reports.

Insurance carriers also might be affected in the transactions. Mortgage insurance companies protect lenders' mortgage investments and might be required to carry part of the ultimate responsibility in cases of loss. More important, hazard insurance carriers might be directly responsible for damages if such coverage was included in the initial policy.

Discovery of Environmental Hazards

Real estate licensees are not expected to have the technical expertise necessary to discover the presence of environmental hazards. However, because they are presumed by the public to have special knowledge about real estate, licensees must be aware both of possible hazards and of where to seek professional help.

The most appropriate people on whom a real estate licensee can rely for sound environmental information are scientific or technical experts. Environmental auditors (or *environmental assessors*) are scientific or technical experts who can provide the most comprehensive studies. Developers and purchasers of commercial and industrial properties often rely on an environmental assessment that includes the property's history of use, a current-use review, and an investigation into the existence of reported or known contamination sources in the subject area that may affect the property. Testing of soil, water, air, and structures can be conducted, if warranted.

Not only do environmental experts detect environmental problems, they can usually offer guidance about how best to resolve the conditions. Although environmental audits or assessments may occur at any stage in a transaction, they are most frequently a contingency that must be satisfied prior to closing.

IN PRACTICE Environmental assessments and tests conducted by environmental consultants can take time. Licensees should be aware of the time involved and contact environmental consultants as soon as they know such tests are needed in order to prevent delays in closing a transaction.

ENVIRONMENTAL SITE ASSESSMENTS

An environmental site assessment is often performed on a property to show that due care was exercised in determining if any environmental impairments exist. The assessment can help prevent parties from becoming involved in contaminated property and work as a defense to liability. It is often requested by a lending institution, developer, or a potential buyer. The assessment is commonly performed in phases, such as Phase 1 or Phase 2. A Phase 1 environmental report is requested first to determine if any potential environmental problems exist at or near the subject property that may cause impairment. Additional phases are performed as warranted and requested.

There are no federal regulations that define what an environmental assessment must include. However, one of the most accepted industry standards is provided by the American Society for Testing Materials International.

A federally funded project requires that an environmental impact statement (EIS) be performed. These statements detail the impact the project will have on the environment. They can include information about air quality, noise, public health and safety, energy consumption, population density, wildlife, vegetation, and need for sewer and water facilities. Increasingly, these statements are also being required for private development.

Disclosure of Environmental Hazards

State laws address the issue of disclosure of known material facts regarding a property's condition. These same rules apply to the presence of environmental hazards. *A real estate licensee may be liable if she should have known about a condition, even if the seller neglected to disclose it.*

SUMMARY

Environmental issues are important to real estate licensees because they have an impact on clients. They may affect real estate transactions by raising issues of health risks or cleanup costs. Some of the principal environmental toxins include asbestos, lead, radon, urea-formaldehyde insulation, formaldehyde gas, and mold.

Asbestos is a mineral composed of fibers that have fireproofing and insulating qualities, and it is a health hazard when those fibers break down and are inhaled. Encapsulation and professional removal are two methods of eliminating its harmful effects.

Lead is found in paint dust, paint chips, and lead pipes, and also may be present in soil or groundwater. Eating or ingesting the chips or dust of lead paint (or drinking water that has passed through lead pipes) can lead to serious health problems, especially mental diminishment and kidney difficulties. Children under the age of six are particularly vulnerable to its effects. Painting over lead paint is of some use, but it is best to have paint removed by qualified professional if children are present. Lead pipes should be replaced. Licensees should be aware of the significance of 1978 for lead and asbestos, after which these materials were not legally used in construction.

Radon is an odorless, tasteless, radioactive gas produced by the natural decay of radioactive substances in the ground and is found throughout the United States. Radon gas may cause lung cancer. Testing for radon in buildings is not a federal requirement. Water pollutants, many from gasoline, can often be filtered out if they are identified. The source of the problem—such as leaking pipes or underground storage tanks—should always be addressed and, ideally, removed.

Mold can be found anywhere and can grow on almost any organic substance, as long as moisture, oxygen, and an organic food source are present. If a moisture problem is not discovered or addressed, mold growth can gradually destroy what it is growing on.

EMFs are generated by the movement of electrical currents.

Improperly constructed or maintained landfills may also present a danger to groundwater that exists under the earth's surface.

CERCLA established the Superfund to finance the cleanup of hazardous waste disposal sites. Liability can be retroactive. The government deals more reasonably with persons who report their own situation as opposed to waiting to be turned in. This is especially true with underground storage tanks, where all or a large part of accumulated fines may be eliminated for citizens who "self-report" and seek assistance in cleanup of a leaking tank.

Licensees and their clients should be aware and on the watch for any possible environmental contamination sources.

In Illinois

The Illinois Radon Awareness Act requires sellers to provide buyers of residential real estate an IEMA pamphlet entitled "Radon Testing Guidelines for Real Estate Transactions" along with the Illinois Disclosure of Information on Radon Hazards form stating that the property may present the potential for exposure to radon. A seller is not required to test or mitigate if test results are elevated. ■

CHAPTER 22 QUIZ

1. Asbestos is MOST dangerous when it
   - a. is used as insulation.
   - b. crumbles and becomes airborne.
   - c. gets wet.
   - d. is wrapped around heating and water pipes.

2. The term *encapsulation* refers to the
   - a. process of sealing a landfill with three to four feet of topsoil.
   - b. way in which asbestos insulation is applied to pipes and wiring systems.
   - c. method of sealing disintegrating asbestos.
   - d. way in which asbestos becomes airborne.

3. A real estate licensee showed a pre-World War I house to a prospective buyer. The buyer has two toddlers and is worried about potential health hazards. Which of the following is TRUE?
   - a. There is a risk that urea-foam insulation was used in the original construction.
   - b. As a real estate licensee, the licensee can offer to inspect for lead and remove any lead risks.
   - c. Because the house was built before 1978, there is a good likelihood of the presence of lead-based paint.
   - d. Removal of lead-based paint and asbestos hazards is covered by standard title insurance policies.

4. Which of the following is TRUE regarding asbestos?
   - a. The removal of asbestos can cause further contamination of a building.
   - b. Asbestos causes health problems only when it is eaten.
   - c. The level of asbestos in a building is affected by weather conditions.
   - d. HUD requires all asbestos-containing materials to be removed from all residential buildings.

5. Which of the following BEST describes the water table?
   - a. Natural level at which the ground is saturated
   - b. Level at which underground storage tanks may be safely buried
   - c. Measuring device used by specialists to measure groundwater contamination
   - d. Always underground

6. Radon poses the greatest potential health risk to humans when it is
   - a. contained in insulation material used in residential properties during the 1970s.
   - b. found in high concentrations in unimproved land.
   - c. trapped and concentrates in inadequately ventilated areas.
   - d. emitted by malfunctioning or inadequately ventilated appliances.

7. Which of the following describes the process of creating a landfill site?
   - a. Waste is liquefied, treated, and pumped through pipes to "tombs" under the water table.
   - b. Waste and topsoil are layered in a pit, mounded up, and then covered with dirt and plants.
   - c. Waste is compacted and sealed into a container, then placed in a "tomb" designed to last several thousand years.
   - d. Waste is buried in an underground concrete vault.

8. Liability under the Superfund is
   - a. limited to the owner of record.
   - b. joint and several and retroactive, but not strict.
   - c. voluntary.
   - d. strict, joint and several, and retroactive.

9. All of the following have been proven to pose health hazards *EXCEPT*
    a. asbestos fibers.
    b. carbon monoxide.
    c. electromagnetic fields.
    d. lead-based paint.

10. Which of the following environmental hazards poses a risk due to particles or fibers in the air?
    a. Carbon monoxide
    b. Radon
    c. UFFI
    d. Asbestos

11. The Residential Lead-Based Paint Hazard Reduction Act sets forth procedures for disclosing the presence of lead in
    a. all residential properties offered for sale.
    b. new residential construction only.
    c. residential properties built prior to 1978.
    d. residential properties built prior to 1990.

12. Which of the following is *NOT* exempt from disclosure regulations of the Residential Lead-Based Hazard Reduction Act?
    a. A duplex built before 1978
    b. Studio apartments where the living area is not separated from the sleeping area
    c. Senior-citizen housing
    d. Residences for the disabled

13. The segment of the population that is most likely to obtain lead poisoning from paint is
    a. the elderly.
    b. children.
    c. teenagers.
    d. all groups

14. Mold and mildew found in the home fall into which category of pollutants?
    a. Pesticides
    b. Formaldehyde
    c. Biological
    d. Hazardous waste

15. All of the following are true about underground water contamination *EXCEPT*
    a. it is a minor problem in the United States.
    b. any contamination of underground water can threaten the supply of pure, clean water from private wells and public water systems.
    c. protective state and federal laws concerning water supply have been enacted.
    d. real estate licensees need to be aware of potential contamination sources.

16. In regulations regarding lead-based paint, HUD requires that
    a. homeowners test for its presence.
    b. paint be removed from surfaces before selling.
    c. known paint hazards be disclosed.
    d. only licensed contracts deal with its removal.

17. A method of sealing off disintegrating asbestos is called
    a. capping.
    b. encapsulation.
    c. containment.
    d. contamination closure.

___In Illinois___

18. The agency primarily responsible for protecting Illinois's natural resources against pollution and other hazards is the
    a. Pollution Control Board of Illinois (PCB).
    b. Illinois Department of Environmental Affairs (IDEA).
    c. Illinois Environmental Protection Agency (IEPA).
    d. Illinois Department of Environmental Regulation (IDER).

19. Environmental regulations in Illinois are
    a. all more stringent than federal regulations.
    b. substantially equivalent to federal regulations.
    c. less restrictive than federal regulations.
    d. not subject to federal regulations.

20. Which are exempt from radon disclosure under the Illinois Radon Awareness Act?
    a. Residential rentals
    b. Properties with six or more units
    c. Transfers between co-owners
    d. Transfers between neighbors

CHAPTER 23

Closing the Real Estate Transaction

■ **LEARNING OBJECTIVES** *When you've finished reading this chapter, you should be able to*

■ **identify** the issues of particular interest to the buyer and the seller as a real estate transaction closes;

■ **describe** the steps involved in preparing a closing statement;

■ **explain** the general rules for prorating;

■ **distinguish** the procedures involved in face-to-face closings from those in escrow closings; and

■ **define** the following *key terms*

accrued item	escrow accounts	Real Estate Settlement
closing	good-faith estimate (GFE)	Procedures Act
closing statement	Mortgage Disclosure	(RESPA)
controlled business	Improvement Act	survey
arrangement	(MDIA)	Uniform Settlement
credit	prepaid items	Statement (HUD-1)
debit	prorations	

■ CLOSING THE REAL ESTATE TRANSACTION

The conclusion of the real estate transaction is the **closing**, the culmination of many efforts—finding clients, negotiating offers, solving problems, coordinating inspections, and much more. At the closing, title to the real estate is transferred in exchange for payment of the purchase price. It's also a complicated time because until closing preparations begin, the licensee's relationship is primarily with the buyer or the seller. During the closing period, new players come on the scene: appraisers, inspectors, loan officers, insurance agents, and lawyers. Negotiations continue, sometimes right up until the property is finally transferred. A thorough knowledge of the process is the best defense against the risk of a transaction failing.

■ PRECLOSING PROCEDURES

Closing involves two major events. First, the promises made in the sales contract are fulfilled; second, the mortgage funds are distributed to the buyer. Before the property changes hands, however, important issues must be resolved. Many real estate licensees maintain lists of events that must take place prior to the actual closing in order to avoid surprises that might lead to delays. Each party—buyer and seller—has specific concerns that must be addressed.

Buyer's Issues

Both the buyers and their lenders must be sure that the seller can deliver the title that was promised in the purchase agreement and that the property is now in essentially the same condition it was in when the buyers and the sellers agreed to the sale. This involves inspecting

> **Closing** is the point at which ownership of a property is transferred in exchange for the payment of the selling price.

- the title evidence;
- the seller's deed;
- any documents demonstrating the removal of undesired liens and encumbrances;
- the survey;
- the results of any required inspections, such as termite or structural inspections, or required repairs; and
- any leases, if tenants reside on the premises.

IN PRACTICE   Although the "For Your Protection, Get a Home Inspection" pamphlet is required only for FHA loans, the information is valuable for all buyers. The pamphlet emphasizes the difference between an appraisal and a home inspection. (See Figure 23.1.)

Final property inspection   In the real estate contract, the buyer usually reserves the right to make a *final inspection*, often referred to as a *walk-through*, shortly before the closing takes place. Accompanied by the licensee, the buyer verifies that necessary repairs have been made, that the property has been well maintained, that all fixtures are in place, and that no unauthorized removal or alteration of any part of the improvements has taken place. It is not an opportunity to reopen negotiations.

Survey   A *survey* provides information about the exact location and size of the property. The sales contract specifies who will pay for the survey. Typically, the survey indicates the location of all buildings, driveways, fences, and other improvements located on the premises. Any improvements located on adjoining property that may encroach on the premises being bought also will be noted. The survey

FIGURE 23.1

For Your Protection, Get a Home Inspection

CAUTION

U.S. Department of Housing
and Urban Development
Federal Housing Administration (FHA)

OMB Approval No: 2502-0538
(exp. 07/31/2009)

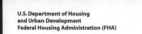

For Your Protection:
Get a Home Inspection

Why a Buyer Needs a Home Inspection

A home inspection gives the buyer more detailed information about the overall condition of the home prior to purchase. In a home inspection, a qualified inspector takes an in-depth, unbiased look at your potential new home to:

- ✔ Evaluate the physical condition: structure, construction, and mechanical systems;
- ✔ Identify items that need to be repaired or replaced; and
- ✔ Estimate the remaining useful life of the major systems, equipment, structure, and finishes.

Appraisals are Different from Home Inspections

An appraisal is different from a home inspection. Appraisals are for lenders; home inspections are for buyers. An appraisal is required to:

- ✔ Estimate the market value of a house;
- ✔ Make sure that the house meets FHA minimum property standards/requirements; and
- ✔ Make sure that the property is marketable.

FHA Does Not Guarantee the Value or Condition of your Potential New Home

If you find problems with your new home after closing, FHA can not give or lend you money for repairs, and FHA can not buy the home back from you. That is why it is so important for you, the buyer, to get an independent home inspection. Ask a qualified home inspector to inspect your potential new home and give you the information you need to make a wise decision.

Radon Gas Testing

The United States Environmental Protection Agency and the Surgeon General of the United States have recommended that all houses should be tested for radon. For more information on radon testing, call the toll-free National Radon Information Line at 1-800-SOS-Radon or 1-800-767-7236. As with a home inspection, if you decide to test for radon, you may do so before signing your contract, or you may do so after signing the contract as long as your contract states the sale of the home depends on your satisfaction with the results of the radon test.

Be an Informed Buyer

It is your responsibility to be an informed buyer. Be sure that what you buy is satisfactory in every respect. You have the right to carefully examine your potential new home with a qualified home inspector. You may arrange to do so before signing your contract, or may do so after signing the contract as long as your contract states that the sale of the home depends on the inspection.

HUD-92564-CN (6/06)

CAUTION

should set out, in full, any existing easements and encroachments. Whether or not the sales contract calls for a survey, lenders frequently require one.

IN PRACTICE   Relying on old surveys is not a good idea; the property should be re-surveyed by a competent surveyor, whether or not the title company or lender requires it. A current survey confirms that the property purchased is exactly what the buyer wants.

Seller's Issues

Naturally, the seller's main interest is to receive payment for the property. Sellers want to be sure that the buyer has obtained the necessary financing and has sufficient funds to complete the sale. Sellers will also want to be certain that they have complied with all the buyer's requirements so the transaction will be completed.

Both parties will want to inspect the closing statement to make sure that all monies involved in the transaction have been accounted for properly. The parties may be accompanied by their attorneys.

IN PRACTICE   Licensees may discuss with clients the approximate expenses involved in closing at the time the listing agreement or buyer agency agreement is entered into but not later than the time when the sales contract is signed.

Title Procedures

Both the buyer and the buyer's lender will want assurance that the seller's title complies with the requirements of the sales contract. Additionally, lenders require title insurance in the event any "clouds" on the title (encumbrances on the real estate or claims on the title) should come up during the course of ownership. The title insurance is not issued until it is clear that such encumbrances from the past are unlikely. A major goal of title procedures is for the new owner to obtain a clear and valid "owner's title policy." Such a policy comes as close as any document can to providing evidence of ownership of a property that is unencumbered by any past liens or potential claims.

> The *title* or *opinion of title* discloses all liens, encumbrances, easements, conditions, and restrictions on the property.

As a first step toward a new owner's title policy, prior to closing and establishment of the new owner's title, the seller usually is required to produce a current abstract of title or title commitment from the title insurance company. When an abstract of title is used, the purchaser's attorney examines it and issues an opinion of title. This opinion, like the title commitment, is a statement of the status of the seller's title. It discloses all liens, encumbrances, easements, conditions, or restrictions that appear on the record and to which the seller's title is subject.

On the date when the sale is actually completed (the date of delivery of the deed), the buyer has a title commitment or an abstract that was issued several days or weeks before the closing. For this reason, there usually are two searches of the public records. The first shows the status of the seller's title on the date of the first search. Usually, the seller pays for this search. The second search, known as a *bring-down*, is made after the closing and generally paid for by the purchaser. The abstract should be reviewed before closing to resolve any problems that might cause delays or threaten the transaction.

As part of this later search, the seller may be required to execute an *affidavit of title*. This is a sworn statement in which the seller assures the title insurance company (and the buyer) that there have been no judgments, bankruptcies, or divorces involving the seller since the date of the title examination. The affidavit promises that no unrecorded deeds or contracts have been made, no repairs or improvements have gone unpaid, and no defects in the title have arisen that the seller knows of. The seller also affirms that he is in possession of the premises. In some areas, this form is required before the title insurance company will issue an owner's policy to the buyer. The affidavit gives the title insurance company the right to sue the seller if his statements in the affidavit are incorrect.

In Illinois

In 2010, the Title Insurance Act was amended by prohibiting title insurance companies, title insurance agents or independent escrowees from making disbursements out of a fiduciary trust account in connection with any escrows, settlements, or closings unless the funds are collected or are good funds. This applies to $50,000 or less from any single party to a transaction or an aggregate amount of $50,000 or greater received from any single party to a transaction.

"Good funds" are in one of the following forms:

- Lawful money of the United States
- Wired funds unconditionally held by the title insurance company, the title insurance agent, or independent escrowee
- Cashier's checks, certified checks, bank money orders, official bank checks, or teller's checks drawn on or issued by a financial institution chartered under the laws of any state of the United States and unconditionally held by the title insurance company, title insurance agent, or independent escrowee
- A personal check or checks in an aggregate amount not exceeding $5,000 per closing, provided that the title insurance company, title insurance agent, or independent escrowee has reasonable grounds to believe that sufficient funds are available for withdrawal in the account upon which the check is drawn at the time of disbursement
- A check drawn on the trust account of any lawyer or real estate broker licensed under the laws of any state, provided that the title insurance company, title insurance agent, or independent escrowee has reasonable grounds to believe that sufficient funds are available for withdrawal in the account upon which the check is drawn at the time of disbursement
- A check issued by Illinois or the United States
- A check drawn on the fiduciary trust account of a title insurance company or title insurance agent, provided that the title insurance company, title insurance agent, or independent escrowee has reasonable grounds to believe that sufficient funds are available for withdrawal in the account upon which the check is drawn at the time of disbursement

Collected funds means funds deposited, finally settled, and credited to the title insurance company, title insurance agent, or independent escrowee's fiduciary trust account. (Source: P.A. 96-645, eff. 1-1-10; 96-1457, eff. 1-1-11.) ■

Whether the purchaser pays cash or obtains a new loan to purchase the property, the seller's existing loan is paid in full and satisfied on record. The exact amount required to pay the existing loan is provided in a current payoff statement from the lender, effective on the date of closing. This payoff statement (also called an estoppel certificate or certificate of no defense) notes the unpaid amount of principal, the interest due through the date of payment, the fee for issuing the certificate of satisfaction or release deed, credits (if any) for tax and insurance reserves, and the amount of any prepayment penalties. Once the borrower has executed the estoppel certificate, the borrower cannot thereafter claim that he did not owe the amount indicated in the payoff or estoppel certificate. The same procedure would be followed for any other liens that must be released before the buyer takes title.

In a transaction in which the buyer assumes the seller's existing mortgage loan, the buyer will want to know the exact balance of the loan as of the closing date. In some areas, it is customary for the buyer to obtain a mortgage reduction certificate from the lender that certifies the amount owed on the mortgage loan, the interest rate, and the last interest payment made.

In some areas, real estate sales transactions customarily are closed through an escrow. In these areas, the escrow instructions usually provide for an extended coverage policy to be issued to the buyer as of the date of closing. The seller has no need to execute an affidavit of title.

IN PRACTICE   Licensees often assist in pre-closing arrangements as part of their service to customers. In some states, licensees are required to advise the parties of the approximate expenses involved in closing when a real estate sales contract is signed. In other states, licensees have a statutory duty to coordinate and supervise closing activities. Aside from state laws on this issue, a licensee without a specific role in the closing may still be the person with the most knowledge about the transaction. Because of this, many licensees feel it is part of their fiduciary duty to be present at a face-to-face closing.

■ CONDUCTING THE CLOSING

Closing is known by many names. For instance, in some areas, closing is called *settlement and transfer*. In other parts of the country, the parties to the transaction sit around a single table and exchange copies of documents, a process known as *passing papers*. ("We passed papers on the new house Wednesday morning.") In other regions, the buyer and seller may never meet at all; the paperwork is handled by an escrow agent in a process known as *closing escrow*. ("We'll close escrow on our house next week.") Whether the closing occurs face-to-face or through escrow, the main concerns are that the buyer receives marketable title and the seller receives the purchase price.

In Illinois

In Illinois, the closing statement is customarily prepared by the buyer's lender, the lender's agent (usually a title insurance company), or the seller's lawyer. Although real estate licensees are prohibited from completing formal closing statements as a result of the Illinois Supreme Court's decision in *Chicago Bar Association, et al., v. Quinlan and Tyson, Inc.*, estimated statements are often needed when preparing a comparative market analysis (CMA), when filling out an offer for a buyer, or when presenting an offer to a seller. For this reason, licensees must understand the preparation of a closing statement, which includes the expenses and prorations of costs to close the transaction. ■

Face-to-Face Closing

> In a *face-to-face closing*, the parties meet face-to-face.

Face-to-face closings may be held at a number of locations, including the offices of the title company, the lending institution, an attorney for one of the parties, the broker, the county recorder, or the escrow company. Those attending a closing *may* include

- the buyer or the buyer's duly authorized agent;
- the seller or the seller's duly authorized agent;
- the real estate licensees (both the buyer's and the seller's agents);
- the seller's and the buyer's attorneys;
- representatives of the lending institutions involved with the buyer's new mortgage loan, the buyer's assumption of the seller's existing loan, or the seller's payoff of an existing loan; and
- a representative of the title insurance company.

Closing agent or closing officer A closing agent may be a representative of the title company, the lender, the real estate broker, or the buyer's or seller's attorney. Some title companies and law firms employ paralegal assistants who conduct closings for their firms.

The closing agent orders and reviews the title insurance policy or title certificate, surveys, property insurance policies, and other items. After reviewing the agreement of sale (purchase agreement), the agent prepares a closing statement indicating the division of income and expenses between the parties. Finally, the time and place of closing must be arranged.

The exchange When the parties are satisfied that everything is in order, the exchange is made. The seller delivers the signed deed to the buyer, who accepts it. All pertinent documents are then recorded in the correct order to ensure continuity of title. For instance, if the seller pays off an existing loan and the buyer obtains a new loan, the seller's satisfaction of mortgage must be recorded *before* the seller's deed to the buyer. The buyer's new mortgage or deed of trust must be recorded *after* the deed because the buyer cannot pledge the property as security for the loan until he owns it.

Closing in Escrow

Although a few states prohibit transactions that are closed in escrow, escrow closings are used to some extent in most states.

> In an *escrow closing*, a third party coordinates the closing activities on behalf of the buyer and seller.

An **escrow** is a method of closing in which a disinterested third party is authorized to act as escrow agent and to coordinate the closing activities. The escrow agent also may be called the *escrow holder*. The escrow agent may be an attorney, a title company, a trust company, an escrow company, or the escrow department of a lending institution. Many real estate firms offer escrow services. However, a real estate licensee cannot be a disinterested party in a transaction from which he expects to collect a commission. Because the escrow agent is placed in a position of great trust, many states have laws regulating escrow agents and limiting who may serve in this capacity.

Escrow procedure   When a transaction will close in escrow, the buyer and seller execute escrow instructions to the escrow agent after the sales contract is signed. One of the parties selects an escrow agent. Which party selects the agent is determined either by negotiation or by state law. Once the contract is signed, the broker turns over the earnest money to the escrow agent, who deposits it in a special trust, or escrow, account.

Buyer and seller deposit all pertinent documents and other items with the escrow agent before the specified date of closing.

The seller usually deposits

- the deed conveying the property to the buyer;
- title evidence (abstract and attorney's opinion of title, certificate of title, title insurance, or Torrens certificate);
- existing hazard insurance policies;
- a letter or mortgage reduction certificate from the lender stating the exact principal remaining (if the buyer assumes the seller's loan);
- affidavits of title (if required);
- a payoff statement (if the seller's loan is to be paid off);
- bill of sale;
- survey;
- transfer tax declarations;
- paid water bill; and
- other instruments or documents necessary to clear the title or to complete the transaction.

The buyer deposits

- the balance of the cash needed to complete the purchase, usually in the form of a certified check;
- loan documents (if the buyer secures a new loan);
- proof of hazard insurance and flood insurance (if required); and
- other necessary documents, such as inspection reports required by the lender.

The escrow agent has the authority to examine the title evidence. When marketable title is shown in the name of the buyer and all other conditions of the escrow agreement have been met, the agent is authorized to disburse the purchase price to the seller, minus all charges and expenses. The agent then records the deed and mortgage or deed of trust (if a new loan has been obtained by the purchaser).

If the escrow agent's examination of the title discloses liens, a portion of the purchase price can be withheld from the seller. The withheld portion is used to pay the liens to clear the title.

If the seller cannot clear the title, or if for any reason the sale cannot be consummated, the escrow instructions usually provide that the parties be returned to their former statuses as if no sale occurred. The escrow agent reconveys title to the seller and returns the purchase money to the buyer. If the seller dies prior to the closing date, but after having given a signed deed to the escrow agent, the closing still may proceed, with the escrow agent transferring title to the buyer and turning the purchase price over to the seller's estate.

IRS Reporting Requirements

Certain real estate closings must be reported to the Internal Revenue Service (IRS) on Form 1099-S. The affected properties include sales or exchanges of

- land (improved or unimproved), including air space;
- an inherently permanent structure, including any residential, commercial, or industrial building;
- a condominium unit and its appurtenant fixtures and common elements (including land); or
- shares in a cooperative housing corporation.

Information to be reported includes the sales price, the amount of property tax reimbursement credited to the seller, and the seller's Social Security number. If the closing agent does not notify the IRS, the responsibility for filing the form falls on the mortgage lender, although the real estate licensees or the parties to the transaction ultimately could be held liable.

Licensee's Role at Closing

Depending on local practice, the licensee's role at closing can vary from simply collecting the commission to conducting the proceedings. Real estate licensees are not authorized to give legal advice or otherwise engage in the practice of law. This means that in some states, a licensee's job is essentially finished as soon as the sales contract is signed. After the contract is signed, the attorneys take over. Even so, a licensee's service generally continues all the way through closing because it is in the licensee's best interest that the transactions move successfully and smoothly to a conclusion. This may mean actively arranging for title evidence, surveys, appraisals, and inspections or repairs for structural conditions, water supplies, sewage facilities, or toxic substances.

Though real estate licensees do not always conduct closing proceedings, they usually attend. Often, the parties look to their agents for guidance, assistance, and information during what can be a stressful experience. Licensees need to be thoroughly familiar with the process and procedures involved in preparing a closing statement, which includes the expenses and prorations of costs to close the transaction.

IN PRACTICE Licensees should avoid recommending sources for any inspection or testing services. If a buyer suffers any injury as a result of a provider's negligence, the licensee might also be named in any lawsuit. The better practice is to give clients the names of several professionals who offer high-quality services. In addition, licensees who receive any compensation or reward from a source they recommend to a client must disclose such an arrangement to the client. Licensees must never receive compensation from an attorney or a lender.

Lender's Interest at Closing

Whether a buyer obtains new financing or assumes the seller's existing loan, the lender wants to protect its security interest in the property. The lender has an interest in making sure the buyer gets good, marketable title and that tax and insurance payments are maintained. Lenders want their mortgage lien to have priority over other liens. They also want to ensure that insurance is kept up-to-date in case property is damaged or destroyed. Therefore, lenders may require a survey, a pest control or another inspection report, or a certificate of occupancy (for a newly constructed building). In order to ensure that the buyer takes good and marketable title at closing, lenders generally require a mortgagee's title insurance policy.

The buyer must also provide a fire and hazard insurance policy (along with a receipt for the premium). A lender usually requests that a reserve account be established for tax and insurance payments so that these payments are maintained. Lenders sometimes even require representation by their own attorneys at closing.

Mortgage Disclosure Improvement Act

Since its effective date of July 31, 2009, the **Mortgage Disclosure Improvement Act (MDIA)** has changed how buyers and sellers, lenders, mortgage brokers, title agents, and real estate licensees prepare for a closing. The timeliness of certain disclosures now affects the date of closings. Lenders and licensees should keep in mind the numbers 3, 7, and 3:

- 3 business days from application to provide the truth-in-lending statement (TIL) and good-faith estimate (GFE)
- 7 business days before the signing of loan documents, after the borrower receives the final truth-in-lending statement and good-faith estimate
- 3 business days to wait for closing if the APR has changed more than 0.125 percent from the original or most recent TIL and GFE

Until the applicant/borrower receives the GFE and the TIL, the lender may collect only a reasonable fee for accessing the applicant's credit history. Plus, the Home Valuation Code of Conduct (HVCC) requires that the borrower be provided with a copy of the home's appraisal within three business days of closing.

Lenders must provide a statement to the applicants indicating that they are not obligated to complete the transaction simply because disclosures were provided or because they applied for a loan. If the annual percentage rate increases more than 0.125 percent from the original TIL, then creditors must provide new disclosures with a revised annual percentage rate (APR) and then wait an additional three business days before closing the loan. Consumers are permitted to accelerate the process if a personal emergency, such as a foreclosure, exists.

The intent of this law is to prevent consumers from receiving an enticing low rate at the initial application and then learning at settlement that the lender is charging more in fees. Licensees should encourage their buyers to discuss all loan options with their lenders before signing a contract so that lenders can provide the disclosures in a timely fashion. Borrowers should lock in interest rates with a date that is about ten days from an anticipated settlement. Any change to the interest rate, loan amount, loan product, or lender's or escrow fees can affect the APR, which may then require a redisclosure. Redisclosures can potentially delay settlement.

Before closing, everyone involved in the real estate transaction should check and double-check that the GFE and TIL forms are consistent with the original application. No one—buyers, sellers, or real estate agents—should schedule closings that do not account for the seven-day waiting period.

■ REAL ESTATE SETTLEMENT PROCEDURES ACT (RESPA)

The **Real Estate Settlement Procedures Act (RESPA)** is a federal consumer law that requires certain disclosures about the mortgage and settlement process and prohibits certain practices that increase the costs of settlement services, such as kickbacks and referral fees that can increase settlement costs for home buyers.

RESPA regulations apply to first-lien residential mortgage loans made to finance the purchases of one- to four-family homes, cooperatives, and condominiums, for either investment or occupancy, as well as second or subordinate liens for home equity loans when a purchase is financed by a federally related mortgage loan. Federally related loans are those made by banks, savings and loan associations, or other lenders whose deposits are insured by federal agencies; loans insured by the FHA and guaranteed by the Department of Veterans Affairs (VA); loans administered by HUD; and loans intended to be sold by the lenders to Fannie Mae, Ginnie Mae, or Freddie Mac. RESPA is administered by HUD.

RESPA does not apply to the following settlements:

- Loans on large properties (i.e., more than 25 acres)
- Loans for business or agricultural purposes
- Construction loans or other temporary financing
- Vacant loans on large properties (i.e., more than 25 acres)
- Loans for business or agricultural purposes
- Construction loans or other temporary financing
- Vacant land (unless a dwelling will be placed on the lot within two years)
- A transaction financed solely by a purchase-money mortgage taken back by the seller
- An installment contract (contract for deed)
- A buyer's assumption of a seller's existing loan (If the terms of the assumed loan are modified, or if the lender charges more than $50 for the assumption, the transaction is subject to RESPA regulations.)

RESPA prohibits certain practices that increase the cost of settlement services:

- **Section 8** prohibits kickbacks and fee-splitting for referrals of settlement services and unearned fees for services not actually performed. Violations are subject to criminal and civil penalties, including fines up to $10,000 and/or imprisonment up to one year. Consumers may privately pursue a violator in court; the violator may be liable for an amount up to three times the amount of the charge paid for the service.
- **Section 9** prohibits homesellers from requiring that homebuyers buy title insurance from a particular company. Buyers may sue the seller for such a violation; violators are liable for up to three times the amount of all charges paid for the title insurance.
- **Section 10** prohibits lenders from requiring excessive escrow account deposits, money set aside to pay taxes, hazard insurance, and other charges related to the property.

Sweeping changes required by January 1, 2010, include the mandatory use of the new Good Faith Estimate (GFE) and the modified HUD-1 form. Although the burden of implementing the new reforms is the responsibility of the lender, real estate licensees should be aware of the requirements because failure to meet the standards can and will delay closings. To make it easier for borrowers to understand costs, the new rules and forms require lenders to provide a standard GFE, provided by HUD, which clearly discloses key loan terms and closing costs. More important, most of these disclosed costs cannot vary greatly between the time that the GFE is issued and closing.

IN PRACTICE   Although RESPA's requirements are aimed primarily at lenders, real estate licensees fall under RESPA when they refer buyers to particular lenders, title companies, attorneys, or other providers of settlement services. Licensees who offer computerized loan origination (CLO) are also subject to regulation. Remember: Buyers have the right to select their own providers of settlement services.

Controlled Business Arrangements

To streamline the settlement process, a real estate firm, title insurance company, mortgage broker, home inspection company, or even a moving company may agree to offer a package of services to consumers, a system known as a **controlled business arrangement (CBA)**. RESPA permits a CBA as long as a consumer is clearly informed of the relationship among the service providers, that participation is not required, that other providers are available, and that the only thing of value received by one business entity from others, in addition to permitted payments for services provided, is a return on ownership interest or franchise relationship.

Fees must be reasonably related to the value of the services provided and not be fees exchanged among the affiliated companies simply for referring business to one another. This referral-fee prohibition may be a particularly important issue for licensees who offer computerized loan origination (CLO) services to their clients and customers. CLOs that provide services to consumers may charge for the services provided; the fees must be disclosed on the HUD-1 or HUD 1A settlement statement. While a borrower's ability to comparison shop for a loan may be enhanced by a CLO system, the range of choices must not be limited. Consumers must be informed of the availability and costs of other lenders. (See Figure 23.2.)

Disclosure Requirements

Lenders and settlement agents have the following disclosure obligations at the time of loan application and loan closing or within three business days of receiving the loan application. If the lender denies the loan within three days, then RESPA does not require that the lender provide the following documents:

Special information booklet   This HUD booklet, which must be given at the time of application or provided within three days of loan application, provides the borrower with general information about settlement (closing) costs. It also explains the various provisions of RESPA, including a line-by-line description of the Uniform Settlement Statement.

FIGURE 23.2

Affiliated Business Arrangement Disclosure

Affiliated Business Arrangement Disclosure

This is to give you notice that _____ (referring Party) has a business relationship with _____ as a loan originator/solicitor. Because of this relationship, this referral may provide (referring party) a financial or other benefit.

[A.] Set forth below is the estimated charge or range of charges for the settlement services listed.

You are **NOT** required to use the listed provider as a condition for settlement of your loan on, or purchase, sale, or refinance of, the subject property. **THERE ARE FREQUENTLY OTHER SETTLEMENT SERVICE PROVIDERS AVAILABLE WITH SIMILAR SERVICES. YOU ARE FREE TO SHOP AROUND TO DETERMINE THAT YOU ARE RECEIVING THE BEST SERVICES AND THE BEST RATE FOR THESE SERVICES.**

[provider] [charge or range of charges]

_____

_____

[B.] Set forth below is the estimated charge or range of charges for the settlement services of an attorney, credit reporting agency, or real estate appraiser that we, as your lender, will require you to use, as a condition of your loan on this property, to represent our interests in the transaction.

[provider and settlement service] [charge or range of charges]

_____

_____

ACKNOWLEDGMENT:

I/we have read this disclosure form, and understand that _____ (referring party) is referring me/us to purchase from the above-described settlement service provider and may receive a financial or other benefit as the result of this referral.

Borrower's Signature   Date

_____   _____

Borrower's Signature   Date

_____   _____

Good-faith estimate of settlement costs The new three-page **Good Faith Estimate (GFE)** must contain the exact language specified by HUD, making it easier for borrowers to compare loan conditions from one lender to another. (See Figure 23.3.)

The only fee that the lender may collect before the applicant receives the GFE is for a credit report. Once the GFE is issued, lenders are committed and may only modify the GFE in certain specific instances. If certain information or circumstances change after the original GFE is issued, then a new GFE must be issued.

FIGURE 23.3

Good Faith Estimate

OMB Approval No. 2502-0265

Good Faith Estimate (GFE)

Name of Originator	Borrower
Originator Address	Property Address
Originator Phone Number	
Originator Email	Date of GFE

Purpose

This GFE gives you an estimate of your settlement charges and loan terms if you are approved for this loan. For more information, see HUD's *Special Information Booklet* on settlement charges, your *Truth-in-Lending Disclosures,* and other consumer information at www.hud.gov/respa. If you decide you would like to proceed with this loan, contact us.

Shopping for your loan

Only you can shop for the best loan for you. Compare this GFE with other loan offers, so you can find the best loan. Use the shopping chart on page 3 to compare all the offers you receive.

Important dates

1. The interest rate for this GFE is available through _____. After this time, the interest rate, some of your loan Origination Charges, and the monthly payment shown below can change until you lock your interest rate.

2. This estimate for all other settlement charges is available through _____.

3. After you lock your interest rate, you must go to settlement within ☐ days (your rate lock period) to receive the locked interest rate.

4. You must lock the interest rate at least ☐ days before settlement.

Summary of your loan

Your initial loan amount is	$
Your loan term is	years
Your initial interest rate is	%
Your initial monthly amount owed for principal, interest, and any mortgage insurance is	$ per month
Can your interest rate rise?	☐ No ☐ Yes, it can rise to a maximum of %. The first change will be in .
Even if you make payments on time, can your loan balance rise?	☐ No ☐ Yes, it can rise to a maximum of $
Even if you make payments on time, can your monthly amount owed for principal, interest, and any mortgage insurance rise?	☐ No ☐ Yes, the first increase can be in and the monthly amount owed can rise to $. The maximum it can ever rise to is $.
Does your loan have a prepayment penalty?	☐ No ☐ Yes, your maximum prepayment penalty is $.
Does your loan have a balloon payment?	☐ No ☐ Yes, you have a balloon payment of $ due in years.

Escrow account information

Some lenders require an escrow account to hold funds for paying property taxes or other property-related charges in addition to your monthly amount owed of $_____.
Do we require you to have an escrow account for your loan?
☐ No, you do not have an escrow account. You must pay these charges directly when due.
☐ Yes, you have an escrow account. It may or may not cover all of these charges. Ask us.

Summary of your settlement charges

A	Your Adjusted Origination Charges *(See page 2.)*	$
B	Your Charges for All Other Settlement Services *(See page 2.)*	$
A + B	Total Estimated Settlement Charges	$

FIGURE 23.3

Good Faith Estimate (continued)

Understanding your estimated settlement charges

Some of these charges can change at settlement. See the top of page 3 for more information.

Your Adjusted Origination Charges

1. Our origination charge
This charge is for getting this loan for you.

2. Your credit or charge (points) for the specific interest rate chosen

☐ The credit or charge for the interest rate of ☐ % is included in "Our origination charge." (See item 1 above.)

☐ You receive a credit of $ ☐ for this interest rate of ☐ %. This credit **reduces** your settlement charges.

☐ You pay a charge of $ ☐ for this interest rate of ☐ %. This charge (points) **increases** your total settlement charges.

The tradeoff table on page 3 shows that you can change your total settlement charges by choosing a different interest rate for this loan.

A Your Adjusted Origination Charges | $

Your Charges for All Other Settlement Services

3. Required services that we select
These charges are for services we require to complete your settlement. We will choose the providers of these services.

Service | *Charge*

4. Title services and lender's title insurance
This charge includes the services of a title or settlement agent, for example, and title insurance to protect the lender, if required.

5. Owner's title insurance
You may purchase an owner's title insurance policy to protect your interest in the property.

6. Required services that you can shop for
These charges are for other services that are required to complete your settlement. We can identify providers of these services or you can shop for them yourself. Our estimates for providing these services are below.

Service | *Charge*

7. Government recording charges
These charges are for state and local fees to record your loan and title documents.

8. Transfer taxes
These charges are for state and local fees on mortgages and home sales.

9. Initial deposit for your escrow account
This charge is held in an escrow account to pay future recurring charges on your property and includes ☐ all property taxes, ☐ all insurance, and ☐ other ☐ .

10. Daily interest charges
This charge is for the daily interest on your loan from the day of your settlement until the first day of the next month or the first day of your normal mortgage payment cycle. This amount is $ ☐ per day for ☐ days (if your settlement is ☐).

11. Homeowner's insurance
This charge is for the insurance you must buy for the property to protect from a loss, such as fire.

Policy | *Charge*

B Your Charges for All Other Settlement Services | $

A + **B** Total Estimated Settlement Charges | $

 Good Faith Estimate (HUD-GFE) 2

FIGURE 23.3

Good Faith Estimate (continued)

Instructions

Understanding which charges can change at settlement

This GFE estimates your settlement charges. At your settlement, you will receive a HUD-1, a form that lists your actual costs. Compare the charges on the HUD-1 with the charges on this GFE. Charges can change if you select your own provider and do not use the companies we identify. (See below for details.)

These charges **cannot increase** at settlement:	The total of these charges **can increase up to 10%** at settlement:	These charges **can change** at settlement:
▪ Our origination charge ▪ Your credit or charge (points) for the specific interest rate chosen *(after you lock in your interest rate)* ▪ Your adjusted origination charges *(after you lock in your interest rate)* ▪ Transfer taxes	▪ Required services that we select ▪ Title services and lender's title insurance *(if we select them or you use companies we identify)* ▪ Owner's title insurance *(if you use companies we identify)* ▪ Required services that you can shop for *(if you use companies we identify)* ▪ Government recording charges	▪ Required services that you can shop for *(if you do not use companies we identify)* ▪ Title services and lender's title insurance *(if you do not use companies we identify)* ▪ Owner's title insurance *(if you do not use companies we identify)* ▪ Initial deposit for your escrow account ▪ Daily interest charges ▪ Homeowner's insurance

Using the tradeoff table

In this GFE, we offered you this loan with a particular interest rate and estimated settlement charges. However:

▪ If you want to choose this same loan with **lower settlement charges,** then you will have a **higher interest rate.**
▪ If you want to choose this same loan with a **lower interest rate,** then you will have **higher settlement charges.**

If you would like to choose an available option, you must ask us for a new GFE.

Loan originators have the option to complete this table. Please ask for additional information if the table is not completed.

	The loan in this GFE	The same loan with lower settlement charges	The same loan with a lower interest rate
Your initial loan amount	$	$	$
Your initial interest rate[1]	%	%	%
Your initial monthly amount owed	$	$	$
Change in the monthly amount owed from this GFE	No change	You will pay $ **more** every month	You will pay $ **less** every month
Change in the amount you will pay at settlement with this interest rate	No change	Your settlement charges will be **reduced** by $	Your settlement charges will **increase** by $
How much your total estimated settlement charges will be	$	$	$

[1] *For an adjustable rate loan, the comparisons above are for the initial interest rate before adjustments are made.*

Using the shopping chart

Use this chart to compare GFEs from different loan originators. Fill in the information by using a different column for each GFE you receive. By comparing loan offers, you can shop for the best loan.

	This loan	Loan 2	Loan 3	Loan 4
Loan originator name				
Initial loan amount				
Loan term				
Initial interest rate				
Initial monthly amount owed				
Rate lock period				
Can interest rate rise?				
Can loan balance rise?				
Can monthly amount owed rise?				
Prepayment penalty?				
Balloon payment?				
Total Estimated Settlement Charges				

If your loan is sold in the future

Some lenders may sell your loan after settlement. Any fees lenders receive in the future cannot change the loan you receive or the charges you paid at settlement.

 Good Faith Estimate (HUD-GFE) 3

Issuing a new GFE triggers a new three-day waiting period; in which case, closing may not occur until after three days have passed.

The new GFE indicates which closing costs may or may not change prior to settlement and, if they do, by how much. The fees are divided into three categories:

- *No tolerance*—fees that may not increase before closing: lender charges for taking, underwriting, and processing the loan application, including points, origination fees, and yield spread premiums
- *10 percent tolerance*—fees that cannot increase by more than 10 percent in any given category: settlement services for which the lender selects the provider or for which the borrower selects the provider from the lender's list, title services and title insurance if the lender selects the provider, and recording fees
- *Unlimited tolerance*—fees for services that are out of the lender's control: services for which the borrower chooses the provider (such as escrow and title insurance), impounds for taxes, mortgage interest, and the cost of homeowners' insurance

Mortgage servicing disclosure statement   This statement tells the borrower whether the lender intends to service the loan or to transfer it to another lender. It will also provide information about resolving complaints.

The last page of the GFE is a worksheet consumers can use to compare different loans and terms to aid in price shopping. The lender is responsible for the accuracy of the GFE and the actual costs that the lender charges on the HUD-1.

Uniform Settlement Statement (HUD-1)   RESPA requires that the Uniform Settlement Statement itemize all charges that are normally paid by a borrower and a seller in connection with settlement, whether required by the lender or another party, or paid by the lender or any other person. Charges required by the lender that are paid before closing are indicated as paid outside of closing (POC). The third page of the new HUD-1 form provides for a comparison of the original GFE estimates to the actual charges appearing on the HUD-1. Lenders are permitted to "correct" any violation of the tolerances by reimbursing the borrower within 30 days of settlement.

RESPA's Consumer Protections:

- CLO regulation
- CBA disclosure
- Settlement cost booklet
- Good-faith estimate of settlement costs
- Uniform Settlement Statement
- Prohibition of kickbacks and unearned fees

RESPA prohibits lenders from requiring borrowers to deposit amounts in escrow accounts for taxes and insurance that exceed certain limits, thus preventing the lenders from taking advantage of the borrowers. While RESPA does not require that escrow accounts be set up, certain government loan programs and some lenders require escrow accounts as a condition of the loan. RESPA places limits on the amounts that a lender may require: on a monthly basis, the lender may require only one-twelfth of the total of the disbursements for the year, plus an amount necessary to cover a shortage in the account. No more than one-sixth of the year's total disbursements may be held as a cushion (a cushion is not required). Once a year, the lender must perform an escrow account analysis and return any amount over $50 to the borrower. (See Table 23.1.)

Item	Paid by Seller	Paid by Buyer
Broker's commission	✗ by agreement	✗ by agreement
Attorney's fees	✗ by agreement	✗ by agreement
Recording expenses	✗ to clear title	✗ transfer charges
Transfer tax	✗ state and county	✗ some municipal taxes
Title expenses	✗ title search	✗ attorney inspection, title insurance
Loan fees	✗ prepayment penalty	✗ origination fee
Tax and insurance reserves (escrow or impound accounts)		✗
Appraisal fees		✗
Survey fees	✗ if required to pay by sales contract	✗ new mortgage financing

* This chart is based on generally applicable practices. Please note that closing practices may be different in your state.

By law, borrowers have the right to inspect a completed HUD-1 form, to the extent that the figures are available, one business day before the closing. (Sellers are not entitled to this privilege.) Lenders must retain these statements for two years after the closing date. In addition, state laws generally require that licensees retain all records of a transaction for a specific period.

Kickbacks and referral fees   RESPA prohibits the payment of kickbacks, or unearned fees, in any real estate settlement service. It prohibits referral fees when no services are actually rendered. The payment or receipt of a fee, kickback, or anything of value for referrals for settlement services includes activities such as mortgage loans, title searches, title insurance, attorney services, surveys, credit reports, and appraisals.

■ PREPARATION OF CLOSING STATEMENTS

A typical real estate transaction requires accounting for the expenses incurred by either party, generally on the HUD-1, a form required for any federally related closing. All expenses must be itemized to arrive at the exact amount of cash required from the buyer and the net proceeds to the seller. These include prorated items—those prepaid by the sellers for which they must be reimbursed and expenses the seller has incurred but for which the buyer will be charged.

How the Closing Statement Works

The completion of a **closing statement** involves an accounting of the parties' debits and credits. A **debit** is an amount that a party owes and must pay at closing. A **credit** is an amount entered in a person's favor—an amount that has already been paid, an amount being reimbursed, or an amount the buyer promises to pay in the form of a loan.

A *debit* is an amount *to be paid* by the buyer or seller; a *credit* is an amount *payable to* the buyer or seller.

To determine the amount a buyer needs at closing, the buyer's debits are totaled. Any expenses and prorated amounts for items prepaid by the seller are added to the purchase price. The buyer's credits are then totaled. These include the earnest money (already paid), the balance of the loan the buyer obtains or assumes, and the seller's share of any prorated items the buyer will pay in the future. (See Table 23.2.) Finally, the total of the buyer's credits is subtracted from the total debits to arrive at the actual amount of cash the buyer must bring to closing. Usually, the buyer brings a cashier's or certified check.

TABLE 23.2

Credits and Debits

Item	Credit to Buyer	Debit to Buyer	Credit to Seller	Debit to Seller	Prorated
Principal amount of new mortgage	✗				
Payoff of existing mortgage				✗	
Unpaid principal balance if assumed mortgage	✗			✗	
Accrued interest on existing assumed mortgage	✗			✗	✗
Tenant's security deposit	✗			✗	
Purchase-money mortgage	✗			✗	
Unpaid water and other utility bills	✗			✗	✗
Buyer's earnest money	✗				
Selling price of property		✗	✗		
Fuel oil on hand (valued at current market price)		✗	✗		✗
Prepaid insurance and tax reserve for mortgage assumed by buyer		✗	✗		✗
Refund to seller of prepaid water charges and similar utility expenses		✗	✗		✗
Accrued general real estate taxes	✗			✗	✗

Note: This chart is based on generally applicable practices. Please note that closing practices may be different in your state.

A similar procedure is followed to determine how much money the seller actually will receive. The seller's debits and credits are each totaled. The credits include the purchase price plus the buyer's share of any prorated items that the seller has prepaid. The seller's debits include expenses, the seller's share of prorated items to be paid later by the buyer, and the balance of any mortgage loan or other lien that the seller pays off. Finally, the total of the seller's debits is subtracted from the total credits to arrive at the amount the seller will receive.

Broker's commission   The responsibility for paying the broker's commission will have been determined by previous agreement. If the broker is the agent for the seller, the seller normally is responsible for paying the commission. If an agency agreement exists between a broker and the buyer, or if two agents are involved, one for the seller and one for the buyer, the commission may be distributed as an expense between both parties or according to some other arrangement.

Attorney's fees   If either of the parties' attorneys will be paid from the closing proceeds, that party will be charged with the expense in the closing statement. This expense may include fees for the preparation or review of documents or for representing the parties at settlement.

Recording expenses   The seller usually pays for recording charges (filing fees) necessary to clear all defects and furnish the purchaser with a marketable title. Items customarily charged to the seller include the recording of release deeds or satisfaction of mortgages, quitclaim deeds, affidavits, and satisfaction of mechanics' liens. The buyer pays for recording charges that arise from the actual transfer of title. Usually, such items include recording the deed that conveys title to the purchaser and a mortgage or deed of trust executed by the buyer.

Transfer tax   Most states require some form of transfer tax, conveyance fee, or tax stamps on real estate conveyances. This expense is most often borne by the seller, although customs vary. In addition, many cities and local municipalities charge transfer taxes. Responsibility for these charges varies according to local practice.

| In Illinois |

In Illinois, state and county transfer taxes are usually paid by the seller in accordance with most sales contracts. Local ordinances usually establish which party is responsible for paying municipal transfer taxes. ■

Title expenses   Responsibility for title expenses varies according to local custom. In most areas, the seller is required to furnish evidence of good title and pay for the title search. If the buyer's attorney inspects the evidence or if the buyer purchases a title insurance policy, the buyer is charged for the expense.

| In Illinois |

Because the seller usually is required by the contract to furnish evidence of good title, the seller customarily pays for the owner's title insurance policy. The buyer customarily pays for the lender's policy, which ensures that the lender has a valid first lien. ■

Loan fees   The discussion of loan fees becomes even more critical with the new good-faith estimate form associated with the new HUD-1 form. For a new loan, the lender generally charges an origination fee and possibly discount points if the borrower wants a below-market interest rate. These lender charges for taking, underwriting, and processing the loan application, including points and origination fees, may not increase prior to closing. If they do, the lender may elect to reissue a new GFE, thereby triggering a three-day waiting period to closing (to allow the buyer time to "shop" for a new loan) or to "correct" the problem with a reimbursement within 30 days of closing. If the buyer assumes the seller's existing financing, the buyer may be required to pay an assumption fee. Also, under the terms of some mortgage loans, the seller may be required to pay a prepayment charge or penalty for paying off the mortgage loan before its due date.

Tax reserves and insurance reserves (escrow or impound accounts)   Most mortgage lenders require that borrowers provide reserve funds or escrow accounts to pay future real estate taxes and insurance premiums. A borrower starts the account at closing by depositing funds to cover at least the amount of unpaid real estate taxes from the date of lien to the end of the current month. (The buyer receives a credit from the seller at closing for any unpaid taxes.) Afterward, an amount equal to one month's portion of the estimated taxes is included in the borrower's monthly mortgage payment.

The borrower is responsible for maintaining adequate fire or hazard insurance as a condition of the mortgage loan. Generally, the first year's premium is paid in full at closing. An amount equal to one month's premium is paid after that. The borrower's monthly loan payment includes the principal and interest on the loan, plus one-twelfth of the estimated taxes and insurance (PITI). The taxes and insurance are held by the lender in the escrow or impound account until the bills are due.

IN PRACTICE   RESPA permits lenders to maintain a cushion equal to one-sixth of the total estimated amount of annual taxes and insurance. However, if state law or mortgage documents allow for a smaller cushion, the lesser amount prevails.

Appraisal fees   The purchaser usually pays the appraisal fees. When the buyer obtains a mortgage, it is customary for the lender to require an appraisal, and the buyer bears the cost. If the fee is paid at the time of the loan application, it is reflected on the closing statement as already having been paid.

Survey fees   The purchaser who obtains new mortgage financing customarily pays the survey fees. The sales contract may require the seller to furnish a survey.

In Illinois

Most real estate contracts in Illinois require that the seller furnish a current survey to the buyer. As a result, the expense of preparing a survey usually is borne by the seller. ■

Additional fees   An FHA borrower owes a lump sum for payment of the *mortgage insurance premium* (MIP) if it is not financed as part of the loan. A VA mortgagor pays a funding fee directly to the VA at closing. If a conventional loan carries private mortgage insurance, the buyer prepays one year's insurance premium at closing.

Accounting for Expenses

Expenses paid out of the closing proceeds are debited only to the party making the payment. Occasionally, an expense item, such as an escrow fee, a settlement fee, or a transfer tax, may be shared by the buyer and the seller. In this case, each party is debited for its share of the expense.

■ PRORATIONS

Most closings involve the division of financial responsibility between the buyer and seller for such items as loan interest, taxes, rents, fuel, and utility bills. These allowances are called **prorations.** Prorations are necessary to ensure that expenses are divided fairly between the seller and the buyer. For example, the seller may owe current taxes that have not been billed; the buyer would want this settled at the closing. Where taxes must be paid in advance, the seller is entitled to a rebate at the closing. If the buyer assumes the seller's existing mortgage or deed of trust, the seller usually owes the buyer an allowance for accrued interest through the date of closing.

> *Accrued items* = buyer credits
> *Prepaid items* = seller credits

Accrued items such as water bills, Illinois real estate taxes, and interest on an assumed mortgage that is paid in arrears are expenses to be prorated that are owed by the seller but later will be paid by the buyer. The seller therefore pays for these items by giving the buyer credits for them at closing.

Prepaid items, such as fuel oil in a tank, are expenses to be prorated that have been prepaid by the seller but not fully used up. They are therefore credits to the seller.

The Arithmetic of Prorating

Accurate prorating involves four considerations:

■ Nature of the item being prorated
■ Whether it is an accrued item that requires the determination of an earned amount
■ Whether it is a prepaid item that requires the determination of an unearned amount (that is, a refund to the seller)
■ What arithmetic processes must be used

The computation of a proration involves identifying a yearly charge for the item to be prorated, then dividing by 12 to determine a monthly charge for the item. Usually, it is also necessary to identify a daily charge for the item by dividing the monthly charge by the number of days in the month. These smaller portions then are multiplied by the number of months or days in the prorated time period to determine the accrued or unearned amount that will be figured in the settlement.

Using this general principle, there are two methods of calculating prorations:

- The yearly charge is divided by a 360-day year (commonly called a *statutory*, or *banking, year*), or 12 months of 30 days each.
- The yearly charge is divided by 365 (366 in a leap year) to determine the daily charge. Then the actual number of days in the proration period is determined, and this number is multiplied by the daily charge.

In Illinois

A third method, the *statutory month variation*, is also acceptable in Illinois. In this method, the yearly charge is divided by 12 to determine a monthly amount. The monthly charge then is divided by the actual number of days in the month in which the closing occurs. This final number is the daily charge for that month. ■

The final proration figure will vary slightly, depending on which computation method is used. The final figure also varies according to the number of decimal places to which the division is carried. All of the computations in this chapter are computed by carrying the division to three decimal places. The third decimal place is rounded off to cents only after the final proration figure is determined.

Accrued Items

When the real estate tax is levied for the calendar year and is payable during that year or in the following year, the accrued portion is for the period from January 1 through the date of closing. If the current tax bill has not yet been issued, the parties must agree on an estimated amount based on the previous year's bill and any known changes in assessment or tax levy for the current year.

Sample proration calculation   Assume a sale is to be closed on September 17. Current real estate taxes of $1,200 are to be prorated. A 360-day year is used. The accrued period, then, is 8 months and 17 days. First determine the prorated cost of the real estate tax per month and day:

$$\frac{\$100 \text{ per month}}{12)\$1,200} \qquad \frac{\$3.333 \text{ per day}}{30)\$100.000}$$
$$\text{months} \qquad\qquad \text{days}$$

Next, multiply these figures by the accrued period and add the totals to determine the prorated real estate tax:

$$\begin{array}{lll} \$100 & \$\ \ 3.333 & \$800.000 \\ \underline{\times\ \ 8 \text{ months}} & \underline{\times\ 17 \text{ days}} & \underline{+\ 56.661} \\ \$800 & \$56.661 & \$856.661 \end{array}$$

Thus, the accrued real estate tax for 8 months and 17 days is $856.66 (rounded off to two decimal places after the final computation). This amount represents the seller's accrued earned tax. It will be a credit to the buyer and a debit to the seller on the closing statement.

To compute this proration using the actual number of days in the accrued period, the following method is used: The accrued period from January 1 to September

17 runs 260 days (January's 31 days plus February's 28 days and so on, plus the 17 days of September).

$1,200 tax bill ÷ 365 days = $3.288 per day
$3.288 × 260 days = $854.880, or $854.88

While these examples show proration as of the date of settlement, the agreement of sale may require otherwise. For instance, a buyer's possession date may not coincide with the settlement date. In this case, the parties could prorate according to the date of possession.

Prepaid Items

A tax proration could be a prepaid item in some locations. Because real estate taxes may be paid in the early part of the year, a tax proration calculated for a closing that takes place later in the year must reflect that the seller has already paid the tax. For example, in the preceding problem, suppose that all taxes had been paid. The buyer, then, would have to reimburse the seller; the proration would be credited to the seller and debited to the buyer.

In figuring the tax proration, it is necessary to ascertain the number of future days, months, and years for which taxes have been paid. The formula commonly used for this purpose is as follows:

	Years	Months	Days
Taxes paid to (Dec. 31, end of tax year)	201X	12	30
Date of closing (Sept. 17, 201X)	201X	−9	−17
Period for which tax must be returned to seller (in "prepay" locale)		3	13

With this formula (using the statutory-month method), we can find the amount the buyer will reimburse the seller for the portion of the real estate tax already paid for time the buyer will live in the house. The prepaid period, as determined using the formula for prepaid items, is 3 months and 13 days. Three months at $100 per month equals $300, and 13 days at $3.333 per day equals $43.329. Add days and months to arrive at $343.329, or $343.33 credited to the seller and debited to the buyer. Where taxes are paid in arrears (2011 is paid in 2012), as in Illinois, the roles reverse (buyer credit, seller debit), but the math is essentially the same.

Sample prepaid item calculation One example of a prepaid item is a water bill. Assume that the water is billed in advance by the city without using a meter. The six months' billing is $60 for the period ending October 31. The sale is to be closed on August 3. Because the water bill is paid to October 31, the prepaid time must be computed. Using a 30-day basis, the time period is the 27 days left in August plus 2 full months: $60 ÷ 6 = $10 per month. For one day, divide $10 by 30, which equals $0.333 per day. The prepaid period is 2 months and 27 days, so

27 days   × $ 0.333 per day = $8.991
2 months × $10   = $20
                                         $28.991, or $28.99

This is a prepaid item; it is credited to the seller and debited to the buyer on the closing statement.

To figure this based on the actual days in the month of closing, the following process would be used:

$10 per month ÷ 31 days in August	=	$0.323 per day
August 4 through August 31	=	28 days
28 days × $0.323	=	$9.044
2 months × $10	=	$20
$9.044 + $20	=	$29.044, or $29.04

General Rules for Prorating

The rules or customs governing the computation of prorations for the closing of a real estate sale vary greatly from state to state. The following are some general guidelines for preparing the closing statement:

- In most states, the seller owns the property on the day of closing, and prorations or apportionments usually are made to and including the day of closing. In a few states, however, it is provided specifically that the buyer owns the property on the closing date. In that case, adjustments are made as of the day preceding the day on which title is closed.
- Mortgage interest, general real estate taxes, water taxes, insurance premiums, and similar expenses usually are computed by using 360 days in a year and 30 days in a month. However, the rules in some areas provide for computing prorations on the basis of the actual number of days in the calendar month of closing. The agreement of sale should specify which method will be used.
- Accrued or prepaid general real estate taxes usually are prorated at the closing. When the amount of the current real estate tax cannot be determined definitely, the proration is usually based on the last obtainable tax bill.
- Special assessments for municipal improvements such as sewers, water mains, or streets usually are paid in annual installments over several years, with annual interest charged on the outstanding balance of future installments. The seller normally pays the current installment, and the buyer assumes all future installments. The special assessment installment generally is not prorated at the closing. A buyer may insist that the seller allow the buyer a credit for the seller's share of the interest to the closing date. The agreement of sale may address the manner in which special assessments will be handled at settlement.
- Rents are usually adjusted on the basis of the actual number of days in the month of closing. It is customary for the seller to receive the rents for the day of closing and to pay all expenses for that day. If any rents for the current month are uncollected when the sale is closed, the buyer often agrees by a separate letter to collect the rents if possible and remit the pro rata share to the seller.
- Security deposits made by tenants to cover the last month's rent of the lease or to cover the cost of repairing damage caused by the tenant generally are transferred by the seller to the buyer.

Real estate taxes   Proration of real estate taxes varies, depending on how the taxes are paid in the area where the real estate is located. In some states, real estate taxes are paid in advance; that is, if the tax year runs from January 1 to December 31, taxes for the coming year are due on January 1. In this case, the seller, who has prepaid a year's taxes, should be reimbursed for the portion of the year remaining after the buyer takes ownership of the property. In other areas, taxes are paid in arrears, on December 31 for the year just ended. In this case, the buyer should be credited by the seller for the time the seller occupied the property. Sometimes, taxes are due during the tax year, partly in arrears and partly in advance; sometimes they are payable in installments. It gets even more complicated if city, state, school, and other property taxes start their tax years in different months. Whatever the case may be in a particular transaction, the licensee should understand how the taxes will be prorated.

In Illinois   Taxes in Illinois are paid in arrears. The buyer must be credited for any taxes that still will be paid in the future for time in the "past" (i.e., up until closing) when the seller occupied the property. If an unpaid installment based on last year has been billed, this specific amount is credited to the buyer and debited to the seller. The buyer must be credited with the current year's taxes to time of closing because those taxes will not be paid until *next* year (again by the buyer/new owner). Consequently, the seller is debited accordingly, to the date of close, and a proration (and often a tax estimate based on last year's tax) is necessary for this latter figure.

The following formula may be used in Illinois:

Last annual tax bill ÷ 360 × Number of days from January 1 to closing date = Tax proration: the amount *seller owes buyer.* ∎

Mortgage loan interest   On almost every mortgage loan the interest is paid in arrears, so buyer and seller must understand that the mortgage payment due on June 1, for example, includes interest due for the month of May. Thus, the buyer who assumes a mortgage on May 31 and makes the June payment pays for the time the seller occupied the property and should be credited with a month's interest. On the other hand, the buyer who places a new mortgage loan on May 31 may be pleasantly surprised to hear that he will not need to make a mortgage payment until a month later.

In Illinois   The terms of some assumed mortgage loans provide that interest is charged at the beginning of the month (in advance); without this provision, interest is always charged at the end of the month (in arrears). When the interest on the existing mortgage to be assumed by the buyer is charged at the beginning of the month, the *unearned portion* (that is, the part that is prepaid from the date of closing to the end of the month) must be credited to the seller and debited to the buyer. When the mortgage interest is charged at the end of the month, the *earned portion* of the mortgage interest through the date of closing is an accrued expense, debited to the seller and credited to the buyer. ∎

■ SAMPLE CLOSING STATEMENT

Settlement computations take many possible forms. A sample transaction follows, using the RESPA Uniform Settlement Statement (HUD-1) in Figure 23.4. Because customs differ in various parts of the country, the way certain expenses are charged in some locations may be different from the illustration.

Basic Information of Offer and Sale

A couple lists their home at 3045 North Racine Avenue in Riverdale, East Dakota, with a real estate brokerage. The listing price is $237,000, and possession will take place within two weeks after all parties have signed the contract. Under the terms of the listing agreement, the sellers agree to pay the licensee a commission of 6 percent of the sales price.

The offer to purchase   On May 18, the real estate brokerage company submits a contract offer to the seller from the buyer, who resides at 22 King Court, Riverdale. The buyer offers $230,000, with earnest money and down payment of $46,000. The buyer expects to obtain a conventional 30-year fixed-rate mortgage for 80 percent of the purchase price and, therefore, will not need private mortgage insurance (PMI). The seller accepts the buyer's offer on May 29, with a closing date of June 15.

In this real estate transaction, taxes are paid in arrears. Taxes for this year, estimated at last year's figure of $3,450, have not been paid. According to the contract, prorations will be made on the basis of 30 days in a month.

The buyer's loan application   The buyer's new loan is for $184,000. The buyer is offered three interest rate options: 4.5 percent with 2 points, 5 percent with 1 point, or 6 percent with ½ point. The rate options would be listed on page 3 of the good-faith estimate (See Figure 23.3.). The buyer's locked-in rate of 6 percent is good until 4 pm June 20, 201X. The buyer will pay interest on the loan for the remainder of the month of closing: 15 days at $25.56 per day ($383.40). The first full payment, including July's interest, will be due on August 1. The loan origination fee is $2,300 and 1 discount point ($1,840). In connection with this loan, the buyer must provide a flood certification ($12), a survey ($395), and a pest inspection ($65).

In connection with this loan, the buyer will be charged $500 to have the property appraised. The buyer is only charged for the credit report at the time of loan application, but the appraisal fee must be paid upon loan approval and before closing. Both items are noted as POC on the settlement statement.

The cost of a one-year hazard insurance policy is $3 per $1,000 of appraised value ($230,000 ÷ 1,000 × 3 = $690) and will be paid at closing to the insurance company. The lender requires a reserve account for property taxes and insurance. The buyer's initial deposit is 7/12 of the anticipated county real estate tax of $3,450 ($2,012.50) and two months of the insurance policy ($115). The lender requires that 1/12 of the annual insurance premium ($57.50) and taxes ($287.50) be included in the monthly payment.

FIGURE 23.4

Uniform Settlement Statement (HUD-1)

OMB Approval No. 2502-0265

A. Settlement Statement (HUD-1)

B. Type of Loan			
1. ☐ FHA 2. ☐ RHS 3. ☐ Conv. Unins. 4. ☐ VA 5. ☐ Conv. Ins.	6. File Number:	7. Loan Number:	8. Mortgage Insurance Case Number:

C. Note: This form is furnished to give you a statement of actual settlement costs. Amounts paid to and by the settlement agent are shown. Items marked "(p.o.c.)" were paid outside the closing; they are shown here for informational purposes and are not included in the totals.

D. Name & Address of Borrower:	E. Name & Address of Seller:	F. Name & Address of Lender:
G. Property Location:	H. Settlement Agent:	I. Settlement Date:
	Place of Settlement:	

J. Summary of Borrower's Transaction		K. Summary of Seller's Transaction	
100. Gross Amount Due from Borrower		**400. Gross Amount Due to Seller**	
101. Contract sales price		401. Contract sales price	
102. Personal property		402. Personal property	
103. Settlement charges to borrower (line 1400)		403.	
104.		404.	
105.		405.	
Adjustment for items paid by seller in advance		**Adjustments for items paid by seller in advance**	
106. City/town taxes to		406. City/town taxes to	
107. County taxes to		407. County taxes to	
108. Assessments to		408. Assessments to	
109.		409.	
110.		410.	
111.		411.	
112.		412.	
120. Gross Amount Due from Borrower		**420. Gross Amount Due to Seller**	
200. Amounts Paid by or in Behalf of Borrower		**500. Reductions In Amount Due to Seller**	
201. Deposit or earnest money		501. Excess deposit (see instructions)	
202. Principal amount of new loan(s)		502. Settlement charges to seller (line 1400)	
203. Existing loan(s) taken subject to		503. Existing loan(s) taken subject to	
204.		504. Payoff of first mortgage loan	
205.		505. Payoff of second mortgage loan	
206.		506.	
207.		507.	
208.		508.	
209.		509.	
Adjustments for items unpaid by seller		**Adjustments for items unpaid by seller**	
210. City/town taxes to		510. City/town taxes to	
211. County taxes to		511. County taxes to	
212. Assessments to		512. Assessments to	
213.		513.	
214.		514.	
215.		515.	
216.		516.	
217.		517.	
218.		518.	
219.		519.	
220. Total Paid by/for Borrower		**520. Total Reduction Amount Due Seller**	
300. Cash at Settlement from/to Borrower		**600. Cash at Settlement to/from Seller**	
301. Gross amount due from borrower (line 120)		601. Gross amount due to seller (line 420)	
302. Less amounts paid by/for borrower (line 220)	( )	602. Less reductions in amount due seller (line 520)	( )
303. Cash ☐ From ☐ To Borrower		**603. Cash** ☐ To ☐ From Seller	

The Public Reporting Burden for this collection of information is estimated at 35 minutes per response for collecting, reviewing, and reporting the data. This agency may not collect this information, and you are not required to complete this form, unless it displays a currently valid OMB control number. No confidentiality is assured; this disclosure is mandatory. This is designed to provide the parties to a RESPA covered transaction with information during the settlement process.

FIGURE 23.4

Uniform Settlement Statement (HUD-1) (continued)

L. Settlement Charges			Paid From Borrower's Funds at Settlement	Paid From Seller's Funds at Settlement
700. Total Real Estate Broker Fees				
Division of commission (line 700) as follows:				
701. $	to			
702. $	to			
703. Commission paid at settlement				
704.				
800. Items Payable in Connection with Loan				
801. Our origination charge	$	(from GFE #1)		
802. Your credit or charge (points) for the specific interest rate chosen $		(from GFE #2)		
803. Your adjusted origination charges		(from GFE A)		
804. Appraisal fee to		(from GFE #3)		
805. Credit report to		(from GFE #3)		
806. Tax service to		(from GFE #3)		
807. Flood certification		(from GFE #3)		
808.				
900. Items Required by Lender to Be Paid in Advance				
901. Daily interest charges from to @ $ /day		(from GFE #10)		
902. Mortgage insurance premium for months to		(from GFE #3)		
903. Homeowner's insurance for years to		(from GFE #11)		
904.				
1000. Reserves Deposited with Lender				
1001. Initial deposit for your escrow account		(from GFE #9)		
1002. Homeowner's insurance months @ $ per month $				
1003. Mortgage insurance months @ $ per month $				
1004. Property taxes months @ $ per month $				
1005. months @ $ per month $				
1006. months @ $ per month $				
1007. Aggregate Adjustment –$				
1100. Title Charges				
1101. Title services and lender's title insurance		(from GFE #4)		
1102. Settlement or closing fee	$			
1103. Owner's title insurance		(from GFE #5)		
1104. Lender's title insurance	$			
1105. Lender's title policy limit $				
1106. Owner's title policy limit $				
1107. Agent's portion of the total title insurance premium	$			
1108. Underwriter's portion of the total title insurance premium	$			
1200. Government Recording and Transfer Charges				
1201. Government recording charges		(from GFE #7)		
1202. Deed $ Mortgage $ Releases $				
1203. Transfer taxes		(from GFE #8)		
1204. City/County tax/stamps Deed $ Mortgage $				
1205. State tax/stamps Deed $ Mortgage $				
1206.				
1300. Additional Settlement Charges				
1301. Required services that you can shop for		(from GFE #6)		
1302.	$			
1303.	$			
1304.				
1305.				
1400. Total Settlement Charges (enter on lines 103, Section J and 502, Section K)				

FIGURE 23.4

Uniform Settlement Statement (HUD-1) (continued)

Comparison of Good Faith Estimate (GFE) and HUD-1 Charges		Good Faith Estimate	HUD-1
Charges That Cannot Increase	**HUD-1 Line Number**		
Our origination charge	# 801		
Your credit or charge (points) for the specific interest rate chosen	# 802		
Your adjusted origination charges	# 803		
Transfer taxes	#1203		

Charges That in Total Cannot Increase More Than 10%		Good Faith Estimate	HUD-1
Government recording charges	# 1201		
	#		
	#		
	#		
	#		
	#		
	#		
	#		
Total			
Increase between GFE and HUD-1 Charges		$ or %	

Charges That Can Change		Good Faith Estimate	HUD-1
Initial deposit for your escrow account	#1001		
Daily interest charges	# 901 $ /day		
Homeowner's insurance	# 903		
	#		
	#		
	#		

Loan Terms

Your initial loan amount is	$
Your loan term is	years
Your initial interest rate is	%
Your initial monthly amount owed for principal, interest, and and any mortgage insurance is	$ includes ☐ Principal ☐ Interest ☐ Mortgage Insurance
Can your interest rate rise?	☐ No. ☐ Yes, it can rise to a maximum of %. The first change will be on and can change again every after . Every change date, your interest rate can increase or decrease by %. Over the life of the loan, your interest rate is guaranteed to never be **lower** than % or **higher** than %.
Even if you make payments on time, can your loan balance rise?	☐ No. ☐ Yes, it can rise to a maximum of $.
Even if you make payments on time, can your monthly amount owed for principal, interest, and mortgage insurance rise?	☐ No. ☐ Yes, the first increase can be on and the monthly amount owed can rise to $. The maximum it can ever rise to is $.
Does your loan have a prepayment penalty?	☐ No. ☐ Yes, your maximum prepayment penalty is $.
Does your loan have a balloon payment?	☐ No. ☐ Yes, you have a balloon payment of $ due in years on .
Total monthly amount owed including escrow account payments	☐ You do not have a monthly escrow payment for items, such as property taxes and homeowner's insurance. You must pay these items directly yourself. ☐ You have an additional monthly escrow payment of $ that results in a total initial monthly amount owed of $. This includes principal, interest, any mortgage insurance and any items checked below: ☐ Property taxes ☐ Homeowner's insurance ☐ Flood insurance ☐ ☐

Note: If you have any questions about the Settlement Charges and Loan Terms listed on this form, please contact your lender.

Closing costs   The unpaid balance of the seller's mortgage as of June 1, 201X, will be $115,500. Payments are $825 per month, with interest at 7 percent per year on the unpaid balance.

The seller submits evidence of title in the form of a title insurance binder at a cost of $30. The title insurance policy, to be paid by the buyer at the time of closing, costs an additional $540, which includes $395 for the lender's coverage and $145 for the owner's coverage. The seller must pay $20 for the recording of two instruments to clear defects in the seller's title. The seller must also pay an attorney's fee of $600 for preparing the deed and for legal representation, which will be paid from the closing proceeds.

The buyer has agreed to pay for the state transfer tax stamps in the amount of $115 ($0.50 per $500 of the sales price or fraction thereof). The buyer must pay an attorney's fee of $500 for examining the title evidence and for legal representation. The buyer must pay $20 to record the deed and $50 to record the mortgage.

Computing the prorations and charges   The following list illustrates the various steps in computing the prorations and other amounts to be included in the settlement to this point:

- Closing date: June 15
- Commission: 6% (0.06) × $230,000 sales price = $13,800
- Seller's mortgage interest: 7% (0.07) × $115,400 principal due after June 1 payment = $8,078 interest per year; $8,078 ÷ 360 days = $22.44 interest per day; 15 days of accrued interest to be paid by the seller × $22.44 = $336.60 interest owed by the seller; $115,400 + $336.60 = $115,736.60 payoff of seller's mortgage
- Real estate taxes (estimated at $3,450): $3,450 ÷ 12 months = $287.50 per month; $287.50 ÷ 30 days = $9.58 per day
- The earned period, from January 1 to and including June 15 (5 months, 15 days): $287.50 × 5 months = $1,437.50; $9.58 × 15 days = $143.70; $1437.50 + $143.70 = $1,581.20 seller owes buyer
- Transfer tax ($0.50 per $500 of consideration, or fraction thereof): $230,000 ÷ $500 = $460; $460 × $0.50 = $230 transfer tax owed by seller
- Buyer's tax reserve payment: $2,012.50 paid to separate account (7/12 of the anticipated county real estate taxes of $3,450)
- Buyer's one-year hazard insurance payment: $3 per $1,000 of appraised value ($230,000 ÷ 1,000 × 3 = $690 paid in advance to insurance company)
- Buyer's first full payment, including July's interest due (15 days × $25.56 = $383.40) on August 1
- The seller's loan payoff is $115,736.60. The seller must pay an additional seller's fee of $25 to record the mortgage release, as well as $100 for a pest inspection and $200 for a survey, as negotiated between the parties.

The Uniform Settlement Statement

The **Uniform Settlement Statement (HUD-1)** used for most residential closings consists of three pages. Sections J and K on the first page are a summary of the borrower's and the seller's transactions. At the bottom of the first page, line

303 indicates the total amount of cash due from (or to) the borrower. Line 603 indicates the cash to (or from) the seller.

The second page itemizes the settlement charges to be paid from the borrower's funds or from the seller's funds at settlement. A number of the costs to the buyer must correlate to the GFE that the buyer received within three business days of loan application. All items in the borrower's column are added up and transferred to line 103 on the first page. All items in the seller's column are added up and transferred to line 502 on the first page.

■ SUMMARY

Closing a real estate sale involves both title procedures and financial matters. The clients' real estate agents are often present at the closing to see that the sale is actually concluded, to lend support to valued clients, and to account for the earnest money deposit (which has normally been held in escrow by the real estate office).

Closings must be reported to the IRS on Form 1099-S.

The federal Real Estate Settlement Procedures Act (RESPA) requires disclosure of all settlement costs when a residential real estate purchase is financed by a federally related mortgage loan. RESPA requires lenders to use a Uniform Settlement Statement to detail the financial particulars of a transaction.

The actual amount to be paid by a buyer at closing is computed on a closing statement form or settlement statement. This lists the sales price, earnest money deposit, and all adjustments and prorations due between buyer and seller. The purpose of this statement is to determine the net amount due the seller at closing. The buyer reimburses the seller for prepaid items like unused taxes or fuel oil. The seller credits the buyer for bills the seller owes, but the buyer will have to pay accrued items such as unpaid water bills.

The closing statement is customarily prepared by the buyer's lender, the lender's agent, or the seller's lawyer. State and county transfer taxes are usually paid by the seller, who also customarily pays for the survey and the owner's title insurance policy. The buyer usually pays for the lender's title insurance policy.

In Illinois

Illinois permits proration by the statutory month variation method.

Real estate taxes in Illinois are paid in arrears; in other words, in the year after they become a lien. ■

CHAPTER 23 QUIZ

1. All encumbrances and liens shown on the report of title other than those waived or agreed to by the purchaser and listed in the contract must be removed so that the title can be delivered free and clear. The removal of such encumbrances is the duty of the
   a. buyer.
   b. seller.
   c. broker.
   d. title company.

2. Legal title *ALWAYS* passes from seller to buyer
   a. on the date of execution of the deed.
   b. when the closing statement has been signed.
   c. when the deed is placed in escrow.
   d. when the deed is delivered.

3. Which of the following would a lender generally require at the closing?
   a. Title insurance
   b. Market value appraisal
   c. Application
   d. Credit report

4. The RESPA Uniform Settlement Statement (HUD-1) must be used to illustrate all settlement charges for
   a. every real estate transaction.
   b. transactions financed by VA and FHA loans only.
   c. residential transactions financed by federally related mortgage loans.
   d. all transactions involving commercial property.

5. The principal amount of a purchaser's new mortgage loan is a
   a. credit to the seller.
   b. credit to the buyer.
   c. debit to the seller.
   d. debit to the buyer.

6. The earnest money left on deposit with the seller's real estate broker is a
   a. credit to the seller.
   b. credit to the buyer.
   c. balancing factor.
   d. debit to the buyer.

7. If a seller collected rent of $1,400, payable in advance, from an attic tenant on August 1, which of the following is *TRUE* at the closing on August 15?
   a. Seller owes buyer $1,400
   b. Buyer owes seller $1,400
   c. Seller owes buyer $700
   d. Buyer owes seller $700

8. Security deposits should be listed on a closing statement as a credit to the
   a. buyer.
   b. seller.
   c. lender.
   d. broker.

9. A building was purchased for $285,000, with 10 percent down and a loan for the balance. If the lender charged the buyer two discount points, how much cash did the buyer need to come up with at closing if the buyer incurred no other costs?
   a. $31,700
   b. $28,500
   c. $33,630
   d. $30,200

   $285K \times 10\% = 28500$
   $256,500 \times 2\% = 5130$

10. A buyer of a $300,000 home has paid $22,000 as earnest money and has a loan commitment for 70 percent of the purchase price. How much more cash does the buyer need to bring to the closing, provided the buyer has no closing costs?
    a. $68,000
    b. $30,000
    c. $58,000
    d. $61,600

    Loan 210K

11. At closing, the listing broker's commission usually is shown as a
    a. credit to the seller.
    b. credit to the buyer.
    c. debit to the seller.
    d. debit to the buyer.

12. At the closing of a real estate transaction, the person performing the settlement gave the buyer a credit for certain accrued items. These items were
    a. bills relating to the property that have already been paid by the seller.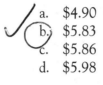
    b. bills relating to the property that will have to be paid by the buyer.
    c. all of the seller's real estate bills.
    d. all of the buyer's real estate bills.

13. The purpose of the Real Estate Settlement Procedures Act (RESPA) is to
    a. make sure buyers do not borrow more than they can repay.
    b. make real estate licensees more responsive to buyers' needs.
    c. help buyers know how much money is required.
    d. see that buyers know all settlement costs.

14. The document that provides borrowers with general information about settlement costs, RESPA provisions, and the Uniform Settlement Statement is the
    a. HUD-1 form.
    b. special information booklet.
    c. good-faith estimate of settlement costs.
    d. closing statement.

15. Which charge noted on the Good Faith Estimate (GFE) must be the same or less than the charge noted on the HUD-1 form?
    a. Cost of settlement service when the lender selects the provider
    b. Lender charges for taking and underwriting the loan
    c. Cost of settlement services when the borrower elects the provider from the list provided by the lender
    d. Cost of homeowners' insurance

16. Under the new Mortgage Disclosure Improvement Act (MDIA), a lender must extend the closing how many days if the APR is increased prior to closing?
    a. Two
    b. Three
    c. Four
    d. Five

In Illinois

17. If the annual real estate taxes on a property were $2,129 last year, what would be the per diem amount for prorations this year using the actual-number-of-days method?
    a. $4.90
    b. $5.83
    c. $5.86
    d. $5.98

18. In Illinois, which party customarily prepares the closing statement?
    a. Buyer's attorney
    b. Listing broker
    c. Buyer's lender
    d. Seller's lender

19. Which of the following formulas BEST expresses the statutory month variation method of calculating a daily prorated charge for an annual prepaid expense?
    a. (Total charge ÷ 12) ÷ Actual days in month of closing = Daily prorated charge
    b. (Total charge ÷ 360) × 12 = Daily prorated charge
    c. (Total charge ÷ 360) × Actual days in month of closing = Daily prorated charge
    d. (Total charge ÷ 365 = y) (y ÷ 12) × Actual days in closing month = Daily prorated charge

20. In Illinois, which party usually pays the state and county transfer taxes?
    a. Buyer
    b. Buyer pays state taxes; seller pays county and municipal taxes
    c. Whichever party is specified in the local ordinance
    d. Seller

Math FAQs

Answers to Your Most Frequently
Asked Real Estate Math Questions

Measurement Problems

■ WHAT ARE LINEAR MEASUREMENTS?

Linear measurement is line measurement. When the terms

■ *per foot,*
■ *per linear foot,*
■ *per running foot,* or
■ *per front foot*

are used, you are being asked to determine the *total length* of the object whether measured in a straight line, crooked line, or curved line. The abbreviation for feet is '. Thus, 12 feet could be written as 12'. The abbreviation for inches is ". Thus, 12 inches could be written as 12".

■ WHAT DOES THE PHRASE "FRONT FOOT" REFER TO?

When the term *per front foot* is used, you are dealing with the number of units on the **frontage** of a lot. The frontage is normally the street frontage, but it could be the water frontage if the lot is on a river, lake, or ocean. If two dimensions are given for a tract of land, the first dimension given is the frontage if the dimensions are not labeled.

■ HOW DO I CONVERT ONE KIND OF LINEAR MEASUREMENT TO ANOTHER?

12 inches = 1 foot

Inches ÷ 12 = Feet (144 inches ÷ 12 = 12 feet)
Feet × 12 = Inches (12 feet × 12 = 144 inches)

36 inches = 1 yard

Inches ÷ 36 = Yards (144 inches ÷ 36 = 4 yards)
Yards × 36 = Inches (4 yards × 36 = 144 Inches)

3 feet = 1 yard

Feet ÷ 3 = Yards (12 feet ÷ 3 = 4 yards)
Yards × 3 = Feet (4 yards × 3 = 12 feet)

5,280 feet = 1 mile

> Feet ÷ 5,280 = Miles (10,560 feet ÷ 5,280 = 2 miles)
> Miles × 5,280 = Feet (2 miles × 5,280 = 10,560 feet)

16.5 feet = 1 rod

> Feet ÷ 16.5 = Rods (82.5 feet ÷ 16.5 = 5 rods)
> Rods × 16.5 = Feet (5 rods × 16.5 = 82.5 feet)

320 rods = 1 mile

> Rods ÷ 320 = Miles (640 rods ÷ 320 = 2 miles)
> Miles × 320 = Rods (2 miles × 320 = 640 rods)

■ **FOR EXAMPLE**   A rectangular lot is 50 feet × 150 feet. The cost to fence this lot is priced per linear/running foot. How many linear/running feet will be used to calculate the price of the fence?

	150'	
50'		50'
	150'	

50 Feet + 150 Feet + 50 Feet + 150 Feet = 400 Linear/Running Feet

400 Linear/Running Feet is the answer.

■ **FOR EXAMPLE**   A parcel of land that fronts on Interstate 90 in Elgin, Illinois, is for sale at $5,000 per front foot. What will it cost to purchase this parcel of land if the dimensions are 150' by 100'?

150 is the frontage because it is the first dimension given.

150 Front Feet × $5,000 = $750,000 Cost

$750,000 Cost is the answer.

■ HOW DO I SOLVE FOR AREA MEASUREMENT?

Area is the two-dimensional surface of an object. Area is quoted in *square units* or in *acres*. We will look at calculating the area of squares, rectangles, and triangles. Squares and rectangles are four-sided objects. All four sides of a square are the same. Opposite sides of a rectangle are the same. A triangle is a three-sided object. The three sides of a triangle can be the same dimension or three different dimensions.

MATH TIP   When two dimensions are given, we assume it to be a rectangle unless told otherwise.

■ HOW DO I CONVERT ONE KIND OF AREA MEASUREMENT TO ANOTHER?

144 square inches = 1 square foot

Square Inches ÷ 144 = Square Feet (14,400 square inches ÷ 144 = 100 square feet)
Square Feet × 144 = Square Inches ÷ (100 square feet × 144 = 14,400 square inches)

1,296 square inches = 1 square yard

Square Inches ÷ 1,296 = Square Yards (12,960 ÷ 1,296 = 10 square yards)
Square Yards × 1,296 = Square Inches (10 square yards × 1,296 = 12,960 square yards)

9 square feet = 1 square yard

Square Feet ÷ 9 = Square Yards (90 square feet ÷ 9 = 10 square yards)
Square Yards × 9 = Square Feet (10 square yards × 9 = 90 square feet)

43,560 square feet = 1 acre

Square Feet ÷ 43,560 = Acres (87,120 ÷ 43,560 = 2 acres)
Acres × 43,560 = Square Feet (2 acres × 43,560 = 87,120 square feet)

640 acres = 1 section = 1 square mile

Acres ÷ 640 = Sections (Square Miles) (1,280 acres ÷ 640 = 2 sections)
Sections (Square Miles) × 640 = Acres (2 sections × 640 = 1,280 acres)

■ HOW DO I DETERMINE THE AREA OF A SQUARE OR RECTANGLE?

Length × Width = **Area of a Square or Rectangle**

■ **FOR EXAMPLE**   How many square feet are in a room 15'6" × 30'9"?

Remember, we must use like dimensions, so the inches must be converted to feet.

6" ÷ 12 = 0.5' + 15' = 15.5' wide
9" ÷ 12 = 0.75' + 30' = 30.75' long
30.75' × 15.5' = 476.625 Square Feet

476.625 Square Feet is the answer.

■ **FOR EXAMPLE**   If carpet costs $63 per square yard to install, what would it cost to carpet the room in the previous example?

476.625 Square Feet ÷ 9 = 52.958333 Square Yards × $63 per Square Yard = $3,336.375 or $3,336.38 rounded

$3,336.38 Carpet Cost is the answer.

■ **F O R   E X A M P L E**   How many acres are there in a parcel of land that measures 450' × 484'?

484' × 450' = 217,800 Square Feet ÷ 43,560 = 5 Acres

5 Acres of Land is the answer.

■ HOW DO I DETERMINE THE AREA OF A TRIANGLE?

½ Base   ×   Height   =   Area of a Triangle

or

Base   ×   Height   ÷   2   =   Area of a Triangle

■ **F O R   E X A M P L E**   How many square feet are contained in a triangular parcel of land that is 400 feet on the base and 200 feet high?

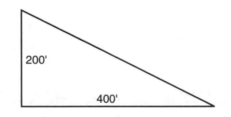

400' × 200' ÷ 2 = 40,000 Square Feet

40,000 Square Feet is the answer.

■ **F O R   E X A M P L E**   How many acres are in a three-sided tract of land that is 300' on the base and 400' high?

300' × 400' ÷ 2 = 60,000 Square Feet ÷ 43,560 = 1.377 Acres

1.377 Acres is the answer.

■ HOW DO I SOLVE FOR VOLUME?

Volume is the space inside a three-dimensional object. Volume is quoted in cubic units. We will look at calculating the volume of boxes and triangular prisms.

■ HOW DO I CONVERT FROM ONE KIND OF VOLUME MEASUREMENT TO ANOTHER?

1,728 cubic inches = 1 cubic foot

Cubic Inches ÷ 1,728 = Cubic Feet
(17,280 cubic inches ÷ 1,728 = 10 cubic feet)

Cubic Feet × 1,728 = Cubic Inches
(10 cubic feet × 1,728 = 17,280 cubic inches)

46,656 cubic inches = 1 cubic yard

Cubic Inches ÷ 46,656 = Cubic Yards
(93,312 cubic inches ÷ 46,656 = 2 cubic yards)

Cubic Yards × 46,656 = Cubic Inches
(2 cubic yards × 46,656 = 93,312 cubic inches)

27 cubic feet = 1 cubic yard

Cubic Feet ÷ 27 = Cubic Yards (270 cubic feet ÷ 27 = 10 cubic yards)
Cubic Yards × 27 = Cubic Feet (10 cubic yards × 27 = 270 cubic feet)

■ HOW DO I DETERMINE THE VOLUME OF A ROOM?

For purposes of determining volume, think of a room as if it were a box.

Length × Width × Height = **Volume of a Box**

■ **FOR EXAMPLE**   A building is 500 feet long, 400 feet wide, and 25 feet high. How many cubic feet of space are in this building?

500' × 400' × 25' = 5,000,000 Cubic Feet

5,000,000 Cubic Feet is the answer.

■ **FOR EXAMPLE**   How many cubic yards of concrete would it take to build a sidewalk measuring 120 feet long; 2 feet, 6 inches wide; and 3 inches thick?

6" ÷ 12' = .5' + 2' = 2.5' Wide

3" ÷ 12' = .25' Thick

120' × 2.5' × .25' = 75 Cubic Feet ÷ 27 = 2.778 Cubic Yards (rounded)

2.778 Cubic Yards is the answer.

■ HOW DO I DETERMINE THE VOLUME OF A TRIANGULAR PRISM?

The terms *A-frame*, *A-shaped*, or *gable roof* on an exam describe a triangular prism.

½ Base × Height × Width = **Volume of a Triangular Prism**

or

Base × Height × Width ÷ 2 = **Volume of a Triangular Prism**

■ **FOR EXAMPLE** An A-frame cabin in the mountains is 50 feet long and 30 feet wide. The cabin is 25 feet high from the base to the highest point. How many cubic feet of space does this A-frame cabin contain?

50' × 30' × 25' ÷ 2 = 18,750 Cubic Feet

18,750 Cubic Feet is the answer.

■ **FOR EXAMPLE** A building is 40 feet by 25 feet with a 10-foot-high ceiling. The building has a gable roof that is 8 feet high at the tallest point. How many cubic feet are in this structure, including the roof?

40' × 25' × 10' = 10,000 Cubic Feet in the Building

40' × 25' × 8' ÷ 2 = 4,000 Cubic Feet in the Gable Roof

10,000 Cubic Feet + 4,000 Cubic Feet = 14,000 Total Cubic Feet

14,000 Cubic Feet is the answer.

Fractions, Decimals, and Percentages

■ WHAT ARE THE PARTS OF A FRACTION?

The **denominator** shows the number of equal parts in the whole or total. The **numerator** shows the number of those parts with which you are working. In the example below, the whole or total has been divided into eight equal parts, and you have seven of those equal parts.

$\dfrac{7}{8}$ $\dfrac{\text{Numerator}}{\text{Denominator}}$ $\dfrac{\text{(Top Number)}}{\text{(Bottom Number)}}$

■ WHAT IS MEANT BY A "PROPER FRACTION"?

⅞ is an example of a **proper fraction.** In a proper fraction the numerator is less than the whole or less than 1.

■ WHAT IS AN "IMPROPER FRACTION"?

$\dfrac{11}{8}$ $\dfrac{\text{Numerator}}{\text{Denominator}}$

This is an example of an **improper fraction.** In an improper fraction, the numerator is greater than the whole or greater than 1.

■ WHAT IS A MIXED NUMBER?

11½ is a **mixed number.** You have a whole number plus a fraction. A mixed number is greater than the whole or greater than 1.

■ HOW DO I MULTIPLY FRACTIONS?

When multiplying fractions, the numerator is multiplied by the numerator, and the denominator by the denominator. Let's start with an easy question. What is ½ × ¾?

First multiply the numerators (top numbers) $1 \times 3 = 3$; then the denominators (bottom numbers) $2 \times 4 = 8$. Thus, $\frac{1}{2} \times \frac{3}{4} = \frac{3}{8}$.

What is $4\frac{2}{3} \times 10\frac{5}{8}$? The first step is to convert the whole number 4 into thirds. This is done by multiplying $4 \times 3 = 12$. (Multiply the whole number, 4, by the denominator of the fraction, 3.) Thus, the whole number 4 is equal to $\frac{12}{3}$.

$4\frac{2}{3}$ is equal to $\frac{12}{3} + \frac{2}{3} = \frac{14}{3}$.

The next step is to convert the whole number 10 into eighths. This is done by multiplying $10 \times 8 = 80$. (Multiply the whole number, 10, by the denominator of the fraction, 8.) Thus, the whole number 10 is equal to $\frac{80}{8}$. $\frac{80}{8} + \frac{5}{8} = \frac{85}{8}$.

So, what is $\frac{14}{3} \times \frac{85}{8}$? First multiply $14 \times 85 = 1{,}190$. Then, $3 \times 8 = 24$. $\frac{1{,}190}{24} = 49.58$. (That is, $1{,}190 \div 24 = 49.58$.)

An easier way to work the question is to convert the fractions to decimals.

$\frac{2}{3}$ is equal to $2 \div 3$ or .67.

$\frac{5}{8}$ is equal to $5 \div 8$ or .625.

$4.67 \times 10.625 = 49.62$.

Whenever working with fractions or decimals equivalents, the answers will be close but not exact.

■ HOW DO I DIVIDE BY FRACTIONS?

Dividing by fractions is a two-step process. What is $\frac{3}{4} \div \frac{1}{4}$?

First, invert the $\frac{1}{4}$ to $\frac{4}{1}$. Then, multiply $\frac{3}{4} \times \frac{4}{1} = \frac{12}{4}$. Finally, $12 \div 4 = 3$.

You may also convert $\frac{3}{4}$ to the decimal .75 and $\frac{1}{4}$ to the decimal .25.

$.75 \div .25 = 3$. (There are three .25 in .75.)

What is $100\frac{7}{8} \div \frac{3}{4}$?

$100 \times 8 = 800$.

$800 + 7 = \frac{807}{8}$.

$\frac{3}{4}$ is inverted to $\frac{4}{3}$.

$\frac{807}{8} \times \frac{4}{3} = 807 \times 4 = 3{,}228$; $8 \times 3 = 24$. $\frac{3{,}228}{24} = 3{,}228 \div 24 = 134.5$

Or $7 \div 8 = .875$ and $3 \div 4 = .75$.

$100.875 \div .75 = 134.50$.

■ HOW DO I CONVERT FRACTIONS TO DECIMALS?

Fractions will sometimes be used in real estate math problems. Since calculators may be used on most licensing examinations, it is best to convert fractions to decimals.

M A T H   T I P   To convert a fraction to a decimal, the top number, called the numerator, is divided by the bottom number, the denominator.

For example:

$$\tfrac{7}{8} = 7 \div 8 = \mathbf{0.875}$$

$$\tfrac{11}{8} = 11 \div 8 = \mathbf{1.375}$$

$$11\tfrac{1}{2} = 1 \div 2 = 0.5 + 11 = \mathbf{11.5}$$

Once fractions have been converted to decimals, other calculations can be easily completed using the calculator. Note that many calculators automatically add the zero before the decimal point as in the first two examples above.

■ HOW DO I ADD OR SUBTRACT DECIMALS?

Line up the decimals, add or subtract, and bring the decimal down in the answer. You may add zeros if necessary as place holders. For example, 0.5 is the same as 0.50, or .5.

```
   0.50          8.20
  +3.25         -0.75
   3.75          7.45
```

M A T H   T I P   When you use a calculator, the decimal will be in the correct place in the answer.

0.5 + 3.25 = 3.75, and 8.2 − 0.75 = 7.45

■ HOW DO I MULTIPLY DECIMALS?

Multiply the numbers, then count the number of decimal places in each number. Next, start with the last number on the right and move the decimal the total number of decimal places to the left in the answer.

Multiply as you normally would to get the 1,500, then count the four decimal places in the numbers (.20 and .75). In the 1,500, start at the last zero on the right, and count four decimal places to the left. The decimal is placed to the left of the **1**.

```
     0.20
   × 0.75
     100
     140
   .1500 or .15
```

Note: When you use a calculator, the decimal will be in the correct place in the answer (0.2 × 0.75 = **0.15**).

■ HOW DO I DIVIDE DECIMALS?

Divide the **dividend** (the number being divided) by the **divisor** (the number you are dividing by) and bring the decimal in the dividend straight up in the **quotient** (answer). If the divisor has a decimal, move the decimal to the right of the divisor and move the decimal the same number of places to the right in the dividend. Now divide as stated above.

$$
\begin{array}{r}
= 0.75 \\
2\overline{)1.5} \\
\underline{1.4} \\
10 \\
\underline{10} \\
0
\end{array}
\qquad
0.5\overline{)15.5} \;=\;
\begin{array}{r}
= 31 \\
5\overline{)155.} \\
\underline{15} \\
05 \\
\underline{5} \\
0
\end{array}
$$

M A T H   T I P   When you use a calculator, you can have a decimal in the divisor and the decimal will be in the correct place in the answer.

1.5 ÷ 2 = 0.75, and 15.5 ÷ 0.5 = 31

■ WHAT IS A PERCENTAGE?

Percent (%) means *per hundred* or *per hundred parts*. The whole or total always represents 100 percent.

5% = 5 parts of 100 parts, or 5 ÷ 100 = 0.05 or ¹⁄₂₀

75% = 75 parts of 100 parts, or 75 ÷ 100 = 0.75 or ¾

120% = 120 parts of 100 parts, or 120 ÷ 100 = 1.2 or 1⅕

■ HOW CAN I CONVERT A PERCENTAGE TO A DECIMAL?

Move the decimal *two places* to the *left* and *drop* the % sign.

20% = 2 ÷ 100 = 0.20 or **0.2**

1% = 1 ÷ 100 = **0.01**

12¼% = 12.25%, 12.25 ÷ 100 = **0.1225**

See Figure 2.1.

FIGURE 2.1

**Converting Decimal
to Percentage and
Percentage to Decimal**

Decimal to Percentage

.10 ⟹ **10%**

Move decimal **two places right**
to find the percentage

Percentage to Decimal

.10 ⟸ **10%**

Move percentage **two places left**
to find the decimal

■ HOW CAN I CONVERT A DECIMAL TO A PERCENTAGE?

Move the decimal *two places* to the *right* and *add* the % sign.

0.25 = **25%**

0.9 = **90%**

0.0875 = **8.75%** or 8¾%

See Figure 2.1.

■ HOW DO I MULTIPLY BY PERCENTAGES?

$500 \times 25\% = 500 \times {}^{25}\!/_{100} = {}^{12,500}\!/_{100} = $ **125**

or

$500 \times 25\% = 125$, or $500 \times .25 = $ **125**

■ HOW DO I DIVIDE BY PERCENTAGES?

$100 \div 5\% = 100 \div 5/100 = 100 \times {}^{100}\!/_{5} = {}^{10,000}\!/_{5} = $ **2,000**

or

$100 \div 5\% = 2,000$, or $100 \div .05 = $ **2,000**

■ IS THERE ANY EASY WAY TO REMEMBER HOW TO SOLVE PERCENTAGE PROBLEMS?

The following three formulas are important for solving all percentage problems:

TOTAL × RATE = PART
PART ÷ RATE = TOTAL
PART ÷ TOTAL = RATE

There is a simple way to remember how to use these formulas:

■ *MULTIPLY* when PART is UNKNOWN.
■ *DIVIDE* when PART is KNOWN.
■ When you divide, always enter PART into the calculator first.

■ WHAT IS THE "T-BAR" METHOD?

The T-Bar is another tool to use to solve percentage problems. For some people, the "three-formula method" is more difficult to remember than the visual image of a *T*.

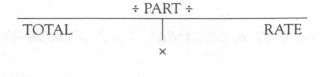

÷ PART ÷

TOTAL | RATE

×

■ HOW DO I USE THE T-BAR?

The procedure for using the T-Bar is as follows:

1. Enter the two *known* items in the correct places.
2. If the line between the two items is *vertical*, you *multiply* to equal the missing item.
3. If the line between the two items is *horizontal*, you *divide* to equal the missing item. When you divide, the top **(Part)** always goes into the calculator first and is divided by the bottom **(Total** or **Rate).**

See Figure 2.2.

The following examples show how the T-Bar can be used to solve percentage problems. These examples deal with discounts because everyone can relate to buying an item that is on sale. Later we will see how the T-Bar can be used for many types of real estate problems.

■ **FOR EXAMPLE**   A man purchased a new suit that was marked $500. How much did he save if it was on sale for 20 percent off?

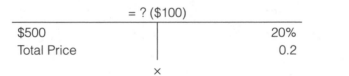

= ? ($100) $100 Saved

$500 | 20%
Total Price | 0.2

×

$500 × 20% (.20) = $100

How much did the man pay for the suit?

$500 Total Price – $100 Discount   **$400 Paid**
or
100% Total Price – 20% Discount = 80% Paid

FIGURE 2.2

Using the T-Bar

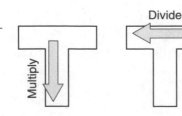

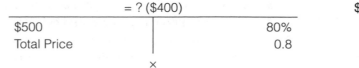

$500 × 80% (.80) = $400

■ **FOR EXAMPLE**   A woman paid $112.50 for a dress that was reduced 25 percent. How much was it originally marked?

100% Original Price – 25% Discount = 75% Paid

$112.50 Paid ÷	
= ? ($150)	75%
	0.75

$150 Original Price

$112.50 ÷ 75% (.75) = $150

■ **FOR EXAMPLE**   A man paid $127.50 for a coat that was marked down from the original price of $150. What percent of discount did the man receive?

$150 Original Price – $127.50 Discount Price = $22.50 Discount

÷ 22.50 Discount	
$150	= ? (0.15 = 15%)
Original Price	

15% Discount

$22.50 ÷ $150 = .15 or 15%

or

÷ $127.50 Paid	
$150	= ? (0.85 = 85%)

85% of Original Price Paid

$127.50 ÷ $150 = .85 or 85%

85% was the percent paid; therefore

100% Original Price – 85% Paid = **15% Discount**

■ WORD PROBLEMS CAN BE TRICKY. HOW SHOULD I DEAL WITH THEM?

There are five important steps that must be taken to solve word problems.

1. **Read** the problem carefully and completely. Never touch the calculator until you have read the entire problem.
2. **Analyze** the problem to determine what is being asked, what facts are given that will be needed to solve for the answer, and what facts are given that will not be needed to solve for the answer. Eliminate any information and/or numbers given that are not needed to solve the problem. Take the remaining information and/or numbers and determine which will be needed first, second, etc., depending on the number of steps it will take to solve the problem.

3. **Choose** the proper formula(s) and steps it will take to solve the problem.

4. **Insert** the known elements and calculate the answer.

5. **Check** your answer to be sure you keyed in the numbers and functions properly on your calculator. Be sure you finished the problem. For example, when the problem asks for the share of the commission a sponsored licensee would receive, do not stop at the sponsoring broker's share of the commission and mark that answer just because it is one of the choices.

Percentage Problems

■ HOW DO I WORK COMMISSION PROBLEMS?

The full **commission** is a percentage of the sales price unless stated differently in the problem. Remember that full commission rates, commission splits between real estate companies, and commission splits between the sponsoring broker and her sponsored licensees are always negotiable. Always read a problem carefully to determine the correct rate(s).

÷ Full Commission ÷	
Sales Price	Full Commission Rate

×

Sales Price × Full Commission Rate = **Full Commission**
Full Commission ÷ Full Commission Rate = **Sales Price**
Full Commission ÷ Sales Price = **Full Commission Rate**

÷ Broker's Share of the Commission ÷	
Full Commission	% of Full Commission to the Broker

×

Full Commission	×	% of Full Commission to the Broker	=	**Broker's Share of the Commission**
Broker's Share of the Commission	÷	% of Full Commission to the Broker	=	**Full Commission**
Broker's Share of the Commission	÷	Full Commission	=	**% of Full Commission to the Broker**

÷ Sponsored Licensee's Share of the Commission ÷	
Broker's Share of the Commission	Sponsored Licensee's % of the Broker's Share

×

Broker's Share of the Commission	×	Sponsored Licensee's % of the Broker's Share	=	**Sponsored Licensee's Share of the Commission**
Sponsored Licensee's Share of the Commission	÷	Sponsored Licensee's % of the Broker's Share	=	**Broker's Share of the Commission**
Sponsored Licensee's Share of the Commission	÷	Broker's Share of the Commission	=	**Sponsored Licensee's % of the Broker's Share**

■ **FOR EXAMPLE**   A seller listed a home for $200,000 and agreed to pay a full commission rate of 5 percent. The home sold four weeks later for 90 percent of the list price. The listing real estate company agreed to give the selling real estate company 50 percent of the commission. The listing broker paid her sponsored licensee 50 percent of her share of the commission, and the selling broker paid his sponsored licensee 60 percent of his share of the commission. How much commission did the selling salesperson receive?

= $180,000 Sales Price

$200,000 List Price		90% or 0.9
	×	

$200,000 × 90% (.90) = $180,000

= $9,000 Full Commission

$180,000 Sales Price		5% or 0.05
	×	

$180,000 × 5% (.05) = $9,000

= $4,500 Broker's Share of the Commission

$9,000 Full Commission		50% or 0.5
	×	

$9,000 × 50% (.50) = $4,500

= $2,700 Selling Sponsored Licensee's
Commission

$4,500	60%
Broker's Share of Comm.	or 0.6

×

4,500 × 60% (.60) = $2,700

$2,700 Selling Sponsored Licensee's Commission is the answer.

■ WHAT IS MEANT BY "SELLER'S DOLLARS AFTER COMMISSION"?

The first deduction from the sales price is the real estate commission. For example, if a house sold for $100,000 and a 7 percent commission was paid, that means $7,000 was paid in commissions. The seller still has 93 percent or $93,000. The seller's dollars after commission will be used to pay the seller's other expenses and hopefully will leave some money for the seller.

÷ Seller's Dollars after Commission ÷

Sales Price	Percent after Commission

×

Remember, the sales price is 100%. Thus 100% − Commission % = Percent after Commission.

Sales Price	×	Percent after Commission	=	**Seller's Dollars after Commission**
Seller's Dollars after Commission	÷	Percent after Commission	=	**Sales Price**
Seller's Dollars after Commission	÷	Sales Price	=	**Percent after Commission**

■ **FOR EXAMPLE**   After deducting $5,850 in closing costs and a 5 percent broker's commission, the sellers received their original cost of $175,000 plus a $4,400 profit. What was the sales price of the property?

$5,850 Closing Costs + $175,000 Original Cost + $4,400 Profit = $185,250 Seller's Dollars after Commission

100% Sales Price − 5% Commission = 95% Percent after Commission

$185,250 Seller's Dollars after Commission ÷

=	**$195,000**	95%
	Sales Price	or 0.95

$185,250 ÷ 95% (.95) = $195,000

$195,000 Sales Price is the answer.

■ HOW DO I DETERMINE INTEREST?

Interest is the cost of using money. The amount of interest paid is determined by the agreed-on annual interest rate, the amount of money borrowed (loan amount) or amount of money still owed (loan balance), and the period of time the money is held. When a lender grants a loan for real estate, the loan-to-value (LTV) ratio is the percentage of the sales price or appraised value, whichever is less, that the lender is willing to lend.

÷ Loan Amount ÷

Sales Price or Appraised Value (whichever is less)	Loan-to-Value Ratio (LTV)

×

Sales Price or Appraised Value (whichever is less)	×	Loan-to-Value Ratio (LTV)	=	**Loan Amount**
Loan Amount	÷	Loan-to-Value Ratio (LTV)	=	**Sales Price or Appraised Value** (whichever is less)
Loan Amount	÷	Sales Price or Appraised Value (whichever is less)	=	**Loan-to-Value Ratio** (LTV)

÷ Annual Interest ÷

Loan Amount (Principal)	Annual Interest Rate

×

Loan Amount	×	Annual Interest Rate	=	**Annual Interest**
Annual Interest	÷	Annual Interest Rate	=	**Loan Amount**
Annual Interest	÷	Loan Amount	=	**Annual Interest Rate**

■ **FOR EXAMPLE**   A parcel of real estate sold for $335,200. The lender granted a 90 percent loan at 7.5 percent for 30 years. The appraised value on this parcel was $335,500. How much interest is paid to the lender in the first monthly payment?

= $301,680 Loan Amount

$335,200 Sales Price	90% or 0.9

×

$335,200 × 90% (.90) = $301,680 Loan

= $22,626 Annual Interest

$301,680		7.5%
Loan Amount		or 0.075

×

$301,680 × 7.5% (.075) = $22,626

$22,626 Annual Interest ÷ 12 Months = $1,885.50 Monthly Interest

$1,885.50 Interest in the First Monthly Payment is the answer.

■ HOW DO I DETERMINE MONTHLY PRINCIPAL AND INTEREST PAYMENTS?

A **loan payment factor** can be used to calculate the monthly principal and interest (PI) payment on a loan. The factor represents the monthly principal and interest payment to amortize a $1,000 loan and is based on the annual interest rate and the term of the loan.

See Table 16.3 for a loan factor chart found on page 357.

Loan Amount ÷ $1,000 × Loan Payment Factor = **Monthly PI Payment**

Monthly PI Payment ÷ Loan Payment Factor = **Loan Amount**

■ **FOR EXAMPLE**   If the lender in the previous example uses a loan payment factor of $6.99 per $1,000 of loan amount, what will be the monthly PI (principal and interest) payment?

$301,680 Loan Amount ÷ $1,000 × $6.99 = $2,108.74 Monthly PI Payment

$2,108.74 Monthly PI Payment is the answer.

■ HOW DO I WORK PROBLEMS ABOUT POINTS?

One **point** equals 1 percent of the loan amount.

÷ Amount for Points ÷		
Loan Amount		Points Converted to a Percent

×

Loan Amount	×	Points Converted to a Percent	=	**Amount for Points**
Amount of Points	÷	Points Converted to a Percent	=	**Loan Amount**
Amount of Points	÷	Loan Amount	=	**Points Converted to a Percent**

■ **FOR EXAMPLE**   The lender will charge 3½ loan discount points on an
$80,000 loan. What will be the total amount due?

$$= \$2,800 \text{ for Points}$$

$80,000 Loan Amount		3.5% or 0.035
	×	

$80,000 × 3.5% (.035) = $2,800

$2,800 for Points is the answer.

■ HOW DO I DETERMINE PROFIT?

A **profit** is made when we sell something for more than we paid for it. If we sell
something for less than we paid, we have suffered a **loss.**

Sales Price – Cost = Profit

	÷ Profit ÷	
Cost		Percent of Profit
	×	

Cost	×	Percent of Profit	=	**Profit**
Profit	÷	Percent of Profit	=	**Cost**
Profit	÷	Cost	=	**Percent of Profit**
Cost	+	Profit	=	**Sales Price**

	÷ Sales Price ÷	
Cost		Percent Sold of Cost
	×	

(100% Cost + % Profit = % Sales Price)

Cost	×	Percent Sold of Cost	=	**Sales Price**
Sales Price	÷	Percent Sold of Cost	=	**Cost**
Sales Price	÷	Cost	=	**Percent Sold of Cost**

■ **FOR EXAMPLE**   Your home listed for $285,000 and sold for $275,000, which gave you a 10 percent profit over the original cost. What was the original cost?

100% Original Cost + 10% Profit = 110% Sales Price

$275,000 Sales Price	
= $250,000	110%
Original Cost	or 1.1

×

$275,000 ÷ 110% (1.1) = $250,000

$250,000 Original Cost is the answer.

■ WHAT IS THE DIFFERENCE BETWEEN APPRECIATION AND DEPRECIATION?

Appreciation is increase in value. **Depreciation** is decrease in value. Both are based on the original cost. We will only cover the **straight-line method**, which is what should be used in math problems unless you are told differently. The straight-line method means that the value is increasing (appreciating) or decreasing (depreciating) the same amount each year. The amount of appreciation or depreciation is based on the original cost.

■ HOW DO I SOLVE APPRECIATION PROBLEMS?

÷ Annual Appreciation ÷

Cost	Annual Appreciation Rate

×

Cost	×	Annual Appreciation Rate	=	**Annual Appreciation**
Annual Appreciation	÷	Annual Appreciation Rate	=	**Cost**
Annual Appreciation	÷	Cost	=	**Annual Appreciation Rate**

Annual Appreciation Rate × Number of Years = **Total Appreciation Rate**
100% Cost + Total Appreciation Rate = **Today's Value as a Percent**

	÷ Today's Value (Appreciated Value) ÷	
Cost		Today's Value as a Percent

$\times$

Cost	$\times$	Today's Value as a Percent	$=$	**Today's Value (Appreciated Value)**
Today's Value (Appreciated Value)	$\div$	Today's Value as a Percent	$=$	**Cost**
Today's Value (Appreciated Value)	$\div$	Cost	$=$	**Today's Value as a Percent**

■ HOW DO I SOLVE DEPRECIATION PROBLEMS?

	÷ Annual Depreciation ÷	
Cost		Annual Depreciation Rate

$\times$

Cost	$\times$	Annual Depreciation Rate	$=$	**Annual Depreciation**
Annual Depreciation	$\times$	Annual Depreciation Rate	$=$	**Cost**
Annual Depreciation	$\div$	Cost	$=$	**Annual Depreciation Rate**

Annual Depreciation Rate × Number of Years = **Total Depreciation Rate**
100% Cost ÷ Total Depreciation Rate = **Today's Value as a Percent**

	÷ Today's Value (Depreciated Value) ÷	
Cost		Today's Value as a Percent

$\times$

Cost	$\times$	Today's Value as a Percent	$=$	**Today's Value (Depreciated Value)**
Today's Value (Depreciated Value)	$\div$	Today's Value as a Percent	$=$	**Cost**

$$\text{Today's Value (Depreciated Value)} \div \text{Cost} = \textbf{Today's Value as a Percent}$$

■ **FOR EXAMPLE**   Seven years ago you purchased a piece of real estate for $93,700, including the original cost of the land, which was $6,700. What is the total value of the land today using an appreciation rate of 8 percent per year?

8% Appreciation per Year × 7 Years = 56% Total Appreciation Rate
100% cost + 56% Appreciation = 156% Today's Value

= $10,452 Today's Value	
$6,700 Original Cost	156% or 1.56

×

$6,700 × 156% (1.56) = $10,452

$10,452 Today's Value is the answer.

■ **FOR EXAMPLE**   The value of a house without the lot at the end of four years is $132,300. What was the original cost of the house if the yearly rate of depreciation was 2.5 percent?

2.5% depreciation per year × 4 years = 10% total depreciation rate

100% cost − 10% depreciation = 90% today's value

$132,300 Today's Value ÷	
$147,000 Original Cost	90% or 0.9

×

$132,300 ÷ 90% (.90) = $147,000

$147,000 Original Cost is the answer.

■ HOW DO I ESTIMATE VALUE FOR INCOME-PRODUCING PROPERTIES?

When appraising income-producing property, the value is estimated by using the annual net operating income (NOI) and the current market rate of return or capitalization rate. Annual scheduled gross income is adjusted for vacancies and credit losses to arrive at the annual effective gross income. The annual operating expenses are deducted from the annual effective gross income to arrive at the annual NOI. Vacancy/credit loss is usually expressed as a percentage of the scheduled gross.

$$\text{Annual Scheduled Gross Income} - \text{Vacancies and Credit Losses} = \textbf{Annual Effective Gross Income}$$

| Annual Effective Gross Income | − | Annual Operating Expenses | = | **Annual NOI** |

÷ Annual NOI ÷

| Value | | Annual Rate of Return or Annual Capitalization Rate |

×

| Annual NOI | ÷ | Annual Rate of Return | = | **Value** |

| Value | × | Annual Rate of Return | = | **Annual NOI** |

| Annual NOI | ÷ | Value | = | **Annual Rate of Return** |

■ **FOR EXAMPLE** An office building produces $132,600 annual gross income. If the annual expenses are $30,600 and the appraiser estimates the value using an 8.5 percent rate of return, what is the estimated value?

$132,600 Annual Gross Income − $30,600 Annual Expenses = $102,000 Annual NOI

$102,000 Annual NOI ÷

| = $1,200,000 Value | | 8.5% or 0.085 |

×

$102,000 ÷ 8.5% = $1,200,000

$1,200,000 Value is the answer.

The above formulas also can be used for investment problems. The total becomes *original cost* or *investment* instead of value.

■ **FOR EXAMPLE** You invest $335,000 in a property that should produce a 9 percent rate of return. What monthly NOI will you receive?

= $30,150 Annual NOI

| $335,000 Investment | | 9% or 0.09 |

×

$335,000 × 9% (.09) = $30,150

$30,150 Annual NOI ÷ 12 Months = $2,512.50

$2,512.50 Monthly NOI is the answer.

■ HOW DO I SOLVE PROBLEMS INVOLVING PERCENTAGE LEASES?

When establishing the rent to be charged in a lease for retail space, the lease may be a **percentage lease** instead of a lease based on dollars per square foot. In the percentage lease, there is normally a base or minimum monthly rent plus a percentage of the gross sales in excess of an amount set in the lease. The percentage lease also can be set up as a percentage of the total gross sales or of the base/minimum rent, whichever is larger. We shall look at the minimum plus percentage lease only.

$$\text{Gross Sales} \quad - \quad \begin{array}{c}\text{Gross Sales Not}\\ \text{Subject to the}\\ \text{Percentage}\end{array} \quad = \quad \begin{array}{c}\textbf{Gross Sales}\\ \textbf{Subject to the}\\ \textbf{Percentage}\end{array}$$

$$\div \text{ Percentage Rent } \div$$

Gross Sales Subject to the Percentage		% in the Lease
	×	

$$\begin{array}{c}\text{Gross Sales}\\ \text{Subject to the}\\ \text{Percentage}\end{array} \quad \times \quad \text{\% in the Lease} \quad = \quad \textbf{Percentage Rent}$$

$$\text{Percentage Rent} \quad \div \quad \text{\% in the Lease} \quad = \quad \begin{array}{c}\textbf{Gross Sales}\\ \textbf{Subject to the}\\ \textbf{Percentage}\end{array}$$

$$\text{Percentage Rent} \quad \div \quad \begin{array}{c}\text{Gross Sales}\\ \text{Subject to the}\\ \text{Percentage}\end{array} \quad = \quad \textbf{\% in the Lease}$$

$$\text{Percentage Rent} \quad + \quad \begin{array}{c}\text{Base/Minimum}\\ \text{Rent}\end{array} \quad = \quad \textbf{Total Rent}$$

■ **FOR EXAMPLE**   A lease calls for monthly minimum rent of $900 plus 3 percent of annual gross sales in excess of $270,000. What was the annual rent in a year when the annual gross sales were $350,600?

$900 Monthly Minimum Rent × 12 Months = $10,800 Annual Minimum Rent

$350,600 Annual Gross Sales – $270,000 Annual Gross Sales Not Subject to the Percentage = $80,600 Annual Gross Sales Subject to the Percentage

= $2,418 Annual Percentage Rent

$80,600 Annual Gross Subject to the Percentage	3% or 0.03
×	

$80,600 × 3% = $2,418 Annual Percentage Rent
$10,800 Annual Minimum Rent + $2,418 Annual Percentage Rent = $13,218
$13,218 Total Annual Rent is the answer.

Proration Problems

Prorate means to divide proportionately. Some expenses and income may be prorated for the closing of a real estate transaction. We will look at prorating interest on a loan, ad valorem taxes on a property, homeowners' insurance on a property, and rent on income-producing property.

■ WHAT ARE THE DIFFERENT CALENDARS USED FOR PRORATING?

When we prorate, we calculate the number of days owed for the expense or the rental income. The days may be calculated using a *banker's year*, *statutory year*, or *calendar year*. The **banker's year** and **statutory year** are the same because they both contain 12 months with 30 days in each month. The total number of days in both a banker's year and a statutory year is 360 days. The **calendar year** contains 12 months with 28 to 31 days in each month. The total number of days in a calendar year is 365. The total number of days in a calendar *leap* year is 366. The following chart shows the days in each month.

FIGURE 4.1

Proration Calendar

	Banker's or Statutory Year	Calendar Year	Calendar Leap Year
January	30	31	31
February	30	28	29
March	30	31	31
April	30	30	30
May	30	31	31
June	30	30	30
July	30	31	31
August	30	31	31
September	30	30	30
October	30	31	31
November	30	30	30
December	30	31	31
Total days in a year	360	365	366

■ WHAT IS THE DIFFERENCE BETWEEN PRORATING *THROUGH* AND PRORATING *TO* THE DAY OF CLOSING?

In a proration problem, we will be told whether to prorate *through* the day of closing or *to* the day of closing. **This is very important when calculating the days owed.** When we prorate *through* the day of closing, the *seller* is responsible for the day of closing. When we prorate *to* the day of closing, the *buyer* is responsible for the day of closing.

■ HOW DO I CALCULATE PRORATION PROBLEMS?

Once we know the number of days owed, we then need to know the amount of the expense or income per day. We take either the annual amount divided by the total days in the year to get the daily amount or the monthly amount divided by the total days in the month to get the daily amount.

MATH TIP　Be sure you use the correct type of year (banker's or statutory year of 360 days, calendar year of 365 days, or calendar leap year of 366 days) when computing the daily amount.

The final step is to multiply the amount per day by the number of days owed to get the prorated amount.

■ WHAT IS THE DIFFERENCE BETWEEN DEBIT AND CREDIT IN A PRORATION PROBLEM?

To calculate a proration problem, you need to know how expenses and income are posted on the closing statement. **Debit** takes money from a person. **Credit** gives money to a person. (See Figure 4.2.) When the prorated amount involves both the buyer and the seller, there will always be a double entry (i.e., it appears twice, once as a debit to one party and once as a credit to the other party). If the seller owes the buyer, the prorated amount will be debited to the seller and credited to the buyer. If the buyer owes the seller, the prorated amount will be debited to the buyer and credited to the seller. When the prorated amount involves the buyer and someone other than the seller, there will be only a single entry. When the prorated amount involves the seller and someone other than the buyer, there will be only a single entry. We will discuss debits and credits as we learn to prorate each expense.

The five questions to ask when prorating are as follows:

- What calendar do we use?
- Is the expense paid in arrears or in advance?
- Who has or will pay the expense?
- Who has earned or received income?
- When will the expense be paid?

FIGURE 4.2

The Debit/Credit Flow

	Buyer	Seller
Sales Price	DEBIT	CREDIT
Tenants' Security Deposits	CREDIT	DEBIT
Fuel Oil (in tank)	DEBIT	CREDIT
Prorated Accrued Water Bill	CREDIT	DEBIT
Unearned Rents	CREDIT	DEBIT
Tax Reserve Account	DEBIT	CREDIT

Different items are treated differently as credits or debits to the buyer or seller on a closing statement.

■ HOW DO I CALCULATE INTEREST IN A PRORATION PROBLEM?

When a loan is assumed or paid off, the accrued interest for the month of closing must be prorated. Interest is paid in arrears; therefore, the monthly payment made on the first day of the month pays interest for the entire previous month. The payment includes interest *up to but not including* the day of the payment unless specified otherwise. Not all payments are due on the first day of the month; therefore, pay attention when you are told what day the interest has been paid through. The sellers owe unpaid interest (also called accrued, earned, or current interest) from the date of the last payment to or through the closing date.

If the prorations are to be calculated *through* the day of closing, the seller will owe payments *including* the day of closing. If the prorations are to be calculated *to* the day of closing, the seller will *owe up to but not including* the day of closing. Remember to use the correct type of year. A banker's or statutory year has 360 days. A calendar year has 365 days. A calendar leap year has 366 days. When a loan is paid off, unpaid interest is calculated and added to the outstanding loan balance and is a **debit** *to the seller only*. Loan payoff is the sum of the principal balance and the accrued interest. On an assumption of the loan, the interest proration is a **debit** to the *seller* and a **credit** to the *buyer*.

■ **FOR EXAMPLE** A home was purchased on April 4, 2010, for $110,000, and the closing was set for May 8, 2010. The buyer assumed the balance of the seller's $93,600 loan with 11.5 percent interest and monthly payments of $990.29 due on the first day of each month. How much will the interest proration be, using a banker's year and prorating through the day of closing? Who will be debited and who will be credited?

Banker's Year/Statutory Year

Step 1. Find the exact number of days of earned or accrued interest.

Seller owes 8 days (May 1 *through* May 8).

Note: It would be 7 days (8 days minus 1 day) if the problem had said prorate *to* the day of closing.

Step 2.
Find the daily interest charge. Outstanding loan balance ×
Annual interest rate = Annual interest ÷ 360 days per year = Daily interest.

$93,600 × 11.5% (0.115) = $10,764 annual interest ÷ 360 days =
$29.90 daily interest

Step 3.
Compute the total amount of accrued interest. Daily interest × Days owed =
Interest proration.

$29.90 daily interest × 8 days = $239.20

$239.20 debit seller, credit buyer is the answer.

Calendar Year (if the problem had said to use a calendar year)

Step 1. Find the exact number of days of earned or accrued interest.

Seller owes 8 days (May 1 *through* May 8).

Note: It would be 7 days (8 days minus 1 day) if the problem had said prorate *to* the
day of closing.

Step 2.
Find the daily interest charge. Outstanding loan balance × Annual interest rate =
Annual interest ÷ 365 days per year = Daily interest.

$93,600 × 11.5% (0.115) = $10,764 annual interest ÷ 365 days =
$29.49041096 daily interest

Step 3.
Compute the total amount of accrued interest. Daily interest × Days owed =
Interest proration.

$29.49041096 daily interest × 8 days = $235.92 rounded

$235.92 debit seller, credit buyer is the answer.

■ HOW DO I PRORATE TAXES?

Real estate taxes are normally assessed from January 1 through December 31. The
tax rate is *always* applied *to the assessed value of the property* instead of the market
value. Taxes are usually paid in arrears; therefore, the seller will owe the buyer for
accrued taxes from January 1 *through* the day of closing or *to* the day of closing.
The most recent tax bill is used to compute the proration, and this is usually the
past year's tax bill. Remember to use the correct type of year. A banker's or statutory year has 360 days. A calendar year has 365 days. A calendar leap year has 366
days.

If the taxes are paid in arrears, the tax proration will be a **debit** to the *seller* and a **credit** to the *buyer*. If the taxes are paid in advance, the tax proration will be a **debit** to the *buyer* and a **credit** to the *seller*.

■ **FOR EXAMPLE**   The market value of a home is $115,000. For tax purposes, the home is assessed at 90 percent of the market value. The annual tax rate is $2.50 per $100 of assessed value. If the closing is on March 13, 2010, what is the prorated amount? Prorations are calculated through the day of closing and using a statutory year.

Banker's Year/Statutory Year

Step 1.
Find the exact number of days of accrued taxes from the beginning of the tax period (January 1, 2010) up to and including the day of closing (March 13, 2010).

> 2 months (January and February) × 30 days per month = 60 days + 13 days in March
> = 73 days

Note: It would be 72 days (73 days minus 1 day) if the problem had said prorate *to* the day of closing.

Step 2.
Calculate the annual taxes. Market value × Assessment ratio = Assessed value ÷ $100 × Tax rate per hundred = Annual taxes.

> $115,000 × 90% = $103,500 ÷ $100 × $2.50 = $2,587.50 annual taxes

Step 3.
Find the tax amount per day. Annual taxes ÷ 360 days per year = Daily taxes.

> $2,587.50 ÷ 360 days = $7.1875 daily taxes

Step 4.
Compute the prorated tax amount. Daily taxes × Days owed = Tax proration.

> $7.1875 per day × 73 days = $524.69 rounded

> **$524.69 debit seller, credit buyer** is the answer.

Calendar Year (if the problem had said to use a calendar year)

Step 1.
Find the exact number of days of accrued taxes from the beginning of the tax period (January 1, 2010) up to and including the day of closing (March 13, 2010).

> 31 days in January + 28 days in February + 13 days in March = 72 days

Note: It would be 71 days (72 days minus 1 day) if the problem had said prorate *to* the day of closing.

Step 2.
Calculate the annual taxes. Market value × Assessment ratio = Assessed value ÷ $100 × Tax rate per hundred = Annual taxes.

$115,000 × 90% = $103,500 ÷ $100 × $2.50 = $2,587.50 annual taxes

Step 3.
Find the tax amount per day. Annual taxes ÷ 365 days per year = Daily taxes.

$2,587.50 ÷ 365 days = $7.089041096 daily taxes

Step 4.
Compute the prorated tax amount. Daily taxes × Days owed = Tax proration.

$7.089041096 per day × 72 days = $510.41 rounded

$510.41 debit seller, credit buyer is the answer.

■ IS INSURANCE ALWAYS PRORATED?

When buying a home, insurance coverage must be provided by the owners if they have a loan. The buyers normally purchase their own insurance policy. There will *not* be a proration if the buyers purchase a new policy because the sellers will cancel their existing policy effective the day of closing and the buyer's new policy will become effective the day of closing.

■ IF INSURANCE IS PRORATED, HOW DO I CALCULATE IT?

If the insurance company will allow a policy to be assumed and the buyers choose to do so, an insurance proration is necessary. Today, insurance policies are written for one year. The premiums are payable in advance; therefore, the sellers have paid the entire yearly premium. If the policy is transferred to the buyers, the buyers owe the sellers for the unused portion of the policy. If you are to prorate *through* the day of closing, the buyers owe the sellers from the day after closing until the expiration of the policy. If you are to prorate *to* the day of closing, the buyers owe the sellers starting with the day of closing until the expiration of the policy. Insurance policies become effective at 12:01 AM and expire exactly one year later at 12:01 AM; therefore, no coverage is counted on the day of expiration of the insurance policy. Remember to use the correct type of year. A banker's or statutory year has 360 days. A calendar year has 365 days. A calendar leap year has 366 days. The insurance proration will be a **debit** to the *buyer* and a **credit** to the *seller*.

■ **FOR EXAMPLE**   A one-year fire insurance policy expires on August 20, 2010. The total premium for this policy was $800 and was paid in full in 2009. The house was sold, and the closing date was set for January 25, 2010. The proration is to be calculated through the day of closing using a banker's year. What will be the total credit to the seller to transfer the insurance policy to the buyer?

Banker's Year/Statutory Year

Step 1.
Compute the number of days of insurance coverage that the buyer assumed.

	30	days in January
–	25	day of closing
	5	days left in January
+	180	days (6 months × 30 days per month/February–July)
+	19	days coverage in August
	204	days left on the policy

Note: It would be 205 days (204 days plus 1 day) if the problem had said prorate *to* the day of closing.

Step 2. Compute the amount of the policy cost per day. Annual insurance premium ÷ 360 days per year = Daily insurance.

$800 insurance premium ÷ 360 days = $2.2222222 daily insurance

Step 3.
Calculate what the buyer owes. Daily insurance × Days left on the policy = Insurance proration.

$2.2222222 daily insurance × 204 days = $453.33 rounded

$453.33 credit seller, debit buyer is the answer.

Calendar Year (if the problem had said to use a calendar year)

Step 1.
Compute the number of days of insurance coverage that the buyer assumed.

	31	days in January
–	25	day of closing
	6	days left in January
+	28	days in February
+	31	days in March
+	30	days in April
+	31	days in May
+	30	days in June
+	31	days in July
+	19	days coverage in August
	206	days left on the policy

Note: It would be 207 days (206 days plus 1 day) if the problem had said prorate *to* the day of closing.

Step 2.

Compute the amount of the policy cost per day. Annual insurance premium ÷ 365 days per year = Daily insurance.

$800 Insurance premium ÷ 365 days = $2.1917808 daily insurance

Step 3.

Calculate what the buyer owes. Daily insurance × Days left on the policy = Insurance proration.

$2.1917808 daily insurance × 206 days = $451.51 rounded

$451.51 credit seller, debit buyer is the answer.

■ HOW DO I PRORATE RENT?

When prorating rents, the amount of rent collected for the month of closing is the only amount prorated. The seller owes the buyer for the unearned rent start-ing with the day after closing through the end of the month if you are prorating *through* the day of closing. The seller owes the buyer for the unearned rent start-ing with the day of closing through the end of the month if you are prorating *to* the day of closing. If security deposits are being held by the seller, they are not prorated; therefore, the entire amount of the security deposits are transferred to the buyer. Always use the actual number of days in the month of closing for rent prorations, unless you are told differently. Both the rent proration and the security deposit amount will be a **debit** to the *seller* and a **credit** to the *buyer*.

■ **FOR EXAMPLE**   A man is purchasing an apartment complex that contains 15 units that rent for $450 per month. A $450 security deposit is being held on each unit. The sale is to close on March 14, and the March rent has been received for all 15 units. Compute the rent proration by prorating through the day of closing. Compute the security deposit.

Calendar Days (remember to use actual days in the month unless specified differently)

Step 1. Compute the unearned days of rent for the month of closing.

```
  31   days in March
- 14   day of closing
  17   days of unearned rent
```

Note: It would be 18 days (17 days plus 1 day) if the problem had said prorate *to* the day of closing.

Step 2.

Compute the daily rent. Monthly rent × Number of units paid = Total rent collected ÷ Number of actual days in the month of closing = Daily rent.

$450 × 15 units = $6,750 monthly rent collected ÷ 31 days in March = $217.7419355 daily rent

Step 3. Compute the prorated rent amount. Daily rent × Days of unearned rent.

$217.7419355 daily rent × 17 days = $3,701.61 rounded

Step 4. Compute the security deposit.

$450 per unit × 15 units = $6,750

$3,701.61 rent proration and **$6,750 security deposit** are the answers. They are both **debit seller** and **credit buyer.**

Real Estate Math Practice Problems

1. The value of your house, not including the lot, is $91,000 today. What was the original cost if it has depreciated 5 percent per year for the past seven years?
   a. $67,407.41
   b. $95,789.47
   c. $122,850.00
   d. $140,000.00

2. What did the owners originally pay for their home if they sold it for $98,672, which gave them 12 percent profit over their original cost?
   a. $86,830
   b. $88,100
   c. $89,700
   d. $110,510

3. What would you pay for a building producing $11,250 annual net income and showing a minimum rate of return of 9 percent?
   a. $125,000
   b. $123,626
   c. $101,250
   d. $122,625

4. An owner agrees to list his property on the condition that he will receive at least $47,300 after paying 5 percent broker's commission and paying $1,150 in closing costs. At what price must it sell?
   a. $48,450
   b. $50,815
   c. $50,875
   d. $51,000

5. A gift shop pays rent of $600 per month plus 2.5 percent of gross annual sales in excess of $50,000. What was the average monthly rent last year if gross annual sales were $75,000?
   a. $1,125.00
   b. $756.25
   c. $600.00
   d. $652.08

6. If your monthly rent is $1,050, what percent would this be of an annual income of $42,000?
   a. 25 percent
   b. 30 percent
   c. 33 percent
   d. 40 percent

7. Two managing brokers split the 6 percent commission on a $73,000 home. The selling licensee was paid 70 percent of his broker's share. The listing licensee was paid 30 percent of her broker's share. How much did the listing licensee receive?
   a. $657
   b. $4,380
   c. $1,533
   d. $1,314

8. The buyer has agreed to pay $175,000 in sales price, 2.5 loan discount points, and a 1 percent origination fee. If the buyer receives a 90 percent loan-to-value ratio, how much will the buyer owe at closing for points and the origination fee?
   a. $1,575.00
   b. $3,937.50
   c. $5,512.50
   d. $6,125.00

9. Calculate eight months' interest on a $5,000 interest-only loan at 9.5 percent.
   a. $475.00
   b. $316.67
   c. $237.50
   d. $39.58

10. A 100-acre farm is divided into lots for homes. The streets require one-eighth of the whole farm, and there are 140 lots. How many square feet are in each lot?
    a. 43,560
    b. 35,004
    c. 31,114
    d. 27,225

11. What is the monthly net income on an investment of $115,000 if the rate of return is 12.5 percent?
    a. $1,150.00
    b. $1,197.92
    c. $7,666.67
    d. $14,375.00

12. A licensee sells a property for $58,500. The contract he has with his managing broker is 40 percent of the full commission earned. The commission due the managing broker is 6 percent. What is the licensee's share of the commission?
    a. $2,106
    b. $1,404
    c. $3,510
    d. $2,340

13. What is the interest rate on a $10,000 loan with semiannual interest of $450?
    a. 7 percent
    b. 9 percent
    c. 11 percent
    d. 13.5 percent

14. A warehouse is 80 feet wide and 120 feet long with ceilings 14 feet high. If 1,200 square feet of floor surface has been partitioned off from floor to ceiling for an office, how many cubic feet of space will be left in the warehouse?
    a. 151,200
    b. 134,400
    c. 133,200
    d. 117,600

15. The lot you purchased five years ago for $30,000 has appreciated 3.5 percent per year. What is it worth today?
    a. $30,375
    b. $33,525
    c. $34,500
    d. $35,250

16. A lease calls for $1,000 per month minimum plus 2 percent of annual sales in excess of $100,000. What is the annual rent if the annual sales were $150,000?
    a. $12,000
    b. $13,000
    c. $14,000
    d. $15,000

17. There is a tract of land that is 1.25 acres. The lot is 150 feet deep. How much will the lot sell for at $65 per front foot?
    a. $9,750
    b. $8,125
    c. $23,595
    d. $8,725

18. A woman earns $20,000 per year and can qualify for a monthly PITI payment equal to 25 percent of her monthly salary. If the annual tax and insurance is $678.24, what is the loan amount she will qualify for if the monthly PI payment factor is $10.29 per $1,000 of loan amount?
    a. $66,000
    b. $43,000
    c. $40,500
    d. $35,000

19. You pay $65.53 monthly interest on a loan bearing 9.25 percent annual interest. What is the loan amount rounded to the nearest hundred dollars?
    a. $1,400
    b. $2,800
    c. $6,300
    d. $8,500

20. What percentage of profit would you make if you paid $10,500 for a lot, built a home on the lot that cost $93,000, and then sold the lot and house together for $134,550?
    a. 13 percent
    b. 23 percent
    c. 30 percent
    d. 45 percent

21. An income-producing property has $62,500 annual gross income and monthly expenses of $1,530. What is the appraised value if the appraiser uses a 10 percent capitalization rate?
    a. $441,400
    b. $625,000
    c. $183,600
    d. $609,700

22. A man pays $2,500 each for four parcels of land. He subdivides them into six parcels and sells each of the six parcels for $1,950. What was his percentage of profit?
    a. 14.5 percent
    b. 17 percent
    c. 52 percent
    d. 78 percent

23. A property sells for $96,000. If it has appreciated 4 percent per year straight line for the past five years, what did the owner pay for the property five years ago?
    a. $76,800
    b. $80,000
    c. $92,300
    d. $115,200

24. If you purchase a lot that is 125 feet by 150 feet for $6,468.75, what price did you pay per front foot?
    a. $23.52
    b. $43.13
    c. $51.75
    d. $64.69

25. Calculate the amount of commission earned by a broker on a property selling for $61,000 if 6 percent is paid on the first $50,000 and 3 percent is paid on the remaining balance.
    a. $3,330
    b. $3,830
    c. $3,600
    d. $3,930

Answer Key for Real Estate Math Practice Problems

1. **d** **$140,000.00 Original Cost**

   5% Depreciation per Year × 7 Years = 35% Total Depreciation

   100% Original Cost − 35% Total Depreciation = 65% Today's Value

$91,000 Today's Value ÷	
= $140,000 **Original Cost**	65% or 0.65

   $91,000 ÷ 65% (.65) = **$140,000 Original Cost**

2. **b** **$88,100 Original Cost**

   100% Original Cost + 12% Profit = 112% Sales Price

$98,672 Sales Price ÷	
= $88,100 **Original Cost**	112% or 1.12

   $98,672 ÷ 112% (1.12) = **$88,100 Original Cost**

3. **a** **$125,000 Price**

$11,250 Annual Net Income ÷	
= $125,000 **Price**	9% or 0.09

   $11,250 ÷ 9% (.09) = **$125,000 Price**

4. **d** **$51,000 Sales Price**

   $47,300 Net to Seller + $1,150 Closing Costs =
   $48,450 Seller's Dollars after Commission

   100% Sales Price − 5% Commission =
   95% Seller's Percent after Commission

$48,450 Seller's Dollars after Commission ÷	
= $51,000 **Sales Price**	95% or 0.95

   $48,450 ÷ 95% (0.95) = **$51,000 Sales Price**

5. **d $652.08 Average Monthly Rent**

$75,000 Gross Annual Sales – $50,000 =
$25,000 Gross Annual Sales Subject to 2.5%

= $625 Annual Percentage Rent	
$25,000	2.5%
Gross Annual Sales	or 0.025

×

$25,000 × 2.5% (.025) = $625

$625 Annual Percentage Rent ÷ 12 Months =
$52.08 Monthly Percentage Rent

$600 Monthly Minimum Rent + $52.08 Monthly Percentage Rent =
$652.08 Average Monthly Rent

6. **b 30%**

$1,050 Monthly Rent × 12 Months = $12,600 Annual Rent

÷ $12,600 Annual Rent	
$42,000 Annual Income	**= 0.3 or 30%**

$12,600 ÷ $42,000 = .30 or **30%**

7. **a $657 Commission to the Listing Licensee**

= $4,380 Full Commission	
$73,000	6%
Sales Price	0.06

×

$73,000 × 6% (.06) = $4,380

$4,380 Full Commission ÷ 2 Managing Brokers =
$2,190 Managing Broker's Share of the Commission

= $657 Listing Licensee's Commission	
$2,190 Managing Broker's	30%
Share of the Commission	0.3

×

$2,190 × 30% (.30) = **$657 Commission**

8. c   **$5,512.50 for Points and the Origination Fee**

2.5 Points Loan Discount + 1 Point Origination Fee = 3.5 Points

= $157,500 Loan	
$175,000 Sales Price	90% or 0.9

×

$175,000 × 90% or (.90) = $157,500

$5,512.50 for Points and Origination Fees	
$157,500 Loan	3.5% or 0.035

×

$157,500 × 3.5% (.035) = **$5,512.50 for Points and Origination Fees**

9. b   **$316.67 Interest**

= $475 Annual Interest	
$5,000 Loan	9.5% or 0.095

×

$5,000 × 9.5% (.095) = $475

$475 Annual Interest ÷ 12 Months × 8 Months = **$316.67 Interest**

10. d   **27,225 Square Feet per Lot**

⅛ = 1 ÷ 8 = 0.125 for Streets

100 Acres × 0.125 = 12.5 Acres for Streets

100 Acres – 12.5 Acres for Streets = 87.5 Acres for Lots × 43,560 = 3,811,500 Square Feet ÷ 140 Lots = **27,225 Square Feet per Lot**

11. b   **$1,197.92 Monthly Net Operating Income**

= $14,375 Annual Net Operating Income	
$115,000 Investment	12.5% or 0.125

×

$115,000 × 12.5% (.125) = $14,375

$14,375 Annual Net Operating Income ÷ 12 Months =
$1,197.92 Monthly Net Operating Income

12. **b $1,404 Licensee's Commission**

$$\frac{= \$3,510 \text{ Full Commission}}{\$58,500 \text{ Sales Price} \quad \Big| \quad \begin{array}{r} 6\% \\ \text{or } 0.06 \end{array}}$$

$$\times$$

$58,500 × 6% (.06) = $3,510

$$\frac{= \$1,404 \text{ Licensee's Commission}}{\$3,510 \text{ Full Commission} \quad \Big| \quad \begin{array}{r} 40\% \\ \text{or } 0.4 \end{array}}$$

$$\times$$

$3,510 × 40% (.40) = **$1,404 Licensee's Commission**

13. **b   9% Annual Interest Rate**

$450 × 2 = $900 Annual Interest

$$\frac{\div \$900 \text{ Annual Interest}}{\$10,000 \text{ Loan} \quad \Big| \quad = 0.09 \text{ or } 9\%}$$

$$\times$$

$900 ÷ $10,000 = **0.09 or 9% Interest Rate**

14. **d   117,600 Cubic Feet**

120 Feet × 80 Feet = 9,600 Square Feet in Building − 1,200 Square Feet for Office = 8,400 Square Feet Left in Warehouse × 14-Foot Ceiling = **117,600 Cubic Feet Left in Warehouse**

15. **d $35,250 Today's Value**

3.5% Appreciation per Year × 5 Years = 17.5% Total Appreciation

100% Cost + 17.5% Total Appreciation = 117.5% Today's Value

$$\frac{= \$35,250 \text{ Today's Value}}{\$30,000 \text{ Original Cost} \quad \Big| \quad \begin{array}{r} 117.5\% \\ \text{or } 1.175 \end{array}}$$

$$\times$$

$30,000 × 117.5% (1.175) = **$35,250 Today's Value**

16. **b $13,000 Annual Rent**

$1,000 Monthly Minimum Rent × 12 Months =
$12,000 Annual Minimum Rent

$150,000 Annual Sales − $100,000 = $50,000 Annual Sales Subject to 2%

$$\frac{\text{= \$1,000 Annual Percentage Rent}}{}$$

$50,000 Annual Sales Subject to 2%	2% or 0.02
×	

$50,000 × 2% (.02) = $1,000

$12,000 Annual Minimum Rent + $1,000 Annual Percentage Rent = **$13,000 Annual Rent**

17. **c $23,595 Sales Price**

1.25 Acres × 43,560 Square Feet = 54,450 Square Feet ÷ 150 Feet Deep =
363 Feet Frontage × $65 per Front Foot = **$23,595 Sales Price**

18. **d $35,000 Loan**

$20,000 Annual Salary ÷ 12 Months = $1,666.67 Monthly Salary

$$\frac{\text{= \$416.67 Monthly PITI Payment}}{}$$

$1,666.67 Monthly Salary	25% or 0.25
×	

$1,666.67 × 25% = $416.67

$678.24 Annual Tax and Insurance ÷ 12 Months =
$56.52 Monthly Tax and Insurance

$416.67 Monthly PITI Payment − $56.52 Monthly TI =
$360.15 Monthly PI Payment

$360.15 Monthly PI Payment ÷ $10.29 × $1,000 = **$35,000 Loan**

19. **d $8,500 Loan**

$65.53 Monthly Interest × 12 Months = $786.36 Annual Interest

$$\frac{\text{\$786.36 Annual Interest ÷}}{}$$

= 8,501.19 or **$8,500 Loan**	9.25% or 0.0925

$786.36 ÷ 9.25% (.0925) = **$8501.19 Loan**

20. **c   30%**

$10,500 Cost of Lot + $93,000 Cost of Home = $103,500 Total Cost

$134,550 Sales Price − $103,500 Total Cost = $31,050 Profit

÷ $31,050 Profit	
$103,500 Total Cost	**= 0.3 or 30%**

$31,050 ÷ $103,500 = **0.3 or 30%**

21. **a $441,400 Value**

$1,530 Monthly Expenses × 12 Months = $18,360 Annual Expenses

$62,500 Annual Gross Income − $18,360 Annual Expenses = $44,140 Annual Net Operating Income

$44,140 Annual Net Operating Income ÷	
= $441,400 Value	10% or 0.1

$44,140 ÷ 10% (.10) = **$441,400 Value**

22. **b   17% Profit**

$2,500 Cost × 4 Parcels = $10,000 Total Cost

$1,950 Sales Price × 6 Parcels = $11,700 Sales Price

$11,700 Sales Price − $10,000 Cost = $1,700 Profit

÷ $1,700 Profit	
$10,000 Cost	**= 0.17 or 17% Profit**

$1,700 ÷ $10,000 Cost = 0.17 or **17% Profit**

23. **b $80,000 Original Cost**

4% Annual Appreciation × 5 Years = 20% Total Appreciation

100% Cost + 20% Total Appreciation = 120% Today's Value

$96,000 Today's Value ÷	
= $80,000 Original Cost	120% 1.2

$96,000 ÷ 120% (1.20) = **$80,000 Original Cost**

24. **c $51.75 per Front Foot**

$6,468.75 Price ÷ 125 Front Feet = **$51.75 per Front Foot**

25. a $3,330 Total Commission

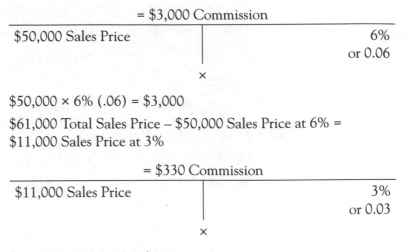

$= \$3,000$ Commission

| $50,000 Sales Price | 6%
or 0.06 |

$\times$

$50,000 \times 6\%$ (.06) = $3,000

$61,000 Total Sales Price – $50,000 Sales Price at 6% =
$11,000 Sales Price at 3%

$= \$330$ Commission

| $11,000 Sales Price | 3%
or 0.03 |

$\times$

$11,000 \times 3\%$ (.03) = $330

$3,000 Commission + $330 Commission = **$3,330 Total Commission**

Sample Illinois Real Estate Licensing Examinations

Modern Real Estate Practice in Illinois, Seventh Edition, is designed to prepare you for a career in real estate. However, before you can become a broker, a leasing agent, or an instructor, you must, under Illinois law, obtain a license. Passing the real estate licensing examination plays a large part in determining your eligibility to become licensed. The examination is designed to test your knowledge of real estate laws, principles, and practices.

The state test is currently prepared and administered by Applied Measurement Professionals, Inc. (AMP), an independent testing company under the sanction of the Illinois Department of Financial & Professional Regulation ("Department"). You can contact AMP to determine the right test site and time for you. The site also provides current, *in-depth* topic outlines, exact procedures for establishing an examination appointment, and rules for the examination. Sample AMP-designed questions are available at *www.goAMP.com*.

■ WHAT TO EXPECT FROM THE EXAM

Illinois broker, managing broker, leasing agent, and instructor candidates are given separate examinations. Questions for the exams involve two broad areas: knowledge of material and application of knowledge in the real estate professions.

The broker exams consist of 140 questions: 100 questions devoted to general knowledge (national real estate practices and principles that apply everywhere in the United States), and 40 questions devoted to the state (Illinois-specific practice and licensing issues). At least 10 percent of the questions involve some sort of mathematical calculations. The questions are multiple-choice in format, with four answer choices for each question.

The rules for taking the exam are set by the Department and the AMP testing service and are detailed in the *AMP Illinois Candidate Handbook*. The state exam must be completed within the allotted time. AMP provides computer monitors equipped with a clock that shows you exactly how much time you have remaining to complete the exam. Once the test begins, you are not allowed to leave the test site until you have completed the exam. *Guessing is not penalized; be sure to answer every question.*

You must pass *both* the national and state sections of the exam to qualify for your real estate license. They are scored separately.

Candidates who pass only one portion must retake and pass the other portion within one year of passing the first portion. Failure to do so will result in having to take the entire examination again. Candidates need a score of 75 percent on each portion of the examination.

Candidates are allowed up to four attempts to pass the examination. After the fourth attempt, you are required to retake the education coursework. Candidates also must not let their coursework lapse for more than four years before taking the examination or they will need to retake the education coursework.

Broker Examination

Approximately 70 percent of the questions in the broker's exam are devoted to national real estate topics, and the remainder are devoted to Illinois-specific real estate topics. Broker candidates are expected to solve basic problems in real estate mathematics related to such topics as commissions, interest, prorations, and square footage. When you review the *AMP Illinois Candidate Handbook*, it will include an outline of the subject areas that are tested on the national section of the test and the approximate number of questions coming from each area.

Examination Outline

The following is the most recent AMP Detailed National Content Outline, along with the chapters of *Modern Real Estate Practice in Illinois*, *Seventh Edition*, in which the subjects are covered.

Topic Headings–National Portion	Chapter
1. Agency Relationships and Contracts 28%	
A. Agency Relationships	
1. Creating Agency	4
2. Types of Agency (including implied agency)	4
3. Rights, Duties and Obligations of the Parties	4
4. Termination and Remedies for Non-Performance	11
5. Disclosure (related to representation)	4
B. General Legal Principles, Theory, and Concepts about Contracts	
1. Unilateral / Bilateral	11
2. Validity	11
3. Void and Voidable	11
4. Notice of Delivery / Acceptance	11
5. Executory / Executed	11
6. Enforceability	11
7. Addenda to Contracts	11
C. Purchase Contracts (contracts between seller and buyer)	
1. General Principles and Legal Concepts	11
2. Purchase Contract (contract of sale, purchase and sale agreement, etc	11
3. Options (contractual right to buy)	11
4. Basic Provisions / Purpose / Elements	11
5. Conditions for Termination / Breach of Contract	11
6. Offer and Acceptance (counteroffers, multiple offers, negotiation, earnest money)	11

Cognitive Level Approximately 30% of the items will require recall on the part of the candidate, 60% will require application of knowledge, and 10% will require analysis.

Pretest Items In addition to the 100 items used to compute candidate scores, unscored items will be included for pretesting.

Illinois-Specific Topics

The following is the most recent AMP Detailed Content Outline for the Illinois-specific portion of the examination, along with the chapters of *Modern Real Estate Practice in Illinois*, *Seventh Edition*, in which the subjects are covered.

Topic Headings	# of Items Broker	Chapter
1. **Licensing Requirements**	10	
A. License exemptions		14
B. Activities requiring a license		14
C. Types of licenses		14
1. Broker		14
2. Managing Broker		14
3. Leasing Agent		14
D. Personal assistants		5, 14
E. Eligibility for licensing, including sponsor card		14
F. Examination		14
G. License renewal		14
H. Continuing education		14
I. Change in licensee information		14
J. Reciprocity		14
K. Real Estate Recovery Fund		14
2. **Laws and Rules Regulating Real Estate Practice**	20	
A. Purpose of license law		14
B. Advertising (other than disclosure)		14
C. Broker/Managing Broker relationship		4, 14
D. Commissions		
1. Finder's fee/referral fee		14
2. Rental finding services		14, 17
E. Ownership issues		
1. Land trust		8
2. Homestead		8
3. Land Sales Registration Act/Time share		8
F. Handling of monies		
1. Escrow accounts		1
2. Security deposits		17
G. Handling of documents		5, 14
H. Performing activities exceeding scope of real estate licensing		
1. Law		14
2. Securities		14
I. Transfer tax stamps/affordable housing		12
J. Intestacy		13

■ MULTIPLE-CHOICE QUESTIONS: TEST-TAKING STRATEGIES

There are many different ways to prepare for and take multiple-choice examinations. Before you try the following sample exams, take some time to read this brief overview of test-taking strategies. While no one can tell you which method will work best for you, it's always a good idea to think about what you're going to do before you do it.

One of the most important things to remember about multiple-choice test questions is this: they always give you the correct answer. You don't have to remember how words are spelled, and you don't have to try to guess what the question is about. The answer is always there right in front of you.

Of course, if it was as easy as that, it wouldn't be much of a test. The key to success in taking multiple-choice examinations is actually twofold: First, know the correct answer. You do that by going to class, paying attention, taking good notes, and studying the material. Then, if you don't know the correct answer, be able to analyze the questions and answers effectively, so you can apply the second key: be able to make a reasonable guess. Even if you don't know the answer, you will probably know which answers are clearly wrong and which ones are more likely than the others to be right.

If you can eliminate one answer as wrong, you have improved your odds of "guessing correctly" from 4-to-1 to 3-to-1. If you can eliminate two wrong answers, you have a 50/50 shot at a correct guess. Of course, if you can eliminate three wrong answers, your chance of a correct response is 100 percent. In any case, there is no secret formula: the only sure way to improve your odds of a correct answer is to study and learn the material.

Structure of the Question

A multiple-choice question has a basic structure. It starts with what test writers call the stem. That's the text of the question that sets up the need for an answer. The stem may be an incomplete statement that is finished by the correct answer; it may be a story problem or hypothetical example (called a fact-pattern) about which you will be asked a question. Or it may be a math problem in which you are given basic information and asked to solve a mathematical issue, such as the amount of a commission or capital gain.

The stem is always followed by options: four possible answers to the question presented by the stem. Depending on the structure and content of the stem, the options may be single words or numbers, phrases, or complete sentences. Three of the options are distractors: incorrect answers intended to "distract" you from the correct choice. One of the options is the correct answer, called the key.

Reading a Multiple-Choice Question

Here are three suggestions for how to read a multiple-choice test question:

1. The Traditional Method.   Read the question through from start to finish then read the options. When you get to the correct answer, mark it and move on. This method works best for short questions, such as those that require completion or simply define a term. For longer, more-complicated questions or those that are not quite so clear, however, you may miss important information.

2. The Focus Method.   As we've seen, multiple-choice questions have different parts. In longer math or story-type questions, the last line of the stem will contain the question's focus: the basic issue the item asks you to address. That is, the question is always in the last line of the stem. In the focus method, when you come to a longer item, read the last line of the stem first. This will clue you in to what the question is about. Then go back and read the stem from beginning to end. The advantage is this: while you are reading the complicated facts or math elements, you know what to look for. You can watch for important items and disregard unnecessary information. It's a sad fact of multiple-choice exams that sometimes test writers include distracting elements in the stem itself. If you check for the question's focus first, you'll spot the test-writer's tricks right away.

3. The Upside-Down Method.   This technique takes the focus method one step further. Here, you do just what the name implies: you start reading the question from the bottom up. By reading the four options first, you can learn exactly what the test writer wants you to focus on. For instance, a fact-pattern problem might include several dollar values in the stem, leading you to believe you're going to have to do a math calculation. You'll be trying to

recall all the equations you've memorized, only to find at the end of the stem that you're only expected to define a term. If you've read the options first, you would have known what to look for.

■ TAKING THE SAMPLE EXAMINATIONS

The following three sample examinations have been designed to help you test your knowledge in preparation for the actual licensing exam. The first two exams are in two parts: 90 questions on general, national real estate principles, and 60 covering Illinois-specific law and practice. Note that proration calculations are based on a 30-day month unless otherwise specified.

The third practice exam consists of 100 Illinois-specific questions, with emphasis on the Illinois Real Estate License Act of 2000.

EXAM ONE PART ONE—GENERAL REAL ESTATE PRACTICE AND PRINCIPLES

1. Which of the following is a lien on real estate?
   a. Recorded easement
   b. Recorded mortgage
   c. Encroachment
   d. Deed restriction

2. A sales contract was signed under duress. Which of the following describes this contract?
   a. Voidable
   b. Breached
   c. Discharged
   d. Void

3. A **sponsoring** broker receives a check for earnest money from a buyer and deposits the money in the **sponsoring** broker's personal interest-bearing checking account over the weekend. This action exposes the **sponsoring** broker to a charge of
   a. commingling.
   b. novation.
   c. subrogation.
   d. accretion.

4. A borrower takes out a mortgage loan that requires monthly payments of $875.70 for 20 years and a final payment of $24,095. This is what type of loan?
   a. Wraparound
   b. Accelerated
   c. Balloon
   d. Variable

5. When demand for a commodity decreases and supply increases,
   a. price is not affected.
   b. price tends to rise.
   c. price tends to fall.
   d. the market becomes stagnant.

6. A **sponsoring** broker signs a contract with a buyer. Under the contract, the **sponsoring** broker agrees to help the buyer find a suitable property and to represent the buyer in negotiations with the seller. Although the buyer may not sign an agreement with any other broker, she may look for properties on her own. The **sponsoring** broker is entitled to payment only if the **sponsoring** broker locates the property that is purchased. What kind of agreement has this **sponsoring** broker signed?
   a. Exclusive buyer agency agreement
   b. Exclusive-agency buyer agency agreement
   c. Open buyer agency agreement
   d. Option contract

7. A woman conveys property to a man by delivering a deed. The deed contains five covenants. This is MOST likely a
   a. warranty deed.
   b. quitclaim deed.
   c. grant deed.
   d. deed in trust.

8. A real estate licensee does not show non-Asian clients any properties in several traditionally Asian neighborhoods. She bases this practice on the need to preserve the valuable cultural integrity of Asian immigrant communities. Which of the following statements is TRUE regarding the licensee's policy?
   a. The licensee's policy is steering and violates the fair housing laws regardless of her motivation.
   b. Because the licensee's is not attempting to restrict the rights of any single minority group, the practice does not constitute steering.
   c. The licensee's policy is steering, but it does not violate the fair housing laws because she is motivated by cultural preservation, not by exclusion or discrimination.
   d. The licensee's policy has the effect, but not the intent, of steering.

9. A grandmother grants a life estate to her grandson and stipulates that on the grandson's death, the title to the property will pass to her son-in-law. This second estate is known as a(n)

   a. remainder.
   b. reversion.
   c. estate at sufferance.
   d. estate for years.

10. What is the effect of property held in joint tenancy?

    a. A maximum of two people can own the real estate
    b. The fractional interests of the owners can be different
    c. Additional owners may be added later
    d. There is always the right of survivorship

11. A real estate licensee has a written contract with his sponsoring broker that specifies that he will not be treated as an employee. The licensee's entire income is from sales commissions rather than an hourly wage. For federal income taxes, the licensee is considered a(n)

    a. real estate assistant.
    b. employee.
    c. subagent.
    d. independent contractor.

12. The states in which the lender holds title to mortgaged real estate are known as

    a. title-theory states.
    b. lien-theory states.
    c. statutory title states.
    d. strict title forfeiture states.

13. The form of tenancy that expires on a specific date is a

    a. joint tenancy.
    b. tenancy for years.
    c. tenancy in common.
    d. tenancy by the entirety.

14. A suburban home that lacks indoor plumbing suffers from which of the following?

    a. Functional obsolescence
    b. Curable physical deterioration
    c. Incurable physical deterioration
    d. External obsolescence

15. If a developer wants to build a commercial building closer to the street than is permitted by the local zoning ordinance because the shape of the lot makes a standard setback impossible, the developer should seek a

    a. variance.
    b. nonconforming use permit.
    c. conditional use permit.
    d. density zoning permit.

16. A licensee showed an owner-occupied property that had window screens, custom venetian blinds, and a wall bed to a buyer. The owner accepted the buyer's offer. What may the seller remove prior to closing?

    a. All of the identified items because they are trade fixtures
    b. Only the venetian blinds as personal property
    c. Only the wall bed because it is real property
    d. None of these identified items

17. A real estate broker specializes in helping both buyers and sellers with the necessary paperwork involved in transferring property. Since the broker is an agent of both parties, he may not disclose either party's confidential information to the other. The broker is

    a. a buyer's agent.
    b. an independent contractor.
    c. a transactional broker.
    d. a dual agent.

18. The portion of the value of owners' property that exceeds the amount of their mortgage debt is called

    a. equality.
    b. escrow.
    c. surplus.
    d. equity.

19. In a 28/36 ratio, the 36 means
    a. recurring long-term debts and housing payment combined may not exceed 36 percent of gross monthly income.
    b. recurring long-term debts and housing payment combined may not exceed 36 percent of net monthly income.
    c. housing payment may not exceed 36 percent of net income.
    d. credit card debt and other monthly (non-house) payments may not exceed 36 percent of gross monthly income.

20. Police powers include which of the following?
    a. Deed restrictions
    b. Zoning
    c. Restrictive covenants
    d. Taxation

21. A seller wants to net $165,000 from the sale of her house after paying the **sponsoring** broker's fee of 5 percent. The seller's gross sales price will be
    a. $155,750.
    b. $156,750.
    c. $173,248.
    d. $173,684.

22. How many square feet are in three acres?
    a. 43,560
    b. 130,680
    c. 156,840
    d. 27,878,400

23. A purchaser obtains financing from a local savings association to purchase a condominium unit. In this situation, which of the following BEST describes the purchaser?
    a. Vendor
    b. Mortgagor
    c. Grantor
    d. Lessor

24. The current value of a property is $240,000. The property is assessed at 40 percent of its current value for real estate tax purposes with an equalization factor of 1.5 applied to the assessed value. If the tax rate is $4 per $100 of assessed valuation, what is the amount of tax due on the property?
    a. $2,500
    b. $3,840
    c. $5,760
    d. $214,400

25. A building was sold for $360,000, with the purchaser putting 10 percent down and obtaining a loan for the balance. The lending institution charged a 1 percent loan origination fee. What was the total cash used for the purchase?
    a. $3,240
    b. $6,500
    c. $39,240
    d. $39,600

26. Several brokerage firms were accused of violating antitrust laws. Of the following, they were MOST likely accused of
    a. not having an equal housing opportunity sign in an office window.
    b. undisclosed dual agencies.
    c. price fixing.
    d. dealing in unlicensed exchange services.

27. What is a capitalization rate?
    a. Amount determined by the gross rent multiplier
    b. Present value based on rate of return a property will produce
    c. Mathematical value determined by a sales price
    d. Rate at which the amount of depreciation in a property is measured

28. The National Do Not Call Registry provides that
    a. licensees may never contact consumers without written authorization.
    b. consumers with whom a licensee has had a business relationship can be contacted for up to 12 months after the purchase.
    c. licensees may not contact a previous customer if they are on the registry.
    d. consumers who have made an inquiry to a licensee may be contacted up to three months later.

29. If a house was sold for $140,000 and the buyer obtained an FHA-insured mortgage loan for $133,700, how much money would the buyer pay in discount points if the lender charged two points?
    a. $495
    b. $2,674
    c. $2,800
    d. $3,800

30. The commission rate is 7¾ percent on a sale of $250,000. What is the dollar amount of the commission?
    a. $17,500
    b. $19,375
    c. $20,425
    d. $22,925

31. A buyer makes an offer on a property and the seller accepts. Three weeks later, the buyer announces that "the deal's off" and refuses to go through with the sale. If the seller is entitled to keep the buyer's earnest money deposit, it is MOST likely because there is what kind of clause in the sales contract?
    a. Liquidated damages clause
    b. Contingent damages clause
    c. Actual damages clause
    d. Revocation clause

32. Until the land contract is paid in full, what is the status of the purchaser's interest in the property?
    a. Purchaser holds legal title to the premises.
    b. Purchaser has no legal interest in the property.
    c. Purchaser possesses a legal life estate in the premises.
    d. Purchaser has equitable title in the property.

33. After signing a five-year lease, the business outgrew its rental space within three years. The business would like another company to take on the responsibility for the remaining two years. A second business can do this through
    a. an assignment.
    b. a novation.
    c. a substitution.
    d. a rescission.

34. An ownership interest that is based on annual occupancy intervals is a
    a. leasehold.
    b. time-share.
    c. condominium.
    d. cooperative.

35. For an offer to purchase real estate to become a contract, whose signature is necessary?
    a. Buyer's only
    b. Buyer's and seller's
    c. Seller's only
    d. Seller's and seller's broker's

36. A borrower just made the final payment on a mortgage loan. Regardless of this fact, the records will still show a lien on the mortgaged property until which of the following events occur?
    a. A satisfaction of the mortgage document is recorded.
    b. A reconveyance of the mortgage document is delivered to the mortgage holder.
    c. A novation of the mortgage document takes place.
    d. An estoppel of the mortgage document is filed with the clerk of the county in which the mortgagee is located.

37. If the annual net income from a commercial property is $22,000 and the capitalization rate is 8 percent, what is the value of the property using the income approach?

a. $176,000
b. $183,000
c. $200,000
d. $275,000

38. A **sponsoring** broker enters into a listing agreement with a seller in which the seller will receive $120,000 from the sale of a vacant lot and the **sponsoring** broker will receive any sale proceeds exceeding that amount. This is what type of listing?

a. Exclusive agency
b. Net
c. Exclusive right to sell
d. Multiple

39. An individual sold her house and moved into a cooperative apartment. Under the cooperative form of ownership, the individual will

a. become a shareholder in the corporation.
b. not lose her apartment if she pays her share of the expenses.
c. have to take out a new mortgage loan on her unit.
d. receive a fixed-term lease for her unit.

40. A defect or a cloud on title to property may be cured by

a. obtaining quitclaim deeds from all appropriate parties.
b. bringing an action to register the title.
c. paying cash for the property at the settlement.
d. bringing an action to repudiate the title.

41. A buyer signed an exclusive-agency buyer agency agreement with a **sponsoring** broker. If the buyer finds a suitable property with no assistance from any licensee, the **sponsoring** broker is entitled to

a. full compensation from the buyer, regardless of who found the property.
b. full compensation from the seller.
c. partial compensation as generally required under this type of agreement.
d. no compensation under the terms of this type of agreement.

42. Under the terms of a net lease, a commercial tenant usually would be responsible for paying

a. principle debt service.
b. real estate taxes.
c. income tax payments.
d. mortgage interest expense.

43. The Civil Rights Act of 1866 prohibits discrimination based on

a. sex.
b. religion.
c. race.
d. familial status.

44. If a borrower must pay $6,000 for points on a $150,000 loan, how many points is the lender charging for this loan?

a. 3
b. 4
c. 5
d. 6

45. What is the difference between a general lien and a specific lien?

a. A general lien cannot be enforced in court, while a specific lien can.
b. A specific lien is held by only one person, while a general lien must be held by two or more people.
c. A general lien is a lien against personal property, while a specific lien is a lien against real estate.
d. A specific lien is a lien against a certain parcel of real estate, while a general lien covers all of a debtor's property.

46. In an option to purchase real estate, which of the following statements is *TRUE* of the optionee?

a. The optionee must purchase the property but may do so at any time within the option period.
b. The optionee is limited to a refund of the option consideration if the option is exercised.
c. The optionee cannot obtain third-party financing on the property until after the option has expired.
d. The optionee has no obligation to purchase the property during the option period.

47. In 2001, an owner constructed a building that was eight stories high. In 2011, the municipality changed the zoning ordinance and prohibited buildings taller than six stories. Which of the following statements is *TRUE* regarding the existing eight-story building?

    a. The building must be demolished.
    b. The building is a conditional use.
    c. The building is a nonconforming use.
    d. The owner must obtain a variance.

48. How many acres are there in the N½ of the SW¼ and the NE¼ of the SE¼ of a section?

    a. 20
    b. 40
    c. 80
    d. 120

49. A home is the smallest in a neighborhood of large, expensive houses. The effect of the other houses on the value of this particular home is known as

    a. regression.
    b. progression.
    c. substitution.
    d. contribution.

50. What kind of lien is created as a result of a judgment, estate or inheritance taxes, the decedent's debts, or federal taxes?

    a. Specific
    b. General
    c. Voluntary
    d. Equitable

51. A broker received a deposit along with a written offer from a buyer. The offer stated "The offeror will leave this offer open for the seller's acceptance for a period of ten days." On the fifth day, and before acceptance by the seller, the offeror notified the broker that the offer was withdrawn and demanded the return of the deposit. Under these circumstances, the offeror

    a. cannot withdraw the offer; it must be held open for the full ten-day period, as promised.
    b. has the right to withdraw the offer and secure the return of the deposit any time before being notified of the seller's acceptance.
    c. can withdraw the offer, and the seller and the broker will each retain one-half of the forfeited deposit.
    d. offeror can withdraw the offer, the broker is legally entitled to declare the deposit forfeited and retain all of it in lieu of the lost commission.

52. A man and a woman own property as joint tenants. The woman sells her interest to another woman. What is the relationship between the man and the second woman regarding the property?

    a. Joint tenants
    b. Tenants in common
    c. Tenants by the entirety
    d. No relationship exists because the first woman cannot sell her joint tenancy interest

53. A property owner and a tenant verbally enter into a six-month lease. If the tenant defaults, the property owner may

    a. not bring a court action because six-month leases must be in writing under the parol evidence rule.
    b. not bring a court action because the statute of frauds governs six-month leases.
    c. bring a court action because six-month leases need not be in writing to be enforceable.
    d. bring a court action because the statute of limitations does not apply to oral leases, regardless of their term.

54. On Monday, a woman offers to sell her vacant lot to a man for $35,000. On Tuesday, the man counteroffers to buy the lot for $25,500. On Friday, the man withdraws his counteroffer and accepts the woman's original price of $35,000. Under these circumstances

   a. a valid agreement exists because the man accepted the woman's offer exactly as it was made, regardless of the fact that it was not accepted immediately.

   b. a valid agreement exists because the man accepted before the woman advised him that the offer was withdrawn.

   c. no valid agreement exists because the woman's offer was not accepted within 72 hours of its having been made.

   d. no valid agreement exists because the man's counteroffer was a rejection of the woman's offer, and once rejected, it need not be accepted later.

55. A property owner's neighbors use her driveway to reach their garage, which is on their property. The property owner's attorney explains that the neighbors have an easement appurtenant that gives them the right to use her driveway. The property owner's property is the

   a. dominant tenement.
   b. servient tenement.
   c. prescriptive tenement.
   d. appurtenant tenement.

56. What action returns the parties to a contract to their original positions, before the contract, including the return of any deposit?

   a. Cancellation
   b. Substitution
   c. Rescission
   d. Subordination

57. A deed conveys ownership to the grantee "as long as the existing building is not torn down." What type of estate does this deed create?

   a. Determinable fee estate
   b. Fee simple absolute estate
   c. Nondestructible estate
   d. Life estate *pur autre vie*, with the measuring life being that of the building

58. Taxes levied on a property owner to pay for installation of sidewalks or sewers are called

   a. ad valorem taxes.
   b. general assessments.
   c. special property taxes.
   d. special excise taxes.

59. What do local zoning ordinances regulate?

   a. Environmental penalties
   b. Deed restrictions
   c. Restrictive covenants
   d. Permitted land uses

60. A sponsoring broker took a listing and later discovered that a court had previously declared the client incompetent. At this point, the status of the listing

   a. is unaffected because the sponsoring broker acted in good faith as the owner's agent.

   b. is of no value to the sponsoring broker because the contract is void.

   c. is the basis for recovery of a commission from the client's guardian or trustee if the sponsoring broker produces a buyer.

   d. is on hold, and may be renegotiated between the broker and the client, based on the new information.

61. A borrower defaulted on his home mortgage loan payments, and the lender obtained a court order to foreclose on the property. At the foreclosure sale, the property sold for $164,000; the unpaid balance on the loan at the time of foreclosure was $178,000. What must the lender do to recover the $14,000 that the borrower still owes?

   a. Sue for specific performance
   b. Sue for damages
   c. Seek a deficiency judgment
   d. Seek a judgment by default

62. Which of the following is exempt to the federal Fair Housing Act of 1968?

a. The sale of listed, owner-occupied single-family home when the listing broker does not advertise the property.

b. The restriction of noncommercial lodgings by a private club to non-members of the club.

c. The rental by the owner who lives in a three-family dwelling who does not advertise the vacancy.

d. The restriction of non-commercial housing where a certified statement has not been filed with the government.

63. When compared with a 30-year payment period, taking out a loan with a 20-year payment results in

a. lower equity buildup.

b. greater impound requirements.

c. lower monthly payments.

d. higher monthly payments.

64. A licensee arrives to present a purchase offer to an older man, who is seriously ill, and finds the man's son and daughter-in-law also present. The son and daughter-in-law angrily urge the man to accept the offer, even though it is much less than the asking price for the property. If the man accepts the offer, the man may later claim that

a. the licensee improperly presented an offer that was less than the asking price.

b. the licensee's failure to protect the man from the son and daughter-in-law constituted a violation of the licensee's fiduciary duties.

c. The man's rights under the ADA have been violated by the son and daughter-in-law.

d. The man was under undue influence from the son and daughter-in-law, so the contract is voidable.

65. A deed of conveyance contained only the following guarantee: "This property was not encumbered during the time the grantor owned it except as noted in this deed." What type of deed did the grantor give to the grantee?

a. General warranty

b. Special warranty

c. Bargain and sale

d. Quitclaim

66. An unmarried couple owns a parcel of real estate. Each owns an undivided interest, with the man owning one-third and the woman owning two-thirds. The form of ownership under which the couple owns their property is

a. severalty.

b. joint tenancy.

c. tenancy at will.

d. tenancy in common.

67. A man agrees to purchase a house for $84,500. He pays $2,000 as earnest money and obtains a new mortgage loan for $67,600. The purchase contract provides for a March 15 settlement. He and the sellers prorate the present year's real estate taxes of $1,880.96, which have been prepaid. The man has additional closing costs of $1,250, and the sellers have other closing costs of $850. Using the actual number of days method, how much cash must the man bring to the settlement?

a. $16,389

b. $17,650

c. $17,840

d. $19,639

68. A broker advertised a house he had listed for sale at the price of $247,900. An African-American saw the house and was interested in it. When the prospect asked the broker the price of the house, the broker told the prospect $253,000. Under the federal Fair Housing Act of 1968, such a statement is

    a. legal because the law requires only that the African-American be given the opportunity to buy the house.
    b. legal because the representation was made by the broker and not directly by the owner.
    c. illegal because the difference in the offering price and the quoted price was greater than 10 percent.
    d. illegal because the terms of the potential sale were changed for the African-American.

69. An owner placed her farm in a trust, naming herself as the beneficiary. When the owner died, her will directed the trustee to sell the farm and distribute the proceeds of the sale to her heirs. The trustee sold the farm in accordance with the will. What type of deed was delivered at settlement?

    a. Trustee's deed
    b. Trustor's deed
    c. Deed in trust
    d. Reconveyance deed

70. An appraiser has been hired to prepare an appraisal report of a property for loan purposes. The property is an elegant old mansion that is now leased out as a restaurant. To which approach to value should the appraiser probably give the greatest weight when making this appraisal?

    a. Income
    b. Sales comparison
    c. Replacement cost
    d. Reproduction cost

71. An applicant applies for a mortgage, and the loan officer suggests that she might consider a term mortgage loan. Which of the following statements BEST explains what the loan officer means?

    a. All of the interest is paid at the end of the term.
    b. The debt is partially amortized over the life of the loan.
    c. The length of the term is limited by state law.
    d. The entire principal amount is due at the end of the term.

72. A condominium community offers a swimming pool, tennis courts, and a biking trail. These facilities are MOST likely owned by the

    a. the condominium board.
    b. corporation in which the unit owners hold stock.
    c. unit owners in the form of proportional divided interests.
    d. unit owners in the form of percentage undivided interests.

73. On a closing statement in a typical real estate transaction, the buyer's earnest money deposit is reflected as a

    a. credit to buyer only.
    b. credit to seller, debit to buyer.
    c. credit to buyer and seller.
    d. debit to buyer only.

74. Prepaid insurance and tax reserves, in which the buyer assumes the mortgage, will appear on a typical closing statement as a

    a. credit to buyer, debit to seller.
    b. credit to seller only.
    c. debit to seller only.
    d. debit to buyer, credit to seller.

75. Real property can become personal property by the process known as

    a. attachment.
    b. severance.
    c. hypothecation.
    d. accretion.

76. Property owners give a neighbor permission to park a camper in their yard for a few weeks. The property owners do not charge rent for the use of the yard. The property owners have given the neighbor a(n)

    a. easement.
    b. estate for years.
    c. license.
    d. permissive encroachment.

77. A tenant's lease has expired, but the tenant has not vacated the premises or negotiated a renewal lease. The landlord has declared that the tenant is not to remain in the building. This situation is an example of

    a. an estate for years.
    b. an estate from year to year.
    c. tenancy at will.
    d. tenancy at sufferance.

78. A property owner signs a listing agreement with a sponsoring broker. A second broker obtains a buyer for the house, and the sponsoring broker does not receive a commission. The sponsoring broker does not sue the seller. The listing agreement between the seller and the sponsoring broker was most likely a(n)

    a. exclusive right to sell.
    b. open.
    c. exclusive agency.
    d. dual agency.

79. A sponsoring broker established the following office policy: "All listings taken by any licensee associated with this real estate brokerage must include compensation based on a 5 percent commission. No lower commission rate is acceptable." If the sponsoring broker attempts to impose this uniform commission requirement, which of the following statements is *TRUE?*

    a. A homeowner may sue the sponsoring broker for violating the antitrust law's prohibition against price-fixing.
    b. The licensees associated with the brokerage will not be bound by the requirement and may negotiate any commission rate they choose.
    c. The sponsoring broker must present the uniform commission policy to the local professional association for approval.
    d. The sponsoring broker may, as a matter of office policy, legally set the minimum commission rate acceptable for the firm.

80. Because the owner of an apartment building failed to perform routine maintenance, the apartment building's central heating plant broke down in the fall. The owner neglected to have the heating system repaired, and the tenant had no heat in her apartment for the first six weeks of winter. Although eight months remained on the tenant's lease, she moved out of the apartment and refused to pay any rent. If the owner sues to recover the outstanding rent, which of the following would be the tenant's *BEST* defense?

    a. Because the tenant lived in the apartment for more than 25 percent of the lease term, she was entitled to move out at any time without penalty.
    b. The tenant was entitled to vacate the premises because the landlord's failure to repair the heating system constituted abandonment.
    c. Because the apartment was made uninhabitable, the landlord's actions constituted actual eviction.
    d. The landlord's actions constituted constructive eviction.

81. A buyer purchased a parcel of land and immediately sold the mineral rights to an oil company. The buyer gave up which of the following?

    a. Air rights
    b. Surface rights
    c. Subsurface rights
    d. Occupancy rights

82. A developer built a six-story structure. Several years later, an ordinance was passed in that area banning any building six stories or higher. This building is a

    a. nonconforming use.
    b. situation in which the structure would have to be demolished.
    c. conditional use.
    d. violation of the zoning laws.

83. What is the maximum capital gains tax exclusion allowable for a married couple, filing jointly, who have lived in their home for the past 3½ years?

    a. $100,000
    b. $250,000
    c. $500,000
    d. $750,000

84. Statements by a real estate licensee that somewhat exaggerate the intangibles of a property without committing fraud are called

    a. polishing.
    b. puffing.
    c. prospecting.
    d. marketing.

85. When planning a subdivision, a developer should determine the kinds of land uses to be involved and the amounts of land to be allocated to each use by considering

    a. which are the most profitable types of buildings to construct.
    b. what he considers an ideal development.
    c. the comprehensive plan of the local government.
    d. the customs of the area and what other developers have already done.

86. Which of the following is TRUE regarding condominiums?

    a. If a unit owner does not pay the monthly maintenance fee, the entire community will be foreclosed.
    b. The covenants and restrictions define the responsibilities of the owners and declare how the homeowner's association will operate the condo community.
    c. Balconies and assigned parking spaces are examples of limited fee simple interests.
    d. They are a blend of severalty and tenancy in common ownership.

87. Which of the following is a legal practice?

    a. To refuse to sell, rent, or negotiate with a person because of race
    b. As a property manager, to check the credit of females only
    c. To display the Equal Housing Opportunity poster
    d. To refuse to let persons with a disability, at their expense, modify a dwelling

88. Which of the following is a voidable contract?

    a. A contract with no contingencies.
    b. A contract entered into on a legal holiday.
    c. A contract that has not been recorded with the recorder of deeds.
    d. A contract entered into by a minor.

89. An owner has entered into a three-month listing agreement with a sponsoring broker. Last week, the owner also entered into the same three-month listing agreement with two separate brokers. The owner has negotiated

    a. exclusive-right-to-sell listings.
    b. exclusive agency listings.
    c. open listings.
    d. net listings.

90. An appraiser has been contracted to determine the value of a large apartment building for a potential investor client. Which appraisal method is the MOST useful for this type of property?

    a. Comparative market analysis
    b. The square foot method
    c. Income approach
    d. Cost approach

EXAM ONE PART TWO—ILLINOIS REAL ESTATE LAW AND PRACTICE

1. A large manufacturing company agrees to relocate to an economically depressed neighborhood of Chicago if the city can provide suitable property in a short period of time. The property needed is a large vacant lot-owned by an investment partnership that refuses to sell. If the City of Chicago wants to relieve unemployment in the neighborhood and improve commercial conditions in the city by bringing in the manufacturer immediately, what can the city legally do?
   a. Nothing. Private real property is exempt from the power of eminent domain
   b. Obtain title to the property by escheat through the provisions of Article I, Section 15, of the Illinois Constitution
   c. Obtain title to the property through a court action seeking condemnation of the property
   d. Obtain immediate rights of possession and use by depositing a sum of money that a court preliminarily considers to be just compensation with the county treasurer through a process known as a quick-take

2. Illinois law requires that a preprinted offer to purchase that is intended to become a binding contract have which of the following headings?
   a. Real Estate Sales Contract
   b. Offer to Purchase
   c. Standard Purchase Offer and Contract
   d. Purchase Offer Form

3. In 1971, a developer conveyed a motel and restaurant to an investor "on condition that no liquor is ever served on the property." The conveyance provided that if liquor was served on this property, ownership would revert to the developer. In 2011, the investor sold the motel and restaurant to his son. Based on these facts, which statement is *TRUE*?
   a. The sale of the motel and restaurant in 2011 extinguished the developer's right of reverter.
   b. Both the developer's right of reverter and the condition expired by operation of Illinois statute in 2000; the investor is free to sell the motel and restaurant without condition.
   c. While the condition continues forever, the developer's right of reverter automatically expired in 2011.
   d. Both the condition and the developer's right of reverter automatically expired in 2005.

4. A couple is married and both Illinois residents. If their co-owned home is sold to satisfy their unpaid credit card debts, what is the maximum the creditors will receive if the property sells for $165,000?
   a. Nothing. By statute, an Illinois resident's home may not be sold except to satisfy a mortgage debt or real estate taxes
   b. $135,000
   c. $157,500
   d. $163,600

5. Which of the following statements in a deed would establish a valid tenancy by the entirety in Illinois?
   a. "To A and B, a lawfully married couple, as tenants by the entirety"
   b. "To A and B, husband and wife, not as joint tenants or tenants in common but as tenants by the entirety"
   c. "To A and B jointly, as married tenants by the entirety"
   d. "To A and B as tenants by the entirety in accordance with Illinois law"

6. An ownership arrangement in which the purchaser receives a fee simple ownership in real property for longer than three years but the right to actually use the property for a specific period of less than one year (on a recurring basis) is a
   a. time-share use.
   b. time-share estate.
   c. public offering statement.
   d. membership camp.

7. Which of the following would be required to be surveyed and have a plat recorded under the Illinois Plat Act?
   a. An owner divides a 30-acre parcel into five equal lots.
   b. An owner divides a 20-acre parcel into five equal lots.
   c. An owner conveys a single 20-acre parcel.
   d. An owner divides a single 20-acre parcel into two 6-acre lots and an 8-acre lot.

8. The general datum plane referred to by surveyors throughout Illinois is the
   a. Chicago City Datum.
   b. New York Harbor Datum.
   c. United States Geological Survey Datum.
   d. Centralia Datum.

9. While the identity of the beneficiary of a land trust is not usually disclosed without the beneficiary's written permission, under what conditions may the trustee be compelled to do so?
   a. When the information is demanded by the Illinois Department of Revenue
   b. During the discovery process of a lawsuit or criminal action not involving the property
   c. When a private request is filed in the public records office
   d. When applying to a state agency for a license or permit affecting the property

10. An owner paid the first installment of her Illinois general real estate tax on July 1. The amount due was $2,380. If the county assessor issued the owner's bill 30 days before the penalty date of June 1, does the owner owe any penalty?
   a. No. The penalty date for the payment of all Illinois general real estate taxes is September 1.
   b. Yes. The owner will have to pay $35.70 as a penalty in addition to the real estate tax owed.
   c. No. The assessor is required by statute to issue tax bills 60 days before any penalty date.
   d. Yes. The owner will have to pay $71.40 as a penalty in addition to the real estate tax owed.

11. A judgment issued by an Illinois court is a
   a. general, involuntary legal lien on all of a debtor's real property and an equitable, specific lien on the debtor's personal property.
   b. general, involuntary, equitable lien on both real and personal property owned by the debtor.
   c. specific lien on the debtor's real and personal property, effective for a nonrenewable period of five years.
   d. general, involuntary, equitable lien on both real and personal property, effective for renewable five-year periods.

12. A man owned property in Peoria prior to his marriage. The wife has no ownership interest in the property. The owner and his wife live in Chicago, and a tenant occupies the house in Peoria. If the owner wants to sell the property, who is required by law to sign the listing agreement?

   a. Both the owner and his wife because they are a married couple
   b. The owner only, because he and his wife do not live in the house
   c. The owner and the tenant as tenant in possession
   d. The owner, his wife, and the tenant

13. A common item appearing in an Illinois listing agreement is

   a. a statement that the property must be shown only to certain prospective buyers because of race, color, religion, national origin, sex, handicap, or familial status.
   b. the time duration of the listing.
   c. the complete legal description of the property being sold.
   d. the proposed net sales price of the property.

14. In Illinois, which agency is responsible for licensing leasing agents?

   a. Division of Professional Regulation
   b. Department of Financial Institutions
   c. Illinois Department of Financial and Professional Regulation
   d. Department of Insurance Registration

15. In Illinois, when a sponsoring broker is taking a listing and asks the seller to complete a disclosure of property conditions,

   a. the disclosures are optional, and the seller may avoid liability by refusing to make any disclosures about the condition of the property.
   b. the standard disclosures cover a narrow range of structural conditions only.
   c. the sponsoring broker should give the seller advice regarding which property conditions to disclose and which to ignore.
   d. seller disclosure of known property conditions is required by Illinois statute.

16. How long must a claimant hold adverse, exclusive, continuous, and uninterrupted use of a property under claim of right in Illinois in order to obtain a prescriptive easement in Illinois?

   a. 10 years
   b. 17 years
   c. 20 years
   d. 30 years

17. An Illinois real estate licensee is the listing agent for a home. After one month of the three-month listing has gone by without any offers on the property, the licensee becomes concerned. At the time the listing agreement was signed, the licensee and the sellers orally agreed that if no offers were received after one month, the price of the property would be reduced by 10 percent. Because the sellers are out of town, the licensee crosses out the old listing price, writes in the new one, and then updates the information on the computerized listing service. Three days later, a prospective buyer comes into the listing licensee's office to make an offer on the property. Based on these facts, which of the following statements is TRUE?

   a. Illinois licensees are prohibited by law from making any addition to, deletion from, or other alteration of a written listing agreement without the written consent of the principal.
   b. Although Illinois law usually prohibits altering a written listing agreement, the listing licensee acted properly in this situation because the sellers were out of town.
   c. Changing the listing price of a property is a matter of professional discretion, and Illinois licensees are permitted to make alterations to only that aspect of a listing agreement without the written consent of the principal.
   d. Although Illinois law usually prohibits altering a written listing agreement, the listing licensee acted properly in this situation because of the prior oral agreement with the sellers.

18. A sponsoring broker signs a listing agreement with a seller. The agreement contains the following clause: "If the property has not been sold after three months from the date of this signing, this agreement will automatically continue for additional three-month periods thereafter until the property is sold." Based on these facts, which of the following statements is *TRUE*?

    a. The agreement is legal under Illinois law, because it contains a reference to a specific time limit.
    b. This agreement is illegal in Illinois.
    c. Illinois law will automatically apply a statutory six-month listing period to this open listing.
    d. This agreement is legal under Illinois law because the time periods are for less than six months each.

19. Under a land contract in Illinois, what type of title does the purchaser have until the "final" closing when the obligation to seller is paid in full?

    a. Equitable title
    b. Full legal title
    c. Land title
    d. No title

20. How are members of the Illinois Real Estate Administration and Disciplinary Board selected?

    a. Appointed by the Governor
    b. Appointed by the Commissioner of Real Estate
    c. Elected by licensees
    d. Elected in statewide elections every six years

21. What is the advantage of seeking an injunction against a licensee who is violating the Illinois Real Estate License Act of 2000?

    a. The statute of limitations no longer applies.
    b. When the injunction is granted, it doubles the penalty for violations of the Act.
    c. It increases the offense to a felony.
    d. It stops the violation from continuing.

22. An Illinois licensee's license may be suspended or revoked for which of the following actions?

    a. Giving earnest money to his or her sponsoring broker rather than depositing it directly
    b. Being declared mentally incompetent
    c. Disclosing agency
    d. Displaying a For Sale sign on a property with the owner's consent

23. In Illinois, which of the following is a required element of a valid deed?

    a. Specifically identified grantee
    b. Notarization of grantees' signature
    c. Hold harmless clause
    d. Name of the lender

24. An approximately straight line (except for corrections) connecting Rockford and Cairo is the

    a. Second Principal Meridian.
    b. Third Principal Meridian.
    c. Fourth Principal Meridian.
    d. Centralia Base Line.

25. A sponsoring broker received an earnest money deposit along with a sales contract from a buyer. Under Illinois law, what must the sponsoring broker do with the money?

    a. Open a special, separate escrow account that will contain funds for this transaction only, separate from funds received in any other transaction
    b. Deposit the money in an existing special noninterest-bearing escrow account in which all earnest money received from buyers may be held at the same time
    c. Immediately (or by the next business day) commingle the funds by depositing the earnest money in his personal interest-bearing checking or savings account
    d. Hold the earnest money deposit in a secure place in his real estate brokerage office until the offer is accepted

26. *Chicago Bar Association, et al. v. Quinlan and Tyson, Inc.* established what principle in Illinois real estate law?

a. Real estate sponsoring brokers must establish a special escrow account for earnest money deposits.

b. The seller must bear any losses that occur before title to property passes or before the buyer takes possession.

c. Real estate licensees may only fill in blanks and make appropriate deletions on pre-printed standard form contracts.

d. Once a contract is signed, a real estate licensee may not make any additions, deletions, or insertions without the written consent of the parties.

27. Under Illinois law, what is the statutory usury ceiling on loans secured by real estate?

a. 10 percent

b. 15 percent

c. 22 percent

d. There is no limit

28. A real estate licensee is aware that certain areas of the city are particularly unfriendly to members of certain minority groups. For these groups' own protection, the licensee shows members of such groups homes for sale only in "friendly" neighborhoods into which members of their minority group have moved in the past. Based on these facts, which of the following statements is *TRUE*?

a. The Real Estate License Act of 2000 does not prohibit the licensee's actions, because the licensee is being protective rather than discriminatory.

b. The critical element in this type of activity is profit motive; if the licensee's actions are not driven by increased profits, the licensee will not be subject to discipline under the Real Estate License Act of 2000.

c. While the licensee's actions are clearly prohibited by Illinois statute, the Real Estate License Act of 2000 does not address blockbusting or steering.

d. The licensee's actions are expressly prohibited by the Real Estate License Act of 2000.

29. The sale price of the property is $250,000. What is the Illinois state transfer tax on this transaction?

a. $125

b. $250

c. $500

d. $1,250

30. In the previous question, how much of the state transfer tax payable will go to fund affordable housing under the Illinois Affordable Housing Act?

a. 10 percent

b. 25 percent

c. 50 percent

d. None

31. In Illinois, how must the real property transfer tax be paid?

a. By personal check, made out to the Illinois Department of Revenue

b. By certified check, made out to the Illinois Housing Development Authority

c. By purchasing transfer tax stamps from the county recorder or appropriate local authority

d. In monthly payments to the lender during the first five years of ownership

32. In Illinois, which property is totally exempt from paying general real estate taxes?

a. Retirement housing for the elderly

b. Properties financed with FHA funds

c. Private schools

d. Housing owned by a disabled veteran

33. A landlord has a "no pets" policy in his apartment building. If a visually impaired person wants to rent an apartment from the landlord, but owns a guide dog, which of the following statements is *TRUE*?

a. If the landlord's "no pets" policy is applied uniformly, in a nondiscriminatory manner, it may be legally applied to the guide dog as well.

b. The Illinois Human Rights Act specifically prohibits the landlord from refusing to rent the apartment to the visually impaired person on the basis of the landlord's "no pets" policy.

c. Under the Illinois Human Rights Act, the landlord may not discriminate against the visually impaired person on the basis of a "no pets" policy, but the landlord may require the tenant to pay an additional damage fee.

d. The Illinois Human Rights Act does not address the issue of guide, hearing, or support dogs.

34. Real property was conveyed for $185,000. What amount will have to be paid in county transfer tax?

a. $37.00
b. $92.50
c. $185.00
d. $1,850.00

35. Which of the following statements is *TRUE* of an Illinois county having fewer than 60,000 residents?

a. The recorder of deeds must be elected.

b. Deeds are recorded by the elected recorder of deeds in the nearest county having a population over 60,000.

c. The city clerk of the largest population center acts as recorder of deeds.

d. The county clerk also serves as recorder of deeds.

36. Which is a requirement for a deed to be recorded in Illinois?

a. The name of the grantee must be typed or printed below the grantee's signature

b. Payment of required tax stamps

c. A blank page for use by the recorder

d. The name, address, and age of the grantee

37. The purpose of the Real Estate Recovery Fund is to

a. permit licensees to reestablish their businesses after a natural or financial disaster.

b. reward consumers for identifying licensees who are engaged in violations of the real estate license law or other wrongful acts.

c. compensate individuals who suffer losses due to the wrongful acts of a licensee.

d. pay for the court costs and legal fees required to defend licensees against accusations of wrongdoing.

38. Which activity requires a real estate license?

a. MLS providing listing information to members

b. A resident manager who collects rent on behalf of a building owner

c. A service that, for a fee, matches individuals who want to buy and sell properties

d. An executor selling a decedent's building

39. An Illinois real estate broker is also a part-owner of a title insurance company. The broker has registered with the appropriate state agency and has disclosed the relationship to the owner of a farm. Under these facts, can the broker recommend that this title insurance company produce the title insurance policy when the farm sells?

a. Yes. The broker has fully complied with the requirements of the Illinois Title Insurance Act.

b. No. The broker must also obtain the written permission of her client.

c. Yes. Because the broker is only a part owner of the title insurance company, the provisions of the Illinois Title Insurance Act do not apply.

d. Yes. If the broker also fills out and provides state disclosure forms to both her clients.

40. What is the name of the act that requires that Illinois developers file statements of record with HUD before they offer unimproved lots for sale in interstate commerce via telephone?
    a. HUD Registration Act
    b. Interstate Land Sales Full Disclosure Act
    c. Interstate Undeveloped Land Act
    d. NAFA

41. In Illinois, if an owner defaults on a mortgage loan and the property is ordered sold at a foreclosure sale, the owner may redeem the property
    a. prior to the sale, under the statutory right of redemption.
    b. prior to the sale, under the equitable right of redemption.
    c. after the sale, under the statutory right of redemption.
    d. after the sale, under the statutory right of reinstatement.

42. For three days, a man watched from his kitchen window as a small construction crew built an attractive gazebo in his backyard. The man had not contracted with anyone to build a gazebo and in fact had never given much thought to having one. But the man liked what he saw. When the contractor presented the man with a bill for the work, the man refused to pay, pointing out that he'd never signed a contract to have the work done. Can the contractor impose a mechanic's lien on the man's property under Illinois law?
    a. No. In Illinois a mechanic's lien attaches on the date the contract is signed or the work is ordered, and neither event occurred here.
    b. No. The man cannot be forced to pay for the contractor's mistake.
    c. Yes. If a landowner knows of work being done on the property and does not object or disclaim responsibility, a mechanic's lien may be create
    d. Yes. The man should have mailed a notice of nonresponsibility to the contractor's main place of business.

43. A woman's property in Peoria has an assessed value of $175,000. The local tax rate is 3 percent, and no equalization factor is used. If the tax was levied in April 2011, the woman had to pay
    a. $5,250 on June 1, 2011.
    b. $2,625 on September 1, 2011.
    c. $2,625 on January 1, 2012.
    d. $2,625 on June 1, 2012.

44. In Illinois, real estate licensees may
    a. complete a bill of sale after a sales contract has been signed.
    b. fill in blanks on preprinted form contracts customarily used in their community.
    c. suggest additional language to be added to a preprinted sales contract by a buyer or seller.
    d. explain the legal significance of specific preprinted contract clauses to a buyer or seller.

45. For which of the following acts is the Department required to suspend or revoke a licensee's license?
    a. Failing to perform as promised in a guaranteed sales plan
    b. Having been found liable in a civil trial for illegal discrimination
    c. Commingling others' money or property with the licensee's own
    d. Failing to provide information requested by the Department within 30 days of the request as part of a complaint or audit procedure

46. Three weeks before a man begins his Illinois real estate prelicense class, he offers to help his neighbor sell her house. The neighbor agrees to pay him a 5 percent commission. An offer is accepted while the man is taking the class and closes the day before the man passes the examination and receives his real estate license. The neighbor refuses to pay the man the agreed commission. Can the man sue to recover payment?

   a. Yes. Because the man was formally enrolled in a course of study intended to result in a real estate license at the time an offer was procured and accepted, the commission agreement is binding.

   b. No. In Illinois, a real estate licensee must be sponsored by a broker who has a permanent office in affiliate licenses are displayed in order to collect a commission from a seller.

   c. Yes. While the statute of frauds forbids recovery on an oral agreement for the conveyance of real property, Illinois law permits enforcement of an oral commission contract under these facts.

   d. No. Illinois law prohibits lawsuits to collect commissions unless the injured party is a real estate licensee and the license was in effect before the agreement was reached.

47. An Illinois real estate licensee may lawfully collect compensation from

   a. either a buyer or a seller.
   b. a sponsoring broker only.
   c. any party to the transaction or the party's representative.
   d. a licensed real estate broker only.

48. A woman has a mortgage loan secured by real property. Under recent law, the woman may terminate the loan's escrow account when the remaining balance is equal to or less than what percentage of the original amount?

   a. 35 percent
   b. 50 percent
   c. 65 percent
   d. 75 percent

49. Three people decide to form a partnership to buy and sell real estate. One partner plans to specialize in residential real estate, the second in commercial real estate, and the third does not plan to list, sell, or rent, but to supervise the office décor and to plan holiday parties. Under these facts, which of the general partners needs to be licensed for the partnership to qualify for a managing broker's license in Illinois?

   a. None. Under Illinois law, a partnership is an independent entity that may obtain a managing broker's license regardless of the status of any individual partner.

   b. Either of the two who are listing and selling, depending on whether the partnership's emphasis will be residential or commercial properties.

   c. Both licensees who are listing and selling residential and commercial real estate must be licensed managing brokers, but the person who oversees the office decor need not be licensed.

   d. All three partners must be licensed real estate managing brokers.

50. With regard to mortgages, Illinois is most accurately described as a(n)

   a. intermediate mortgage theory state.
   b. lien-theory state.
   c. title-theory state.
   d. equitable-theory state.

51. Which of the following is legal in Illinois?

   a. Offering finder's fees to consumers
   b. Giving referral fees to other licensees
   c. Using a lottery to convey the property
   d. Indicating a "standard commission" when asked

52. Regarding security deposits, what difference is there between requirements for the landlord of a three-unit apartment building and the landlord of a 30-unit apartment building?

    a. Both landlords must give tenants an item-ized statement of alleged damages before they can withhold any part of the security deposit as compensation.

    b. Only the landlord of the 30-unit building is required to pay interest on security deposits.

    c. Only the landlord of the three-unit build-ing is required to give tenants an itemized statement of alleged damages before any part of the security deposit may be withheld as compensation.

    d. Both landlords are required to pay interest on security deposits at a rate linked to mini-mum deposit passbook savings accounts at Illinois's largest commercial bank.

53. How many members are on the Illinois Real Estate Administration and Disciplinary Board?

    a. 6
    b. 8
    c. 9
    d. 12

54. In Illinois, how much written notice is a land-lord required to give a tenant to pay overdue rent prior to terminating the lease, when the tenant is in default only for failing to pay rent on time?

    a. 0 days
    b. 3 days
    c. 5 days
    d. 10 days

55. In Illinois, if a home rule county has an ordi-nance that conflicts with that of a home rule city, whose ordinance will prevail?

    a. The county's ordinance
    b. The city's ordinance
    c. The relevant township ordinance
    d. The dispute is constitutional in nature and so may be resolved only by the Illinois Supreme Court.

56. A non-possessory interest in real property is also called a(n)

    a. encumbrance.
    b. leasehold estate.
    c. license.
    d. servient tenement.

57. When a broker is representing her client, she is MOST likely acting as a(n)

    a. universal agent.
    b. ostensible agent.
    c. special agent.
    d. dual agent.

58. Which lien has priority in a foreclosure sale?

    a. First lien recorded
    b. Mechanics or materialmen who file a timely notice after commencing work on the property
    c. Delinquent property taxes
    d. Mortgagee or original lender

59. The individual appointed to the position of Real Estate Coordinator

    a. may not have held a real estate license in the past.
    b. must surrender the real estate license for during the appointment.
    c. must hold an active real estate license.
    d. must sign a statement that she will not pursue real estate activities that require a license during the appointment.

60. What is the penalty if a person is convicted of practicing real estate without first obtaining a real estate license?

    a. Fine of up to $5,000 and/or up to six months imprisonment
    b. Fine up to $10,000 but no prison
    c. Up to $25,000 for each offense
    d. Minimum of six months but no more than one year imprisonment

EXAM TWO PART ONE—GENERAL REAL ESTATE PRACTICE AND PRINCIPLES

1. A landlord sold an apartment building so that a freeway can be built. The tenant's lease has expired, but the landlord permits him to stay in the apartment until the building is torn down. The tenant continues to pay the rent as prescribed in the lease. What kind of tenancy does the tenant have?
   a. Holdover tenancy
   b. Month-to-month tenancy
   c. Tenancy at sufferance
   d. Tenancy at will

2. The owner of a house wants to fence the yard for her dog. When the fence is erected, the fencing materials are converted to real estate by
   a. severance.
   b. subrogation.
   c. adaptation.
   d. attachment.

3. A man is interested in selling his house as quickly as possible and believes that the best way to do this is to have several brokers compete against each other for the commission. The man's listing agreements with four different brokers specifically promise that if one of them finds a buyer for his property, the man will be obligated to pay a commission to that broker. What type of agreement has the man entered into?
   a. Executed
   b. Discharged
   c. Unilateral
   d. Bilateral

4. In some states, by paying the debt after a foreclosure sale, a borrower has the right to regain the property under which of the following?
   a. Novation
   b. Redemption
   c. Reversion
   d. Recovery

5. A woman enters into a sale-leaseback agreement with a man, under which the man will become the owner of the woman's ranch. Which of the following statements is *TRUE* of this arrangement?
   a. The woman retains title to the ranch.
   b. The man receives possession of the property.
   c. The man is the lessor.
   d. The woman is the lessor.

6. An investor hires a real estate licensee to locate suitable properties for investment purposes. When the licensee finds a property that the investor might be interested in buying, she is careful to find out as much as possible about the property's owners and why their property is on the market. The licensee's efforts to keep the investor informed of all facts that could affect a transaction is the common-law duty of
   a. care.
   b. loyalty.
   c. obedience.
   d. disclosure.

7. A parcel of vacant land 80 feet wide and 200 feet deep was sold for $200 per front foot. How much money would a broker receive for her 60 percent share in the 10 percent commission?
   a. $640
   b. $960
   c. $1,600
   d. $2,400

8. Which situation violates the federal Fair Housing Act of 1968?

    a. The refusal of a property manager to rent an apartment to a Catholic couple who is not otherwise qualified

    b. The general policy of a loan company to grant home improvement loans to qualified individuals living in transitional neighborhoods

    c. A widowed woman's insistence on renting her spare bedroom only to another widowed woman

    d. The intentional neglect of a broker to show an Asian family any property listings in all-white neighborhoods

9. If a storage tank that measures 12 feet by 9 feet by 8 feet is designed to store a gas that costs $1.82 per cubic foot, what does it cost to fill the tank to one-half of its capacity?

    a. $685
    b. $786
    c. $864
    d. $1,572

10. A condo was purchased for $125,000. It appraised for $120,500 and previously sold for $118,250. Based on these facts, if the purchaser applies for an 80 percent mortgage, what will be the amount of the loan the purchaser will receive?

    a. $94,600
    b. $96,400
    c. $100,000
    d. $106,750

11. A buyer and a seller both sign a purchase contract. What kind of title interest, if any, does the buyer have in the property at this point?

    a. Legal
    b. Equitable
    c. Defeasible
    d. The buyer has no title interest at this point.

12. Which of the following federal laws requires that finance charges be stated as an annual percentage rate?

    a. Truth in Lending Act
    b. Real Estate Settlement Procedures Act (RESPA)
    c. Equal Credit Opportunity Act (ECOA)
    d. Federal Fair Housing Act

13. A seller signed a 90-day listing agreement with a sponsoring broker. Two weeks later, the seller was killed in an accident. What is the present status of the listing?

    a. The listing agreement is binding on the seller's estate for the remainder of the 90 days.

    b. Because the seller's intention to sell was clearly defined, the listing agreement is still in effect and the sponsoring broker may proceed to market the property on behalf of the seller's estate.

    c. The listing agreement is binding on the seller's estate only if the sponsoring broker can produce an offer to purchase the property within the remainder of the listing period.

    d. The listing agreement was terminated automatically when the seller died.

14. A woman conveys the ownership of an office building to a nursing home. The nursing home agrees that the rental income will pay for the expenses of caring for the woman's parents. When the woman's parents die, ownership of the office building will revert to the woman. The estate held by the nursing home is a

    a. remainder life estate.
    b. legal life estate.
    c. life estate pur autre vie.
    d. temporary leasehold estate.

15. A purchaser signs a buyer's brokerage agreement under which the real estate broker will help the purchaser find a three-bedroom house in the $285,000 to $300,000 price range. A seller comes into the licensee's office and signs a listing agreement to sell the seller's two-bedroom condominium for $170,000. Based on these facts, which of the following statements is *TRUE*?

    a. The purchaser is the licensee's client; the seller is the licensee's customer.
    b. The purchaser is the licensee's customer; the seller is the licensee's client.
    c. While both the purchaser and the seller are clients, the licensee owes the fiduciary duties of an agent only to the seller.
    d. Because both Stan and James are the licensee's clients, the licensee owes the fiduciary duties of an agent to both.

16. In a township of 36 sections, which of the following statements is *TRUE*?

    a. Section 31 lies to the east of Section 32.
    b. Section 18 is by law set aside for school purposes.
    c. Section 6 lies in the northeast corner of the township.
    d. Section 16 lies to the north of Section 21.

17. A lawyer represented the seller in a transaction. Her client informed her that he did not want to recite the actual consideration that was paid for the house. Based on these instructions, the lawyer

    a. must inform her client that only the actual price of the real estate may appear on the deed.
    b. may prepare a deed that shows only nominal consideration of $10.
    c. should inform the seller that either the full price should be stated in the deed or all references to consideration should be removed from it.
    d. may show a price on the deed other than the actual price, provided that the variance is not greater than 10 percent of the purchase price.

18. A sponsoring broker obtained a listing agreement to act as the listing agent in the sale of the client's home. When a buyer was found for the property, all agreements were signed. As an agent for the seller, the sponsoring broker is responsible for

    a. completing the buyer's loan application.
    b. making sure that the buyer receives copies of all documents the seller is required to deliver to the buyer.
    c. ensuring that the buyer is qualified for the new mortgage loan.
    d. scheduling the buyer's inspection of the property.

19. What is a real estate broker's share of the commission when the sales price of a property was $195,000 and the broker is entitled to 65 percent of the 7.5 percent commission?

    a. $950.63
    b. $8,872.50
    c. $9,506.25
    d. $95,062.50

20. An appraiser estimates the value of a property using the cost approach. Which of the following describes what the appraiser should do?

    a. Estimate the replacement cost of the improvements
    b. Deduct the depreciation of the land and buildings
    c. Determine the original cost and adjust for depreciation
    d. Review the sales prices of comparable properties

21. Before the closing of a real estate transaction, a mortgage loan originator (MLO) provides the buyer and seller with statements of all fees and charges they will incur. In doing this, the MLO complies with the

    a. Equal Credit Opportunity Act (ECOA).
    b. Truth in Lending Act (Regulation Z).
    c. Real Estate Settlement Procedures Act (RESPA).
    d. Fair Housing Act.

22. The landlord of an apartment building neglected to repair the building's plumbing system. As a result, the apartments did not receive water, as provided by the leases. If a tenant's unit becomes uninhabitable, which of the following would MOST likely result?

    a. Suit for possession
    b. Claim of constructive eviction
    c. Tenancy at sufferance
    d. Suit for negligence

23. A man conveys a life estate to his sister. Under the terms of the man's conveyance, the property will pass to his niece upon his sister's death. Which of the following BEST describes the niece's interest in the property during the sister's lifetime?

    a. Remainder
    b. Reversion
    c. Life estate pur autre vie
    d. Redemption

24. On a settlement statement, prorations for real estate taxes paid in arrears are shown as a

    a. credit to the seller and a debit to the buyer.
    b. debit to the seller and a credit to the buyer.
    c. credit to both the seller and the buyer.
    d. debit to both the seller and the buyer.

25. What type of lease establishes a rental payment and requires that the lessor pay for the taxes, insurance, and maintenance on the property?

    a. Percentage
    b. Net
    c. Expense only
    d. Gross

26. A conventional loan was closed on July 1 for $57,200 at 13.5 percent interest amortized over 25 years at $666.75 per month. On September 1, what would the principal amount be after the monthly payment was made?

    a. $56,533.25
    b. $56,556.50
    c. $57,065.35
    d. $57,176.75

27. In the preceding question, what would the interest portion of the payment be?

    a. $610.65
    b. $620.25
    c. $643.50
    d. $666.75

28. When the seller listed her home with the sponsoring broker for $190,000, the seller told the broker, "I have to sell quickly because of a job transfer. If necessary, I can accept a price as low as $175,000." The broker tells a prospective buyer to offer $180,000 "because the seller is desperate to sell." The seller accepts the buyer's offer. Based on these facts, the broker

    a. did not violate his agency relationship with the seller because the broker did not reveal the seller's lowest acceptable price.
    b. violated his agency relationship with the seller.
    c. acted properly to obtain a quick offer on the seller's property, in accordance with the seller's instructions.
    d. violated his duties toward the buyer by failing to disclose that the seller would accept a lower price than the buyer offered.

29. Which of the following BEST describes the capitalization rate under the income approach to estimating the value of real estate?

    a. Rate at which a property increases in value
    b. Rate of return a property earns as an investment
    c. Rate of capital required to keep a property operating most efficiently
    d. Maximum rate of return allowed by law on an investment

30. On a settlement statement, the cost of the lender's title insurance policy required for a new loan is usually shown as which of the following?

    a. Credit to the seller
    b. Credit to the buyer
    c. Debit to the seller
    d. Debit to the buyer

31. An FHA-insured loan for $57,500 at 8.5 percent for 30 years was closed on July 17, 2011. The first monthly payment is due on September 1. Because interest is paid monthly in arrears, what was the amount of the interest adjustment the buyer owes at the settlement, using the statutory method?

    a. $190.07
    b. $230.80
    c. $407.29
    d. $4,887.50

32. If a home that originally cost $142,500 three years ago is now valued at 127 percent of its original cost, what is its current market value?

    a. $164,025
    b. $172,205
    c. $174,310
    d. $180,975

33. A woman has a contract to paint her brother's garage door for $1,200. Before starting the project, the woman has a skiing accident and breaks both arms. She asks a friend to take over the job. The friend paints the brother's garage door, and the brother pays the friend $1,200 for the work. This scenario is an example of

    a. assignment.
    b. acceptance.
    c. novation.
    d. revocation.

34. When searching the public record regarding title to a specific property, what is the researcher MOST likely to find?

    a. Encroachments
    b. Rights of parties in possession
    c. Inaccurate survey
    d. Judgments

35. A rectangular lot is worth $193,600. This value is the equivalent of $4.40 per square foot. If one lot dimension is 200 feet, what is the other dimension?

    a. 110 feet
    b. 220 feet
    c. 400 feet
    d. 880 feet

36. A sponsoring broker listed a seller's property at an 8 percent commission rate. After the property was sold and the settlement had taken place, the seller discovered that the broker had been listing similar properties at 6 percent commission rates. Based on this information alone, which of the following statements is TRUE?

    a. The broker has done nothing wrong because a commission rate is always negotiable between the parties.
    b. If the broker inflated the usual commission rate for the area, the broker may be subject to discipline by the state real estate commission.
    c. The seller is entitled to rescind the transaction based on the principle of lack of reality of consent.
    d. The seller is entitled to a refund from the broker of 2 percent of the commission.

37. A woman has six months remaining on her apartment lease. Her monthly rent is $1875. The woman moves out of the apartment, and her friend moves in. The friend pays the woman a monthly rental of $1700, and the woman continues paying the full rental amount under her lease to the landlord. When the woman's lease term expires, her friend will either move out or sign a new lease with the landlord. This is an example of

    a. assignment.
    b. subletting.
    c. rescission and renewal.
    d. surrender.

38. One broker asked another, "Will I have to prove that I was the procuring cause if my seller sells the property himself?" The other broker answers, "No, not if you have an

    a. option listing."
    b. open listing."
    c. exclusive-agency listing."
    d. exclusive-right-to-sell listing."

39. The capitalization rate on a property reflects which of the following factors?

    a. Risk of the investment
    b. Replacement cost of the improvements
    c. Real estate taxes
    d. Debt service

40. An investment property worth $180,000 was purchased seven years ago for $142,000. At the time of the purchase, the land was valued at $18,000. Assuming a 31½-year life for straight-line depreciation purposes, what is the present book value of the property?

a. $95,071
b. $113,071
c. $114,444
d. $126,000

41. A person who dies without having made a will is said to be

a. a testate.
b. a testator.
c. in probate.
d. intestate.

42. A farmer owns the W½ of the NW¼ of the NW¼ of a section. The remainder of the NW¼ can be purchased for $300 per acre. Owning all of the NW¼ of the section would cost the farmer

a. $6,000.
b. $12,000.
c. $42,000.
d. $48,000.

43. In a standard sales contract, several words were crossed out or inserted by the parties. To eliminate future controversy as to whether the changes were made before or after the contract was signed, the usual procedure is to

a. write a letter to each party listing the changes.
b. have each party write a letter to the other approving the changes.
c. redraw the entire contract.
d. have both parties initial or sign in the margin near each change.

44. The manager of an apartment building receives an 8½ percent commission for each new tenant that he signs, based on the unit's annualized rent. In one year, the manager signed five new tenants. Three of the apartments rented for $795 per month; one rented for $1,200 per month; and one rented for $900 per month. What was the total amount of the manager's new-tenant commissions for that year?

a. $381.23
b. $2,952.90
c. $3,685.47
d. $4,574.70

45. The monthly rent on a warehouse is $1 per cubic yard. Assuming the warehouse is 36 feet by 200 feet by 12 feet high, what would the annual rent be?

a. $3,200
b. $9,600
c. $38,400
d. $115,200

46. A veteran wishes to refinance his home with a VA-guaranteed loan. The lender is willing, but insists on 3½ discount points. In this situation, the veteran can

a. refinance with a VA loan, provided the lender charges no discount points.
b. refinance with a VA loan, provided the lender charges no more than two discount points.
c. be required to pay a maximum of 1 percent of the loan as an origination fee.
d. proceed with the refinance loan and pay the discount points.

47. A father owns two properties. He conveys one property to his daughter with no restrictions; The daughter holds all rights to this property forever. The man then conveys the second property to his son "so long as no real estate licensee ever sets foot on the property." If a licensee visits the second property, ownership will revert to the father. Based on these two conveyances, which of the following statements is TRUE?

    a. The daughter holds the first property in fee simple; the son holds the second property in fee simple determinable.
    b. The daughter holds the first property in fee simple absolute; the son holds the second property in fee simple defeasible, subject to a condition subsequent.
    c. The son may not transfer ownership of the second property without his father's permission.
    d. The father has retained a right of reentry with regard to the second property.

48. A real estate transaction had a closing date of November 15. The seller, who was responsible for costs up to and including the date of settlement, paid the property taxes of $1,116 for the calendar year. On the closing statement, the buyer would be

    a. debited $139.50.
    b. debited $976.50.
    c. credited $139.50.
    d. credited $976.50.

49. An agreement that ends all future lessor-lessee obligations under a lease is known as a(n)

    a. assumption.
    b. surrender.
    c. novation.
    d. breach.

50. A man buys a house for $234,500. He makes a $25,000 cash down payment and takes out a $209,500 mortgage for 30 years. The lot value is $80,000. If the man wants to depreciate the property over a period of 27½ years, how much will the annual depreciation amount be, using the straight-line method?

    a. $3,818.18
    b. $4,709.09
    c. $5,618.18
    d. $8,527.27

51. A property manager leased a store for three years. The first year, the store's rent was $1,000 per month, and the rent was to increase 10 percent per year thereafter. The manager received a 7 percent commission for the first year, 5 percent for the second year, and 3 percent for the balance of the lease. The total commission earned by the property manager was

    a. $840.
    b. $1,613.
    c. $1,936.
    d. $2,785.

52. Against a recorded deed from the owner of record, the party with the weakest position is a

    a. person with a prior unrecorded deed who is not in possession.
    b. person in possession with a prior unrecorded deed.
    c. tenant in possession with nine months remaining on the lease.
    d. painter who is half-finished painting the house at the time of the sale and who has not yet been paid.

53. An individual bought a home in 2011 for $346,000. Three years later, he sold the home for $374,800 and moved into an apartment. In computing the individual's income tax, what amount of this transaction is taxable?

    a. $11,320
    b. $16,980
    c. $28,800
    d. Nothing is taxable; the individual's capital gain is within the exemption guidelines.

54. A man moved into an abandoned home and installed new cabinets in the kitchen. When the owner discovered the occupancy, the owner had the man ejected. What is the status of the kitchen cabinets?

   a. The man has no right to the cabinets.
   b. The cabinets remain because they are trade fixtures.
   c. Although the cabinets stay, the man is entitled to the value of the improvements.
   d. The man can keep the cabinets if they can be removed without damaging the real estate.

55. A man, his nephew, and his niece are joint tenants. The man sells his interest to his sister, and then this nephew dies. As a result, which of the following statements is *TRUE*?

   a. The nephew's heirs are joint tenants with the man and his sister.
   b. The nephew's heirs and the man are joint tenants, but the sister is a tenant in common.
   c. The man is a tenant in common with his sister's and nephew's heirs.
   d. The man and his sister are tenants in common.

56. In a settlement statement, the selling price *ALWAYS* is

   a. a debit to the buyer.
   b. a debit to the seller.
   c. a credit to the buyer.
   d. greater than the loan amount.

57. The state wants to acquire a strip of farmland to build a highway. Does the state have the right to acquire privately owned land for public use?

   a. Yes: the state's right is called condemnation.
   b. Yes: the state's right is called eminent domain.
   c. Yes: the state's right is called escheat.
   d. No: Under the U.S. Constitution, state or federal governments may never acquire private property.

58. A woman's estate was distributed according to her will as follows: 54 percent to her husband, 18 percent to her children, 16 percent to her grandchildren, and the remainder to her college. The college received $79,000. How much did the woman's children receive?

   a. $105,333
   b. $118,500
   c. $355,500
   d. $658,333

59. Which of the following is an example of external obsolescence?

   a. Numerous pillars supporting the ceiling in a store
   b. Leaks in the roof of a warehouse, making the premises unusable and therefore unrentable
   c. Coal cellar in a house with central heating
   d. Vacant, abandoned, and run-down buildings in an area

60. Which of the following phrases, when placed in a print advertisement, would comply with the requirements of the Truth in Lending Act (Regulation Z)?

   a. "12 percent interest"
   b. "12 percent rate"
   c. "12 percent annual interest"
   d. "12 percent annual percentage rate"

61. If an office building lease does not prohibit assignment or subletting, under what conditions, if any, may the tenant assign the space?

   a. Only to an associated corporation
   b. Only with any rent increase being split with the owner.
   c. After hiring legal counsel to obtain full rights to the lease.
   d. Freely

62. The Equal Credit Opportunity Act makes it illegal for lenders to refuse credit to or otherwise discriminate against which of the following applicants?

   a. Parent of twins who receives public assistance and who cannot afford the monthly mortgage payments
   b. New homebuyer who does not have a favorable credit history
   c. Single person who receives public assistance
   d. Unemployed person with no job prospects and no identifiable source of income

63. When a woman died, a deed was found in her desk drawer. While the deed had never been recorded, it was signed, dated, and acknowledged. The deed gave the woman's house to a local charity. The woman's will, however, provided as follows: "I leave all of the real and personal property that I own to my beloved nephew." In this situation, the house MOST likely will go to the

   a. charity because acknowledgment creates a presumption of delivery.
   b. charity because the woman's intent was clear from the deed.
   c. nephew because the woman still owned the house when she died.
   d. nephew because the deed had not been recorded.

64. If a woman takes out a $90,000 loan at 7½ percent interest to be repaid at the end of 15 years with interest only paid annually, what is the total interest that the woman will pay over the life of the loan?

   a. $10,125
   b. $80,000
   c. $101,250
   d. $180,000

65. After an offer is accepted, the seller finds that the sponsoring broker was the undisclosed agent for the buyer as well as the agent for the seller. The seller may

   a. withdraw without obligation to sponsoring broker or buyer.
   b. withdraw but would be subject to liquidated damages.
   c. withdraw but only with the concurrence of the buyer.
   d. refuse to sell but would be subject to a suit for specific performance.

66. To net the owner $90,000 after a 6 percent commission is paid, the selling price would have to be

   a. $95,400.
   b. $95,745.
   c. $95,906.
   d. $96,000.

67. Which of the following would MOST likely be legal under the provisions of the Civil Rights Act of 1968?

   a. A lender refuses to make loans in areas in which more than 25 percent of the population is Hispanic.
   b. A private country club development ties home ownership to club membership, but due to local demographics, all club members are white.
   c. A church excludes African Americans from membership and rents its nonprofit housing to church members only.
   d. A licensee directs prospective buyers away from areas where they are likely to feel uncomfortable because of their race.

68. It is discovered after a sale that the land parcel is 10 percent smaller than the owner represented it to be. The broker who passed this information on to the buyer is

   a. not liable as long as he only repeated the seller's data which he knew to be misrepresented.
   b. not liable if the misrepresentation was unintentional.
   c. not liable if the buyer actually inspected what she was getting.
   d. liable if he knew or should have known of the discrepancy.

69. On a residential lot 70 feet square, the side yard building setbacks are 10 feet, the front yard setback is 25 feet, and the rear yard setback is 20 feet. The maximum possible size for a single-story structure would be how many square feet?

    a. 1,000
    b. 1,200
    c. 1,250
    d. 4,900

70. What is the purpose of the Real Estate Settlement Procedures Act (RESPA)?

    a. Ensure that buyers know all settlement costs that will be charged to them
    b. Make real estate brokers more responsive to buyers' needs
    c. Require a particular title insurance company
    d. Accept a fee or charge for services that were not performed

71. The rescission provisions of the Truth in Lending Act apply to which of the following transactions?

    a. Agricultural loans
    b. Construction lending
    c. Business financing
    d. Consumer credit

72. A property has a net income of $30,000. An appraiser decides to use a 12 percent capitalization rate rather than a 10 percent rate on this property. What is the result of using the higher cap rate?

    a. 2 percent increase in the appraised value
    b. $50,000 increase in the appraised value
    c. $50,000 decrease in the appraised value
    d. No change in the appraised value

73. The section of a purchase contract that provides for the buyer to forfeit any earnest money if the buyer fails to complete the purchase is known as the provision for

    a. liquidated damages.
    b. punitive damages.
    c. hypothecation.
    d. subordination.

74. In one commercial building, the tenant intends to start a health food shop using her life savings. In an identical adjacent building is a showroom leased to a major national retailing chain. Both tenants have long-term leases with identical rents. Which of the following statements is correct?

    a. If the values of the buildings were the same before the leases, the values will be the same after the leases.
    b. An appraiser would most likely use a higher capitalization rate for the store leased to the national retailing chain.
    c. The most accurate appraisal method an appraiser could use would be the sales comparison approach to value.
    d. The building with the health food shop will probably appraise for less than the other building.

75. A builder wants to offer financial assistance to prospective buyers but does not want to lower the price of the homes. Instead the builder agrees to pay a lump sum in cash to the lender at closing so that the buyers will enjoy a lower interest rate. What type of loan is this?

    a. Equity
    b. Participation
    c. Open-end
    d. Buydown

76. A $100,000 loan at 12 percent could be amortized with monthly payments of $1,200.22 on a 15-year basis or payments of $1,028.63 on a 30-year basis. The 30-year loan results in total payments of what percent of the 15-year loan's total payments?

    a. 146 percent
    b. 158 percent
    c. 171 percent
    d. 228 percent

77. According to a broker's CMA, a property is worth $125,000. The homeowner bought the property for $90,000 and added $50,000 in improvements, for a total of $140,000. The property sold for $122,500. Which of these amounts represents the property's market price?

   a. $90,000
   b. $122,500
   c. $125,000
   d. $140,000

78. What will be the amount of tax payable where the property's assessed value is $85,000 and the tax rate is 4 percent in a community in which an equalization factor of 110 percent is used?

   a. $2,337.50
   b. $3,090.91
   c. $3,700.40
   (d.) $3,740.00 ✓

79. In a settlement statement, how will a proration of prepaid water, gas, and electric charges be reflected?

   a. Debit to the seller, credit to the buyer
   b. Debit to the buyer, credit to the seller
   c. Debit to the buyer only
   d. Credit to the seller only

80. An apartment manager decides not to purchase flood insurance. Instead, the manager installs raised platforms in the basement storage areas and has the furnace placed on eight-inch legs. This form of risk management is known as

   a. avoiding the risk.
   b. controlling the risk.
   c. retaining the risk.
   d. transferring the risk.

81. A real estate broker was responsible for a chain of events that resulted in the sale of one of his client's properties. The broker is legally referred to as the

   a. initiating factor.
   b. procuring cause.
   c. responsible party.
   d. compensable cause.

82. A characteristic of real estate licensees who are independent contractors is that they commonly receive

   a. more than 50 percent of income in the form of a monthly salary or hourly wage.
   b. company-provided health insurance and other benefits.
   c. reimbursement for documented travel and business expenses.
   d. more than 90 percent of income based on sales production.

83. In the cost approach to value, the appraiser makes use of the

   a. owner's original cost of the building.
   b. estimated current replacement cost of the building.
   c. sales prices of similar buildings in the area.
   d. assessed value of the building.

84. A buyer enters into an exclusive-agency buyer agency agreement with a real estate broker. Based on these facts, which of the following statements is TRUE?

   a. The buyer is obligated to pay the broker's compensation regardless of who finds a suitable property.
   b. If the buyer finds a suitable property without the broker's assistance, she is under no obligation to pay the broker.
   c. The buyer may enter into other, similar agreements with other brokers.
   d. If the buyer finds a suitable property without the broker's assistance, the buyer will have to pay the broker's compensation.

85. An owner is usually concerned about how much money she can get when she sells her home. A competitive market analysis may help the seller determine a realistic listing price. Which of the following is TRUE of a CMA?

   a. A competitive market analysis is the same as an appraisal.
   b. A sponsoring broker, not an affiliate, is permitted to prepare a competitive market analysis.
   c. A certified real estate appraiser prepares a competitive market analysis.
   d. A competitive market analysis contains a compilation of other similar properties that have sold.

86. An owner sells his fourplex. In regard to this situation, which of the following is *TRUE?*

    a. The tenants may void their leases.
    b. The lender may void the leases.
    c. The current leases must be honored by the new landlord.
    d. The current leases may be discharged by the previous landlord.

87. When appraising a single-family home, the appraiser would consider which of the following in determining the value of a property?

    a. Racial demographics
    b. Date sold
    c. Properties located within a 10-mile radius
    d. Pending property sales

88. Under the Mortgage Disclosure Improvement Act, a lender must extend the closing how many days if the APR is increased prior to closing?

    a. Three
    b. Two
    c. Five
    d. Seven

89. One general rule of the federal do-not-call regulations is that

    a. states must maintain separate do-no-call lists.
    b. the national registry must be searched once a year.
    c. real estate offices are exempt from the laws because they are not telemarketers.
    d. it is illegal to make an unsolicited phone call to a number listed on the national registry.

90. Federal regulations on unsolicited e-mail

    a. require commercial e-mails to include a physical address for the sender.
    b. require prior permission of recipients in order to send e-mail to them.
    c. require that e-mail lists be scrubbed every 31 days.
    d. exempt phone calls to individuals with whom the office has a prior business relationship.

EXAM TWO PART TWO—ILLINOIS REAL ESTATE LAW AND PRACTICE

1. A transaction is closing on May 2 in a non-leap year. Which of the following is the correct proration of an annual charge of $560, using the statutory variation method?
   a. $188.78
   b. $189.68
   c. $190.78
   d. $191.98

2. Under Illinois law, what is the statutory ceiling on the prepayment penalty a lender may charge on loans secured by real estate that bear more than 8 percent annual interest?
   a. 1 percent
   b. 3 percent
   c. 8 percent
   d. There is none

3. A tenant agrees to rent an apartment for nine months under a verbal agreement with the landlord. If the tenant defaults, the landlord may
   a. not bring court action because of parol evidence rule.
   b. not bring court action because of the statute of frauds.
   c. bring a court action because one-year leases need not be in writing to be enforced.
   d. bring a court action because the statute of limitations does not apply to verbal leases.

4. What principle of landlord-tenant relations was established by the Illinois Supreme Court in 1972?
   a. Interest payments required on all security deposits
   b. Landlord damages for a tenant's failure to vacate the premises
   c. Implied warranty of habitability in residential tenancies
   d. Landlord may forcibly remove a tenant without court action under the doctrine of "self-help"

5. In Illinois, if a landlord purposely fails to maintain an apartment building's furnace and plumbing, what option is available to a tenant whose apartment is without heat and water during the first three months of winter?
   a. Suit for constructive eviction
   b. Suit for actual eviction
   c. Suit for forcible detainer
   d. Suit for negligent default

6. A woman pays $1,250 per month for her apartment. If she refers three new tenants to the building's owner during the year, how much is she entitled to receive under the Real Estate License Act of 2000 if the landlord's normal referral fee is $500 per new tenant?
   a. Nothing, unless she is a licensed real estate broker, managing broker, or rental-finding agent
   b. $1,500
   c. $1,250
   d. $1,000

7. Which of the following properties are exempt from paying real estate taxes?
   a. Apartment complexes.
   b. Industrial parks.
   c. Shopping centers.
   d. Educational institutions.

8. Under the Illinois Human Rights Act, an "elderly person" is defined as any person who is older than
   a. 40.
   b. 55.
   c. 62.
   d. 65.

9. The Illinois Human Rights Act specifically exempts which of the following?

   a. Gender-based discrimination in housing intended for multi-gender occupancy.

   b. Religious organizations giving preference in housing to nonmembers.

   c. A five-unit apartment building with a resident property manager living in one of the units.

   d. A three-unit apartment building with the owner living in one of the units.

10. Many of the residents of the landlord's apartment building are elderly, and some are in poor health. To ensure that they are not disturbed, the landlord politely declines to rent units to families or individuals who have young children. However, the landlord provides such persons with a printed list of nearby apartment buildings that welcome children. Based on these facts, which of the following statements is *TRUE*?

    a. By providing a printed list of alternative comparable housing, the landlord is in full compliance with the Illinois Human Rights Act.

    b. Because the landlord's primary intent is to protect existing tenants' quality of life, and not to discriminate against prospective tenants who have young children, the Illinois Human Rights Act does not apply to this situation.

    c. The landlord's policy violates the Illinois Human Rights Act.

    d. While the landlord's policy, as stated, violates the Illinois Human Rights Act, he could add a "no children" provision to leases offered to new tenants and avoid violating the act.

11. What is the relationship between the Illinois agency statutes and the common law of agency?

    a. Illinois agency statutes supersede the common law of agency in Illinois.

    b. Illinois agency statutes and the common law of agency both govern agency relationships in Illinois.

    c. Agency statutes are simply an administrative codification of the common law of agency.

    d. The Illinois agency statutes govern managing broker's relationships with clients, while the common law of agency applies to broker relationships.

12. Which of the following is an example of a "ministerial act" under the Illinois agency law?

    a. Arguing the merits of an offer on behalf of a prospective buyer

    b. Helping prospective buyers determine an appropriate price range and geographic location for their home search

    c. Responding to general questions about the price and location of a specific property

    d. Assisting a buyer through the closing process

13. A real estate sponsoring broker commonly names individual sponsored licensees in her brokerage office as the exclusive agents of certain clients, leaving the other sponsored licensees free to represent other parties in a transaction. Which of the following statements is *TRUE* regarding this practice?

    a. Because it is a common office practice, it is permitted as an exception to the general statutory prohibition against such arrangements.

    b. Illinois agency law specifically permits designated agency arrangements such as this.

    c. This is an example of designated agency, which is an illegal relationship under the Illinois agency law.

    d. The sponsoring broker will be considered an undisclosed dual agent under these facts and will be in violation of Illinois law.

14. A sponsoring broker decides to "sweeten" an MLS listing for a property by making a blanket offer of subagency. Is the sponsoring broker's action acceptable?

a. Yes, because Illinois law permits the creation of subagency relationships only through multiple listing services.

b. Yes, because a subagency relationship may be created by either a blanket offer in an MLS or through a specific agreement between parties.

c. No, because subagency is illegal under Article 15 of the Real Estate License Act of 2000.

d. No, because subagency relationships may not be offered through an MLS in Illinois.

15. A broker represents the seller in a transaction. When prospective buyers ask to look at the property, which of the following must the broker do?

a. Tell them that they must first enter into a buyer representation agreement with another licensee.

b. Clearly disclose in writing that the broker represents the seller's interests.

c. Inform them that if a transaction results, a dual agency may be the best course of action.

d. Show them the property without making any disclosures about the broker's relationship with the seller because the best time to close is at contract signing.

16. Several years ago, a unit in a condominium community was the site of a brutal and highly publicized murder. The unit was sold to an elderly woman who contracted the AIDS virus in a blood transfusion and died in the unit last year. As the agent for the woman's estate, what are the disclosure responsibilities to prospective purchasers of this unit?

a. Agents must disclose both the murder and the AIDS-related death.

b. Agents are specifically required to disclose the AIDS death and may (at seller discretion) disclose the murder.

c. Agents are specifically prohibited by federal law from disclosing AIDS.

d. Agents must not disclose the murder, but should disclose the AIDS-related death.

17. In Illinois, an unlicensed real estate assistant may perform which activity?

a. Negotiate commission

b. Prepare legal documents required for a closing

c. Prepare and distribute flyers and promotional materials

d. Explain simple contract documents to prospective buyers

18. Illegal discrimination might result in which of the following actions?

a. Loss of license

b. Nothing

c. Unlimited civil fines by the Department

d. Reduced errors and omissions insurance premiums

19. An unlicensed assistant worked late nights and weekends to help ensure the successful closing of a difficult transaction. At the licensee's direction, the assistant's extra work included making several phone calls to the prospective buyers, encouraging them to accept the seller's counteroffer. Largely because of the assistant's efforts, the sale went through with no problem. The licensee wants to pay the assistant a percentage of the commission, "because the assistant has really earned it." Under Illinois law, what should the licensee do?

a. Illinois law permits the licensee to compensate the assistant in the form of a commission under the circumstances described here because the assistant was clearly directed to do the work described.

b. While the licensee may not pay the assistant a cash commission, the licensee is permitted to make a gift of tangible personal property.

c. The licensee should pay no commission to the assistant. The licensee's direction and the assistant's work violated Illinois law. Payment of commission would also violate the law.

d. The licensee may pay a commission to the assistant only if the assistant is an independent contractor.

20. A buyer wants to have a clause included in the sales contract under which the seller offers assurances that no one has died in the home. Which of the following statements is *TRUE* in Illinois?

   a. The licensee may include the clause because such standard disclosures are in general usage.

   b. Only the buyer or a licensed attorney may prepare the clause for inclusion in the sales contract.

   c. In Illinois, licensees are permitted to add additional clauses to blank form contracts, such as the clause described here, that do not directly involve the conveyance of title to real property.

   d. Under Illinois law, a clause such as the one described here is not permitted and any contract containing such a clause will be void.

21. A broker lists the seller's home. Under the terms of the agreement, when the property sells, the seller will receive a guaranteed $75,000. Any amount left over after the seller's $75,000 will constitute the broker's compensation. Based on these facts, which of the following statements is *TRUE* in Illinois?

   a. This type of arrangement, called a guaranteed sales agreement, is illegal in Illinois, and the broker will be disciplined for entering into it.

   b. This type of arrangement, called a net listing, is illegal in Illinois, and the broker will be disciplined for entering into it.

   c. This is an example of a guaranteed sales agreement, which is permissible in Illinois if the broker provides the seller with the necessary disclosures.

   d. This is an example of a net listing, which is discouraged (but not illegal) in Illinois.

22. In Illinois, which of the following in a listing agreement would result in the suspension or revocation of a licensee's license to practice real estate?

   a. A specified commission rate

   b. No specific termination date

   c. No broker protection clause

   d. A specific termination date

23. Which disclosure must be included in a listing contract under Illinois law?

   a. Anticipated seller closing costs

   b. Tax identification number

   c. Seller's net return

   d. Disposition of earnest money in the event of a purchaser default

24. A married couple lives in Springfield, Illinois. The wife is the owner of their home. If the couple decide to sell their home and move to Wisconsin, who is required to sign the listing agreement?

   a. Both the husband and the wife must sign the listing.

   b. Because the wife is the sole owner of their home, she is the only party legally required to sign the listing.

   c. Because the husband and wife are married, the signature of either spouse is legally sufficient.

   d. The husband is required to sign the listing only if the wife plans to use the capital gains exclusion.

25. From what source do Illinois local units of government receive their powers of eminent domain?

   a. A grant of authority signed by the governor

   b. Article 5 of the U.S. Constitution

   c. The Illinois Statehood Charter of 1818 and the Code of Administrative Procedure

   d. The Illinois Constitution and Code of Civil Procedure

26. A person dies without leaving a will. If the deceased owns real property in Illinois and has no heirs, what will happen to her real property?

   a. The deceased's real property will be taken by the county in which it is located under the power of eminent domain.

   b. Ownership of the deceased's real property will go to the state of Illinois through escheat.

   c. The deceased's property will escheat to the county in which it is located.

   d. The deceased's property will escheat to the county in which she last resided prior to her death.

27. Is there any limitation on an original grantor's right of reverter in Illinois?

    a. Yes. Both an original grantor's right of reverter and the enforceability of the underlying condition expire by law after 20 years.

    b. Yes. The original grantor's right of reverter continues for 40 years, although the underlying condition remains enforceable.

    c. Yes. Both the original grantor's right of reverter and the underlying condition automatically expire after 99 years.

    d. No. Under Illinois law there is no limitation on an original grantor's future interest.

28. Which of the following legal life estates could be available to a surviving husband in Illinois?

    a. Homestead

    b. Dower

    c. Curtesy

    d. A marital easement

29. How much of an estate of homestead is an individual entitled to in Illinois?

    a. $3,250

    b. $5,000

    c. $15,000

    d. $10,000

30. A couple living in Moline, Illinois, were married on July 10, 2011. On June 15, 2006, the husband purchased a motel. On July 15, 2012, the wife inherited an apartment building. On August 5, 2011, the husband purchased a farm. On August 10, the wife sold her inherited apartment building and bought strip shopping center. Based on these facts, which of the following best describes the interests held by the husband and the wife under Illinois law in the event the marriage is dissolved?

    a. Under the Illinois community property laws, the husband and wife are equal co-owners of all three properties.

    b. The motel and strip shopping center are nonmarital property; the farm is marital property.

    c. The motel is nonmarital property; the farm is marital property; strip shopping center is marital property by transmutation.

    d. All three properties are considered marital property.

31. Real property locations in Illinois are described by their geographic relation to which of the following?

    a. Fifth Principal Meridian.

    b. Government check.

    c. Correction line F.

    d. Second, third, and fourth Principal Meridian.

32. How often is the assessed valuation of all real estate in Illinois adjusted by county authorities?

    a. Quarterly

    b. Annually

    c. Biennially

    d. Every three years

33. An Illinois resident was born on March 6, 2011. When will this person become of legal age?

    a. March 6, 2029

    b. March 7, 2032

    c. March 6, 2032

    d. March 7, 2029

34. If a minor enters into a contract in Illinois, what is the statutory period within which the minor may legally void the contract after reaching the age of majority?

    a. 6 months

    b. 1 year

    c. The contract may be voided only up to the date when the minor reaches the age of majority; after that date, the contract is binding.

    d. There is no statutory period.

35. Which of the following is essential to the validity of a deed in Illinois?

    a. A seal (or the word seal)

    b. Acknowledgment

    c. Granting clause

    d. Recording

36. In Illinois, the amount of consideration used to determine transfer taxes must be shown on a special form. What is the name of that form?

    a. The "Recording Form"

    b. The "Real Estate Declaration of Transfer"

    c. The "Blue Sheet"

    d. The "Tax Code Sheet"

37. How far back in time does a normal Illinois title search go?

   a. 15 years
   b. 40 years
   c. 75 years
   d. 125 years

38. Which of the following are exempt from the provisions of the Real Estate License Act of 2000?

   a. Property owners who sell or lease property on behalf of others since they are familiar with the process
   b. Individual who is employed as a resident property manager
   c. Individual who engages in fee based management services
   d. Resident lessee who receives the equivalent of $2,000 as a "finder's fee" for referring a new tenant to the owner

39. Which is a requirement for obtaining an Illinois broker's license?

   a. Having successfully completed 90 hours of approved real estate courses
   b. Being at least 21 years of age
   c. Being of good moral character
   d. Having been actively engaged as a licensed salesperson for at least five years

40. A person who successfully completed her Illinois real estate education requirement on November 1, 2011, may take the state license exam no later than

   a. December 31, 2014
   b. November 1, 2015
   c. October 31, 2014
   d. October 31, 2015

41. What is the expiration date of every broker's license in Illinois?

   a. The broker's birthday, every other year
   b. April 30 of each even-numbered year
   c. May 31 of each odd-numbered year
   d. Every other anniversary date of the individual broker's license

42. An Illinois sponsoring broker wants to open a branch office in a neighboring town. The sponsoring broker applies for a branch office license and gives the branch a name that clearly identifies its relationship with his main office. The sponsoring broker names a licensed Illinois leasing agent, as the branch office manager. Under these facts, will the sponsoring broker receive approval for the branch office?

   a. Yes. The sponsoring broker has fully complied with the requirements of the Real Estate License Act of 2000.
   b. No. Under the Real Estate License Act of 2000, sponsoring brokers cannot have branch offices in more than one municipality.
   c. No. Branch office management requires a special license.
   d. No. The manager of a branch office must hold a managing broker's license.

43. A licensee could tell that a prospective buyer would probably not make an offer if she knew the previous occupant of a property had died from complications due to AIDS and did not disclose that fact. An Illinois real estate broker set up a "microbrokerage" real estate services outlet in a convenience store by placing a desk at the end of the snack food aisle. A managing broker waited outside an AMP testing facility and handed out brochures to prospective licensees on their way in to take the real estate exam, encouraging them to apply for a job at his office. Which, if any, of these individuals is subject to disciplinary action for violating the Real Estate License Act of 2000?

   a. The licensee only
   b. The managing broker only
   c. All three licensed individuals
   d. Only the two brokers

44. Which would be grounds for a disciplinary action?

    a. Being convicted of a felony in Illinois

    b. Advertising in a magazine that the broker is a member of the Chicago Association of REALTORS® when the broker is not

    c. Depositing escrow money into a personal account

    d. All of the above would be grounds for disciplinary action.

45. A licensee engaged in activities that constitute violations of the Illinois Human Rights Act, including blockbusting and discrimination on the basis of disability. The licensee also cashed a $25,000 earnest money check from a prospective buyer and used the proceeds to buy a new car. The licencee's sponsoring broker was completely unaware of all of these activities. When the licensee's violations are brought to the attention of the Department, which of the following statements is *TRUE*?

    a. The sponsoring broker will not have his license revoked as a result of the licensee's violations.

    b. The licensee's sponsoring broker will be required to pay any fine imposed against the licensee out of his own personal funds.

    c. The licensee's violations are legally the responsibility of the sponsoring broker, who will be subject to the same disciplinary action as the licensee, regardless of whether he knew the violations had occurred.

    d. The licensee's sponsoring broker will be held liable for the Human Rights Act violations only.

46. A broker is convicted of a crime involving fraud in Wisconsin on November 9. On February 1 of the following year, the Wisconsin licensing agency notifies the Department of the conviction. Based on this information, which is *TRUE*?

    a. The broker should have called the Department first.

    b. The Department may refuse to renew the broker's license based on his Wisconsin conviction for a crime involving fraud.

    c. Because the conviction was not in Illinois, no discipline will occur.

    d. A conviction due to fraud does not constitute a violation of the Illinois Real Estate License Act of 2000.

47. Which of the following accurately describes the review process for a final administrative decision of the Department?

    a. The accused may appeal a final administrative decision of the Department directly to the Illinois Supreme Court.

    b. The accused may petition the circuit court of the county in which the accused resides. The circuit court's decision may be appealed directly to the Illinois Supreme Court.

    c. The accused may petition the circuit court of the county in which the property involved in the transaction that gave rise to the violation is located. The circuit court's decision may be appealed directly to the federal district court.

    d. The accused may request a rehearing by the Department, but administrative decisions may not be appealed to any court.

48. Which of the following is required to adopt a company policy manual?

    a. Sole proprietorship with no other sponsored licensees

    b. Brokerage companies are not required to have a policy manual

    c. Brokerage company with sponsored licensees

    d. Self-sponsored broker with no sponsored licensees

49. Every Illinois broker who applies for renewal of a license must successfully complete a certain number of hours of continuing education courses in each two-year license renewal period. How many hours are required by Illinois law?

   a. Six
   b. Eight
   c. Nine
   d. Twelve

50. With regard to mortgage theory, Illinois is usually described as a(n)

   a. title-theory state.
   b. lien-theory state.
   c. intermediate mortgage theory state.
   d. security-theory state.

51. Twenty years ago, a man obtained a 30-year mortgage loan to purchase a home. The interest rate on the loan was 9.275 percent. Today, the man is prepared to pay off the loan early. Based on these facts, which of the following statements is *TRUE* in Illinois?

   a. The man's lender is entitled by statute to charge the man a prepayment penalty equal to one year's interest on the current balance of the loan.
   b. The man's lender is permitted by Illinois statute to charge the man a prepayment penalty of no more than 8 percent of the current outstanding balance of the loan.
   c. Illinois does not take an official statutory position on the issue of prepayment penalties.
   d. Because the man's interest rate is greater than 8 percent, the lender may not charge a prepayment penalty under Illinois law.

52. In Illinois, if a landlord wants to terminate a year-to-year tenancy, how much notice must the tenant receive?

   a. 7 days
   b. 30 days
   c. 60 days
   d. 4 months

53. In Illinois, which of the following is *TRUE* of an individual who wishes to engage only in the leasing of residential real property?

   a. The individual must obtain a broker's license and be employed by a broker who specializes in residential leases.
   b. The individual may obtain a certified leasing-agent designation by passing a test.
   c. The individual may obtain a limited leasing-agent license by completing 15 hours of instruction and passing a written examination.
   d. The individual may engage in residential leasing activities without obtaining a license or other certification.

54. In Illinois, disclosure includes which of the following?

   a. Stigmatized property
   b. Multiple clients represented by the same agent
   c. Registered sex offenders
   d. Single agency

55. If an annual charge of $560 is prorated in October using the statutory variation method, which of the following will be the resulting daily charge?

   a. $1.51
   b. $1.53
   c. $1.54
   d. $1.56

56. Who does the real estate licensee represent?

   a. The seller
   b. The buyer
   c. Both the seller and the buyer
   d. Whoever hired the real estate licensee

57. Zoning ordinances may regulate which of the following?

   a. Water usage
   b. Deed restrictions
   c. Restrictive covenants
   d. Density

58. Which of the following is *TRUE* regarding option contracts?

a. An option contract is classified as a unilateral contract.

b. An option contract that has been exercised is classified as a bilateral contract.

c. The option money may not be applied toward the purchase price.

d. The seller is the optionee and the buyer is the optionor.

59. Grounds for discipline under the License Act include

a. disclosing dual agency.

b. representing a broker other than the sponsoring broker.

c. advertising the sponsoring broker's name in the advertisement.

d. maintaining an escrow account to hold earnest money deposits.

60. Which of the following would terminate a listing contract?

a. Only the seller agreeing to cancel since it is a unilateral decision of the client

b. Foreclosure of the neighbor's property

c. Death of the sponsoring broker

d. There is no cancellation provision in listing contracts

EXAM THREE—ILLINOIS LICENSE LAW AND PRACTICE

1. Under the Real Estate License Act of 2000, what does "Advisory Council" refer to?
   a. The Real Estate Education Advisory Council
   b. The Advisory Council that enforces the Rules
   c. The framers of the license act itself
   d. A business management consulting body for local Associations of REALTORS®

2. Under the Real Estate License Act of 2000, what body does the director oversee?
   a. Department of Real Estate Regulation
   b. The Real Estate Education Association
   c. Legislators Concerned for Real Estate
   d. The Division of Professional Regulation

3. Under the Real Estate License Act of 2000, which of the following need to be licensed?
   a. Personal assistants who only sit at public open houses
   b. An owner's agent who does not collect rents on more than 25 units
   c. Those who work only with buyers (never take listings)
   d. All of the above

4. What is the primary purpose of the Real Estate Recovery Fund?
   a. It is a legal defense fund for REALTORS® who cannot pay their legal debts.
   b. It is to reimburse consumers who have been wronged by a licensee's actions.
   c. It is for the Department to use at will when a current year's budget is exceeded.
   d. It is used for recovery of unpaid commissions.

5. Which of the following statements regarding broker licensing is *TRUE*?
   a. They need to take 90 hours of education.
   b. They have to take 30 hours of post-licensing education.
   c. They may take prelicensing classes online if the courses are approved.
   d. All of the above are true.

6. What is the composition of the Real Estate Administration and Disciplinary Board?
   a. Nine members appointed by the governor
   b. Eight members elected by local REALTOR® associations
   c. Eight members appointed by the director
   d. Six members elected by the public

7. How long are the membership terms on "The Board"?
   a. Three-year staggered terms
   b. Two years each
   c. Four-year staggered terms
   d. Three years with a possible three-year renewal

8. The Real Estate Research and Education Fund each year receives what amount, and from what source?
   a. $100,000 from the state of Illinois
   b. $50,000 from voluntarily collected funds of licensees
   c. $125,000 from the Real Estate License Administration Fund
   d. $80,000 from licensees' fines placed in a Research and Education Fund escrow

9. Under the Real Estate License Act of 2000, who among the following could work in a limited way indefinitely without a specific license?
   a. Personal assistant hired by a sponsored broker
   b. Leasing agent hired by a property management company
   c. Leasing agent working independently
   d. Broker working independently

10. The number of hours of continuing education that can be taken in one day
    a. is not regulated by the law.
    b. cannot be more than six hours.
    c. cannot be more than nine hours.
    d. can be up to twelve hours.

11. When does a leasing agent's license expire?

    a. On the date it was first acquired, every two years

    b. On July 31 of each even-numbered year

    c. On April 30 of each odd-numbered year

    d. On January 1, every third year

12. Why is early discussion of agency so important under the Real Estate License Act of 2000?

    a. Working with a consumer may now be construed as an implied agency if nothing else has been stated.

    b. Working with a consumer may compel the consumer to pay a commission, whether a written agreement exists or not.

    c. If nothing is stated, subagency may be in effect.

    d. If nothing is stated, a minimum hourly fee may be demanded after the fact.

13. A licensee does not receive a license renewal form in the mail. In this situation, the licensee

    a. must respond within three months of the date of the scheduled renewal.

    b. must respond by the scheduled renewal date or the licensee will only have two additional weeks grace period.

    c. may renew the license up to six months later with a $25 fine.

    d. must no longer practice real estate after the expiration date on the license.

14. Prelicense courses will have to be taken again if a license has been expired for more than

    a. six months.

    b. one year.

    c. eighteen months.

    d. two years.

15. Who would *NOT* need a signed written employment agreement in Illinois for working with a sponsoring broker?

    a. Leasing agent

    b. Licensed broker

    c. Other brokers employed in the firm

    d. Co-op broker

16. Under the Real Estate License Act of 2000, a buyer to whom a licensee is showing houses under a buyer-brokerage agreement is considered to be

    a. without a formal relationship.

    b. a customer.

    c. a client.

    d. a possible client.

17. Which statement could an Illinois buyer's agent appropriately make to a buyer client?

    a. "Here are the CMAs. I think they suggest the highest range you should pay is about $110,000–$120,000, but that's up to you."

    b. "The listing agent said the floors underneath the carpet are oak. Isn't that great?"

    c. "I know this neighborhood. Don't worry about radon."

    d. "There really isn't any way to get a list of released sex offenders' addresses in Illinois."

18. Employment agreements with a sponsoring broker must cover at least

    a. supervision, duties, referral fees, and MLS requirements.

    b. referral fees, commission splits, and cooperation with other brokers.

    c. supervision, duties, compensation, and termination.

    d. salary and benefits agreed on.

19. Who needs to disclose material facts related to a transaction in Illinois?

    a. Listing agent

    b. Buyer's agent

    c. Sellers

    d. All of the above, if they have material information

20. What is always *TRUE* of licensed personal assistants under the Real Estate License Act of 2000?

   a. They must be licensed as brokers.
   b. They need an employment agreement with the broker with whom they work day to day.
   c. They are usually paid directly by the person who selected them and with whom they work most closely.
   d. They need an employment agreement with the sponsoring broker and must be paid by the sponsoring broker.

21. What is *TRUE* about real estate advertising in Illinois under the Real Estate License Act of 2000?

   a. The company name must appear in a print ad for houses.
   b. Whenever the company name does appear, it must be in letters larger than the sponsored broker's name.
   c. Links on a broker's real estate Web site must routinely be approved by the Department.
   d. On an Internet site, the company name is usually not needed.

22. Which of the following does *NOT* need to be disclosed in Illinois?

   a. To a buyer: the fact that the seller is also a client
   b. To a seller's agent: the fact that the buyer client qualifies for the purchase price with only $5,000 to spare
   c. To a customer who is just starting to work with the licensee: he is a customer, but that agency is possible and may very quickly be presumed in Illinois if nothing else is said
   d. To a buyer client: the fact that the licensee hold a 1.1 percent interest in a property he wants to buy

23. What is *TRUE* about the typeface of ads under the Real Estate License Act of 2000?

   a. The name of the licensee should always be smaller than the name of the company.
   b. The name of the company should always be at least as large as the name of the licensee.
   c. The name of the company must appear first.
   d. There is no statement or rule regarding relative size of agent name and company name.

24. Who may pay compensation to a broker in Illinois?

   a. Listing agent in the office
   b. Sponsoring broker
   c. Title company
   d. Mortgage company

25. Who may sue for commission in Illinois?

   a. The listing broker
   b. The client
   c. The sponsoring broker
   d. Only the sponsored broker directly involved

26. Which of the following may *NOT* be offered to consumers in Illinois?

   a. Coupons to the local grocery store if they list
   b. Discounts on commission if they list
   c. A new television if they buy
   d. A finder's fee for referring client prospects

27. Which of the following may be offered to an Illinois licensee for referring business to a lawyer or loan officer?

   a. A weekend in Peoria
   b. A small stereo
   c. A cash amount less than $200
   d. None of the above

28. What would *NOT* happen under the Real Estate License Act of 2000 for offenses noted in the Act?

   a. License revoked
   b. $25,000 fine
   c. $5,000 fine
   d. Commissions seized

29. For which of the following could a licensee be late in Illinois without affecting license renewal?
    a. Student loans
    b. Illinois income tax
    c. Child support
    d. Mortgage payment

30. Dual agency conflict of interest is best avoided in Illinois by way of
    a. implied dual agency.
    b. designated agency.
    c. special agency.
    d. co-op agency.

31. Under the Real Estate License Act of 2000, when the license of any sponsoring broker is suspended or revoked, what is *TRUE* with regard to sponsored licensees' agreements with that sponsoring broker?
    a. They expire on the date of suspension.
    b. Each licensee has ten days in which to find another sponsoring broker.
    c. A licensee can continue to work through the suspension.
    d. The licensee has 30 days in which to finish all deals.

32. A sponsored licensee can now sell "by owner"
    a. if the broker agrees.
    b. with the changes in the new license act.
    c. only if she lives in the home.
    d. only once per year.

33. An Illinois sponsoring broker has been showing other agents' listings to a buyer but that buyer has not signed an agency agreement. Nothing else has been said. The buyer is
    a. unrepresented.
    b. client.
    c. a consumer.
    d. a customer.

34. Real estate licensees are frequently referred to as agents. This is technically correct in Illinois because they are *ALWAYS*
    a. general agents for the sponsoring broker.
    b. universal agents for the seller.
    c. special agents for the lender.
    d. general agents for consumers.

35. Which of the following licensee statements would be appropriate in Illinois?
    a. Licensee answering a call-in customer's question: "The standard commission is 6 percent."
    b. Listing agent to buyer's agent: "List price is $200,000, but my seller will probably sell for about $195,000."
    c. Buyers' agent to listing agent: "My buyers need to buy this weekend, so I think we can get this deal together."
    d. Licensee to a licensed personal assistant: "Thanks for your help on this transaction, but I can't cut you a check."

36. How are the terms *statutory law* and *common law* intertwined historically in the law of agency in Illinois?
    a. Illinois real estate law actively cites both common law and statutory law, but in a real estate conflict common law always supercedes.
    b. Illinois real estate law is historically grounded in common law; the current statutory laws were influenced by it.
    c. Common law dominates and supersedes statutory law in most real estate situations, but the statutes apply in all other cases.
    d. Common law is federal law; statutory law is state law.

37. An unlicensed individual who engages in activities for which a real estate license is required is subject to which of the following penalties?
    a. A fine not to exceed $1,000
    b. A fine not to exceed $5,000 and one-year imprisonment
    c. A civil penalty of $25,000 in addition to possible other penalties stipulated by law
    d. A civil penalty not to exceed $25,000 and a mandatory prison term not to exceed five years

38. When a broker passes the license examination, the first proof of the eligibility to engage in real estate activities in Illinois is a
    a. sponsor card.
    b. pocket card.
    c. license.
    d. pass card.

39. Of the following types of insurance policies used in this state, which is MOST likely to meet full replacement cost of a destroyed property (possibly exceeding the stated policy value)?

a. Actual cash value
b. Cash value with coinsurance
c. Basic "plus"
d. Guaranteed replacement cost

40. Under the Real Estate License Act of 2000, the exception to the rule that a licensee may accept compensation only from a sponsoring broker occurs

a. if the buyer chooses to pay the agent directly.
b. when assisting a FSBO and the FSBO wishes to compensate the agent.
c. when a transaction closes that was put together while the agent worked for a previous sponsoring broker.
d. when none of the above happens.

41. To qualify for a nonresident license, an out-of-state sponsoring broker must do which of the following?

a. Be an active sponsoring broker for at least five years immediately preceding application
b. Open a definite, permanent, and conspicuous place of business within Illinois
c. Take and pass the entire sponsoring broker exam
d. Be licensed in a state that has enacted a reciprocal licensing agreement with Illinois

42. What should a buyer's agent check first if a buyer indicates he does NOT want to buy a home in a floodplain?

a. The listings in the MLS computer
b. The seller disclosure form for a given home
c. Floodplain maps for the area(s) in which the buyer is interested
d. House addresses available through FEMA

43. An Illinois agent's errors and omissions insurance will NOT cover

a. an agent who is being sued for failure to disclose urea-formaldehyde insulation.
b. an agent who is being sued because a client fell down the stairs at a showing.
c. an agent who obeyed seller instructions not to show a house to a certain ethnic group.
d. an agent who poorly handled a dual agency situation.

44. The Real Estate License Act of 2000 provides for fines up to

a. $5,000.
b. $10,000.
c. $25,000.
d. $50,000.

45. In Illinois, which of the following would be inappropriate?

a. An attorney providing a cash referral directly to a salesperson for recommending the attorney in a transaction
b. A buyer's agent for a client preparing multiple CMAs for the buyer
c. A tenant receiving $1,000 in one year for referrals of tenants
d. A licensed personal assistant showing a property

46. What is the guideline for when agency should be disclosed in Illinois?

a. No later than 48 hours after meeting a customer
b. No later than 72 hours after meeting a customer
c. As early as possible
d. During negotiations

47. How is the problem of dual agency often avoided today in Illinois?

a. Companies must refer the buyer to another company.
b. Companies do not disclose dual agency.
c. One designated agent is assigned to each client.
d. A transactional arbitrator is brought in.

48. What is the status of disclosed dual agency in Illinois in the first few years of the 21st century?

    a. Void
    b. Legal
    c. Illegal
    d. Voidable

49. Under the Real Estate License Act of 2000, what must be in writing?

    a. Grantee's signature on the deed
    b. All listings
    c. Exclusive-agency and exclusive-right-to-sell listings
    d. Agency between a buyer and a broker

50. A broker placed the following order with the telephone company: "List my name in the directory under the heading 'Real Estate,' as 'My name, Real Estate Broker, Residential Property is My Specialty.'" The broker is also required to include

    a. her license number.
    b. the expiration date of her license.
    c. her street address.
    d. the name of her employing (sponsoring) broker.

51. Who designates a sponsored broker in Illinois to act as a "designated agent"?

    a. The state
    b. The seller or buyer
    c. The broker himself, in signing a client agreement
    d. The sponsoring broker

52. Actions being brought against licensees under Article 15 (Agency Relationships) of the Real Estate License Act of 2000 must be taken

    a. within two years after the facts become known.
    b. within one year after the facts become known.
    c. any time after the closing if negligence can be proven.
    d. within six months after closing.

53. Which one of the following situations would be allowed by Illinois law?

    a. An offer of subagency through the MLS
    b. Showing homes after one's license has expired, so long as one doesn't write the contract
    c. A listing agent refusing to present an offer to the sellers because it is a low offer
    d. A buyer's agent choosing not to mention to the listing agent that the buyers plan to tear down the house after purchase

54. In Illinois, licensees working through an MLS are NOT legally

    a. special agents to clients.
    b. general agents of their sponsoring broker.
    c. designated by their sponsoring broker as agents to clients.
    d. subagents.

55. Under the Real Estate License Act of 2000, which statement is TRUE?

    a. The person with whom a licensee works is always a customer if nothing else is said.
    b. The person with whom a licensee works is a client if nothing else is said.
    c. The person who works with buyers who do not want client status is called their agent.
    d. A client becomes a client only when the agency agreement is signed.

56. Who pays a licensed leasing agent?

    a. The owner of the properties being rented
    b. The tenant
    c. The sponsoring broker
    d. The previous tenant

57. How long may a leasing agent work without a license in Illinois, provided the agent is working to obtain a license and has a proper sponsor?

    a. 30 days
    b. 130 days
    c. 90 days
    d. 120 days

58. An Illinois licensee has listed a property whose owner had AIDS. The licensee should
    a. note that the owner had AIDS at the bottom of the disclosure sheet, per federal law.
    b. note that the owner had AIDS at the bottom of the disclosure sheet, per state law.
    c. do what seems right. There is no specific obligation to disclose, but if the agent feels it is best for all parties, the agent may do so.
    d. not mention this to anyone, unless the owner directs the agent to do so.

59. Which of the following is *TRUE* about leasing agents in Illinois?
    a. Leasing agents in Illinois may operate independently as long they are approved by the Department.
    b. While leasing agents are not licensed, a test indicating basic competence must be passed to work as a leasing agent.
    c. Leasing agents must have a sponsoring broker.
    d. Leasing agents may work without a license for 130 days if properly supervised.

60. A Champaign, Illinois, buyer's agent is showing properties to a young mother of three children whose safety is paramount to her. Which one of the following would *NOT* be appropriate?
    a. The agent tells the mother she can check addresses of convicted but released sex offenders on the Internet.
    b. The agent decides to show only certain neighborhoods.
    c. The licensee checks properties surrounding an interesting subject property carefully for any signs of oil leaks, USTs, formaldehyde odors, gas odors, bogs, or fire/explosion hazards.
    d. The buyer's agent recommends radon testing, carbon monoxide detectors, and water testing.

61. Which of the following is outside the bounds of what an Illinois buyer's agent may do under law?
    a. Tell a seller (the seller's agent) that a buyer "qualifies" without mentioning the buyer barely qualifies for the seller's home.
    b. Check recent sales prices of homes in the area, mention the low ones to the listing agent, and use them as a basis to negotiate down.
    c. Indicate to seller that a buyer has new work with a company in the area when the buyer is just interviewing for a job.
    d. Threaten to report a listing agent to the local Association if a low offer isn't presented to the seller.

62. Under the Real Estate License Act of 2000, which statement describes how a licensed personal assistant is paid?
    a. Whichever broker the personal assistant works for on a daily basis pays the assistant.
    b. Fees usually come straight from any closings in which the licensed assistant has participated.
    c. The cooperative broker fee covers the personal assistant.
    d. The sponsoring broker pays the licensed personal assistant.

63. In most transactions of residential real estate in Illinois, who pays for the local transfer tax stamps?
    a. The seller
    b. The seller or buyer, depending on rules of the municipality
    c. Buyer's attorney
    d. The buyer

64. In determining Illinois taxation, at what stage is property value equalized?
    a. After determining assessed value
    b. Just after locating or determining fair market value
    c. After subtracting exemptions
    d. After the tax rate is applied to the property value

65. How much do local (city or town) tax stamps in Illinois cost?

   a. Vary by street
   b. $1.50 per $1,000
   c. $2.00 per $500
   d. Vary by town

66. Under the Real Estate License Act of 2000, who among the following would need to work under a sponsoring broker in Illinois?

   a. An appraiser
   b. A home inspector
   c. Another broker who is not a sponsoring broker
   d. An unlicensed personal assistant to a broker

67. In Illinois, if a sponsored broker leaves one firm to go to another, the broker's listings

   a. automatically go with the agent.
   b. stay with the sponsoring broker unless the employment agreement stipulates otherwise.
   c. are canceled.
   d. are left to the discretion of the sellers.

68. If you lived in Galena, Illinois, where would it be best to record a judgment?

   a. In the county where the property is located
   b. In all counties where the person owns both real and personal property
   c. In the county where the judgment was obtained
   d. The Department of Financial and Professional Regulation

69. Who would receive a co-op fee in Illinois?

   a. The broker with the buyer (through the sponsoring broker)
   b. The listing sponsoring broker only
   c. No broker because there is no co-op fee
   d. A dual agent (through the sponsoring broker)

70. If a broker is found guilty of violating the Real Estate License Act of 2000, a sponsoring broker also may be disciplined by the Department if the

   a. broker was a convicted criminal.
   b. sponsoring broker had prior knowledge of the violation.
   c. sponsoring broker failed to conduct the four-step pre-employment investigation of the broker's background and character required by the license law.
   d. sponsoring broker failed to keep all local business licenses current.

71. A licensee must have written consent of the owners to advertise their house

   a. in the newspapers.
   b. by putting up a yard sign.
   c. on the Internet.
   d. in all of the above ways.

72. What projects does the transfer tax pay for in Illinois?

   a. Key state and county medical projects
   b. Illinois Department of Transportation (usually road projects)
   c. REALTORS® Defense Fund
   d. Affordable housing and land preservation

73. A will must include which heirs?

   a. Sisters and brothers
   b. Children
   c. Spouse
   d. Parents

74. What has replaced dower and curtesy in Illinois?

   a. Uniform Probate Code
   b. Spousal right of first choice
   c. Real estate by devise
   d. Life estate pur autre vie

75. Which type of ownership can be used only by a married couple in Illinois?

   a. Tenancy in common
   b. Joint tenancy
   c. Life estate
   d. Tenancy by the entirety

76. Which type of seller liens would a buyer MOST likely agree to at an Illinois closing?

a. Any liens existing at closing
b. Mechanics' liens, because these often cannot be discovered prior to close
c. Second mortgage liens, because these benefit the buyers
d. An assumed mortgage

77. In Illinois, which type of contract might be considered held to be enforceable if entered into by someone under 18?

a. Listing contract
b. Sales contract
c. Lease contract
d. Land contract

78. Which type of will is enforceable in Illinois?

a. Oral, so long as a person was there to hear it
b. Holographic will
c. Noncupative will
d. Written will, signed and witnessed

79. In Illinois, which type of deed becomes null and void after one year if it is not recorded?

a. General warranty deed
b. Special warranty deed
c. Bargain and sale deed
d. Tax deed

80. An expired real estate license may be renewed in Illinois for how long?

a. One year
b. Two years
c. Three years
d. Five years

81. Which of the following is exempt from licensure?

a. A hotel operator registered with the Illinois Department of Revenue
b. A licensed auctioneer selling real estate at auction
c. A time-share owner who refers no more than 20 prospective purchasers in any one year
d. All of the above are exempt

82. Which of the following licenses expire on July 31, even years?

a. Leasing agent license
b. Broker license
c. Managing broker license
d. Appraiser license

83. Which of the following escrow records must be kept by a broker?

a. Journal
b. Ledger
c. Monthly reconciliation statements
d. All of the above must be kept

84. The principal to whom a real estate agent gives advice and counsel is a

a. subagent.
b. customer.
c. client.
d. fiduciary.

85. Who of the following is charged with the responsibility of administering the day-to-day activities of the Department?

a. Secretary of State
b. Real Estate Coordinator
c. Secretary of the Illinois Department of Financial & Professional Regulation
d. Division Director of the Office of Banks and Trusts

86. The Real Estate Recovery Fund was

a. established to provide a means of compensating people who have been harmed by a licensee's negligence.
b. created to provide licensees with errors and omissions insurance.
c. established to provide up to $100,000 for losses.
d. created to recover escrow losses.

87. A sponsoring broker who deposits earnest money in an escrow account must make sure that

a. the account is state-insured.
b. either buyer or seller has signed a written request form identifying who is to receive the interest.
c. the money, when released, is at the direction of either principal.
d. the account is FDIC insured.

88. A real estate developer who lives in Mississippi and is selling lots located in Mississippi from his company office in Illinois must be in compliance with which act?

a. Illinois Interstate Commerce Act
b. Illinois Development Act
c. Illinois Land Plat Act
d. Illinois Land Sales Registration Act

89. The most important purpose of the Real Estate License Act of 2000 is to

a. protect the public.
b. protect the real estate industry from fraudulent practices.
c. regulate real estate businesses.
d. regulate real estate practitioners.

90. Real estate licensees in Illinois must disclose which of the following?

a. Minor problems in the neighborhood of which they have knowledge
b. Designated agency
c. Special compensation found outside the scope of their agency relationship
d. All are required disclosures.

91. Which appraisal licensing category allows an appraiser to appraise residential property of one unit to four units without regard to transaction value or complexity?

a. Associate trainee real estate appraiser
b. Certified residential appraiser
c. Certified general real estate appraiser
d. None of the above

92. Appraisal licensing is required for which of the following?

a. All federally related transactions
b. For-sale-by-owner transactions
c. Only commercial property transactions
d. Commercial and industrial property transactions

93. Which of the following shows the receipt and disbursement of funds affecting a single particular transaction?

a. Journal
b. Ledger
c. Reconciliation worksheet
d. Master escrow account log

94. Which of the following shows the chronological sequence in which funds are received and disbursed for all transactions?

a. Journal
b. Ledger
c. Reconciliation worksheet
d. Master escrow account log

95. Which of the following identifies all escrow bank account numbers and bank name and address?

a. Journal
b. Ledger
c. Reconciliation worksheet
d. Master escrow account log

96. Escrow records must be maintained for at least

a. three years.
b. five years.
c. seven years.
d. ten years.

97. Illinois has reciprocity with which of the following states?

a. Indiana
b. Iowa
c. Georgia
d. All of the above

98. Which of the following is TRUE about the members of the Disciplinary Board?

a. Members have no term limits.
b. Members must be appointed by the Department secretary.
c. Six members must have real estate licenses.
d. The governor appoints seven members.

99. Illinois recognizes which of the following estates?

a. Homestead
b. Curtesy
c. Dower
d. Community property

100. In Illinois, in order to be eligible for a homestead estate, an owner must

a. file an eligibility form with the state agency.
b. have an equity interest in the property.
c. be married.
d. reside in the property.

Web Links

■ CHAPTER 1

American Society of Home Inspectors: *www.ashi.org*
Building Owners and Managers Association International: *www.boma.org*
Commercial Investment Real Estate Institute: *www.ccim.com*
Counselors of Real Estate: *www.cre.org*
Fannie Mae: *www.fanniemae.com*
Federal Reserve Board: *www.federalreserve.gov*
Freddie Mac: *www.freddiemac.com*
Ginnie Mae: *www.ginniemae.gov*
Institute of Real Estate Management: *www.irem.org*
National Association of Exclusive Buyer Agents: *www.naeba.org*
National Association of Independent Fee Appraisers: *www.naifa.com*
National Association of Real Estate Brokers: *www.nareb.com*
National Association of REALTORS®:   *www.realtor.org*
Real Estate Buyer's Agent Council: *www.rebac.net*
Real Estate Educators Association: *www.reea.org*
U.S. Department of Housing and Urban Development (HUD):   *www.hud.gov*

■ CHAPTER 2

Manufactured Housing Institute: *www.manufacturedhousing.org*

■ CHAPTER 3

Comprehensive Loss Underwriting Exchange (CLUE):   *www.choicetrust.com*
Federal Emergency Management Agency: *www.fema.gov*
U.S. Department of Housing and Urban Development (HUD):   *www.hud.gov*
U.S. Department of Housing and Urban Development: Housing:
    http://portal.hud.gov/hudportal/HUD?src=/program_offices/housing
U.S. Department of Veterans Affairs: *www.va.gov*

■ CHAPTER 4

Chicago Association of REALTORS® (CAR):   *www.chicagorealtor.com*
Illinois Association of REALTORS® (IAR):   *www.illinoisrealtor.org*

■ CHAPTER 5

Association of Real Estate License Law Officials: *www.arello.org*
Electronic Signatures in Global and National Commerce Act (E-Sign):
   www.ftc.gov/os/2001/06/esign7.htm
National Do Not Call Registry: *www.donotcall.gov/default.aspx*
Uniform Electronic Transaction Act (UETA):   *www.law.upenn.edu/bll/archives/*
   ulc/fnact99/1990s/ueta99.htm
U.S. Department of Internal Revenue: *www.irs.gov*
U.S. Department of Justice, Antitrust Division: *www.justice.gov/atr/*

■ CHAPTER 6

Illinois Department of Human Rights: *www.state.il.us/dhr/*

■ CHAPTER 8

Illinois Condominium Property Act: *www.condorisk.com/content/condoact/*
   property_act.htm

■ CHAPTER 10

Illinois General Assembly: *www.ilga.gov*
U.S. Department of Internal Revenue Service: *www.irs.gov*

■ CHAPTER 14

Applied Measurement Professionals, Inc.:   *www.goamp.com*
Illinois Division of Professional Regulation: Real Estate: *www.idfpr.com/*
   realestate
Illinois Real Estate License Act of 2000:   *www.ilga.gov/legislation/ilcs/ilcs3.*
   asp?ActID=1364&ChapterID=24
Legal Information Institute: Mortgage: *http://topics.law.cornell.edu/wex/mortgage*

■ CHAPTER 16

Fannie Mae: *www.fanniemae.com*
Farm Credit: *www.farmcredit.com*
Farmer Mac: *www.farmermac.com*
Federal Reserve Board: *www.federalreserve.gov*
Freddie Mac: *www.freddiemac.com*
Ginnie Mae: *www.ginniemae.gov*
National Reverse Mortgage Lenders Association: *www.reversemortgage.org*
U.S. Department of Agriculture— Farm Service Agency: *www.fsa.usda.gov*
U.S. Department of Housing and Urban Development (HUD):   *www.hud.gov*
U.S. Department of Veterans Affairs: Home Loans: *www.homeloans.va.gov*

■ CHAPTER 17

Americans with Disabilities Act Home Page: *www.ada.gov*
Legal Information Institute: Landlord-Tenant Law: *http://topics.law.cornell.edu/ wex/landlord-tenant_law*
U.S. Department of Housing and Urban Development: Healthy Homes and Lead Hazard Control: *http://portal.hud.gov/hudportal/HUD?src=/ program_offices/healthy_homes*

■ CHAPTER 18

American Management Association: *www.amanet.org*
Building Owners and Managers Association International: *www.boma.org*
Building Owners and Managers Institute International: *www.bomi.org*
Equifax: *www.equifax.com*
Experian: *www.experian.com*
Illinois Department of Insurance: *http://insurance.illinois.gov/*
Institute of Real Estate Management: *www.irem.org/home.cfm*
National Association of Home Builders: *www.nahb.com*
National Association of Residential Property Managers: *www.narpm.org*
TransUnion: *www.tuc.com*
U.S. Department of Justice: Disability Rights Section: *www.justice.gov/crt/ about/drs/*

■ CHAPTER 19

American Society of Appraisers: *www.appraisers.org*
American Society of Farm Managers and Rural Appraisers: *www.asfmra.org*
Appraisal Foundation: *www.appraisalfoundation.org*
Appraisal Institute: *www.appraisalinstitute.org*
Illinois General Assembly: *www.ilga.gov*
International Right of Way Association: *www.irwaonline.org*
National Association of Independent Fee Appraisers: *www.naifa.com*
National Association of Master Appraisers: *www.masterappraisers.org*

■ **CHAPTER 20**

Illinois Department of Human Rights: *www.state.il.us/dhr/*

Illinois Division of Professional Regulation—Timeshare/Land Sales: *www.idfpr.com/DPR/RE/TSLS.asp*

International Code Council: *www.iccsafe.org*

U.S. Department of Housing and Urban Development: Housing: *http://portal.hud.gov/hudportal/HUD?src=/program_offices/housing*

U.S. Department of Housing and Urban Development: Interstate Land Sales: *http://portal.hud.gov/hudportal/HUD?src=/program_offices/housing/rmra/ils/ilshome*

U.S. Department of Housing and Urban Development: Land Sales Complaints: *www.hud.gov/complaints/landsales.cfm*

■ **CHAPTER 21**

Americans with Disabilities Act Home Page: *www.ada.gov*

U.S. Department of Justice: Housing and Civil Enforcement: *www.justice.gov/crt/about/hce/*

National Association of REALTORS® Code of Ethics: *www.realtor.org/mempolweb.nsf/pages/code*

National Fair Housing Advocate Online: *www.fairhousing.com*

U.S. Department of Housing and Urban Development: Fair Housing: *http://portal.hud.gov/hudportal/HUD?src=/program_offices/fair_housing_equal_opp*

U.S. Department of Housing and Urban Development: Fair Housing Accessibility Guidelines: *http://portal.hud.gov/hudportal/HUD?src=/program_offices/fair_housing_equal_opp/disabilities/fhefhag*

U.S. Department of Housing and Urban Development: Fair Housing Laws and Presidential Executive Orders: *http://portal.hud.gov/hudportal/HUD?src=/program_offices/fair_housing_equal_opp/FHLaws*

U.S. Department of Housing and Urban Development: Fair Housing Library: *www.hud.gov/library/bookshelf08/index.cfm*

U.S. Department of Housing and Urban Development: Housing Discrimination: *http://portal.hud.gov/hudportal/HUD?src=/topics/housing_discrimination*

U.S. Department of Housing and Urban Development: Fair Housing Ad Campaign: *http://portal.hud.gov/hudportal/HUD?src=/program_offices/fair_housing_equal_opp/adcampaign*

■ **CHAPTER 22**

Illinois Emergency Management Agency Radon Program: *www.radon.illinois.gov*

U.S. Environmental Protection Agency: *www.epa.gov*

U.S. Environmental Protection Agency: Asbestos: *www.epa.gov/oppt/asbestos/*

U.S. Environmental Protection Agency: Carbon Monoxide: *www.epa.gov/iaq/co.html*

U.S. Environmental Protection Agency: CERCLA Overview: *www.epa.gov/superfund/policy/cercla.htm*

U.S. Environmental Protection Agency: Compliance and Enforcement: *www.epa.gov/compliance*

U.S. Environmental Protection Agency: Formaldehyde: *www.epa.gov/iaq/formalde.html*

U.S. Environmental Protection Agency: Lead: *www.epa.gov/lead/*

U.S. Environmental Protection Agency: Lead-Based Paint Disclosure Forms: *http://www.epa.gov/lead/pubs/brochure.htm*

U.S. Environmental Protection Agency: Indoor Air Quality: Mold: *www.epa.gov/mold/*

U.S. Environmental Protection Agency: Indoor Air Quality: Radon: *www.epa.gov/radon/*

U.S. Environmental Protection Agency: Mold Remediation: *www.epa.gov/mold/mold_remediation.html*

U.S. Environmental Protection Agency: Water: *http://water.epa.gov/*

■ CHAPTER 23

U.S. Department of Housing and Urban Development: RESPA: *http://portal.hud.gov/hudportal/HUD?src=/program_offices/housing/rmra/res/respa_hm*

U.S. Department of Housing and Urban Development: RESPA: Frequently Asked Questions: *http://portal.hud.gov/hudportal/HUD?src=/program_offices/housing/rmra/res/respafaq*

NAR Code of Ethics

Code of Ethics and Standards of Practice
of the NATIONAL ASSOCIATION OF REALTORS®
Effective January 1, 2011

Where the word REALTORS® is used in this Code and Preamble, it shall be deemed to include REALTOR-ASSOCIATE®s.

While the Code of Ethics establishes obligations that may be higher than those mandated by law, in any instance where the Code of Ethics and the law conflict, the obligations of the law must take precedence.

Preamble

Under all is the land. Upon its wise utilization and widely allocated ownership depend the survival and growth of free institutions and of our civilization. REALTORS® should recognize that the interests of the nation and its citizens require the highest and best use of the land and the widest distribution of land ownership. They require the creation of adequate housing, the building of functioning cities, the development of productive industries and farms, and the preservation of a healthful environment.

Such interests impose obligations beyond those of ordinary commerce. They impose grave social responsibility and a patriotic duty to which REALTORS® should dedicate themselves, and for which they should be diligent in preparing themselves. REALTORS®, therefore, are zealous to maintain and improve the standards of their calling and share with their fellow REALTORS® a common responsibility for its integrity and honor.

In recognition and appreciation of their obligations to clients, customers, the public, and each other, REALTORS® continuously strive to become and remain informed on issues affecting real estate and, as knowledgeable professionals, they willingly share the fruit of their experience and study with others. They identify and take steps, through enforcement of this Code of Ethics and by assisting appropriate regulatory bodies, to eliminate practices which may damage the public or which might discredit or bring dishonor to the real estate profession. REALTORS® having direct personal knowledge of conduct that may violate the Code of Ethics involving misappropriation of client or customer funds or property, willful discrimination, or fraud resulting in substantial economic harm, bring such matters to the attention of the appropriate Board or Association of REALTORS®. *(Amended 1/00)*

Realizing that cooperation with other real estate professionals promotes the best interests of those who utilize their services, REALTORS® urge exclusive representation of clients; do not attempt to gain any unfair advantage over their competitors; and they refrain from making unsolicited comments about other practitioners. In instances where their opinion is sought, or where REALTORS® believe that comment is necessary, their opinion is offered in an objective, professional manner, uninfluenced by any personal motivation or potential advantage or gain.

The term REALTOR® has come to connote competency, fairness, and high integrity resulting from adherence to a lofty ideal of moral conduct in business relations. No inducement of profit and no instruction from clients ever can justify departure from this ideal.

In the interpretation of this obligation, REALTORS® can take no safer guide than that which has been handed down through the centuries, embodied in the Golden Rule, "Whatsoever ye would that others should do to you, do ye even so to them."

Accepting this standard as their own, REALTORS® pledge to observe its spirit in all of their activities whether conducted personally, through associates or others, or via technological means, and to conduct their business in accordance with the tenets set forth below. *(Amended 1/07)*

Duties to Clients and Customers

Article 1

When representing a buyer, seller, landlord, tenant, or other client as an agent, REALTORS® pledge themselves to protect and promote the interests of their client. This obligation to the client is primary, but it does not relieve REALTORS® of their obligation to treat all parties honestly. When serving a buyer, seller, landlord, tenant or other party in a non-agency capacity, REALTORS® remain obligated to treat all parties honestly. *(Amended 1/01)*

- **Standard of Practice 1-1**
  REALTORS®, when acting as principals in a real estate transaction, remain obligated by the duties imposed by the Code of Ethics. *(Amended 1/93)*

- **Standard of Practice 1-2**
  The duties imposed by the Code of Ethics encompass all real estate-related activities and transactions whether conducted in person, electronically, or through any other means.

  The duties the Code of Ethics imposes are applicable whether REALTORS® are acting as agents or in legally recognized non-agency capacities except that any duty imposed exclusively on agents by law or regulation shall not be imposed by this Code of Ethics on REALTORS® acting in non-agency capacities.

  As used in this Code of Ethics, "client" means the person(s) or entity(ies) with whom a REALTOR® or a REALTOR®'s firm has an agency or legally recognized non-agency relationship; "customer" means a party to a real estate transaction who receives information, services, or benefits but has no contractual relationship with the REALTOR® or the REALTOR®'s firm; "prospect" means a purchaser, seller, tenant, or landlord who is not subject to a representation relationship with the REALTOR® or REALTOR®'s firm; "agent" means a real estate licensee (including brokers and sales associates) acting in an agency relationship as defined by state law or regulation; and "broker" means a real estate licensee (including brokers and sales associates) acting as an agent or in a legally recognized non-agency capacity. *(Adopted 1/95, Amended 1/07)*

- **Standard of Practice 1-3**
  REALTORS®, in attempting to secure a listing, shall not deliberately mislead the owner as to market value.

- **Standard of Practice 1-4**
  REALTORS®, when seeking to become a buyer/tenant representative, shall not mislead buyers or tenants as to savings or other benefits that might be realized through use of the REALTOR®'s services. *(Amended 1/93)*

NATIONAL
ASSOCIATION *of*
REALTORS®

- **Standard of Practice 1-5**

  REALTORS® may represent the seller/landlord and buyer/tenant in the same transaction only after full disclosure to and with informed consent of both parties. *(Adopted 1/93)*

- **Standard of Practice 1-6**

  REALTORS® shall submit offers and counter-offers objectively and as quickly as possible. *(Adopted 1/93, Amended 1/95)*

- **Standard of Practice 1-7**

  When acting as listing brokers, REALTORS® shall continue to submit to the seller/landlord all offers and counter-offers until closing or execution of a lease unless the seller/landlord has waived this obligation in writing. REALTORS® shall not be obligated to continue to market the property after an offer has been accepted by the seller/landlord. REALTORS® shall recommend that sellers/landlords obtain the advice of legal counsel prior to acceptance of a subsequent offer except where the acceptance is contingent on the termination of the pre-existing purchase contract or lease. *(Amended 1/93)*

- **Standard of Practice 1-8**

  REALTORS®, acting as agents or brokers of buyers/tenants, shall submit to buyers/tenants all offers and counter-offers until acceptance but have no obligation to continue to show properties to their clients after an offer has been accepted unless otherwise agreed in writing. REALTORS®, acting as agents or brokers of buyers/tenants, shall recommend that buyers/tenants obtain the advice of legal counsel if there is a question as to whether a pre-existing contract has been terminated. *(Adopted 1/93, Amended 1/99)*

- **Standard of Practice 1-9**

  The obligation of REALTORS® to preserve confidential information (as defined by state law) provided by their clients in the course of any agency relationship or non-agency relationship recognized by law continues after termination of agency relationships or any non-agency relationships recognized by law. REALTORS® shall not knowingly, during or following the termination of professional relationships with their clients:

  1) reveal confidential information of clients; or
  2) use confidential information of clients to the disadvantage of clients; or
  3) use confidential information of clients for the REALTOR®'s advantage or the advantage of third parties unless:
     a) clients consent after full disclosure; or
     b) REALTORS® are required by court order; or
     c) it is the intention of a client to commit a crime and the information is necessary to prevent the crime; or
     d) it is necessary to defend a REALTOR® or the REALTOR®'s employees or associates against an accusation of wrongful conduct.

  Information concerning latent material defects is not considered confidential information under this Code of Ethics. *(Adopted 1/93, Amended 1/01)*

- **Standard of Practice 1-10**

  REALTORS® shall, consistent with the terms and conditions of their real estate licensure and their property management agreement, competently manage the property of clients with due regard for the rights, safety and health of tenants and others lawfully on the premises. *(Adopted 1/95, Amended 1/00)*

- **Standard of Practice 1-11**

  REALTORS® who are employed to maintain or manage a client's property shall exercise due diligence and make reasonable efforts to protect it against reasonably foreseeable contingencies and losses. *(Adopted 1/95)*

- **Standard of Practice 1-12**

  When entering into listing contracts, REALTORS® must advise sellers/landlords of:

  1) the REALTOR®'s company policies regarding cooperation and the amount(s) of any compensation that will be offered to subagents, buyer/tenant agents, and/or brokers acting in legally recognized non-agency capacities;
  2) the fact that buyer/tenant agents or brokers, even if compensated by listing brokers, or by sellers/landlords may represent the interests of buyers/tenants; and
  3) any potential for listing brokers to act as disclosed dual agents, e.g., buyer/tenant agents. *(Adopted 1/93, Renumbered 1/98, Amended 1/03)*

- **Standard of Practice 1-13**

  When entering into buyer/tenant agreements, REALTORS® must advise potential clients of:

  1) the REALTOR®'s company policies regarding cooperation;
  2) the amount of compensation to be paid by the client;
  3) the potential for additional or offsetting compensation from other brokers, from the seller or landlord, or from other parties;
  4) any potential for the buyer/tenant representative to act as a disclosed dual agent, e.g., listing broker, subagent, landlord's agent, etc., and
  5) the possibility that sellers or sellers' representatives may not treat the existence, terms, or conditions of offers as confidential unless confidentiality is required by law, regulation, or by any confidentiality agreement between the parties. *(Adopted 1/93, Renumbered 1/98, Amended 1/06)*

- **Standard of Practice 1-14**

  Fees for preparing appraisals or other valuations shall not be contingent upon the amount of the appraisal or valuation. *(Adopted 1/02)*

- **Standard of Practice 1-15**

  REALTORS®, in response to inquiries from buyers or cooperating brokers shall, with the sellers' approval, disclose the existence of offers on the property. Where disclosure is authorized, REALTORS® shall also disclose, if asked, whether offers were obtained by the listing licensee, another licensee in the listing firm, or by a cooperating broker. *(Adopted 1/03, Amended 1/09)*

Article 2

REALTORS® shall avoid exaggeration, misrepresentation, or concealment of pertinent facts relating to the property or the transaction. REALTORS® shall not, however, be obligated to discover latent defects in the property, to advise on matters outside the scope of their real estate license, or to disclose facts which are confidential under the scope of agency or non-agency relationships as defined by state law. *(Amended 1/00)*

- **Standard of Practice 2-1**

  REALTORS® shall only be obligated to discover and disclose adverse factors reasonably apparent to someone with expertise in those areas required by their real estate licensing authority. Article 2 does not impose upon the REALTOR® the obligation of expertise in other professional or technical disciplines. *(Amended 1/96)*

- **Standard of Practice 2-2**

  (Renumbered as Standard of Practice 1-12 1/98)

- **Standard of Practice 2-3**

  (Renumbered as Standard of Practice 1-13 1/98)

- **Standard of Practice 2-4**

  REALTORS® shall not be parties to the naming of a false consideration in any document, unless it be the naming of an obviously nominal consideration.

- **Standard of Practice 2-5**

  Factors defined as "non-material" by law or regulation or which are expressly referenced in law or regulation as not being subject to disclosure are considered not "pertinent" for purposes of Article 2. *(Adopted 1/93)*

Article 3

REALTORS® shall cooperate with other brokers except when cooperation is not in the client's best interest. The obligation to cooperate does not include the obligation to share commissions, fees, or to otherwise compensate another broker. *(Amended 1/95)*

- **Standard of Practice 3-1**

  REALTORS®, acting as exclusive agents or brokers of sellers/landlords, establish the terms and conditions of offers to cooperate. Unless expressly indicated in offers to cooperate, cooperating brokers may not assume that the offer of cooperation includes an offer of compensation. Terms of compensation, if any, shall be ascertained by cooperating brokers before beginning efforts to accept the offer of cooperation. *(Amended 1/99)*

- **Standard of Practice 3-2**

  To be effective, any change in compensation offered for cooperative services must be communicated to the other REALTOR® prior to the time that REALTOR® submits an offer to purchase/lease the property. *(Amended 1/10)*

- **Standard of Practice 3-3**

  Standard of Practice 3-2 does not preclude the listing broker and cooperating broker from entering into an agreement to change cooperative compensation. *(Adopted 1/94)*

- **Standard of Practice 3-4**

  REALTORS®, acting as listing brokers, have an affirmative obligation to disclose the existence of dual or variable rate commission arrangements (i.e., listings where one amount of commission is payable if the listing broker's firm is the procuring cause of sale/lease and a different amount of commission is payable if the sale/lease results through the efforts of the seller/landlord or a cooperating broker). The listing broker shall, as soon as practical, disclose the existence of such arrangements to potential cooperating brokers and shall, in response to inquiries from cooperating brokers, disclose the differential that would result in a cooperative transaction or in a sale/lease that results through the efforts of the seller/landlord. If the cooperating broker is a buyer/tenant representative, the buyer/tenant representative must disclose such information to their client before the client makes an offer to purchase or lease. *(Amended 1/02)*

- **Standard of Practice 3-5**

  It is the obligation of subagents to promptly disclose all pertinent facts to the principal's agent prior to as well as after a purchase or lease agreement is executed. *(Amended 1/93)*

- **Standard of Practice 3-6**

  REALTORS® shall disclose the existence of accepted offers, including offers with unresolved contingencies, to any broker seeking cooperation. *(Adopted 5/86, Amended 1/04)*

- **Standard of Practice 3-7**

  When seeking information from another REALTOR® concerning property under a management or listing agreement, REALTORS® shall disclose their REALTOR® status and whether their interest is personal or on behalf of a client and, if on behalf of a client, their relationship with the client. *(Amended 1/11)*

- **Standard of Practice 3-8**

  REALTORS® shall not misrepresent the availability of access to show or inspect a listed property. *(Amended 11/87)*

- **Standard of Practice 3-9**

  REALTORS® shall not provide access to listed property on terms other than those established by the owner or the listing broker. *(Adopted 1/10)*

- **Standard of Practice 3-10**

  The duty to cooperate established in Article 3 relates to the obligation to share information on listed property, and to make property available to other brokers for showing to prospective purchasers/tenants when it is in the best interests of sellers/landlords. *(Adopted 1/11)*

Article 4

REALTORS® shall not acquire an interest in or buy or present offers from themselves, any member of their immediate families, their firms or any member thereof, or any entities in which they have any ownership interest, any real property without making their true position known to the owner or the owner's agent or broker. In selling property they own, or in which they have any interest, REALTORS® shall reveal their ownership or interest in writing to the purchaser or the purchaser's representative. *(Amended 1/00)*

- **Standard of Practice 4-1**

  For the protection of all parties, the disclosures required by Article 4 shall be in writing and provided by REALTORS® prior to the signing of any contract. *(Adopted 2/86)*

Article 5

REALTORS® shall not undertake to provide professional services concerning a property or its value where they have a present or contemplated interest unless such interest is specifically disclosed to all affected parties.

Article 6

REALTORS® shall not accept any commission, rebate, or profit on expenditures made for their client, without the client's knowledge and consent.

When recommending real estate products or services (e.g., homeowner's insurance, warranty programs, mortgage financing, title insurance, etc.), REALTORS® shall disclose to the client or customer to whom the recommendation is made any financial benefits or fees, other than real estate referral fees, the REALTOR® or REALTOR®'s firm may receive as a direct result of such recommendation. *(Amended 1/99)*

- **Standard of Practice 6-1**

  REALTORS® shall not recommend or suggest to a client or a customer the use of services of another organization or business entity in which they have a direct interest without disclosing such interest at the time of the recommendation or suggestion. *(Amended 5/88)*

Article 7

In a transaction, REALTORS® shall not accept compensation from more than one party, even if permitted by law, without disclosure to all parties and the informed consent of the REALTOR®'s client or clients. *(Amended 1/93)*

Article 8

REALTORS® shall keep in a special account in an appropriate financial institution, separated from their own funds, monies coming into their possession in trust for other persons, such as escrows, trust funds, clients' monies, and other like items.

Article 9

REALTORS®, for the protection of all parties, shall assure whenever possible that all agreements related to real estate transactions including, but not limited to, listing and representation agreements, purchase contracts, and leases are in writing in clear and understandable language expressing the specific terms, conditions, obligations and commitments of the parties. A copy of each agreement shall be furnished to each party to such agreements upon their signing or initialing. *(Amended 1/04)*

- **Standard of Practice 9-1**

  For the protection of all parties, REALTORS® shall use reasonable care to ensure that documents pertaining to the purchase, sale, or lease of real estate are kept current through the use of written extensions or amendments. *(Amended 1/93)*

- **Standard of Practice 9-2**

  When assisting or enabling a client or customer in establishing a contractual relationship (e.g., listing and representation agreements, purchase agreements, leases, etc.) electronically, REALTORS® shall make reasonable efforts to explain the nature and disclose the specific terms of the contractual relationship being established prior to it being agreed to by a contracting party. *(Adopted 1/07)*

Duties to the Public

Article 10

REALTORS® shall not deny equal professional services to any person for reasons of race, color, religion, sex, handicap, familial status, national origin, or sexual orientation. REALTORS® shall not be parties to any plan or agreement to discriminate against a person or persons on the basis of race, color, religion, sex, handicap, familial status, national origin, or sexual orientation. *(Amended 1/11)*

REALTORS®, in their real estate employment practices, shall not discriminate against any person or persons on the basis of race, color, religion, sex, handicap, familial status, national origin, or sexual orientation. *(Amended 1/11)*

- **Standard of Practice 10-1**

  When involved in the sale or lease of a residence, REALTORS® shall not volunteer information regarding the racial, religious or ethnic composition of any neighborhood nor shall they engage in any activity which may result in panic selling, however, REALTORS® may provide other demographic information. *(Adopted 1/94, Amended 1/06)*

- **Standard of Practice 10-2**

  When not involved in the sale or lease of a residence, REALTORS® may provide demographic information related to a property, transaction or professional assignment to a party if such demographic information is (a) deemed by the REALTOR® to be needed to assist with or complete, in a manner consistent with Article 10, a real estate transaction or professional assignment and (b) is obtained or derived from a recognized, reliable, independent, and impartial source. The source of such information and any additions, deletions, modifications, interpretations, or other changes shall be disclosed in reasonable detail. *(Adopted 1/05, Renumbered 1/06)*

- **Standard of Practice 10-3**

  REALTORS® shall not print, display or circulate any statement or adver-tisement with respect to selling or renting of a property that indicates any preference, limitations or discrimination based on race, color, religion, sex, handicap, familial status, national origin, or sexual ori-entation. *(Adopted 1/94, Renumbered 1/05 and 1/06, Amended 1/11)*

- **Standard of Practice 10-4**

  As used in Article 10 "real estate employment practices" relates to employees and independent contractors providing real estate-related services and the administrative and clerical staff directly supporting those individuals. *(Adopted 1/00, Renumbered 1/05 and 1/06)*

Article 11

The services which REALTORS® provide to their clients and customers shall conform to the standards of practice and competence which are reasonably expected in the specific real estate disciplines in which they engage; specifically, residential real estate brokerage, real property management, commercial and industrial real estate brokerage, land brokerage, real estate appraisal, real estate counseling, real estate syndication, real estate auction, and international real estate.

REALTORS® shall not undertake to provide specialized professional services concerning a type of property or service that is outside their field of competence unless they engage the assistance of one who is competent on such types of property or service, or unless the facts are fully disclosed to the client. Any persons engaged to provide such assistance shall be so identified to the client and their contribution to the assignment should be set forth. *(Amended 1/10)*

- **Standard of Practice 11-1**

  When REALTORS® prepare opinions of real property value or price, other than in pursuit of a listing or to assist a potential purchaser in formulating a purchase offer, such opinions shall include the following unless the party requesting the opinion requires a specific type of report or different data set:

  1) identification of the subject property
  2) date prepared
  3) defined value or price
  4) limiting conditions, including statements of purpose(s) and intended user(s)
  5) any present or contemplated interest, including the possibility of representing the seller/landlord or buyers/tenants
  6) basis for the opinion, including applicable market data
  7) if the opinion is not an appraisal, a statement to that effect
  (Amended 1/10)

- **Standard of Practice 11-2**

  The obligations of the Code of Ethics in respect of real estate disciplines other than appraisal shall be interpreted and applied in accordance with the standards of competence and practice which clients and the public reasonably require to protect their rights and interests considering the complexity of the transaction, the availability of expert assistance, and, where the REALTOR® is an agent or subagent, the obligations of a fiduciary. *(Adopted 1/95)*

- **Standard of Practice 11-3**

  When REALTORS® provide consultive services to clients which involve advice or counsel for a fee (not a commission), such advice shall be rendered in an objective manner and the fee shall not be contingent on the substance of the advice or counsel given. If brokerage or transaction services are to be provided in addition to consultive services, a separate compensation may be paid with prior agreement between the client and REALTOR®. *(Adopted 1/96)*

- **Standard of Practice 11-4**

  The competency required by Article 11 relates to services contracted for between REALTORS® and their clients or customers; the duties expressly imposed by the Code of Ethics; and the duties imposed by law or regulation. *(Adopted 1/02)*

Article 12

REALTORS® shall be honest and truthful in their real estate communications and shall present a true picture in their advertising, marketing, and other representations. REALTORS® shall ensure that their status as real estate professionals is readily apparent in their advertising, marketing, and other representations, and that the recipients of all real estate communications are, or have been, notified that those communications are from a real estate professional. *(Amended 1/08)*

- **Standard of Practice 12-1**

REALTORS® may use the term "free" and similar terms in their advertising and in other representations provided that all terms governing availability of the offered product or service are clearly disclosed at the same time. *(Amended 1/97)*

- **Standard of Practice 12-2**

REALTORS® may represent their services as "free" or without cost even if they expect to receive compensation from a source other than their client provided that the potential for the REALTOR® to obtain a benefit from a third party is clearly disclosed at the same time. *(Amended 1/97)*

- **Standard of Practice 12-3**

The offering of premiums, prizes, merchandise discounts or other inducements to list, sell, purchase, or lease is not, in itself, unethical even if receipt of the benefit is contingent on listing, selling, purchasing, or leasing through the REALTOR® making the offer. However, REALTORS® must exercise care and candor in any such advertising or other public or private representations so that any party interested in receiving or otherwise benefiting from the REALTOR®'s offer will have clear, thorough, advance understanding of all the terms and conditions of the offer. The offering of any inducements to do business is subject to the limitations and restrictions of state law and the ethical obligations established by any applicable Standard of Practice. *(Amended 1/95)*

- **Standard of Practice 12-4**

REALTORS® shall not offer for sale/lease or advertise property without authority. When acting as listing brokers or as subagents, REALTORS® shall not quote a price different from that agreed upon with the seller/landlord. *(Amended 1/93)*

- **Standard of Practice 12-5**

REALTORS® shall not advertise nor permit any person employed by or affiliated with them to advertise real estate services or listed property in any medium (e.g., electronically, print, radio, television, etc.) without disclosing the name of that REALTOR®'s firm in a reasonable and readily apparent manner. This Standard of Practice acknowledges that disclosing the name of the firm may not be practical in electronic displays of limited information (e.g., "thumbnails", text messages, "tweets", etc.). Such displays are exempt from the disclosure requirement established in this Standard of Practice, but only when linked to a display that includes all required disclosures. *(Adopted 11/86, Amended 1/11)*

- **Standard of Practice 12-6**

REALTORS®, when advertising unlisted real property for sale/lease in which they have an ownership interest, shall disclose their status as both owners/landlords and as REALTORS® or real estate licensees. *(Amended 1/93)*

- **Standard of Practice 12-7**

Only REALTORS® who participated in the transaction as the listing broker or cooperating broker (selling broker) may claim to have "sold" the property. Prior to closing, a cooperating broker may post a "sold" sign only with the consent of the listing broker. *(Amended 1/96)*

- **Standard of Practice 12-8**

The obligation to present a true picture in representations to the public includes information presented, provided, or displayed on REALTORS®' websites. REALTORS® shall use reasonable efforts to ensure that information on their websites is current. When it becomes apparent that information on a REALTOR®'s website is no longer current or accurate, REALTORS® shall promptly take corrective action. *(Adopted 1/07)*

- **Standard of Practice 12-9**

REALTOR® firm websites shall disclose the firm's name and state(s) of licensure in a reasonable and readily apparent manner.

Websites of REALTORS® and non-member licensees affiliated with a REALTOR® firm shall disclose the firm's name and that REALTOR®'s or non-member licensee's state(s) of licensure in a reasonable and readily apparent manner. *(Adopted 1/07)*

- **Standard of Practice 12-10**

REALTORS®' obligation to present a true picture in their advertising and representations to the public includes the URLs and domain names they use, and prohibits REALTORS® from:
1) engaging in deceptive or unauthorized framing of real estate brokerage websites;
2) manipulating (e.g., presenting content developed by others) listing content in any way that produces a deceptive or misleading result; or
3) deceptively using metatags, keywords or other devices/methods to direct, drive, or divert Internet traffic, or to otherwise mislead consumers. *(Adopted 1/07)*

- **Standard of Practice 12-11**

REALTORS® intending to share or sell consumer information gathered via the Internet shall disclose that possibility in a reasonable and readily apparent manner. *(Adopted 1/07)*

- **Standard of Practice 12-12**

REALTORS® shall not:
1) use URLs or domain names that present less than a true picture, or
2) register URLs or domain names which, if used, would present less than a true picture. *(Adopted 1/08)*

- **Standard of Practice 12-13**

The obligation to present a true picture in advertising, marketing, and representations allows REALTORS® to use and display only professional designations, certifications, and other credentials to which they are legitimately entitled. *(Adopted 1/08)*

Article 13

REALTORS® shall not engage in activities that constitute the unauthorized practice of law and shall recommend that legal counsel be obtained when the interest of any party to the transaction requires it.

Article 14

If charged with unethical practice or asked to present evidence or to cooperate in any other way, in any professional standards proceeding or investigation, REALTORS® shall place all pertinent facts before the proper tribunals of the Member Board or affiliated institute, society, or council in which membership is held and shall take no action to disrupt or obstruct such processes. *(Amended 1/99)*

- **Standard of Practice 14-1**

REALTORS® shall not be subject to disciplinary proceedings in more than one Board of REALTORS® or affiliated institute, society, or council in which they hold membership with respect to alleged violations of the Code of Ethics relating to the same transaction or event. *(Amended 1/95)*

- **Standard of Practice 14-2**

  REALTORS® shall not make any unauthorized disclosure or dissemination of the allegations, findings, or decision developed in connection with an ethics hearing or appeal or in connection with an arbitration hearing or procedural review. *(Amended 1/92)*

- **Standard of Practice 14-3**

  REALTORS® shall not obstruct the Board's investigative or professional standards proceedings by instituting or threatening to institute actions for libel, slander, or defamation against any party to a professional standards proceeding or their witnesses based on the filing of an arbitration request, an ethics complaint, or testimony given before any tribunal. *(Adopted 11/87, Amended 1/99)*

- **Standard of Practice 14-4**

  REALTORS® shall not intentionally impede the Board's investigative or disciplinary proceedings by filing multiple ethics complaints based on the same event or transaction. *(Adopted 11/88)*

Duties to REALTORS®

Article 15

REALTORS® shall not knowingly or recklessly make false or misleading statements about competitors, their businesses, or their business practices. *(Amended 1/92)*

- **Standard of Practice 15-1**

  REALTORS® shall not knowingly or recklessly file false or unfounded ethics complaints. *(Adopted 1/00)*

- **Standard of Practice 15-2**

  The obligation to refrain from making false or misleading statements about competitors, competitors' businesses, and competitors' business practices includes the duty to not knowingly or recklessly publish, repeat, retransmit, or republish false or misleading statements made by others. This duty applies whether false or misleading statements are repeated in person, in writing, by technological means (e.g., the Internet), or by any other means. *(Adopted 1/07, Amended 1/10)*

- **Standard of Practice 15-3**

  The obligation to refrain from making false or misleading statements about competitors, competitors' businesses, and competitors' business practices includes the duty to publish a clarification about or to remove statements made by others on electronic media the REALTOR® controls once the REALTOR® knows the statement is false or misleading. *(Adopted 1/10)*

Article 16

REALTORS® shall not engage in any practice or take any action inconsistent with exclusive representation or exclusive brokerage relationship agreements that other REALTORS® have with clients. *(Amended 1/04)*

- **Standard of Practice 16-1**

  Article 16 is not intended to prohibit aggressive or innovative business practices which are otherwise ethical and does not prohibit disagreements with other REALTORS® involving commission, fees, compensation or other forms of payment or expenses. *(Adopted 1/93, Amended 1/95)*

- **Standard of Practice 16-2**

  Article 16 does not preclude REALTORS® from making general announcements to prospects describing their services and the terms of their availability even though some recipients may have entered into agency agreements or other exclusive relationships with another REALTOR®. A general telephone canvass, general mailing or distribution addressed to all prospects in a given geographical area or in a given profession, business, club, or organization, or other classification or group is deemed "general" for purposes of this standard. *(Amended 1/04)*

Article 16 is intended to recognize as unethical two basic types of solicitations:

First, telephone or personal solicitations of property owners who have been identified by a real estate sign, multiple listing compilation, or other information service as having exclusively listed their property with another REALTOR® and

Second, mail or other forms of written solicitations of prospects whose properties are exclusively listed with another REALTOR® when such solicitations are not part of a general mailing but are directed specifically to property owners identified through compilations of current listings, "for sale" or "for rent" signs, or other sources of information required by Article 3 and Multiple Listing Service rules to be made available to other REALTORS® under offers of subagency or cooperation. *(Amended 1/04)*

- **Standard of Practice 16-3**

  Article 16 does not preclude REALTORS® from contacting the client of another broker for the purpose of offering to provide, or entering into a contract to provide, a different type of real estate service unrelated to the type of service currently being provided (e.g., property management as opposed to brokerage) or from offering the same type of service for property not subject to other brokers' exclusive agreements. However, information received through a Multiple Listing Service or any other offer of cooperation may not be used to target clients of other REALTORS® to whom such offers to provide services may be made. *(Amended 1/04)*

- **Standard of Practice 16-4**

  REALTORS® shall not solicit a listing which is currently listed exclusively with another broker. However, if the listing broker, when asked by the REALTOR®, refuses to disclose the expiration date and nature of such listing, i.e., an exclusive right to sell, an exclusive agency, open listing, or other form of contractual agreement between the listing broker and the client, the REALTOR® may contact the owner to secure such information and may discuss the terms upon which the REALTOR® might take a future listing or, alternatively, may take a listing to become effective upon expiration of any existing exclusive listing. *(Amended 1/94)*

- **Standard of Practice 16-5**

  REALTORS® shall not solicit buyer/tenant agreements from buyers/tenants who are subject to exclusive buyer/tenant agreements. However, if asked by a REALTOR®, the broker refuses to disclose the expiration date of the exclusive buyer/tenant agreement, the REALTOR® may contact the buyer/tenant to secure such information and may discuss the terms upon which the REALTOR® might enter into a future buyer/tenant agreement or, alternatively, may enter into a buyer/tenant agreement to become effective upon the expiration of any existing exclusive buyer/tenant agreement. *(Adopted 1/94, Amended 1/98)*

- **Standard of Practice 16-6**

  When REALTORS® are contacted by the client of another REALTOR® regarding the creation of an exclusive relationship to provide the same type of service, and REALTORS® have not directly or indirectly initiated such discussions, they may discuss the terms upon which they might enter into a future agreement or, alternatively, may enter into an agreement which becomes effective upon expiration of any existing exclusive agreement. *(Amended 1/98)*

- **Standard of Practice 16-7**

The fact that a prospect has retained a REALTOR® as an exclusive representative or exclusive broker in one or more past transactions does not preclude other REALTORS® from seeking such prospect's future business. *(Amended 1/04)*

- **Standard of Practice 16-8**

The fact that an exclusive agreement has been entered into with a REALTOR® shall not preclude or inhibit any other REALTOR® from entering into a similar agreement after the expiration of the prior agreement. *(Amended 1/98)*

- **Standard of Practice 16-9**

REALTORS®, prior to entering into a representation agreement, have an affirmative obligation to make reasonable efforts to determine whether the prospect is subject to a current, valid exclusive agreement to provide the same type of real estate service. *(Amended 1/04)*

- **Standard of Practice 16-10**

REALTORS®, acting as buyer or tenant representatives or brokers, shall disclose that relationship to the seller/landlord's representative or broker at first contact and shall provide written confirmation of that disclosure to the seller/landlord's representative or broker not later than execution of a purchase agreement or lease. *(Amended 1/04)*

- **Standard of Practice 16-11**

On unlisted property, REALTORS® acting as buyer/tenant representatives or brokers shall disclose that relationship to the seller/landlord at first contact for that buyer/tenant and shall provide written confirmation of such disclosure to the seller/landlord not later than execution of any purchase or lease agreement. *(Amended 1/04)*

REALTORS® shall make any request for anticipated compensation from the seller/landlord at first contact. *(Amended 1/98)*

- **Standard of Practice 16-12**

REALTORS®, acting as representatives or brokers of sellers/landlords or as subagents of listing brokers, shall disclose that relationship to buyers/tenants as soon as practicable and shall provide written confirmation of such disclosure to buyers/tenants not later than execution of any purchase or lease agreement. *(Amended 1/04)*

- **Standard of Practice 16-13**

All dealings concerning property exclusively listed, or with buyer/tenants who are subject to an exclusive agreement shall be carried on with the client's representative or broker, and not with the client, except with the consent of the client's representative or broker or except where such dealings are initiated by the client.

Before providing substantive services (such as writing a purchase offer or presenting a CMA) to prospects, REALTORS® shall ask prospects whether they are a party to any exclusive representation agreement. REALTORS® shall not knowingly provide substantive services concerning a prospective transaction to prospects who are parties to exclusive representation agreements, except with the consent of the prospects' exclusive representatives or at the direction of prospects. *(Adopted 1/93, Amended 1/04)*

- **Standard of Practice 16-14**

REALTORS® are free to enter into contractual relationships or to negotiate with sellers/landlords, buyers/tenants or others who are not subject to an exclusive agreement but shall not knowingly obligate them to pay more than one commission except with their informed consent. *(Amended 1/98)*

- **Standard of Practice 16-15**

In cooperative transactions REALTORS® shall compensate cooperating REALTORS® (principal brokers) and shall not compensate nor offer to compensate, directly or indirectly, any of the sales licensees employed by or affiliated with other REALTORS® without the prior express knowledge and consent of the cooperating broker.

- **Standard of Practice 16-16**

REALTORS®, acting as subagents or buyer/tenant representatives or brokers, shall not use the terms of an offer to purchase/lease to attempt to modify the listing broker's offer of compensation to subagents or buyer/tenant representatives or brokers nor make the submission of an executed offer to purchase/lease contingent on the listing broker's agreement to modify the offer of compensation. *(Amended 1/04)*

- **Standard of Practice 16-17**

REALTORS®, acting as subagents or as buyer/tenant representatives or brokers, shall not attempt to extend a listing broker's offer of cooperation and/or compensation to other brokers without the consent of the listing broker. *(Amended 1/04)*

- **Standard of Practice 16-18**

REALTORS® shall not use information obtained from listing brokers through offers to cooperate made through multiple listing services or through other offers of cooperation to refer listing brokers' clients to other brokers or to create buyer/tenant relationships with listing brokers' clients, unless such use is authorized by listing brokers. *(Amended 1/02)*

- **Standard of Practice 16-19**

Signs giving notice of property for sale, rent, lease, or exchange shall not be placed on property without consent of the seller/landlord. *(Amended 1/93)*

- **Standard of Practice 16-20**

REALTORS®, prior to or after their relationship with their current firm is terminated, shall not induce clients of their current firm to cancel exclusive contractual agreements between the client and that firm. This does not preclude REALTORS® (principals) from establishing agreements with their associated licensees governing assignability of exclusive agreements. *(Adopted 1/98, Amended 1/10)*

Article 17

In the event of contractual disputes or specific non-contractual disputes as defined in Standard of Practice 17-4 between REALTORS® (principals) associated with different firms, arising out of their relationship as REALTORS®, the REALTORS® shall submit the dispute to arbitration in accordance with the regulations of their Board or Boards rather than litigate the matter.

In the event clients of REALTORS® wish to arbitrate contractual disputes arising out of real estate transactions, REALTORS® shall arbitrate those disputes in accordance with the regulations of their Board, provided the clients agree to be bound by the decision.

The obligation to participate in arbitration contemplated by this Article includes the obligation of REALTORS® (principals) to cause their firms to arbitrate and be bound by any award. *(Amended 1/01)*

- **Standard of Practice 17-1**

The filing of litigation and refusal to withdraw from it by REALTORS® in an arbitrable matter constitutes a refusal to arbitrate. *(Adopted 2/86)*

- **Standard of Practice 17-2**

Article 17 does not require REALTORS® to arbitrate in those circumstances when all parties to the dispute advise the Board in writing that they choose not to arbitrate before the Board. *(Amended 1/93)*

- **Standard of Practice 17-3**

  REALTORS®, when acting solely as principals in a real estate transaction, are not obligated to arbitrate disputes with other REALTORS® absent a specific written agreement to the contrary. *(Adopted 1/96)*

- **Standard of Practice 17-4**

  Specific non-contractual disputes that are subject to arbitration pursuant to Article 17 are:

  1) Where a listing broker has compensated a cooperating broker and another cooperating broker subsequently claims to be the procuring cause of the sale or lease. In such cases the complainant may name the first cooperating broker as respondent and arbitration may proceed without the listing broker being named as a respondent. When arbitration occurs between two (or more) cooperating brokers and where the listing broker is not a party, the amount in dispute and the amount of any potential resulting award is limited to the amount paid to the respondent by the listing broker and any amount credited or paid to a party to the transaction at the direction of the respondent. Alternatively, if the complaint is brought against the listing broker, the listing broker may name the first cooperating broker as a third-party respondent. In either instance the decision of the hearing panel as to procuring cause shall be conclusive with respect to all current or subsequent claims of the parties for compensation arising out of the underlying cooperative transaction. *(Adopted 1/97, Amended 1/07)*

  2) Where a buyer or tenant representative is compensated by the seller or landlord, and not by the listing broker, and the listing broker, as a result, reduces the commission owed by the seller or landlord and, subsequent to such actions, another cooperating broker claims to be the procuring cause of sale or lease. In such cases the complainant may name the first cooperating broker as respondent and arbitration may proceed without the listing broker being named as a respondent. When arbitration occurs between two (or more) cooperating brokers and where the listing broker is not a party, the amount in dispute and the amount of any potential resulting award is limited to the amount paid to the respondent by the seller or landlord and any amount credited or paid to a party to the transaction at the direction of the respondent. Alternatively, if the complaint is brought against the listing broker, the listing broker may name the first cooperating broker as a third-party respondent. In either instance the decision of the hearing panel as to procuring cause shall be conclusive with respect to all current or subsequent claims of the parties for compensation arising out of the underlying cooperative transaction. *(Adopted 1/97, Amended 1/07)*

  3) Where a buyer or tenant representative is compensated by the buyer or tenant and, as a result, the listing broker reduces the commission owed by the seller or landlord and, subsequent to such actions, another cooperating broker claims to be the procuring cause of sale or lease. In such cases the complainant may name the first cooperating broker as respondent and arbitration may proceed without the listing broker being named as a respondent. Alternatively, if the complaint is brought against the listing broker, the listing broker may name the first

  cooperating broker as a third-party respondent. In either instance the decision of the hearing panel as to procuring cause shall be conclusive with respect to all current or subsequent claims of the parties for compensation arising out of the underlying cooperative transaction. *(Adopted 1/97)*

  4) Where two or more listing brokers claim entitlement to compensation pursuant to open listings with a seller or landlord who agrees to participate in arbitration (or who requests arbitration) and who agrees to be bound by the decision. In cases where one of the listing brokers has been compensated by the seller or landlord, the other listing broker, as complainant, may name the first listing broker as respondent and arbitration may proceed between the brokers. *(Adopted 1/97)*

  5) Where a buyer or tenant representative is compensated by the seller or landlord, and not by the listing broker, and the listing broker, as a result, reduces the commission owed by the seller or landlord and, subsequent to such actions, claims to be the procuring cause of sale or lease. In such cases arbitration shall be between the listing broker and the buyer or tenant representative and the amount in dispute is limited to the amount of the reduction of commission to which the listing broker agreed. *(Adopted 1/05)*

- **Standard of Practice 17-5**

  The obligation to arbitrate established in Article 17 includes disputes between REALTORS® (principals) in different states in instances where, absent an established inter-association arbitration agreement, the REALTOR® (principal) requesting arbitration agrees to submit to the jurisdiction of, travel to, participate in, and be bound by any resulting award rendered in arbitration conducted by the respondent(s) REALTOR®'s association, in instances where the respondent(s) REALTOR®'s association determines that an arbitrable issue exists. *(Adopted 1/07)*

The **Code of Ethics** *was adopted in 1913. Amended at the Annual Convention in 1924, 1928, 1950, 1951, 1952, 1955, 1956, 1961, 1962, 1974, 1982, 1986, 1987, 1989, 1990, 1991, 1992, 1993, 1994, 1995, 1996, 1997, 1998, 1999, 2000, 2001, 2002, 2003, 2004, 2005, 2006, 2007, 2008, 2009, and 2010.*

Explanatory Notes

The reader should be aware of the following policies which have been approved by the Board of Directors of the National Association:

In filing a charge of an alleged violation of the Code of Ethics by a REALTOR®, the charge must read as an alleged violation of one or more Articles of the Code. Standards of Practice may be cited in support of the charge.

The Standards of Practice serve to clarify the ethical obligations imposed by the various Articles and supplement, and do not substitute for, the Case Interpretations in *Interpretations of the Code of Ethics.*

Modifications to existing Standards of Practice and additional new Standards of Practice are approved from time to time. Readers are cautioned to ensure that the most recent publications are utilized.

166-288 (12/10 JBK)

430 North Michigan Avenue • Chicago, IL 60611-4087
800.874.6500 • www.REALTOR.org

Glossary

abstract of title   The condensed history of a title to a particular parcel of real estate, consisting of a summary of the original grant and all subsequent conveyances and encumbrances affecting the property and a certification by the abstractor that the history is complete and accurate.

acceleration clause   The clause in a mortgage or deed of trust that can be enforced to make the entire debt due immediately if the borrower defaults on an installment payment or other covenant.

accession   Acquiring title to additions or improvements to real property as a result of the annexation of fixtures or the accretion of alluvial deposits along the banks of streams.

accretion   The increase or addition of land by the deposit of sand or soil washed up naturally from a river, lake, or sea.

accrued items   On a closing statement, items of expense that are incurred but not yet payable, such as interest on a mortgage loan or taxes on real property.

acknowledgment   A formal declaration made before a duly authorized officer, usually a notary public, by a person who has signed a document.

acre   A measure of land equal to 43,560 square feet, 4,840 square yards, 4,047 square meters, 160 square rods, or 0.4047 hectares.

actual eviction   The legal process that results in the tenants being physically removed from the leased premises.

actual notice   Express information or fact; that which is known; direct knowledge.

addendum   Any provision added to an existing contract without altering the content of the original; it must be signed by all parties.

adjustable-rate mortgage (ARM)   A loan characterized by a fluctuating interest rate, usually one tied to a bank or savings and loan association cost-of-funds index.

adjusted basis   *See* basis.

ad valorem tax   A tax levied according to value, generally used to refer to real estate tax. Also called the *general tax*.

adverse possession   The actual, open, notorious, hostile, and continuous possession of another's land under a claim of title. Possession for a statutory period may be a means of acquiring title.

affidavit of title   A written statement, made under oath by a seller or grantor of real property and acknowledged by a notary public, in which the grantor (1) identifies himself and indicates marital status, (2) certifies that since the examination of the title on the date of the contract no defects have occurred in the title and (3) certifies that he is in possession of the property (if applicable).

affiliated business disclosure   A disclosure that a company or individual referring settlement services has either an affiliate relationship with or a direct or beneficial ownership interest of more than 1 percent in a provider of settlement services and who then refers business to that provider or in some way influences the selection of that provider.

agency   The relationship between a principal and an agent wherein the agent is authorized to represent the principal in certain transactions.

agency coupled with an interest   An agency relationship in which the agent is given an estate or interest in the subject of the agency (the property).

agent   One who acts or has the power to act for another. A fiduciary relationship is created under the law of agency when a property owner, as the principal, executes a listing agreement or management contract authorizing a licensed sponsoring broker to be his agent.

air lot   A designated airspace over a piece of land. An air lot, like surface property, may be transferred.

air rights   The right to use the open space above a property, usually allowing the surface to be used for another purpose.

alienation   The act of transferring property to another. Alienation may be voluntary, such as by gift or sale, or involuntary, as through eminent domain or adverse possession.

alienation clause   The clause in a mortgage or deed of trust that states that the balance of the secured debt becomes immediately due and payable at the lender's option if the property is sold by the borrower. In effect, this clause prevents the borrower from assigning the debt without the lender's approval.

allodial system   A system of land ownership in which land is held free and clear of any rent or service due to the government; commonly contrasted to the feudal system. Land is held under the allodial system in the United States.

amendment A change to an existing contract.

American Land Title Association (ALTA) policy A title insurance policy that protects the interest in a collateral property of a mortgage lender who originates a new real estate loan.

Americans with Disabilities Act (ADA) Legislation that prohibits discrimination against the physically or mentally impaired as it relates to employment opportunities and public accommodations.

amortized loan A loan in which the principal as well as the interest is payable in monthly or other periodic installments over the term of the loan.

annual percentage rate (APR) The relationship of the total finance charges associated with a loan. This must be disclosed to borrowers by lenders under the Truth in Lending Act.

anticipation The appraisal principle that holds that value can increase or decrease based on the expectation of some future benefit or detriment produced by the property.

antitrust laws Laws designed to preserve the free enterprise of the open marketplace by making illegal certain private conspiracies and combinations formed to minimize competition. Most violations of antitrust laws in the real estate business involve either price-fixing (real estate companies conspiring to set fixed compensation rates) or allocation of customers or markets (real estate companies agreeing to limit their areas of trade or dealing to certain areas or properties).

appraisal An estimate of the quantity, quality, or value of something. The process through which conclusions of property value are obtained; also refers to the report that sets forth the process of estimation and conclusion of value.

appraiser An independent person trained to provide an unbiased opinion of value in an impartial and objective manner according to the appraisal process.

appreciation An increase in the worth or value of a property due to economic or related causes, which may prove to be either temporary or permanent; opposite of depreciation.

appurtenance A right, privilege, or improvement belonging to, and passing with, the land.

appurtenant easement An easement that is annexed to the ownership of one parcel and allows the owner the use of the neighbor's land.

asbestos A mineral once used in insulation and other materials that can cause respiratory diseases.

assemblage The combining of two or more adjoining lots into one larger tract to increase their total value.

assessment The imposition of a tax, charge, or levy, usually according to established rates.

assignment The transfer in writing of interest in a bond, mortgage, lease, or other instrument.

assumption of mortgage Acquiring title to property on which there is an existing mortgage and agreeing to be personally liable for the terms and conditions of the mortgage, including payments.

attachment The act of taking a person's property into legal custody by writ or other judicial order to hold it available for application to that person's debt to a creditor.

attorney's opinion of title An abstract of title that an attorney has examined and has certified to be, in his opinion, an accurate statement of the facts concerning the property ownership.

automated underwriting Computer systems that permit lenders to expedite the loan approval process and reduce lending costs.

automatic extension A clause in a listing agreement that states that the agreement will continue automatically for a certain period of time after its expiration date. In many states, use of this clause is discouraged or prohibited.

avulsion The sudden tearing away of land, as by earthquake, flood, volcanic action, or the sudden change in the course of a stream.

balance The appraisal principle that states that the greatest value in a property will occur when the type and size of the improvements are proportional to each other as well as to the land.

balloon payment A final payment of a mortgage loan that is considerably larger than the required periodic payments because the loan amount was not fully amortized.

bargain and sale deed A deed that carries with it no warranties against liens or other encumbrances but that does imply that the grantor has the right to convey title. The grantor may add warranties to the deed at his discretion.

base line The main imaginary line running east and west and crossing a principal meridian at a definite point, used by surveyors for reference in locating and describing land under the rectangular (government) survey system of legal description.

basis The financial interest that the Internal Revenue Service attributes to an owner of an investment property for the purpose of determining annual depreciation and gain or loss on the sale of the asset. If a property was acquired by purchase, the owner's basis is the cost of the property plus the value of any capital expenditures for improvements to the property, minus any depreciation allowable or actually taken. This new basis is called the adjusted basis.

benchmark A permanent reference mark or point established for use by surveyors in measuring differences in elevation.

beneficiary (1) The person for whom a trust operates or on whose behalf the income from a trust estate is drawn. (2) A lender in a deed of trust loan transaction.

bequest A gift of personal property under a will.

bilateral contract *See* contract.

bill of sale A legal document that transfers personal property.

binder An agreement that may accompany an earnest money deposit for the purchase of real property as evidence of the purchaser's good faith and intent to complete the transaction.

blanket loan A mortgage covering more than one parcel of real estate, providing for each parcel's partial release from the mortgage lien on repayment of a definite portion of the debt.

blind ad An advertisement whereby the sponsoring broker's name is not identified in the advertisement.

blockbusting The illegal practice of inducing homeowners to sell their properties by making representations regarding the entry or prospective entry of persons of a particular race or national origin into the neighborhood.

blue-sky laws Common name for those state and federal laws that regulate the registration and sale of investment securities.

boot Money or property given to make up any difference in value or equity between two properties in an exchange.

boycott Occurs when two or more businesses conspire against another business or agree to withhold their patronage to reduce competition.

branch office A secondary place of business apart from the principal or main office from which real estate business is conducted. A branch office usually must be run by a licensed real estate managing broker working on behalf of the sponsoring broker.

branch office license In Illinois, a separate license that must be obtained for each branch office a sponsoring broker wishes to establish.

breach of contract Violation of any terms or conditions in a contract without legal excuse; for example, failure to make a payment when it is due.

broker One who acts as an intermediary on behalf of others for a fee or commission.

brokerage The bringing together of parties interested in making a real estate transaction.

brokerage agreement A written or oral agreement between a sponsoring broker and a consumer for licensed activities to be provided to a consumer in return for compensation or the right to receive compensation from another. They may constitute either a bilateral or unilateral agreement between the sponsoring broker and the sponsoring broker's client depending upon the content of the brokerage agreement. All exclusive brokerage agreements must be in writing.

brownfields Defunct, derelict, or abandoned commercial or industrial sites; many have toxic wastes.

Brownfields Legislation Provides federal funding to states and localities to clean up brownfields sites.

buffer zone A strip of land, usually used as a park or designated for a similar use, separating land dedicated to one use from land dedicated to another use (e.g., residential from commercial).

building code An ordinance that specifies minimum standards of construction for buildings to protect public safety and health.

building permit Written governmental permission for the construction, alteration, or demolition of an improvement, showing compliance with building codes and zoning ordinances.

bundle of legal rights The concept of land ownership that includes ownership of all legal rights to the land— for example, possession, control within the law, and enjoyment.

buydown A financing technique used to reduce the monthly payments for the first few years of a loan. Funds in the form of discount points are given to the lender by the builder or seller to buy down or lower the effective interest rate paid by the buyer, thus reducing the monthly payments for a set time.

buyer-agency agreement A principal-agent relationship in which the sponsoring broker is the agent for the buyer, with fiduciary responsibilities to the buyer.

buyer's agent A real estate licensee who represents the prospective purchaser in a transaction. The buyer's agent owes the buyer/principal the statutory agency duties.

buyer's broker A real estate licensee who represents prospective residential buyers exclusively. As the buyer's agent, the licensee owes the buyer/principal the common-law or statutory agency duties.

CAN-SPAM Act of 2003 Establishes requirements for commercial e-mail, spells out penalties for e-mail senders, and gives consumers the right to have e-mailers stop sending e-mails to them.

capital gain Profit earned from the sale of an asset.

capitalization A mathematical process for estimating the value of a property using a proper rate of return on the investment and the annual net operating income expected to be produced by the property. The formula is expressed as Net income ÷ Rate = Value.

capitalization rate The rate of return a property will produce on the owner's investment.

cash flow The net spendable income from an investment, determined by deducting all operating and fixed expenses from the gross income. When expenses exceed income, a negative cash flow results.

cash rent In an agricultural lease, the amount of money given as rent to the landowner at the outset of the lease, as opposed to sharecropping.

caveat emptor A Latin phrase meaning "let the buyer beware."

certificate of reasonable value (CRV) A form indicating the appraised value of a property being financed with a VA loan.

certificate of sale The document generally given to the purchaser of delinquent property taxes at a tax foreclosure sale.

certificate of title A statement of opinion on the status of the title to a parcel of real property based on an examination of specified public records.

chain of title The succession of conveyances, from some accepted starting point, whereby the present holder of real property derives title.

change The appraisal principle that holds that no physical or economic condition remains constant.

chattel *See* personal property.

chlorofluorocarbons Nontoxic, nonflammable chemicals containing atoms of carbon, chlorine, and fluorine. Most often used in air conditioners, refrigerators, paints, solvents, and foam-blowing applications.

Civil Rights Act of 1866 An act that prohibits racial discrimination in the sale and rental of housing.

client A person who is being represented by a licensee; the principal.

closing The point at which ownership of a property is transferred in exchange for the selling price.

closing statement A detailed cash accounting of a real estate transaction showing all cash received, all charges and credits made, and all cash paid out in the transaction.

cloud on title Any document, claim, unreleased lien, or encumbrance that may impair the title to real property or make the title doubtful; usually revealed by a title search and removed by either a quitclaim deed or suit to quiet title.

clustering The grouping of homesites within a subdivision on smaller lots than normal, with the remaining land used as common areas.

code of ethics A written system of standards for ethical conduct.

codicil A supplement or an addition to a will, executed with the same formalities as a will, that normally does not revoke the entire will.

coinsurance clause A clause in insurance policies covering real property that requires that the policyholder maintain fire insurance coverage generally equal to at least 80 percent of the property's actual replacement cost.

collateral Something having value that is given to secure repayment of a debt.

commingling The illegal act by a real estate licensee of placing client or customer funds with personal funds.

commission Payment to a licensee for services rendered, such as in the sale or purchase of real property; usually a percentage of the selling price of the property.

common elements Parts of a property that are necessary or convenient to the existence, maintenance, and safety of a condominium or are normally in common use by all of the condominium residents. Each condominium owner has an undivided ownership interest in the common elements.

common law The body of law based on custom, usage, and court decisions.

common law of agency The traditional law governing the principal-agent relationship, superseded by statute in Illinois.

Community Association Manager Licensing & Disciplinary Act Legislation created to provide for the regulation of managers of community association management and provide for high standards of professional conduct by those licensed. Anyone acting under this license cannot perform any activities for which a real estate managing broker's license is required under the Illinois Real Estate License Act of 2000.

community property A system of property ownership based on the theory that each spouse has an equal interest in the property acquired by the efforts of either spouse during marriage.

Community Reinvestment Act (CRA) Under the act, financial institutions are expected to meet the deposit and credit needs of their communities; participate and invest in local community development and rehabilitation projects; and participate in loan programs for housing, small businesses, and small farms.

comparables Properties used in an appraisal report that are substantially equivalent to the subject property.

comparative market analysis (CMA) A comparison of the prices of recently sold homes that are similar to a listing seller's home in terms of location, style, and amenities.

compensation The valuable consideration given by one person or entity to another person or entity in exchange for the performance of some activity or service.

competition The appraisal principle that states that excess profits generate competition.

Comprehensive Environmental Response, Compensation, and Liability Act (CERCLA) A federal law administered by the Environmental Protection Agency that establishes a process for identifying parties responsible for creating hazardous waste sites, forcing liable parties to clean up toxic sites, bringing legal action against responsible parties, and funding the abatement of toxic sites. *See* Superfund.

Comprehensive Loss Underwriting Exchange (CLUE) A database of consumer claim history that allows insurance companies to access prior claim information in the underwriting and rating process.

comprehensive plan *See* master plan.

condemnation A judicial or administrative proceeding to exercise the power of eminent domain, through which a government agency takes private property for public use and compensates the owner.

conditional-use permit Written governmental permission allowing a use inconsistent with zoning but necessary for the common good, such as locating an emergency medical facility in a predominantly residential area.

condominium The absolute ownership of a unit in a multiunit building based on a legal description of the airspace the unit actually occupies, plus an undivided interest in the ownership of the common elements, which are owned jointly with the other condominium unit owners.

confession of judgment clause Permits judgment to be entered against a debtor without the creditor's having to institute legal proceedings.

conformity The appraisal principle that holds that the greater the similarity among properties in an area, the better they will hold their value.

consideration (1) That received by the grantor in exchange for his deed. (2) Something of value that induces a person to enter into a contract.

construction loan *See* interim financing.

constructive eviction Actions of a landlord that so materially disturb or impair a tenant's enjoyment of the leased premises that the tenant is effectively forced to move out and terminate the lease without liability for any further rent.

constructive notice Notice given to the world by recorded documents. All people are charged with knowledge of such documents and their contents, whether or not they have actually examined them. Possession of property is also considered constructive notice that the person in possession has an interest in the property.

consumer A person or entity seeking or receiving licensed activities.

contemporaneous offers When a buyer's agent is acting as designated agent for more than one prospective buyer who the designated agent has reason to believe is making or preparing to make contemporaneous offers to purchase the property located at a specific address, the buyers have the option of being referred to another designated agent who will serve as the agent of the buyer.

contingency A provision in a contract that requires a certain act to be done or a certain event to occur before the contract becomes binding.

contract A legally enforceable promise or set of promises that must be performed and for which, if a breach of the promise occurs, the law provides a remedy. A contract may be either unilateral, by which only one party is bound to act, or bilateral, by which all parties to the instrument are legally bound to act as prescribed.

contribution The appraisal principle that states that the value of any component of a property is what it gives to the value of the whole or what its absence detracts from that value.

conventional loan A loan that requires no government insurance or guarantee.

conversion The wrongful appropriation of property belonging to another; also, the process of changing a property's status from rental to condominium.

conveyance A term used to refer to any document that transfers title to real property. The term is also used in describing the act of transferring.

cooperating broker *See* listing broker.

cooperative A residential multiunit building whose title is held by a trust or corporation that is owned by and operated for the benefit of persons living within the building, who are the beneficial owners of the trust or stockholders of the corporation, each possessing a proprietary lease.

co-ownership Title ownership held by two or more persons.

corporation An entity or organization, created by operation of law, whose rights of doing business are essentially the same as those of an individual. The entity has continuous existence until it is dissolved according to legal procedures.

correction lines   Provisions in the rectangular survey (government survey) system made to compensate for the curvature of the earth's surface. Every fourth township line (at 24-mile intervals) is used as a correction line on which the intervals between the north and south range lines are remeasured and corrected to a full six miles.

cost approach   The process of estimating the value of a property by adding to the estimated land value the appraiser's estimate of the reproduction or replacement cost of the building, less depreciation.

cost recovery   An Internal Revenue Service term for *depreciation*.

counteroffer   A new offer made in response to an offer received. It has the effect of rejecting the original offer, which cannot be accepted thereafter unless revived by the offeror.

covenant   A written agreement between two or more parties in which a party or parties pledge to perform or not perform specified acts with regard to property; usually found in such real estate documents as deeds, mortgages, leases, and contracts for deed.

covenants, conditions, and restrictions (CC&R)   Private rules set up by the developer that set standards for all the parcels within a defined subdivision.

covenant of quiet enjoyment   The covenant implied by law by which a landlord guarantees that a tenant may take possession of leased premises and that the landlord will not interfere in the tenant's possession or use of the property.

credit   On a closing statement, an amount entered in a person's favor—either an amount the party has paid or an amount for which the party must be reimbursed.

curtesy   A life estate, usually a fractional interest, given by some states to the surviving husband in real estate owned by his deceased wife. Most states have abolished curtesy.

customer   The third party or non-represented consumer for who some level of service is provided.

datum   A horizontal plane from which heights and depths are measured.

debit   On a closing statement, an amount charged; that is, an amount that the debited party must pay.

decedent   A person who has died.

dedication   The voluntary transfer of private property by its owner to the public for some public use, such as for streets or schools.

deed   A written instrument that, when executed and delivered, conveys title to or an interest in real estate.

deed in lieu of foreclosure   A deed given by the mortgagor to the mortgagee when the mortgagor is in default under the terms of the mortgage. This is a way for the mortgagor to avoid foreclosure.

deed in trust   An instrument that grants a trustee under a land trust full power to sell, mortgage, and subdivide a parcel of real estate. The beneficiary controls the trustee's use of these powers under the provisions of the trust agreement.

deed of trust   *See* trust deed.

deed of trust lien   *See* trust deed lien.

deed restrictions   Clauses in a deed limiting the future uses of the property.

default   The nonperformance of a duty, whether arising under a contract or otherwise; failure to meet an obligation when due.

defeasance clause   A clause used in leases and mortgages that cancels a specified right upon the occurrence of a certain condition, such as cancellation of a mortgage on repayment of the mortgage loan.

defeasible fee estate   An estate in which the holder has a fee simple title that may be divested on the occurrence or nonoccurrence of a specified event. There are two categories of defeasible fee estates: fee simple on condition precedent (fee simple determinable) and fee simple on condition subsequent.

deficiency judgment   A personal judgment levied against the borrower when a foreclosure sale does not produce sufficient funds to pay the mortgage debt in full.

demand   The amount of goods people are willing and able to buy at a given price; often coupled with the term *supply*.

density zoning   Zoning ordinances that restrict the maximum average number of houses per acre that may be built within a particular area, generally a subdivision.

Department of Housing and Urban Development (HUD)   Government agency that administers the Fair Housing Act, governs RESPA, and provides standardized forms such as the 1003 loan application, the HUD-1 settlement statement, and the good-faith estimate (GFE).

depreciation   (1) In appraisal, a loss of value in property due to any cause, including physical deterioration, functional obsolescence, and external obsolescence. (2) In real estate investment, an expense deduction for tax purposes taken over the period of ownership of income property.

descent   Acquisition of an estate by inheritance in which an heir succeeds to the property by operation of law.

designated agent   A licensee authorized by a sponsoring broker to act as the agent for a specific principal in a particular transaction.

developer One who attempts to put land to its most profitable use through the construction of improvements.

devise A gift of real property by will. The donor is the devisor, and the recipient is the devisee.

divisor A number or quantity divided into another.

discount point A unit of measurement used for various loan charges; one point equals 1 percent of the amount of the loan.

discount rate The interest rate set by the Federal Reserve that member banks are charged when they borrow money through the Fed.

doctrine of prior appropriation The right to use any water, with the exception of limited domestic use, is controlled by the state rather than by the landowner adjacent to the water.

dominant tenement A property that includes in its ownership the appurtenant right to use an easement over another person's property for a specific purpose.

dower The legal right or interest, recognized in some states, that a wife acquires in the property her husband held or acquired during their marriage. During the husband's lifetime the right is only a possibility of an interest; on his death, it can become an interest in land.

dual agency Representing both parties to a transaction. In Illinois, this is illegal unless both parties agree to it in writing.

due-on-sale clause A provision in the mortgage that states that the entire balance of the note is immediately due and payable if the mortgagor transfers (sells) the property.

duress Unlawful constraint or action exercised on a person whereby the person is forced to perform an act against his will. A contract entered into under duress is voidable.

earnest money Money deposited by a buyer under the terms of a contract, to be forfeited if the buyer defaults but applied to the purchase price if the sale is closed.

easement A right to use the land of another for a specific purpose, such as for a right-of-way or utilities; an incorporeal interest in land.

easement by condemnation An easement created by the government or government agency that has exercised its right under eminent domain.

easement by necessity An easement allowed by law as necessary for the full enjoyment of a parcel of real estate; for example, a right of ingress and egress over a grantor's land.

easement by prescription An easement acquired by continuous, open, and hostile use of the property for the period of time prescribed by state law.

easement in gross An easement that is not created for the benefit of any land owned by the owner of the easement but that attaches personally to the easement owner. For example, a right granted by Eleanor Franks to Joe Fish to use a portion of her property for the rest of his life would be an easement in gross.

economic life The number of years during which an improvement will add value to the land.

electromagnetic fields Physical areas generated by the movement of electrical currents.

emblements Growing crops, such as grapes and corn, that are produced annually through labor and industry; also called *fructus industriales*.

eminent domain The right of a government or municipal quasi-public body to acquire property for public use through a court action called *condemnation*, in which the court decides that the use is a public use and determines the compensation to be paid to the owner.

employee Someone who works as a direct employee of an employer and has employee status. The employer is obligated to withhold income taxes and Social Security taxes from the compensation of employees. *See also* independent contractor.

employment contract A document evidencing formal employment between employer and employee or between principal and agent. In the real estate business, this generally takes the form of a listing agreement or management agreement.

enabling acts State legislation that confers zoning powers on municipal governments.

encapsulation A method of controlling environmental contamination by sealing off a dangerous substance.

encroachment A building or some portion of it—a wall or fence, for instance—that extends beyond the land of the owner and illegally intrudes on some land of an adjoining owner or a street or alley.

encumbrance Anything—such as a mortgage, tax, or judgment lien; an easement; a restriction on the use of the land; or an outstanding dower right—that may diminish the value or use and enjoyment of a property.

Equal Credit Opportunity Act (ECOA) The federal law that prohibits discrimination in the extension of credit because of race, color, religion, national origin, sex, age, or marital status.

equalization The raising or lowering of assessed values for tax purposes in a particular county or taxing district to make them equal to assessments in other counties or districts.

equalization factor A factor (number) by which the assessed value of a property is multiplied to arrive at a value for the property that is in line with statewide tax assessments. The ad valorem tax is based on this adjusted value.

equitable lien *See* statutory lien.

equitable right of redemption The right of a defaulted property owner to recover the property prior to its sale by paying the appropriate fees and charges.

equitable title The interest held by a vendee under a contract for deed or an installment contract; the equitable right to obtain absolute ownership to property when legal title is held in another's name.

equity The interest or value that an owner has in property over and above any indebtedness.

Equity in Eminent Domain Act Legislation that provides protections for private property owners when government seeks to acquire land for economic development projects.

erosion The gradual wearing away of land by water, wind, and general weather conditions; the diminishing of property by the elements.

errors and omissions insurance Business liability insurance that helps protect real estate professionals, individuals, or companies from bearing the full cost of the defense for lawsuits relating to an error or omission in providing covered professional services.

escheat The reversion of property to the state or county, as provided by state law, in cases where a decedent dies intestate without heirs capable of inheriting or when the property is abandoned.

escrow The closing of a transaction through a third party called an *escrow agent*, or *escrowee*, who receives certain funds and documents to be delivered on the performance of certain conditions outlined in the escrow instructions.

escrow account The trust account established by a sponsoring broker under the provisions of the license law for the purpose of holding funds on behalf of the sponsoring broker's principal or some other person until the consummation or termination of a transaction.

escrow instructions A document that sets forth the duties of the escrow agent, as well as the requirements and obligations of the parties, when a transaction is closed through an escrow.

escrow moneys All moneys, promissory notes, or any other type or manner of legal tender or financial consideration deposited with any person for the benefit of the parties to the transaction.

estate (tenancy) at sufferance The tenancy of a lessee who lawfully comes into possession of a landlord's real estate but who continues to occupy the premises improperly after his lease rights have expired.

estate (tenancy) at will An estate that gives the lessee the right to possession until the estate is terminated by either party; the term of this estate is indefinite.

estate (tenancy) for years An interest for a certain, exact period of time in property leased for a specified consideration.

estate (tenancy) from period to period An interest in leased property that continues from period to period—week to week, month to month, or year to year.

estate in land The degree, quantity, nature, and extent of interest a person has in real property.

estate taxes Federal taxes on a decedent's real and personal property.

estoppel Method of creating an agency relationship in which someone states incorrectly that another person is his agent, and a third person relies on that representation.

estoppel certificate A document in which a borrower certifies the amount owed on a mortgage loan and the rate of interest.

ethics The systems of moral principles and rules that become standards for professional conduct.

eviction A legal process to oust a person from possession of real estate.

evidence of title Proof of ownership of property; commonly a certificate of title, an abstract of title with lawyer's opinion, title insurance, or a Torrens registration certificate.

exchange A transaction in which all or part of the consideration is the transfer of like-kind property (such as real estate for real estate).

exclusive-agency listing A listing contract under which the owner appoints a sponsoring broker as his exclusive agent for a designated period of time to sell the property on the owner's stated terms for a commission. The owner reserves the right to sell without paying anyone a commission if he sells to a prospect who has not been introduced or claimed by the sponsoring broker.

exclusive-right-to-sell listing A listing contract under which the owner appoints a sponsoring broker as his exclusive agent for a designated period of time to sell the property on the owner's stated terms. The owner agrees to pay the sponsoring broker a commission when the property is sold, whether by the sponsoring broker, the owner, or another broker.

executed contract A contract in which all parties have fulfilled their promises and thus performed the contract.

execution The signing and delivery of an instrument. Also, a legal order directing an official to enforce a judgment against the property of a debtor.

executory contract A contract under which something remains to be done by one or more of the parties.

express agreement An oral or written contract in which the parties state the contract's terms and express their intentions in words.

express contract *See* express agreement.

external depreciation Reduction in a property's value caused by outside factors (those that are off the property).

facilitator *See* nonagent.

Fair Housing Act The federal law that prohibits discrimination in housing based on race, color, religion, sex, handicap, familial status, and national origin.

Fannie Mae A quasi-government agency established to purchase any kind of mortgage loans in the secondary mortgage market from the primary lenders. Formerly called Federal National Mortgage Association (FNMA).

Federal Deposit Insurance Corporation (FDIC) An independent federal agency that insures the deposits in commercial banks.

Federal Home Loan Mortgage Corporation (FHLMC) A corporation established to purchase primarily conventional mortgage loans in the secondary mortgage market.

Federal National Mortgage Association (FNMA) *See* Fannie Mae.

Federal Open Market Committee (FOMC) A component of the Federal Reserve System; buys and sells U.S. government securities on the open market.

Federal Reserve System The country's central banking system, which controls the nation's monetary policy by regulating the supply of money and interest rates.

fee simple absolute The maximum possible estate or right of ownership of real property, continuing forever.

fee simple defeasible *See* defeasible fee estate.

feudal system A system of ownership usually associated with precolonial England, in which the king or other sovereign is the source of all rights. The right to possess real property was granted by the sovereign to an individual as a life estate only. On the death of the individual, title passed back to the sovereign, not to the decedent's heirs.

FHA loan A loan insured by the Federal Housing Administration and made by an approved lender in accordance with the FHA's regulations.

fiduciary One in whom trust and confidence is placed; a reference to a sponsoring broker employed under the terms of a listing contract or buyer agency agreement.

fiduciary standard A legal standard that holds a licensee to the highest ethical standards that the law provides.

fiduciary relationship A relationship of trust and confidence, as between trustee and beneficiary, attorney and client, or principal and agent.

Financial Institutions Reform, Recovery, and Enforcement Act (FIRREA) This act restructured the savings and loan association regulatory system; enacted in response to the savings and loan crisis of the 1980s.

financing statement *See* Uniform Commercial Code.

fiscal policy The government's policy in regard to taxation and spending programs. The balance between these two areas determines the amount of money the government will withdraw from or feed into the economy, which can counter economic peaks and slumps.

fixture An item of personal property that has been converted to real property by being permanently affixed to the realty.

foreclosure A legal procedure whereby property used as security for a debt is sold to satisfy the debt in the event of default in payment of the mortgage note or default of other terms in the mortgage document. The foreclosure procedure brings the rights of all parties to a conclusion and passes the title in the mortgaged property to either the holder of the mortgage or a third party, who may purchase the realty at the foreclosure sale, free of all encumbrances affecting the property subsequent to the mortgage.

fractional section A parcel of land less than 160 acres, usually found at the edge of a rectangular survey.

fraud Deception intended to cause a person to give up property or a lawful right.

Freddie Mac *See* Federal Home Loan Mortgage Corporation (FHLMC).

freehold estate An estate in land in which ownership is for an indeterminate length of time, in contrast to a leasehold estate.

front footage The measurement of a parcel of land by the number of feet of street or road frontage.

functional obsolescence A loss of value to an improvement to real estate arising from functional problems, often caused by age or poor design.

future interest A person's present right to an interest in real property that will not result in possession or enjoyment until some time in the future, such as a reversion or right of reentry.

gap A defect in the chain of title of a particular parcel of real estate; a missing document or conveyance that raises doubt as to the present ownership of the land.

general agent One who is authorized by a principal to represent the principal in a specific range of matters.

general lien The right of a creditor to have all of a debtor's property—both real and personal—sold to satisfy a debt.

general partnership *See* partnership.

general warranty deed A deed in which the grantor fully warrants good clear title to the premises. Used in most real estate deed transfers, a general warranty deed offers the greatest protection of any deed.

Ginnie Mae *See* Government National Mortgage Association (GNMA).

good-faith estimate (GFE) A document that indicates what a buyer's estimated closing costs will be prior to closing. Once the GFE is issued, lenders are committed and may only modify the GFE in certain instances. If information or circumstances change after the original GFE is issued, a new GFE must be issued.

government check The 24-mile-square parcels composed of 16 townships in the rectangular (government) survey system of legal description.

government lot Fractional sections in the rectangular (government) survey system that are less than one quarter-section in area.

Government National Mortgage Association (GNMA) A government agency that plays an important role in the secondary mortgage market. It sells mortgage-backed securities that are backed by pools of FHA and VA loans.

government survey system *See* rectangular (government) survey system.

graduated-payment mortgage (GPM) A loan in which the monthly principal and interest payments increase by a certain percentage each year for a certain number of years and then level off for the remaining loan term.

grantee A person who receives a conveyance of real property from a grantor.

granting clause Words in a deed of conveyance that state the grantor's intention to convey the property at the present time. This clause is generally worded as "convey and warrant"; "grant"; "grant, bargain, and sell"; or the like.

grantor The person transferring title to or an interest in real property to a grantee.

gross income multiplier (GIM) A figure used as a multiplier of the gross annual income of a property to produce an estimate of the property's value.

gross lease A lease of property according to which a landlord pays all property charges regularly incurred through ownership, such as repairs, taxes, insurance, and operating expenses. Most residential leases are gross leases.

gross rent multiplier (GRM) The figure used as a multiplier of the gross monthly income of a property to produce an estimate of the property's value.

ground lease A lease of land only, on which the tenant usually owns a building or is required to build as specified in the lease. Such leases are usually long-term net leases; the tenant's rights and obligations continue until the lease expires or is terminated through default.

groundwater The water that exists under the earth's surface within the tiny spaces or crevices in geological formations.

growing-equity mortgage (GEM) A loan in which the monthly payments increase annually, with the increased amount being used to directly reduce the principal balance outstanding and thus shorten the overall term of the loan.

guaranteed sales plan Any real estate purchase or sales plan in which a sponsoring broker enters into an unconditional written contract with a seller, promising to purchase the seller's property for a specified price if the property has not sold within an agreed period of time on terms acceptable to seller.

habendum clause That part of a deed beginning with the words "to have and to hold," following the granting clause and defining the extent of ownership the grantor is conveying.

heir One who might inherit or succeed to an interest in land under the state law of descent when the owner dies without leaving a valid will.

highest and best use The possible use of a property that would produce the greatest net income and thereby develop the highest value.

holdover tenancy A tenancy whereby a lessee retains possession of leased property after the lease has expired and the landlord, by continuing to accept rent, agrees to the tenant's continued occupancy as defined by state law.

holographic will A will that is written, dated, and signed in the testator's handwriting.

home equity loan A loan (sometimes called a *line of credit*) under which a property owner uses his residence as collateral and can then draw funds up to a prearranged amount against the property.

Home Mortgage Disclosure Act Requires that all institutional mortgage lenders with assets in excess of $36 million and with one or more offices in a given geographic area make annual reports.

homeowners' insurance policy A standardized package insurance policy that covers a residential real estate owner against financial loss from fire, theft, public liability, and other common risks.

homestead Land that is owned and occupied as the family home. In many states, a portion of the area or value of this land is protected or exempt from judgments for debts.

hypothecate To pledge property as security for an obligation or loan without giving up possession of it.

Illinois Department of Financial and Professional Regulation (the Department) The entity responsible for administering and enforcing the Illinois Real Estate License Act of 2000.

Illinois Human Rights Act Legislation that prohibits discrimination on the basis of race, color, religion, sex, national origin, ancestry, familial status, physical or mental disability, age, marital status, unfavorable military discharge, sexual orientation, and order of protection status.

Illinois Radon Awareness Act Legislation that requires a seller to provide to a buyer, before the buyer is obligated under any contract to purchase residential real property, a disclosure of information on radon hazards along with a pamphlet entitled "Radon Testing Guidelines for Real Estate Transactions" stating that the property may present the potential for exposure to radon.

implied agreement A contract under which the agreement of the parties is demonstrated by their acts and conduct.

implied contract *See* implied agreement.

implied warranty of habitability A theory in landlord/tenant law in which the landlord renting residential property implies that the property is habitable and fit for its intended use.

improvement (1) Any structure, usually privately owned, erected on a site to enhance the value of the property—for example, building a fence or a driveway. (2) A publicly owned structure added to or benefiting land, such as a curb, sidewalk, street, or sewer.

income approach The process of estimating the value of an income-producing property through capitalization of the annual net income expected to be produced by the property during its remaining useful life.

incorporeal right A nonpossessory right in real estate; for example, an easement or a right-of-way.

independent contractor Someone who is retained to perform a certain act but who is subject to the control and direction of another only as to the end result and not as to the way in which the act is performed. Unlike an employee, an independent contractor pays for all expenses, Social Security, and income taxes, and receives no employee benefits. Most real estate salespeople are independent contractors.

index method The appraisal method of estimating building costs by multiplying the original cost of the property by a percentage factor to adjust for current construction costs.

inflation The gradual reduction of the purchasing power of the dollar, usually related directly to the increases in the money supply by the federal government.

inheritance taxes State-imposed taxes on a decedent's real and personal property.

inoperative status In Illinois, a license status that prohibits a licensee from engaging in real estate activities because he is unsponsored or his license has lapsed or been suspended or revoked.

installment contract A contract for the sale of real estate whereby the purchase price is paid in periodic installments by the purchaser, who is in possession of the property even though title is retained by the seller until all payments are received in full. Also called a *contract for deed* or *articles of agreement for warranty deed.*

installment sale A transaction in which the sales price is paid in two or more installments over two or more years. If the sale meets certain requirements, a taxpayer can postpone reporting such income until future years by paying tax each year only on the proceeds received that year.

interest A charge made by a lender for the use of money.

interim financing A short-term loan usually made during the construction phase of a building project.

intermediate mortgage theory Theory based on the principles of title theory states but still requiring the mortgagee to formally foreclose to obtain legal title.

Interstate Land Sales Full Disclosure Act Federal law that regulates the sale of certain real estate in interstate commerce.

intestate The condition of a property owner who dies without leaving a valid will. Title to the property will pass to the decedent's heirs as provided in the state law of descent.

intrinsic value An appraisal term referring to the value created by a person's personal preferences for a particular type of property.

investment Money directed toward the purchase, improvement, and development of an asset in expectation of income or profits.

involuntary alienation *See* alienation.

involuntary lien A lien placed on property without the consent of the property owner.

joint tenancy Ownership of real estate between two or more parties who have been named in one conveyance as joint tenants. Upon the death of a joint tenant, the decedent's interest passes to the surviving joint tenant or tenants by the right of survivorship.

joint venture   The joining of two or more people to conduct a specific business enterprise. A joint venture is similar to a partnership in that it must be created by agreement between the parties to share in the losses and profits of the venture. It is unlike a partnership in that the venture is for one specific project only rather than for a continuing business relationship.

judgment   The formal decision of a court on the respective rights and claims of the parties to an action or suit. After a judgment has been entered and recorded with the county recorder, it usually becomes a general lien on the property of the defendant.

judicial foreclosure   Type of foreclosure that allows the property to be sold by court order after the lender has given sufficient public notice to the defaulting borrower.

judicial precedent   In law, the requirements established by prior court decisions.

Junk Fax Prevention Act of 2005   Prohibits faxing unsolicited fax advertisements or solicitations and does allow for an established business relationship exception.

junior lien   An obligation, such as a second mortgage, that is subordinate in right or lien priority to an existing lien on the same realty.

laches   An equitable doctrine used by courts to bar a legal claim or prevent the assertion of a right because of undue delay or failure to assert the claim or right.

land   The earth's surface, extending downward to the center of the earth and upward infinitely into space, including things permanently attached by nature, such as trees and water.

land contract   *See* installment contract.

landfill   An enormous hole, either excavated for the purpose of waste disposal or left over from surface mining operations.

latent defect   A hidden structural defect that could not be discovered by ordinary inspection and that threatens the property's soundness or the safety of its inhabitants. Some states impose on sellers and licensees a duty to inspect for and disclose latent defects.

law of agency   *See* agency.

Lead-Based Paint Hazard Reduction Act   Persons selling or leasing residential housing constructed before 1978 must disclose the presence of known lead-based paint and provide purchasers or tenants with any relevant records or reports.

lease   A written or oral contract between a landlord (the *lessor*) and a tenant (the *lessee*) that transfers the right to exclusive possession and use of the landlord's real property to the lessee for a specified period of time and for a stated consideration (rent). By state law leases for longer than a certain period of time (generally one year) must be in writing to be enforceable.

leasehold estate   A tenant's right to occupy real estate during the term of a lease, generally considered to be a personal property interest.

lease option   A lease under which the tenant has the right to purchase the property either during the lease term or at its end.

lease purchase   The purchase of real property, the consummation of which is preceded by a lease, usually long term. Typically done for tax or financing purposes.

leasing agent license   In Illinois, a limited license for individuals who wish to engage only in activities related to leasing residential property.

legacy   A disposition of money or personal property by will.

legal description   A description of a specific parcel of real estate complete enough for an independent surveyor to locate and identify it.

legally competent parties   People who are recognized by law as being able to contract with others; those of legal age and sound mind.

legatee   *See* beneficiary.

lessee   *See* lease.

lessor   *See* lease.

leverage   The use of borrowed money to finance an investment.

levy   To assess; to seize or collect. To levy a tax is to assess a property and set the rate of taxation. To levy an execution is to officially seize the property of a person to satisfy an obligation.

license   (1) A privilege or right granted to a person by a state to operate as a real estate broker, managing broker, or salesperson. (2) The revocable permission for a temporary use of land—a personal right that cannot be sold.

lien   A right given by law to certain creditors to have their debts paid out of the property of a defaulting debtor, usually by means of a court sale.

lien theory   Some states interpret a mortgage as being purely a lien on real property. The mortgagee thus has no right of possession but must foreclose the lien and sell the property if the mortgagor defaults.

life cycle costing In property management, comparing one type of equipment with another based on both purchase cost and operating cost over its expected useful lifetime.

life estate An interest in real or personal property that is limited in duration to the lifetime of its owner or some other designated person or persons.

life tenant A person in possession of a life estate.

limited liability company (LLC) A business structure that combines the most attractive features of limited partnerships and corporations. The members of an LLC enjoy the limited liability offered by a corporate form of ownership and the tax advantages of a partnership.

limited partnership *See* partnership.

liquidated damages An amount predetermined by the parties to a contract as the total compensation to an injured party should the other party breach the contract.

liquidity The ability to sell an asset and convert it into cash, at a price close to its true value, in a short period of time.

lis pendens A recorded legal document giving constructive notice that an action affecting a particular property has been filed in either a state or a federal court.

listing agreement A contract between an owner (as principal) and a real estate sponsoring broker (as agent) by which the sponsoring broker is employed as agent to find a buyer for the owner's real estate on the owner's terms, for which service the owner agrees to pay a commission.

listing broker The sponsoring broker in a multiple listing situation from whose office a listing agreement is initiated, as opposed to the cooperating sponsoring broker, from whose office negotiations leading up to a sale are initiated. The listing sponsoring broker and the cooperating sponsoring broker may be the same person.

littoral rights (1) A landowner's claim to use water in large navigable lakes and oceans adjacent to her property. (2) The ownership rights to land bordering these bodies of water up to the high-water mark.

loan origination fee A fee charged to the borrower by the lender for making a mortgage loan. The fee is usually computed as a percentage of the loan amount.

loan-to-value ratio The relationship between the amount of the mortgage loan and the value of the real estate being pledged as collateral.

location *See* situs.

lot-and-block (recorded plat) system A method of describing real property that identifies a parcel of land by reference to lot and block numbers within a subdivision, as specified on a recorded subdivision plat.

management agreement A contract between the owner of income property and a management firm or individual property manager that outlines the scope of the manager's authority.

managing broker A broker who has supervisory responsibilities for licensees in one or, in the case of a multioffice company, more than one office and who has been appointed as such by the sponsoring broker.

manufactured housing Dwellings that are built off-site and trucked to a building lot where they are installed or assembled.

market A place where goods can be bought and sold and a price established.

marketable title Good or clear title, reasonably free from the risk of litigation over possible defects.

market price The price a property actually sells for; also called *sales price*.

market value The most probable price property would bring in an arm's-length transaction under normal conditions on the open market.

master plan A comprehensive plan to guide the long-term physical development of a particular area.

material fact Any fact that, if known, might reasonably be expected to affect the course of events.

mechanic's lien A statutory lien created in favor of contractors, laborers, and materialmen who have performed work or furnished materials in the erection or repair of a building.

medium of advertising Any method of communication intended to influence the general public to use or purchase a particular good or service or real estate.

Megan's Law Federal legislation that promotes the establishment of state registration systems to maintain residential information on every person who kidnaps children, commits sexual crimes against children, or commits sexually violent crimes.

meridian One of a set of imaginary lines running north and south and crossing a base line at a definite point, used in the rectangular (government) survey system of property description.

meta tag A special HTML tag that is used to store information about a Web page but is not displayed in a Web browser.

metes-and-bounds description A legal description of a parcel of land that begins at a well-marked point and follows the boundaries, using directions and distances around the tract, back to the point of beginning.

minimum services A provision of the Real Estate License Act of 2000 that requires licensees to perform a minimum level of service to clients.

ministerial acts In Illinois, acts that a licensee may perform for a consumer that are informative and do not constitute active representation.

minor Someone who has not reached the age of majority and therefore does not have legal capacity to transfer title to real property.

mold Fungi that grows in the form of multicellular filaments called *hyphae*. Some mold can cause disease, and others play a role in biodegradation or in the production of antibiotics and enzymes.

monetary policy Governmental regulation of the amount of money in circulation through such institutions as the Federal Reserve Board.

month-to-month tenancy A periodic tenancy under which the tenant rents for one month at a time. In the absence of a rental agreement (oral or written), a tenancy is generally considered to be month to month.

monument A fixed natural or artificial object used to establish real estate boundaries for a metes-and-bounds description.

mortgage A conditional transfer or pledge of real estate as security for the payment of a debt. Also, the document creating a mortgage lien.

mortgage banker Mortgage loan companies that originate, service, and sell loans to investors.

mortgage broker An agent of a lender who brings the lender and borrower together. The broker receives a fee for this service.

Mortgage Disclosure Improvement Act Legislation that creates a timeline for the lender to provide the GFE and the TIL. The intent is to prevent consumers from receiving an enticing low rate at the initial loan application and then learning at settlement that the lender is charging more in fees.

mortgagee A lender in a mortgage loan transaction.

mortgage insurance An insurance policy that protects a lender or title holder in the event that the borrower defaults.

mortgage insurance premium (MIP) An up-front premium charged at closing for all FHA loans.

mortgage lien A lien or charge on the property of a mortgagor that secures the underlying debt obligations.

mortgage loan originators (MLOs) Anyone who, for compensation or expectation of compensation, takes a residential mortgage loan by phone or in person.

mortgagor A borrower in a mortgage loan transaction.

multiperil policies Insurance policies that offer protection from a range of potential perils, such as those of a fire, hazard, public liability, and casualty.

multiple listing clause A provision in an exclusive listing for the authority and obligation on the part of the listing broker to distribute the listing to other brokers in the multiple listing organization.

multiple listing service (MLS) A marketing organization composed of member brokers who agree to share their listing agreements with one another in the hope of procuring ready, willing, and able buyers for their properties more quickly than they could on their own. Most multiple listing services accept exclusive-right-to-sell or exclusive-agency listings from their member brokers.

mutual assent A meeting of the minds between parties.

National Do Not Call Registry A registry managed by the Federal Trade Commission that lists the phone numbers of consumers who have indicated their preference to limit the telemarketing calls they receive.

Nationwide Mortgage Licensing System (NMLS) Mortgage loan originators (MLOs) in Illinois are required to register in this system.

negotiable instrument A written promise or order to pay a specific sum of money that may be transferred by endorsement or delivery. The transferee then has the original payee's right to payment.

net lease A lease requiring that the tenant pay not only rent but also costs incurred in maintaining the property, including taxes, insurance, utilities, and repairs.

net listing A listing based on the net price the seller will receive if the property is sold. Under a net listing the sponsoring broker can offer the property for sale at the highest price obtainable to increase the commission. This type of listing is legal in Illinois.

net operating income (NOI) The income projected for an income-producing property after deducting losses for vacancy, collection, and operating expenses.

nonagent An intermediary between a buyer and seller, or landlord and tenant, who assists both parties in a transaction without representing either.

nonconforming use A use of property that is permitted to continue after a zoning ordinance prohibiting it has been established for the area.

nonhomogeneity A lack of uniformity; dissimilarity. Because no two parcels of land are exactly alike, real estate is said to be non-homogeneous.

note *See* promissory note.

novation Substituting a new obligation for an old one or substituting new parties to an existing obligation.

nuncupative will An oral will declared by the testator in her final illness, made before witnesses and afterward reduced to writing.

obsolescence   The loss of value due to factors that are outmoded or less useful. Obsolescence may be functional or economic.

occupancy permit   A permit issued by the appropriate local governing body to establish that the property is suitable for habitation by meeting certain safety and health standards.

offer and acceptance   Two essential components of a valid contract; a "meeting of the minds."

offeror/offeree   The person who makes the offer is the *offeror*; the person to whom the offer is made is the *offeree*.

Office of Thrift Supervision (OTS)   Monitors and regulates the savings and loan industry. OTS was created by FIRREA (the Department).

open buyer agency agreement   An agreement that permits the buyer to enter into multiple agreements with an unlimited number of sponsoring brokers, and the sponsoring broker receives compensation only if she locates the property the buyer ultimately purchases; also called a nonexclusive buyer agency agreement.

open-end loan   A mortgage loan that is expandable by increments up to a maximum dollar amount, the full loan being secured by the same original mortgage.

open listing   A listing contract under which the sponsoring broker's commission is contingent on the sponsoring broker producing a ready, willing, and able buyer before the property is sold by the seller or another sponsoring broker.

option   An agreement to keep open for a set period an offer to sell or purchase property.

option listing   Listing with a provision that gives the listing sponsoring broker the right to purchase the listed property.

ostensible agency   A form of implied agency relationship created by the actions of the parties involved rather than by written agreement or document.

package loan   A real estate loan used to finance the purchase of both real property and personal property, such as in the purchase of a new home that includes carpeting, window coverings, and major appliances.

parol evidence rule   A rule of evidence providing that a written agreement is the final expression of the agreement of the parties, not to be varied or contradicted by prior or contemporaneous oral or written negotiations.

participation mortgage   A mortgage loan wherein the lender has a partial equity interest in the property or receives a portion of the income from the property.

partition   The division of cotenants' interests in real property when the parties do not all voluntarily agree to terminate the co-ownership; takes place through court procedures.

partnership   An association of two or more individuals who carry on a continuing business for profit as co-owners. Under the law a partnership is regarded as a group of individuals rather than as a single entity. A general partnership is a typical form of joint venture in which each general partner shares in the administration, profits and losses of the operation. A limited partnership is a business arrangement whereby the operation is administered by one or more general partners and funded, by and large, by limited or silent partners who are, by law responsible for losses only to the extent of their investments.

party wall   A wall that is located on or at a boundary line between two adjoining parcels of land and is used or is intended to be used by the owners of both properties.

patent   A grant or franchise of land from the United States government.

payment cap   The limit on the amount the monthly payment can be increased on an adjustable-rate mortgage when the interest rate is adjusted.

payoff statement   *See* reduction certificate.

percentage lease   A lease, commonly used for commercial property, whose rental is based on the tenant's gross sales at the premises; it usually stipulates a base monthly rental plus a percentage of any gross sales above a certain amount.

percolation test   A test of the soil to determine if it will absorb and drain water adequately to use a septic system for sewage disposal.

periodic estate (tenancy)   *See* estate (tenancy) from period to period.

personal property   Items, called *chattels*, that do not fit into the definition of real property; movable objects.

personalty   *See* personal property.

physical deterioration   A reduction in a property's value resulting from a decline in physical condition; can be caused by action of the elements or by ordinary wear and tear.

PITI (principle, interest, taxes, and insurance)   Expenses that comprise an owner's monthly payment.

planned unit development (PUD)   Planned combination of diverse land uses, such as housing, recreation, and shopping, in one contained development or subdivision.

plat map   A map of a town, section, or subdivision indicating the location and boundaries of individual properties.

plottage The increase in value or utility resulting from the consolidation (*assemblage*) of two or more adjacent lots into one larger lot.

pocket card The card issued by the Department to signify that the person named on the card is currently licensed under the Real Estate License Act of 2000.

point of beginning (POB) In a metes-and-bounds legal description, the starting point of the survey, situated in one corner of the parcel; all metes-and-bounds descriptions must follow the boundaries of the parcel back to the point of beginning.

police power The government's right to impose laws, statutes, and ordinances, including zoning ordinances and building codes, to protect the public health, safety, and welfare.

polychlorinated biphenyls Used as an insulating material in dielectric oil and may be present in electrical equipment.

power of attorney A written instrument authorizing a person, the attorney-in-fact, to act as agent for another person to the extent indicated in the instrument.

prepaid items On a closing statement, items that have been paid in advance by the seller, such as insurance premiums and some real estate taxes, for which she must be reimbursed by the buyer.

prepayment penalty A charge imposed on a borrower who pays off the loan principal early. This penalty compensates the lender for interest and other charges that would otherwise be lost.

price-fixing *See* antitrust laws.

primary mortgage market The mortgage market in which loans are originated, consisting of lenders such as commercial banks, savings and loan associations, and mutual savings banks.

principal (1) A sum loaned or employed as a fund or an investment, as distinguished from its income or profits. (2) The original amount (as in a loan) of the total due and payable at a certain date. (3) A main party to a transaction—the person for whom the agent works.

principal meridian The main imaginary line running north and south and crossing a base line at a definite point, used by surveyors for reference in locating and describing land under the rectangular (government) survey system of legal description.

prior appropriation A concept of water ownership in which the landowner's right to use available water is based on a government-administered permit system.

priority The order of position or time. The priority of liens is generally determined by the chronological order in which the lien documents are recorded; tax liens, however, have priority even over previously recorded liens.

private mortgage insurance (PMI) Insurance provided by private carrier that protects a lender against a loss in the event of a foreclosure and deficiency.

probate A legal process by which a court determines who will inherit a decedent's property and what the estate's assets and liabilities are.

procuring cause The effort that brings about the desired result. Under an open listing the sponsoring broker who is the procuring cause of the sale receives the commission.

professional real estate services Services that require a person to have an Illinois real estate license in order to perform those services on behalf of clients, customers, and consumers.

progression An appraisal principle that states that, between dissimilar properties, the value of the lesser-quality property is favorably affected by the presence of the better-quality property.

promissory note A financing instrument that states the terms of the underlying obligation, is signed by its maker, and is negotiable (transferable to a third party).

property management agreement An agreement between the property owner and sponsoring broker. It sets forth the nature of the relationship between the two parties. The agreement covers such items as time period, property manager's responsibilities, extent of property manager's authority, compensation, and reporting to name a few.

property manager Someone who manages real estate for another person for compensation. Duties include collecting rents, maintaining the property, and keeping up all accounting.

property reports The mandatory federal and state documents compiled by subdividers and developers to provide potential purchasers with facts about a property prior to their purchase.

proprietary lease A lease given by the corporation that owns a cooperative apartment building to the shareholder for the shareholder's right as a tenant to an individual apartment.

prorations Expenses, either prepaid or paid in arrears, that are divided or distributed between buyer and seller at the closing.

protected class Any group of people designated as such by the Department of Housing and Urban Development (HUD) in consideration of federal and state civil rights legislation. Currently includes ethnic minorities, women, religious groups, the handicapped, and others.

puffing Exaggerated or superlative comments or opinions.

pur autre vie A life estate *pur autre vie* is a life estate that is measured by the life of a person other than the grantee.

purchase-money mortgage (PMM) A note secured by a mortgage or deed of trust given by a buyer, as borrower, to a seller, as lender, as part of the purchase price of the real estate.

quantity-survey method The appraisal method of estimating building costs by calculating the cost of all of the physical components in the improvements, adding the cost to assemble them and then including the indirect costs associated with such construction.

quiet title A court action to remove a cloud on the title.

quitclaim deed A conveyance by which the grantor transfers whatever interest she has in the real estate, without warranties or obligations.

race The inclusion of ancestral and ethnic characteristics, including certain physical, cultural, or linguistic characteristics that are shared by a group with a common nation origin.

radon A naturally occurring gas that is suspected of causing lung cancer.

range A strip of land six miles wide, extending north and south and numbered east and west according to its distance from the principal meridian in the rectangular (government) survey system of legal description.

rate cap The limit on the amount the interest rate can be increased at each adjustment period in an adjustable-rate loan. The cap also may set the maximum interest rate that can be charged during the life of the loan.

ratification Method of creating an agency relationship in which the principal accepts the conduct of someone who acted without prior authorization as the principal's agent.

ready, willing, and able buyer One who is prepared to buy property on the seller's terms and is ready to take positive steps to consummate the transaction.

real estate Land; a portion of the earth's surface extending downward to the center of the earth and upward infinitely into space, including all things permanently attached to it, whether naturally or artificially.

real estate assistant A licensed or unlicensed individual who assists a licensee in the real estate business.

real estate investment trust (REIT) Trust ownership of real estate by a group of individuals who purchase certificates of ownership in the trust, which in turn invests the money in real property and distributes the profits back to the investors free of corporate income tax.

Real Estate License Act 2000 State law enacted to protect the public from fraud, dishonesty, and incompetence in the purchase and sale of real estate. It was amended in 2011.

real estate mortgage investment conduit (REMIC) A tax entity that issues multiple classes of investor interests (securities) backed by a pool of mortgages.

real estate recovery fund A fund established to cover claims of aggrieved parties who have suffered monetary damage through the actions of a real estate licensee.

Real Estate Settlement Procedures Act (RESPA) The federal law that requires certain disclosures to consumers about mortgage loan settlements. The law also prohibits the payment or receipt of kickbacks and certain kinds of referral fees.

real property The interests, benefits, and rights inherent in real estate ownership.

REALTOR® A registered trademark term reserved for the sole use of active members of the National Association of REALTORS®.

reconciliation The final step in the appraisal process, in which the appraiser combines the estimates of value received from the sales comparison, cost, and income approaches to arrive at a final estimate of market value for the subject property.

reconveyance deed A deed used by a trustee under a deed of trust to return title to the trustor.

recording The act of entering or recording documents affecting or conveying interests in real estate in the recorder's office established in each county. Until it is recorded, a deed or mortgage ordinarily is not effective against subsequent purchasers or mortgagees.

rectangular (government) survey system System established in 1785 by the federal government, providing for surveying and describing land by reference to principal meridians and base lines.

redemption The right of a defaulted property owner to recover her property by curing the default.

redemption period A period of time established by state law during which a property owner has the right to redeem her real estate from a foreclosure or tax sale by paying the sales price, interest, and costs. Many states do not have mortgage redemption laws.

redlining The illegal practice of a lending institution denying loans or restricting their number for certain areas of a community.

reduction certificate (payoff statement) The document signed by a lender indicating the amount required to pay a loan balance in full and satisfy the debt; used in the settlement process to protect both the seller's and the buyer's interests.

regression An appraisal principle that states that, between dissimilar properties, the value of the better-quality property is affected adversely by the presence of the lesser-quality property.

regular employee A person working an average of 20 hours per week for a person or entity who would be considered as an employee under the Internal Revenue Service.

Regulation Z Implements the Truth in Lending Act requiring that credit institutions inform borrowers of the true cost of obtaining credit.

reinstatement The activation of a suspended, revoked, or inoperative license.

release deed A document, also known as a *deed of reconveyance*, that transfers all rights given a trustee under a deed of trust loan back to the grantor after the loan has been fully repaid.

remainder interest The remnant of an estate that has been conveyed to take effect and be enjoyed after the termination of a prior estate, such as when an owner conveys a life estate to one party and the remainder to another.

rent A fixed, periodic payment made by a tenant of a property to the owner for possession and use, usually by prior agreement of the parties.

rent schedule A statement of proposed rental rates, determined by the owner or the property manager or both, based on a building's estimated expenses, market supply and demand, and the owner's long-range goals for the property.

replacement cost The construction cost at current prices of a property that is not necessarily an exact duplicate of the subject property but serves the same purpose or function as the original.

reproduction cost The construction cost at current prices of an exact duplicate of the subject property.

Resolution Trust Corporation The organization created by FIRREA to liquidate the assets of failed savings and loan associations.

restrictive covenants A clause in a deed that limits the way the real estate ownership may be used.

reverse mortgage A loan under which the homeowner receives monthly payments based on her accumulated equity rather than a lump sum. The loan must be repaid at a prearranged date or on the death of the owner or the sale of the property.

reversionary interest The remnant of an estate that the grantor holds after granting a life estate to another person.

reversionary right The return of the rights of possession and quiet enjoyment to the lessor at the expiration of a lease.

right of survivorship *See* joint tenancy.

right-of-way The right given by one landowner to another to pass over the land, construct a roadway, or use as a pathway, without actually transferring ownership.

riparian rights An owner's rights in land that borders on or includes a stream, river, or lake. These rights include access to and use of the water.

risk management Evaluation and selection of appropriate property and other insurance.

rules and regulations Real estate licensing authority orders that govern licensees' activities; they usually have the same force and effect as statutory law.

sale and leaseback A transaction in which an owner sells her improved property and, as part of the same transaction, signs a long-term lease to remain in possession of the premises.

sales comparison approach The process of estimating the value of a property by examining and comparing actual sales of comparable properties.

salesperson A person who performs real estate activities while employed by or associated with a licensed real estate sponsoring broker.

satisfaction of mortgage A document acknowledging the payment of a mortgage debt.

secondary mortgage market A market for the purchase and sale of existing mortgages, designed to provide greater liquidity for mortgages.

Secretary Refers to the Secretary of the Department of Financial and Professional Regulation or a person authorized by the Secretary to act in the Secretary's stead.

section A portion of a township under the rectangular (government) survey system. A township is divided into 36 sections, numbered 1 through 36. A section is a square with mile-long sides and an area of one square mile, or 640 acres.

Secure and Fair Enforcement for Mortgage Licensing Act of 2008 (SAFE Act) Act requires that each individual state must license and register mortgage loan originators (MLOs).

security deposit A payment by a tenant, held by the landlord during the lease term and kept (wholly or partially) on default or destruction of the premises by the tenant.

seisin Possession of real property under claim of freehold estate (fee simple).

seller disclosure form Sellers are required to provide this form to buyers, identifying any property defects that the seller may be aware of.

separate property Under community property law, property owned solely by either spouse before the marriage, acquired by gift or inheritance after the marriage, or purchased with separate funds after the marriage.

servient tenement Land on which an easement exists in favor of an adjacent property (called a *dominant estate*); also called a *servient estate*.

setback The amount of space local zoning regulations require between a lot line and a building line.

severalty Ownership of real property by one person only, also called *sole ownership*.

severance Changing an item of real estate to personal property by detaching it from the land; for example, cutting down a tree.

sharecropping In an agricultural lease, the agreement between the landowner and the tenant farmer to split the crop or the profit from its sale.

short sale A sale of real estate in which the sale proceeds fall short of the balance owed on the property's mortgage loan.

Sherman Antitrust Act This act prohibits monopolies and any contracts, combinations, and conspiracies that unreasonably restrain trade.

single agency The representation of a single principal.

situs The personal preference of people for one area over another.

social networking The practice of expanding the number of one's business and or social contacts by making connections through individuals.

special agent One who is authorized by a principal to perform a single act or transaction; a real estate broker is usually a special agent authorized to find a ready, willing, and able buyer for a particular property.

special assessment A tax or levy customarily imposed against only those specific parcels of real estate that will benefit from a proposed public improvement like a street or sewer.

special service area (SSA) A taxing mechanism that can be used to fund a wide range of special or additional services and/or physical improvements in a defined geographic area within a municipality or jurisdiction.

special warranty deed A deed in which the grantor warrants, or guarantees, the title only against defects arising during the period of her tenure and ownership of the property and not against defects existing before that time.

specific lien A lien affecting or attaching only to a certain, specific parcel of land or piece of property.

specific performance A legal action to compel a party to carry out the terms of a contract.

sponsor card In Illinois, a card that certifies a new licensee's relationship with a sponsoring broker and serves as a temporary permit to practice until a permanent pocket card is received.

sponsoring broker The broker who has issued a sponsor card to a licensed broker, managing broker, or leasing agent.

square-foot method The appraisal method of estimating building costs by multiplying the number of square feet in the improvements being appraised by the cost per square foot for recently constructed similar improvements.

statute of frauds The part of a state law that requires that certain instruments, such as deeds, real estate sales contracts, and certain leases, be in writing to be legally enforceable.

statute of limitations That law pertaining to the period of time within which certain actions must be brought to court.

statutory lien A lien imposed on property by statute—a tax lien, for example; in contrast to an equitable lien, which arises out of common law.

statutory redemption The right of a defaulted property owner to recover the property after its sale by paying the appropriate fees and charges.

steering The illegal practice of channeling homeseekers to particular areas, either to maintain the homogeneity of an area or to change the character of an area, which limits their choices of where they can live.

stigmatized property A property that has acquired an undesirable reputation due to an event that occurred on or near it, such as violent crime, gang-related activity, illness, or personal tragedy. Some states restrict the disclosure of information about stigmatized properties.

straight-line method A method of calculating depreciation for tax purposes, computed by dividing the adjusted basis of a property by the estimated number of years of remaining useful life.

straight (term) loan A loan in which only interest is paid during the term of the loan, with the entire principal amount due with the final interest payment.

subagent One who is employed by a person already acting as an agent.

subdivider One who buys undeveloped land, divides it into smaller, usable lots, and sells the lots to potential users.

subdivision A tract of land divided by the owner, known as the subdivider, into blocks, building lots, and streets according to a recorded subdivision plat, which must comply with local ordinances and regulations.

subdivision and development ordinances Municipal ordinances that establish requirements for subdivisions and development.

subdivision plat *See* plat map.

sublease *See* subletting.

subletting The leasing of premises by a lessee to a third party for part of the lessee's remaining term. *See also* assignment.

subordination Relegation to a lesser position, usually in respect to a right or security.

subordination agreement A written agreement between holders of liens on a property that changes the priority of mortgage, judgment, and other liens under certain circumstances.

subrogation The substitution of one creditor for another, with the substituted person succeeding to the legal rights and claims of the original claimant. Subrogation is used by title insurers to acquire from the injured party rights to sue to recover any claims the insurers have paid.

substitution An appraisal principle that states that the maximum value of a property tends to be set by the cost of purchasing an equally desirable and valuable substitute property, assuming that no costly delay is encountered in making the substitution.

subsurface rights Ownership rights in a parcel of real estate to the water, minerals, gas, oil, and so forth that lie beneath the surface of the property.

suit for possession A court suit initiated by a landlord to evict a tenant from leased premises after the tenant has breached one of the terms of the lease or has held possession of the property after the lease's expiration.

suit for specific performance A court action in which the defaulting party is sued to perform under the terms and conditions agreed to in the contract.

suit to quiet title A court action intended to establish or settle the title to a particular property, especially when there is a cloud on the title.

Superfund Popular name of the hazardous-waste cleanup fund established by the Comprehensive Environmental Response, Compensation, and Liability Act (CERCLA).

Superfund Amendments and Reauthorization Act (SARA) An amendatory statute that contains stronger cleanup standards for contaminated sites, increased funding for Superfund, and clarifications of lender liability and innocent landowner immunity. *See* Comprehensive Environmental Response, Compensation, and Liability Act (CERCLA).

supply The amount of goods available in the market to be sold at a given price. The term is often coupled with the term *demand*.

supply and demand The appraisal principle that follows the interrelationship of the supply of and demand for real estate. As appraising is based on economic concepts, this principle recognizes that real property is subject to the influences of the marketplace just as is any other commodity.

surety bond An agreement by an insurance or bonding company to be responsible for certain possible defaults, debts, or obligations contracted for by an insured party. In the real estate business a surety bond is generally used to ensure that a particular project will be completed at a certain date or that a contract will be performed as stated.

surface rights Ownership rights in a parcel of real estate that are limited to the surface of the property and do not include the air above it (air rights) or the minerals below the surface (subsurface rights).

survey The process by which boundaries are measured and land areas are determined; the on-site measurement of lot lines, dimensions, and position of a house on a lot, including the determination of any existing encroachments or easements.

syndicate A combination of people or firms formed to accomplish a business venture of mutual interest by pooling resources. In a real estate investment syndicate, the parties own and/or develop property, with the main profit generally arising from the sale of the property.

tacking Adding or combining successive periods of continuous occupation of real property by adverse possessors. This concept enables someone who has not been in possession for the entire statutory period to establish a claim of adverse possession.

taxation The process by which a government or municipal quasi-public body raises monies to fund its operation.

tax credit An amount by which tax owed is reduced directly.

tax deed An instrument given to a purchaser after the expiration of the redemption rights. *See also* certificate of sale.

tax lien A charge against property, created by operation of law. Tax liens and assessments take priority over all other liens.

tax sale A court-ordered sale of real property to raise money to cover delinquent taxes.

tenancy by the entirety The joint ownership of property acquired by husband and wife during marriage. Upon the death of one spouse, the survivor becomes the owner of the property.

tenancy in common A form of co-ownership by which each owner holds an undivided interest in real property as if she were sole owner. Each individual owner has the right to partition. Unlike joint tenants, tenants in common have right of inheritance.

tenant One who holds or possesses lands or tenements by any kind of right or title.

tenant improvements Alterations to the interior of a building to meet the functional demands of the tenant.

testate   Having made and left a valid will.

testator   A person who has made a valid will.

tier (township strip)   A strip of land six miles wide, extending east and west and numbered north and south according to its distance from the base line in the rectangular (government) survey system of legal description.

time is of the essence   A phrase in a contract that requires the performance of a certain act within a stated period of time.

time-share   A form of ownership interest that may include an estate interest in property and that allows use of the property for a fixed or variable time period.

time-share estate   A fee simple interest in a time-share property.

time-share use   A right of occupancy in a time-share property, less than a fee simple interest.

title   (1) The right to or ownership of land. (2) The evidence of ownership of land.

title insurance   A policy insuring the owner or mortgagee against loss by reason of defects in the title to a parcel of real estate, other than encumbrances, defects, and matters specifically excluded by the policy.

title search   The examination of public records relating to real estate to determine the current state of the ownership.

title theory   Some states interpret a mortgage to mean that the lender is the owner of mortgaged land. On full payment of the mortgage debt, the borrower becomes the landowner.

township   The principal unit of the rectangular (government) survey system. A township is a square with six-mile sides and an area of 36 square miles.

township strips   *See* tier.

trade fixture   An article installed by a tenant under the terms of a lease and removable by the tenant before the lease expires.

transfer tax   Tax stamps required to be affixed to a deed by state and/or local law.

trust   A fiduciary arrangement whereby property is conveyed to a person or institution, called a *trustee*, to be held and administered on behalf of another person, called a *beneficiary*. The one who conveys the trust is called the *trustor*.

trust account   *See* escrow account

trust deed   An instrument used to create a mortgage lien by which the borrower conveys title to a trustee, who holds it as security for the benefit of the note holder (the lender); also called a *deed of trust*.

trust deed lien   A lien on the property of a trustor that secures a deed of trust loan.

trustee   The holder of bare legal title in a deed of trust loan transaction.

trustee's deed   A deed executed by a trustee conveying land held in a trust.

trustor   A borrower in a deed of trust loan transaction.

tying agreements   Agreements to sell one product only if the buyer purchases another product as well. The sale of the first product is "tied" to the purchase of a second product.

unauthorized practice of law   Persons or entities who engage in the practice of law but are not authorized to practice law pursuant to state law.

undivided interest   *See* tenancy in common.

unenforceable contract   A contract that has all the elements of a valid contract, yet neither party can sue the other to force performance of it.

Uniform Settlement Statement (HUD-1)   A special form that itemizes all charges to be paid by buyer and seller in connection with settlement.

Uniform Vendor and Purchaser Risk Act   This act states that the seller bears any loss that occurs before the title passes or the buyer takes possession.

unilateral contract   A one-sided contract wherein one party makes a promise so as to induce a second party to do something. The second party is not legally bound to perform; however, if the second party does comply, the first party is obligated to keep the promise.

unit-in-place method   The appraisal method of estimating building costs by calculating the costs of all of the physical components in the structure, with the cost of each item including its proper installation, connection, and so forth; also called the *segregated cost method*.

unit of ownership   The four unities that are traditionally needed to create a joint tenancy—unity of title, time, interest, and possession.

unsecured debt   Any type of debt or general obligation that is not collateralized by a lien on specific assets of the borrower in the case of bankruptcy or liquidation.

usury   Charging interest at a higher rate than the maximum rate established by state law.

valid contract   A contract that complies with all the essentials of a contract and is binding and enforceable on all parties to it.

VA loan   A mortgage loan on approved property made to a qualified veteran by an authorized lender and guaranteed by the Department of Veterans Affairs to limit the lender's possible loss.

value The power of a good or service to command other goods in exchange for the present worth of future rights to its income or amenities.

variance Permission obtained from zoning authorities to build a structure or conduct a use that is expressly prohibited by the current zoning laws; an exception from the zoning ordinances.

vendee A buyer, usually under the terms of a land contract.

vendor A seller, usually under the terms of a land contract.

voidable contract A contract that seems to be valid on the surface but may be rejected or disaffirmed by one or both of the parties.

void contract A contract that has no legal force or effect because it does not meet the essential elements of a contract.

voluntary alienation *See* alienation.

voluntary lien A lien placed on property with the knowledge and consent of the property owner.

walk-through The final property inspection by the buyer, a few days prior to closing, to ensure that the property is in the same condition that it was in at the time the sales contract was written.

waste An improper use or an abuse of a property by a possessor who holds less than fee ownership, such as a tenant, life tenant, mortgagor, or vendee. Such waste ordinarily impairs the value of the land or the interest of the person holding the title or the reversionary rights.

water table The natural level at which the ground is saturated.

will A written document, properly witnessed, providing for the transfer of title to property owned by the deceased, called the *testator*.

workers' compensation acts Laws that require an employer to obtain insurance coverage to protect her employees who are injured in the course of their employment.

wraparound loan A method of refinancing in which the new mortgage is placed in a secondary, or subordinate, position; the new mortgage includes both the unpaid principal balance of the first mortgage and whatever additional sums are advanced by the lender.

zoning ordinance An exercise of police power by a municipality to regulate and control the character and use of property.

Answer Key

Following are the correct answers to the review questions included in each chapter of the text. *In parentheses following the correct answers are references to the pages where the question topics are discussed or explained.* Suggested math calculations for some of the review questions can be found on pages 695 and 696. *If you have answered a question incorrectly, be sure to go back to the page or pages noted and restudy the material until you understand the correct answer.* The references for the practice examinations are to chapter numbers.

CHAPTER 1

Introduction to the Real Estate Business

1. b (2)
2. b (6)
3. c (7)
4. c (8)
5. b (2, 3)
6. d (4)
7. b (8)
8. a (3)
9. d (2)
10. a (5)
11. b (6)
12. b (2)
13. a (7)
14. b (5)
15. d (7)
16. c (6)
17. d (3)
18. a (6)
19. c (2)
20. b (8)

CHAPTER 2

Real Property and the Law

1. a (16)
2. b (19)
3. c (20)
4. c (16)
5. d (16)
6. b (14, 15)
7. a (18)
8. d (19)
9. b (17, 18)
10. a (18)
11. b (16)
12. c (18)

13. d (14)
14. a (14)
15. a (15)
16. b (14)
17. b (15, 16)
18. c (19)
19. b (20)
20. d (16)

CHAPTER 3

Concepts of Home Ownership

1. d (29)
2. d (31)
3. b (30)
4. a (27)
5. b (27)
6. b (28)
7. b (30)
8. d (30)
9. a (32)
10. c (30)
11. c (31)
12. b (35)
13. c (30)
14. c (31)
15. b (27)
16. d (30)
17. d (29)
18. d (32)
19. b (33)
20. d (30)

CHAPTER 4

Real Estate Agency

1. c (42)
2. a (54)
3. a (43)
4. b (42)

5. c (54)
6. b (54)
7. d (40)
8. c (41)
9. c (48)
10. c (58)
11. b (55)
12. a (42)
13. d (49)
14. b (55)
15. b (50)
16. d (42)
17. b (45)
18. a (58)
19. b (58)
20. d (55)

CHAPTER 5

Real Estate Brokerage

1. b (92)
2. b (76)
3. b (93)
4. b (92)
5. c (91)
6. c (92)
7. d (79)
8. c (97)
9. a (95)
10. a (95)
11. c (98)
12. d (99)
13. c (100)
14. c (79)
15. b (79)
16. d (76)
17. a (94)
18. c (93)
19. b (93)
20. d (98)

CHAPTER 6
Brokerage Agreements

1. a (108)
2. c (109)
3. c (112)
4. a (109)
5. a (115)
6. d (109)
7. a (109)
8. d (113)
9. a (108)
10. d (115)
11. b (122)
12. b (113)
13. a (115)
14. c (115)
15. c (109)
16. b (109)
17. c (111)
18. a (132)
19. b (112)
20. a (108)

CHAPTER 7
Interests in Real Estate

1. c (141)
2. a (145)
3. c (145)
4. d (150)
5. d (144)
6. d (152)
7. c (154)
8. a (151)
9. d (145)
10. b (150)
11. c (145)
12. b (147)
13. b (153)
14. a (149)
15. d (153)
16. b (148)
17. a (152)
18. c (152)
19. c (143)
20. a (151)

CHAPTER 8
Forms of Real Estate Ownership

1. d (165)
2. d (163, 164)
3. b (164)
4. a (169)
5. c (177)
6. c (178)
7. c (172)
8. d (164)
9. d (166)
10. b (164)
11. c (176)
12. b (165, 167)
13. a (164)
14. d (179)
15. b (171)
16. a (166)
17. a (172)
18. b (164)
19. d (166)
20. a (175)

CHAPTER 9
Legal Descriptions

1. b (191)
2. d (188)
3. b (187)
4. c (191)
5. c (191)
6. a (191)
7. a (191)
8. d (191)
9. c (188)
10. d (193)
11. b (193)
12. b (198)
13. b (200)
14. b (200)
15. c (191)
16. a (188)
17. c (189)
18. b (197)
19. c (197)
20. c (197)

CHAPTER 10
Real Estate Taxes and Other Liens

1. d (207)
2. b (208)
3. b (215)
4. c (207)
5. b (208)
6. d (212)
7. c (209)
8. c (217)
9. d (213)
10. c (216)
11. d (218)
12. c (208)
13. b (216)
14. d (216)
15. d (207)
16. b (209)
17. b (211)
18. a (218)
19. c (214)
20. a (213)

CHAPTER 11
Real Estate Contracts

1. c (229)
2. b (232)
3. d (228)
4. b (228)
5. d (234)
6. d (235)
7. a (252)
8. a (252)
9. d (232)
10. d (255)
11. c (227)
12. b (230)
13. b (229)
14. d (234)
15. b (228)
16. a (235)
17. c (252)
18. b (235)
19. b (236)
20. b (255)

CHAPTER 12
Transfer of Title

1. a (262)
2. a (262)
3. d (263)
4. a (264)
5. c (266, 267)
6. d (266)
7. b (267)
8. c (265)
9. b (265)
10. b (271)
11. d (271)
12. a (266)
13. d (273)
14. c (273)
15. c (271)
16. b (273)
17. b (268)
18. d (270)
19. c (273)
20. c (274)

CHAPTER 13
Title Records

1. a (281)
2. a (282)
3. c (281)
4. a (283)
5. a (283)
6. d (266)
7. d (285, 286)
8. d (283)
9. c (284)
10. a (284)
11. c (285)
12. d (286)
13. c (287)
14. b (287)
15. a (286)
16. b (282)
17. b (282)
18. d (281)
19. c (281)
20. b (281)

CHAPTER 14
Illinois Real Estate License Law

1. a (296, 297)
2. c (298)
3. c (305)
4. b (306)
5. a (320)
6. d (322)
7. c (304)
8. a (300)
9. d (308)
10. b (319)
11. b (296, 297)
12. d (317)
13. b (323)
14. a (319)
15. b (317)
16. d (313)
17. a (305)
18. c (299)
19. b (321)
20. a (301)

CHAPTER 15
Real Estate Financing: Principles

1. b (332)
2. a (334)
3. c (334)
4. a (334)
5. d (339)
6. d (335)
7. a (336)
8. a (340)
9. b (332)
10. a (330)
11. b (331)
12. b (332)
13. b (331)
14. c (343)
15. c (337)
16. b (344)
17. c (337)
18. d (332)
19. d (341)
20. c (330)

CHAPTER 16
Real Estate Financing: Practice

1. d (365)
2. d (367)
3. c (353)
4. c (358)
5. a (356)
6. b (352)
7. c (358)
8. b (366)
9. c (361)
10. b (355)
11. b (353)
12. b (354)
13. b (355)
14. b (355)
15. c (359)
16. c (355)
17. a (359)
18. b (368)
19. a (368)
20. c (365)

CHAPTER 17
Leases

1. c (391)
2. c (391)
3. d (388)
4. c (391)
5. b (389)
6. d (378)
7. c (378)
8. b (379)
9. b (394)
10. b (378)
11. b (380)
12. b (391)
13. c (392)
14. a (377)
15. c (386)
16. c (379)
17. b (386)
18. a (393)
19. c (379)
20. c (396)

Property Management

1. b (415)
2. c (409)
3. c (414)
4. d (409)
5. c (415)
6. c (407)
7. b (414)
8. d (412)
9. b (412)
10. c (408)
11. a (408)
12. c (415)
13. c (415)
14. c (408)
15. b (412)
16. b (405)
17. c (413)
18. a (409)
19. d (403)
20. b (410)

Real Estate Appraisal

1. c (430, 431)
2. b (423)
3. b (425)
4. b (423)
5. d (425)
6. a (425)
7. d (429, 430)
8. c (435)
9. a (431, 432)
10. c (432)
11. c (431)
12. c (423)
13. b (432)
14. c (429)
15. d (431)
16. d (426)
17. b (430)
18. b (430)
19. b (430)
20. c (421)

Land-Use Controls and
Property Development

1. a (455)
2. a (451)
3. b (455)
4. c (449)
5. c (552)
6. a (448)
7. a (451)
8. d (451)
9. b (456)
10. a (456)
11. a (453)
12. c (453)
13. b (454)
14. b (455)
15. b (453)
16. a (455)
17. a (457)
18. a (447)
19. c (450)
20. b (447)

Fair Housing and Ethical
Practices

1. c (466)
2. a (466)
3. d (466)
4. b (474)
5. b (475)
6. a (476)
7. b (471)
8. b (475)
9. c (472)
10. b (481)
11. a (471)
12. b (481)
13. d (478)
14. c (469)
15. d (475)
16. d (469)
17. b (470)
18. a (479)
19. a (479)
20. c (471)

Environmental Issues and the
Real Estate Transaction

1. b (490)
2. c (491)
3. c (491)
4. a (491)
5. a (501)
6. c (495)
7. b (504)
8. d (506)
9. c (500)
10. d (491)
11. c (492)
12. a (494)
13. b (491)
14. c (500)
15. a (501)
16. c (492)
17. b (491)
18. c (489)
19. b (489)
20. c (497)

Closing the Real Estate
Transaction

1. b (517)
2. d (520)
3. a (517)
4. c (524)
5. b (532)
6. b (532)
7. c (538)
8. a (532)
9. c (540)
10. a (540)
11. c (533)
12. b (535)
13. d (524)
14. b (525)
15. b (525)
16. b (523)
17. b (539)
18. c (519)
19. a (536)
20. d (533)

■ MATH CALCULATIONS FOR REVIEW QUESTIONS

CHAPTER 3

12. $9,500 + $800 + $1,000 = $11,300

CHAPTER 5

21. $8,200 ÷ 0.06 = $136,666.67
22. $2,520 × 2 = $5,040 ÷ $72,000 = 0.07 or 7%

CHAPTER 6

5. $12,925 ÷ $235,000 = 0.055 or 5.5%
10. 0.065 × 0.40 = 0.026
    $9,750 ÷ 0.026 = $375,000
13. $153,500 × 0.06 × 0.40 = $3,684
14. $387,000 × 0.055 = $21,285. $387,000 − $21,285 = $365,715

CHAPTER 9

8. 43,560 × $2.15 = $93,654
12. 4.5 × 43,560 = 196,020
    $78,400 ÷ 196,020 = 0.40
    150 × 100 = 15,000
    0.40 × 15,000 = $6,000
13. 10 × 43,560 − 26,000 ÷ 5,000 = 81.92, rounded to 81
14. 400 × 640 ÷ 2 = 128,000 ÷ 43,560 = 2.94

CHAPTER 10

6. $160,000 × 0.75 × 0.040 = $4,800
9. $47,250 × 1.25 × 0.025 = $1,477

CHAPTER 15

1. $120,000 × 0.03 = $3,600
9. $2,700 ÷ $90,000 = 0.03 or 3 points

CHAPTER 16

13. $100,000 × 0.075 = $7,500 ÷ 12 = $625 interest
    $902.77 − $625.00 = $277.77
    $100,000 − $277.77 = $99,722.23
14. $85,000 × 0.115 = 9,775 ÷ 12 = $814.58
    $823.76 − $814.58 = $9.18
15. $114,500 × 0.80 = $91,600

CHAPTER 17

13. $1,200 × 12 = $14,400
    $19,200 − 14,400 = 4,800 ÷ 0.04 = $120,000
    $120,000 + 150,000 = $270,000

9. $24,000 ÷ $300,000 = 0.08 or 8 percent
15. $112,000 – $53,700 ÷ $542,000 = 10.75 percent
17. $240,000 ÷ 65 × 5 = $18,462
18. $240,000 – $18,462 = $221,538

9. $285,000 × 0.10 = $28,500
 $285,000 – $28,500 = $256,500
 $256,500 × 0.02 = $5,130 + $28,500 = $33,630
10. $300,000 × 0.30 = $90,000
 $90,000 – $22,000 = $68,000
23. $2,129 ÷ 365 = $5.83

Practice Exam One

The number in the parentheses refers to the chapter in the text where information pertaining to the answer is located. * See Math Calculations beginning on page 700.

(P A R T   O N E)

1. b (10)
2. a (11)
3. a (11)
4. c (16)
5. c (1)
6. b (6)
7. a (12)
8. a (21)
9. a (7)
10. d (8)
11. d (5)
12. a (15)
13. b (17)
14. a (19)
15. a (21)
16. d (2)
17. c (4)
18. d (3)
19. a (3)
20. b (7)
21. d (5)*
22. b (9)*
23. b (15)
24. b (10)*
25. c (15)*
26. c (5)*
27. b (19)
28. d (5)
29. b (15)*
30. b (6)*
31. a (11)
32. d (11)
33. a (11)
34. b (3)
35. b (12)
36. a (15)
37. d (19)*
38. b (6)
39. a (3)
40. a (12)
41. d (6)
42. b (17)
43. c (21)

44. b (15)*
45. d (10)
46. d (11)
47. c (20)
48. d (9)*
49. b (19)
50. b (10)
51. b (6)
52. b (8)
53. c (17)
54. d (11)
55. b (7)
56. c (11)
57. a (7)
58. c (10)
59. d (20)
60. b (11)
61. c (15)
62. c (21)
63. d (16)
64. d (11)
65. b (12)
66. d (8)
67. b (23)*
68. d (21)
69. a (12)
70. a (19)
71. d (16)
72. d (3)
73. a (23)
74. d (23)
75. b (2)
76. c (7)
77. d (17)
78. b (6)
79. d (5)
80. d (17)
81. c (2)
82. a (20)
83. c (3)
84. b (4)
85. c (20)
86. d (8)
87. c (21)

88. d (11)
89. c (6)
90. c (19)

(P A R T   T W O)

1. d (7)
2. a (11)
3. c (20)
4. b (7)*
5. b (8)
6. b (8)
7. b (9)
8. c (9)
9. a (8)
10. b (10)
11. b (10)
12. b (8)
13. b (6)
14. c (2)
15. d (6)
16. c (7)
17. a (11)
18. b (6)
19. a (11)
20. a (14)
21. d (14)
22. b (14)
23. a (12)
24. b (9)
25. b (4)
26. c (11)
27. d (15)
28. d (21)
29. b (12)
30. c (12)
31. c (12)
32. c (10)
33. b (17)
34. b (12)*
35. d (13)
36. b (12)
37. c (14)
38. c (14)
39. d (14)

40. b (20)
41. b (15)
42. c (10)
43. d (10)*
44. b (11)
45. b (14)
46. d (14)
47. b (5)
48. c (15)
49. c (14)
50. a (15)
51. b (5)
52. b (17)
53. c (14)
54. c (17)
55. b (20)
56. a (7)
57. c (4)
58. d (10)
59. b (14)
60. c (14)

Practice Exam Two

(P A R T   O N E)

1. d (17)
2. d (2)
3. c (11)
4. b (10)
5. c (16)
6. d (4)
7. b (*)
8. d (21)
9. b (*)
10. b (16)*
11. b (11)
12. a (23)
13. d (4)
14. c (7)
15. d (4)
16. d (9)
17. b (12)
18. b (23)
19. c (6)*
20. a (19)
21. c (23)
22. b (17)
23. a (7)

24. b (23)
25. d (17)
26. d (16)*
27. c (16)*
28. b (4)
29. b (19)
30. d (23)
31. a (23)*
32. d*
33. a (11)
34. d (10)
35. b*
36. a (6)
37. b (11)
38. d (6)
39. a (19)
40. c (19)*
41. d (12)
42. c (9)*
43. d (11)
44. d (14)*
45. c*
46. d (16)
47. a (7)
48. a (23)*
49. b (17)
50. c (19)*
51. c (6)*
52. a (13)
53. d (3)
54. a (2)
55. d (8)
56. a (23)
57. b (7)
58. b (Section 2)*
59. d (19)
60. d (16)
61. d (17)
62. c (21)
63. c (13)
64. c*
65. a (4)
66. b (6)*
67. b (21)
68. d (4)
69. c*
70. a (23)
71. d (16)
72. c (19)*

73. a (11)
74. d (19)
75. d (16)
76. c (Section 3)*
77. b (18)
78. d (10)*
79. b (23)
80. b (18)
81. b (5)
82. d (5)
83. b (19)
84. b (6)
85. d (6)
86. c (17)
87. b (19)
88. a (23)
89. d (5)
90. a (5)

(P A R T   T W O)

1. b (23)*
2. d (15)
3. c (17)
4. c (17)
5. a (17)
6. c (17)
7. d (10)
8. a (21)
9. d (21)
10. c (21)
11. a (2)
12. c (4)
13. b (4)
14. d (4)
15. b (4)
16. c (14)
17. c (5)
18. a (21)
19. c (5)
20. b (4)
21. d (6)
22. b (6)
23. d (6)
24. a (6)
25. d (7)
26. c (7)
27. b (7)
28. a (6)
29. c (6)

30. c (8)
31. d (9)
32. b (10)
33. a (11)
34. d (11)
35. c (11)
36. b (12)
37. b (13)
38. b (14)
39. c (14)
40. d (14)
41. b (14)
42. d (14)
43. d (14)
44. d (14)
45. a (14)
46. b (14)
47. b (14)
48. c (5)
49. d (14)
50. d (15)
51. d (15)
52. c (17)
53. c (14)
54. b (4)
55. a (23)*
56. d (4)
57. d (20)
58. d (11)
59. b (14)
60. c (6)

Practice Exam Three

1. a (14)
2. d (14)
3. d (5)
4. b (14)
5. d (14)
6. a (14)
7. c (14)
8. c (14)
9. a (5)
10. b (14)
11. b (14)
12. a (4)
13. d (5)
14. d (14)
15. d (14)

16. c (14)
17. a (6)
18. c (14)
19. d (4, 6)
20. d (14)
21. a (14)
22. b (4)
23. d (14)
24. b (1)
25. c (14)
26. d (14)
27. d (14)
28. d (14)
29. d (14)
30. b (14)
31. a (14)
32. b (14)
33. b (4)
34. a (4)
35. d (5)
36. b (14)
37. c (14)
38. a (14)
39. d (3)
40. c (14)
41. d (14)
42. c (3)
43. c (4)
44. c (14)
45. a (14)
46. c (4)
47. c (14)
48. b (4)
49. c (6)
50. d (14)
51. d (14)
52. a (14)
53. d (6)
54. d (4)
55. b (4)
56. c (14)
57. d (14)
58. d (4)
59. c (14)
60. b (21)
61. c (4)
62. d (14)
63. b (12)
64. a (10)

65. d (12)
66. c (5)
67. b (1, 2)
68. b (10)
69. b (14)
70. b (14)
71. d (14)
72. d (12)
73. c (12)
74. a (7)
75. d (8)
76. d (10)
77. c (11)
78. d (12)
79. d (10)
80. b (14)
81. d (8)
82. a (14)
83. d (14)
84. c (4)
85. b (14)
86. a (14)
87. d (11)
88. d (20)
89. a (2)
90. b (4)
91. b (19)
92. a (19)
93. b (14)
94. a (14)
95. d (14)
96. b (14)
97. d (14)
98. c (14)
99. a (7)
100. d (7)

Practice Exam One

(PART ONE)

18. $10\,\frac{3}{8} - 9\,\frac{6}{8} = \frac{5}{8}$
    5 points will increase yield by $\frac{5}{8}$

21. $\$65,000 \div 0.94 = \$69,149$

22. $3 \times 43,560 = 130,680$ sq. ft.

24. $\$40,000 \times 0.40 \times 1.5 \times 0.04 = \$960$

25. $\$60,000 \times 0.90 = \$54,000 \times 0.01 = \$540$
    $\$60,000 \times 0.10 = \$6,000 + \$540 = \$6,540$

26. $\$274,550 \div 0.85 = \$323,000$

28. $640 \div 4 = 160$
    $640 \div 4 = 160$
    $160 + 160 = 320$ acres $\times \$875 = \$280,000 \times 0.05 = \$14,000$

29. $\$38,500 \times 0.04 = \$1,540$

30. $\$50,000 \times 0.0775 = \$3,875$

37. $\$22,000 \div 0.08 = \$275,000$

44. $\$6,000 \div \$150,000 = 0.04$ or 4 points

48. $2 \times 4 = 8.$ $640 \div 8 = 80$
    $4 \times 4 = 16.$ $640 \div 16 = 40$
    $80 + 40 = 120$ acres

56. $\$562.50 \times 4 = \$2,250$
    $\$2,250 \div 0.075 = \$30,000$

58. $\$460 \times 12 = \$5,520 \div 0.08 = \$69,000$ loan
    $\$69,000 \div 0.80 = \$86,250$

63. $\$37,000 \times 0.25 = \$9,250 - \$3,000 = \$6,250$

67. Count the actual number of days from March 16 through December 31: 291 days.
    $\$1,880.96 \div 365 = \$5.153 \times 291 = \$1,500$
    $\$84,500 - 67,600 = \$16,900$ down $- \$2,000$ paid $= \$14,900$
    $\$14,900 + 1,500 + 1,250 = \$17,650$

77. $90' + 175' + 90' + 175' = 540' \times \$1.25 = \$662.50$
    $530' \times 6.5' = 3,445$ sq. ft. $\times \$.825 = \$2,842$
    $\$662.50 + 2,842 = \$3,505$

85. $\$157,000 \times 0.06 \times 0.10 = \$942$

Practice Exam One

4. $165,000 – $30,000 (their total homestead) = $135,000

29. $250,000 ÷ $500 = 500 × $.50 = $250

34. $185,000 ÷ $500 = 370 × $.25 = $92.50

43. $175,000 × 0.030 ÷ 2 = $2,625 on June 1

Practice Exam Two

7. 80' × $200 = $16,000 × 0.10 × 0.60 = $960

9. 9' × 12' × 8' = 864 cubic feet × $1.82 = $1,572 ÷ 2 = $786

10. $120,500 × 0.80 = $96,400

19. $195,000 × 0.075 × 0.65 = $9,506.25

26. $57,200 × 0.135 = $7,722 ÷ 12 = $643.50
    $666.75 – 643.50 = $23.25
    $57,200 – 23.25 = $57,176.75

27. $57,200 × 0.135 = $7,722 ÷ 12 = $643.50

31. $57,500 × 0.085 = $4,887.50 ÷ 360 = 13.576 × 14 = 190.07
    The bank will add interest on the day of closing.

32. $142,500 × 1.27 = $180,975

35. $193,600 ÷ $4.40 = 44,000 sq. ft. ÷ 200' = 220 feet

40. $142,000 – 18,000 = $124,000 value of building ÷ 31.5 years = $3,936.51
    $3,936.51 × 7 years = $27,556 depreciation
    $142,000 – 27,556 = $114,444

42. 2 × 4 × 4 = 32
    640 ÷ 32 = 20 acres that he owns.
    He wants to own 160 acres. 160 – 20 = 140 acres × $300 = $42,000

44. $795 × 3 = $2,385
    $2,385 + 1,200 + 900 = $4,485 × 12 = $53,820 × 0.085 = $4,574.70

45. 36' × 200' × 12' = 86,400 cubic feet ÷ 27 = 3,200 cubic yards × $1 × 12 = $38,400

48. 45 days to the end of the year.
    $1,116 ÷ 360 = $3.10 × 45 days = $139.50

50. $234,500 – 80,000 = $154,500 value of building ÷ 27.5 = $5,618.18

51. $1,000 × 12 × 0.07 = $840
    $1,100 × 12 × 0.05 = 660
    $1,210 × 12 × 0.03 = 435.60
    $840 + 660 + 435.60 = $1,936

58. 54% + 18% + 16% = 88%
    100% − 88% = 12% to the college
    $79,000 ÷ 0.12 = $658,333 × 0.18 = $118,500

64. $90,000 × 0.075 = $6,750 × 15 = $101,250

66. $90,000 ÷ 0.94 = $95,745

69. Subtract front setback 25' and rear setback 20' from 70': 70' − 45' = 25'
    Subtract side setback 10' and side setback 10' from 70': 70' − 20' = 50'
    50' × 25' = 1,250 sq. ft.

72. $30,000 ÷ 0.10 = $300,000
    $30,000 ÷ 0.12 = $250,000
    $300,000 − 250,000 = $50,000

76. $1,200.22 × 12 × 15 = $216,040
    $1,028.63 × 12 × 30 = $370,307
    $370,307 ÷ 216,040 = 1.71 or 171%

78. $85,000 × 1.10 × 0.040 = $3,740

Practice Exam Two

(P A R T   T W O)

1. January 1 to May 2 is 4 months and 2 days
   $560 ÷ 12 = $46.667 × 4 months = $186.667
   $46.667 ÷ 31 × 2 days = $3.011
   $186.667 + 3.011 = $189.68

55. $560 ÷ 12 ÷ 31 = $1.505 or $1.51

Index

Notes

Notes

Notes

Notes

Notes